# THE ROUTLEDGE COMPANION TO MEDIA INDUSTRIES

Bringing together 49 chapters from leading experts in media industries research, this major collection offers an authoritative overview of the current state of scholarship while setting out proposals for expanding, re-thinking, and innovating the field.

Media industries occupy a central place in modern societies, producing, circulating, and presenting the multitude of cultural forms and experiences we encounter in our daily lives. The chapters in this volume begin by outlining key conceptual and critical perspectives while also presenting original interventions to prompt new lines of inquiry. Other chapters then examine the impact of digitalization on the media industries, intersections formed between industries or across geographic territories, and the practices of doing media industries research and teaching. General ideas and arguments are illustrated through specific examples and case studies drawn from a range of media sectors, including advertising, publishing, comics, news, music, film, television, branded entertainment, live cinema experiences, social media, and music video.

Making a vital and significant contribution to media research, this volume is essential reading for students and academics seeking to understand and evaluate the work of the media industries.

**Paul McDonald** is Professor of Media Industries at King's College London. He recently co-edited *Digital Media Distribution: Portals, Platforms, Pipelines* (2021 with Courtney Brannon Donoghue and Timothy Havens). Alongside authoring or editing major works in the field, he's contributed to advancing critical studies of media industries by launching the Media Industries conferences, being a founding member of the Editorial Collective for the journal *Media Industries*, co-editing (with Michael Curtin) the International Screen Industries book series from the British Film Institute, and establishing specialized media industries networks within the Society for Cinema and Media Studies (SCMS) and the European Network of Cinema and Media Studies (NECS). Before entering academia, he worked in various areas of the media industries, with periods spent as an actor, media analyst, and in aspects of animated film production, art book publishing, film exhibition, and studio photography.

# THE ROUTLEDGE COMPANION TO MEDIA INDUSTRIES

*Edited by Paul McDonald*

LONDON AND NEW YORK

First published 2022
by Routledge
2 Park Square, Milton Park, Abingdon, Oxon OX14 4RN

and by Routledge
605 Third Avenue, New York, NY 10158

*Routledge is an imprint of the Taylor & Francis Group, an informa business*

*British Library Cataloguing-in-Publication Data*
A catalogue record for this book is available from the British Library

*Library of Congress Cataloging-in-Publication Data*
Names: McDonald, Paul, 1963– editor.
Title: The Routledge companion to media industries /
edited by Paul McDonald.
Description: Abingdon, Oxon; New York, NY: Routledge, 2022. |
Includes bibliographical references and index.
Identifiers: LCCN 2021010346 (print) | LCCN 2021010347 (ebook) |
ISBN 9780367225261 (hardback) | ISBN 9781032065342 (paperback) |
ISBN 9780429275340 (ebook)
Subjects: LCSH: Mass media.
Classification: LCC P90 .R6728 2022 (print) |
LCC P90 (ebook) | DDC 302.23–dc23
LC record available at https://lccn.loc.gov/2021010346
LC ebook record available at https://lccn.loc.gov/2021010347

ISBN: 978-0-367-22526-1 (hbk)
ISBN: 978-1-032-06534-2 (pbk)
ISBN: 978-0-429-27534-0 (ebk)

DOI: 10.4324/9780429275340

Typeset in Bembo
by Newgen Publishing UK

# CONTENTS

# FIGURES

# TABLES

# CONTRIBUTORS

**Georgia Aitaki** is Senior Lecturer in Media and Communication Studies at Örebro University. Her research focuses on critical approaches to television and popular culture and, specifically, questions of inclusions/exclusions, with an empirical focus on Greek, Swedish, and US media. Her work has appeared in journals such as *Media, Culture and Society*, *Social Semiotics*, and *Screen*, and in a number of anthologies.

**Sarah Atkinson** is Professor of Screen Media in the Department for Culture, Media and Creative Industries at King's College London and co-editor of *Convergence: The International Journal of Research into New Media Technologies*. She has published widely on the impacts of digital technologies on cinema audiences and film production practices.

**Henrik Bødker** is Associate Professor in the Media and Journalism Studies Department at Aarhus University. His most recent work focuses on how digital technologies are transforming the circulation and temporality of journalism. He is currently working on a monograph titled *Journalism, Time and the Digital: Continuity and Disruption* and has just finished co-editing (with Hanna Morris) a volume titled *Climate Change and Journalism: Negotiating Rifts of Time*. He has, among other journals, published in *Media History*, *Critical Studies in Media Communication*, *Journalism*, *Journalism Studies*, and *Digital Journalism*.

**Courtney Brannon Donoghue** is an Assistant Professor in the Department of Media Arts at the University of North Texas. Her publications include *Localising Hollywood* (2017) as well as articles in *Cinema Journal*, *Feminist Media Studies*, *Media, Culture and Society*, and various edited collections. Brannon Donoghue's upcoming books include an examination of gender inequity and the barriers for female-driven projects in the film industry, and co-editing the collection *Digital Media Distribution: Portals, Platforms, Pipelines* (2021 with Paul McDonald and Timothy Havens).

**Emily Caston** is Professor of Screen Industries and director of PRISM at the University of West London. Previously a board member Film London (2008–2015), Emily has produced over 100 music videos and commercials for artists ranging from Madonna to U2, with directors including Spike Jonze and Chris Cunningham, and was previously Executive Producer of Black Dog Films for Ridley Scott Associates. She is a member of the British Academy of Film and Television Arts (BAFTA), has held research grants from the Arts and Humanities Research Council, and contributes regularly to the Sky Arts series *Video Killed the Radio Star*. She has published in *Music, Sound, and the Moving Image*, *Journal of British Cinema and Television*, and *Alphaville: Journal of Film and Screen Media*. Her books include *Celluloid Saviors: Angels and Reform Politics in Hollywood Film* (2009) and *British Music Videos 1966–2016: Genre, Authenticity and Art* (2020). She recently curated the Thunderbird DVD collection *Power to the People: 200 Landmark British Music Videos* (2018).

**Georgia H. N. Chik** currently serves as a Research Assistant in the Centre for Youth Studies, Hong Kong Institute of Asia-Pacific Studies at the Chinese University of Hong Kong. She received a BA in cultural management from the same university and a Juris Doctor from the University of Hong Kong. Her research interests focus on creative industries, intellectual property, and cultural policy.

**Erin Copple Smith** is Associate Professor of Media Studies at Austin College in Sherman, Texas, where she teaches courses on the media industries, youth media, gender and sexuality, television, and stardom, among others. Her work has been published in *Very Special Episodes: Televising Industrial and Social Change* (2021), *From Networks to Netflix: A Guide to Changing Channels* (2018), and *Beyond Prime Time: TV Formats in the Post-Network Era* (2009).

**David Craig** is a Clinical Professor at the University of Southern California (USC) in the Annenberg School for Communication and Journalism. In the graduate program for communication management, he has taught courses in media industries and management for over a decade. His books include co-authoring *Social Media Entertainment* (2019) and *Wanghong as Social Media Entertainment in China* (2021), and co-editing *Creator Culture: An Introduction to Global Social Media Entertainment* (2021). Prior to USC, he was a veteran Hollywood producer and former television executive responsible for over 30 projects that garnered in excess of 70 Emmy, Peabody, and Golden Globe nominations.

**Stuart Cunningham** is Distinguished Emeritus Professor, Queensland University of Technology. He is well known for his research on topics such as emerging social media industries, the creative industries, and media and cultural policy. Recent books are *Media Economics* (with Terry Flew and Adam Swift, 2015) *Social Media Entertainment: The New Intersection of Hollywood and Silicon Valley* (with David Craig, 2019), *A Research Agenda for Creative Industries* (edited with Terry Flew, 2019), *Wanghong as Social Media Entertainment in China* (with David Craig and Jian Lin, 2021) and *Creator Culture: Studying the Global Social Media Entertainment Industry* (edited with David Craig, 2021). In 2015, he was invested as a Member of the Order of Australia for "significant service to higher education, particularly to the study of media and communications, as an academic and researcher."

**Roei Davidson** is Senior Lecturer in the Department of Communication at the University of Haifa. He studies how economic forces and technological infrastructures are implicated in cultural production. His recent publications include: "Proactive Ephemerality: How Journalists Use Automated and Manual Tweet Deletion to Minimize Risk and Its Consequences for Social Media as a Public Archive" (2020, with Sharon Ringel) in *New Media and Society*, and "The

Role of Platforms in Fulfilling the Potential of Crowdfunding as an Alternative Decentralized Arena for Cultural Financing" (2019) in *Law and Ethics in Human Rights*.

**Gillian Doyle** is Professor of Media Economics at the Centre for Cultural Policy Research, University of Glasgow where she directs the MSc in Media Management. Her research on media economics and policy and on digitization has been published in several languages. Gillian is a former President of the Association for Cultural Economics International. A member of the European Expert Network on Culture and Audiovisual, she has carried out, supervised, and contributed to a number of studies on media economics and media policy funded by bodies including the UK Research Councils, the European Commission, the Organisation for Economic Co-operation and Development (OECD), and the Council of Europe.

**Philip Drake** is Professor of Media and Creative Industries and Head of Education in the Faculty of Arts and Humanities at Manchester Metropolitan University. He has published widely on media industries, including recently on film distribution, video-on-demand, European co-productions, independent film, and policy and practice in the creative industries, as well as co-editing *Hollywood and Law* (2015). He has also advised the Council of Europe on film funding and recently directed a collaborative media industry research project on independent film distribution and video-on-demand.

**Andrea Esser** is Emerita Professor of Media and Globalization at Roehampton University, and is a Visiting Professor at King's College London and Director of the *Media Across Borders* network funded by the Arts and Humanities Research Council. Her research considers all aspects of television's inter- and transnationalization: production networks, program distribution, TV format adaptation, and the consumption and reception of screen content across borders. She has published widely in peer-reviewed journals and anthologies and has edited three special journal issues on television formats along with the collection *Media Across Borders: Localising TV, Film and Video Games* (2016, with Iain R. Smith, Miguel Á. Bernal-Merino).

**Elizabeth Evans** is Associate Professor of Film and Television Studies at the University of Nottingham. Her research examines the social, industrial, and technological factors that shape (and are shaped by) audiences' experiences of media texts. She is the author of *Understanding Engagement in Transmedia Culture* (2019) and *Transmedia Television: Audiences, New Media and Daily Life* (2011).

**Matthew Freeman** is Reader in Multiplatform Media at Bath Spa University. He is Co-Director of the Centre for Media Research. His research concentrates on cultures of media production across the borders of platforms, cultures, industries, and history, publishing extensively on the cultural histories and industrial workings of transmediality. He has also published on such topics as media branding, convergence cultures, and methodological approaches to media industry studies.

**Anthony Y. H. Fung** is a Professor in the School of Journalism and Communication at the Chinese University of Hong Kong. He is also a Professor in the School of Art and Communication at Beijing Normal University. His research interests and teaching focus on popular culture and cultural studies, popular music, gender and youth identity, cultural industries and policy, and digital media studies. He has published widely in international journals and authored or edited more than 20 Chinese and English books. His most recent books are *Youth*

*Cultures in China* (2016, with Jeroen de Kloet), *Global Game Industries and Cultural Policy* (2016), *Cultural Policy and East Asian Rivalry: The Hong Kong Game Industry* (2018), and *Made in Hong Kong: Studies in Popular Music* (2020).

**Tejaswini Ganti** is Associate Professor of Anthropology and core faculty in the Program in Culture and Media at New York University. She has been conducting research about the social world and filmmaking practices of the Hindi film industry since 1996 and is the author of *Producing Bollywood: Inside the Contemporary Hindi Film Industry* (2012) and *Bollywood: A Guidebook to Popular Hindi Cinema* (2004 and 2013, 2nd ed.). Her current research examines the politics of language and translation within the Mumbai media world; the formalization and professionalization of film training through film schools in India; and a social history of Indian cinema in the United States.

**Paul Grainge** is Professor of Film and Television Studies at the University of Nottingham. His books include *TV and Cars* (2022), *Promotional Screen Industries* (2015, with Catherine Johnson), *Brand Hollywood: Selling Entertainment in a Global Media Age* (2008), and *Monochrome Memories* (2002), and the edited collections *Ephemeral Media: Transitory Screen Culture from Television to YouTube* (2011), *Film Histories* (2007, with Mark Jancovich and Sharon Monteith), and *Memory and Popular Film* (2003). His current project examines media industry metaphor.

**Jonathan Hardy** is Professor of Communications and Media at the University of the Arts London. He writes and comments on media industries, media and advertising, communications regulation, and international media systems. His books include *Branded Content: the Fateful Merging of Media and Marketing* (2021), *Critical Political Economy of the Media* (2014), *Cross-Media Promotion* (2010), and *Western Media Systems* (2008). He is co-editor of *The Advertising Handbook* (2018) and is series editor of Routledge Critical Advertising Studies. He is a member of the editorial boards of *Digital Journalism*, *Political Economy of Communication*, *Mediterranean Journal of Communication*, and *TripleC: Communication, Capitalism & Critique*.

**David Hesmondhalgh** is Professor of Media, Music, and Culture at the University of Leeds. He is the author of *The Cultural Industries* (2019, 4th ed.), *Why Music Matters* (2013), and coauthor of *Creative Labor: Media Work in Three Cultural Industries* (2010, with Sarah Baker) and *Culture, Economy and Politics: The Case of New Labour* (2015, with Kate Oakley, David Lee, and Melissa Nisbett). He is also editor or co-editor of eight other books or special journal issues, including: a 2014 special issue of *Popular Communication* (with Anamik Saha) on "Race, Ethnicity and Cultural Production", *The Media and Social Theory* (2008, with Jason Toynbee), and *Media and Society* (2019, 6th ed., with James Curran).

**Annette Hill** is a Professor of Media and Communication at Lund University and Visiting Professor at King's College London. Her research focuses on audiences and popular culture, with interests in media engagement, everyday life, genres, production studies, and cultures of viewing. She is the author of nine books and many articles and book chapters that address varieties of engagement with reality television, news and documentary, television drama, entertainment formats, live events and sports entertainment, film violence, and media ethics.

**Jennifer Holt** is Associate Professor of Film and Media Studies at the University of California, Santa Barbara, and a Fellow with the Center for Democracy and Technology in Washington, DC. She is the author of *Empires of Entertainment: Media Industries and the Politics of Deregulation,*

*1980–1996* (2011) and co-editor of *Distribution Revolution: Conversations about the Digital Future of Film and Television* (2014, with Michael Curtin and Kevin Sanson), *Connected Viewing: Selling, Streaming and Sharing Media in the Digital Age* (2013, with Kevin Sanson), and *Media Industries: History, Theory, Method* (2009, with Alisa Perren). She is also a co-founder of the *Media Industries* journal.

**Deborah L. Jaramillo** is Associate Professor of Television Studies in the Department of Film and Television at Boston University. She is the author of *The Television Code: Regulating the Screen to Safeguard the Industry* (2018), an examination of the circumstances that prompted the National Association of Broadcasters to implement a document of self-regulatory standards in 1952. Her first book, *Ugly War, Pretty Package: How CNN and Fox News Made the Invasion of Iraq High Concept* (2006), studied the narrativization, stylization, and marketing of the United States military's invasion of Iraq in 2003.

**Catherine Johnson** is Professor of Media and Communications at the University of Huddersfield. She is the author of *Online TV* (2019), *Promotional Screen Industries* (2015, with Paul Grainge), *Branding Television* (2012), and *Telefantasy* (2005), and the co-editor of *Transnational Television History* (2012, with Andreas Fickers) and *ITV Cultures* (2005, with Rob Turnock).

**Michael Keane** is Distinguished Professor in the State Key Laboratory of Media Convergence and Communication, Chinese University of Communication, and Adjunct Professor of Chinese Media at Queensland University of Technology. His key research interests are digital transformation in China; East Asian cultural and media policy; television in China; and creative industries and cultural export strategies in China and East Asia.

**Helen W. Kennedy** is Professor of Creative and Cultural Industries at Nottingham University. Her research interests are feminist interventions into digital games culture, live cinema, and the broader ludification of cultural experiences. She has been awarded significant UK Research Council funding to investigate new technologies and new creative practices in immersive experience design.

**Finola Kerrigan** is Professor of Marketing and Director of the Fashion Business Research Centre at the London College of Fashion, University of the Arts. Her research on marketing and consumption in the arts has been published in leading international journals. She is the author of *Film Marketing* (2010 and 2017, 2nd ed.) and has edited a number of collections on arts marketing.

**Geoff King** is Professor of Film Studies at Brunel University London. He is the author of books on American independent cinema including *American Independent Cinema* (2005), *Indiewood, USA: Where Hollywood Meets Independent Cinema* (2009), and *Indie 2.0: Continuity and Change in Contemporary American Indie Film* (2014). His most recent books are *Quality Hollywood: Markers of Distinction in Contemporary Studio Film* (2016), *Positioning Art Cinema: Film and Cultural Value* (2019), and *The Cinema of Discomfort: Disquieting, Awkward and Uncomfortable Experiences in Contemporary Art and Indie Film* (2021).

**Andrew Leyshon** is Emeritus Professor of Economic Geography at the University of Nottingham. Research has focused on money and finance, the musical economy, and the emergence of diverse economies. His books include: *Reformatted: Code, Networks and the Transformation of the Music Industry* (2014) explores how peer-to-peer (P2P) networks and MP3 software helped remake the musical economy; *Money/Space: Geographies of Monetary Transformation* (1997, with Nigel Thrift) argued that not only does money have a geography, but that it is inherently geographical, and *Alternative Economic Spaces* (2003, with Roger Lee and Colin Williams) sought to account for the diverse ways in which "alternative" economies have emerged within contemporary capitalism.

**Ramon Lobato** is Associate Professor in the School of Media and Communication at RMIT University, Melbourne. His research interests include video services, digital distribution, and piracy. Ramon is the author of *Shadow Economies of Cinema* (2012), *The Informal Media Economy* (2015, with Julian Thomas), and *Netflix Nations: The Geography of Digital Distribution* (2019).

**Paul McDonald** is Professor of Media Industries at King's College London. He recently co-edited *Digital Media Distribution: Portals, Platforms, Pipelines* (2021 with Courtney Brannon Donoghue and Timothy Havens). Alongside authoring or editing major works in the field, he's contributed to advancing critical studies of media industries by launching the *Media Industries* conferences, being a founding member of the Editorial Collective for the journal *Media Industries*, co-editing (which Michael Curtin) the International Screen Industries book series from the British Film Institute, and establishing specialized media industries networks within the Society for Cinema and Media Studies (SCMS) and the European Network of Cinema and Media Studies (NECS). Before entering academia, he worked in various areas of the media industries, with periods spent as an actor, media analyst, and in aspects of animated film production, art book publishing, film exhibition, and studio photography.

**Lee McGuigan** is an Assistant Professor in the Hussman School of Journalism and Media at the University of North Carolina at Chapel Hill. His research on various entanglements of information, technology, markets, and culture appears in venues such as *New Media & Society*, *Critical Studies in Media Communication*, the *Journal of Consumer Culture*, *Media, Culture, & Society*, and *Television & New Media*. He is co-editor of *The Audience Commodity in a Digital Age*, published in 2014 by Peter Lang. Lee completed a PhD at the University of Pennsylvania's Annenberg School for Communication in 2018.

**Oren Meyers** is Associate Professor and Chair of the Department of Communication, University of Haifa. His main areas of research include journalistic work, collective memory, and media representations of civil–military relations. His recent publications include: "Mnemonic Newswork: Exploring the Role of Journalism in the Rereading of National Pasts" (2018) and "The Critical Potential of Commemorative Journalism" (2019).

**Maria Michalis** is Reader in Communication Policy and Deputy Director of the Communication and Media Research Institute (CAMRI) at the University of Westminster, London. Her main research interests are television, telecommunications, and internet policy. She is author of *Governing European Communications* (2007) and has published numerous refereed academic articles and book chapters. Her recent work focuses on the convergence between television and the internet, and the future of public service broadcasting. She also recently completed working on the European Union (EU)-funded project NetCommons, which examined network infrastructure as commons and looked into community networks. Maria has presented her research at national, European, and international policy fora.

**Jade L. Miller** is Associate Professor of Communication Studies at Wilfrid Laurier University in Waterloo, Ontario, Canada. She works on the political economy of creative production, global media flows, and media industries. Her first book, *Nollywood Central* (2016), was on the industrial structure and global connections of the Nigerian video industry.

**Graham Murdock** is Emeritus Professor of Culture and Economy at Loughborough University. He was a founding member of the pioneering Leicester Centre for Mass Communication Research where he helped develop a distinctive critical political economy of media industries and production. He has held visiting professorships at the Universities of Auckland, California at San Diego, Mexico City, Curtin, Bergen, the Free University of Brussels, and Stockholm, and taught widely across China. His work has been translated into 21 languages. His recent books include, as co-editor, *Money Talks: Media, Markets, Crisis* (2015, with Jostein Gripsrud) and *Carbon Capitalism and Communication: Confronting Climate Change* (2017, with Benedetta Brevini).

**Lydia Papadimitriou** is Reader in Film Studies at Liverpool John Moores University. She has published extensively on different aspects of Greek and Balkan cinema, often with an emphasis on film industry-related questions. She is principal editor of the *Journal of Greek Media and Culture*. Most recently, she co-edited *Contemporary Balkan Cinema: Transnational Exchanges and Global Circuits* (2020).

**Alisa Perren** is Associate Professor in the Department of Radio-Television-Film and Co-Director of the Center for Entertainment and Media Industries at the University of Texas at Austin. She is author of *Indie, Inc.: Miramax and the Transformation of Hollywood in the 1990s* (2012), co-author of *The American Comic Book Industry and Hollywood* (2021, with Gregory Steirer), co-editor of *Media Industries: History, Theory, and Method* (2009, with Jennifer Holt), and co-founder and editorial collective member of the journal *Media Industries*.

**Angus Phillips** is Professor of Publishing and Director of the Oxford International Centre for Publishing at Oxford Brookes University. He formerly worked in the publishing industry as a trade editor at Oxford University Press. He has delivered talks and lectures about publishing all over the world including across Europe and in China and South America, and has carried out consultancy and training work with international publishers. He is on the European Advisory Board of Princeton University Press and was a judge for *The Bookseller* industry awards for four years in a row. With Michael Bhaskar, he is the editor of *The Oxford Handbook of Publishing* (2019) and author of a number of books including *Turning the Page* (2014) and *Inside Book Publishing* (2019, 6th ed., with Giles Clark). He is the editor of the journal *Logos* and in 2015 published a book of selected articles from the journal's history – *The Cottage by the Highway and Other Essays on Publishing: 25 Years of Logos*.

**Jennifer Porst** is an Assistant Professor in the Department of Media Arts at the University of North Texas. Her work has appeared in publications such as *Television and New Media* and *Hollywood and the Law* (2015). She is the author of *Broadcasting Hollywood: The Struggle Over Feature Films on Early TV* (2021), and co-editor (with Jonathan Cohn) of *Very Special Episodes: Televising Industrial and Social Change* (2021).

**Anna Potter** is Associate Professor in the School of Business and Creative Industries at the University of the Sunshine Coast, Queensland, Australia. She is the author of *Creativity, Culture,* *and Commerce: Producing Australian Children's Television with Public Value* (2015) and *Producing Children's Television in the On-Demand Age* (2020).

**Eva Novrup Redvall** is Associate Professor at the University of Copenhagen where she is head of the Section for Film Studies and Creative Media Industries. Her research focuses on film and television screenwriting and production, particularly in the Nordic media industries. She has published widely in the field of media industry studies, including the monograph *Writing and Producing Television Drama in Denmark: From* The Kingdom *to* The Killing (2013) and co-editing the collection *European Film and Television Co-production: Policy and Practice* (2018, with Julia Hammett-Jamart and Petar Mitric).

**Ulrike Rohn** is Professor of Media Management and Economics at Tallinn University, Estonia, where she works at the Baltic Film, Media, Arts and Communication School (BFM), and where she co-leads the Centre of Excellence in Media Innovation and Digital Culture (MEDIT). Dr. Rohn is the President of the *European Media Management Association* (emma, 2016–2021) and Associate Editor of the *Journal of Media Business Studies*. She is also the co-editor for the *Springer Series in Media Industries*. Dr. Rohn leads the ScreenME-Net, an international consortium with the aim to improve scholarship on screen media entrepreneurship that is funded through the European Commission's Horizon2020/Twinning framework.

**Anamik Saha** is Senior Lecturer in the Department of Media, Communications and Cultural Studies at Goldsmiths, University of London. His research interests are in race and the media, with a particular focus on cultural production and the cultural industries, and issues of "diversity." He is the author of *Race and the Cultural Industries* (2018). In 2019, he received an Arts and Humanities Research Council Leadership Fellow grant for a project titled "Rethinking Diversity in Publishing", which led to a report of the same name published by Goldsmiths Press in June 2020. Anamik is an editor of the *European Journal of Cultural Studies*. His latest book titled *Race, Culture, Media* was published in Spring 2021.

**Kevin Sanson** is Associate Professor in the School of Communication and a Chief Investigator in the Digital Media Research Centre's Transforming Media Industries Research Group at Queensland University of Technology. He also serves as co-founder and editor of *Media Industries*, the first open access, peer-reviewed academic journal for critical media industries research. His own research focuses on the film and television industries, especially labor practices and globalization.

**Steven Secular** is Faculty Associate in Film and Media Studies at Arizona State University. His research focuses on the globalization and digitization of the sports media industry. His upcoming book, *The House That Hoops Built* (University of Illinois Press), examines the evolving relationship between sports and media through the case of the National Basketball Association and its global investments in emerging media technologies.

**Paul Smith** is Associate Professor of Media and Communication at the Leicester Media School, De Montfort University, Leicester. He has published widely on sports rights, including articles in the *European Journal of Communication* and *Media, Culture and Society*, and the book *The Political Economy of Television Sports Rights* (2013, with Petros Iosifidis and Tom Evens).

**Andrew Spicer** is Professor of Cultural Production at the University of the West of England. His books include *The Man Who Got Carter: Michael Klinger, Independent Production and the*

*British Film Industry 1960–1980* (2013, with A. T. McKenna). He co-edited *Beyond the Bottom Line: The Producer in Film and Television Studies* (2014, with A. T. McKenna and Christopher Meir), and is currently working on *Sean Connery: Acting, Stardom and National Identity* and leading a research project investigating regional screen industries.

**Jeanette Steemers** is Professor of Culture, Media, and Creative Industries at King's College London where she is Vice Dean Research in the Faculty of Arts and Humanities. After working for CIT Research, a research company, and HIT Entertainment, an international distributor of children's content, she joined academia in 1993. Her many publications on children's media include *Creating Preschool Television* (2010), *Children's TV and Digital Media in the Arab World* (2017, with Naomi Sakr), and *Screen Media for Arab and European Children* (2019, with Naomi Sakr). Her work has been funded by the British Academy, the Leverhulme Trust, and the Arts and Humanities Research Council.

**Gregory Steirer** is Associate Professor of English and Film and Media Studies at Dickinson College. He is currently completing a monograph, funded in part by the National Endowment for the Humanities, on US intellectual property law and the origins of the narrative-based franchise. He is coauthor of *The American Comic Book Industry and Hollywood* (2021, with Alisa Perren).

**Katharina Stolley** is a doctoral researcher in the Department of Marketing at the Birmingham Business School, University of Birmingham. She holds a BA (Hons) in Business Studies and International Management and an MSc in Consumer Behaviour. Her research interests lie in the areas of marketing within the creative and cultural industries, the production and consumption of cultural artifacts, marketing communications, and branding. She is currently investigating how branded entertainment and new product placement modalities are transforming the creative industries. Prior to commencing her studies, she worked in the creative industries and in marketing across a range of industries.

**Wendy Su** is Associate Professor of the Department of Media and Cultural Studies at the University of California Riverside. She is the author of *China's Encounter with Global Hollywood: Cultural Policy and the Film Industry, 1994–2013* (2016) and co-editor of *Asia-Pacific Film Co-productions: Theory, Industry and Aesthetics* (2019, with Dal Yong Jin).

**Petr Szczepanik** is an Associate Professor at Charles University in Prague. His current research focuses on East-Central European screen industries, production cultures, and public service media in the internet era. His historical research on the state socialist mode of film production was published in *Behind the Screen: Inside European Production Culture* (2013, co-edited with Patrick Vonderau).

**Yannis Tzioumakis** is Reader in Film and Media Industries at the University of Liverpool. He is the author of five books, most recently *Acting Indie: Industry, Aesthetics, Performance* (2020, co-authored with Cynthia Baron) and co-editor of six collections of essays, most recently *United Artists* (2020, co-edited with Peter Krämer, Gary Needham, and Tino Balio). Yannis also co-edits two book series: the Routledge Hollywood Centenary and Cinema and Youth Cultures.

**Pieter Verdegem** is Senior Lecturer in Media Theory in the Westminster School of Media and Communication and a member of the Communication and Media Research Institute (CAMRI), University of Westminster. His research investigates the political economy of digital media and the impact of digital technologies on society. He has published in journals such as *New Media & Society, Information, Communication & Society, European Journal of Communication, Telecommunications Policy, Government Information Quarterly.* He is editor of *AI for Everyone? Critical Perspectives*, published in 2021 by University of Westminster Press. He is a Senior Fellow of the Higher Education Academy.

**M. Bjørn von Rimscha** is Professor of Media Business and Head of the Communication Department at the Johannes Gutenberg University Mainz, Germany. His research interest is in structural, organizational, and individual drivers of (entertainment-)media production. His work has been published in communication as well as in media business journals. He has served on the board of the European Media Management Association and is associate editor of the *Journal of Media Business Studies*.

**Patrick Vonderau** is Professor of Media and Communication Studies at the University of Halle. His most recent book publications include the co-authored *Advertising and the Transformation of Screen Cultures* (2021, with Bo Florin and Yvonne Zimmermann) and *Spotify Teardown: Inside the Black Box of Streaming Music* (2019, with Maria Eriksson, Rasmus Fleischer, Anna Johansson, and Pelle Snickars). He is a co-founder of the European Network for Cinema and Media Studies (NECS).

**Janet Wasko** is Professor in Media Studies at the University of Oregon. She is author or editor of 22 books including *MEDIA: A Trandisciplinary Inquiry* (2021, with Jeremy Swartz), *Understanding Disney: The Manufacture of Fantasy* (2020, 2nd ed.), *A Companion to Television* (2020, 2nd ed., with Eileen R. Meehan), *Global Media Giants* (2017, with Benjamin Birkinbine and Rodrigo Gómez), and *The Handbook of Political Economy of Communications* (2011, with Graham Murdock and Helena Sousa). She served as President of the International Association for Media and Communication Research (2012–2020).

**Allan Watson** is a Senior Lecturer in Human Geography at Loughborough University and the theme lead for Culture, Economy, and Policy in the University's Centre for Research in Communication and Culture. Allan has published widely in leading journals on the economic geography and cultural economy of the music industry, with his most recent research focusing on platformization and the development of a MusicTech innovation ecosystem. Allan is author of *Cultural Production in and Beyond the Recording Studio* (2014), and co-editor of *Rethinking Creative Cities Policy: Invisible Agents and Hidden Protagonists* (2015, with Calvin Taylor) and *Music Cities: Evaluating a Global Policy Concept* (2020, with Christina Ballico).

**Justin Wyatt** is Associate Professor of Film/Media, Journalism and Communication Studies at the University of Rhode Island. He is the author of *High Concept: Movies and Marketing in Hollywood* (1994) and *The Virgin Suicides: Reverie, Sorrow and Young Love* (2018) and co-editor of *Contemporary American Independent Film: From the Margins to the Mainstream* (2004, with Chris Holmlund), and *ReFocus: The Later Films and Legacy of Robert Altman* (2021, with Lisa Dombrowski). From 2000 to 2015, he worked professionally in the television industry leading media market research initiatives.

**Cagri Yalkin** is Associate Professor of Marketing at Middle East Technical University, Northern Cyprus. Her research on consumer behavior, digital marketing, and brand management has been published in journals such as the *Journal of Business Research, European Management Review,*

*New Media and Society*, and the *Journal of Marketing Management*. She has a PhD in marketing from Warwick Business School.

**Anna Zoellner** is a Lecturer at the School of Media and Communication, University of Leeds, with a professional background in film and television production. Her research interests lie at the intersection of media industries, media production studies, cultural labor research, and television studies with a methodological interest in ethnography and internationally comparative research. She has published in journals such as *Mass Communication and Society*, *Journal for the Study of British Cultures*, *Journal of Media Practice* and the *International Journal of Communication*, and in several anthologies.

# ACKNOWLEDGMENTS

Everyone who input to this volume did so in extraordinary circumstances as we tackled working around the everyday impacts of the COVID-19 pandemic. Faced with these challenges, the commitment of authors in getting this volume through to completion is truly remarkable. A great many thanks to all the contributing authors; it was a pleasure working with you and I learnt so much from your scholarship. Your expertise and insight have made the *Companion* such a valuable project. At Routledge, I'm deeply grateful to Natalie Foster for the invite to put together the *Companion* in the first place, and to Jennifer Vennall for coordinating production of the finished text. And no part of this whole venture would have been possible without the love, support, and continuing patience of the ever wonderful Tamar.

Paul

# MEDIA, INDUSTRIES, RESEARCH

## Problematizing the field

*Paul McDonald*

Media industries research addresses an object that is expansive, heterogeneous, and forever changeable. A composite of two plural nouns, "media industries" immediately communicates the need to contemplate multiplicity. It is a label commonly applied to collectively classify the industries of publishing, journalism (or what in the not-too-distant past would sometimes be called "the press"), cinema, radio, television, video, electronic games, and social media. What differentiates these from other industry sectors is how they form a sphere of creative, communicative, and commercial activity focused on the production, dissemination, and offering of *cultural outputs*: e.g. books, newspapers, and radio or television programs. It is this defining characteristic, the production of cultural forms, that places media industries within the wider gamut of the "cultural industries." Any sense of the media as forming a coherent sector, however, immediately disappears once differences between and within industries are observed with regard to things like their structural organization, forms of output, skills specializations, or business models.

Media industries provide an unstable object for research for they become meeting points where the interests of multiple stakeholders – consumers, labor, owners, et cetera – congregate and compete. They represent an arena of cultural and economic power, enacted at micro- and macro-scales, in which participants contest the range of cultural expressions and meanings generated, and how the commercial value of culture should be accumulated and invested. Furthermore, the object shifts as contextual factors distinguish the conditions in which media industries operate. Spatial factors site or locate media industries within differing economic and political systems, and spaces of cultural practice. Equally, at any moment, temporal factors see industries negotiating the double pull of continuity and change. Media change cannot be generalized because the causes, outcomes, and scales are always multifarious and multilayered, occurring unevenly and asynchronously across industries.

Media industries research therefore constantly addresses the fundamental challenge of understanding, analytically interrogating, and critically evaluating a mutable target. It is unsurprising, therefore, that the associated body of scholarship is characterized by conceptual, perspectival, analytical, and methodological diversity. Reading key overviews (e.g., Albarran, Jung, and Mierzejewskam 2018; Deuze and Prenger 2019; Doyle 2013; Herbert, Lotz, and Punathambekar 2020; Holt and Perren 2009; Mayer, Banks, and Caldwell 2009; Paterson,

DOI: 10.4324/9780429275340-1

Lee, Saha, and Zoellner 2016; Rohn and Evens 2020; Szczepanik and Vonderau 2013), it is immediately clear that research on media industries does not cohere into a "discipline," and nor should it, for one of the key strengths of studies conducted in this area is how these represent interdisciplinary inquiry. Researchers examining media industries adopt interdisciplinary ways of working, more from pragmatic necessity than a principled intellectual commitment to extending the scope of knowledge, for no one set of concepts or explanatory frameworks can universally account for how and why media industries work in the ways they do. Researchers take inspiration and mix insights gleaned from anthropology, business and management, computer science, economics, history, human and urban geography, law, languages and literatures, politics, and sociology. Methodologically, researchers might work with interviews, physical world or online ethnography, archival documentation, data scraping, and discourse analysis. These influences and ways of working have variously coalesced in forming different traditions of inquiry, including the critical political economy of communications, media economics, media management, studies of production cultures, policy studies, and media industry historiography. Research examining media industries is therefore to be found in many of branches of knowledge, even if researchers don't necessarily self-identify their work under label such as "media industries research" or "media industry studies."

Within these traditions, differences inevitably arise over the chosen foci. Points of emphasis can be placed on the organizing logics and structures of industries; policy and regulation; work worlds of media labor; trends in media markets; the practices and processes of producing, disseminating, and offering media; the environmental impacts of media output; technological innovation and disruption; transnational flows of media products; or the spatial clustering of media businesses. Given the diversities at play, therefore, it can be best to think of media industries research as a "field," a particular space of scholarly inquiry in which differing research perspectives and agendas congregate but without cohering. As the preceding discussion no doubt suggests, this is a field that is certainly not "settled."

The *Routledge Companion to Media Industries* therefore provides a route into grasping just some of the research directions taken in this field. Contributors bring particular areas of expertise to their analyses and arguments, representing something of the intellectual diversity characterizing the field. Chapters vary between the media examined and the perspectives taken. Setting the stage for the chapters that follow, and in the interests of encouraging future work, the following discussion problematizes the respective contours of "media," "industries," and "research." This is done in the spirit that there is everything to gain from ensuring media industries research does not seek to settle and stabilize, but rather maintains itself as a dynamic field of inquiry that is self-reflexively critical of its foci and purposes.

## Media industries in the digital economy

What are the "media" of media industries research? Among the wealth of literature, industry-specific studies have addressed book publishing, news, adult entertainment, advertising, music, radio, film, television, home video, and digital gaming. In some cases, studies explore industries as sites of cross-media interactions, for example the film music industry of Bollywood, and junctures between Hollywood film and the industries of digital games and comics.

This suggests the field is broad, and yet research interventions can productively expose its limits. Revisionist histories may draw attention to how the body of scholarship has constructed absences, for example by focusing on the otherwise overlooked presences of people of color (Chambers 2008) or women (Hill 2016) in the media workforce. Companies and organizations inevitably feature as key points of reference in media industries research, so that things like industry structures, market dynamics, business models, and regulatory frameworks become the subject of inquiry. By focusing on those employed in the media, however, critical studies of media labor push our understandings of media industries beyond stories of corporations (Curtin and Sanson 2016; Hesmondhalgh and Baker 2011), including making visible forms of "invisible labor" (Mayer 2011). Similarly, work on "production cultures" or "production studies" view media industries from below, emphasizing the human, the everyday and "ordinary" rather than the corporate, the exceptional, and elite (Caldwell 2008; Szczepanik and Vonderau 2013). These and other forms of intervention do more than simply enlarge the field: they test the parameters of knowledge, and in so doing contribute toward fundamentally recasting how "industry" and "media" are constituted as objects of inquiry.

Challenges to those terms particularly come into play whenever research seeks to conceptualize and assess change, moments when the composition and meanings of industry and media are transformed. Given the mutability of the media industries and the breadth of work produced, any generalization becomes a hostage to fortune. Yet in the most abstract terms, the field has generated a sizable body of scholarship from a common conception of media-as-industry resting on a few premises. First, while the forms vary, media industries operate as contexts for producing, disseminating, and exploiting certain types of cultural output – for example, novels, music recordings, radio, or television programs – and so in other terms media industries might be described as "content industries." Second, although key areas of media production operate by public service or non-profit principles, otherwise the media are presumed to follow commercial principles, "monetizing" content by either direct sales of individualized goods (e.g., books, music downloads), paid access to one-off events (e.g., cinema tickets) or bundles of content (e.g., pay-TV subscriptions), and packaging the attention of media consumers for sale to advertisers. Third, intellectual property laws, specifically copyright, provide the statutory mechanism for controlling the circulation and commercial exploitation of content, so that in legal terms, media industries are implicitly "copyright industries." Fourth, media industries form distinct business communities of small, medium, and large enterprises, becoming participants in the "the media" because their work is principally directed toward making and marketizing media content. Fifth, media industries represent a sphere of professionalized labor, peopled by creative, administrative, and managerial specialists hired and remunerated for their skills and knowledges. Finally, in media markets, members of the public become "consumers," reached through a one-way, one-to-many model of communication by either the reproduction of artifacts or communication signals, and creating the collective constructs of a "readership," "listenership," "audience" or "users," even if these can take the forms of tightly defined "niches" rather than an undifferentiated "mass."

This version of media-as-industry has provided the stimulus for a significant body of excellent research, and as the characteristics remain fully applicable to many aspects of the media today, they continue to inform future work. Significant developments in the media landscape, however, have challenged certain of these premises, so that the field must undergo processes of reconfiguring and retheorization. In recent years, this has been most evident with how media industries research has developed an agenda addressing the changes brought about by the integration of digital technologies into media industries. Here, the challenge has been to think through and assess how technological change, *digitization*, relates to industry change, *digitalization*, and more specifically, how a digitally mediated media economy is illustrative of a broader digital economy.

Accounts vary, but in the most general of terms, the digital economy is understood as how digital information and communication technologies (ICTs) create an environment for multiple forms of economic activity, with that environment largely conducted through the online space of the Internet. On the technical side, the "digital" is marked by the convergence of computing technologies (e.g., personal and business computers, software, servers, data storage), communication devices (e.g., smartphones), and fixed and mobile telecommunication networks. On the business side, the "economy" facilitated through this environment is seen to extend into many sectors, of which media industries represent but one. Still, ambiguities persist over how the digital economy might be theorized. As Tim Jordan (2020: 2) asks:

> When referring to the "new" digital economy are we referring to changes that digital and internet socio-technologies have brought to the existing economy, turning the whole economy into a "digital economy," or does the latter refer to a new kind of economic activity that can be labelled digital.

This is an important consideration, for if thinking about these options just in relation to the media industries, is the research task to understand a wholesale digital makeover of the media economy, or rather to narrow the scope toward recognizing specific and particular ways in which media industries have gone digital?

Jordan cautions that

> Any analysis that effectively collapses the digital economy into the whole economy will have a strong tendency to miss two things: first, the distinctiveness of the digital compared to prior economic processes; second, how much of the preceding economy remains non-digital. The danger is of a kind of selective blindness that sees digital processes everywhere but misses already existing practices.
>
> *p. 2*

Situating media industries within the digital economy, therefore, the test is to recognize distinctiveness – how digital technologies have changed fundamental aspects of the operational conduct and economic activity of media industries – while at the same time noting the persistence and continuation of established practices and players.

When placing media industries in the digital economy, a core consideration is how these industries engage with the online space of the Internet. During the 1990s, popular adoption of the World Wide Web was largely driven by email and a one-way model of information publishing whereby users browsed text and images posted on static webpages. Bandwidth limitations technically hampered opportunities for large-scale relays of sound and images to consumers. During the following decade, several developments came together to change the reach and functionality of the Internet. Fixed broadband improved data speeds to homes, allowing users to be "always online." Speeds also increased in mobile telephony, with commercial third and fourth generation technologies incrementally improving wireless Internet access. Improved data speeds enabled consumer-orientated services for downloading or streaming music, film, television, and games. Furthermore, the Internet of Things (IoT) extended connectivity beyond computers to other "smart" domestic devices, including heating, lighting, and security systems, but also the media-related devices of television receivers, games consoles, and audio speakers. Finally, online communications moved beyond the publishing model, becoming "social" with software tools enabling two-way interactive, collaborative, and participatory activity. This was most visible with the creative, communicative, community-building, and sharing activities afforded by tools for social networking, microblogging, and the posting of text, image, or video user-generated content (UGC).

Engaging with this context has reset the research agenda, triggering numerous lines of inquiry that cumulatively reconceptualize the media industries object. Changes to the corporate landscape are noted as companies from the information technology sector have not only entered the media industries but consolidated positions of power that surpass even the major traditional media incumbents (Barwise and Watkins 2018; de Bustos and Izquierdo-Castillo 2019; Fuchs 2016; Hesmondhalgh and Meier 2018). In many cases, these companies are diversified across multiple types of service and product, variously including cloud storage, operating systems, streaming hardware, and virtual and augmented reality. Their prominence in the digital economy, however, is centered around how they've achieved brand recognition through the provision of software for accessing specific categories of service: web search (Google, Baidu), social media (Facebook, WeChat), video-sharing (YouTube (acquired by Google in 2006), Douyin/TikTok), microblogging (Twitter, Sina Weibo), electronic commerce (Amazon, Alibaba), photo sharing (Instagram (acquired by Facebook in 2012)), or instant messaging (Tencent QQ).

As leading manufacturers of computing and communication devices (smartphones, tablets, etc.), Apple and Xiaomi are regarded as further evidence of how the IT sector asserts influence over the media. Google and Apple's role in intermediating access to media also extends to online stores for downloading software apps for use in their proprietary Android, iOS, and macOS operating systems. Although their main lines of business position them outside the media sector, IT companies may own valuable media assets, for example Tencent's online gaming and video and music offerings, Apple's iTunes download store and Music streaming service, Facebook's video-on-demand outlet Watch, and Amazon's ownership of the live video game streaming service Twitch. Furthermore, it is increasingly difficult to view these companies as somehow distinct from conventional media content industries as they embark on producing original content through subsidiary ventures such as Amazon Studios, Tencent Pictures, or Alibaba Pictures. These developments unsettle the media business community, as some of the most influential players now operating in media remain centered around lines of business that predominantly position them outside the sector.

Although the sources of value previously described still pertain in the media industries, critiques of "datafication" evaluate the new forms of value generated from the large-scale systematic quantification of human life (Mejias and Couldry 2019: 3). Media industries have always gathered market data to represent and commodify members of the public as consumers or audiences, with divergences inevitably arising between audience representations and actual audiences. Multiplication of media technologies and service offerings fragment audiences, further straining the capacity of tradition measurement techniques to convincingly capture the identities and behaviors of media consumers (Napoli 2010). With social media platforms harvesting and monetizing user data on a massive scale, however, attention has turned to data as a key form of capital underpinning the digital economy. In the media industries, predictive analytics for example can inform data-driven decision making in relation to content (assessing the likely market success of creative elements such as script or key talent) or advertising (placement and targeted groups). This in turn expands the corporate landscape of media in another direction, with media companies contracting the specialized services of external firms to gather, process, or store data on their behalf. In large part, the value of data as capital is sustained by media industries adopting collective scientist faith in "big data services [to] raise the possibility if not the reality of giving audiences more concrete forms" (Arsenault 2017: 12).

A further meeting point between information technology and media is what Stuart Cunningham and David Craig (2019: 5) describe as "social media entertainment" (SME), "an emerging proto-industry fueled by professionalizing, previously amateur content creators using new entertainment and communicative formats, including vlogging, gameplay, and do-it-yourself (DIY), to develop potentially sustainable businesses based on significant followings that can exist across multiple platforms." SME is the outcome of "*an interdependent clash of industrial cultures*" (original emphasis, p. 22). On the one hand, from the information technology sector, strategies are adopted of aggressive disruption, rapid prototyping and iteration, advanced measurement metrics and programmatic advertising. On the other, screen industries, in the forms of Hollywood film and television, broadcasting networks, and cable providers, prioritize talent-driven mass media and premium professionally produced content. SME combines technical with commercial affordances. Technically, online services such as YouTube, Facebook, Instagram, Twitter, Snapchat, and Vimeo provide software that integrates social networking features with the posting of video, photo, or text content. These services are then made openly and freely accessible but on condition that users allow data on their personal profiles and behavior to be collected, processed, and sold to third parties for targeted advertising exposure.

SME content may come from several sources, including established media companies, but Cunningham and Craig foreground the importance of "creators" in this context. Creators are "amateurs" in the sense they may have turned to producing media content without any formalized program of skills acquisition or training. In many cases, a creator may at least start out as a one-person operation, individually performing all productive and promotional tasks without the specialized divisions of labor employed in conventional media industries. At the same time, creators become "professional" if their output leads to them earning levels of remuneration to make SME their main or sole livelihood. This depends on a partnership model of remuneration, so that rather than receiving payment for assigning copyright in their work, creators take a share of revenues from the paid advertising appearing on the platforms carrying their content. For the platforms themselves, the absence of intellectual property rights has enabled them to extend services globally, for by avoiding the territorial licensing arrangements applied in conventional media, "SME content is largely 'born global'" (p. 15). SME therefore departs from and tests the vision of media that has underpinned so much media industries research. Not only does SME emerge from a hybrid entertainment business community, in which the IT sector holds equal if not greater influence than media players, but the status of creators confuses distinctions between professionals and amateurs, and the partnership model supports a commercially viable and valuable media market segment which has no dependence on monetizing copyright-controlled content.

In the midst of these changes, however, it is important to recognize the persistence of industry activities based on producing and monetizing established categories of media content. Still, applications of digital technology have changed the forms and status of the media content commodity. With digitization, content becomes code. By transferring things into files, digitization dematerializes content, suggesting a media economy based on exchanging non-physical intangibles. Yet, as data always subsists in material forms, the digital commodity actually rematerializes content (Morris 2015: 14), taking marketable forms as digital artifacts such CDs (Daniel 2019) or file formats like MP3 (Sterne 2012). Pushing this point to a broader level, the digitalization of the media industries might also be understood as a process of rematerialization, as digital technologies have become adopted, integrated, and applied to creative and business practices.

While the Internet proliferates the volume and forms of cultural contents publicly circulated, at the same time the centrality of content as a source of value is to a certain extent demoted. For example, among the most visible signs of how media industries have migrated to the Internet is the provision of streaming services that bundle or aggregate music recordings, television programs, or films. With these, business models have been based around offering consumers paid *access* to, rather than ownership of, content (Spilker 2017). Proliferation of studies examining streaming services should be read as indicative of how the media industries research agenda has broadly turned from addressing conditions of content production, and towards analyzing the conditions shaping access to content.

Distribution has always been key to the monetization of media, yet with the popularization of social media, plus streaming and download services, attention to distributive activities in the media industries has intensified (e.g., Braun 2015; Crisp 2015; Elkins 2019; Johnson 2019; McDonald, Brannon Donoghue, and Havens 2021; Spilker and Colbjørnsen 2020). Instead of regarding distribution simply as a functional bridge between production and consumption, critical studies focus on the processes of, and participants in, distribution as shaping forces in the dissemination of culture. Debates address "distribution" according to its twin meanings: the actions of getting media to end users (how are media distributed?) and the resulting condition of dissemination (when, where, and to whom are media distributed?).

In a closely related line of inquiry, a sizable body of work has focused on theorizing "platforms" as a new breed of corporate entity occupying a central mediating role in the digital economy. This work critically assesses the distinctive logics and consequences of "platformization" (e.g., Evens and Donders 2018; Gillespie 2010; Helmond 2015; Poell, Nieborg, and Van Dijck 2019; Van Dijck, Poell, and De Waal 2018), in some cases examining in depth how specific platforms exemplify those logics (e.g., Eriksson, Fleischer, Johansson, Snickars and Vonderau 2019; Lobato 2019). Studies of platforms not only set out original and important conceptual ground for media industries research but are also representative of how the digital economy problematizes the meanings of media and industry.

While platforms are regarded from many subject fields as central definers of the digital economy, there is considerable slipperiness over just what they define. In part, this is a problem arising from the expansiveness of the term, which is equally deployed to describe online media-related services as varied as social media (Facebook, WeChat), video hosting and sharing (YouTube, Youku), and music or video streaming (Tencent Video, Netflix, Spotify), but also other things like massive open online courses (Coursera), e-commerce marketplaces (Ebay, Etsy), accommodation bookings (AirBnB) and taxi hailing, home food delivery, and cycle or scooter rentals (Uber). Platforms problematize the object of media industries research, for not only do they represent a quite different techno-economic-cultural form to the conventional vision of media previously outlined, but considerable difficulties persist in how to define and conceptualize that form, and then how media platforms might hold a distinctive presence in a more general platformized digital economy.

Definitions of platforms focusing on computational properties highlight web services that combine a user interface – allowing members of the public to create personal profiles and to connect with others – with a programmable Application Programming Interface (API), that is software tools enabling third-party developers to build and run their own applications on top of the platform. If the former connects humans, the latter connects services. When considered in relation to social media, it is the programmability of APIs that marks "the shift from social network *sites* to social media *platforms*" (original emphasis Helmond 2015: 1). Alternatively, economic and business orientated definitions focus on platforms as markets, specifically how platforms function as two-sided and multi-sided markets mediating between users and other parties (e.g., advertisers or developers), plus the network effects obtained as benefits increase for all parties as more people interact (Poell, Nieborg, and Van Dijck 2019: 7). "Platformization" has therefore been described as: "the rise of the platform as the dominant infrastructural and economic model of the social web and its consequences … entail[ing] the extension of social media platforms into the rest of the web and their drive to make external data 'platform ready'"

(Helmond 2015: 1); or, "*the penetration of the infrastructures, economic processes, and governmental frameworks of platforms in different economic sectors and spheres of life*" and "*the reorganization of cultural practices and imaginations arounds platforms*" (original emphasis; Poell, Nieborg and Van Dijck 2019: 5–6).

This definitional work valuably helps toward resolving the question "what is a platform?" yet the all-encompassing pervasiveness of platformization obscures what might be distinctive about platforms in relation to the media industries. Historically tracing how concepts of platform were initially articulated in Japan and the United States, Marc Steinberg (2019) arrives at a tripartite typology. Usages of the term across instances as varied as car manufacturing, computers and game consoles carried a shared meaning: *product-technology platforms* that enable the layering of one product on top of another. *Transactional and mediation platforms* rest on an economic meaning, describing services which act as intermediaries for bringing together money, people, and commodities in multi-sided markets, and generating direct and in-direct network effects (pp. 97–98). In this case, platforms are not intrinsically technological entities, although the Internet is regarded as boosting opportunities for operating services of this type.

With *content platforms*, however, meaning shifts to services facilitating the sharing of UGC, represented by social media networks and video-sharing sites. A platform is understood as "a distribution channel for contents" (p. 90). It is this category that is generally being invoked when platformization is discussed in relation to the media industries. Steinberg finds an elaboration of this usage in a 2015 book from Kawakami Nobuo, founder and CEO of the Japanese video-sharing service Niconico, where a content platform is understood to combine a business model, user base, and means of promotion for advertisers, forming a framework in which to circulate content and control the quality of that content. With their circulatory and quality control functions, platforms implicitly hold power over content (pp. 90–91). As Steinberg emphasizes, the three categories are not mutually exclusive, and so any one example might evince elements from all categories.

When seeking to apply the platform concept to the media industries, there remains considerable potential for confusion. If a content platform is generalized as "a distribution channel for contents," then a wide range of media services can be classified under the heading. Strictly referring to the distribution of UGC, however, usage becomes limited to social media and video-sharing platforms, thereby excluding Internet-enabled channels distributing professionally produced content. As an alternative to platform, to discuss developments in television distribution, Amanda Lotz (2017: 8) proffers "portal" as a descriptor for "the crucial intermediary services that collect, curate, and distribute television programming via internet distribution." As Lotz notes, "internet-distributed television" departs from the linearity of broadcast schedules, instead offering aggregated bundles of programming that can be accessed on-demand, supported by a subscriber business model. Yet internet television distribution is not intrinsically tied to that financial model, and so a broader understanding is offered by Catherine Johnson when she describes "online television" as "*services that facilitate the viewing of editorially selected audiovisual content through internet-enabled devices*" (original emphasis, 2019: 1; see also Johnson in this volume).

In their respective ways, Lotz and Johnson are describing a form of television distribution that is not only distinguishable from that of broadcasting and cable channels, but by disseminating long-form, professional-produced, IP-protected content, is also distinguishable from the types of short-form, amateur-produced, non-IP content that most frequently characterize UGC. Furthermore, subscription-video-on-demand services and the online television portals offered by broadcast networks or cable/satellite providers represent only part of the online distributive environment. In addition to these options, Ramon Lobato (2019: 7–8) points out that television programming or television like content is now disseminated across a broader "distribution ecology," including services offering transactional models for short-term renting or purchasing content, free and advertising-supported sharing of professional and amateur-produced video, unauthorized streaming or file-hosting, and linear live streaming.

Lobato is certainly not suggesting any or all of these options be regarded as platforms, and yet they fulfill a basic definition of content platforms. Considerably terminological confusion therefore persists over what "platform" specifically refers to when applied to media. Returning to the caveats raised by Jordan, attention to the form of platforms certainly provides theoretical ground (maybe a "platform"?) for recognizing the distinctiveness of a digitally mediated media economy. Yet, while distinctions between product technology, transactional/mediation, and content help to disambiguate the meanings of "platform," the content platform category alone might be stretched so far that it loses sight of distinctive differences in distributive channels. In which case, there is continuing value in not only asking "what is a platform?" but in also querying "how is a platform being understood in this specific context?"

The intervention of platform studies into media industries research necessitates a larger reflection on how industry change is conceptualized. Again, with Jordan's cautions in mind, an approach to media industries research focused on seeing digital innovation everywhere can lead to selective disregard for the continuance and resilience of existing industry practices. With terms like "digitization," "digitalization," or "platformization," the "-ization" suffix not only implies a causal relationship – X is "-ized" by Y – but also a larger narrative of linear transition from one state to a new state. Newspapers, publishing, advertising, recorded music, radio, film, and television industries all developed over extended pre-digital existences. In some commentaries, therefore, these get to be labelled "legacy media," contrasting with the "new media" of "born digital" industries. Such terms simplistically and confusingly bifurcate the industrial landscape. "Legacy" implies industries frozen in a past, ignoring how these adapt to coexist and compete with digital entrants. Calling anything "new" is so historically contingent that the term cannot substantively describe anything. It assumes that individually or collectively, media industries change en masse, with the new inevitably and wholly replacing the "old." This ignores a basic lesson from media theory, which is that emergent media forms never entirely displace existing media. Inspired by Marshall McLuhan's (1964: 23) aphorism that "the 'content' of any medium is always another medium," Jay David Bolter and Richard Grusin (1999: 273) advanced "remediation" as a way of conceptualizing "the formal logic by which new media refashion prior media forms." Social media platforms might be widely regarded as the epitome of a new online digital media universe, but by synthesizing text, image, and video, they've created businesses based on remediating forms with origins in printing, photography, and numerous moving image media.

When describing services offering televisual content over the web, Lotz (2017: 8) chose the label "internet-distributed television" to emphasize

> the consistency of television's defining attributes regardless of the development of a new mechanism of distribution with some new capabilities. Early belief of [sic] the "internet" as a form of "new media" and narratives of technological replacement concealed the reality of what has transpired – that the most desired application for distributing video via internet protocol has been accessing legacy television content outside its linear [broadcast] delivery.

What is described can be read as just one particular case of how the "old" persists in permeating the "new." When situating media industries in the digital economy, if there is no discreet break between what existed before or after the coming of the digital, then channeling McLuhan, we might say the contents of media industries – if "contents" is understood in a generous manner to describe not only communicative outputs but also the entire logics structuring industry processes, practices, and belief systems – are always to some extent other media industries. For the media industries research field then, part of the challenge of grasping the mutability of "media" requires finding a balance that recognizes how the distinctive and innovative remains infused with the persistive and remediative.

## From media industries to the industrial existences of media

So far, the discussion has considered how changes in both the landscape of the media industries and the accompanying body of research have problematized the meanings of "media." But what about "industry"? When researching media industries, referring to entities such as the "digital games industry" or "music industry" becomes a necessity. Indeed, similar labels appear within this chapter and throughout the collection. Yet what is being referred to when describing media as industry.

Dictionary definitions of "industry" vary in their details but commonly understand the term to mean companies engaging together in activities toward producing particular categories of goods or services for a market. Consequently, media industries are frequently labelled by the type of output generated. This seems fair enough, for what is the film industry if not the industry that makes, supplies, and presents films? Such innocent acts of labelling, however, set conceptual horizons that, if unchecked, can frame the object of inquiry in ways that can be both limiting and misleading. Using the singular *industry* (so, "the [insert relevant media] industry") implicitly conceptualizes any sector of industrial activity as a coherent totality. Several problems can emerge from this. First, it can encourage a kind of *industry essentialism*, where a particular form of output and the activities associated with its production and circulation, are presumed to stand for the whole or at least the core of an industry, and thereby ignoring how any industry produces multiple forms. For example, frequently discussions of the "film industry" unconsciously assume the narrative feature film industry. This then creates a second problem, for in privileging a particular form of output, there is a danger of industry-*generalization*, obscuring internal diversity by eliding divisions between specialized sub-sectors and hierarchical relations. Furthermore, essentialism and generalization can shade into industry-*enclosure*, compartmentalizing one industry off from other industries. This creates problems at two levels. It overlooks the *cross-media* interactions routinely enacted between media industries, but also ignores the *cross-sector* interactions that arise as media link with and often depend on non-media industries.

Any and all of these problems can emerge in how we conceptualize a media industry. When Williamson and Cloonan (2007: 316) argue "'the music industry' is … a complete misnomer," or Sterne (2014: 53) declares "There is no 'music industry,'" they are not dismissing the existence of such an industry. Rather they are provoking wider appreciation of "music industri*es* rather than an industry" (original emphasis; Williamson and Cloonan 2007: 313), and how "There are many industries with relationships to music" (Sterne 2014: 53). It is commonplace to see accounts of the music industry essentialized around what Sterne calls the "monetization-of-recordings construct" (p. 50), taking recorded music as standing for the entirety of business activities conducted around music. Centering the recorded music commodity results in a partial account that not only excludes additional for-profit activities related to live performance, concert promotion, and education or training (Williamson and Cloonan 2007: 310–311), but also overlooks the numerous other commodities "sold through, with, or around music, ranging from musical instruments, to hardware and software, to smartphones, to speakers and room architectures" (Sterne 2014: 52).

With an article asking "Is There a Comic Book Industry?" Benjamin Woo (2018) questions the presumed coherence of the American comic industry through drawing attention to its internal diversity. To many eyes, a single form defines the comics business, the superhero genre, most usually associated with the publishers Marvel Comics and DC Comics, and whose predominance has been boosted by big budget Hollywood franchise films. While this part of the industry might be taken as epitomizing the mainstream, there is a far wider spectrum of production extending to alternative or independent comics. Even once this breadth is recognized, however, Woo provides reasons for questioning such a bifurcated conceptualization of the industry. Not only are terms such as "mainstream," "alternative," or "independent" definitionally ambiguous, even with the popularity of the superhero genre, "comic books are now principally orientated toward a relatively restricted, subcultural audience of fans and collectors" (p. 32). In which case, the comics mainstream is in itself alternative, sitting outside mainstream mass taste: "even … best sellers do not sell all that well" (p. 38).

Internal divisions exist, between comic book and graphic novels publishing, between the leading "premier" publishers and small presses, and in sales channels between general trade bookstores and the direct market system selling to a network of specialty comic bookstores. To recognize rather than overlook this diversity, Woo advises "we have to keep in view the range of different models in different formats and channels addressing different audiences that characterize the field of American comic books" (p. 38). Further problematizing conceptualizations of the business is how the comic commodity intersects with the book publishing and film industries (see Perren and Steirer's contribution to this collection, Chapter 12).

Interrogating the essentializing and homogenizing tendencies in industry conceptualizations not only expands the scope and complexity of the object analyzed, but moreover reveals the politics of how media industries are *represented*, both in the sense of speaking for someone, and of portraying something. Returning to music for a moment, trade organization the International Federation of the Phonographic Industry (IFPA) is committed to "representing the global recording industry worldwide." While the organization's name and mission make openly clear the IFPA only represents the *recording* business, at the same time there is a sense of mission creep wherever the Federation presumes to speak for music industries more generally. Campaigning to "creat[e] a sustainable environment in which the whole music community can grow and develop," the IPFA claims broader representational authority, although the partiality of this goal is clear from how the pillars of the campaign focus on fair terms for the licensing of recordings by online distribution services, and the strengthening of copyright protections (IFPI n.d.). Furthermore, with 8,000 members, the IFPI speaks for the interests of many, but with the membership drawn from only 70 countries, claims to "global" or "worldwide" representativeness appear overstated. As this example shows, when

> single interest/industry representative organisations … present themselves as representing "the music industry" [they] are doing so in order to elicit public and political support for campaigns which may be in the interests of only *parts* of the industries and may not be in fans' interests.
>
> *Williamson and Cloonan 2007: 309; original emphasis*

What the IPFI actually represents is a globally restricted part of the "whole music community," one centered on (to use Sterne's terminology) the "monetization-of-recordings construct" in certain international territories.

Reading music industries through the recorded music commodity essentializes and generalizes the music business, and yet equally offers a point of departure for problematizing industry enclosure. Easily deployable, music recordings get to be integrated into the operations of multiple other industries. Indeed, the system of music rights provides a legal mechanism that is precisely directed as dispersing music across media and other business sectors. "Synchronization rights" license recordings for use by audiovisual industries, granting permission to "sync" music in adverts, films, television programs, and games. Managing catalogs of recordings on behalf of rights owners, performance rights organizations issue "blanket licenses," permitting radio and television broadcasters, shops, clubs, bars, restaurants, hotels, and airlines to play any works from a licensed catalog, creating efficiencies by avoiding piecemeal negotiations over the uses of individual recordings. In these cases, the rights system controls the deployments of recordings, but elsewhere, music touches many other areas of industry activity. Sterne (2014: 52) argues music playback is a consideration for "sound design in high-end automobiles … sound insulation in trendy condo developments … [and] the vast consumer electronics, computing and bandwidth industries," and although these lines of business "don't sell music, they sell music experiences."

As these examples suggest, "music industry" or even "music industries" don't comprehensively encompass the multifarious sites of industry activity where the recorded and performative commodity forms of music are produced and commercially exploited. This point extends to media overall. Media industries alone do not explain how media forms come to exist, nor the contexts in which they exist. When taking the media industries as an object of research inquiry, it is important to recognize these industries only partially represent what might be called the *industrial existences of media*. Connections between media and other industries pull in two directions. Centrifugal connections are formed as media industries reach outwards to access the outputs of other industries: think of how the consumer electronics and computer technology industries have researched, developed, and manufactured the devices on which much of the media we encounter now appears; or how telecommunication companies install fixed immobile wiring to households and other spaces to enable mobile "wireless" listening, viewing, or gaming. At the same time, centripetal connections form when, through corporate diversification or ownership structures, external industries become not only active participants in the media but also some of the most high-profile players in the sector. As the previous section already suggested, media represent meeting points for multiple industries, not all of which might be immediately assumed to be "media."

Noting how any mention of "industry" or "industries" sets conceptual limits on the object of inquiry certainly does not mean the terms should be jettisoned. Not only would this be deeply disabling, it would lose the considerable communicative value of using a language that straightforwardly and immediately connotes a regard for media-as-business. Either term works perfectly well if we consciously reflect on and interrogate what is being presumed in their usages. As Woo (2018: 40) highlights, industries are representational constructions:

> Industries are not a given. As a collective concept, industries are theoretical rather than empirical objects, although they obviously have empirical effects. What we perceive as an industry is itself the result of boundary-drawing practices imposed on a fluid, complex field of social practices. It must be constructed before it can be analyzed, but such processes of construction are never neutral.

This has implications for media industries research, for the field does not simply find an object to be analyzed but rather actively constructs its object. When analyzing industry discourse, but also academic discourse, there is a need to query the meanings of "industry," inviting such questions as: what version of the industry is proffered, why is it deployed in this context, and what interests are thereby represented and excluded?

On this note, we might consider how terms other than "industry" shift the conceptualization of media business activity. Displacing essentialist conceptualizations of industry, "network" connotes a sense of numerous components and participants engaged in cognate activities and linked through multiple lines of intersection without a center or core. For example, Andrew Leyshon (2001: 20–31) proposes a model of the music economy comprising four connected and partially overlapping networks. *Creativity* relates to music composition, performance, and recording. While this includes the familiar elements of the recorded music business (recording companies, recording studios legal services, and artists' management agencies), it also includes musical instruments and supplies, and performance venues. Sharing some of the same ground, *reproduction* encompasses the same elements of music recording while also extending to manufacturing and music publishing. In *distribution*, recording companies again feature, as does manufacturing, but by covering the dissemination of copyrighted products to final markets, this network also includes promotional activities, physical distribution of copies, and retail outlets. Finally, *consumption* represents those retail outlets, for example what at the time Leyshon was writing would have been largely represented by bricks-and-mortar shops and mail order.

Certain elements are missing from Leyshon's model that should be counted as part of the music economy: collecting societies, music education and training organizations, and most crucially, the consumption network does not include consumers, the end users of music received in any form. Also, since Leyshon originally posed his model, popularization of paid downloads, and subsequently streaming services, demands some reconceptualization of this network. However, the point here is not to query the detail but rather to recognize how the network concept refigures the industrial existences of media. By not essentializing the business around music recordings, a network perspective recognizes how music features in the production of other commercial outputs, for example, live performances, or musical instruments. Additionally, activity is not anchored around a particular center. In Leyshon's model, recording companies appear in three of the four networks, and so exercise more power and influence than other participants, yet they do not define the entire system. Thinking of media industries as sets of network arrangements provides a means for appreciating a fuller range of participants and the various activities they engage in.

Another means of conceptualizing the industrial existences of media is suggested by the term "ecosystem". Adopting an explicitly ecological metaphor for organizational research, James F. Moore (1996: 26) described a "business ecosystem" as "[a]n economic community supported by a foundation of interacting organizations and individuals … This economic community produces goods and services of value to customer, who are themselves members of the ecosystem." Moore's concept gained traction in business studies but also among business practitioners. Separately, references to "ecosystems" have appeared in some studies of media, although often without explanation or lacking theoretical elaboration. Addressing precisely this conceptual gap, Ivana Kostovska, Tim Raats, Karen Donders, and Pieter Ballon (2021: 13) survey the relevant literature to arrive at a definition of "media ecosystem" as "a multi-layered and dynamic structure of interdependent organisations and stakeholders that interact and co-evolve around one or several local firms, that provide media products or services, to create a joint value proposition." In this account, it is that joint commitment to a "value proposition," the value promised to customers who acquire a product or service, that links participants in a media ecosystem.

Concepts of business and media ecosystem share some common ground. First, by inhabiting an ecosystem, participants are separate actors but are brought together in relations of interaction, interdependence, and coevolution. Second, while ecosystems include actors conventionally thought of as participants in an industry (i.e., companies and their competitors and suppliers), the system also involves multiple categories of non-industry actor: Moore included government agencies, regulators, standards organizations, and most crucially, consumers. In an ecosystem, multiple stakeholders therefore come together, not all of whom might be defined as "industry." Third, just as a natural ecosystem has no set spatial limits, so Moore (1996: 28) argued a "business ecosystem does not respect traditional industry boundaries," for any company might be seen as participating in multiple ecosystems that cross industries, but also an ecosystem exceeds national borders. On the latter, with regard to media ecosystems, Kostovska et al. (Kostovska, Raats, Donders, and Ballon 2021: 12–13) offer a corrective, for geographic boundaries can still hold sway wherever the conduct of media industries is influenced by policy formation at national and regional levels. Also, we might further add how the technologies of regional lockout (region coding for DVDs and games consoles, and now geo-blocking online entertainment services) circumscribe media ecosystems within electronic boundaries (Elkins 2019).

Adopting an ecosystem approach can therefore help avoid tendencies to essentialize, generalize and enclose media industries, yet certain conceptual problems still arise from the ecosystem metaphor. In order to provide some analytical parameters, we might ask what is the scope or scale of an ecosystem? Moore (1996: 28) saw the scale of an ecosystem as flexible, equally referring "to small business initiatives or to vast collections of enterprises," and similarly Kostovska et al. (2021: 8) regard ecosystems as having "scale-independence." This elasticity gives the concept broad currency while at the same making it nebulous. Linking back to the previous section, how effectively can the concept guide analysis if one particular online television platform, or the full range of options for distributing television programming online, can equally be regarded as ecosystems? Also, due to the multiple interdependencies enacted between participants, control of an ecosystem is viewed as dispersed and decentralized, yet Kostovska et al.'s modeling of actors into "core," secondary and tertiary levels, implies centers of influence still operate. For example, the core level is occupied by "ecosystem orchestrators" and "focal firms" (p. 14). If the "overarching aim of the media ecosystem is to succeed in creating a common ecosystem value proposition" (p. 15), actors are being viewed as joining in a unity of purpose, yet this seems to downplay the potential for competition and discord between participants. For example, labor unions, positioned in the model at the tertiary level, rightly feature in media ecosystems, but their goal of securing value in terms of a better settlement for members could be quite a different objective to that of say a production company seeking to make a film within budget. For union representatives and their members, the goals of organized labor are "core" not subordinate to whatever the overall ecosystem is seeking to achieve.

Whatever the terms applied, the research field benefits from recognizing and assessing the presumptions locked up in how we conceive of and represent media as industries. Thinking beyond essentializing and enclosing representations provides ground for theorizing more broadly the industrial existences of media. As representational lenses, ecosystem or network metaphors provide conceptual coordinates for thinking through *intra-* and *inter-*industry relations. Again reflecting on the previous section, taking an ecosystem perspective gives some ground for looking beyond "the media" to encourage recognition of how the information technology sector has become integral to media in the digital economy. By thinking beyond the boundedness of industries while foregrounding multi-stakeholderism and interdependencies among industry and non-industry actors, with some conceptual and analytical refinement the ecosystem metaphor can effectively encourage more expansive imaginings of the industry landscape in which media exist.

## Research practice and the production of media industries

Previous sections addressed two problematics. First, how the integration of media industries into the digital economy tests certain premises that have defined a version of media informing much research in the field. Among the most notable challenges are the inroads made by technology companies into the media sector, the revalorization of data as capital, the de/rematerialization of content, the intermediary roles of platforms, and an emergent industry of social media entertainment. These developments encourage the need to address large-scale digital transformation, and yet it is equally important to heed the caveat that any analysis of contemporary media industries will fundamentally misunderstand change if overlooking the resilience and persistence of established industry practices.

Second, the discussion highlighted how essentializing, generalizing, and enclosing accounts of "industry" obscure the industrial existences of media, the broader set of industrialized activities and actors that extend beyond "the media," but which are not only necessary to producing media but to also utilizing media as sources of value. As a way of consciously addressing the broader industry "scape," concepts of "network" or "ecosystem," if used with some critical reflection, can productively encourage forms of analysis attentive to how media exist in and through complexes of intra- and inter-industry relationships, where the interests converge of multiple categories of actor or stakeholder, not all of whom might be immediately regarded as participants in a specifically media industry community.

For researchers working on media industries, these problematics raise ontological concerns – what exists as media and industry in the context of a study? Of equal importance, however, is the epistemological problematic – in what ways, and by what means or techniques, are media industries known? As noted at the opening, media industries research necessarily draws on insights from multiple other fields, and so is thoroughly interdisciplinary. Yet arguably, only sporadically do contributions to the field actually reflect back on how and why interdisciplinary choices are made. In other words, interdisciplinarity is practiced but not always with conscious consideration of why, or with what benefits. Advocating an interdisciplinary approach to media policy research, Holt and Secular's contribution to this collection provides something of a rare case of such reflection (see Chapter 39).

Given the mutability of media industries as an object for research inquiry, continuing commitment to interdisciplinary rejuvenation and expansion is required. For example, if media industries research is to deal in an informative way with the implications of digitalization, there is a pragmatic need for the field to become at least selectively cognizant of how computing processes relate to cultural production. This is a task that might not come naturally for researchers schooled in traditions of humanist and social science research, although it does not necessitate thorough reschooling in computer science. Digitalization does not completely reset media industries, and similarly, the act of researching the processes of digital change requires balancing disciplinary innovation with continuity.

Platformization extends beyond the media industries, but for how it provides some perspective on how the contemporary media environment is constituted, then to grasp its complexities, media industries research might do well to heed proposals for adopting insights from software studies, business studies, critical political economy, and cultural studies for how these respectively aid understanding of platforms as technological infrastructures, multi-sided markets, instruments of governance, and sites of cultural practices (Poell, Nieborg, and Van Dijck 2019: 4–5). While the latter three represent familiar ground for studies of media industries, connecting with the former involves intersecting with another field of interdisciplinary working concerned with the consequences of how software is implemented in social and cultural life.

What might critical engagements with information technology bring to media industries research? In some contexts, the phrase "black box" is used to communicate how technological devices or systems represent closed entities whose inner workings remain opaque and essentially unknown. Focusing on the Swedish music streaming service Spotify, a project conducted by Maria Erikksson, Rasmus Fleischer, Anna Johansson, Pelle Snickars, and Patrick Vonderau (2019) opened up the black box of one of the leading names in the platform-mediated media economy. This interdisciplinary team conducted a "teardown," "to disassemble the way Spotify's product is commonly conceptualized" (p. 9). To this end, mixed methods were applied in a series of subsidiary projects described as "interventions." For example, to study the back-end processes by which artists and labels get music placed on Spotify, particularly how the gatekeeping role of "aggregators" filters what music gets accepted onto the service, the team created a new record company, submitting its own modest repertoire of self-produced recordings to the standard vetting procedures. Placing themselves within the processes examined, the researchers conducted an autoethnographic "breaching experiment" (p. 71). Among the findings, this work showed genre categories as holding continued importance for categorizing recordings, but also how the production of metadata, particularly artist biographies, was outsourced to and controlled by a mini industry of specialized companies (pp. 73–74).

One of the most notable features of the project was how software could be employed to analytically disassemble the platform. Using "bots" to simulate human listening activity, an experiment tested the workings of Spotify's royalty payment system (pp. 76–77). Software for conducting network protocol analysis ("packet sniffers") was repurposed as a research tool for "eavesdropping" to follow the data traffic generated by the researchers' own manually actioned plays. Any play proliferated data beyond music data, triggering connections that spread between backbone network providers, Content Delivery Networks, services for programmatic advertising, and the data centers of Google Cloud platform (where the requested music was most likely stored). "When pushing play on Spotify," the team concluded, "music is heard – amid a cacophony of other data" (p. 113). It might be imagined that applying digital methods to research digital phenomena delivers greater rigor and systematicity, avoiding the human limits or messiness of manual methods, yet some interventions generated a superfluity of data but without delivering useful data, thereby leaving certain research assumptions unproven (pp. 139–147).

Here, interdisciplinary working and methodological innovation combine to expose and productively disrupt the construction of an industry formation. Spotify might be easily viewed as a major player in the "music industry," and indeed it is, yet tracking the data showed Spotify could not be essentialized or enclosed in these terms. Combining manual and computer-enabled methods accreted insights that cumulatively rendered visible and tangible how Spotify, far from being a closed system, is better understood as an ecosystem involving multiple categories of corporate actor. In this sense, the data transmissions initiated by individual plays showed how Spotify's existences extended way beyond the recorded music commodity.

By chasing the data, the project could be interpreted as undertaking a digitally enabled form of what Charles Acland (drawing on Harold Innis) (2014: 9) metaphorically calls "dirt" research:

> media commodities are but a surface manifestation of a deep structure of materials and their movement. Our analytic capabilities would be impoverished if they only charted the topsoil and ignored the geological layers beneath. Pursing the dirt and depth of cultural economies should not dissolve medium specificity, but should help

us conceptualize and understand the full systemic entwinement of our media objects with resource economies.

Following Innis, Acland is thinking of how the industrial existences of media outputs can be traced downward to the industries responsible for mineral extraction, chemicals, the production of basic materials or electronics components, creating a "model of economic depth" (p. 8). Although taking a different line of inquiry, Eriksson et al. (2019) still posed a model of industry depth, chasing data to dig below the "topsoil" of a particular media service to excavate the "geological layers" of platformatization. Striking a geological analogy does not sound too contrived when it is considered that platform developers already invoke depth metaphors when they describe building applications by combining multiple technological services to create a "tech *stack*." On the one hand, rummaging around in "dirt" can imply becoming immersed in *impurities*, things that shouldn't really concern media industries research, and yet on the other hand can also mean getting down to the very *substance* of the research object.

When presenting these arguments, this chapter has been concerned with recognizing how the object or objects of media/industries/research are not simply found but rather created in acts of inquiry. Nitin Govil (2013: 173) notes:

> One of the entrenched yet underexamined presumptions of Media Industries Studies … is the obviousness of its object. After all, most studies proceed from a general understanding of what an industry comprises, with a tacit sense of its boundaries and capacities. However, instead of taking industries as pre-given and stable formations, Film and Media Studies might take up a more foundational conceptual challenge. What are the provisional forms, sites and practices that constitute media industries? What are the social, textual, political, and cultural infrastructures and interactions assembled under the sign of "industry"? What are these formal and informal processes of assembly, and how do exchange practices move in and out of industry status? In other words, how are industries "made up"?

Anchoring these questions, Govil looks at how the film business in India became formally rationalized as an industry, a process that in part involved representation through statistical enumeration. Recognizing the Indian industry did not pre-exist but was given form through representation, Govil argues the critical challenge is to "depart from understanding industry simply as a form of production and focus instead on the production of 'industry' itself" (p. 176). This proposal might be taken more broadly as a guiding principle for media industries research. To fruitfully problematize the production of "industry," in the processes of research we might come to existing literature with an eye to asking what versions of "media" and "industry/ies" are produced here, and in the resulting process of inquiry, to then ask of ourselves what versions are we producing?

For the following parts, chapters are grouped around five concerns. Initially, authors survey key perspectives and traditions in media industries research. With Part II, chapters propose ways for revising or innovating the conceptual and methodological parameters of the field. In Part III, a range of studies look at how digitalization relates to different industries. For Part IV, authors unsettle industry enclosures with case studies looking at how industries operate across national boundaries or media. Finally, chapters address the activity of conducting media industries inquiries, both in terms of methodological procedures and pedagogical practice. These concerns are elaborated on in the introductions that precede the various parts. Each chapter makes distinct interventions and arguments, so that the diversity of voices combines to express something of the scope and vibrancy of the field.

# References

Acland, C. R. (2014) "Dirt Research for Media Industries," *Media Industries,* 1 (1): 6–10.

Albarran, A. B., Jung, J., and Mierzejewskam, B. I. (eds) (2018) *Handbook of Media Management and Economics,* New York: Routledge.

Arsenault, A. H. (2017) "The Datafication of Media: Big Data and the Media Industries," *International Journal of Media and Cultural Politics,* 13 (1–2): 7–24.

Barwise, P. and Watkins, L. (2018) "The Evolution of Digital Dominance: How and Why We Got to GAFA," in M. Moore and D. Tambini (eds) *Digital Dominance: The Power of Google, Amazon, Facebook, and Apple,* New York: New York University Press: 21–49.

Bolter, J. D. and Grusin, R. (1999) *Remediation: Understanding New Media,* Cambridge, MA: MIT Press.

Braun, J. (2015) *This Program is Brought to You By…: Distributing Television News Online,* New Haven, CT: Yale University Press.

Caldwell, J. T. (2008) *Production Culture: Industrial Reflexivity and Critical Practice in Film and Television,* Durham, NC: Duke University Press.

Chambers, J. (2008) *Madison Avenue and the Color Line: African Americans in the Advertising Industry,* Philadelphia: University of Pennsylvania Press.

Crisp, V. (2015) *Film Distribution in the Digital Age: Pirates and Practitioners,* New York: Palgrave Macmillan.

Cunningham, S. and Craig, D. (2019) *Social Media Enterainment: The New Intersection of Hollywood and Silicon Valley,* New York: New York University Press.

Curtin, M. and Sanson, K. (eds) (2016) *Precarious Creativity: Global Media, Local Labor,* Oakland, CA: University of California Press.

Daniel, R. (2019) "Digital Disruption in the Music Industry: The Case of the Compact Disc," *Creative Industries Journal,* 12 (2): 159–166.

de Bustos, J. C. and Izquierdo-Castillo, J. (2019) "Who Will Control the Media? The Impact of GAFAM on the Media Industries in the Digital Economy," *Revista Latina de Comunicación Social,* 74: 803–821.

Deuze, M. and Prenger, M. (eds) (2019) *Making Media: Production, Practices, and Professions,* Amsterdam: Amsterdam University Press.

Doyle, G. (2013) *Understanding Media Economics,* 2nd ed., London: Sage.

Elkins, E. (2019) *Locked Out: Regional Restrictions in Digital Entertainment Culture,* New York: New York University Press.

Eriksson, M., Fleischer, R., Johansson, A., Snickars, P., and Vonderau, P. (2019) *Spotify Teardown: Inside the Black Box of Streaming Music,* Cambridge, MA: MIT Press.

Evens, T. and Donders, K. (2018) *Platform Power and Policy in Transforming Television Markets,* Cham: Palgrave Macmillan.

Fuchs, C. (2016) "Baidu, Weibo and Renren: The Global Political Economy of Social Media in China," *Asian Journal of Communication,* 26 (1): 14–41.

Gillespie, T. (2010) "The Politics of 'Platforms'," *New Media and Society,* 12 (3): 347–364.

Govil, N. (2013) "Recognizing 'Industry'," *Cinema Journal,* 52 (3): 172–176.

Helmond, A. (2015) "The Platformization of the Web: Making Web Data Platform Ready," *Social Media + Society,* 1 (2): 1–11.

Herbert, D., Lotz, A. D. and Punathambekar, A. (2020) *Media Industry Studies,* Cambridge: Polity.

Hesmondhalgh, D. and Baker, S. (2011) *Creative Labour: Media Work in Three Cultural Industries,* Abingdon: Routledge.

Hesmondhalgh, D. and Meier, L. M. (2018) "What the Digitalisation of Music Tells Us About Capitalism, Culture and the Power of the Information Technology Sector," *Information, Communication and Society,* 21 (11): 1555–1570.

Hill, E. (2016) *Never Done: A History of Women's Work in Media Production,* New Brunswick, NJ: Rutgers University Press.

Holt, J. and Perren, A. (eds) (2009) *Media Industries: History, Theory, and Method,* Malden, MA: Wiley-Blackwell.

IFPI (n.d.) "Creating a Fair Environment for Music," available at www.ifpi.org/ifpi-priorities/creating-a-fair-environment-for-music/ (accessed March 12, 2021).

Johnson, C. (2019) *Online TV,* Abingdon: Routledge.

Jordan, T. (2020) *The Digital Economy,* Cambridge: Polity.

Kostovska, I., Raats, T., Donders, K., and Ballon, P. (2021) "Going Beyond the Hype: Conceptualising 'Media Ecosystem' for Media Management Research," *Journal of Media Business Studies,* 18 (1): 6–26.

Leyshon, A. (2001) "Time–Space (and Digital) Compression: Software Formats, Musical Networks, and the Reorganisation of the Music Industry," *Environment and Planning A: Economy and Space,* 33 (1): 49–77.

Lobato, R. (2019) *Netflix Nations: The Geography of Digital Distribution,* New York: New York University Press.

Lotz, A. D. (2017) *Portals: A Treatise on Internet-distributed Television,* Ann Arbor, MI: Maize.

Mayer, V. (2011) *Below the Line: Producers and Production Studies in the New Television Economy,* Durham, NC: Duke University Press.

Mayer, V., Banks, M. J., and Caldwell, J. T. (eds) (2009) *Production Studies: Cultural Studies of Media Industries,* New York: New York.

McDonald, P., Brannon Donoghue, C., and Havens, T. (eds) (2021) *Digital Media Distribtion: Portals, Platforms, Pipelines,* New York: New York University Press.

McLuhan, M. (1964) *Understanding Media: The Extensions of Man,* New York: Signet.

Mejias, U. A. and Couldry, N. (2019) "Datafication," *Internet Policy Review,* 8 (4): 1–10.

Moore, J. F. (1996) *The Death of Competition: Leadership and Strategy in the Age of Business Ecosystems,* New York: HarperBusiness.

Morris, J. W. (2015) *Selling Digital Music, Formatting Culture,* Berkeley, CA: University of California Press.

Napoli, P. M. (2010) *Audience Economics: Media Institutions and the Audience Marketplace,* New York: Columbia University Press.

Paterson, C., Lee, D., Saha, A., and Zoellner, A. (eds) (2016) *Advancing Media Production Research: Shifting Sites, Methods, and Politics,* Houndmills: Palgrave Macmillan.

Poell, T., Nieborg, D., and Van Dijck, J. (2019) "Platformisation," *Internet Policy Review,* 8 (4): 1–13.

Rohn, U. and Evens, T. (eds) (2020) *Media Management Matters: Challenges and Opportunities for Bridging Theory and Practice,* New York: Routledge.

Spilker, H. S. (2017) *Digital Music Distribution: The Sociology of Online Music Streams,* Abingdon: Routledge.

Spilker, H. S. and Colbjørnsen, T. (2020) "The Dimensions of Streaming: Toward a Typology of an Evolving Concept," *Media, Culture and Society,* 42 (7–8): 1210–1225.

Steinberg, M. (2019) *The Platform Economy: How Japan Transformed the Consumer Internet,* Minneapolis, MN: University of Minnesota Press.

Sterne, J. (2012) *MP3: The Meaning of a Format,* Durham, NC: Duke University Press.

Sterne, J. (2014) "There is No Music Industry," *Media Industries,* 1 (1): 50–55.

Szczepanik, P. and Vonderau, P. (eds) (2013) *Behind the Screen: Inside European Production Cultures,* New York: Palgrave Macmillan.

Van Dijck, J., Poell, T., and De Waal, M. (2018) *The Platform Society: Public Values in a Connective World,* New York: Oxford University Press.

Williamson, J. and Cloonan, M. (2007) "Rethinking the Music Industry," *Popular Music,* 26 (2): 305–322.

Woo, B. (2018) "Is There a Comic Book Industry?," *Media Industries,* 5 (1): 27–46.

# PART I

# Perspectives

## Conceptual and critical directions

Media industries research necessarily constitutes a diverse multidisciplinary field of inquiry. As noted in the opening chapter, studies of media industries can be found across a broad spectrum of social science and humanities subject areas. At the same time, the multifaceted make-up of media industries – as locations of economic, technological, social, and cultural activity – but also their transmutability, means no single theoretical framework or methodological approach seems sufficient to grasping how these industries work or the effects they generate. Nonetheless, as the chapters in this part show, certain perspectives and "traditions" are identifiable within the field, each bringing to the object of study their own conceptual credentials and points of critical emphasis.

Initially, two chapters traces histories of formative developments in media industries research. Graham Murdock sees work in Europe from the mid-1960s onward as responding to two contexts: the institutionalization of academic communication research, and the structural transformation of the communication landscape by increased exposure to market forces. Interrogating the latter reinvigorated the critical political economy of communication in the UK and France, while analyses of media organizations and occupations, or situated ethnographies of production practices, examined how broad industry dynamics were being negotiated on the ground. Critiques questioned the deleterious impacts of media marketization on the diversity of available representation, participation in the media, and sustaining the production of a democratic public sphere.

Offering a parallel history, Janet Wasko surveys developments in the United States. Rather than a unified field, media industries research was dispersed across multiple intellectual directions and media. Early work in media management appeared from the 1930s, and during the 1960s a US perspective on the political economy of communication emerged, with the production of culture and production studies denoting more recent approaches. Furthermore, throughout the first decades of the twentieth century, media-specific seams of inquiry concentrated on the newspaper, radio, or film industries, while by the final decades of the century the effects of conglomeration and diversification necessitated work that could trace the intersections formed between media.

Outlining some of the most prominent theoretical and critical perspectives active in media industries research, a range of chapters identify the interventions made by critical political

DOI: 10.4324/9780429275340-2

economy (CPE), policy studies, media economics, media management, and production studies. Noting the contributions, but also criticisms, of CPE, Jonathan Hardy presents proposals for revising CPE to address the contemporary industrial landscape, and specifically the convergence of media and advertising manifested in forms of branded content. To grasp shifting power relationships in this context, Hardy proffers governance as a central concept to address the multiple sites and processes of rule-making active across production, circulation, consumption, and use. Hardy sets out a range of propositions for applying critical governance analysis to integrate attention to the sources of governance represented by formal regulation, industry self-regulation, market power, and civil society action.

As Maria Michalis argues, policy and industry are inseparable in the media. Centrally concerned with forms of power, critical studies of policy probe how the state and other authorities shape the media systems and content we get, while at the same time advocating for reforms that advance the public interest. As Michalis details, media policy finds multiple points of application (e.g., restrictions on ownership, allocation of communication frequencies, technical standards, copyright, or consumer protection) effecting all categories of industry participant, and operating across sub-national, national, regional, or international spheres of influence. Placing the analytic emphasis on process rather than outcome foregrounds policymaking as a contested terrain.

In media economics, application of economic theories, concepts, and methods enhance understanding of how the business of media is conducted. Yet, as Gillian Doyle argues, the distinctive characteristics of media industries partially defy conventional economic thinking: for example, assessments of efficiency can seem meaningless in a sector where objectives are uncertain or divergent, and quantitative economic analysis seems ill suited to evaluating the impacts of media on public welfare. Still, Doyle views media economics as valuably illuminating business strategies and behaviors, including why and how media industries must work to manage risk, plus providing tools for assessing the economic importance of advertising in the media sector, and explaining why media industries so frequently adopt oligopolistic and monopolistic structures.

While noting common ground with media economics, Ulrike Rohn differentiates media management research by its emphasis on corporate and entrepreneurial decision-making and firm performance over concerns with industries and markets. Scoping the breadth of media management research, Rohn sees studies varying by their chosen unit of analysis (individual, firm, or media product), emphasis on forces internal (e.g., leadership, work culture) or external (e.g., technology innovation, audience behavior, competitive environment) to the media firm, theoretical (e.g., strategic management, structure-conduct-performance, organizational culture) or methodological approach, and stakeholder orientation (does the work address industry, policy-makers and/or academia?).

Studies of media production are certainly not new, but as Philip Drake explains, with the growth of "production studies" there has been a concerted drive to develop modes of inquiry aimed at capturing the complexities of production contexts. Drawing eclectically on multidisciplinary insights, there is no unified direction in this field, yet certain commonalities emerge: an emphasis on engaging with media workers, particularly those occupying "below-the-line" roles, through using interview and observational methods to construct "thick" accounts of the lived micro-level realities of working cultures, and critically prioritizing issues of autonomy, precarious employment, and self-exploitation.

In their search for significance and persuasiveness, theoretical and methodological paradigms can frequently assume universal applicability, bypassing reflection on the contextual circumstances from which ideas and arguments are born, or how incongruous these may seem when transferred to other situations. In the interests of recognizing the territorial embedded-ness of research, Georgia Aitaki, Lydia Papadimitriou, and Yannis Tzioumakis offer a case study locating the development of a media industries research agenda in a particular national context. Focusing on studies of media industries conducted in and about Greece, they see the centrality of the state in the nation's media environment as determining the research trajectory, influencing the theoretical traditions applied, media studied, and issues prioritized. If media industries research deals fundamentally with the material specificities of cultural production, then Aitaki, Papadimitriou, and Tzioumakis' account foregrounds a need to be equally cognizant of the conditions shaping knowledge production.

# 1

# ASSEMBLING PRODUCTION STUDIES

## Formative interventions in Britain and Europe

*Graham Murdock*

### Tracking change

The recent resurgence of research on media industries and production to which the present volume testifies, has looked mainly to the United States for conceptual frameworks and models of inquiry. Landmark American studies of Hollywood, network television, and news production continue to offer indispensable resources, but they do not exhaust them. This chapter reviews a second major reference point, represented by the formative work developed in Britain and Europe between 1965 – when communications research began to gather momentum in the universities – and 1995.

This tradition of inquiry has been mostly passed over or recalled selectively, erasing insights that continue to illuminate present conditions. While it addresses many of the same issues, it differs from US research in two ways. First, it is more strongly informed by European social and political theory and, for some authors, by an engagement with Marxism. Second, in contrast to the market-oriented US system, at the outset of the period covered here governments in Britain and Europe played a major role in organizing national communication. Regulation of competition in commercial markets was informed by public interest criteria. Telecommunication networks were nationalized and operated as public utilities. Public service broadcasters, financed by taxation, played a central role in delivering advertising-free television services.

As McDonald (2013) has argued, one of the challenges facing media industry studies is "to situate the now and the new within larger patterns of continuity and change." My cut-off date of 1995 precludes analysis of the impacts of the new business model developed by the major social media corporations, based on free access to their platforms in return for the exclusive right to monetize the personal data generated by users' activities. It also excludes the digital majors' continuing disruption of established communication industries. A concerted focus on technological innovation and new forms of labor and use, however, deflects attention from the fundamental reorganization of contemporary capitalism that gathered momentum from the mid-1980s onward. In Britain and across Europe, we witness the reassertion of markets and profit maximization as the fundamental principles of economic organization. Publicly owned assets were sold to corporate investors (privatization), markets that were previously monopolies or

DOI: 10.4324/9780429275340-3

protected were opened to competition (liberalization), employment was increasingly casualized and worker's rights whittled away, regulations restricting ownership were relaxed, and public institutions pressured to seek additional sources of funding to compensate for reductions in public resource (corporatization).

Despite repeated demands from market advocates, the BBC remained a public corporation, but in 1987, France's leading public television channel TF1 was sold to investors led by the Bouygues group whose interests spanned telecommunications, construction, and real estate. Britain spearhead the privatization of the national post, telegraph, and telephone (PTT) system, converting it from a monopoly public utility to profit-generating company competing with new entrants, a movement later replicated in all the European Union (EU) countries. The arrival of commercial satellite and cable services broke the broadcast monopolies of public service organizations across Europe. In 1972 Britain introduced commercial radio. A decade later, a fourth national UK television channel was launched, publicly owned but financed by advertising. In 1984, cable companies, previously restricted to relaying terrestrial services, were freed to carry as many channels as they wished together with telephone services in competition with the privatized British Telecom. From 1990, a commercial consortium led by Rupert Murdoch's Sky Television secured monopoly control over satellite broadcasting in Britain, originally intended as an extension of the BBC's remit.

Marketization's militant promotion of commercial communications and advertising was accompanied by a relaxation of the regulations governing takeovers and mergers, allowing companies to consolidate their position within their original sphere of operations (through horizontal and vertical acquisitions) and to move into new areas (diversification). Rupert Murdoch's monopoly control of satellite services followed the cementation of his leading position in the national newspaper market through his acquisition of *The Times* and *Sunday Times* to add to his tabloid titles *The Sun* and *The News of the World*. These British interests were incorporated into a business empire with global reach, operating across print and audiovisual media and spanning Australia, Asia, and the United States, typifying the newly dominant corporate form of the global multiple media conglomerate.

This fundamental rebalancing of relations between states and markets, corporate ambitions, and the public interest paved the ways for digital platforms to commercially exploit research and networks originally developed with public funding and to operate with virtually no regulation. This intervention reinforced changes to the organization and operation of the established media industries in response to the first wave of marketization establishing an unbroken chain of reaction and adaptation.

This structural transformation has been underpinned ideologically by a reassertion of liberalism (neoliberalism) redefined as the freedom of entrepreneurs to capitalize on every area of communication with minimum regulatory hindrance and the freedom of consumers to craft identities around purchased goods and services. The ideal of citizenship, anchored in shared membership of a moral and political community with rights to commonly provided cultural resources and responsibilities that contribute to the quality of collective life, has been progressively marginalized. This has posed particular problems for public service broadcasting organizations faced with intensified competition from commercial rivals but required to continue promoting diversity of expression and addressing minority interests.

## Levels of analysis: assembling Russian dolls

Mapping this new media landscape, detailing market concentration, tracking the new forms of corporate organization, investigating the increasing commodification of culture, and exploring their consequences for the organization of production and diversity of public expression were central concerns for a reinvigorated critical political economy of communications. Early contributions in Britain came from Graham Murdock, Peter Golding, and Nicholas Garnham, and in France from the group led by Bernard Miège in Grenoble based around Groupe de recherche sur les enjeux socio-economiques de la communication (GRESEC). Murdock and Golding's (1973) formative essay "For a Political Economy of Mass Communication" was followed by Nicholas Garnham's (1979) "Contribution to a Political Economy of Mass Communication," overlapping with two major overviews from the Grenoble group: the jointly authored *Capitalisme et industries culturelles* (Huet, Ion, Lefrebvre, Miège, and Peron 1978) and Patrice Flichy's (1980a) *Les industries de l'imaginaire*.

These overviews identified changing spaces and pressures, but production studies also needed to look in detail at the ways these structural dynamics are negotiated and responded to by those making media artifacts across a range of settings, from novelists working in their home office, to journalists in the newsroom, production teams assembled on film sets or in recording studios, or volunteers in a community radio station. It is through close attention to their everyday routines, social relations, professional beliefs, and selections from available materials that we gain a fuller understanding of how ideas and information are translated into cultural forms. Where possible explorations of situated action have drawn on ethnographic methods of participant observation developed within anthropology, presenting cultural labor as an active process of assembling meaning, a perspective signaled by including "making," "putting together," or "manufacturing" in the titles of research monographs. Where access to production sites is denied, investigation has fallen back on detailed interviews with production personnel. Both forms of qualitative inquiry were employed in pioneering studies during the period reviewed here.

Production sites are not isolated self-contained enclaves. They are embedded within institutional formations that respond to the shifting pressures and opportunities mapped by critical political economy in different ways depending on their relative position within the cultural economy and the clusters of resources they command. The work reviewed here paid particular attention to three of these intermediate structures: industrial sectors, media organizations, and professions. A novelist contracted to a small independent publisher is working under very different conditions to a scriptwriter for a primetime television soap opera. In an important intervention we will return to. Miège (1987) and his colleagues situated these differences within a general typology of media industries organized around two contrasting modes of operation: "publishing" and "flow" (see below). Communication workers seldom spend their entire career working for one organization. The majority of creative personnel in the audio-visual industries, for example actors, directors, and script writers are employed for a particular production or project with career progression mediated primarily through personal networks and reputation. Journalists are more likely to work for a particular organization but moving to better paid, more prestigious, positions often entails changing employer, as in the classic shift from a provincial to a national newspaper. One of the consequences of intensified marketization has been an increasingly casualized communications labor force with more and more workers operating on a freelance or just-in-time basis. Traditionally, creative workforces have been held together by shared membership of an identifiable profession defined by mastery of a particular set of skills and governed by a code of practice based on an agreed set of values. These professional solidarities operate as both a bulwark against external interference from employers and governments and a mechanism of exclusion. They may be reinforced by membership of a trade union campaigning for improved conditions of work and defending members in dispute with their employers. Unionism, however, has traditionally been at its strongest among workers involved in the multiple technical processes supporting creative production.

These different levels of analysis are most usefully thought of as a set of Russian dolls nested within each other. No single study is likely to include them all, but a comprehensive account needs to look for ways to assemble them into an integrated whole. The interventions introduced in the following sections continue to offer essential resources for pursuing this ambition under contemporary conditions.

## Research nodes and networks

The three research centers that played a formative role in developing British media studies were all located in provincial universities: Leeds, Leicester, and Birmingham. Their position outside the "golden" academic triangle of Oxford, Cambridge, and London reflected the marginal status of communications and popular culture as legitimate areas of academic study. At the time, there were no degree programs in the field in institutions of higher education. In a further signal of marginality, all four formative figures – Joseph Trenaman, Jay Blumler, James Halloran, and Richard Hoggart – began their academic careers in adult education rather than established university departments.

Hoggart's hugely influential *The Uses of Literacy* (1957) had paid particular attention to the shifting relationship between the organic working-class culture he had grown up in between the wars and the increasingly commercialized media culture of the post–World War II years. In 1964 he moved to a professorship at Birmingham University and established the Centre for Contemporary Cultural Studies (CCCS) within the English Department to develop research on the interplay between situated and mediated cultures. Refusing the easy dismissals of production for the "masses" current among defenders of consecrated "high" culture, he insisted that "even the apparently most processed forms of mass art are more complex constructions than the usual formulations suggest, complex in themselves and in their relations to their readers or audiences" (Hoggart 1969: 12). These twin concerns, with the construction of meaning in media texts and the interpretive activities of audiences, defined the Centre's core research agenda. Stuart Hall, who abandoned his planned doctoral thesis on Henry James to teach in London secondary schools while editing the journal *New Left Review*, and who had just published a groundbreaking analysis of popular media – *The Popular Arts* with Paddy Whannel, education officer at the British Film Institute (Hall and Whannel 1964) – was recruited to help develop the research.

In 1969, when Hoggart left Birmingham to move to UNESCO in Paris, Hall became the Centre's director pulling the exploration of mediated meaning more firmly onto the terrain of ideology analysis grounded in Marxism. In 1973, at a conference convened by the Council of Europe, he presented an ambitious model of the communication process based on a schema originally developed by Italy's leading semiotician, Umberto Eco. Titled "Encoding/Decoding," it focused on the ways meaning was encoded in media artifacts and decoded by audiences. He conceded that mediated meanings are assembled by media professionals on the basis of their own sets of judgments and values, and that these occupational codings may be "relatively independent of the dominant code" generating tensions and struggles with political and economic power holders, although he noted that the concrete social practices and conditions that secure compliance or accommodate dissent are "a complex matter which cannot be spelled out here" (Hall 1973:15). This "matter" was never revisited in the CCCS's subsequent work. The result was a research agenda that generated formative studies of media artifacts and the activity of audiences in negotiating and resisting dominant definitions but excluded comparably nuanced research on processes of production. Explorations were being conducted elsewhere, however.

In 1954, the BBC's monopoly control over broadcasting ended with the launch of the advertising supported Independent Television (ITV) network of regionally based companies. Around this time, in 1959 Joseph Trenaman left the BBC Further Education Unit to take up a research fellowship at Leeds University, established by Granada, the company that had won the television franchise for the north of England. The arrival of commercial television added to growing concern that the medium's immediacy and visuality would disrupt political communication by reinforcing an emphasis on personalities rather than policies and displacing informed discussion with staged spectacles. As the country's first televised General Election, the 1959 campaign offered an opportunity to explore these issues empirically and Trenaman's pioneering study, conducted with Denis McQuail (Trenaman and McQail 1961), was the first in a series undertaken at Leeds tracking changes in the television coverage of politics and elections. Following Trenaman's death in 1961, the Granada Fellowship was awarded in 1964 to Jay Blumler, an American born political scientist who had taught social and political theory for over a decade at Ruskin College, Oxford University's adult and workers' education institute, and was a Labour Party activist in the city. His passionate commitment to democratic ideals and public education ensured a continuing focus on television's relations to the political process, but the university refused to grant him the staff and resources he needed to develop his research agenda and he moved to Maryland in 1983.

The Leeds' studies, which we will return to presently, focused on the changing organization of political information and debate during General Elections. A more comprehensive exploration of the dynamics shaping media production's engagement with social experience and issues of common concern was being developed by the research group at Leicester. Prompted by mounting political concern that televised violence may be fermenting teenage delinquency and disorder, in July 1963 the Home Secretary established the Television Research Committee to "initiate and coordinate research into the part which television plays, or could play" in the development of "young peoples' moral concepts and attitudes" (quoted in Halloran 1964b: 7). The Committee was chaired by Fraser Noble, Vice Chancellor of Leicester University, who appointed James Halloran from the university's adult education department as the Committee's Secretary. Halloran had just published *Control or Consent?* (1964a), exploring key issues in media, and under his direction a small research team was recruited. They addressed the Committee's core remit with a major study of *Television and Delinquency* (Halloran, Brown, and Chaney 1970: 179).

From an early point in the Committee's work however, Halloran had insisted on the need to see mass communication as a continuous process in which choices conditioned by the pressures and opportunities generated by particular social situations are made at both ends of the communicative chain, by producers making media artifacts and audience members interpreting and responding to them. However, it was not until the Committee's work was completed and the University agreed to support Halloran's planned research program by establishing the Centre for Mass Communication Research (CMCR) in 1966 that studies of production became a central focus.

Key here were the path-breaking investigations of Phillip Elliott. Arriving at the Centre with an Oxford degree in politics, philosophy, and economics, together with postgraduate training in social anthropology under Max Gluckman at Manchester, Elliott began work on ethnographic studies of two documentaries produced by the Midlands regional commercial television franchise holder, ATV: *The Nature of Prejudice*, a six-part documentary mini-series shot in March 1967, and the one-off documentary *Men against Cancer* made in September that year. These pioneering studies, which we will return to, established a major current of production research at the Leicester Centre, which expanded into studies of news, drama, and participatory community media.

*The Making of a Television Series* (Elliott 1972), the title given to *The Nature of Prejudice* study, referenced Elliott's double training in politics and economics and in anthropology. It underlined the case for studying production as an active process of selecting and assembling meanings embedded in situated webs of social relations, while at the same time insisting that this activity was shaped by its location within organizations and professional communities subject to cross-cutting economic imperatives and political pressures. Later research at Leicester built on this approach, combining a critical political economy of marketized communication with ethnographies of production, including a major comparative study of broadcast news in Sweden, Nigeria, and the Irish Republic (Golding and Elliott 1979). Philip Elliott also acted as informal advisor to Phillip Schlesinger's path-breaking (1978) ethnography of the BBC newsroom and they later collaborated on a study of television's coverage of terrorism (Schlesinger, Murdock, and Elliott 1983).

Explorations of media production were also gathering momentum in university departments of sociology, particularly in the "new" universities created in the 1960s, which were more open to emerging fields of study. Notable examples included Simon Frith's (1978) work at Warwick University on the music industry, drawing on his experiences as a rock journalist and professional sociologist, and the group located in the Sociology department at Essex University that included Jeremy Tunstall, Michael Lane, and Stanley Cohen. Tunstall concentrated on the analysis of occupational communities. After initial research on trawlermen working the fishing grounds of the North Sea, he turned to media occupations exploring the organization of work in advertising (Tunstall 1964) and journalism (Tunstall 1970, 1974). Michael Lane (Lane and Booth 1980) focused on the social and economic organization of the book publishing industry, a relatively neglected area of media at the time. Stanley Cohen's pioneering research on the role of media in fueling a moral panic around teenage violence led to an influential anthology on representation of deviance, *The Manufacture of News*, drawing on work from both the Leicester and Birmingham groups (Cohen and Young 1973). It was left to Cohen's doctoral student, Steve Chibnall (1977), however, to develop the first grounded account of the working lives of crime reporters.

In the early years of period under consideration here, British higher education remained divided between a centrally funded university sector and a polytechnic sector controlled by city councils and charged with vocational training. The country's first undergraduate degree in the subject field, a BA in Media Studies, was launched in 1975 at one of the leading institutions in this second sector, the Polytechnic of Central London (PCL) (later to become the University of Westminster). Under the directorship of Nicholas Garnham, who had worked at the BBC as an editor and producer, and who co-edited a collection of interviews with television personnel reflecting on their changing working environment (Bakewell and Garnham 1970), PCL attracted distinguished staff, a number of whom had practical experience of media production. James Curran was a weekly columnist for *The Times* and Vincent Porter had been an independent documentary maker. These experiences, bolstered by left politics, generated a marked focus on the changing organization and political economy of the communications system, its failings as a space of expressive diversity and open political debate, and a consistent commitment to contributing to policy debates and campaigning for reforms.

Outside of higher education, Manuel Alvarado at the British Film Institute (BFI) played an important role in extending research beyond news and actuality television, conducting, sponsoring, and publishing studies of popular television fiction texts. They included the detective series *Hazell* (1978–79) (Alvarado and Buscombe 1978), the BBC's long-running science fiction series *Doctor Who* (1963–98, 2005–) (Tulloch and Alvarado 1984) and the popular series produced by Euston Films (Alvarado and Stewart 1985)

## Channel crossings

Selective translations of works from European writers, despite being focused primarily on national media systems or contexts, played a major role in shaping British work in communication and cultural studies. The publication of Roland Bathes' (1973) semiotic dissection of French popular culture, *Mythologies*, and the revisionist model of ideology offered by selections from the prison notebooks of Italian communist Antonio Gramsci (1971) offered new resources for investigating the role of popular media in supporting prevailing relations of power that were extensively explored within film and cultural studies.

In contrast, European work on the organization of media industries, production, and labor went largely unnoticed. There were however important points of connection. In 1978 a Political Economy Section was formed within the International Association of Communication Research (IAMCR) drawing in critical researchers working on media industries and production from Britain and across Europe. They included Garnham, Miège, and Murdock. Additionally, in 1979, the PCL group launched the journal *Media, Culture and Society*, which under Garnham's editorship played a pivotal role in making available in English research on communication industries and labor emerging from continental Europe. This was followed in 1986 by the launch of the *European Journal of Communication*, cofounded by Denis McQuail who, unusually for a British academic, had moved to work in Europe, teaching in Amsterdam from 1977. Despite these points of contact however, a degree of national self-enclosure persisted. As Patrice Flichy remarked regretfully, while there is "a certain similarity between some of the work being carried out in France" and the work of British researchers, "French researchers have few contacts with their Anglo-Saxon equivalents" (1980b: 187). Despite this relative lack of regular contact, two currents within the French work had a significant influence on British researchers: the reclassification of media industries developed by Miège and his colleagues, and the revisionist model of resources for action and arenas of competition presented by France's preeminent sociologist, Pierre Bourdieu.

## Working regimes: publishing and flow

Miège and his colleagues situate cultural production within a classification of media sectors based on differential time scales and financial, employment, and reward structures (see Flichy 1980a; Miège 1987) organized around two basic institutional forms of cultural commodification labelled "flow" and "publishing," typified respectively by commercial broadcasting and book publishing. For Miège, both are governed by logics that present the actors working within them with particular arrays of possibilities and constraints. Table 1.1 summarizes their defining features. Newspapers and magazines did not fit easily into this schema. Miège saw them as displaying a unique, third, logic, but critics argued that they were more usefully regarded as variants of the flow model (see Lacroix and Tremblay 1997). The schema also faced challenges from the rise of new communications markets, prompting the construction of a new category, "the club," to accommodate commercial cable services where customers subscribe to packages of channels and pay-per-view opportunities (Tremblay and Lacroix 1991).

Despite its limits, the schema offers a useful starting point for developing systematic comparisons between the opportunities and pressures shaping similar work in different commercial media sectors, but it did not provide a basis for investigating differences in the conditions and practices of media workers in the same sector, such as comparing news and current affairs journalists with fiction writers working in commercial television, for example. Nor did it engage fully with production outside the commercial system. Miège addresses this gap elsewhere, however.

*Table 1.1* Publishing and flow logics

|  | Publishing | Flow |
|---|---|---|
|  | *Production* |  |
| Key sectors | Books, records | Commercial broadcasting |
| Technology | Reproduction | Diffusion |
| Production cycle | Periodic | Continuous |
| Production sites | Dispersed | Integrated |
| Output | Individual copies | Program schedules |
| Finance | Direct sales | Advertising payments |
|  | *Labor* |  |
| Editorial function | Compiling a catalog | Constructing a schedule |
| Creative workforce | Freelance | Contract and freelance |
| Intermediaries | Agents | Professions/trade unions |
| Payments | Royalties/copyright | Wages |

*Source*: Author's analysis based on Miège (1987)

## Commodities, gifts, and public goods

In an early programmatic essay (1979), Miège revisits Marx's distinction between productive and unproductive cultural labor in the first volume of *Capital* (Marx 1990: 1044). For Marx, a singer is only productive if they create a commodity that can be sold for a profit. If they sing at a family birthday party or in a choir supported by public funds, they may bring pleasure and joy to their listeners but are unproductive since they are not generating a return for capital. As Miège points out, "from this perspective whether (cultural) labor is productive or unproductive is not determined by its content, but by the place it occupies in the relations of production" (p. 301).

This perspective generates a map of the cultural field organized around three cultural economies: of commodities, public goods, and gifts (see Murdock 2013). Cultural production in capitalist societies is dominated by commodity economies in which media goods are either sold directly to customers (books, records, cinema tickers) or provide advertising platforms promoting general commodities (commercial television and radio programming), and as we noted earlier, with marketization their reach has expanded. At the same time, the economy of public goods, paid for out of taxation and freely available at the point of use, typified by public service broadcasting, persists as a significant alternative, together with gift economies based on voluntary donations of time and expertise to collaborative projects designed to provide shared common resources. Examples include community radio stations and more recently open software initiatives. This schema releases analysis from an exclusive focus on professionally crafted commodities and public goods and directs attention to the ways amateur vernacular production can become incorporated into the operating strategies of public service organizations as they respond to popular demands for greater representation or is capitalized on by commercial corporations as free labor.

## Rethinking capital and competition

A second challenge to established models of cultural production came from Pierre Bourdieu's redefinition of the forms of capital brought to bear on competitions for advantage and his structural model of fields of action.

In a hugely influential intervention, Bourdieu adds two further forms of capital to possession of financial resources; the cultural capital bestowed by command over valued symbolic expression as defined by legitimated arbiters of excellence, and the social capital derived from membership of networks of support and influence. He deploys this schema to devastating effect in *Distinction* (Bourdieu 1984), his dissection of French cultural tastes, revolutionizing approaches to the class dynamics of taste and consumption and their role in the exercise of power. He does not explore how the three forms of capital are mobilized in cultural production with the same thoroughness, but the value of this typology is illustrated by an early contribution to the British Film Institute's series of studies of television production – Boleslaw Sulik's (1976) account of working as a script writer on an adaptation of Joseph Conrad's short story, *The Shadow Line*, commissioned by Thames television, the franchise holder for London's commercial television services. Sulik asks why a British company, primarily oriented to profit maximization, should be interested in making a film from a director whose name "smacks of minority tastes, of obscure, foreign, subtitled art-film" (p. 43). His answer was that one of the company's board members, Jeremy Issacs, had himself garnered enormous prestige within the industry for his monumental 26-part documentary series *World at War* (1973–74) and was "a voice ... not adverse to seeking prestige for the company with the occasional ambitious 'art project'" (p. 43). The additional symbolic capital accumulated by demonstrating a commitment to expressive diversity and catering to minority tastes required by their public service remit could then be converted into political capital when the franchise came up for renewal.

The majority of Bourdieu's own research on cultural production centered around the "restricted" literary and artistic artifacts governed by a "professional ideology of production for producers" (1993:127) and presents symbolist poetry as the "most perfectly autonomous sector of the field of cultural production where the only audience aimed at is other producers" (Bourdieu 1993: 39). The importance of peer esteem emerged as a central theme in Philip Elliott's pioneering ethnographies. He draws a critical distinction between the production team responsible for assembling a program, and the technical studio crew operating a production system (Elliott 1972 128). Different crews, employed by the company on a continuing basis, worked on different programs in a series and had little investment in the eventual outcome. In contrast, members of the production team were employed for specific projects and looked to the finished programs as calling cards for future employment. The opinion of their peers and accumulated professional reputation played crucial roles in securing future contracts.

Studies of media production have often passed over technical staff as simply skilled support for creative activity, but as Antione Hennion and Jean-Pierre Vignolle (1978) demonstrate in their study of the French record industry, technicians may play a more central role. Based on three years of research across 12 companies, combining interviews and observations with documentary research, they linked critical political economy with situated ethnography to provide a detailed portrait of both the organization of the industry and the work of producing recorded music. After observing studio recording sessions, Hennion and Vignolle argued that far from being "a simple process of 'packaging' already fixed sounds," the professional skills of sound engineers were "integral [to] active production," with the finished recording emerging from the different sound possibilities the engineers presented to singers and musicians (1980: 87). A similar argument can be made for the lighting camera person on a film set, or the editor in post-production, which in their respective ways challenge the auteur theory's elevation of the director as the primary creative force.

As Nicholas Garnham and Raymond Williams noted when introducing Bourdieu to English readers, while rejecting all attempt to see cultural artifacts as the product of creative biographies, Bourdieu has little to say about "the increased intervention of economic capital into the production of symbolic goods" (1980: 222) or the changing technologies of production, absences that lead him to see "creative liberty and the laws of the market" (Bourdieu 1993: 127) as governing entirely separate domains of cultural production rather than as permanent points of tension within mainstream media production. Witnessing the aggressive promotion of marketization late in his life, however, Bourdieu became a vocal critic of major media companies, denouncing their "pursuit of maximum *short-term* profit and the 'aesthetic' that derives from that pursuit" as "ever more intensely and widely imposed" across the full range of creative activity (original emphasis 2010: 224–225). In developing his analysis, Bourdieu draws on his long standing characterization of cultural production as a "field" of play, simultaneously an arena of competition in which actors devise strategies "to defend or improve their position" and "a network of objective relations" governed by rules of the game (1993:30). This model assumes that most "players" will devote themselves to jockeying for advantage within the prevailing system but leaves open the possibility that some may seek to alter the terms of competition and the layout of the field.

Observing the increasing concentration of corporate power, the critical political economy of communications developed in Britain arrived earlier at the same conclusion by a different route. The power of media owners to determine the organization and direction of production within the companies they controlled had been a major focus of research from the outset. Studies had focused on two dimensions of owner power: direct interventions in production to advance their business interests or political views (instrumental power), and the impact on diversity of expression and employment from decisions over the allocation of company resources and staffing, shifting from investigative journalism to celebrity and life style coverage for example (allocative control) (see Murdock 1982). Steven Lukes' influential (1974) revisionist account of power had added a third dimension, structural power, the ability of dominant firms to reset the terms of competition. Rupert Murdoch's interventions provided British observers with a case study of structural power in action. There was ample evidence that Murdoch mobilized his newspaper titles to promote his favored ideological positions and secure political support for his business ambitions (see McKnight 2012), but it was equally clear that he was intent on reordering the field of competition by capitalizing on the potentials for cost cutting and market entry offered by new production technologies.

Under the hot metal linotype system, compositors had enjoyed a historic monopoly over making up newspaper pages. Murdoch's decision to move his London-based national newspaper production from his central Fleet Street location to cheaper premises at Wapping and to introduce computer typesetting precipitated a bitter year-long strike that ended with the abolition of a craft skill, paving the way for mass redundancies among national print workers and allowing journalists to input copy directly. Additionally, his successful bid for monopoly control of the British satellite market rewrote the rules of competition in the television industry increasing the costs of securing broadcast rights to major sporting events and maintaining audience share. Surveying the French cultural marketplace, Bourdieu (2005: 195) belatedly comes to the same conclusion, noting that "the dominant firms exert their pressure on the dominated firms and on their strategies ... modifying the entire environment of other firms and the system of constraints that bear on them or the space of possibles offered to them." His observation confirms the crucial role of critical political economy in mapping the shifting balance of forces shaping the organization and direction of activity within specific production sites.

## Producing the public sphere: mediating citizenship

The term "political" in political economy points to a second enduring focus of analysis; the role of mass media in providing the cultural resources that support the informed and empathetic social participation on which democracy's promise of full and equal citizenship ultimately rests. Access to accurate information, sustained analysis of causes and consequences, and open debate on available options for action are essential prerequisites for active participation in public deliberations on issues of common concern that inform decisions in legislative assemblies. In his landmark (1962) contribution to political theory, *The Structural Transformation of the Public Sphere*, Jurgen Habermas offers a sustained lament for the unfulfilled ideal of a vibrant public sphere comprised of multiple social and mediated sites of deliberation. Although German broadcasting at the time was ordered around regional public service organizations, he saw a cultural landscape where "the laws of the market ... have come to guide production in the wide fields of a culture of consumers" (1991: 165), and where citizenship is equated with a civic duty to contribute to collective well-being by boosting consumption and "the state has to 'address' its citizens like consumers" (p. 195). Habermas did not pursue this argument empirically, but his vision of democracy in decline exerted a powerful influence on British research, directing concerted attention to television's changing presentation of political events and issues.

As the point in the political cycle when deliberation on issues is at its most concentrated, the conduct of General Elections had long been seen as a test of representative democracy's viability and vitality. Jay Blumler's studies of how television covered UK General Elections during 1966 and 1979 pointed to important changes as political parties developed strategies for directing and orchestrating coverage designed to provide media outlets with readymade content that fitted their institutional and presentational requirements. In contrast to the coverage of the 1966 election offered by commercial broadcaster ITV, which relied more heavily on extracts from politician speeches, the BBC introduced debates between party spokespeople and leaders and filmed reports of the campaign in the country. However, their inclusion in the newly introduced current affairs program *24 Hours*, distinguished by its "lively pace" and "reliance on immediate viewer appeal" (Blumler 1969: 101), was seen by some members of the production team as a departure from straight reporting. This difference of opinion marked, Blumer argues, a moment of transition between journalists' "daily relations with party representatives and rival styles of political coverage thought appropriate for the intended audience" (p. 111).

Blumler returned to the BBC to observe the Corporation's coverage of the 1979 election to find a highly routinized operation, tellingly called "the factory," focused primarily on the "limited number of predesignated action stations" offered by parties' press conferences and the party leaders' speeches and walkabouts (Gurevitch and Blumler 1982: 184). It was, he argued, "a far cry from the more 'old-fashioned' notion of election coverage in which alert reporters roam the field to see where the action is" (p. 189). Professionalism had come to be equated with skillful packaging, "sifting through the materials provided by politicians" to assemble an engaging narrative enlivened with the drama of oppositional remarks (p. 199). This closure of discursive space was accompanied by a more presidential style of campaigning with over 60 percent of the coverage of the main parties devoted to their leaders' statements (p. 201), a finding that supported Habermas's (1991: 195) contention that modern politics was taking on "feudal features" as leaders sought to project the "aura and supernatural authority" once bestowed on kings and emperors, positioning voters as spectators in a staged political theater rather than active participants in a deliberative process.

Faced with resurgent social movements, Habermas later revised his original account of the public sphere modelled on the town hall meeting, conceding that "sometimes the support of ... mass protests and incessant campaigning is required before an issue can make its way into the core of the political system" (Habermas 1992: 381). October 1968 saw the largest mass demonstration in postwar Britain as a broadly based coalition of groups marched through central London to protest against the American war in Vietnam. The research team at the Leicester

Centre took a snap decision to investigate the news coverage of the event as a case study in the reporting and public responses to contentious issues. The resulting study combined observational research in television and press newsrooms, textual analysis of the coverage, and studies of differential audience responses (Halloran, Elliot, and Murdock 1970). It opened the black box of production practices left unopened in the encoding/decoding model to detail how journalists' professional ideologies and selections relayed and reinforced official accounts.

The demonstration was framed by the "events" in Paris in May 1968 and the clashes outside the American embassy in London during an earlier demonstration. Drawing on information supplied by the security services (later proved to be inaccurate), *The Times* headline for September 5 announced "Militant Plot Feared in London," claiming that "extremists," led by overseas agitators, planned to use the march to attack police and public buildings. On the day 70,000 marched peacefully through the center of London to a rally in Hyde Park. An estimated 3,000 peeled off to demonstrate outside the American embassy in Grosvenor Square with around 50 attempting to breach the police cordon around the embassy. In line with the original framing, the ensuing confrontation dominated the coverage in the right of center dailies. The left-leaning *Daily Mirror* and *Guardian* devoted less space, but both carried a photograph of a policeman apparently being kicked in the face by a demonstrator in the Square on the front page.

Members of the research team observed editorial decision-making in both papers' newsrooms and at the BBC as staff negotiated the tensions between acknowledging the political significance of the event, professional judgments of newsworthiness, and the inferential structure established by coverage to the build up to the march. As the researchers argue, the prior expectation of violence created an "unwitting bias" where even "reporting on the peaceful main march suggested disorder and quasi-violence," effectively constructing the story as "simply one of violence or no-violence," delegitimizing direct political action and marginalizing alternative perspectives (p. 237).

The BBC's unique position within the British political system generates additional tensions. As the national broadcaster funded out of the public purse, the Corporation is caught in a permanent tension between serving the public interest by providing comprehensive information and analysis, and pressure to promote the "national interest" as defined by the government of the day. The founding moment in this abrasive relation, the General Strike of 1926, had been examined in Michael Tracey's doctoral thesis at the Leicester Centre (Tracey 1978), but in the period under review here, it was particularly evident in decisions around the coverage of the "Troubles" in Northern Ireland.

Defining and engaging with terrorism presents particularly difficult dilemmas for democratic states. Official discourses promoting a "war" against terror clash with alternative discourses insisting that state action must remain within the rule of law and the political claims of insurgent groups themselves. In the Leicester study, *Televising "Terrorism,"* Schlesinger, Elliott, and Murdock (1983) drew attention to the crucial role of cultural forms and genres in organizing this discursive field. They present television programming as arranged along a continuum of relative openness and closure depending on which discourses are brought into play and how the relations between them are arranged and resolved. News is relatively closed since, as multiple studies have confirmed, it is primarily organized around the agendas and discourses of legitimate power holders. In contrast, current affairs and documentary programs may be more open to questioning official accounts and offering space to alternative and oppositional discourses. In October 1985, the BBC produced *At the Edge of Union*, featuring extended portraits of two elected politicians at opposite ends of the political spectrum in Northern Ireland; Gregory Campbell, a hardline Unionist, and Martin McGuiness from the main

Republican party, Sinn Fein, widely thought to be the chief of staff of the Irish Republican Army, then engaged in armed conflict with the British state. The Home Secretary sent a letter to the BBC's Board of Governors asking for the scheduled broadcast to be cancelled, arguing that it was "damaging to security and therefore to the public interest to provide a boost to the morale of terrorists in this way" (quoted in Murdock 1991:109). In response, BBC journalists staged a one-day strike defending editorial independence. Eventually, the program was broadcast without cuts but with minor additions.

## The lives of others: fabricating fictions

Democracies rest on negotiated social settlements rooted in empathy and respect for those holding different views and the ability to see the world through their eyes. Television drama plays a central role in cultivating these essential dispositions. Its ability to present multiple experiences and perspectives depends on the balance struck between the creative ambitions of authors and the constraints imposed by the economics of production and the organization of different generic conventions.

Single plays are arguably the most open, while continuing serials set in a particular location the least flexible, with a mid-point occupied by series based around a central character's encounters with successive challenges. Traditionally, single plays broadcast in primetime had been a major presence in the schedules with ITV's *Armchair Theatre* (1956–1974), and the BBC's *Wednesday Play* (1964–1970) and its successor, *Play for Today* (1970–1984). Productions frequently drew on the new social realism in popular novels and film to probe the bleak underside of the emerging consumer society, typified by *Cathy Come Home*, Ken Loach's harrowing 1966 depiction of homelessness. In UK television, intensification of competition from the mid-1980s onward, however, saw a decline in support for single plays and increasing reliance on the opportunities to build audience loyalty and ratings offered by engagement with the continuing characters featured in series and serials.

The dynamics of popular series production were explored in Alvarado and Buscombe's path-breaking BFI-sponsored study of the private eye series *Hazell* made by the ITV London franchise holder, Thames Television. The aim was to produce a detailed "behind the scenes" account of program making for use in teaching. As Buscombe (2010: 450) later noted, it didn't "spend too much time reflecting on more abstract research issues governing the relationship between authorial creativity and institutional dynamics. It wasn't intended to be that kind of book." Licensed to move between social milieu, the central character in the series – private detective James Hazell – encounters a range of situations but these are always seen primarily through his eyes excluding sustained attention to other points of view. This generic limitation is an economic advantage. By encouraging viewers to identify with a character, they get to know it helps build audience loyalty and ratings.

The economics of series were explored in a second BFI study detailing to development of the Thames production subsidiary, Euston Films (Alvarado and Stewart 1985). Here the research highlighted the increasing importance of overseas program sales in commercial calculations, although time limitations prevented the authors from pursuing this analytical thread. They subsequently began work on a book provisionally titled *Selling Television* but never completed it. The need to cultivate export markets was not confined to the commercial television companies. Under increasing political pressure to become more commercially minded and supplement its license fee income by exploiting market opportunities, in 1979 the BBC launched a commercial division, BBC Enterprises, selling finished programs and formats to overseas markets and increasing the range of associated merchandise The hugely successful science fiction series

*Doctor Who,* whose production had been detailed in another early BFI-sponsored study (Tulloch and Alvarado 1984) offered the ideal vehicle for both ambitions: stateless and featuring multiple archetypal villains and monsters, it was sold into over 50 markets, supporting an extensive range of games and toys based on the characters. Increasing attention to export potential developed alongside a concerted search for co-production agreements designed to reduce costs and ensure entry to key markets. Series are tradeable commodities in export markets. They meet the need for multiple episodes to fill set slots in the schedules (and more recently for "box sets") but crossing geographical boundaries imposes cultural costs. Constructing "Englishness" around internationally known motifs – the Royal Family, Jane Austen, Sherlock Holmes, and the Elizabethan era – may play well in international markets but pushed less familiar but decisive moments for a fuller understanding of national history out of the frame, the continuing neglect of the English Civil War being a case in point.

In 1985, in another major reallocation of production resources, the BBC launched a primetime soap opera, *EastEnders,* to rival Granada's high-rating *Coronation Street* introduced in 1960. Both were set in working-class neighborhoods, but their fixed locations limited the situations and issues that could be plausibly introduced. The balance between the shifting political economy of broadcasting and the range of drama production was explored at the Leicester Centre through interviews with a range of executive and creative personnel (Murdock 1980a, 1980b, 1981; Murdock and Halloran 1979).

Engagement with the stark realities of Britain's de-industrialization, though less concerted than in the heyday of the single play, still found a place in the schedules. One of the most watched sole-authored series *Boys from the Blackstuff* (1982) detailed the human costs of unemployment, then reaching record levels. Research on its production (Millington and Nelson 1986) highlighted the continuing importance of taking account of institutional dynamics. The drama secured resources because it fitted with the commitment to find new northern voices then underway in the BBC's regional production in Birmingham. This initiative was part of a wider move to address issues around representation.

## Participation and professionalism: openings and closings

The increasing marketization of the British media coincided with a deepening crisis of representation in both senses that term carries in English. Questions were increasingly asked about the range of experiences and viewpoints presented in the dominant media and about who was entitled to speak about other people's lives. These concerns were driven first by the overcentralized structure of British broadcasting, and second by demands from social movements around ethnicity, gender, sexuality, and social issues that had been gathering momentum since the late 1960s. Increasingly viewers and listeners were pressing for their voices and views to be given space on the major broadcast channels and demanding to speak for themselves rather than being spoken about by professional program makers.

Space to accommodate these demands opened up unexpectedly in 1972 when the Conservative government licensed experimental community cable ventures in five cities. Three folded before their licenses were due to expire in 1979 but two survived, in Greenwich, South London, and Swindon. Both were extensively researched by members of the Leicester Centre (Croll and Husband 1975; Negrine 1977). The Greenwich organizers recorded "a far greater demand for program time than our resources can cater" and claimed to be attracting up to 12 percent of the viewing audience (quoted in Lewis 1978: 23), but with no government grant, lack of funding forced it to close. Swindon Viewpoint, originally owned by the entertainment major, EMI, and later supported by a modest grant from the local council, survived for longer with 85 percent of programming being made on the suggestion of viewers and 18 percent involved in production and 57 percent in editing (Croll and Husband 1975). Production continued on a reduced basis until 1980, relying entirely on volunteers. Again, funding failed to match demand. In 1984, the government granted the first fully commercial franchises translating cable from a potential space of participation to a conduit for popular professionally made programming. Studies of community cable's promise of animating local communities and providing expressive spaces for marginalized groups were also conducted in France (Beaud, Millard, and Willener 1976); the results recorded dashed hopes. As Augustin Girard (1978: 89) concluded, reasserting the primacy of professional production, "enthusiasts" could not cite a single enduring example of audiences preferring the "remarkable talents to be discovered among thirteen-year-old amateurs" to "over-polished and artificial programmes from capital cities."

Even when successful, community broadcasting was limited by its local reach and failed to satisfy demands for greater visibility on the main broadcast channels. The BBC's newly created Community Programming Unit responded in April 1973 by launching *Open Door*, offering marginalized groups the opportunity to make their own programs. Since the margins extended to both ends of the political spectrum, entries included a group campaigning to stop immigration alongside a group of black teachers and the Transex Liberation Group. The program marked a fundamental break with the professional monopoly over program making for national channels translating audiences into potential producers. In 1991 the BBC launched a new access initiative, *Video Diaries*, capitalizing on the easy-to-use portable camcorder and video equipment to allow people to tell their own stories in their own way. Participants exercised substantial control over content and editing but were selected by the production team and an increasingly competitive broadcast environment pulled decisions toward the quirky typified by a man's year-long vigil at Loch Ness hoping to see the fabled monster. In 1993, with the launch of *Video Nation,* the selection of contributors was limited to 55 people chosen to represent a diversity of social situations and experiences, but as Richard Kilborn's (1998: 228) research revealed, what they produced was "subject to a rigorous filtering and editing process."

This consolidation of access to the national screen was reinforced by the transformation of Channel 4 in Britain. After a heated debate, in 1982 the channel had been assigned to a new broadcast organization, which for the first time in Britain uncoupled production from distribution offering an alternative to the vertically integrated system that had dominated BBC and ITV keeping virtually all production "in-house." The new channel opened access to multiple small and specialized program makers with close ties to groups outside of the mainstream. Channel 4 began broadcasting in November 1982, but from 1990 was allowed to sell its own advertising, precipitating a shift toward more mainstream programming. That same year a new Broadcasting Act required both the BBC and ITV to acquire at least a quarter of their programming from independents. This neoliberal opening of previously protected markets had two major impacts on the diversity of production. It led to the disappearance of many small companies, increasing the consolidation of independent production in the hands of major concerns. Second, a tracking survey of creative personnel conducted by the BFI confirmed the social and cultural capital generated by relational contacts and professional reputation became indispensable resources for ensuring a steady flow of commissions (Patterson 2017).

This narrowing of the terms of participation over the period covered here intersected with the structural tendency toward professional closure within the broadcasting and media industries. As Tom Burns noted in his pioneering (1977) organizational study of the BBC, claims to professionalism allowed members to resist "external" control from audience demands as well as from management and government agencies, reinforcing a persistent pull toward enclosure within the "small, exotic plural society" of the production team (Burns 1972: 291). One of the reasons why ethnographies of production are relatively rare is that "outsiders" who may raise awkward questions that are unwelcome within these enclaves. Personal recommendation and shared background and experience can help to open doors, however. Philip Elliott (1972: 171) recounts how his relations with the production team were facilitated by the Oxford University background he shared with three of its members. Similarly, Philip Schlesinger's entry to the BBC newsroom was eased by an approach from his doctoral supervisor to a colleague married to a BBC announcer (1980: 342). They arrived to find occupational enclaves where social background and networks were central to recruitment and advancement, and as Elliott (1972) discovered, working practices which drew heavily on personal contacts for sources, supplemented by approaches to people who had previously featured in media coverage. The resulting self-reinforcing circle led him to conclude that mass communication was a "contradiction in terms" since the more an occupational group develops its own routines, criteria, and standards the more it becomes enclosed within them and detached from audience experience.

## Logging continuities

In the years since the period covered here, digital media have experienced exponential growth, exercising increasing command over both advertising revenues and audience attention, and undermining the political economies of established media, now often designated as "legacy" media, suggesting that these increasing belong to a rapidly disappearing past. As I argued at the outset however, the digital age is also the age of marketization and since the fundamental impacts of marketization on media production have intensified the studies reviewed here continue to provide indispensable resources. They direct analysis to three continuing processes: increasing corporate concentration, the reorganization of creative labor, and the crisis of representation.

Bernard Miege's model of publishing and flow, typified by book production and commercial television, assumed that these sectors were separate, but with the accelerating pace of mergers and acquisitions they are increasingly integrated into broadly based media conglomerates. In 2020 the German communications major Bertelsmann successfully bid for the major publishing house, Simon & Schuster. When added to Bertelsmann's existing publishing interests centered on Penguin Random House, the acquisition gave the company a 30 percent share of global English book sales. Bertelsmann already enjoyed market strength in other media sectors, represented by control of a major European television and radio broadcaster-producer, RTL, and the BMG music publishing and recording division. In 2019 the company established a Creative Alliance to look for ways of maximizing the benefits of this diversification by developing joint formats and synergies, basing programs on best-selling books for example. How these new integrated corporate structures reorder production decisions merits sustained research.

The argument around the exercise and impact of structural power, outlined earlier in relation to Rupert Murdoch's monopoly control of satellite broadcasting in Britain, has assumed new relevance with the rise of streaming services, led by Netflix, and the altered production and distribution strategies being developed by terrestrial broadcasters in response to a radically changed competitive environment. As studies have consistently demonstrated, the marketization of employment that began in the period covered here has accelerated substantially altering the conditions of creative labor, entry to journalism and television production is increasingly conditional on holding a university degree and having unpaid work experience through intern opportunities, the kinds of opportunities that as Bourdieu points out, largely depend on access to the financial support, contact networks, and cultural capital provided by already advantaged families. The result is a continuing class bias. Recent surveys of British journalists found that 54 percent of senior figures had attended either Oxford or Cambridge (Kirby 2016) and 98 percent of those joining the profession in recent years held a bachelor's degree (Thurman, Cornia, and Kunert 2016: 8–13). While there was less discrimination in entry to the profession according to gender, with women making up 45 percent of the profession, frequently this was to less well-paid and junior positions. Only 0.2 percent of journalists came from the Black British community.

These persistent social biases and exclusions are intensifying the crisis of representation. Early utopian hopes that the internet would provide a universally accessible space of collective expression, bypassing the editorial selectivity exercised by established media, have been comprehensively undermined by the virtual monopolies exercised by the dominant social media platforms. Control over representation informed by professional values has passed to unaccountable algorithms supplemented by poorly paid human evaluators. The result is a fundamental deconstruction of the public sphere as a shared space of encounter as audiences are sorted into polarized political and cultural silos. In searching for alternatives, the early experiments in access television, based on collaborative partnerships between professionals and amateurs in the service of maximizing diversity of representation, merit sustained reevaluation as part of a wider reconsideration of the relations between the cultural economies of public goods and gifts, and the future of public service broadcasting as the central hub in a non-commercial digital commons. Media industries, and the questions we ask about their organization or the artifacts they produce, remain as they have always been, central to the future of democratic life.

# References

Alvarado, M. and Buscombe, E. (1978) *Hazell: The Making of a TV Series*, London: British Film Institute.

Alvarado, M. and Stewart, J. (1985) *Euston Films Ltd*, London: Methuen.

Bakewell, J. and Garnham, N. (eds) (1970) *The New Priesthood: British Television Today*, London: Allen Lane.

Barbier-Bouvet J. P., Beaud, P., and Flichy, P. (1979) *Communication et Pouvoir-Media de Masse et Media Communautaires au Quebec*, Paris: Editions Anthropos.

Barthes, R. (1973) *Mythologies*, London: Paladin.

Beaud, P., Millard, G., and Willener, A. (1976) *Télévision Locale et Animation Urbaine*, Celta Vevey: Éditions Delta.

Blumler, J. G. (1969) "Producers Attitudes towards Television Coverage of an Election Campaign: A Case Study," in P. Halmos (ed.) *The Sociology of Mass Communicators*, Keele: Keele University, 85–115.

Bourdieu, P. (1984) *Distinction: A Social Critique of the Judgement of Taste*, London: Routledge.

Bourdieu, P. (1993) *The Field of Cultural Production*, Cambridge: Polity.

Bourdieu, P. (2005) "The Principles of an Economic Anthropology," in P. Bourdieu, *The Social Structures of the Economy*, Cambridge: Polity, 193–222.

Bourdieu, P. (2010) "Culture is in Danger," in G. Sapiro (ed.), *Sociology Is a Martial Art: Political Writings by Pierre Bourdieu*, New York: The New Press, 222–233.

Burns, T. (1972) "Commitment and Career in the BBC," in D. McQuail (ed.), *Sociology of Mass Communications*, Harmondsworth: Penguin, 281–310.

Burns, T. (1977) *The BBC: Public Institution and Private World*, London: Macmillan.

Buscombe, E. (2010) "Writing Hazel," *Television and New Media*, 11 (6): 448–450.

Chibnall, S. (1977) *Law and Order News: An Analysis of Crime Reporting in the British Press*, London: Tavistock.

Cohen, S. and Young, J. (eds) (1973) *The Manufacture of New: Deviance, Social Problems and the Mass Media*, London: Constable.

Croll, P. and Husband, C. (1975) *Communication and Community: A Study of the Swindon Community Television Experiment*, unpublished report, Leicester: University of Leicester, Centre for Mass Communication Research.

Elliott, P. (1972) *The Making of a Television Series: A Case Study in the Sociology of Culture*, London: Constable.

Flichy, P. (1980a) *Les Industries de L'Imaginaire*, Grenoble: Presse Universitaires de Grenoble/Institut national de L'audiovisuel.

Flichy, P. (1980b) "Current Approaches to Mass Communication Research in France," *Media, Culture and Society*, 2 (2): 179–188.

Frith, S. (1978) *The Sociology of Rock*, London: Constable.

Garnham, N. (1979) "Contribution to a Political Economy of Mass-communication," *Media, Culture and Society*, 1 (1): 123–146.

Garnham, N. and Williams, R. (1980) "Pierre Bourdieu and the Sociology of Culture: An Introduction," *Media, Culture and Society*, 2 (3): 209–223.

Girard, A. (1978) "Cable Television and Cultural Policy," in J. Caughie (ed.), *Television Ideology and Exchange*, London: British Film Institute, 86–91.

Golding, P. and Elliott, P. (1979) *Making the News*, London: Longman.

Golding, P. and Harris, P. (eds) (1997) *Beyond Cultural Imperialism: Globalization, Communication and the New World Order*, London: Sage.

Gramsci, A (1971) *Selections from the Prison Notebooks*, London: Lawrence and Wishart.

Gurevitch, M. and Blumler, J. G. (1982) "The Construction of Election News: An Observation Study at the BBC," in J. S. Ettema and D. C. Whitney (eds), *Individuals in Mass Media Organizations: Creativity and Constraint*, Beverly Hills, CA: Sage Publications, 179–204.

Habermas, J. (1991) *The Structural Transformation of the Public Sphere*, Cambridge, MA: MIT Press.

Habermas, J. (1992) *Between Facts and Norms: Contributions to a Discourse Theory of Law and Democracy*, Cambridge, MA: MIT Press.

Hall, S. (1973) *Encoding and Decoding the Television Discourse*, paper CCC/DC (73) 104, Strasbourg: Council of Europe Committee for Out-of-School Education and Cultural Development.

Hall, S. and Whannel, P. (1964) *The Popular Arts*, London: Hutchinson Educational.

Halloran, J. D. (1964a) *Control or Consent? A Study of the Challenges of Mass Communication*, London: Sheed and Ward.

Halloran, J. D. (1964b) *The Effects of Mass Communication with Special Reference to Television*, Leicester: Leicester University Press.

Halloran, J. D., Brown, R. L., and Chaney, D. C (1970) *Television and Delinquency*, Leicester: Leicester University Press.

Halloran, J. D., Elliot, P., and Murdock, G. (1970) *Demonstrations and Communication: A Case Study*, Harmondsworth: Penguin.

Hennion, A. and Vignolle, J-P. (1978) *L'economie du disque en France*, Paris: La Documentation Francaise.

Hennion, A. and Vignolle, J-P. (1980) "Mixing Genres and Reaching the Public: The Production of Popular Music," *Social Science Information*, 19 (1): 79–105.

Hoggart, R. (1957) *The Uses of Literacy*, London: Chatto and Windus.

Hoggart, R. (1969) *Contemporary Cultural Studies: An Approach to the Study of Literature and Society*, Birmingham: Birmingham University, Centre for Contemporary Cultural Studies.

Huet, A., Ion, J., Lefrebvre, A., Miège, B., and Peron, R. (1978) *Capitalisme et industries culturelles*, Grenoble. Presse Universitaires de Grenoble.

Kilborn, R. W. (1998) "Shaping the Real: Democratization and Commodification in UK Factual Broadcasting," *European Journal of Communication*, 13 (2). 201–218.

Kirby, P. (2016) *Leading People 2016: The Educational Background of the UK Professional Elite*, London: The Sutton Trust.

Lacroix, J-G. and Tremblay, G. (1997) "The Institutionalization of Cultural Commodification: Logics and Strategies," *Current Sociology*, 45 (4): 39–69.

Lane, M. and Booth, J. (1980) *Books and Publishers: Commerce against Culture in Postwar Britain*, Lexington, KY: Lexington Books.

Lewis, P. M. (1978) *Community Television Cable in Britain*, London: British Film Institute.

Lukes, S. (1974) *Power: A Radical View*, London: Macmillan.

McDonald, P. (2013) "Studies of Media Industries: Four Challenges," *In Media Res: A Media Commons Project*, May 27, available at http://mediacommons.org/imr/2013/05/25/studies-media-industries-four-challenges (accessed August 8, 2020).

McKnight, D. (2012) *Rupert Murdoch: An Investigation of Political Power*, Sydney: Allen & Unwin.

Marx, K. (1990) *Capital: Volume 1*, London: Penguin.

Miège, B. (1979) "The Cultural Commodity," *Media, Culture and Society*, 1 (3): 297–311.

Miège, B. (1987) "The Logics at Work in the New Cultural Industries," *Media, Culture and Society*, 9 (3): 273–289.

Millington, B. and Nelson, R. (1986) *Boys from the Blackstuff: The Making of a TV Drama*, London: Comedia.

Murdock, G. (1980a) "Authorship and Organisation," *Screen Education,* 35: 19–34.

Murdock, G. (1980b) "Radical Drama, Radical Theatre," *Media, Culture and Society,* 2 (2): 149–168.

Murdock, G. (1981) "Organising the Imagination: Sociological Perspectives on Radio Drama," in P. Lewis (ed.), *Radio Drama,* London: Longman, 143–163.

Murdock, G. (1982) "Large Corporations and the Control of the Communication Industries," in M. Gurevitch, T. Bennett, J. Curran, and J. Woollacott (eds), *Culture, Society and the Media,* London: Methuen, 118–150.

Murdock, G. (1991) "Patrolling the Border: British Broadcasting and the Irish Question in the 1980's," *Journal of Communication,* 41 (4): 104–115.

Murdock, G. (2013) "Political Economies as Moral Economies: Commodities, Gifts and Public Goods," in J. Wasko, G. Murdock, and H. Sousa (eds), *The Handbook of Political Economy of Communication,* Oxford: Blackwell, 13–40.

Murdock, G. and Golding, P. (1973) "For a Political Economy of Mass Communication," in R. Miliband and J. Saville (eds), *The Socialist Register 1973: A Survey of Movements and Ideas,* London: Merlin Press, 205–234.

Murdock, G. and Halloran, J. D. (1979) "Contexts of Creativity in Television Drama: An Exploratory Study in Britain," in H-D. Fischer and S. R. Melnik (eds), *Entertainment: A Cross-Cultural Examination,* New York: Hastings House, 273–285.

Negrine, R. (1977) *Cable Television and Community Access,* unpublished doctoral thesis, Leicester: Leicester University, Centre for Mass Communication Research.

Patterson, R. (2017) "Early Independent Production Entrepreneurs in UK Television," *International Journal of Entrepreneurial Venturing,* 9 (3): 280–298.

Schlesinger, P. (1978) *Putting 'Reality' Together: BBC News,* London: Constable.

Schlesinger, P. (1980) "Between Sociology and Journalism," in H. Christian (ed.), *The Sociology of Journalism and the Press,* Keele: Keele University, 341–369.

Schlesinger, P., Murdock, G. and Elliott, P. (1983) *Televising 'Terrorism': Political Violence in Popular Culture,* London: Comedia.

Sulik, B. (1976) *A Change of Tack: Making the Shadow Line,* London: British Film Institute.

Thurman, N., Cornia, A., and Kunert, J (2016) *Journalists in the UK.* Oxford: Reuters Institute for the Study of Journalism.

Tracey, M. (1978) *The Production of Political Television,* London: Routledge & Kegan Paul.

Tremblay, G. and Lacroix, J-G. (1991) *Télévision: Deuxième dynastie,* Québec: Presse de l'Universite du Québec.

Trenaman, J. and McQuail, D. (1961) *Television and the Political Image: A Study of the Impact of Television on the 1959 General Election,* London: Methuen.

Tulloch, J. and Alvarado, M. (1984) *Dr Who: The Unfolding Text,* London: St Martins.

Tunstall, J. (1964) *The Advertising Man in London Advertising Agencies,* London: Chapman Hall

Tunstall, J. (1970) *The Westminster Lobby Correspondents,* London: Routledge & Kegan Paul.

Tunstall, J. (1974) *Journalists at Work,* London: Constable.

# 2

# ORIGINS OF RESEARCH INTO MEDIA INDUSTRIES CONDUCTED IN THE UNITED STATES

*Janet Wasko*

Once upon a time, it was rare to find much interest by media scholars in research on media industries. Times have changed, indeed. The study of media industries has been recognized as a legitimate and more popular approach to the study of media, despite lingering issues relating to its definitions, scope, and motivations. The proliferation of studies that fit under this umbrella is a clear sign of this development, as is the large number of Society for Cinema and Media Studies (SCMS) scholars who identified with the Media Industries Scholarly Interest Group when it was formed in 2011. This is not to say that the field of media industries is necessarily new as research has been done in the past that has provided groundwork for such inquiry.

To explore the origins of media industries research in the United States, this chapter will review some of the relevant approaches and sample studies that fit this description from the turn of the nineteenth century through to the early 2000s when "Media Industries Studies" began to be identified as a distinct and new field or sub-discipline. The aim is to present a picture of the *breadth* of industries research conducted historically in the United States, and not to explore in *depth* or detail any or all of these studies for the insights they contribute, toward offering a cumulative picture of the multiplicity of research directions characterizing studies of media industries. The development of particular ideas or arguments will not be explored, but a review of the historical emergence and shaping of a body of scholarship is offered. General approaches will be discussed first, followed by studies of single industries and then research working across industries.

## Defining media industries studies

First, it is important to establish what media and theoretical approaches have been included in the study of media industries. For instance, this volume encompasses contributions looking at publishing, print, advertising, comics, music, film, television, and social media industries. However, the new Media Industries Studies approach seems to focus mostly on what Michelle Hilmes has called "sound and screen" media[1]:

DOI: 10.4324/9780429275340-4

In the United States, the most extended and well-established body of work examining the function of the media industry in its most popular and widely disseminated forms has arisen around the "sound and screen" media: radio, television, and film now extending to new digital venues.

*(2009: 21)*

As Hilmes (and others) have explained, the study of print media and journalism (as well as advertising and telecommunications) have different histories than sound and screen media, and often have drawn from different epistemological traditions. Organization of academic study related to these various media has also often diverged, with separate degree programs, departments, schools, and different professional organizations. Thus, print, publishing, and journalism, as well as other media industries, have not always been included as part of the newly defined Media Industry Studies.[2] As media industries and technologies have increasingly converged, becoming part of diversified conglomerates or converged industries, they have increasingly been analyzed and referred to collectively in popular and critical discussions as "the media." This makes it possible to consider the collective significance and impacts of media – in other words, moving beyond sound/screen media. It also might be noted that the notion of media has been expanded beyond all of these forms. For instance, contributors to Swartz and Wasko (2021) present a transdisciplinary notion of medium/media, exploring media as technology and as environment, with special attention to material, historical, and ecological ramifications.

The discussion that follows will briefly identify various approaches to the study of the traditional media industries as developed in the United States, providing some examples of early research on the press, broadcasting, film, and advertising, as well as highlighting some of the historical work on mass communications or the media industry as a whole.

## Approaches to the study of media industries in the United States

Before specific academic programs developed for the study of media and communication, media industries were analyzed by scholars in other disciplines. Some of the most notable research was by academics associated with law and economics, but important work was also offered by scholars from political science, sociology, and anthropology. While there is still research on media industries from within these various disciplines, more distinct approaches have developed as the academic study of media has grown.

### *Political economy*

Academic study of media and communication has not always embraced economic analysis, much less a political economic approach. During the 1940s and 1950s, US communication scholars focused primarily on individual effects and psychologically oriented research, with little concern for the economic context in which media are produced, distributed, and consumed. However, studying the political economy of communication/media grew as a distinct approach in the United States. Although different forms of political economy developed, including conservative versions such as public choice theory (also known as the new or positive political economy), most of the work related to media has drawn from more radical, critical, or Marxian versions. In the United States, Dallas Smythe, Herbert Schiller, and Thomas Guback focused their research and teaching around the political economy of communication during the 1960s, influenced by the general political and economic developments of the period. Since that time, more scholars have adopted this approach, influenced not only by these "founding fathers," but also by British and European scholarship.

While a general overview of the approach was offered by Smythe in 1960, Vincent Mosco's texts (1996, 2009) became common references. Mosco defined the study of political economy as "the study of *the social relations, particularly power relations, that mutually constitute the production, distribution and consumption of resources*" (2009: 24; original emphasis). He explains that political economy is about survival and control, or how societies are organized to produce what is necessary to survive, and how order is maintained to meet societal goals. Mosco further delineated four central characteristics of critical political economy, including social change and history, social totality, moral philosophy, and praxis. The study of the political economy of the media has often focused on issues related to competition, concentration, commodification, commercialization, labor and trade unions, intellectual property, globalization, and relationships with the state and other institutions.

## Media economics

While economists offered studies of individual media industries from a variety of economic theories, the introduction of television in the 1950s spurred increasing attention to media, and media economics emerged as a distinct focus of research activity in the 1980s. Several books appeared setting out the basics of this approach (e.g., Gomery 1989; Picard 1989), and the *Journal of Media Economics* was launched in 1988. Addressing the media economics community, the *Journal* now describes the field as concerned with "the economics and policy of mediated communication, focusing on firms, markets, and institutions" (Taylor & Francis 2020). For Albarran (2004: 291),

> media economics involves the application of economic theories, concepts, and principles to study the macroeconomic and microeconomic aspects of mass media companies and industries. Concomitant with the increasing consolidation and concentration across the media industries, media economics emerged as an important area of study for academicians, policymakers, and industry analysts.

Early work from this perspective focused on microeconomic concepts, examining specific media industries. Later attention was given to macroeconomic issues, including ownership and concentration across media industries, although seldom presenting an explicit critique of capitalist media systems as in critical political economy.

Generally, media economics texts and the journals have echoed the concerns of mainstream (neoclassical) economics and positivist approaches. An industrial organization model has been used by many media economists, with analysis of market structure, conduct, and performance, and employing the theory of the firm. Studies have considered media products, dual-product marketplaces, branding, competition, economies of scale and scope, mergers and acquisitions, and labor (Albarran 2004).

## Media management

Other research in the United States focused on media industries has utilized media management theories related to strategic management; technology, innovation, creativity; contingency/efficiency; organizational or professional cultures; and leadership and media labor force research (for overviews, see Ferguson 1997; Mierzjewska and Hollifield 2005; Albarran,

Chan-Olmsted, and Wirth 2006). The media management approach has been described as the study of "how media organizations use scarce resources to meet the needs and wants of a given society. In other words, it is interested in the effective management of media outlets" (Muñoz 2018). The roots of media management studies can be found in communication and business, with early work published in the 1930s mostly by industry professionals. From the 1960s, scholars focused on business and economic aspects of the media, and by the 1990s, the approach included media/communication scholars as well. A single example would be Ferguson (1997), who presented a theoretical framework for media management, noting five reasons why media industries are different from others. He proposed that media industries are: (1) often larger than life; (2) operate in a fishbowl; (3) lack unique expertise in the eye of consumers; (4) manage creativity; and (5) serve as webs of gatekeeping (pp. 180–181).

## Production of culture

Another more recent approach that might be considered under the umbrella of media industries research is the production of culture, which has been developed with a broad scope encompassing areas beyond media. Richard Peterson is said to have formally "launched" this perspective in 1974, drawing on his previous work on the sociology of music (for instance, Peterson and Berger 1971). Other early explications of a distinct research area were offered in collections by Coser (1978) and DiMaggio (1982). In 1992, Crane summarized the study of the production of culture, arguing that cultural forms cannot be understood "apart from the context in which they are produced and consumed" (p. vii). More recently, Peterson and Anand (2004: 311) outlined the development of the approach:

> The production of culture perspective focuses on how the symbolic elements of culture are shaped by the systems within which they are created, distributed, evaluated, taught, and preserved. Initially, practitioners of this perspective focused on the fabrication of expressive-symbol elements of culture, such as art works, scientific research reports, popular culture, religious practices, legal judgments, journalism … and other parts of what are now called the culture or creative industries. Recently, the perspective has been successfully applied to a range of quite different situations in which the manipulation of symbols is a by-product rather than the purpose of the collective activity.

Peterson and Anand present a model of six "facets" which contribute to the producing of culture: technology, law and regulation, industry structure, organizational structure, occupational careers, and market.

## Production studies

Even more recently, another version somewhat related to this approach emerged as production studies, which attempts to stretch across the humanities (film and television studies, English, cultural studies) and social sciences (sociology, political economy, communication, anthropology, geography). Proposing a cultural studies approach to media production, John Caldwell (2008) emphasized the value of "on the ground" microlevel analyses of media workers and labor rather than focusing on those occupying elite managerial or creative roles. More specifically, Mayer, Banks, and Caldwell (2009: 2) describe production studies as the examination of the unique cultural practices of media production, "the notion of production as a culture," requiring interest

> in how media producers make culture, and in the process, make themselves into particular kinds of workers in modern, mediated societies ... look[ing] up and down the food chains of production hierarchies, to understand how people work through professional organizations and informal networks to form communities of shared practices, languages, and cultural understandings of the world.

While production studies developed as a distinct research area from the first decade of the twenty-first century, in the previous century some earlier studies had laid the groundwork, for instance Hortense Powdermaker's study of *Hollywood, the Dream Factory* (1950) and Julie D'Acci's *Defining Women* (1994).

## Creative industries

And, finally, a good deal of attention also has been directed to the notion of "creative industries," which has developed rapidly in the UK, Europe, and Australia, but to a lesser extent, in the United States. One of the most popular definitions of creative industries was offered by Britain's Department for Culture, Media and Sport: "those industries which have their origin in individual creativity, skill and talent and which have a potential for wealth and job creation through the generation and exploitation of intellectual property" (DCMS 2001: 5). This definition has been adopted in policy discussions and scholarly literature beyond the UK. However, in the United States, this approach emanated from Richard Florida's (2002) work, which focused more specifically on various workers in this sector, which he called the "creative class." Florida's thesis was that the cities that were thriving were doing so because of the success of those in the creative economy and that success would *trickle down* to all sectors of the urban economy.

A wide range of industries beyond the media industries have been called "creative" and, depending on the definition, have included design (product, graphic, and fashion), architecture, crafts, visual and performing arts, museums, and galleries, as well as (less often) education, engineering, and research and development. It might also be noted that discussions of creative industries often focus on the potential for economic growth, wealth creation, increased employment, and the extension of intellectual property rights (see Garnham 2005; Caves 2000).

## Individual industry studies

As noted above, the academic study of media industries has mostly focused on a few industries – newspapers, film, and broadcasting – media that have been central to mass communication in the United States, as well as setting the stage for other media. Thus, the abbreviated discussion that follows focuses mostly on what Hilmes (2009) notes as "industrial production" or "sites of production." The focus here is on some foundational studies of the structures and policies of media industries, as well as the various implications of those structures.

## Newspapers

Academic study of the newspaper industry in the United States has a long tradition, emanating from a range of disciplines, becoming institutionalized from the early 1900s as the first journalism schools emerged in the country around that time. Early analyses of the industry by economists, media researchers, and others focused especially on concentration in the owner- ship of newspapers: Lee (1938: 126), for example, discussed "independence and financial sta- bility, monopoly, and 'one-newspaper places.'" These themes continued over the years in studies such as Kinter (1945) and Ray (1951), as well as attention to the influence of advertising on newspapers (Kinter 1947). In the 1960s and 1970s, even more attention was directed at the com- mercialization of the newspaper industry, as well as ongoing concentration, by researchers such as Ferguson (1963), Nixon (1968, 1971), Bagdikian (1973), and Udell (1978). Compaine (1980) focused on the newspaper industry in the 1980s using an early version of media economics. More recently, the decline of the newspaper industry, in light of newer media technologies, has prompted analysis by media economic scholars such as Picard (1988) and Lacy and Davenport (1994), as well as political economic studies (George and Waldfogel 2003) and other approaches.

## Film

While the study of the film as an industry has not always been a priority for film/cinema studies, several early works provided insights into the evolution of commercial motion pictures in the United States, and subsequently served as groundings for the expansion of media industry studies. Classic studies of film production, distribution, and exhibition in the United States were published during the 1930s and 1940s. Research by Hampton (1970, originally written in 1931), Lewis (1933), and Huettig (1944) presented useful discussions of trends, such as con- centration and monopolistic practices in the emerging Hollywood film industry. Work eman- ating from a variety of disciplines also provided historical foundations for the study of film industries. In *Hollywood, the Dream Factory*, Powdermaker (1950) looked at Hollywood from an anthropological perspective, revealing a lot about the business of film in the United States. And Conant (1960) provided a clear and insightful legal analysis of the details and consequences of the Paramount decrees for the US film industry in the years following the 1948 Supreme Court decision. As film and media studies emerged in a more formally coordinated manner from the 1960s, key texts on the US film industry emerged. Guback's *The International Film Industry* (1969) was one of the first studies of film by a media scholar employing a political economic per- spective. Guback drew attention to the role of the state in Hollywood's international activities, clearly showing us that globalization of the US film industry was not a new phenomenon, and detailing Hollywood's domination of foreign markets. As cinema and media studies grew in the 1970s and 1980s, scholars such as Balio (1976), Gomery (1986), Kindem (1982), Schatz (1988), and others gave more attention to the industrial policies and structures of the film industry.

Markets for film were enhanced and expanded by the development and proliferation of screen technologies, with broadcast, satellite and cable television, and home video formats such as video cassette recorders (VCRs) and digital versatile discs (DVDs). Consequently, many different types of experts, from academics to industry representatives, offered analyses of these developments involving a complex mix of historical, economic, political, and cultural factors. A few examples might include Wasko (1994) and Wasser (2001). Equally, international film markets continued to be studied by film scholars employing historical approaches to provide essential foundations for understanding media globalization (e.g., Thompson 1985; Pendakur 1990; and Segrave 1997).

## Broadcasting

Given the commercial nature and public role of American broadcasting, it is perhaps not sur- prising that the industries of radio and television have been studied extensively by university researchers, as well as government and industry representatives. As early as 1925, the economics of the radio industry were analyzed by Jome (1925), who described radio's early history, especially related to the Radio Corporation of America (RCA). Also, a plethora of research on the radio industry was produced by the government. One interesting example is a US Department of Labor report on employment in the radio industry, especially focusing on women who worked at companies producing radio sets and tubes (Manning 1931). An early study undertaken by the radio industry itself was written by Weinberger (1939), who was associated with the License Laboratory at RCA, and reviewed long-term economic trends, including markets and demand for receivers and other equipment.

While a wide range of academic studies focused on the radio and television industries from the 1950s and onward, Barnouw's (1966a, 1968, 1970) detailed history of broadcasting in the United States emphasized issues relating to industrial and commercial organization, providing a model for future researchers. As television expanded, academic study of the television industry appeared, including focus on economic issues (e.g., Owen, Beebe and Manning 1974; Noll, Peck, and McGowan 1973; Litman 1979a, 1979b), as well as legal developments (for instance, Long 1973). Critical assessments of television have been offered from a critical political economy perspective, including Wells (1972), Melody (1973), Bunce (1976), and Downing (1990), while Guback and Dombkowski (1976) considered relationships between television and film industries in the United States.

## General media industries studies

As media industries multiplied and the media's significance grew, more research was conducted across industries, as well as addressing the media sector as a whole. This kind of work increased as patterns of diversification, synergy, and convergence intensified in US media.

Researchers looked at the media industries from particular disciplinary perspectives, such as economics (Stigler 1961; Rosse and Dertouzos 1978), and/or considered specific issues, such as Mahaffie's (1968) study of mergers and diversification in the newspaper, broadcasting, and information industries, and also Johnson and Hoak's (1970) examination of media concentration. Meanwhile, Sterling and Haight (1978) offered a useful compendium of statistics and trends relating to the media industries. In 1983, Compaine, Guback, Sterling, and Noble (1983) posed the question, who owns the media, as they examined newspaper, book publishing, magazine, theatrical film, broadcasting, cable and pay television industries. Starting in 1983, journalist, news media critic, and academic Ben Bagdikian published the first of what became seven editions of his widely hailed study *The Media Monopoly*. Over successive editions, Bagdikian traced increasing corporate concentration: at the time of the 1983 edition, 50 corporations controlling most US media, shrinking to just five companies by the 2004 version. This work then inspired other media critics and critical media scholars to conduct similar analyses.

Several scholars who studied the political economy of communication in the United States produced work embracing the entire media sector. One of the first examples was Smythe, who in a 1960 article in *Journalism Quarterly* outlined a wide range of research questions related to studying mass communication. Touching on newspaper, magazine, film, radio, and television media, Smythe argued the priorities of political economic analysis were to critically interrogate policy in three areas: services or goods produced; allocation of goods or services; and capital, organization, and control. Taking a broad view of the sector, Schiller looked at trends in mass communication research in the United States (1974) and the corporatization of culture (1989), while Ewen (1976) explored advertising's role in consumer culture. This kind of work has continued through the turn of the century, focusing on issues related to media concentration and commercialization, as well as ongoing attention to globalization.

## Summary

The conceptual approaches and scholars mentioned in this chapter have contributed to media industries research in the United States. An effort has been made to offer a wide range of examples and influences, highlighting intellectual and methodological diversity from various research traditions. As might be noted, these approaches adopt varying views on which media should be addressed and how these industries should be studied. A major distinction might also be perceived in terms of research motivations, as well as positions taken vis-à-vis the industries themselves. While research orientations have emerged that are critical of media industries in various ways, some researchers in the United States have avoided explicit critique or offer celebratory accounts (sometimes from an "aca-fan" position) that accept the media landscape as inevitable. Despite ongoing technological, economic, and political changes, the media industries continue to contribute significantly to our societies and require the scrutiny that is possible from scholarly inquiry. The multiplicity of research approaches outlined in this chapter would seem to be necessary grounding to fully analyze and understand these ongoing continuities and changes for future media industries research.

## Notes

1 This emphasis on the primacy of sound and screen media is also to be found elsewhere, for example the University of Wisconsin's graduate program in Media and Cultural Studies (https://commarts.wisc.edu/graduate/media-cultural-studies/) and is used as well as by the Society for Cinema and Media Studies (SCMS) in defining the scope of their members' scholarship (www.cmstudies.org/page/about_us).
2 The evolution of disciplinary divisions related to the study of media and communication in the United States is a complex saga in itself and cannot be fully addressed here. See, for instance, Simonson and Peters (2008) or Simonson (2015).

## References

Albarran, A. B. (2004) "Media Economics," in J. D. H. Downing, D. McQuail, P. Schlesinger, and E. Wartella (eds), *The Sage Handbook of Media Studies*, Thousand Oaks, CA: Sage, 291–308.
Albarran, A. B., Chan-Olmsted, S. M., and Wirth, M. O. (eds) (2006) *Handbook of Media Management and Economics*, Mahwah, NJ: Erlbaum.
Baer, W. S., Geller, H., Grundfest, J. A., and Possner, K. B. (1974) *Concentration of Mass Media Ownership: Assessing the State of Current Knowledge*, Santa Monica, CA: Rand.
Bagdikian, B. (1973) "The Myth of Newspaper Poverty," *Columbia Journalism Review*, 11 (6): 19–25.
Bagdikian, B. (1983) *The Media Monopoly*, Boston, MA: Beacon Press.
Bagdikian, B. (2004) *The New Media Monopoly*, Boston, MA: Beacon Press.
Balio, T. (1976) *The American Film Industry*, Madison, WI: University of Wisconsin Press.
Barnouw, E. (1966a) *A Tower in Babel: A History of Broadcasting in the United States to 1933*, New York: Oxford University Press.
Barnouw, E. (1968) *The Golden Web: A History of Broadcasting in the United States 1933 to 1953*, New York: Oxford University Press.
Barnouw, E. (1970) *The Image Empire: A History of Broadcasting in the United States From 1953*, New York: Oxford University Press.
Bunce, R. (1976) *Television in the Corporate Interest*, New York: Praeger.
Caldwell, J. T. (2008) *Production Culture: Industrial Reflexivity and Critical Practice in Film and Television*, Durham, NC: Duke University Press.
Caves, R. E. (2000) *Creative Industries: Contracts Between Art and Commerce*, Cambridge, MA: Harvard University Press.

Compaine, B. M. (1980) *The Newspaper Industry in the 1980s: An Assessment of Economics and Technology*, White Plains, NY: Knowledge Industry Publications.

Compaine, B. M., Sterling, C. H., Guback, T., and Noble Jr., J. K. (1983) *Anatomy of the Communication Industry: Who Owns the Media?* White Plains, NY: Knowledge Industries Publications.

Conant, M. (1960) *Antitrust in the Motion Picture Industry*, Berkeley, CA: University of California Press.

Coser, L. A. (issue editor) (1978) "The Production of Culture," *Social Research*, 48 (2).

Crane, D. (1992) *The Production of Culture: Media and the Urban Arts*, London: Sage.

D'Acci, J. (1994) *Defining Women: Television and the Case of Cagney and Lacey*, Chapel Hill, NC: University of North Carolina Press.

DCMS (2001) *Creative Industries Mapping Document 2001*, 2nd ed., London: Department of Culture, Media and Sport, available at https://web.archive.org/web/20080727021512/http://www.culture.gov.uk/reference_library/publications/4632.aspx (accessed October 21, 2020).

De Beukelaer, C. and Spence, K-M. (2018) *Global Cultural Economy*, New York: Routledge.

DiMaggio, P. (1982) "Cultural Entrepreneurship in Nineteenth Century Boston, I: The Creation of an Organizational Basis for High Culture in America," *Media, Culture and Society*, 4 (1): 33–50.

Downing, J. (1990) "The Political Economy of U.S. Television," *Monthly Review*, 42 (1): 30–41.

du Gay, P. and Pryke, M. (eds) (2002) *Cultural Economy: Cultural Analysis and Commercial Life*, London: Sage Publications.

Ewen, S. (1976) *Captains of Consciousness: Advertising and the Social Roots of the Consumer Culture*, New York: McGraw-Hill.

Ferguson, D. (1997) "The Domain of Inquiry for Media Management Researchers," in C. Warner (ed.), *Media Management Review*, Mahwah, NJ: Erlbaum, 177–183.

Ferguson, J. M. (1963) *The Advertising Rate Structure in the Daily Newspaper Industry*, Englewood Cliffs, NJ: Prentice Hall.

Florida, R. (2002) *The Rise of the Creative Class: And How It's Transforming Work, Leisure and Everyday Life*, New York: Basic Books.

Garnham, N. (2005) "From Cultural to Creative Industries," *International Journal of Cultural Policy*, 11 (1): 15–29.

George, L. and Waldfogel, J. (2003) "Who Affects Whom in Daily Newspaper Markets?" *Journal of Political Economy*, 111 (4): 765–784.

Gomery, D. (1989) "Media Economics: Terms of Analysis," *Critical Studies in Media Communication*, 6 (1): 43–60.

Gomery, D. (1986) *The Hollywood Studio System*, New York: Palgrave Macmillan.

Guback, T. H. (1969) *The International Film Industry: Western Europe and America Since 1945*, Bloomington, IN: Indiana University Press.

Guback, T. H. and Dombkowski, D. J. (1976) "Television and Hollywood: Economic Relations in the 1970s," *Journal of Broadcasting and Electronic Media*, 20 (4): 511–526.

Hampton, B. (1970) *History of the American Film Industry from Its Beginnings to 1931*, New York: Dover Press.

Hartley, J. (2005) "Creative Industries," in J. Hartley (ed.), *Creative Industries*, Malden, MA: Blackwell, 1–41.

Hilmes, M. (2009) "Nailing Mercury: The Problem of Media Industry Historiography," in J. Holt and A. Perren (eds), *Media Industries: History, Theory, and Method*, Malden, MA: Wiley-Blackwell, 21–33.

Huettig, M. D. (1944) *Economic Control of the Motion Picture Industry*, Philadelphia, PA: University of Pennsylvania Press.

Johnson, N. and Hoak Jr, J. M. (1970) "Media Concentration: Some Observations on the United States' Experience," *Iowa Law Review*, (56): 267–291.

Jome, H. L. (1925) *Economics of the Radio Industry*, Chicago, IL: AW Shaw Company.

Kinter, C. V. (1945) "The Changing Pattern of the Newspaper Publishing Industry," *The American Journal of Economics and Sociology*, 5 (1): 43–63.

Kinter, C. V. (1947) "Cyclical Influences on Newspaper Advertising," *The American Journal of Economics and Sociology*, 7 (1): 81–92.

Lacy, S. and Davenport, L. (1994) "Daily Newspaper Market Structure, Concentration, and Competition," *Journal of Media Economics*, 7 (3): 33–46,

Lee, A. M. (1938) "Recent Developments in the Daily Newspaper Industry," *Public Opinion Quarterly*, 2 (1): 126–133.

Lewis, H. T. (1933) *The Motion Picture Industry*, New York: D. Van Nostrand.

Litman, B. R. (1979a) "The Television Networks, Competition and Program Diversity," *Journal of Broadcasting and Electronic Media*, 23 (4): 393–409.

Litman, B. R. (1979b) *The Vertical Structure of the Television Broadcasting Industry*, East Lansing: Michigan State University.

Long, S. (1973) "Antitrust and the Television Networks: Restructuring Via Cable TV," *Antitrust Law and Economics Review*, 6 (4): 99–108.

Kindem, G. (1982) *The American Movie Industry: The Business of Motion Pictures*, Carbondale, IL: Southern Illinois University Press.

Mahaffie Jr, C. D. (1968) "Mergers and Diversification in the Newspaper, Broadcasting and Information Industries," *The Antitrust Bulletin*, 13 (3): 927–936.

Manning, C. (1931) *Fluctuation of Employment in the Radio Industry*, Washington, DC: United States Government Printing Office.

Mayer, V., Banks, M. J., and Thornton Caldwell, J. T. (2009) "Introduction – Production Studies: Roots and Routes," in V. Mayer, M. J. Banks, and J. T. Caldwell (eds) (2009) *Production Studies: Cultural Studies of Media Industries,* New York: Routledge, 1–12.

Melody, W. (1973) *Children's Television: The Economics of Exploitation*, New Haven, NJ: Yale University Press.

Mierzjewska, B. I. and Hollifield, A. (2005) "Theoretical Approaches in Media Management Research," in A. B. Albarran, S. M. Chan-Olmsted and M. O. Wirth (eds), *Handbook of Media Management and Economics*, Abingdon: Routledge, 37–66.

Mosco, V. (1996) *The Political Economy of Communication: Rethinking and Renewal*, London: Sage.

Mosco, V. (2009) *The Political Economy of Communication*, 2nd ed., London: Sage.

Muñoz, J. P. A. (2018) "Media Management," *Oxford Bibliographies*, October 19, available at https://www.oxfordbibliographies.com/view/document/obo-9780199756841/obo-9780199756841-0089.xml (accessed October 21, 2020).

Nixon, R. B. (1968) "Trends in US Newspaper Ownership: Concentration with Competition," *Gazette*, 14 (3): 181–193.

Nixon, R. B. and Hahn, T. Y. (1971) "Concentration of Press Ownership: A Comparison of 32 Countries," *Journalism Quarterly*, 48 (1): 5–16.

Noll, R. G., Peck, M. J., and McGowan, J. J. (1973) *Economic Aspects of Television Regulation*, Washington, DC: Brookings Institution.

Owen, B. M., Beebe, J. H., and Manning, W. G. (1974) *Television Economics*, Lexington, MA: Lexington Books.

Pendakur, M. (1990) *Canadian Dreams and American Control: The Political Economy of the Canadian Film Industry,* Toronto: University of Toronto Press.

Peterson, R. A. and Anand, N. (2004) "The Production of Culture Perspective," *Annual Review of Sociology*, (30): 311–334.

Peterson, R. A. and Berger, D. G. (1971) "Entrepreneurship in Organizations: Evidence from the Popular Music Industry," *Administrative Science Quarterly*, 16 (1): 97–106.

Picard, R. G. (1989) *Media Economics: Concepts and Issues,* Beverly Hills, CA: Sage Publications.

Picard, R. G. (1988) "Measures of Concentration in the Daily Newspaper Industry," *Journal of Media Economics*, 1 (1): 61–74.

Powdermaker, H. (1950) *Hollywood, the Dream Factory*, Boston, MA: Little, Brown.

Ray, R. H. (1951) "Competition in the Newspaper Industry," *Journal of Marketing*, 15 (4): 444–456.

Rosse, J. N. and Dertouzos, J. N. (1978) "Economic Issues in Mass Communication Industries," *Proceedings of the Symposium on Media Concentration vol. 1*, Washington, DC: Bureau of Competition Federal Trade Commission, 40–192.

Schatz, T, (1988) *The Genius of the System: Hollywood Filmmaking in the Studio Era,* New York: Pantheon Books,

Schiller, H. I. (1974) "Waiting for Orders: Some Current Trends in Mass Communications Research in the United States," *Gazette*, 20 (1): 11–21.

Schiller, H. I. (1989) *Culture, Inc.: The Corporate Takeover of Public Expression,* New York: Oxford University Press.

Segrave, K. (1997) *American Films Abroad: Hollywood's Domination of the World's Movie Screens from the 1890s to the Present,* Jefferson, NC: McFarland.

Simonson, P. (2015) "Communication and Media Studies, History Since 1968," in *The International Encyclopedia of Communication,* Wiley Online Library, available at https://doi.org/10.1002/9781405186407.wbiecc086.pub3 (accessed October 21, 2020).

Simonson, P. and Peters, J. D. (2008) "Communication and Media Studies, History to 1968," in *The International Encyclopedia of Communication,* Wiley Online Library, available at https://winwithguinn.files.wordpress.com/2014/10/comm-media-history-to-19681.pdf (accessed October 21, 2020).

Smythe, D. W. (1960) "On the Political Economy of Communications," *Journalism Quarterly,* 37 (4): 563–572.

Springer (n.d.) "Journal of Cultural Economics," available at www.springer.com/journal/10824 (accessed October 23, 2020).

Sterling, C. H. and Haight, T. R. (1978) *The Mass Media: Aspen Institute Guide to Communication Industry Trends,* New York: Praeger.

Stigler, G. J. (1961) "The Economics of Information," *Journal of Political Economy,* 69 (3): 213–225.

Swartz, J. and Wasko, J. (2021) *MEDIA: A Transdisciplinary Inquiry,* Bristol and Chicago, IL: Intellect and University of Chicago Press.

Taylor & Francis (2020) "*Journal of Media Economics*: Aims and Scope," available at www.tandfonline.com/action/journalInformation?show=aimsScope&journalCode=hmec20 (accessed December 12, 2020).

Thompson, K. (1985) *Exporting Entertainment: America in the World Film Market 1907–1934,* London: British Film Institute.

Udell, J. G. (ed.) (1978) *The Economics of the American Newspaper,* New York: Hastings House.

Wasko, J. (1994) *Hollywood in the Information Age: Beyond the Silver Screen,* Cambridge: Polity.

Wasser, F. (2001) *Veni, Vidi, Video: The Hollywood Empire and the VCR,* Austin, TX: University of Texas Press.

Weinberger, J. (1939) "Basic Economic Trends in the Radio Industry," *Proceedings of the IRE,* 27 (11): 704–715.

Wells, A. (1972) *Picture-Tube Imperialism? The Impact of U.S. Television on Latin America,* Maryknoll, NY: Orbis Books.

# 3

# MEETING THE CHALLENGES OF MEDIA AND MARKETING CONVERGENCE

## Revising critical political economy approaches

*Jonathan Hardy*

This chapter illustrates how critical political economic (CPE) analysis can be revised to address media industries in a manner that satisfies the core objectives of proponents and addresses valid criticisms of deficiencies. It does so by advancing critical governance analysis as a means to integrate and advance the study of media industries practices, rule-shaping processes, and societal engagements. These arguments are developed at both a general level and in relation to a specific topic, the convergence of media and marketing communications as it is occurring across Western media.

## Critical political economy of media

The study of media industries has been influenced by a tradition of critical scholarship that took institutional form at the end the 1960s and was catalyzed by global radicalism across that decade (Wasko 2004). In media and communication studies, critical political economy approaches are characterized by a central claim: that different ways of organizing and financing communications have implications for the range and features of media content, and the ways in which these are consumed and used (Murdock and Golding 2005; Mosco 2009; Hardy 2014). Critical political economy refers to approaches that examine the unequal distribution of power and resources across societies and are critical of arrangements whereby such inequalities are sustained and reproduced, including by, and within, media industries. This approach calls for attention to the interplay between the symbolic and economic dimensions of the production of meaning. One direction of enquiry leads from media production arrangements to meaning-making and consumption; another considers the relationship of media and communication systems to wider forces and processes in society. In exploring these relationships, CPE approaches are not reliant on specific concepts or methods: rather the ongoing justification for CPE rests on the quality and salience of its analysis of *problems* in communication and social systems. My own short definition is as follows: "Critical political economic of communications is a critical realist approach that investigates problems connected with the political and economic organization of communication resources" (Hardy 2014: 14).

DOI: 10.4324/9780429275340-5

I have argued for a CPE that is reflexive, revising, adaptive, and porous (Hardy 2014, 2016). Yet the task of advancing a mobile CPE, with indistinct borders, is undoubtedly made harder by sustained efforts to displace CPE within self-styled "new," or "critical," media industries studies (Havens, Lotz, and Tinic 2009; Havens and Lotz 2012). Three overlapping approaches have emerged: "convergence culture" (Jenkins 2006), "creative industries" (Hartley, Potts, Cunningham, Flew, Keane, and Banks 2013), and "critical media industries" research. These differ in the degree to which a critical mantle is advanced but have in common an anchorage in cultural studies and repudiation of more explicitly Marxian or anti-capitalist critical work as rigid, reductive, and outdated. These approaches place justified analytical emphasis on complexity and contradiction in the practices and positionality of media workers. Yet, the three culturalist media studies (CMS) perspectives advocate adopting a more positive account of capitalist accumulation as a mechanism for cultural innovation, diversity, and empowerment. This amounts to a repositioning toward a more affirmative account of commercial media provision and arrangements in what I call market pluralism.

We can identify gaps and deficiencies in scholarship in a generous manner, acknowledging the contexts and contribution of particular researchers' work, while highlighting the need to address new conditions and data, neglected concerns, promising concepts, and insights. Doing so is what I mean by regarding CPE as necessarily a reflexive, revising approach. However, the critiques made in the CMS literature above go further, seeking to persuade readers that CPE has inherent, insurmountable limitations: economism, Marxist influence, and insufficiency in social theory. Researchers are warned that CPE approaches are crude and outdated, representing an exhausted tradition that offers limited value or contemporary salience (for a review, see Wasko and Meehan 2013; Hardy 2016). The culturalist critique makes some valid points but the attack is lopsided, and CPE is misrepresented. This chapter argues that ongoing revision of critical scholarship is needed but that this can build on and integrate work from within as well as without the critical political economy tradition.

## CPE approaches to media and advertising

The advertising industry "involves two interconnected systems of activity that are crucial to Western society": systems of ideology and of media support (Turow and McAllister 2009: 2). Critical political economists have made contributions to analysis across the full range of industry arrangements and practices, yet a distinctive contribution has been to address how advertising finance influences media content, provision, and access to communication services. Classic CPE contributions examine advertisers' influence on non-advertising content and media firms' behavior, with debates on the salience of instrumentalist (purposeful action, e.g., leveraging ad spending to influence media content decisions) and structuralist (impersonal forces, e.g., the outcome of myriad decisions on cost-effective ad placement) explanations (Baker 1994; Curran 1986). Advertising influence depends on such factors as economic dependency: the proportion of a media provider's income derived from advertising, reliance on particular advertisers, and wider market conditions. Factors include the acceptability of advertising influence on content decisions (and the "cost" of consumer or other stakeholder disapproval), which varies according to the media institutional arrangements and user expectations.

Many of the problems CPE analysts addressed in the latter half of the twentieth century remain salient today, but critical scholars have also updated theory and analysis to deal with transformations in the ways marketing communications are produced and circulated, and the changing dynamics of media–advertising relationships. Key features include the expansion of marketers' self-promotion ("owned" media), the "disaggregation" of media and advertising as marketers bypass media to target and reach consumers directly through online behavioral advertising, and the "integration" of media and advertising through product placement, native advertising, and various other forms of branded content (Turow 2011; Hardy 2017, 2018; Einstein 2016).

## Challenges of media and marketing convergence

Media and marketing communications are converging across digital platforms, communication forms and spaces, with profound implications for academic domains as well as for industry arrangements and practices. Increasingly, brands are involved in the production of media content. This branded content takes various forms, from material that is self-published by brands, through to "publisher-hosted" content, where brands supply or fund content carried by third-party publishers. Many of these forms have long histories, from nineteenth-century reading notices and twentieth-century advertorials in print publishing, to product placement, coterminous with the birth of cinema, but now extending across entertainment, news, games, post-production virtual placement (Dagnino 2020), and on to influencer marketing by (micro) celebrities and artificial intelligence (AI) assistants (Yesiloglu and Costello 2020).

The characteristic relationship of media and advertising in the mid-twentieth century was *integration with separation*: ads were physically integrated with the media product but separated from editorial content. The emergent forms are *integration without separation*, notably forms of branded content, but this coexists with trends toward the *disaggregation* of media and advertising. Marketers are less dependent on the intermediary role of media publishers, can track and target consumers directly, and demand to reduce their subsidy to media by paying only the costs of delivering an advert onto a selected platform. These contrary tendencies, toward embeddedness and disaggregation, both manifest in the increased dependency of advertiser-financed media on marketers and represent a power shift from media to marketers. However, analysis of the shifting power dynamics between marketers, marketing agencies, platforms, media, and consumers is always complex, since so many factors are potentially influential in any given context. Marketers and media are also both in positions of dependence toward regionally dominant platforms, such as Google and Facebook, who together took more than half of total global internet advertising revenue in 2018 (Sinclair 2020) and dominate advertising technology or adtech, that is, the software, tools and processes used to select, create, bid for, purchase, and place digital advertising opportunities.

Advertising has long been the major patron of commercial media. Yet various regulatory and market mechanisms set limits on that patronage. Regulations and industry norms upheld principles of the separation of advertising and editorial across mass media. Market arrangements tended to work against advertisers exercising direct, instrumental power over editorial content. Marketers controlled adverts (paid media) but not the content around them. Public relations professionals pursued "earned" media coverage that they could not fully control. The separation principle was generally upheld by self-regulatory codes across media and advertising industries, with stronger, statutory regulation in sectors such as European broadcasting. The shifts we are seeing certainly pre-date digitalization but increasingly marketers' control is extending from advertising forms to integrated editorial forms. This involves a mix of instrumental and structural power by advertisers, but also complex attenuation, as decision-making spreads across digital advertising networks and into programmatic advertising buying and other forms of automation, such as the content recommendation engines used to place branded content onto news media and other publishers' websites. How branded content is developing in different national and regional contexts is influenced by formal laws and regulations, corporate decision-making, and by the cultures and practices of media and marketing practitioners and users alike. The next section outlines a framework for analysis of governance and proposes this as a way to advance the integrated study of media and marketing industries.

## Governance analysis

Governance refers to all processes of governing and rule wherever they occur (Bevir 2012). For Rosenau (1992: 4), governance "embraces governmental institutions, but it also subsumes informal, non-governmental mechanisms .... Governance is thus a system of rule that is as dependent on intersubjective meanings as on formally sanctioned constitutions and charters." One attraction of governance as a concept is that it encompasses the range of informal as well as formal processes by which practices are ordered, enabled, and constrained. Such a mix of laws, regulatory agencies, industry, and professional self-regulation, evolving standards, and looser "rulemaking" is a general feature of contemporary media industries, situated within dynamic, adaptive digital communications systems.

Governance analysis examines how practices and processes shape, and are shaped by, the distribution of resources and power. A criticism made of some governance studies is that they attend to specific "micro" operations of power without an adequate account of the macro-level influences of state–capital relationships. To remedy this, critical governance analysis draws on efforts to theorize and examine the interacting relations of power across macro–meso–micro levels, without reproducing a deterministic account. Analysis, argues Benson (1977: 5), "must deal with the complex interlocking through which components are built into each other. This involves a search for dominant forces or components without resort to a deterministic argument." Benson's dialectical network analysis has influenced more contemporary analyses by Jessop (2007), Davies (2011) and others, whose work demonstrates efforts to examine how practices are organized materially and discursively, and trace connections between the influences of political and economic forces on those practices.

Applied to branded content, this includes the task of examining power shifts between marketers, marketing agencies and intermediaries, media, platforms, and consumers. It also requires analysis of the broader influence of neoliberalism on the organization and liberalizing re-regulation of communications markets, and on increasing "hyper-commercialism" (McChesney 2013), marketization, financialization, and commodification affecting communication services and content (Berry 2019). The discussion below illustrates some resources for critical governance analysis, including the influence of new institutionalism, and concepts of path dependency (Mahoney 2000), path shaping (Jessop 2007), and neo-Gramscian analysis of hegemony (Davies 2011) to study processes of normalization and contestation.

In recent years, communication scholars have developed governance analysis, especially within media policy studies (Puppis 2010) but also comparative media systems analysis (Ginosar 2013). Freedman (2008: 14) defines media governance as "the sum total of mechanisms, both formal and informal, national and supranational, centralized and dispersed, that aim to organize media systems according to the resolution of media policy debates." The concept has been most developed in media policy analysis to encompass the dynamic range of rule-shaping activities and the significance of the discursive production and ordering of power, drawing on discursive institutionalist approaches (Schmidt 2008). The critical governance analysis proposed here follows these insightful approaches but argues, inter alia, for an expansion beyond the policy domain to engage with wider discursive production within practitioner/professional and public-mediated communications.

The task of mapping governance requires examining the range of actors and processes through which relations of power are produced, sustained, and contested. The main sources of governance are:

- formal regulation (regulatory agencies directed by state or supranational law; independent regulatory agencies; co-regulation between public authorities and industries)
- industry self-regulation (codes and standards; technology-assisted rule application)
- market power (including consumer action)
- civil society action (including protest)

The following illustrates how such sources interact in the governance of branded content.

## *Formal regulation*

Most countries have regulations concerning the labelling and identification of communications that are paid for or otherwise sponsored by a trader (GALA 2018; European Parliament and Council 2005). The UK regulatory system, while particular, illustrates wider issues in governance. There are a range of regulatory agencies including statutory agencies (the communications regulator Ofcom, and the Competition and Markets Authority (CMA)), non-statutory self-regulatory organizations (SROs) (notably the Advertising Standards Authority (ASA)), and various industry professional bodies. In accordance with the principle of transparency, and European Union regulation, the ASA warns against any labelling that disguises advertising or is otherwise unclear to consumers. However, the ASA applies a dual test of whether the brand pays and also exercises control over content. This lacks transparency and provides a means whereby if publishers and advertisers have an interest *not* to disclose sponsored content, they can rest upon a claim of the publisher retaining editorial control that is difficult for regulators, much less readers, to assess. ASA rules apply to paid advertising but not public relations, and so do not cover so-called organic mentions in "earned" rather than "paid" content (CAP 2014). Yet that division is becoming increasingly blurred as reciprocal deals, bartering and other transactional arrangements abound across digital publishing and influencer marketing. European Union (EU) countries are required to alert consumers to product placement, the paid presence of brands in audiovisual production (European Parliament and Council 2018). Users must be informed about brand payment through a standardized sign, which in the UK takes the form of a P-sign. Yet, no such standardization is required for publications, platforms, or other content providers carrying editorial-like content produced in association with third-party marketers.

Despite ongoing regulatory convergence, a diverse range of agencies regulate, and self-regulate, branded content, reflecting historical, institutional differences across publishing, broadcasting and audiovisual, public relations, and advertising. This legacy of separate regulation, and demarcation of content, has been ill-equipped for rapid convergence across marketing communications and media publishing, with regulatory arrangements lagging behind industry practices and benefiting market expansion. Yet, heightened attention to issues of fake news and misinformation, undisclosed political advertising, influencer marketing and online harms, digital literacy, and communication rights is resulting in pressure for more regulatory intervention. The outcome will depend on corporate lobbying power, the mobilization of civil society interests, discursive ordering across mediated communications, and on self-regulatory responses across the industries involved.

## *Industry self-regulation*

Leading professional associations, such as the Interactive Advertising Bureau, advise their members on complying with regulations on labelling and disclosure of branded content, and advocate good practice principles, including through codes of practice. Yet, they and other bodies also lobby against stronger regulation. The IAB (2015) criticized the US Federal Trade Commission's (2015) updated disclosure requirements for native advertising as "overly prescriptive," arguing "the guidelines could impinge on commercial speech protections" (see also Lynch 2018: 18, 20). Industry perspectives represent a complex and volatile mix, however, engaging with business, operational, and ethical problems to varying degrees, although rarely attacking underlying premises for commercial expansion. Where there are risks to "brand safety" and reputation, as there are when ads appear in contexts that damage brands, such as next to hate speech or misinformation, there can be incentives for firms and sectors to differentiate themselves as responsible actors from the damaging practices committed by others. Increasingly, self-regulation also takes technological form, where behavior is constrained or encouraged by automated rules. For instance, Instagram offers marketers the incentive of accessing richer data analytics if they use its sub-headers on posts to declare that they are sponsored. In 2020, following investigations by the UK Competition and Markets Authority highlighting widespread non-disclosure, Instagram announced a new prompt requiring influencers to confirm if they have received incentives to promote content and updated algorithms to detect potential advertising content (CMA 2020). Yet, industry compliance with existing regulations generally remains low. Research indicates that a significant proportion of publishers do not identify branded content in accordance with the relevant regulatory standards: the Native Advertising Institute (Eliasson 2018) found that 11 percent of news media publishers were not labelling native ads at all. Labelling in many countries remains inconsistent and confusing. *The Guardian* (2017) newspaper's divisions between "Advertiser content," "Paid content," and "Supported by" requires a sophisticated understanding of publishing to decode. So, it is unsurprising that audiences are often confused and annoyed, especially when they discover only after viewing content that it was sponsored. Research by the Reuters Institute for the Study of Journalism (2015) found that a third of UK adults felt disappointed or deceived in this way.

## *Market power and civil society*

After regulation and self-regulation, a third key source of governance is the market. The behavior of firms is shaped by competitors, consumers, suppliers, and other market actors. Consumer activity has influence, from the aggregation of individual purchasing decisions, to discussion and feedback, to more collective responses such as boycotts. For branded content governance, ad-blocking is a powerful instance of consumers exercising market power, with 36 percent of users in the UK and an estimated 26 percent of users in the United States in 2020 using app and browser ad-blocking tools (Statista 2020a, 2020b).

The final source of governance agency is civil society, including health and children's non-governmental organizations (NGOs), trades unions, and communications reform groups. Governance through civil society includes campaigns such as Stop Hate for Profit in the United States, and culture jamming, brandalism, and subvertising initiatives that parody corporate or other advertising. It extends into more "disorganized" movements and citizen-consumer action, aided by social media, such as the protests against the Kendall Jenner Pepsi ad in 2017, challenging Pepsi's appropriation of the Black Lives Matter movement. To date, there has been limited campaigning against branded content and native advertising, yet a combination of initiatives on quality standards, consumer protection, and policy advocacy by civil society groups challenges industry practices and governance arrangements. There are also signs of growing criticism of influencer marketing, with a commercial survey of European audiences finding that more than half (55 percent) felt that influencer sponsored content "takes advantage of impressionable audiences by being too materialistic ... and misrepresenting real life," with 49 percent advocating stricter content rules (*Bazaarvoice* 2018).

## Normalization and contestation

Communications policy and regulation predominantly comprises specialized negotiations between industry stakeholders and core policy leadership actors. For other civil society stakeholders to have influence there usually has to be a combination of powerful interest groups, such as the lobbies on behalf of health and children, and widespread public coverage of the issues, including discussion of problems and solutions, increasing pressure on politicians, regulators, and industries to act. Accordingly, governance analysis must encompass the many ways in which rules and norms are established, and how they are subject to discursive construction and contestation (Davies 2011). This requires an expansive policy network analysis that can identify the range of stakeholders involved, the diversity of communicative activities they use to promote and advance interests, and the ordering of that discursive space. While such analysis must always be circumscribed for practical purposes, it is in keeping with this conception of critical governance to question where such boundary points are set and to look for actors and communication exchanges that may otherwise be ignored. A study of influencer marketing governance, for instance, would need to consider multiple sites of discursive engagement, from public and performative interactions, to relatively confidential and concealed contractual discussions among microcelebrities, marketing agencies, and intermediaries.

Governance is analytically encompassing, inviting attention to the multiple sites and processes of rulemaking and ordering across production, circulation, consumption, and use. This reconnects the study of media policy and regulation, a specialist subfield, with analysis of production arrangements and practices across media and marketing industries. The study of governance includes examining how professional attitudes change, how norms are formed and challenged, and how industry practitioners and trade bodies engage with contestation from within and outside their domains. For instance, Carlson (2015) identifies a process of norm entrepreneurship in news publishing whereby separation norms are supplanted by a "curatorial" norm that embraces the collation of editorial and paid content for readers. Hanusch, Banjac, and Maares (2020) examine how organizational and individual factors, including employment status, age, and media sector, are among key determinants for how lifestyle journalists perceive commercial influences from public relations (PR) and advertising interests.

Governance analysis requires study of the organization of practices and social arrangements, including power dynamics arising from ownership and control, commercial and other managerial pressures, employment status, and other factors affecting decision-making power, and their working out in the practices and perceptions of actors. This requires theories of the relationship, and synthesis, of structure and agency. Giddens (1984) proposes three kinds of structure–action rules in social systems: signification, where meaning is coded in discourse; legitimation, the embedding of normative perspectives; and, domination, the way power is exercised, particularly over resources. While there are ongoing debates concerning the interaction of agentic and structural elements across Gidden's structuration theory, Jessop's (2007) strategic relational analysis, and others, these approaches can be complemented by theories of the maintenance of professional domains and boundaries, such as Bourdieu's field theory

(Bourdieu 1988; Vos 2019), boundary work (Carlson 2019), and social identity theory (Harwood 2016). Governance analysis faces a further challenge of addressing the influence of automated processes on rule-shaping. The structuralist account of advertiser influence discussed earlier identifies impersonal forces, yet these are aggregations of human decision-making. Now, automated decisions occur across all stages of marketing communications, including the buying, selling, assembling, and displaying of programmatic advertising. While it is essential to recover the human activity at all points, from highly paid programmers to low-paid piece workers, the ramifications of datafication need to be addressed. In turn, these technosocial processes need to be reincorporated into critical analysis of how capitalist economic and social forces shape the social orders emerging through datafication (Couldry 2020).

Governance offers a means to integrate political economic, policy, and cultural analysis, by addressing connections across macro-meso-micro levels, including: state–capital–market relations; industrial organization and arrangements; regulatory institutions and processes; socio-cultural practices, norms and attitudes across producers, users and other actors; and communicative action and discursive interaction across all relevant stakeholders and media. We might approach this with a holistic awareness of the influence of all these elements in the dynamic ordering of multiple forms of power, even if we select specific areas of interaction for manageable research design. Drawing on Foucault and Gramsci, Serazio (2013) examines the governance of the consumer subject in relations between marketers and communication users. This approach addresses vital elements of the broader governance analysis I have outlined, yet even in expanded form, governance analysis inevitably privileges some features over others, so the aspiration to recognize, if never fully deliver, a holistic account, means continually connecting with other phenomena and explanations.

The governance of branded content is multidimensional and multilevel but is ordered by the relationships between leading capitalist enterprises and state power. Capitalist states are oriented to support arrangements that favor wealth creation and market expansion for owners of capital and serve nationally inscribed interests within an overarching globally integrated capitalist system. States are not neutral terrain for competing interests but have structurally inscribed strategic priorities, favoring some interests, forces, and initiatives over others (Jessop 2007). Countervailing forces exist at all levels and shape outcomes, but are weaker, and can usually influence policy action only within the boundaries of state, or supranational, selectivities, unless the balance of forces shifts to challenge these and provide access to state power for excluded interests. The interaction between the interests and capabilities of political authorities and capitalist enterprises opens up space whereby underlying capitalist dynamics of data extraction and commodification are subject to regulatory action. Social action can influence this regulatory space but also change the outcomes across all domains of governance. The critical governance approach outlined seeks to consider the ordering and interconnections between various levels, without determinism.

Earlier studies of factors affecting advertiser influence on media tended to regard media and advertisers as separate entities, whereas we must now examine integration across corporate ownership, practices, and norms. To update studies (see Hardy 2017), we can include the range of actors and processes through which governance arrangements are produced and sustained across material-discursive spaces:

1. Level of economic dependence on advertising finance and support
2. Formal regulatory arrangements (legal-regulatory authorities)
3. Industry self-regulatory arrangements (sector(s)-wide; organization-level)
4. Professional norms of relevant media workers and managers

5. Behavior and influence of media owners
6. Influence of relevant institutional traditions of media-advertiser relations
7. Influence of users (direct and indirect, including anticipated consumer responses)
8. Influence of other stakeholders across policy networks and in communications spaces (including media reporting and commentary)
9. Norms and practices across all intermediary agencies
10. Automated processes and human–computer interaction associated with all of the above.

This chapter has discussed and illustrated the challenges to revise critical political economy (CPE) approaches to media and advertising relationships so that they are adequate for the theoretical, methodological, and empirical investigation of contemporary media industries. Critical governance analysis has been advanced as a tool for integrated analysis of communications practices, environments, rule-shaping, and problems. This can provide renewed resources to address key questions asked by the radical tradition: how is advertiser power strengthened or countered across contemporary communications systems, and what are the consequences?

# References

Baker, C. E. (1994) *Advertising and a Democratic Press*, Princeton, NJ: Princeton University Press.

*Bazaarvoice* (2018) "Content Called Out; 47% of Consumers Fatigued by Repetitive Influencers," August 2, available at www.bazaarvoice.com/uk/press/content-called-out-47-of-consumers-fatigued-by-repetitive-influencers/ (accessed August 4, 2018).

Benson, J. K. (1977) "Organizations: A Dialectical View," *Administrative Science Quarterly*, 22 (1): 1–21.

Berry, M. (2019) "Neo Liberalism and the Media," in J. Curran and D. Hesmondhalgh (eds), *Media and Society*, London: Bloomsbury, 57–82.

Bevir, M. (2012) *Governance: A Very Short Introduction*, Oxford: Oxford University Press.

Bourdieu, P. (1988) *Homo Academicus*, Stanford, CA: Stanford University Press.

Carlson, M. (2015) "When News Sites Go Native: Redefining the Advertising–Editorial Divide in Response to Native Advertising," *Journalism*, 16 (7): 849–865.

Carlson, M. (2019) "Boundary Work," in T. P Vos and F. Hanusch (eds), *The International Encyclopedia of Journalism Studies*, Malden, MA: John Wiley.

CAP (2014) *The CAP Code: The UK Code of Non-broadcast Advertising and Direct and Promotional Marketing* edition 12, London: Committee of Advertising Practice, available at www.asa.org.uk/codes-and-rulings/advertising-codes/non-broadcast-code.html (accessed November 16, 2020).

CMA (Competition and Markets Authority) (2020) "Instagram to Tackle Hidden Advertising After CMA Action," October 16, available at www.gov.uk/government/news/instagram-to-tackle-hidden-advertising-after-cma-action (accessed October 16, 2020).

Couldry, N. (2020) "Recovering Critique in an Age of Datafication," *New Media and Society*, 22 (7): 1135–1151.

Curran, J. (1986) "The Impact of Advertising on the British Mass Media," in R. Collins, J. Curran, N. Garnham, P. Scannel, and C. Sparks (eds), *Media, Culture and Society: A Critical Reader*, London: Sage, 309–333.

Dagnino, G. (2020) *Branded Entertainment and Cinema: The Marketization of Italian Film*, Abingdon: Routledge.

Davies, J. (2011) *Challenging Governance Theory: From Networks to Hegemony*, Bristol: The Policy Press.

Einstein, M. (2016) *Black Ops Advertising Native Ads, Content Marketing, and the Covert World of the Digital Sell*, New York: OR Books.

Eliasson, J. (2018) "Should We Have a Global Standard for How We Label Native Advertising," *Native Advertising Institute*, January 24, available at https://blog.nativeadvertisinginstitute.com/global-standard-label-native-advertising (accessed January 26, 2018).

European Parliament and Council (2005) "Unfair Commercial Practices Directive," Brussels: European Parliament and Council.

European Parliament and Council (2018) "Audiovisual Media Services Directive," Brussels: European Parliament and Council.

Federal Trade Commission (2015) *Enforcement Policy Statement on Deceptively Formatted Advertisements*, available at www.ftc.gov/system/files/documents/public_statements/896923/151222deceptive enforcement.pdf (accessed December 30, 2015).

Freedman, D. (2008) *The Politics of Media Policy*, Cambridge: Polity Press.

GALA (2018) *Advertising Law: A Global Legal Perspective – Volumes 1 and 2*, New York: Global Advertising Lawyers Alliance.

Giddens, A. (1984) *The Constitution of Society: Outline of the Theory of Structuration*, Cambridge: Polity Press.

Ginosar, A. (2013) "Media Governance: A Conceptual Framework or Merely a Buzz Word?" *Communication Theory*, 23 (4): 356–374.

Hardy, J. (2014) *Critical Political Economy of the Media: An Introduction*, Abingdon: Routledge.

Hardy, J. (2016) "Money, (Co)Production and Power," *Digital Journalism*, 5 (1): 1–25.

Hardy, J. (2017) "Marketers' Influence on Media: Renewing the Radical Tradition for the Digital Age," in J. F. Hamilton, R. Bodle, and E. Korin (eds), *Explorations in Critical Studies of Advertising*, New York: Routledge, 13–27.

Hardy, J. (2018) "Branded Content: Media and Marketing Integration," in J. Hardy, H. Powell, and I. MacRury (eds), *The Advertising Handbook*, 4th ed., Abingdon: Routledge, 102–122.

Hartley, J., Potts, J., Cunningham, S., Flew, T., Keane, M. and Banks, J. (2013) *Key Concepts in Creative Industries*, London: Sage.

Harwood, J. (2016) "Social Identity Theory," in K. B. Jensen, E. W. Rothenbuhler, J. D. Pooley, and R. T. Craig (eds), *The International Encyclopedia ˙of Communication Theory and Philosophy*, Malden, MA: John Wiley.

Hanusch, F., Banjac, S. and Maares, P. (2020) "The Power of Commercial Influences: How Lifestyle Journalists Experience Pressure from Advertising and Public Relations," *Journalism Practice*, 14 (9): 1029–1046.

Havens, T., and Lotz, A. (2012) *Understanding Media Industries*, Oxford: Oxford University Press.

Havens, T., Lotz, A., and Tinic, S. (2009) "Critical Media Industry Studies: A Research Approach," *Communication, Culture and Critique* 2: 234–253.

IAB (2015) "IAB Concerned About FTC Guidance on Native Advertising," IAB, December 24, available at www.iab.com/news/iab-concerned-about-ftc-guidance-on-native-advertising/ (accessed January 10, 2016).

Jenkins, H. (2006) *Convergence Culture: Where Old and New Media Collide*, New York: New York University Press.

Jessop, B. (2007) *State Power: A Strategic-Relational Approach*, Cambridge: Polity.

Lynch, L. (2018) *Native Advertising: Advertorial Disruption in the 21st-Century News Feed*, New York: Routledge.

Mahoney, J. (2000) "Path Dependence in Historical Sociology," *Theory and Society* 29 (4): 507–548.

McChesney, R. (2013) *Digital Disconnect: How Capitalism is Turning the Internet against Democracy*, New York: The New Press.

Mosco, V. (2009) *The Political Economy of Communications*, 2nd ed., London: Sage.

Murdock, G. and Golding, P. (2005) "Culture, Communications and Political Economy," in J. Curran and M. Gurevitch (eds), *Mass Media and Society*, 4th ed., London: Hodder Arnold, 60–83.

Puppis, M. (2010) "Media Governance: A New Concept for the Analysis of Media Policy and Regulation," *Communication. Culture and Critique*, 3 (2): 139–149.

Reuters Institute for the Study of Journalism (2015) "Readers Feel Deceived Over Sponsored Content, Posing Significant Risk of Damage to the Reputation of Digital Publishers," June 16, available at https://reutersinstitute.politics.ox.ac.uk/sites/default/files/2017-06/Reuters%20Institute%20 Digital%20News%20Report%202015%20Sponsored%20Content%20Press%20Release.pdf (accessed June 20, 2015).

Rosenau, J. N. (1992) "Governance, order and change in world politics" in J. Rosenau and E. O. Czempiel (eds), *Governance without Government: Order and change in World Politics,* Cambridge: Cambridge University Press, 1–29.

Schmidt, V. A. (2008) "Discursive Institutionalism: The Explanatory Power of Ideas and Discourse," *Annual Review of Political Science,* 11: 303–326.

Serazio, M. (2013) *Your Ad Here. The Cool Sell of Guerrilla Marketing*, New York: New York University Press.

Sinclair, J. (2020) "Cracking Under Pressure: Current Trends in the Global Advertising Industry," *Media International Australia*, 174 (1): 3–16.

Statista (2020a) "Usage of Ad Blocking Software in the United Kingdom (UK) in 2018 and 2020," available at www.statista.com/statistics/874736/ad-blocker-usage-in-united-kingdom/ (accessed 16 November 16, 2020)

Statista (2020b) "Ad Blocking User Penetration Rate in the United States from 2014 to 2021," www.statista.com/statistics/804008/ad-blocking-reach-usage-us/ (accessed November 16, 2020)

*The Guardian* (2017) "Content Funding on the Guardian," May 22, available at www.theguardian.com/info/2016/jan/25/content-funding (accessed November 16, 2020).

Turow, J. (2011) *The Daily You*, New Haven, CT: Yale University Press.

Turow, J. and McAllister, M. (2009) "General Introduction," in J. Turow and M. McAllister (eds), *The Advertising and Consumer Culture Reader*, New York: Routledge.

Vos, T. (2019) "Field Theory and Journalistic Capital," in T. Vos and F. Hanusch (eds), *The International Encyclopedia of Journalism Studies*, Malden, MA: John Wiley.

Yesiloglu, S. and Costello, J. (eds) (2020) *Influencer Marketing: Building Brand Communities and Engagement*, Abingdon: Routledge.

Wasko, J. (2004) "The Political Economy of Communications," in J. Downing (ed.), *The Sage Handbook of Media Studies*, Thousand Oaks, CA: Sage, 309–331.

Wasko, J. and Meehan, E. (2013) "Critical Crossroads or Parallel Routes? Political Economy and New Approaches to Studying Media Industries and Cultural Products," *Cinema Journal* 52 (3): 150–156.

# 4

# WHY SHOULD WE CARE ABOUT MEDIA POLICY?

## Critical directions in media policy research

*Maria Michalis*

Media policy matters because the media matter. The media matter because they have power, the power

> to set an agenda. The power they have to destroy one. The power they have to influence and change the political process. The power to enable, to inform. The power to deceive. The power to shift the balance of power: between state and citizen; between country and country; between producer and consumer. And the power that they are denied: by the state, by the market, by the resistant or resisting audience, citizen, consumer.
>
> *Silverstone 1999: 143*

Media policy and media industries are inextricably interlinked. One cannot study the one without studying the other. In this chapter, contra neoliberal thinking, markets are conceptualized "not [as] natural phenomena but [as] politically constructed and politically maintained" (Gamble 1995: 523; for a historical account see Polyani 1957). Governments make a number of choices related to media – regardless of how well articulated and justified these are – about such diverse matters as who can own or control the media, the allocation of scarce resources such as radio frequencies, the remit and funding of public service broadcasting (a core public policy intervention), public subsidies for the press, regulation of media content and advertising rules, to mention some. These policies are specific to the media and come in addition to the competition rules that apply to all sectors, even though in some cases competition rules, like merger regulations, have been adapted to reflect the significance of the media in societies. For instance, in Britain, the so-called media public interest test allows the Secretary of State to intervene in media mergers to determine whether the merger, even if it does not raise competition concerns as such, might harm the public interest and should therefore be approved with conditions or rejected altogether.

The next section defines media policy, explains why and how it matters, and points to recent challenges. The chapter then moves on to assess ways one can analyze policy critically. This refers to research that does not simply describe policy but rather places policy within the existing technological, socioeconomic, and institutional context of power relations with a view

DOI: 10.4324/9780429275340-6

to advancing policies that promote the public interest. The chapter ends with a summary of the main points.

## Defining media policy and establishing its importance

"Policy is a medium of control acting upon politics and at the same time a product of the political process" (Hanada quoted by Raboy 2002: 5). Put differently, the media are a target of policy themselves and at the same time they can serve as instruments of governance.

Media policy, as Puppis and van den Bulck (2019: 3–4) observe, may not get the level of attention that other policies attract – such as trade, health and migration – yet it lies "at the heart of contemporary society" for it concerns "information, news and cultural production, meaning creation and content curation and the distribution of content and services to individuals." Indeed, Braman (2004: 153) uses the term information policy to denote policies "dealing with an information production chain that includes information creation, processing, flows and use" and as such it is broader than the concept of media policy that focuses on the "technologies, processes and content by which the public itself is mediated."

The term "media policy" refers to policy directed toward a number of distinct sectors, notably broadcasting, the press, and film (Hesmondhalgh 2019: 138). Communication policy has come to denote digitization and the evolving convergence of previously identifiable separate sectors and includes, in addition, the telecommunications and Internet industries, that is the technologies and infrastructures that support the media (Iosifidis 2011: 7). Cultural policy, finally, has expanded from its original narrow meaning referring to the arts and heritage, to include, since the late 1990s, creativity, entrepreneurship and knowledge generation, explaining why one increasingly encounters the term creative industries policy (Hesmondhalgh 2019: 175–196).

Policy sets out the broad objectives to be achieved, the direction of travel for the media industries and the media users. Regulation is narrower. It is responsible for the actual implementation of policies. Policy is typically state-led, whereas regulation is generally assigned to sectoral regulatory authorities, like Ofcom in Britain or the Federal Communications Commission (FCC) in the United States. For example, let us look at policy directed toward pro-competitive market restructuring. From the 1980s onward, an increasing number of countries opted to liberalize their media markets, that is, open them up to competition. Regulation has been responsible for operationalizing the policy aim of liberalization, for addressing the details of how that is going to be achieved in practice with measures that include an array of structural and behavioral rules. Examples of the former are media (cross-)ownership restrictions, while content regulations are an example of behavioral rules. In short, despite the oft-used term "deregulation," the liberalization and privatization processes necessitated more, not less, regulation (Moran 2003).

To understand the media system and industries of a country or region, one needs to understand that country or region's media policies. Media industries and media policies are two sides of the same coin. There is nothing natural about the media we get, be they state-owned and controlled, commercial, public or community.[1] All countries with any political system have media policy (Picard 2020); it is just that the character, tools, and outcomes differ from country to country. As Freedman argues (2008: 1).

> media systems are … purposefully created, their characters shaped by competing political interests that seek to inscribe their own values and objectives on the possibilities facilitated by a complex combination of technological, economic and social factors.

The aim of media policy research then is to explain how policy works, how choices are made and with what effect, why societies get the media they get, with what implications and, in doing so, identify possible opportunities for reform.

Legislation is probably the most obvious element of policy. But policy and rules do not necessarily come from government. In cases of co-regulation, industry typically works together with national regulatory authorities: the industry operates on the basis of commonly agreed principles and guidelines, while the regulator oversees such adherence and has the power to intervene in cases of non-compliance. An example from Britain concerns commercial communications. The Advertising Standards Agency (ASA) is responsible for day-to-day regulation of the content of radio and television advertisements on the basis of an industry code under contract from Ofcom. There is also self-regulation, whereby an industry voluntarily establishes rules to regulate itself, which can raise questions about the effectiveness of those rules. In Britain, the Independent Press Standards Organization (IPSO), which regulates most national newspapers, has been described as too close to the industry to be an effective and accountable regulator (e.g., Barnett 2016). Moreover, especially in the case of the Internet, there are various industry and multistakeholder groupings that work on technical standards and policy issues, like the W3C (World Wide Web Consortium), ICANN (Internet Corporation for Assigned Names and Numbers), and the Internet Governance Forum. Finally, individual media companies too often develop their own rules, like the BBC, which has its own editorial standards. In the sphere of social media, this has become the norm, with the big companies such as Facebook, Twitter, and YouTube setting the rules for their platforms. Puppis (2010: 138) uses the term "media governance" to capture both collective and such organizational governance, hence covering "the entirety of forms of rules that aim to organize media systems."

Governance in political science and international relations has generally been used to denote changes "in the nature of the state" (Treib, Bähr, and Falkner 2007) or what Rhodes (1997) calls the "hollowing out" of the state with the decline of central authority from below (by liberalization and networks), across (by agencies), and above (by international organizations). The fields of media and communication were among the first to establish international regimes of governance, albeit with a narrow focus originally, addressing technical, operational, and commercial cross-border issues. It was later with the gradual process of market liberalization that international organizations moved to policy matters. Media policy then operates at various levels: sub-national, national, regional (e.g., European Union) and international (e.g., ITU, ICANN).

Policy touches all media industry actors in one way or another, from production to distribution and consumption (see Nieminen 2018: 7). For instance, in production, copyright law is significant to content creators. Copyright is relevant to all media industries, including newspapers, magazines, and broadcasting, where laws concerning privacy, defamation, and freedom of speech are also applicable. Legislation and rules governing access to and use of frequencies, and rights of way are some examples that relate to distribution. Retail price controls, network neutrality rules, universal service and rollout obligations, copyright enforcement, and consumer protection rules, among others, concern media consumers.

Media policy and regulation aim to address a variety of technical, economic, social, political, and cultural objectives. Technical regulation has to do with standards, interoperability of equipment, and safety. From an economic perspective, state intervention aims at correcting market failures: tackling media ownership concentration, encouraging positive externalities (e.g., local productions entailing economic and cultural value) while reducing negative externalities (e.g., violent content which might promote anti-social behavior), and supporting the public good elements of the media that private provision may undersupply (Flew 2018: 18).

Policy interventions based on such economic rationales can simultaneously promote non-economic aims, even though that is not their direct intention, like support for local media productions can promote plurality of voices and social cohesion. Similarly, plurality of ownership reduces media power concentration, encouraging the expression of diverse voices and promoting democratic values (Baker 2006). Although there are valid justifications for policy, democratic societies have to strike a balance between intervention and media freedom.

Epistemologically then, media policy research should address "the informative and cultural functions of the media" (Nieminen 2018: 4). This is relevant regardless of the level of analysis (macro, meso, or micro) or indeed the political system of a country. Often, media policy focuses on and is justified in economic terms, but media policy is inextricably linked to political, social, and cultural objectives, as well as being relevant to human rights. Indeed, this link has had a long history in international and national policy debates and is often part of broader geopolitical structures. More recently, in the Internet era and in reaction to neoliberal economic policies, the rise of surveillance capitalism (Zuboff 2019), the concentration of power amongst a handful of global mighty data-driven platforms, as well as strong evidence of mis- and dis-information, has renewed attention in communication rights and in a wider understanding of media policy as social policy (e.g., Ala-Fossi, Alén-Savikko, Hilden, Horowitz, Jääsaari, Karppinen, Lehtisaari, and Nieminen 2019; Calabrese and Burgelman 1999; Irion and Helberger 2017; Kerr, Musiani, and Pohle 2019; Shomron and Schejter 2020).

## Analyzing media policy

Policymaking is a process, not an instance of a decision. Researchers often divide policy into stages, starting from agenda setting and moving through policy formulation, decision-making, and implementation stages. While these categories have analytic value, they may give the false impression that policymaking is linear and moves unproblematically from one stage to the next. But this is not a linear, rational, or methodical process in pursuit of a single universally agreed objective (Bauer 2005; Garnham 2005). Policy is a field of contestation. It tries to address various issues simultaneously on the basis of limited knowledge. It can even result in unintended consequences as one line of (in)action can create new – or aggravate existing – problems. Path dependencies and established power structures further limit policy options. Policymaking is therefore often messy, resembling what Charles Lindblom (1959) calls "muddling through," with small incremental adaptations, and reaching outcomes that can even be accidental (Kingdon 1995).

Media policy is spatial, temporal, and relational. Not only is it country- and time-specific, being embedded in a specific historical context, but it is relational in the sense that it exists in negotiation with other policies, reflecting and often reinforcing existing power relations. For instance, feminist critiques, growing stronger in the Internet era, draw attention to wider systemic gender inequalities (e.g., D'Ignazio and Klein 2020; Noble 2018).

Above all, media policy is about power. Following Lukes (1974), power can be visible but also invisible and structural. We can examine policy decisions, as these are known and visible, being evident in specific policy preferences. Although decisions often provide an obvious focus of analysis, it is equally important, if not more so, to examine the invisible but consequential impacts of inaction and non-decisions. Inaction is as much about power as action is. Inaction is a decision not to address an issue, or often not even to recognize something as a problem, which leaves existing power structures intact. Inaction thereby supports and entrenches the status quo. Non-decisions prevent political demands from being made. The policy agenda is set by sweeping away potential (undesirable) issues. This is what Freedman

(2010: 355) refers to as "policy silences." To examine this second dimension of power, researchers have to focus on the "informal process of agenda-setting within the corridors of power" (Hay 2002: 177). Finally, Lukes has put forward a third radical dimension of power that relates to the shaping of preferences: how hegemonic ideologies and structures can result in distorted and misconceived perceptions and preferences. This is the structural element of Lukes' model of power.

In sum, policy studies tend to focus on visible decisions, overlooking preceding and subsequent developments. While Lukes' first dimension of power draws attention to decisions, the most visible element of power, his second and third dimensions are a call to investigate the agenda-setting and policy formulation stages in particular. Equally, there are few studies on the implementation of policies and the analysis of policy failures, as often the problem is not the absence of policies but rather their lax adherence and enforcement. One can come up with the best policy solution to a problem, but unless those responsible for implementation (notably the media industries) are committed to putting the solution into practice with monitoring mechanisms in place, nothing will have been achieved. Policy implementation and evaluation are therefore important elements of the policymaking process. Indeed, "implementation decisions are ... closely bound up with policy choices," and "usually are policy choices" themselves, so that crucially they often can feed back into the policy process (John 2012: 164). Implementation and policy evaluation contribute to policy learning and policy transfer across borders (e.g., comparative studies and best practice models).

Any policy analysis entails assumptions about the state–market relationship, and corporate and public actions. Policy analyses involve invariably one or a combination of the following elements: institutions (structures); actors' interests (preferences) and networks; political, social, and economic conditions; ideas; and individual actors. All these elements are in constant interaction and the aim of analysis is to use these elements in order to provide a holistic account. The aim is not to describe a policy (change) but to explain policy (non-)options, changes, and variations with a view to advancing policies that promote the public interest.

With their formal and informal rules and processes, institutions are central in understanding policy. New institutionalism draws attention to the role of institutions in policymaking, change, and variation (March and Olsen 1984). Institutions as structures can both enable and constrain action. They can become policy actors in their own right, often in coalition with like-minded networks. They "include the constitutions, laws, procedures, organizations and rules that are central to every political system" (John 2012: 29). At the most basic level, knowing how the political system of a country works gives you an idea of which institutions matter, and how and when they matter, for all these may vary during the course of the policymaking process. It is worth mentioning the historical institutionalist strand of new institutionalism that highlights path dependencies and the influence of past policy (in)action over current policy debates and choices in ways that constrain change. Galperin (2004), for example, explains how institutional factors and the legacies in the broadcasting sector in each country shaped the transition from analog to digital television in the United States and Britain, producing different outcomes.

Alongside institutions, actors (such as media organizations, civil society associations, media device manufacturers, trade unions) have policy preferences that they try to promote in order to influence the policy process. Actors may operate alone, as may be the case with a single big media company, but more often it is the interaction of actors with other actors, including institutions, that matters and can help explain policies. Concepts like policy networks (Rhodes 1997) and policy advocacy coalitions (Sabatier and Jenkins-Smith 1999; and for an application to media policy, see van den Bulck and Donders 2014) draw attention to such formal and informal relationships and patterns of association.

Acknowledging the wider historical, political, social, and economic conditions that form the broader contexts in which media policies operate is crucial. In the media field, there have been accounts of how the larger environment shapes the overall media system of a country, its policy, and regulation. One early example is Siebert, Peterson, and Schramm's (1954) *Four Theories of the Press*, which divides the world into free liberal democracies, Soviet totalitarian regimes, and authoritarian societies. More recently, perhaps the best known, though not unproblematic, account is that by Hallin and Mancini (2004) who identify three models of media-political systems: liberal (e.g., United States, Canada, Britain), democratic corporatist (encountered mostly in Northern and Central Europe), and the polarized pluralist model (found in Southern Europe). Similarly, Syvertsen, Enli, Mjøs, and Moe (2014) examine the media welfare model of the Nordic countries. Curran and Park (2000) aim to de-westernize the typologies and divide the world into authoritarian and democratic societies, each further subdivided into neoliberal and regulated media systems. Although all these accounts suffer from the usual limitations of categorization, they do point to the influence that broader political, social, and economic factors can have upon media systems and the policies which contribute to shaping those systems.

Ideas and discourse matter too (Hay 2002: 194–215). These concern whether and how issues are identified and framed, playing important roles in justifying and legitimating policy (non-)intervention. Since the 1980s, the rise of neoliberalism, strongly identified with the Reagan administration in the United States and the Thatcher government in Britain, and promoting calls for greater reliance on unfettered market forces and the concomitant withdrawal of the state, has spread internationally, rapidly contributing to a radical privatization and pro-competition policy reform program. Media policy is full of examples where neoliberalism, globalization, and technological advances are presented as objective forces that set forth a certain course of (in)action. For example, very often the proposed course of (in)action is presented as technology-driven, non-negotiable, and thus unavoidable. The general argument that one cannot regulate the Internet and international platforms because they operate transnationally is a well-rehearsed one, and yet Internet regulation has many forms and levels. By directing attention to the role of ideas, discourses, knowledge, and beliefs in the construction of reality, constructivist insights highlight how the credibility and acceptability of proposed measures are made appear commonsensical. But ideas always reflect specific interests and can help legitimate certain policy options over others. Ideas, therefore, "have important distributional consequences in influencing problem definition and policy outcomes" (Richardson and Lindley 1994: 3).

Individual actors and their preferences matter. This is not only the case for political leaders but also for individuals within organizations and companies who are crucial in setting the strategy, as well as for policy networks. In recent years, we also have excellent examples of single agency, individual political activists who have shaped the course of policy internationally. One example concerns the revelations of Edward Snowden in 2013 through the leaking of highly classified information from the US National Security Agency about global surveillance perpetrated in cooperation with other, notably European, governments, national security agencies, and telecommunications providers. Similarly, starting in 2013, Max Schrems, an Austrian activist and lawyer, took legal action against Facebook alleging violations of European privacy regulations and rules about the transfer of personal data outside the European Union to the United States. Snowden's revelations and Schrems' legal actions contributed to media policy debates internationally, feeding into the formation of actual policies, such as the European Union's General Data Protection Regulation (GDPR) on data protection and privacy.

What is interesting about these cases and the power of individual agency is that they very clearly demonstrate the unpredictability of the policy process, the role of highly motivated individuals ("policy entrepreneurs") who identify a "policy window," a rare opportunity to act swiftly and influence the policy process. In so doing, they seriously challenge the policy consensus and coalitions, upsetting the established policy equilibrium. Such actions and events can represent exogenous shocks to the policy process and cause policy change, aspects of the policy process that single accounts of policy focusing on one of the elements noted above might well miss, for such accounts tend to describe processes and so give the impression of policy stability, even predictability. Kingdon's model of multiple policy streams aims precisely to address this and provide a dynamic explanatory framework. Based on a study of US public policy, Kingdon explains policy as the result of three sets of streams (processes) converging to present a window of opportunity for a given policy to have a chance for fruition. First, the *problem stream* is about issues perceived as public in the sense that there is public awareness about them, hence they require government attention and action. Second, the *policy stream* refers to plausible solutions which draw upon experience and expertise. Lastly, the *political stream* is the zeitgeist of a period, comprising factors such as executive and legislative changes, and swings in the popular mood. Media policy research has engaged with Kingdon's multiple streams framework. For instance, Herzog and Karppinen (2014) use it to analyze the reforms in public service media funding in Germany and Finland in 2013, while Sundet and Syvertsen (2020) apply the framework to explain policy change and no change in the review processes of public service broadcasting in Britain and Norway between 2013 and 2017.

## Conclusion

The field of media policy has advanced and addressed criticisms that such studies tend to be *a*critical and *a*theoretical (e.g., Picard 2016). Media policy scholars do not need to invent new theoretical tools but can use existing theoretical frameworks and analytical concepts to research media policy. Indeed, depending on the questions asked, there are many fields upon which media policy can draw but also, importantly, to which media policy research can contribute to. Media policy scholars have drawn on anthropology and sociology (e.g., Born 2004), economics and management sciences (e.g., Doyle 2013; Picard, Rohn, and Evens 2020), political science and international relations (e.g., Harcourt 2006; Humphreys and Simpson 2018; Michalis 2007), law (e.g., Edwards 2018; Marsden 2011), philosophy and normative frameworks, interpretive and constructivist approaches, environmental studies (e.g., Maxwell and Miller 2012), psychology, and political economy (e.g., Fuchs 2015; Hardy 2014), to mention some. In terms of methods, media policy research has relied on the methods of the main discipline housing the research. It is also worth noting the recent publication of an edited volume on methods for media policy research (van den Bulck, Puppis, Donders, and van Audenhove 2019) showcasing the richness of available methods attuned to shedding light on the highly complex media policy process, again drawing on fields such as psychology, sociology, political science, computer science, and so forth.

The discussion in this chapter underlined the interconnectedness of media industries and media policy, and examined the main forms, themes, and elements of such policy. It showed that we can never have *the* account of any policy but rather we can form multiple accounts of policies. What is important is that media policy studies do not end up providing a descriptive account but rather strive to offer an explanation of policy (non-)intervention, an analysis of policy within wider historical, socioeconomic, and institutional power frameworks with the aim to promote interventions that advance the public interest.

## Note

1 Community media are from the people, by the people, and for the people. They tend to serve localities. Although public media are similar to community media in that they treat audiences as citizens, not consumers, they are not produced or operated by the people but on their behalf, and they typically serve larger geographical areas.

## References

Ala-Fossi, M., Alén-Savikko, A., Hilden, J., Horowitz, M. A., Jääsaari, J., Karppinen, K., Lehtisaari, K. and Nieminen, H. (2019) "Operationalising Communication Rights: The Case of a "Digital Welfare State," *Internet Policy Review*, 8 (1), available at https://policyreview.info/articles/analysis/operationalising-communication-rights-case-digital-welfare-state (accessed December 14, 2020).

Baker, E. C. (2006) *Media Concentration and Democracy: Why Ownership Matters*, New York: Cambridge University Press.

Barnett, S. (2016) "IMPRESS vs IPSO: A Chasm, Not a Cigarette Paper," *LSE Media Blog*, available at https://blogs.lse.ac.uk/medialse/2016/10/31/impress-vs-ipso-a-chasm-not-a-cigarette-paper/ (accessed December 8, 2020).

Bauer, J. (2005) "Mechanical to Adaptive Policy," in P. Verhoest (ed.), *Contradiction, Confusion and Hubris. A Critical Review of European Information Society Policy*, Brussels: ENCIP, 27–30.

Born, G. (2004) *Uncertain Vision: Birt, Dyke and the Reinvention of the BBC*, London: Vintage.

Braman, S. (2004) "Where Has Media Policy Gone? Defining the Field in the Twenty-First Century," *Communication Law and Policy*, 9 (2): 153–182.

Calabrese, A. and Burgelman, J. C. (1999) *Communication, Citizenship, and Social Policy*, Lanham, MA: Rowman & Littlefield.

Curran, J. and Parks, M. J. (2000) *De-westernizing Media Studies*, London: Routledge.

D'Ignazio, C. and Klein, L. F. (2020) *Data Feminism*, Cambridge, MA: MIT Press.

Doyle, G. (2013) *Understanding Media Economics*, 2nd ed., London: Sage.

Edwards, L. (ed.) (2018) *Law, Policy and the Internet*, Oxford: Hart Publishing.

Flew, T. (2018) *Understanding Global Media* 2nd ed., London: Palgrave.

Freedman, D. (2008) *The Politics of Media Policy*, Cambridge: Polity.

Freedman, D. (2010) "Media Policy Silences: The Hidden Face of Communications Decision Making," *International Journal of Press/Politics*, 15 (3): 344–361.

Fuchs, C. (2015) *Culture and Economy in the Age of Social Media*, New York: Routledge.

Galperin, H. (2004) *New Television, Old Politics: The Transition of Digital TV in the United States and Britain*, Cambridge: Cambridge University Press.

Gamble, A. (1995) "The New Political Economy," *Political Studies*, 43 (3): 516–530.

Garnham, N. (2005) "Contradiction, Confusion and Hubris. A Critical Review of European Information Society Policy," in P. Verhoest (ed.), *Contradiction, Confusion and Hubris. A Critical Review of European Information Society Policy*, Brussels: ENCIP, 6–18.

Hallin, D. C. and Mancini, P. (2004) *Comparing Media Systems: Three Models of Media and Politics*, Cambridge: Cambridge University Press.

Harcourt, A. (2006) *European Union and the Regulation of Media Markets*, Manchester: Manchester University Press.

Hardy, J. (2014) *Critical Political Economy of the Media*, Abingdon: Routledge.

Hay, C. (2002) *Political Analysis: A Critical Introduction*, Basingstoke: Palgrave.

Herzog, C. and Karppinen, K. (2014) "Policy Streams and Public Service Media Funding reforms in Germany and Finland," *European Journal of Communication*, 29 (4): 416–432.

Hesmondhalgh, D. (2019) *The Cultural Industries*, 4th ed., London: Sage.

Humphreys, P. and Simpson, S. (2018) *Regulation, Governance and Convergence in the Media*, Cheltenham: Edward Elgar.

Iosifidis, P. (2011) *Global Media and Communication Policy: An International Perspective*, Basingstoke: Palgrave Macmillan.

Irion, K. and Helberger, N. (2017) "Smart TV and the Online Media Sector: User Privacy in View of Changing Market Realities," *Telecommunications Policy*, 41 (3): 170–184.

John, P. (2012) *Analyzing Public Policy*, 2nd ed., Milton Park, Abingdon: Routledge.

Kerr, A., Musiani, F., and Pohle, J. (2019) "Communication and Internet Policy: A Critical Rights-based History and Future," *Internet Policy Review*, 8 (1), available at https://policyreview.info/articles/analysis/communication-and-internet-policy-critical-rights-based-history-and-future (accessed December 14, 2020).

Kingdon, J. (1995) *Agendas, Alternatives, and Public Policy*, 2nd ed., New York: Harper Collins.

Lindblom, C. E. (1959) "The Science of 'Muddling Through'," *Public Administration*, 19 (2): 79–88.

Lukes, S. (1974) *Power: A Radical View*, London: Macmillan.

March, J. and Olsen, J. (1984) "The New Institutionalism: Organizational Factors in Political Life," *The American Political Science Review*, 78 (3): 734–749.

Marsden, C. T. (2011) *Internet Co-regulation*, Cambridge: Cambridge University Press.

Maxwell, R. and Miller, T. (2012) *Greening the Media*, Oxford: Oxford University Press.

Michalis, M. (2007) *Governing European Communications*, Lanham, MD: Lexington.

Moran, M. (2003) *The British Regulatory State: High Modernism and Hyper-innovation*, Oxford: Oxford University Press.

Nieminen, H. V. (2018) "Why Study Media Policy and Regulation?" in L. D´Haenens, H. Sousa, and J. Trappel (eds), *Comparative Media Policy, Regulation and Governance in Europe: Unpacking the Policy Cycle*, Bristol: Intellect, 1–20.

Noble, S. U. (2018) *Algorithms of Oppression: How Search Engines Reinforce Racism*, New York: New York University Press.

Picard, R. G. (2016) "Isolated and Particularised: The State of Contemporary Media and Communications Policy Research," *Javnost/The Public*, 23 (2): 135-152, available at www.tandfonline.com/doi/abs/10.1080/13183222.2016.1162991 (accessed June 19, 2021).

Picard, R. G. (2020) *Media and Communications Policy Making: Processes, Dynamics and International Variations*, Cham: Palgrave Macmillan.

Polanyi, K. (1957) *The Great Transformation*, Boston, MA: Beacon Press.

Puppis, M. (2010) "Media Governance: A New Concept for the Analysis of Media Policy and Regulation," *Communication, Culture and Critique*, 3: 134–149.

Puppis, M. and van den Bulck, H. (2019) "Introduction: Media Policy and Media Policy Research," in H. van den Bulck, M. Puppis, K. Donders, and L. van Audenhove (eds), *The Palgrave Handbook of Methods for Media Policy Research*, London: Palgrave, 3–21.

Raboy, M. (2002) "Media Policy in the New Communications Environment," in M. Raboy (ed.) *Global Media Policy in the New Millennium*, Luton: University of Luton Press, 3–16.

Rhodes, R. A. W. (1997) *Understanding Governance: Policy Networks, Governance, Reflexivity and Accountability*, Buckingham: Open University Press.

Richardson, J. J. and Lindley, R. M. (1994) "Editorial," *Journal of European Public Policy*, 1 (1): 1–7.

Rohn, U. and Evens, T. (eds) (2020) *Media Management Matters: Challenges and Opportunities for Bridging Theory and Practice*, New York: Routledge.

Sabatier, P. and Jenkins-Smith, H. (1999) "The Advocacy Coalition Framework: An Assessment," in P. Sabatier (ed.), *Theories of the Policy Process*, Boulder, CO: Westview.

Shomron, B. and Schejter, A. (2020) "The Communication Rights of Palestinian Israelis Understood Through the Capabilities Approach," *International Journal of Communication*, available at https://ijoc.org/index.php/ijoc/article/view/13846/3018 (accessed June 19, 2021).

Siebert, E., Peterson, T., and Schramm, W. (1956) *Four Theories of the Press*, Urbana, IL: University of Illinois Press.

Silverstone, R. (1999) *Why Study the Media?* London: Sage.

Sundet, V. S. and Syvertsen, T. (2020) "From Problem to Solution? Why it is Difficult to Restrict the Remit of Public Broadcasters," *International Journal of Cultural Policy*, available at www.tandfonline.com/doi/full/10.1080/10286632.2020.1807522 (accessed December 14, 2020).

Syvertsen, T., Enli, G., Mjøs, O. J., and Moe, H. (2014) *The Media Welfare State: Nordic Media in the Digital Era*, Ann Arbor, MI: University of Michigan Press.

Treib, O., Bähr, H., and Falkner, G. (2007) "Modes of Governance: Towards a Conceptual Clarification," *Journal of European Public Policy*, 14 (1): 1–20.

van den Bulck, H. and Donders, K. (2014) "Analyzing European Media Policy: Stakeholders and Advocacy Coalitions," in K. Donders, C. Pawels, and J. Loisen (eds), *The Palgrave Handbook of European Media Policy*, Basingstoke: Palgrave, 16–35.

van den Bulck, H. Puppis, M., Donders, K., and van Audenhove, L. (eds) (2019) *The Palgrave Handbook of Methods for Media Policy Research*, Cham: Palgrave Macmillan.

Zuboff, S. (2019) *The Age of Surveillance Capitalism*, London: Profile Books.

# 5

# ECONOMIC PERSPECTIVES ON THE CHARACTERISTICS AND OPERATION OF MEDIA INDUSTRIES

*Gillian Doyle*

Whereas academic studies of media have traditionally been dominated by sociology or other non-economic disciplines, the perspectives and frameworks offered by economics are now properly recognized as central to our understanding of the organization and behavior of media industries. Therefore, media economics – the subject area that concerns itself with the economics of making and supplying media – is flourishing. In media economics, the focus is on applying economic theories and concepts to activities such as film-making, news production, print and online publishing, video-on-demand streaming services, and television and radio broadcasting, and on developing models and paradigms for the advancement of economic studies of all aspects of media. As more and more economists have turned their attention to media firms and industries, media economics has developed as a rich and diverse field in its own right. This chapter sets out to give a sense of some of the main concerns that mark this out as a distinctive and lively area of study. The first of the two main sections below identifies some of the defining features of media economics and the main purposes and approaches that characterize the field. The second section elaborates on key themes and questions that have featured in economic studies of media, past and present.

## Purposes of media economics research

Media are unique in many ways and this is reflected in the nature and purposes of economic research into media organizations and industries. For example, one defining aspect of media is that technology is at the heart of the business and because of this there is a constant need for analysis of the effects of changing industrial circumstances. But an even more fundamental defining feature is that the business of producing and distributing media and supplying messages and ideas to audiences involves wider societal and public welfare implications. Many media firms operate as commercial businesses but not all are motivated by profit. So research that falls within the ambit of media economics stems not only from traditional economics, with its concern for efficiency, but also from the perspective called critical political economy. As Gomery argues, "studying the economics of mass communications as though one were trying to make toaster companies run leaner and meaner is far too narrow a perspective" (1993: 198). The

DOI: 10.4324/9780429275340-7

political economy approach, with its emphasis on interrelations between economic, political, and social dimensions of media, allows for a wider and a more normative perspective. As Wasko puts it "[t]hrough studies of ownership and control, political economists document and analyze relations of power, class systems and other structural inequalities" (2014: 260) to critically make sense of the economics of media.

But research in media economics is varied in its roots, purposes, and approaches. As early as the 1950s, some studies which focused on competition in the newspaper industry had emerged in the United States. Other early studies in the field by Steiner (1952) and subsequently Beebe (1977) focused on competitive programming strategies among broadcasters. Some early media economics research owed its existence to the needs of public policymaking. For example, in the UK, the Peacock Report (1986) was tasked with examining the feasibility of alternative funding options to support the BBC but subsequently went well beyond this remit provided the first systematic economic assessment of the UK television industry. More recently, national and international interest in understanding economic aspects of media has grown exponentially, buoyed up the digital revolution and its transformative impacts on media organizations and industries (Küng 2017). Forces encouraging greater demand for research focused on economic aspects of media have included convergence and globalization, the rise of transnational digital platforms, shifts in modes of media consumption and distribution, disruption to business models, deregulation of national media systems and, in many quarters, a growing focus on the economic potential of creative industries (Cunningham, Flew, and Swift 2015; Doyle 2013; Picard and Wildman 2015).

Many areas of media economics research have potential to feed into policy debates: for example, analysis focused on utilization of intellectual property right (IPRs), wealth creation and employment, international trade, ownership, and competition. However, one of the long-standing challenges associated with conducting economic analysis of media, as noted by Alan Peacock (1989) whose work on the economics of broadcasting was seminal, is that the all-important welfare impacts associated with communicating with mass audiences are not easily incorporated within the framework of standard quantitative economic analysis. This is by no means the only peculiarity that bedevils media economics research. Other problems stem from the unusual "public good" aspects of media content, or from dealing with the uncertainties and irrationalities that are naturally inherent to producing creative outputs – analyzed in influential work on arts and contracts by US economist Richard Caves (2000) – or from the impossibility of pinpointing factors that, on account of the persistence of technological change in media industries, are permanently prone to flux and upheaval.

The public good aspect of media refers to the way that media content, in common with many other cultural goods, tends not to be used up or destroyed in the act of consumption. As identified in very early work in the field by Collins, Garnham, and Locksley (1988: 7), broadcast output is non-rivalrous and non-excludable in the sense that broadcast output can be supplied over and over again to additional consumers without being depleted. Media content is not truly "consumable" in the purest sense of this term (Albarran 2002: 28). The essential value of media for audiences, as with many cultural goods, is symbolic and tied up in the messages they convey, rather than with the material carrier of that information (that is, the radio spectrum, the digital file, and so on). The fact that media content is not depleted in the act of consumption is a peculiarity that defies one of the basic tenets of economics – scarcity – without which modelling what constitutes an efficient use of resources becomes very difficult.

Notions of economic efficiency and assessments of whether efficiency is being achieved or not are problematic in the context of media because these partly depend upon clarity about objectives. Such clarity is elusive in industries involved in cultural provision where different constituencies may well have differing but legitimately held views about which priorities and purposes organizations ought to be pursuing. It is widely recognized that, when it comes to organizations involved in making and supplying media, perceived objectives are often multifaceted (Wirth and Bloch 1995; Doyle 2013).

Another well-documented economic feature that distinguishes media industries in the widespread availability of economies of scale. While the costs of producing the "first copy" of, say, a television program are typically high, it then costs relatively little or nothing to reproduce and supply it to extra customers. So media firms enjoy increasing marginal returns as consumption of their output expands (Doyle 2013). Economies of scope are also exceptionally prevalent in media industries, where reformatting or altering of the scope of a media product intended for one audience into a "new" one that extends its consumption releases savings for the firm and generates economies of scope (pp. 16–17). These benefits are magnified by the spread of digital technologies (Lotz 2017). A further distinguishing feature is the fact that media often operate in markets that are "multi-sided" (Rochet and Tirole 2003) where different sorts of output are sold to separate and distinct user groups. For example, content is sold to media audiences while audience attention is sold to advertisers, and the growing complexity of multisided media platforms within digital ecosystems can raise potentially difficult challenges for regulators (Gabszewicz, Resende, and Sonnac 2015: 28).

The distinctive attributes of media may at times add to the complexity of conducting media economics research, but they also contribute to the fascination and appeal of this field. The following section outlines a number of research topics that fall within the ambit of media economics. This is by no means a comprehensive survey, but rather it is intended to provide the reader with a sense of some of the key questions, issues and concerns that mark out this growing area of academic study.

## Research themes

Whereas historically, studies concerned with the economics of media – for example studies of broadcasting or newspaper publishing or competition in media markets – have frequently emerged in response to the needs of industry or policymaking, the field of media economics is now rich and diverse, encompassing a wide array of both applied and theoretical interdisciplinary interests and approaches. The needs of policymakers and industry continue to influence agendas for research and one theme, which recurs frequently is technological change (Martens 2016). In recent times the focus has been on twin forces that have transformed media firms and reshaped market structures and boundaries over recent decades: convergence and globalization. Digital convergence has radically redrawn landscapes of media provision, altering audience consumption behaviors, blurring and extinguishing sectoral and geographic boundaries, and disrupting traditional conceptions of the supply chain while opening up opportunities for innovation across the media industry (Doyle 2013). Many recent research studies have sought to shed light on the economic and strategic implications of these changes (Chan-Olmsted 2006; Cunningham, Flew, and Swift 2015). Much of this work exists within the overlap between media economics and the related discipline of media management studies, focusing on how organizations adapt their strategies to deal with these developments (Achtenhagen, Melin, and Naldi 2013; Anderson, Stromberg, and Waldfogel 2015; Aris and Bughin 2009; Dogruel 2015; Doyle 2015; Küng 2017; Küng, Picard, and Towse 2008; Medina, Herrero, and Guerrero 2015).

Another enduring interest that has shaped research in this field has been the business strategies and behaviors that typify and reflect the unique circumstances of the media industry.

For example, because of inherent uncertainties surrounding the success of any new media product or, as Caves (2000: 5) puts it, the "nobody knows" factor, strategies of risk-spreading are important. The hit-or-miss nature of the business of supplying a product such as a feature film or a television program requires risk mitigation (Picard 2011; Hoskins, McFadyen and Finn 1997) and the use of forecasting models to try and estimate likely demand represents one area of research in media economics (Hofmann-Stölting, Clement, Wu, and Albers 2017). Media economists have also sought to investigate and explain how risks and associated uncertainties can be offset, for example through such strategies as relying on adaptations, sequels, and series that build on prior success. Another risk mitigation strategy is reliance on star actors or directors that help to build up brand loyalty among audiences and therefore to promote higher and more stable revenue streams. In the film business, the ability of the Hollywood majors, through their control over distribution and ability to supply abundant well-funded product, to counteract risk and dominate international trade has been the focus in a number of economic studies of the film industry (De Vany 2004; Jin 2012). More recently, the threat to this model posed by growth in online distribution and illegal copying has provided a new focus for research (Crisp 2015; Hennig-Thurau, and Houston 2019; McDonald 2016; Ulin 2013).

Many media organizations are supported largely through advertising and, as a consequence, patterns of advertising activity exert a very significant influence over the fortunes of the media industry as a whole. Not surprisingly then, audiences and advertising have featured strongly in many economic studies of the media. For example, the economic role played by advertising and the impact it exerts over competitive market structures and consumer decision-making attracted considerable interest in the 1970s and 1980s. Much of that work concerned itself with whether the role played by advertising is helpful in making the market system work more effectively, or whether it is economically detrimental (Schmalensee 1972; Chiplin and Sturgess 1981). Key to this question is the extent to which advertising improves information flows and promotes competition as opposed to, as some would argue, distorting consumer decision-making and impeding market access for potential rivals.

More recently, the many ways in which growth of the internet has affected advertising has been a rich topic for research in media economics. At a macroeconomic level, one area of interest is the relationship between growth rates for the economy and cycles in advertising expenditure, trends that historically have exhibited close correlations. But movements in gross domestic product (GDP) and in advertising expenditure also diverge on occasion (Van der Wurff, Bakker, and Picard 2008) and have tended to do so increasingly in the digital era. Ongoing work in this area is therefore concerned with understanding the exact nature, strength, and consistency of the relationship between economic wealth and advertising activity. More widely, researchers in media economics have been interested in the trade-offs between reliance on advertising revenues versus direct payments from media consumers, and in how digital platforms have changed the ways that audience attention is commoditized and traded. Some studies have sought to unravel the economic implications of targeting behavioral advertising (Athey and Gans, 2010) and the effects on advertising markets of real-time bidding (RTB), while others have examined processes of automated trade or programmatic advertising (Andrew 2019; Chen, Yuan, and Wang 2014).

The ways in which major technology companies such as Facebook and Google have encroached upon the advertising revenues, which at one time were dominated by traditional media, and the associated threats for news and magazine publishers, have been major themes in media economics research. Significant amounts of work have emerged on the implications of new online platforms and changing trends in advertising for media strategies (Küng 2017), innovation (Storsul and Krumsvik 2012), competition (Haucap and Heimeshoff 2014) and processes of industry renewal (Doyle 2015). Some research has flagged up the growing monopol-ization of online advertising by technology giants and such problems associated with advertising on online platforms as fraud, mismeasurement of advertising, and inappropriate placement of advertising messages that may result from automated trade in advertising spaces (Barwise 2017). It may be argued that in the digital advertising environment consumers benefit from more effective targeting and lower prices for online services but, even so, intrusive advertisements and the problem of loss of privacy represent powerful counterbalancing disadvantages (Bourreau, de Streel, and Graef 2017; Evans 2009).

Media industry analysts and media economists have long been interested in examining how demand among advertisers for audience access is converted into revenue streams by media organizations, and how markets for audience attention are evolving (Napoli 2011; Webster, Phelan, and Lichty 2000; Wildman 2003). The issue of audience fragmentation, which featured in the earliest economic studies of television audiences (Barwise and Ehrenberg 1989), has remained an enduring concern over time as attention has turned to the impact of globalized content services such as Netflix (Webster and Ksiazek 2012; Lotz 2014; Jenner 2018). Other key themes over recent years have included the challenges surrounding how to measure audience engagement in a multiplatform environment (Jenkins and Deuze 2008; Napoli 2012; Webster 2014) and how best to integrate analysis of big data into the "essentially human concerns" of audience studies (Athique 2017).

For economists specializing in media, questions around monopolization, competition, and ownership represent a particularly lively area of interest. This reflects the fact that, on account of the prevalence of economies scale and scope, media industries naturally gravitate toward oligopoly and monopoly. An abundance of empirical research has shown how mergers and acquisitions have taken place on a massive scale across media and related communications and technology sectors, resulting in the formation of numerous large transnational media conglomerates that wield significant amounts of market power (Noam 2016). Strategies of expansion and monopolization are propelled not only by pursuit of supply side economies of scale but also, for many online media service providers and intermediaries such as search engines and social networking sites, by the presence of network effects (Srnicek 2016; Belleflamme and Peitz 2018). Network effects or benefits often stem from the fact that higher or wider usage of a network (such as a communications network or a social networking site) confers greater value on all fellow users within the network. Given that the presence of such effects naturally incentivizes service providers in network industries to strive for ever-larger numbers of users, the danger that initial rivalry will eventually give way to monopoly for the dominant system is ever-present.

Despite the arrival and growth of numerous new digital platforms and avenues for dis-tribution of media content in the twenty-first century, concentrations of ownership remain a widespread phenomenon in media (Noam 2016). In industrial economics, strategies of enlargement and diversification are typically attributed to two key incentives related to profit-maximizing behavior: increased efficiency or increased market power. Efficiency gains imply an improved use of resources and are generally seen as beneficial to the economy as a whole but, by contrast, when individual firms accumulate market power this may threaten rivals and consumers alike. A dilemma for policymakers is that proposed mergers and expansion strat-egies in the media and communications industries may often result in both sorts of outcomes (Doyle 2013).

Questions around the rise of digital platforms, the monopolistic nature of technology giants, how they impact on efficiency and competition, and just how policymakers should deal with them are currently important points of focus in media economics (Martens 2016; Moore and

Tambini 2018). Some recent research has aimed at shedding light on the "natural monopoly problem" exacerbated in recent times by network effects (Belleflamme and Peitz 2018: 289) and related problems for policymaking. Promoting innovation and the development of new media firms while also sustaining competition is a problematic challenge, particularly in the context of emerging digital platforms, which often have characteristics of both firms and markets (Coyle 2018).

The role that data may play in building and sustaining positions of market power among emergent technology giants is another area of interest. Although the notion that big data gives firms insurmountable advantages over rivals is disputed by some economists (Evans and Schmalensee 2017), others point to the ways that proprietorial ownership of large amounts of data about consumers or social media participants can support and extend worrying levels of market power (Graef 2018). The potential for big data to generate valuable insights, for example about what audiences like, and to become a source of competitive advantage, has been amply demonstrated by a range of new digital content service providers such as Spotify and Netflix. Although regulatory concerns about the potentially harmful implications of large-scale usage of return path data (or data about the online behavior of subscribers that can be extracted from media software and hardware) have thus far focused primarily on consumer privacy, a growing body of work in media economics has drawn attention to the emergence and implications of asymmetries of power in relation to ownership and use of data, which now represents a key informational resource, particularly in the television industry (Doyle 2018; Schepp and Wambach 2016).

## Conclusion

While the research mentioned in this chapter hopefully gives an indication of the topicality and vitality of media economics as a study area, its coverage is by necessity limited and readers whose appetites have been sharpened will find an array of research on additional worthwhile themes in the range of books and journals and other literature whose focus is economic aspects of media. Interest in the subject now extends across the globe from South America and India to the Far East. Even so, media economics is an area that continues to offer abundant opportunity for researchers to develop new knowledge and to forge new analytical concepts that will help to shape this field in years to come. Research in the future, as in the past, will be driven by the concerns of media industry participants and the needs of media policymaking as well as by the curiosity of academic scholars. Areas offering fertile ground for future economic research include the ongoing transformative effects of advancing technologies and their implications for media markets and organizations; changing relationships between media producers, consumers, distribution outlets, and platforms; negotiating adjustment to the rise of the data economy; and modeling responses to the risks, disruptions, and opportunities that characterize this dynamic and fascinating industry.

## References

Achtenhagen, L., Melin, L., and Naldi, L. (2013) "Dynamics of Business Models: Strategizing, Critical Capabilities and Activities for Sustained Value Creation," *Long Range Planning*, 46 (6): 427–442.

Albarran, A. (2002) *Media Economics: Understanding Markets, Industries and Concepts*, 2nd ed., Ames: Iowa State University Press.

Anderson, S. and Gabszewicz, J. (2006) "The Media and Advertising: A Tale of Two-Sided Markets," in V. A. Ginsburg and D. Throsby (eds), *Handbook of the Economics of Art and Culture*, vol. 1, Oxford: North Holland, 567–614.

Anderson, S., Stromberg, D and Waldfogel, J. (eds) (2015) *Handbook of Media Economics: Volume 1A*, Oxford: North-Holland.

Andrew, D. (2019) "Programmatic Trading: The Future of Audience Economics," *Communication Research and Practice*, 5 (1): 73–87.

Aris, A. and Bughin, J. (2009) *Managing Media Companies*, 2nd ed, Chichester: John Wiley.

Athey, S. and Gans, J. (2010) "The Impact of Targeting Technology on Advertising Markets and Media Competition," *American Economic Review*, 100 (2): 608–613.

Athique, A (2017) "The Dynamics and Potentials of Big Data for Audience Research," *Media, Culture and Society*, 40 (1): 59–74.

Barwise, P. and Ehrenberg, A. (1989) *Television and Its Audience*, London: Sage.

Barwise, P. (2017) "Disrupting the Digital Giants: Advertisers and Traditional Media Push Back," April 5, available at https://blogs.lse.ac.uk/medialse/2017/04/05/disrupting-the-digital-giants-advertisers-and-traditional-media-push-back/ (accessed October 21, 2020).

Beebe, J. H. (1977) "Industrial Structure and Program Choices in Television Markets," *Quarterly Journal of Economics*, 91 (1): 15–37.

Belleflamme, P. and Peitz, M. (2018) "Platforms and Network Effects," in: L. C. Corchón and M. A. Marini (eds) *Handbook of Game Theory and Industrial Organisation, Volume II – Applications*, Cheltenham: Edward Elgar, 286–317.

Bourreau, M., de Streel, A. and Graef, I. (2017) *Big Data and Competition Policy: Market Power, Personalised Pricing and Advertising*, Brussels: Centre on Regulation in Europe.

Caves, R. (2000) *Creative Industries: Contracts Between Art and Commerce*, Cambridge, MA: Harvard University Press.

Chan-Olmsted, S. (2006) "Issues in Media Management and Technology," in A. Albarran and S. Chan-Olmsted and M. Wirth (eds), *Handbook of Media Management and Economics*, Mahwah, NJ: Lawrence Erlbaum Associates, 251–273.

Chen, B., Yuan, S., and Wang, J. (2014) "A Dynamic Pricing Model for Unifying Programmatic Guarantee and Real-Time Bidding in Display Advertising," *Proceedings of the Eighth International Workshop on Data Mining for Online Advertising*, New York: Association for Computing Machinery, 1–9.

Chiplin, B. and Sturgess, B. (1981) *Economics of Advertising*, London: Advertising Association.

Collins, R. Garnham, N., and Locksley, G. (1988) *The Economics of Television: The UK Case*, London: Sage.

Coyle, D. (2018) "Platform Dominance: The Shortcomings of Antitrust Policy," in M. Moore and D. Tambini (eds), *Digital Dominance: The Power of Google, Amazon, Facebook, and Apple*, New York: Oxford University Press, 50–70.

Crisp, V. (2015) *Film Distribution in the Digital Age: Pirates and Professionals*, Basingstoke: Palgrave Macmillan.

Cunningham, S., Flew, T. and Swift, A. (2015) *Media Economics*, London: Palgrave.

De Vany, A. (2004) *Hollywood Economics: How Extreme Uncertainty Shapes the Film Industry*, Abingdon: Routledge.

Dogruel, L. (2015) "Innovation Research in Media Management and Economics: An Integrative Framework," *Journal of Media Business Studies*, 12 (3):153–167.

Doyle, G. (2013) *Understanding Media Economics*, 2nd ed., London: Sage.

Doyle, G (2015) "Multi-platform Media and the Miracle of the Loaves and Fishes," *Journal of Media Business Studies*, 12 (1): 49–65.

Doyle, G. (2018) "Television and the Development of the Data Economy: Data analysis, Power and the Public Interest," *International Journal of Digital Television*, 9 (1): 53–68.

Evans, D. S. (2009) "The Online Advertising Industry: Economics, Evolution, and Privacy," *Journal of Economic Perspectives*, 23 (3): 37–60.

Evans, D. S. and Schmalensee, R. (2017) "Network Effects: March to the Evidence, Not to the Slogans," *Antitrust Chronicle*, September, available at www.competitionpolicyinternational.com/network-effects-march-to-the-evidence-not-to-the-slogans-2/ (accessed October 21, 2020).

Gabszewicz, J., Resende, J., and Sonnac, N. (2015) "Media as Multi-sided Platforms," in R. Picard and S. Wildman (eds), *Handbook on the Economics of the Media*, Cheltenham: Edward Elgar, 3–35.

Graef, I. (2018) "When Data Evolves into Market Power: Data Concentration and Data Abuse Under Competition Law," in M. Moore and D. Tambini (eds), *Digital Dominance: The Power of Google, Amazon, Facebook, and Apple*, Oxford: Oxford University Press, 71–97.

Gomery, D. (1993) "The Centrality of Media Economics," *Journal of Communication*, 43 (3): 190–198.

Haucap, J. and Heimeshoff, U. (2014) "Google, Facebook, Amazon, eBay: Is the Internet Driving Competition or Market Monopolization?" *International Economics and Economic Policy*, 11 (1–2): 49–61.

Hennig-Thurau, T. and Houston, M. (2019) *Entertainment Science: Data Analytics and Practical Theory for Movies, Games, Books, and Music*, Cham: Springer.

Hofmann-Stölting, C., Clement, M., Wu, S., and Albers, S. (2017) "Sales Forecasting of New Entertainment Media Products," *Journal of Media Economics*, 30 (3): 143–171.

Hoskins, C., McFadyen, S., and Finn, A. (1997) *Global Television and Film: An Introduction to the Economics of the Business*, Oxford: Clarendon Press.

Jenkins, H. and Deuze, M. (2008) "Editorial: Convergence Culture," *Convergence*, 14 (1): 5–12.

Jenner, M. (2018) *Netflix and the Re-invention of Television*, Cham: Palgrave Macmillan.

Jin, D. (2012) "Transforming the Global Film Industries: Horizontal Integration and Vertical Concentration Amid Neoliberal Globalization," *International Communication Gazette*, 74 (5): 405–422.

Küng, L. (2017) *Strategic Management in the Media*, 2nd ed., London: Sage.

Küng, L., Picard, R., and Towse, R. (2008) *The Internet and the Mass Media*, London: Sage.

Lotz, A. (2014) *The Television Will Be Revolutionized*, 2nd ed., New York: New York University Press.

Lotz, A. (2017) *Portals: A Treatise on Internet-distributed Television*, Ann Arbor, MI: Maize.

Martens, B. (2016) "An Economic Policy Perspective on Online Platforms," Institute for Prospective Technological Studies Digital Economy Working Paper 2016/05, available at https://papers.ssrn.com/sol3/papers.cfm?abstract_id=2783656 (accessed October 21, 2020).

McDonald, P. (2016) "Hollywood, the MPAA, and the Formation of Anti-piracy Policy," *International Journal of Cultural Policy*, 22 (5): 686–705.

Medina, M., Herrero, M., and Guerrero, E. (2015) "Audience Behaviour and Multiplatform Strategies: The Path Towards Connected TV in Spain," *Austral Comunicación*, 4 (1): 153–172.

Moore, M. and Tambini, D. (eds) (2018) *Digital Dominance: The Power of Google, Amazon, Facebook, and Apple*, Oxford: Oxford University Press.

Noam, E. (ed.) (2016) *Who Owns the World's Media? Media Concentration and Ownership around the World*, New York: Oxford University Press.

Napoli, P. (2011) *Audience Evolution: New Technologies and the Transformation of Media Audiences*, New York: Columbia University Press.

Napoli, P. (2012) "Audience Evolution and the Future of Audience Research, *International Journal on Media Management*, 14 (2): 79–97.

Peacock, A. (1986) *Report of the Committee on Financing the BBC*, London: HMSO.

Peacock, A. (1989) "Introduction," in G. Hughes and D. Vines (eds), *Deregulation and the Future of Commercial Television*, Aberdeen: Aberdeen University Press: 1–8.

Picard, R. (2011) *The Economics and Financing of Media Companies*, 2nd ed., New York: Fordham University Press.

Picard, R. and Wildman, S. (eds) (2015) *Handbook on the Economics of Media*, Cheltenham: Edward Elgar.

Rochet, J. and Tirole, J. (2003) "Platform Competition in Two-Sided Markets," *Journal of the European Economic Association*, 1 (4): 990–1029.

Schmalensee, R. (1972) *The Economics of Advertising*, Amsterdam: North-Holland.

Schepp, N. and Wambach, A. (2016) "On Big Data and its Relevance for Market Power Assessment," *Journal of European Competition Law and Practice*, 7 (2): 120–124.

Srnicek, N. (2016) *Platform Capitalism*, Cambridge: Polity.

Steiner, P. O. (1952) "Program Patterns and Preferences and the Workability of Competition in Radio Broadcasting," *Quarterly Journal of Economics*, 66 (2): 194–223.

Storsul, T. and Krumsvik, A. (eds) (2012) *Media Innovations: A Multidisciplinary Study of Change*, Nordicom: Gothenburg, Sweden.

Ulin, J. (2013) *The Business of Media Distribution: Monetizing Film, TV and Video Content*, 2nd ed, New York: Focal Press.

Van der Wurff, R., Bakker, P., and Picard, R. (2008) "Economic Growth and Advertising Expenditures in Different Media in Different Countries," *Journal of Media Economics*, 21 (1): 28–52.

Wasko, J. (2014) "The Study of the Political Economy of the Media in the Twenty-first Century," *International Journal of Media and Cultural Politics*, 10 (3): 259–271.

Webster, J., Phelan, P., and Lichty, L. (2000) *Ratings Analysis: The Theory and Practice of Audience Research*, 2nd ed, Mahwah, NJ: Lawrence Erlbaum Associates.

Webster, J. (2014) *The Marketplace of Attention: How Audiences Take Shape in a Digital Age*, Cambridge, MA: MIT Press.

Webster, J. and Ksiazek, T. (2012) "The Dynamics of Audience Fragmentation: Public Attention in an Age of Digital Media," *Journal of Communication*, 62 (1): 39–56.

Wildman, S. (2003) "Modeling the Advertising Revenue Potential of Media Audiences: An Underdeveloped Side of Media Economics," *Journal of Media Economics and Culture,* 1 (2): 7–37.

Wirth, M. and Bloch, H. (1995) "Industrial Organization Theory and Media Industry Analysis," *Journal of Media Economics*, 8 (2): 15–26.

# 6

# THE STATE OF MEDIA MANAGEMENT RESEARCH

*Ulrike Rohn*

Media management research aims to understand corporate and entrepreneurial decision-making, conduct, and performance in the media industry. This chapter provides a detailed introduction to media management scholarship.

## The scholarly roots of media management research

Media management scholarship is not the same as management studies applied to the media industry. Instead of taking the media industry as a mere case industry, media management scholarship aims to develop a profound understanding of the special characteristics of the media industry. This not only includes economic and managerial aspects of the media but also, for instance, their important role for culture and society, their particular regulatory environment, the specifics of audience behavior and trends, as well as the applications and developments of the technology used. As such, media management scholarship is very interdisciplinary. Most media management scholars, however, consider themselves as either most closely related to management studies or to media and communication studies. Lowe and Picard (2020) surveyed media management scholars and found most are situated in media-related schools rather than in business and management schools. Few scholars are truly interdisciplinary in their educational as well as institutional background.

Interest in studying the economics and management of media firms started roughly 80 years ago (Albarran 2013), first among economics and management scholars. Only later, in the 1980s, did media and communication scholars take an interest in the economics and business logic of media firms. The *Journal of Media Economics* (*JoME*) was launched in 1987, followed in 1999 by the *International Journal on Media Management* (*IJMM*), and in 2004, by the *Journal of Media Business Studies* (*JoMBS*). The European Media Management Association (emma) was established in 2003 and is the world's largest and most established academic association in the field. Moreover, in the early 2000s, an increasing number of higher education programs on media management were introduced. In response to the growing research output, two new journals were launched to complement the three established journals: the *Journal of Media Management and Entrepreneurship* was launched in 2019 and the *Nordic Journal of Media Management* in 2020.

DOI: 10.4324/9780429275340-8

Many scholars would identify themselves as both media management and media economics researchers. In fact, media management developed in the shade of media economics, and the two scholarly fields are very much intertwined. Unlike media management, which focuses on managerial decision-making and firm performance, media economics is more concerned with industries and markets. Typical research topics include market structure, competition, concentration, policy and regulations, economic growth, employment, and aggregate consumption and production behavior (Albarran 2004, 2014). The connection between media economics and media management is obvious if one considers that one cannot fully understand firm behavior and performance without understanding the context of the markets and industries in which the firms operate. Through media economics and its study of the micro- and macroeconomic conditions in markets and industries, media management is also connected to critical political economy.

The largest conference for both media management and media economics scholars is the biennial World Media Economics and Management Conference, which usually has approximately 200 participants. Emma's annual conference often has between 100 and 200 researchers from various countries, and the association also organizes a biennial doctoral summer school on media management. A somewhat smaller event is the annual gathering of the International Media Management Academic Association (IMMAA), and another popular gathering for media management researchers is the annual meeting of the Media Management, Economics, and Entrepreneurship Division (MMEE) of the Association for Education in Journalism and Mass Communication (AEJMC) in the United States.

In addition to these conferences that specifically target media management scholars, conferences – such as those of the Strategic Management Society (SMS), the European Academy of Management (EURAM), the Academy of Management (AOM), and the European Group for Organizational Studies (EGOS) – attract media management scholars who prefer to identify as management scholars. Those who identify with media and communication studies are more likely to attend conferences organized by, for instance, the International Association for Media and Communication Research (IAMCR), International Communication Association (ICA) or European Communication Research and Education Association (ECREA), and their respective working groups and divisions on media industries.

## Current trends in media management research

Although media management scholarship has no long history, researchers have already witnessed enormous changes in the media industry, which is also reflected in their academic interests and focus. Most prominently, the definition of a media firm has changed in recent years. Traditionally, media management scholars understood media firms as companies "involved in the production and distribution of content intended for a mass audience" (Mierzejewska and Shaver 2014). This publishing-broadcasting approach, however, has been replaced by the so-called platform approach (Hess 2014), encompassing firms that only aggregate, curate, or provide content, including user-created content. As such, companies such as Facebook, YouTube, Apple, and Google are as much of interest to media management scholars as legacy media firms. Ots, Nyilasy, Rohn, and Wikström (2015) go a step further by suggesting that media management studies can be applied to any firm, since digital content strategies have become a key means of creating value for all firms (e.g., Horst, Järventie-Thesleff and Perez-Lattre 2020).

Media management scholars are also becoming increasingly interested in entrepreneurship, since this is now seen as a key variable for success in the media industry. Entrepreneurship includes the founding of startups as well as entrepreneurial ventures within established media organizations (e.g., Hang and van Weezel, 2007; Achtenhagen 2017; Khajeheian 2019). The wider importance of media entrepreneurship studies is that understanding the processes of entrepreneurship in the media helps in identifying processes, activities, and players in the industry before they become significant enough to disrupt existing structures and routines (Rohn 2018). The increasing scholarly attention paid to entrepreneurship in the media has been accompanied by rising interest in research into professional media careers. Entrepreneurship has become a key variable for professional success, including journalism (Achtenhagen 2017; De Cock and De Smaele 2016).

In fact, there are demands for a greater focus to be placed on individual behavior and motives in media management, which would provide a more nuanced understanding of managerial decision-making and behavior, including possible irrational elements (Küng 2017; Picard and Lowe 2016; Rohn 2018).

## Categorizing media management research

Media management research is a broad field. Differences among research projects may be found in the object of study as well as in the theoretical and methodological approaches applied. The following is a list of categories along which research can be differentiated.

### *Unit of analysis*

Dupagne (2018) surveyed articles published in the *JoME* and the *IJMM* between 2004 and 2016 and found that in *IJMM*, 41.2 percent of the articles presented work in which individuals were the unit of analysis, whereas 29.4 percent of the articles focused on the second most frequently used unit of analysis, the firm. In *JoME*, the most common unit of analysis was, in fact, the media product (32.7 percent), followed by the firm (22.0 percent). He also found that in both journals, there was an increase over time in studies on individuals and products, but a decrease on studies on firms.

### *External or internal orientation*

Media management research may also be categorized in terms of whether it looks at external forces in the industry and the market or at the internal forces and processes within a media firm. Research concerning internal processes within media firms includes, for instance, studies on human resource management, leadership, work culture, and organizational restructuring. Studies of external forces on the other hand may look at a firm's decision-making, conduct, and behavior regarding, for instance, technology developments, changes in audience behavior, and competitive and regulatory environments. Where media management research analyzes external market and industry forces, the overlap with media economics is clear.

### *Theories applied*

Media management research does not have its own theories but instead applies theories from related disciplines. This has been criticized as a weakness of the scholarship (Küng 2007; Lowe 2016; Achtenhagen and Mierzejewska 2016; Rohn 2018; Picard and Lowe 2016; Brown 2016). Mierzejewska (2018) surveyed the articles published in the *JoME*, *IJMM*, and *JoMBS* from when each journal was launched until 2016. She found 56 percent of the articles employed management theories, 27 percent used economic theories, and only 6 percent worked with communication theories. Interestingly, Mierzejewska also found that most authors who applied management theories to the media did not, in fact, work in university departments for management and economics, but rather in departments for journalism, advertising, and communication.

Of the articles applying management theory, Mierzejewska observed most used strategic management theories (approximately 50 percent), which mainly included structure-conduct-performance theory (Bain 1968; Porter 1991), the resource-based view (Barney 1991), and niche theory (Dimmick 2003). The next most applied body of theories related to consumer behavior (Mierzejewska 2018), including diffusion and innovation theory (Rogers 1995), the technology acceptance model (Davis, 1989), and theories in the tradition of the classical attitude-behavior paradigm. Many studies also looked at the audience in terms of a product sold to advertisers (Napoli 2012). Third were organizational culture theories (approximately 20 percent) (Mierzejewska 2018), which seek to understand the motivation and control of employees, productivity, and organizational change.

## Methodological approach

Media management research tends to be very practice-oriented, and therefore, much of the research published is based on empirical analysis (see, for example, Ots, Nyilasy, Rohn, and Wikström 2015). Comparing the articles published in the *JoME* and *IJMM* between 2004 and 2016, however, Dupagne (2018) found differences between the two journals. Whereas as many as 90.6 percent of the articles in the *JoME* were based on quantitative studies, only 51.4 percent in the *IJMM* were based on such studies. In addition, 6.3 and 41.2 percent of the articles in these journals, respectively, were based on a qualitative analysis. Due to increasing interest among scholars for a more nuanced understanding of decision-making and processes in firms, methodological approaches, such as ethnography, are becoming more important (Horst, 2020). As such, participant observation increasingly complements the traditionally well-applied data collection methods adopted by media management scholars, involving uses of secondary data, surveys, literature reviews, and field interviews (Dupagne 2018). Furthermore, the overriding methodological approach of action research, in which outside stakeholders are actively integrated into the research process, is becoming increasingly popular among media management scholars (Cook 2020; Whitehead and McNiff 2006).

## Stakeholder orientation

Media management research has three main stakeholders: the media industry, policymakers, and academia (i.e., everyone involved in education, research, or scholarship). With respect to educators, there is a growing interest among media management scholars in publications that reflect on experiences and best practices in the context of teaching media management (such as Graybeal 2020). A survey by Förster and Rohn (2015), for instance, showed that having constantly to stay up-to-date with the most current changes in the industry is perceived as the main challenge for media management educators, especially for those who prepare their students for working in the media.

Commonly, however, the term "stakeholder-oriented media management research" is applied to work that is relevant to the industry or policymakers, both of which can be seen as the main stakeholders outside media management's own scholarly community. Ideally, media management research produces practice-relevant and actionable knowledge (Argyris 2003; Oliver 2020) that informs decision-making by these stakeholders. Both industry and policy makers can benefit from media management research by allowing them to gain a deeper understanding of ongoing changes and processes, and of the possible impact of their decisions and actions. It is widely acknowledged that research collaborations with stakeholders are important, not only because they result in research that actually matters to the stakeholders, but also because stakeholders, especially industry participants, can serve as crucial sources of information about current market and industry dynamics, as well as processes and decisions made within media firms. Lowe and Picard (2020), however, found that industry collaborations were not widespread among media management scholars. The authors noted the structural issues inherent in university incentive systems that prefer traditional scholarly activities, such as publication in peer-reviewed journals and securing research grants from research councils or foundations.

Rohn and Evens (2020b) call for media management scholarship to developed as so-called engaged scholarship (Van de Ven 2007), bridging theory and practice, and being equally motivated by the ambition to advance academic knowledge while addressing and unpacking the "real-world" challenges faced by media firms and policymakers. Engaged scholarship differs from applied market research conducted by, for instance, commercial consultancies, because it is based on theory and has implications for further research. A close dialogue with stakeholders to identify critical research questions and to discuss the relevance and reliability of research findings is generally seen as important (Küng 2016). In order to create truly engaged scholarship, the stakeholder perspective needs to be present at all stages of the research projects, and research results and their implications need to be shared with and clearly communicated to the relevant stakeholders outside academia (Rohn and Evens, 2020a).

Media management research may also be categorized according to Lazarsfeld's (1944) distinction between administrative and critical research. Administrative research is common among media management scholars, and there is a growing demand for more critical research reflecting the implications of firm behavior and policy decisions for the economy, society, and culture that may indicate possible alternative decisions and forms of conduct (Rohn 2018; Brown 2016). The distinction between administrative and critical research does not necessarily have to be a binary split, as shown by contributions to the volume edited by Rohn and Evens (2020b), describing concrete media management research projects conducted in collaboration with media firms and media policymakers. In fact, stakeholder-oriented and administrative research are crucial for informing critical research. What is important, however, is that researchers agree, prior to undertaking a collaborative project, with the stakeholder partners that their academic freedom and independence as researchers will be ensured throughout the project (Rohn and Evens 2020a).

## Types of media management publications

Alongside white papers and market or industry reports that mainly target industry or policy stakeholders (such as Buschow and Wellbrock 2019), media management scholars present their research in academic publications that can be divided into five different groups:

1. Textbooks introducing the logic of the media business and providing rich industry and case study data, which are of interest not only for those who study the media but also for those who work in it (e.g., Noam 2018; Wirtz 2011; Picard 2011; Doyle 2013).
2. Edited volumes and handbooks present a wide selection of key topics in media management research in more detail (e.g., Albarran, Mierzejewska, and Jung 2018; Lowe and Brown 2016; Rohn and Evens 2020b).
3. Monographs and edited volumes on specific topics. Küng's (2017) *Strategic Management in the Media: Theory and Practice* is an essential guide, and Gershon (2017) considers innovation in

the media. The volume edited by Siegert, Förster, Chan-Olmsted, and Ots (2015) offers a guide to media branding, while Altmeppen, Hollifield, and Van Loon (2017) discuss value-oriented media management, and Friedrichsen and Wolfgang (2013) consider social media management, to name just a few examples.

4. Peer-reviewed articles, such as those that appear in the *JoMBS* or *IJMM*, mostly present the results of concrete research projects.

5. Various forms of publications that present reflections on the identity and direction of the scholarship (including Küng 2007, 2016; Mierzejewska and Shaver 2014; Ots, Nyilasy, Rohn, and Wikström 2015; Lowe 2016; Achtenhagen 2016; Achtenhagen and Mierzejewska 2016; Picard and Lowe 2016; Rohn and Evens 2020a; Rohn 2018, 2019).

## Research topics and geographic origin of the research output

The agenda of media management research can be traced through actual examination of published work. In the following, the *Journal of Media Business Studies* (*JoMBS*) serves as a case study. *JoMBS* is the flagship journal of emma, and the keywords used to define articles allow one to draw conclusions about the importance of certain topics to scholars in the community. A study of the articles published between 2010 and 2019 showed the keyword most commonly used by authors to describe their papers was "strategy" (26 mentions), appearing in phrases such as "strategic management," "corporate strategy," "digital strategy," "business strategy," "triple-play strategies," "multiplatform strategies," "emerging strategy," "strategic plan," "communication strategy," "strategic formulation," and "strategic transformation." "Newspaper" (24 mentions) appeared second, occurring in terms such as "newspaper industry," "newspaper market," "family newspapers," "newspaper publishing," and "legacy newspaper," with most articles (13) published between 2010 and 2012. Reflecting increasing convergence in the media landscape and a shift away from the study of industry silos, the more general terms "news" or "news media" (12 mentions) have gradually replaced "newspaper," being included in phrases such as "news outlines," "online news," "news app," "newsroom management," and "news diversity." Third, "advertising" (18 mentions) occurred in phrases such as "mobile advertising," "advertising agencies," "advertising sales," "local advertising," and, more and more, "native advertising."

Other notable terms include: "journalism" (16 mentions, e.g., "digital journalism," "mobile journalism," "online journalism," "professional journalism," "entrepreneurial journalism," "quality journalism," and "not-for-profit journalism") or "policy and regulations" (e.g., "industrial policy," "media policy," "public policy," "media regulations," "privacy regulations," and "regulatory institutions") and "business model" (e.g., "business model innovation"), both mentioned 15 times; "public service media or public service broadcasting," "audience" (e.g., "audience perception," "behavior," and "valuation"), and "content" (e.g., "user-generated content," "content analysis," "content diversity," "content production," "paid content," "sponsored content," "content re-purposing," and "radio content"), each mentioned 11 times; and "brand" (10 mentions, e.g., "brand extension," "brand management," "brand equity," "brand loyalty," "brand trust," and "brand placement").

A similar analysis can also show the international spread of authorship in shaping the research agenda. For articles published between 2010 and 2019 in the *JoMBS*, authors and coauthors were based at institutions in 32 different countries, and for the *IJMM*, from 24 countries. Regionally, in both journals, most authors were from the United States and Canada (42 percent of the 235 in the *IJMM* and 22 percent of the 315 *JoMBS* authors), with the second largest group from Europe (36 percent in *IJMM* and 68 percent in *JoMBS*), and smaller cohorts outside

North America and Europe (22 percent *IJMM*, 9 percent *JoMBS*). Nationally, ten authors or more published in the two journals from institutions in the following countries: United States (165), Germany (65), Finland (57), Sweden (32), Spain (28), UK (27), Belgium (20), Norway (20), the Netherlands (19), Switzerland (19), Denmark (13), Australia (12), China (11), Taiwan (11), and Hong Kong (11).

In summary, there is a clear dominance of US, German, and northern European institutions in media management scholarship. The exception is Spain. It is also apparent that a few of the smaller European countries, such as Belgium and Switzerland, are active in the field, whereas scholars from some larger European nations (Italy (9) and France (4)) have not published frequently in the leading journals addressing the media management scholarly community. In fact, the need for the community to become more international has been a topic among media management scholars (Rohn, 2018). With abstract submissions to the annual conference of emma in 2020 from as many as many as 29 different countries across Europe and the world, change may already be on the way.

## The ongoing meta-discussion of the scholarship about itself

Although still fairly new, media management scholarship has reached the point where it is reflecting on its identity, its output, and its past and future developments. Küng (2007) initiated this meta-discussion, noting how the scholarship remained confused concerning its scope, purpose, and methods. Mierzejewska and Shaver (2014) observe the tremendously fast-changing media industry required new perspectives, research questions, and methods, while Ots, Nyilasy, Rohn, and Wikström (2015) argue media management scholarship should not limit itself to studying the media industry. Lowe (2016) suggest the unique characteristics of management in the media industry legitimate the scholarship. Picard and Lowe (2016) recommended scholars should improve their understanding of the institutional and social forces that impact media management rather than focusing only on internal organizational processes and decision-making practices. Also, they positively noted how media management researchers have started to employ a greater range of theories than before, though they remarked these theories were merely applied to empirical phenomena without expansion or modification to fit the media management context, or further development. Furthermore, they proposed that scholars in the field should extend their networks outside the media management community and engage in multidisciplinary conferences and projects. Similarly, Achtenhagen (2016) criticized media management scholars for mainly staying only within their own community and publishing only in their own journals. She indicated that there was little interaction and acknowledgment between media management researchers and general management researchers. Küng (2016) has pointed out that for media management scholars to produce high-quality research, they need to have a better dialogue with key players inside media organizations, while Rohn and Evens (2020b) have commented on the challenges and opportunities of bridging theory and practice, they showcase research projects in which collaborations with industry and policy stakeholders resulted in practice-relevant knowledge without sacrificing academic independence.

## Positioning media management research in relation to media industry studies

Transformation of the media industry demands research that crosses boundaries between different academic fields. In this context, the formation of media industry studies as "a burgeoning and fully articulated subfield that transcends disciplines and academic societies"

(Arsenault et al. 2016: 2) is a timely response to the growing need for research on the media industry. If the 2009 publication of Holt and Perren's *Media Industries: History, Theory and Method* marks the formation of media industry studies, then media management scholarship is older, with its first journal, the *IJMM*, launched in 1999, and the *JoME* starting in the late 1980s. If we take Herbert, Lotz, and Punathambekar's (2020) definition of media industry studies as the analysis of "how individuals, institutions, and industries produce and circulate cultural forms" (p. 7), then both media industry studies and media management research have the same aims. Media management research, as an interdisciplinary field of research drawing from both management studies and media and communication studies, can, therefore, be seen as an earlier attempt to approach the study of the media industries from an interdisciplinary angle.

Yet, there is a crucial difference between media management research and media industry studies. The latter, by definition, adopts a critical perspective. This has, traditionally, not been the case for media management research, which attempts to understand the media industry, including its products, audiences, and regulations, through the eyes of media firms, including entrepreneurs. Consequently, the work can be more descriptive and less critical. With growing demands for media management researchers to engage in reflective and critical research (Rohn 2018; Brown 2016), however, the overlap between media management scholarship and media industry studies is increasing. Similarities between the two research communities are more likely to be felt by media management scholars from media and communication departments than those from management and business schools. It is the former, after all, who attend the conferences of the ICA, IAMCR, and ECREA, which have divisions and working groups related to media industry studies.

However, although the scholarly community of media management researchers may not yet fully associate itself with the media industry studies community, the research output of both communities is of real relevance to the other. Research conducted under the aegis of media industry studies may support media management scholars in their efforts to contextualize their research, especially in terms of offering critical reflections on industry dynamics. Media industry studies, on the other hand, may benefit from media management research that provides insights into the problems faced by media firms and entrepreneurs, including into the actions they take to solve these problems. Understanding how and why media firms and practitioners make ordinary, everyday decisions may help guide media industry studies toward an improved understanding of the actions and underlying motivations of media firms.

Not only do firms and entrepreneurs react to the changes we see in the industry, they also initiate and promote some of these changes. By providing insights from the perspective of media firms and entrepreneurs, who are at the very center of the dynamics of the industry, media management research, therefore, can also contribute to a broader understanding of the transformational processes in the industry that we are witnessing today. Finally, the perspective of media firms and entrepreneurs can also contribute to achieving a better understanding of the regulatory and policy environment that is most likely to support firms' sustainability and media pluralism. Hence, within the ongoing and increasingly interdisciplinary dialogue taking place under the heading of media industry studies, media management research plays an important role.

## Acknowledgment

The writing of this chapter was supported by a grant from the Estonian Research Council (PUT1674).

# References

Achtenhagen, L. (2016) "Developing Media Management Scholarship: A Commentary to Picard and Lowe's Essay," *Journal of Media Business Studies*, 13 (2): 117–123.

Achtenhagen, L. (2017) "Media Entrepreneurship: Taking Stock and Moving Forward," *International Journal on Media Management*, 19 (1): 1–10.

Achtenhagen, L. and Mierzejewska, B. (2016) "The Development of Media Management as an Academic Field: Tracing the Contents and Impact of its Three Leading Journals," in G. F. Lowe and C. Brown (eds), *Managing Media Firms and Industries: What's So Special About Media Management?* Cham: Springer, 23–42.

Albarran, A. B. (2004) "Media Economics," in J. D. H. Downing, D. McQuail, P. Schlesinger, and E. Wartella (eds), *The SAGE Handbook of Media Studies*, Thousand Oaks: Sage, 291–307.

Albarran, A. B. (2013) "Media Management and Economics Research: The First 75 Years," in A. B. Albarran (ed.), *Media Management and Economics Research in a Transmedia Environment*, New York: Routledge, 5–17.

Albarran, A. B. (2014) "Assessing the Field of Media Management and Economics Research: Looking Back, Looking Forward," *Palabra Clave*, 17 (4): 1025–1040.

Albarran, A. B., Mierzejewska, B., and Jung, J. (eds) (2018) *Handbook of Media Management and Economics*, New York: Routledge.

Altmeppen, K.-D., Hollifield, A. C., and Van Loon, J. (eds) (2017) *Value-oriented Media Management: Decision Making between Profit and Responsibility*, Cham: Springer.

Argyris, C. (2003) "A Life Full of Learning," *Organizational Studies*, 24 (7): 1178–1192.

Arsenault, A., Cunningham, S., Curtin, M., Flew, T., Fung, A., Holt, J., McDonald, P., McNair, B., Perren, A. and Sanson, K. (2016) "Introduction: Welcome to the Media Industries," in A. Arsenault and A. Perren (eds), *Media Industries: Perspectives on an Evolving Field*, Atlanta, GA: Media Industries Editorial Board, 1–4.

Bain, J. S. (1968) *Industrial Organization*, New York: Wiley.

Barney, J. B. (1991) "Firm Resources and Sustained Competitive Advantage," *Journal of Management*, 17 (1): 99–120.

Brown, C. (2016) "Media Management: A Critical Discipline?," in G. F. Lowe and C. Brown (eds), *Managing Media Firms and Industries: What's So Special About Media Management?* Cham: Springer, 83–100.

Buschow, C. and Wellbrock, C-M. (2019) *Money for Nothing and Content for Free? Willingness to Pay for Digital Journalism*, Düsseldorf: Landesanstalt für Medien NRW.

Cook, C. (2020). "Evaluating Action Research to Innovate Digital Journalism Revenue Models." In U. Rohn and T. Evens (eds), *Media Management Matters: Challenges and Opportunties for Bridging Theory and Practice*, New York: Routledge, 93–106.

Davis, F. D. (1989) "Perceived Usefulness, Perceived Ease of Use, and User Acceptance of Information Technology," *MIS Quarterly*, 13 (3): 319–340.

De Cock, R. and De Smaele, H. (2016) "Freelancing in Flemish News Media and Entrepreneurial Skills as Pivotal Elements in Job Satisfaction: Perspectives of Masters or Servants?" *Journalism Practice*, 10 (2): 251–265.

Dimmick, J. (2003) *Media Competition and Coexistence: The Theory of the Niche*, New York: Lawrence Erlbaum.

Doyle, G. (2013) *Understanding Media Economics*, 2nd ed., London: Sage.

Dupagne, M. (2018) "Methodological Approaches in Media Management and Economics," in A. B. Albarran, B. Mierzejewska, and J. Jung (eds), *Handbook of Media Management and Economics*, 2nd ed., New York: Routledge, 368–378.

Förster, K. and Rohn, U. (2015) "Media Management Education: Key Themes, Pedagogies, and Challenges," *Journalism and Mass Communication Educator*, 70 (4): 1–15.

Friedrichsen, M. and Wolfgang, M-B. (eds) (2013) *Handbook of Social Media Management: Value Chain and Business Models in Changing Media Markets*, Heidelberg: Springer.

Gershon, R. A. (2017) *Digital Media and Innovation: Management and Design Strategies in Communication*, Thousand Oaks, CA: Sage.

Graybeal, G. (2020) "Teaching Strategic Management for Media Students," in S. Baumann (ed.), *Teaching Strategic Managment: A Hands-on Guide to Teaching Success*, Cheltenham: Edward Elgar, 220–238.

Hang, M. and van Weezel, A. (2007) "Media Entrepreneurship: What Do We Know and Where Should We Go?" *Journal of Media Business Studies*, 4 (1): 51–70.

Herbert, D., Lotz, A. D., and Punathambekar, A. (2020) *Media Industry Studies: A Short Introduction*, Cambridge: Polity.

Hess, T. (2014) "What is a Media Company? A Reconceptualization for the Online World," *International Journal on Media Management*, 16 (1): 3–8.

Holt, J. and Perren, A. (eds) (2009) *Media Industries: History, Theory, and Method*, Malden, MA: Wiley-Blackwell.

Horst, S-O. (2020) "Conducting Media Management Ethnography," in U. Rohn and T. Evens (eds), *Media Management Matters: Challenges and Opportunities for Bridging Theory and Practice*, New York: Routledge, 75–92.

Horst, S.-O., Järventie-Thesleff, R., and Perez-Lattre, F. (2020) "Entrepreneurial Identity Development through Digital Media," *Journal of Media Business Studies*, 17(2): 87–112.

Khajeheian, D. (2019) "Editorial Preface: Inaugural Issue of Journal of Media Management and Entrepreneurship," *Journal of Media Management and Entrepreneurship*, 1 (1): v–viii.

Küng, L. (2007) "Does Media Management Matter? Establishing the Scope, Rationale and Future Research Agenda for the Discipline," *Journal of Media Business Studies*, 4 (1): 21–39.

Küng, L. (2016) "Why is Media Management Research So Difficult – and What Can Scholars Do to Overcome the Field's Intrinsic Challenges?" *Journal of Media Business Studies*, 13 (4): 276–282.

Küng, L. (2017) *Strategic Management in the Media: Theory and Practice*, London: Sage.

Lazarsfeld, P. F. (1944) "Remarks on Critical and Administrative Communication Research," *Studies in Philosophy and Science*, 9 (1): 2–16.

Lowe, G. F. (2016) "Introduction: What's So Special about Media Management?" in G. F. Lowe and C. Brown (eds), *Managing Media Firms and Industries: What's So Special about Media Management?* Cham: Springer, 1–20.

Lowe, G. F. and Brown, C. (eds.) (2016) *Managing Media Firms and Industries: What's So Special About Media Management?* Cham: Springer.

Lowe, G. F. and Picard, R. G. (2020) "University-industry Collaboration in the Media Management Field," in U. Rohn and T. Evens (eds.), *Media Management Matters: Challenges and Opportunities for Bridging Theory and Practice*, New York: Routledge, 29–45.

Mierzejewska, B. (2018) "Theoretical Approaches in Media Management Research Revisited," in A. B. Albarran, B. Mierzejewska, and J. Jung (eds) *Handbook of Media Management and Economics*, 2nd ed., New York: Routledge, 37–65.

Mierzejewska, B. and Shaver, D. (2014) "Key Changes Impacting Media Management Research," *International Journal on Media Management*, 16 (2): 47–54.

Napoli, P. M. (2012) "Audience Evolution and the Future of Audience Research," *International Journal on Media Management*, 14 (2): 79–97.

Noam, E. M. (2018) *Managing Media and Digital Organizations*, Cham: Palgrave Macmillan.

Oliver, J. (2020) "Case Studies of Practice-led Research, Actionable Knowledge and Instrumental Impact," in U. Rohn and T. Evens (eds), *Media Management Matters: Challenges and Opportunities for Bridging Theory and Practice*, New York: Routledge, 59–73.

Ots, M., Nyilasy, G., Rohn, U., and Wikström, P. (2015) "Media Business Studies as We See It: Why Does It Matter, for Whom, and How Do We Get Published?" *Journal of Media Business Studies*, 12 (2): 103–106.

Picard, R. G. (2011) *The Economics and Financing of Media Companies*, New York: Fordham University Press.

Picard, R. G. and Lowe, G. F. (2016) "Questioning Media Management Scholarship: Four Parables about How to Better Develop the Field," *Journal of Media Business Studies*, 13 (2): 61–72.

Porter, M. (1991) "Towards a Dynamic Theory of Strategy," *Strategic Management Journal*, 12 (S2): 95–117.

Rogers, E. M. (1995) *Diffusion of Innovations*, New York: Free Press.

Rohn, U. (2018) "Media Management Research in the 21st Century," in A. B. Albarran, B. Mierzejewska, and J. Jung (eds) *Handbook of Media Management and Economics*, 2nd ed., New York: Routledge, 425–441.

Rohn, U. (2019) "Industry Organization, Media Management and Media Economics," in A. B. Albarran (ed.), *Research Agenda for Media Economics*, Northampton, MA: Edward Elgar Publishing, 144–158.

Rohn, U. and Evens, T. (2020a) "Media Management as an Engaged Scholarship," in U. Rohn and T. Evens (eds), *Media Management Matters: Challenges and Opportunities for Bridging Theory and Practice*, New York: Routledge, 9–18.

Rohn, U. and Evens, T. (eds.) (2020b) *Media Management Matters: Challenges and Opportunities for Bridging Theory and Practice*, New York: Routledge.

Siegert, G., Förster, K., Chan-Olmsted, S., and Ots, M. (2015) *Handbook of Media Branding*, Heidelberg: Springer International.

Van de Ven, A. H. (2007) *Engaged Scholarship: A Guide for Organizational and Social Research*, Oxford: Oxford University Press.

Whitehead, J. and McNiff, J. (2006) *Action Research: Living Theory*, London: Sage.

Wirtz, B. W. (2011) *Media and Internet Management*, Wiesbaden: Gabler Verlag.

# 7

# CRITICAL AND CULTURAL?

## Production studies as situated storytelling

*Philip Drake*

This chapter aims to explore what it means to study production and producers, to consider "production studies" methods, and to reflect on the ethical issues and practical challenges of such work. In doing so, I am not attempting to present a comprehensive overview of production studies as an academic subdiscipline of media industries research – there is insufficient space for this and similar overviews already exist – nor to trace the historical and geographically specific trajectories of such research, which is well explored by other essays in this volume. Instead, I will explore why the *idea* of production studies as a particular field has been so compelling for scholars in recent years, the benefits and limitations of production studies approaches to media industries research, and finally to consider how production studies produce culturally situated forms of storytelling.

### Production studies as a field of scholarly production

While the study of cultural production and the analysis of the production of culture have been well-established areas of media and cultural studies for over two decades, and the sociological analysis of cultural production for more than twice that, there is no doubt that there has been a surge in interest in production studies within media, communications, and screen studies over the past ten years, with dominant, residual, and emergent approaches. Barely visible at the turn of the millennium, by 2021 the term "production studies" had firmly moved into the mainstream of media industries research itself – as this volume testifies – an expanding area that had gained greater prominence in film and television studies during this period.

At its most simple, production studies offer critical approaches to the study of cultural production. As a field, it draws on cultural studies methods to examine how production itself is a culture that can be analyzed and understood. Emerging from different disciplinary traditions and different continents, the strength of production studies has been to synthesize a range of methodological and theoretical approaches to offer a greater understanding of production through accounts of its workers and their interaction with industrial processes, building deeper accounts of production practices and lived experiences than can be offered through either the top-down analysis of media industries or markets, or the cultural analysis of texts. In doing so, production studies often attempt to illuminate not only specific media industry practices and rituals, but

 DOI: 10.4324/9780429275340-9

also draw out wider conclusions in order to present an understanding of wider industry-social practices and organizational cultures, and potentially provide important correctives to earlier traditions. For example, production studies of film production can challenge the long-standing focus on directorial authorship in film studies by offering detailed accounts of collaborative production practices among writers, designers, producers, and craft workers, and present not only a fuller understanding of the organization of cultural labor but also of the creative process.

Tracking the emergence of any field or subdiscipline risks telling disciplinary history from a particular perspective and place, and it is important to recognize the limitations imposed through cultural and linguistic access. The dominance of English language production studies across key edited collections and journals, and especially in Anglo-American and Western European accounts of media industries, do not adequately reflect the range of international research – a considerable body of which remains untranslated in English – and the dominance of scholarship from the United States and Europe can therefore provide only partial accounts of global media production cultures. As I will elaborate, the emergence of production studies as a field is both productive and limiting; productive as it provides a focal point to consider particular issues via the microanalysis of production practices, yet limiting if it excludes the full "circuit of culture" (Du Gay 1997) that connects cultural production to audiences and their consumption and circulation of cultural meaning. The visibility of media production studies in recent years does not, however, imply it does not draw heavily on previous research methods, often deploying and updating approaches and models that have been well-established in fields such as the sociology of culture and ethnography. Before I engage with more recent trends, I want to briefly turn to production studies before the term itself was in use.

The dominance of, and fascination with, Hollywood cinema produced early production studies in the first half of the twentieth century and many accounts of media production (e.g., Mayer, Banks, and Caldwell 2009) point to the important legacy of studies of Hollywood undertaken by the political scientist Leo Rosten (1941) (who was also a successful screenwriter, so not exactly an outsider in Hollywood) and the pioneering cultural anthropologist Hortense Powdermaker (1950). Fascinatingly full of detail, their accounts of Hollywood and Los Angeles – plus *The New Yorker* columns of Lillian Ross – went beyond popular biographies of known public figures (such as stars and Hollywood moguls) to provide detailed and rich historical accounts of Hollywood workers during the studio era. This work on Hollywood notwithstanding, there is no doubt that media industries research has been reinvigorated by encounters with anthropologically inspired production studies methods, which have generated exciting and sometimes troubling accounts of what workers do at different levels of the media industries and provided researchers with an opportunity to develop new primary research data and applied case studies.

The evolution of the study of the media industries and its related fields is expertly documented by David Hesmondhalgh across a substantial body of his work and can also be traced through the four (so far) editions of his *The Cultural Industries* (2002, 2007, 2012, 2019). Taking the United Kingdom, the context I'm most familiar with, there were clear antecedents to production studies from established scholars in media and sociology. Yet cultural and sociological studies of art worlds, subcultures, music scenes, readers, or audiences, despite often adopting approaches that have informed production studies, such as interviews and ethnography, are rarely acknowledged as antecedents. Graham Murdock's chapter in this volume helpfully outlines the tradition of earlier media research emerging from the UK and its diverse sociological and political economy approaches as well as other European traditions (e.g., Miège 1989) that offered important insights into cultural production studies. Similar earlier work mostly on journalism, television, and popular music pioneered interview-based approaches and ethnographic accounts (Elliott 1972; Tunstall 1974; Frith 1978; Frith 1981; Becker 1982; Schlesinger 1978; Tulloch and Alvarado 1983; Gitlin 1983; Newcomb 1983; Silverstone 1985; Petrie 1991; Negus 1992; Tunstall 1993; D'Acci 1994; Grindstaff 2002; Born 2004). Popular music scholar Simon Frith's career is notable in this regard. A cultural critic for *The Village Voice* and *The Sunday Times*, while also Chair of the Mercury Music Prize and a leading academic within the sociology of popular music, Frith presents a particularly interesting example of walking the line between insider and outsider, with a reflexivity evident in his work as to his own position in the music and journalism industries as commentator, critic, participant, and academic.

For scholars in film and television studies, arriving rather later to production studies theories and methods, much of the groundwork for this shift was therefore already in place through preceding work in media, journalism, sociology, and cultural studies, and to some extent organizational and management studies. While many scholars had identified a need for a more nuanced understanding of the creative process through a deeper engagement with industry practitioners, few new academic studies followed up on the work of these earlier researchers and interview-based research with media practitioners rarely ventured beyond interviews with elites: directors and, to a lesser extent, actors, writers, producers, and above-the-line talent (e.g., Ohmann 1996; Zucker 2002). Such a focus on above-the-line roles and formal interviews with star actors and directors effaced the role of collaborators and craftworkers, as well as intermediaries such as publicists, managers, and agents, and the relationships, processes, and networks involved in producing the work. However, recent scholarly uptake of the term "production studies" has at least in part been produced by a turn in film and television studies (and more lately games and digital industries research) toward a greater attention to microstudies of industries and the politics of media work and creative labor. All of this has helped to shift the analysis of production cultures to the center of film and television studies, and in particular to focus on the experiences of production workers and below-the-line production labor rather than elites.

John T. Caldwell's influential and generative *Production Culture* (2008) argues for a more sophisticated account of media production that understands media industries as a "production culture," drawing on self-reflexive anthropological and ethnographic methods to understand the culture in which production takes place. His research, involving extensive industry fieldwork and participant observation over a decade, considers the development of reflexive practices within the US film and television industries and Caldwell presents a rich, detailed, and lengthy analysis of the "cultural self-performances" of workers and the layering of industry practices and knowledge in which they then make sense of their work. In doing so, he shows not only how workers create their sense of self-identity but also how this is embedded within reflexive industry rituals and processes. He describes his approach as an "integrated cultural-industrial analysis" that draws on four modes: (1) textual analysis of trade or worker artifacts, (2) interviews with film/ television workers, (3) ethnographic field observation of production spaces and professional gatherings, and (4) economic/industrial analysis (Caldwell 2008: 4). Importantly, for Caldwell, the term "production culture" indicates that industry workers are themselves theorists, not texts to be interpreted by the researcher, and they also engage in what he calls "critical industrial practices" to make sense of their work. This marks a departure from earlier approaches that either describe or critique industry practices or analyze media industries through a particular theoretical lens applied by the researcher. In addition, Caldwell is also interested in studying below-the-line creative labor, an important corrective to then prevalent "studying up" approaches focused on elites such as above-the-line directors, writers, and stars.

The following year brought two collections of essays that took up and extended a number of Caldwell's points. *Media Industries: History, Theory and Method*, edited by Jennifer Holt and

Alisa Perren (2009), presented a mapping of diverse recent developments in the study of media industries – or what they termed "media industry studies." *Production Studies: Cultural Studies of Media Industries* edited by Vicki Mayer, Miranda Banks, and Caldwell (2009) offered an important range of essays that drew upon and extended Caldwell's approach to argue, through varied studies of production, that a new range of tools are required in order to map the complex structures of production and creative work, revising the director and star auteur-based accounts so long dominant in film and, to a lesser extent, television studies. Mayer, Banks, and Caldwell suggested that production studies instead "take the lived realities of people involved in media production as the subjects for theorizing production as culture" (2009: 4). Such accounts were followed by other major production studies such as Vicki Mayer (2011), Eva Novrup Redvall (2013), Bridget Conor (2014), and Miranda Banks (2015).

Across these often quite different studies are key questions exploring how media workers make sense of their work, understanding how professionals reflect on their industry and their place within it, exploring industrial hierarchies and economies of labor, and bringing out a deeper understanding of industry rituals and practices. I will explore methodological questions around these approaches more shortly, but it's worth noting that these accounts turn traditional industry accounts around by not focusing on production to better understand media texts, but instead to better understand media workers, the industries, and cultures in which they work, and the lives they lead. The so-called ethnographic turn in production studies research means that the texts of production studies tend to be oral accounts and interviews, fieldwork observation notes, and participant observation. Building on Clifford Geertz (1973) and his concept of "thick description," Mark Peterson (2003: 8) argues that ethnography is "based on intimate, long-term reflexive encounters between scholars and the peoples they are studying." Many, and possibly most, production studies do not, however, provide "long-term reflexive encounters" but rather rely on shorter-term negotiated access, for instance through a series of interviews, time spent observing on a production set or in meetings, or a period of observation (and occasionally participant observation) in order to produce situated knowledge and thickly descriptive accounts of media work and practices. As production studies has become established, there is, as Nightingale (1989) reminded scholars researching audiences, an important need to distinguish between brief encounters, such as conducting a series of interviews, and longer-term media production ethnographies.

Although ethnography is not in itself necessarily focused on questions of power, a number of scholars draw on ethnographic research to produce broader social theories and critiques of media industries and in particular their conditions of work (see Hesmondhalgh and Baker 2008, 2010; Deuze 2007, 2010). Reflecting this attention to the politics of cultural production, the term "production studies" itself has been variously called "critical production studies," "production cultures," and related to wider discussions around the term "media industry studies" and "critical media industries" research (for a discussion, see Havens, Lotz, and Tinic 2009; Hesmondhalgh 2019). Unlike classic ethnography, such research draws on wider cultural studies approaches and retains an interest in power and agency, as well as theory. Subsequently the study of production cultures has extended its methods and reach, including collections on screen production cultures from European scholars, *Behind the Screen: Inside European Production Cultures* (Szczepanik and Vonderau 2013) and a sequel to *Production Studies* presenting analysis from a wider and more global range of media industries (Banks, Mayer, and Conor 2016).

While production studies might well have now built up a sufficient body of work to be justifiably considered a field, albeit not marked by a single approach, methodology or object of study (see Paterson, Lee, Saha and Zoellner 2016), it has continued to draw on and benefit from related cognate areas of scholarship – indeed a defining feature of production studies research has been its willingness to traverse disciplinary boundaries and to provide complimentary "micro" accounts to "macro" analyses from other areas. Banks, Mayer, and Conor suggest production studies offers "grounded analyses of media makers' experiences, observations, conversations, and interactions" and "specific sites and fabrics of media production as distinct interpretative communities, each with its own organizational structures, professional practices, and power dynamics" (2016: x). As this volume attests, analysis of media production is addressed in different ways, including within media management, economic geography and urban studies, organizational studies, sociology, and science and technology studies. Work from the perspective of economic geography, such as Allen J. Scott (2005) or Jennifer Johns (2006), also offer useful comparative cross-disciplinary insights and a productive critical dialogue over theory and method.

## Production studies methods and issues

Methodological approaches in production studies include conducting interviews, observation/participant observation, reflexive ethnography, and less commonly methods such as conversation analysis and social network analysis. These are often placed alongside and in dialogue with other methods, including macro industry and policy analysis, as well the analysis of texts, contexts, and, more rarely, audiences. As I have outlined above, there is not a single approach to production studies, or for that matter even a single approach to media ethnography. While some researchers focus on observation fieldwork and being unobtrusive, others become participants in the work they observe, and other studies primarily involve limited encounters via interviews. For most research, negotiating access to media production takes a great deal of time and effort, and often that access is regulated and can be easily denied, indirectly regulating the research space. Sherry Ortner (2009, 2010), an established cultural anthropologist and former student of Geertz, offers a fascinating account of the struggle to gain access to undertake ethnographic research in the Hollywood film industry. Ortner proposes what she calls "interface ethnography" (2009|:179), attending and studying events in which the media industries present themselves to the public, as a way of addressing lack of access.

Recent production studies research has been informed by work on the politics of cultural production and work/creative labor, and a number of significant studies (e.g., Hesmondhalgh and Baker 2010; Mayer 2011) are concerned with understanding the status of above- and below-the-line-workers and the critical industrial practices in which they make sense of their work. At the heart of these studies is a need to understand the often challenging and precarious positions of labor typifying the media industries (Ursell 2000; Blair 2001; Kerr 2006; Banks 2007; Randle and Culkin 2009; Ross 2009; Deuze 2011; McRobbie 2016; Curtin and Sanson 2016; Banks 2017; Deuze and Prenger 2019). In their examination of creative labor in the television industries, Hesmondhalgh and Baker (2008, 2010) discuss how such jobs frequently exploit those who wish to enter these industries. In critically examining the types of work characterizing magazine journalism, music, and television, they found a prevalence of short-term jobs and employment precarity, lack of autonomy, and significant possibility of burnout, yet accompanied by positive experiences of how working in the creative sector produced a sense of professional identity and the pleasures of creating good work. Yet for many workers in the media industries, the only chance to build a longer-term career is through accepting long hours, low pay, and a lack of job security. The rise of the unpaid or minimum wage intern in these sectors is a particular concern, reducing the diversity of applicants. Media industries offer many examples of such exploited labor, as there is an oversupply of individuals willing to accept below-par working conditions and low pay in order to break into these industries and to try to build a career. Rosalind Gill, Angela McRobbie, Mark Banks, and Doris Ruth Eikof, among others, have produced a body of research that examines how the media and creative industries not only lead to overworking and exploitation but also to systemic discrimination according to gender and ethnicity (see Gill 2002; McRobbie 2002; McRobbie 2016; Gill and Pratt 2008; Gill 2011; Gill, Banks, and Taylor 2013; Eikof, Newsinger, Rudloff, Luchinskaya, and Banks 2018; Eikof and Marsden 2019; Saha 2017; Nwonka and Malik 2018). Such research demonstrates the attrition in the media workforce experienced by women in their mid-thirties and older, often due to the difficulties of balancing family life and irregular working hours, and a persistent lack of opportunity for minority ethnic workers.

Underpinning a number of production studies on media labor is work on exploitation and emotional labor. Sociologist Arlie Russell Hochschild's (1983) influential book *The Managed Heart: Commercialization of Human Feeling* developed the concept of "emotional labor" to describe how workers in certain professions (e.g., flight attendants, nurses, teachers) are required to demonstrate emotional qualities when conducting their work. In the media industries, much creative work can be understood as emotion work, involving a level of emotional investment that helps to explain why workers might accept forms of exploitation. In my own interviews conducted with media workers, I noted their passion for working on specific projects, often for no or little money, and also how media workers connected and formed identities in multiple ways with the wider arts sector, supporting other cultural activities and engaging in other forms of employment and cultural activities, often unpaid and unrecognized by economic surveys (Drake 2013). These interviews also suggested the importance of creative autonomy (being able to choose what one does) and place (where one does it). For some interviewees, they felt they had greater autonomy in a more precarious role, and therefore had to work hard to balance job security against job satisfaction. In such analysis, "exploitation" is an interesting but often under-specified concept. As Hesmondhalgh (2015) notes, it relies on a conceptualization of systemic unjust advantage and suffering. Whether such exploitation is distinctive to the media industries seems less clear – the precarity and exploitation of cultural labor may be more typical of our current age than exceptional to cultural work (Ross 2009; Standing 2011).

A focus on production processes as well as labor is often also foregrounded in many production studies. One such example is the research of Eva Novrup Redvall (2013) who explores the collaborative creative process of screenwriting for Danish television through observation and interviews while placing herself clearly in the position of researcher in the study. Other studies importantly illuminate the practices of below-the-line workers, often women, who have been written out of media histories (Mayer 2011; Conor 2014; Warner 2018). This work can involve interviews with women who held media roles (Cobb and Williams 2020) and analyses of archival materials, documents, and oral histories to map the presence and absence of women in media professions (Bell 2017). Beyond Western media industries, emerging work in production studies considers media workers in transnational media industries, such as Nigeria (Miller 2016) and between Nigeria and India (Jedlowski 2017), as well as the local presence of Hollywood in international territories (Brannon Donoghue 2017).

Although production studies have primarily focused on production workers and processes, a small number of scholars have considered how such processes might be applied to distribution or exhibition, alongside a larger group addressing media infrastructures and platforms. Alisa Perren, in an article titled "Rethinking Distribution for the Future of Media Industry Studies," asks "do industry workers tend to identify themselves as part of the distribution process? How often are such roles denied or elided? Does a specific type of responsibility or power come by self-identifying as a distributor?" (2013: 170). Attempting to answer this, during 2014–2016 colleagues and myself conducted a collaborative project with the public film agency Film London and a newly launched video-on-demand (VOD) platform. The project generated a range of qualitative and quantitative data through observation and interviews with Film London's "Build Your Audience" program (16 film business professionals and projects with 28 filmmakers, producers, writers, and directors spread across 11 feature film projects), plus focus groups, in depth interviews with ten film industry professionals including sales and distribution specialists. Taking on board Perren's suggestions for adapting Caldwell's approach to distribution studies, we looked at how independent filmmakers themselves drew distinctions between production and distribution, and distribution and exhibition, and their understandings of sales agents and distributors. (Drake, Franklin, Sathe, and Tierney 2015). As a partnership, the project was driven in part by need: funding (for the VOD platform to develop), information (for Film London to provide to independent filmmakers) and research (for the academic team to develop new knowledge). However, the project also demonstrated the difficulties of agreeing a three-way "knowledge exchange" that fulfilled the needs of all three partners and their objectives, alongside requirements for commercial confidentiality and restrictive contractual agreements.

Reflecting on this example, I propose a tentative typology of collaborative media production studies research: (1) research looking critically *at* media industries, (2) research collaborating *with* and providing research *to* the media industries, and (3) research primarily *directed by* the priorities of media industries and focused on their business support. Balancing the needs of researchers and those individuals and organizations who are being researched is clearly of major importance to production studies and would seem deserving of more analysis.

## Conclusion: production studies as storytelling

In this chapter I have discussed production studies as a field, drawing broadly from other disciplines, and explored a number of production studies methods and concerns. Emerging from this is a sense of how media production studies need to be understood as forms of situated, relational storytelling, providing scholars with contextualized and reflexive micro accounts of the cultures of media industries and their workers. The situational stories produced by production studies require careful contextualization – emanating from a specific time and place, posing conclusions that cannot be easily generalized – yet they are also rich in insight and, in Geertz's terms, constitute thick descriptions. Inevitably, as has been outlined, media production studies have deployed different methods and prioritized certain research questions, and to date larger comparative studies crossing either industry sectors or international cultural boundaries have yet to be substantially undertaken. As many of those undertaking production studies acknowledge, media researchers are mostly untrained as ethnographers or anthropologists, and so we need to reflect deeply on the ethics of the research process. This includes considering the place of the researcher, how we gain access to and treat key informants, and attention to questions of unconscious bias and forms of gatekeeping. Equally, there is the need to always recognize the limits of studies, for example Anglophone bias, providing accounts that are only relevant to some sectors, or focusing on production over cultures of distribution or circulation. Furthermore, it is often left unspecified what happens after a production studies research project concludes: has there been consideration of how the research might impact on the culture studied and how do precariously employed industry participants feel about the research and its afterlife? As production studies proliferate, we need to share our methods and approaches, to archive and historicize our work, and to produce production studies not only of production labor but also of distribution and exhibition labor. I'd like to briefly return to

Caldwell, and to his own painting *Semper Fi Panavision* on the cover of the original *Production Studies* collection (Mayer, Banks, and Caldwell 2009) – an image of heroic production workers carrying a camera, knowingly recreating the famous photograph of US soldiers *Raising the Flag on Iwo Jima* (1945). This heroic valorization of physical labor mimics the heavy lifting undertaken by media workers and the difficulty of their toil. However, the silent, less heroic, invisible aspects of production cultures are also important, and all those workers – the caterers, assistants, cleaners, drivers, marketeers that ultimately support media production to happen – require our consideration too, not just those at the production summit. Caldwell reflects the changes in production cultures in the sequel collection (Banks, Conor, and Mayer 2016), with its own cover painting, *Insurgent Crowd-Sourcing*, presenting a more reflexive and variegated image of media workers.

In concluding, I propose a set of important questions and challenges which this single chapter cannot, in itself, fully answer, but which reading this volume as a whole may bring into relief. First, what gains are there in thinking about "production studies" as a unified field of enquiry? Does the idea of a field facilitate and legitimize approaches from a wide range of perspectives, or does it hive off the study of production cultures from related media industries research? Second, how do media production studies account for different cultural contexts and scale – for instance, are the same methods applicable when researching production labor in Hollywood and a small regional media industry? Third, does media specificity matter or are the same approaches for film production also suitable for radio or sound or games industries? Fourth, what are the relative statuses of texts, theory, and analysis in production studies? Fifth, how do we do historical production studies, or historicize the production studies that are already done? And finally, how might we use production studies to not only describe and understand cultures of media production, but also address their systemic inequalities and to change those industries? Many of these questions are yet to be adequately answered, however with its diversity of approaches and methods, concern to address social inequalities, and ambition to use research to lead the charge toward more diverse, ethical, and sustainable industries, production studies will continue to be of importance to our understanding of and relationship with media industries and their workers.

# References

Banks, M. (2007) *The Politics of Cultural Work*, London: Palgrave Macmillan.

Banks, M. (2017) *Creative Justice: Cultural Industries, Work and Inequality*, London: Rowman & Littlefield.

Banks, M. (2009) "Gender Below-the-Line: Defining Feminist Production Studies," in V. Mayer, M. J. Banks, and J. T. Caldwell (eds), *Production Studies: Cultural Studies of Media Industries*, New York: Routledge, 87–98.

Banks, M. (2015) *The Writers*, New Brunswick, NJ: Rutgers University Press.

Banks, M., Mayer, V., and Conor, B. (eds) (2016) *Production Studies, The Sequel! Cultural Studies of Global Media Industries*, New York: Routledge.

Bell, M. (2017) "Learning to Listen: Histories of Women's Soundwork in the British Film Industry," *Screen*, 58 (4): 437–457.

Blair, H. (2001) "'You're Only as Good as Your Last Job': The Labour Process and Labour Market in the British Film Industry," *Work, Employment and Society*, 15 (1): 149–169.

Becker, H. S. (1982) *Art Worlds*, Berkeley, CA: University of California Press.

Born, G. (2004) *Uncertain Vision: Birt, Dyke and the Reinvention of the BBC*, London: Secker & Warburg.

Brannon Donoghue, C. (2017) *Localising Hollywood*, London: British Film Institute.

Caldwell, J. T. (2008) *Production Culture. Industrial Reflexivity and Critical Practice in Film and Television*, Durham, NC: Duke University Press.

Cobb, S. and Williams, L. R. (2020) "Histories of Now: Listening to Women in British Film," *Women's History Review*, 29 (5): 890–902.

Conor, B. (2014) *Screenwriting: Creative Labor and Professional Practice*, Abingdon: Routledge.

Curtin, M. and Sanson, K. (eds) (2016) *Precarious Creativity: Global Media, Local Labor*, Berkeley, CA: University of California.

Curtin, M. and Vanderhoef, J. (2014) "A Vanishing Piece of the Pi: The Globalization of Visual Effects Labor," *Television and New Media*, 16 (3): 219–239.

Deuze, M. (2007) *Media Work*, Cambridge: Polity Press.

Deuze, M. (ed.) (2011) *Managing Media Work*, London: Sage.

Deuze, M. and Prenger, M. (eds) (2019) *Making Media: Production, Practices, and Professions*, Amsterdam: Amsterdam University Press.

D'Acci, J. (1994) *Defining Women: Television and the Case of Cagney and Lacey*, Chapel Hill, NC: University of North Carolina Press.

Drake, P. (2013) "Policy and Practice: Deconstructing the Creative Industries," in P. Szczepanik and P. Vonderau (eds), *Behind the Screen: Inside European Production Cultures*, London: Palgrave Macmillan.

Drake, P., Franklin, M., Sathe, D., and Tierney, S. (2015) *We Are Colony: Digital VOD Distribution for Independent Film*, London: Nesta.

Du Gay, P. (ed.) (1997) *Production of Culture/Cultures of Production*, London: Sage/Open University.

Eikhof, D. R., Newsinger, J., Rudloff, D., Luchinskaya, D., and Banks, M. (2018) *Workforce Diversity in the UK Screen Sector: Evidence Review*, Leicester: University of Leicester.

Eikhof, D. R. and Marsden, S. (2019) "Diversity and Opportunity in the Media industries," in M. Deuze and M. Prenger (eds), *Making Media: Production, Practices, and Professions*, Amsterdam: Amsterdam University Press: 247–258.

Elliott, P. (1972) *The Making of a Television Series: A Case Study in the Sociology of Culture*, London: Constable.

Frith, S. (1978) *The Sociology of Rock*, London: Constable.

Frith, S. (1981) *Sound Effects: Youth, Leisure, and the Politics of Rock,* New York: Pantheon.

Geertz, C. (1973) *The Interpretation of Cultures*, New York: Basic Books.

Goldsmith, B., Ward, S., and O'Regan, T. (2010) *Local Hollywood: Global Film Production and the Gold Coast*, St. Lucia: University of Queensland Press.

Gill, R. (2002) "Cool Creative and Egalitarian? Exploring Gender in Project-based New Media Work in Europe," *Information, Communication and Society*, 5 (1): 70–89.

Gill, R. (2011) "Life is a Pitch: Managing the Self in New Media Work," in M. Deuze (ed.), *Managing Media Work*, London: Sage: 249–262.

Gill, R., Banks, M., and Taylor, S. (eds) (2013) *Theorizing Cultural Work: Labour, Continuity and Change in the Creative Industries*, London: Routledge.

Gill, R. and Pratt, A. (2008) "In the Social Factory? Immaterial Labour, Precariousness and Cultural Work," *Theory, Culture and Society*, 25 (7–8): 1–30.

Gitlin, T. (1983) *Inside Prime Time*, New York: Pantheon.

Grindstaff, L. (2002) *The Money Shot: Trash, Class, and the Making of TV Talk Shows*, Chicago, IL: University of Chicago Press.

Havens, T., Lotz, A. D., and Tinic, S. (2009) "Critical Media Industry Studies: A Research Approach," *Communication, Culture and Critique*, 2 (2): 234–253.

Hesmondhalgh, D. (2002) *The Cultural Industries*, London: Sage.

Hesmondhalgh, D. (2007) *The Cultural Industries*, 2nd ed., London: Sage.

Hesmondhalgh, D. (2012) *The Cultural Industries*, 3rd ed., London: Sage.

Hesmondhalgh, D. (2015) "Exploitation and Media Labor," in R. Maxwell (ed.), *The Routledge Companion to Labor and Media*, New York: Routledge: 30–39.

Hesmondhalgh, D. (2019) *The Cultural Industries*, 4th ed., Los Angeles, CA: Sage.

Hesmondhalgh, D. and Baker, S. (2008) "Creative Work and Emotional Labour in the Television Industry," *Theory, Culture and Society*, 25 (7): 97–118.

Hesmondhalgh, D. and Baker, S. (2010) *Creative Labour: Media Work in the Cultural Industries*, Abingdon: Routledge.

Holt, J. and Perren, A. (eds) (2009) *Media Industries: History, Theory and Method*, Malden, MA: Wiley Blackwell.

Hochschild, A. R. (1983) *The Managed Heart: Commercialization of Human Feeling*, Berkeley, CA: University of California Press.

Jedlowski, A. (2017) "Post-imperial Affinities and Neoliberal Convergences: Discourses and Practices of Collaboration Between the Nigerian and the Indian Film Industries," *Media, Culture and Society*, 40 (1): 23–40.

Johns, J. (2006) "Video Games Production Networks: Value Capture, Power Relations and Embeddedness," *Journal of Economic Geography*, 6 (2): 151–180.

Kerr, A. (2006) *The Business and Culture of Digital Games: Gamework/Gameplay*, London: SAGE.

Mayer, V. (2011) *Below the Line: Producers and Production Studies in the New Television Economy*, Durham, NC: Duke University Press.

Mayer, V., Banks, M. J., and Caldwell, J. T. (eds) (2009) *Production Studies: Cultural Studies of Media Industries*, New York: Routledge.

McRobbie, A. (2002) "From Holloway to Hollywood: Happiness at Work in the New Cultural Economy," in P. du Gay and M. Pryke (eds), *Cultural Economy*, London: Sage, 97–114.

McRobbie, A. (2016) *Be Creative*, Cambridge: Polity Press.

Miège, B. (1989) *The Capitalization of Cultural Production*, New York: International General.

Miller, J. (2016) *Nollywood Central: The Nigerian Videofilm Industry*, London: British Film Institute.

Negus, K. (1992) *Producing Pop: Culture and Conflict in the Popular Music Industry*, London: Arnold.

Newcomb, H. (1983) *The Producer's Medium: Conversations with Creators of American TV*, Oxford: Oxford University Press.

Nightingale, V. (1989) "What's Ethnographic about 'Ethnographic' Audience Research?" *Australian Journal of Communication*, 16: 50–63.

Nwonka, C. and Malik, S. (2018) "Cultural Discourses and Practices of Institutionalised Diversity in the UK Film Sector: 'Just Get Something Black Made'," *The Sociological Review*, 66 (6): 1111–1127.

Ortner, S. (2009) "Studying Sideways: Ethnographic Access in Hollywood," in V. Mayer, M. J. Banks, and J. T. Caldwell (eds), *Production Studies: Cultural Studies of Media Industries*, New York: Routledge: 175–189.

Ortner, S. (2010) "Access: Reflections on Studying Up in Hollywood," *Ethnography*, 11 (2): 211–233.

Ohmann, R. (ed.) (1996) *Making and Selling Culture Making and Selling Culture*, Hanover: Wesleyan University Press.

Paterson, C., Lee, D., Saha, A. and Zoellner, A. (eds) (2016) *Advancing Media Production Research: Shifting Sites, Methods, and Politics*, Basingstoke: Palgrave.

Perren, A. (2013) "Rethinking Distribution for the Future of Media Industry Studies," *Cinema Journal*, 52 (3): 165–171.

Peterson, M. A. (2003) *Anthropology and Mass Communication: Media and Myth in the New Millennium*, New York: Berghahn.

Petrie, D. (1991) *Creativity and Constraint in the British Film Industry*, London: Macmillan Press.

Powdermaker, H. (1950) *Hollywood, the Dream Factory: An Anthropologist Looks at the Movie-makers*, Hollywood, CA: Little, Brown.

Randle, K. and Culkin, C. (2009) "Getting in and Getting on in Hollywood: Freelance Careers in an Uncertain Industry," in A. McKinlay and C. Smith (eds), *Creative Labour: Working in the Creative Industries*, Basingstoke: Palgrave Macmillan, 93–115.

Redvall, E. N. (2013) *Writing and Producing Television Drama in Denmark: From The Kingdom to The Killing*, London: Palgrave Macmillan.

Ross, A. (2009) *Nice Work If You Can Get It: Life and Labor in Precarious Times*, New York: New York University Press.

Rosten, L. (1941) *Hollywood: The Movie Colony, The Movie Makers*, New York: Harcourt, Brace and Company.

Saha, A. (2017) *Race and the Cultural Industries*, Cambridge: Polity Press.

Scott, A. J. (2005) *On Hollywood: The Place, the Industry*, Princeton, NJ: Princeton University Press.

Schlesinger, P. (1978) *Putting 'Reality' Together: BBC News*, London: Constable.

Silverstone, R. (1985) *Framing Science: The Making of a BBC Documentary*. London: British Film Institute.

Szczepanik, P. and Vonderau, P. (eds) (2013) *Behind the Screen: Inside European Production Cultures*, London: Palgrave Macmillan.

Standing, G. (2011) *The Precariat: The New Dangerous Class*, London: Bloomsbury Academic.

Tulloch, J. and Alvarado, M. (1983) *Dr Who: An Unfolding Text*, London: Macmillan Press.

Tunstall, J. (1974) *Journalists at Work*, London: Constable.

Tunstall, J. (1993) *Television Producers*, London: Routledge.

Ursell, G. (2000) "Television Production: Issues of Exploitation, Commodification and Subjectivity in UK Television Labour Markets," *Media, Culture and Society*, 22 (6): 805–825.

Warner, H. (2018) "Below-the-(Hem)line: Storytelling as Collective Resistance in Costume Design," *Feminist Media Histories,* 4 (1): 37–57.

Zucker, C. (2002) *Conversations with Actors on Film, Television and Stage Performance*, Portsmouth, NH: Heinemann.

# 8

# LOCATING AND LOCALIZING MEDIA INDUSTRY STUDIES

## The case of Greece

*Georgia Aitaki, Lydia Papadimitriou, and Yannis Tzioumakis*

This chapter throws a spotlight on the globally peripheral case study of Greek media industry studies. By taking this focus, the chapter has two aims: *locating* the relevant research trajectory in and about the country and arguing for the significance of *localizing* media industries research within the broader context of Media Industry Studies. Media Industry Studies (MIS) emerged in Anglo-American scholarship in the late 2000s as an umbrella term, a "big tent" (Herbert, Lotz, and Punathambekar 2020: 7), that aims to bring together the study of diverse and historically distinct media industries through a variety of disciplinary and methodological traditions. MIS's multidisciplinary agenda embraces aspects of both the humanities and social sciences. One of its key contributions thus far has been to highlight the role that arts, humanities, and cultural studies can play in expanding and enriching our understanding of media industries. In celebrating plurality, however, MIS has faced difficulty in establishing common ground with certain media-related disciplines whose research agenda was incompatible with others.[1] Central to this has been the prioritization or not of issues related to culture, and the concomitant methodological implications of such a choice.

In retrospectively locating MIS in and about Greece, this chapter will trace the expansion of media industries research agenda beyond the political economy-driven social sciences research that predominated until recently, toward a more methodologically mixed and qualitatively oriented humanities-inspired agenda. Such a shift in approaches also reflects the expansion of the objects of research beyond information-providing to entertainment-orientated media: from an almost exclusive focus on such issues as the print press, television news, or online journalism, to film, television fiction, or video games. The chapter will also argue for the significance of localizing media industries research, in other words, of taking into account the specific socio-political, economic, and cultural factors in which the particular media industries operate, before defining a research agenda appropriate and relevant to the media context it aims to analyze.

By taking this route, the chapter aims to interrogate the extent to which MIS is transferable and applicable to contexts outside the United States, the UK, and certain other countries that have contributed to the emergence of this research field as a distinct interdisciplinary school of thought. For the most part, MIS has been situated within traditions that are not only Western in terms of their geopolitical specificity, but which are also by and large based in work available in the English language. This is evident in the account of the development of MIS in a recent

DOI: 10.4324/9780429275340-10

study that positions the field within a distinctly Western scholarly tradition that ranges from the Frankfurt School of the 1930s to debates around media convergence in the twenty-first century (Herbert, Lotz, and Punathambekar 2020: 12–30). While such an account provides some examples of early work in non-Western contexts, notably in India and Latin America, it is only when MIS became firmly established in the 2010s that a more concerted effort took place to examine such contexts.

In some ways, the Greek case exemplifies this development. Although there has been research on Greek media industries since the 1980s in both Greek and English languages, such work was rarely noted internationally or informed broader debates on media industries research. Part of the reason for this was the small size of the country and its peripheral position in the global media economy, rendering the country's media industries virtually invisible. Another reason was, arguably, the inward-looking focus of most Greek media research, which focused on the relationship between media and the often-obstructive state, a focus that *hyper-localized* the research agenda and did not engage with concerns shared with the remit of a dominant agenda that was often tied to the US media environment due to its sheer size and global presence. This environment is characterized, among others, by the historical dominance of private capital, the firm control of media markets by a cadre of major corporations, the commercial orientation of most media industries from inception, their ever-growing operation on a global scale, the development of regulative regimes aimed at increasing competition, and the relative absence of the US government from the media sector. In this sense, the prevalence of US media in MIS has shaped many research questions and methods, as showcased by Holt and Perren's (2009) field-defining volume, which may not be at the core of studies in other (national) contexts.

By focusing on a globally peripheral case study, this chapter points to a number of questions that highlight the significance of localizing MIS research: how far do specific sociopolitical, economic, and cultural contexts impact on the research questions asked when analyzing particular media industries? Do some approaches have more validity and relevance (and/or more shortcomings) than others because of such particular contexts? And does technological change, increased globalization, and the (perceived) democratization of production and dissemination reduce the significance of such contexts, or not?

The rest of the chapter will begin to point to how answers can be formulated with reference to Greece, its media industries, and the nature and scope of research that has been conducted on them. As we argue, the research agenda of what can be retrospectively labelled "Greek Media Industry Studies" has been affected by the specific ways in which media have grown in the country, characterized, primarily, though not exclusively, by the involvement of the state as a key stakeholder. While there are significant variations among different Greek media industries regarding the extent and means of the state's participation in their operations, the extensive presence of the state in activities that have elsewhere been in the realm of civil society has impacted heavily on the research agenda. This chapter will briefly explain the state's involvement in the Greek media industries and the historical reasons for its extent and its nature, before offering a summary review of the body of work that has focused on this and highlighting how this work came to be considered the dominant paradigm in Greek media industries research. It will then point to newer developments in the Greek media industries landscape that revolve around the introduction of digital technologies, the impact of the post-2008 financial crisis, and the country's increasing participation in transnational practices and global markets which have changed significantly the relationship between the state and the media. To address these developments, more recent work has been evidencing a variety of media practices and embracing a multitude of methodological approaches and analytical perspectives.

## The Greek media industries environment: the state and the media

Unlike the United States, with its multibillion dollar and globally dominant media industries, Greece is a small media market that operates almost exclusively within national boundaries. As such, it shares a number of "structural peculiarities" (Puppis 2009: 10) with other similarly sized countries/markets, that include, among others, limited production resources, restricted commercial potential, and a high proportion of imported media (Papadimitriou 2020: 182). Aside from stressing its small size and its globally peripheral status, in order to understand the development of media industries research in the country, it is important to frame the development of Greek media industries in a wider historical and sociopolitical context.

Established as a sovereign nation-state in 1829 after a war of independence from the Ottoman Empire and with the support of the then European powers, Greece, like other "new" countries that emerged in similar circumstances, found itself negotiating sovereignty with external interference. As all its institutions were new and modelled more or less directly on European examples, an ambivalent relationship toward the state emerged from the start. While the promise of belonging to the West was embraced, established modes of "behind the scenes" operations focusing around clientelist networks also persisted (Mouzelis 1980: 242, 249). Within the Greek context, such operations took the form of direct political patronage, whereby a small cadre of oligarchic families maintained control of local voters and were therefore able to exert influence on the government, and the state apparatus more broadly (Mouzelis 1980: 242). In many regards, the development of the Greek state displayed characteristics typical to postcolonial states, including "overdevelopment," a "new and relatively autonomous economic role," and a "significant ideological function" (Ziemann and Lanzendorfer 1977: 143). According to sociologist Nikos Mouzelis, the state quickly became "the functioning axis of the Greek social formation" to the detriment of an atrophied bourgeois civil society (1980: 247–248) and its remarkable presence in Greek society continued well into its capitalist era (post-1920s).

Speaking of the state's "overdevelopment" refers to the extent to which it repeatedly subsidized industrial sectors, which elsewhere would have advanced as a result of private enterprise. State involvement with such industries, however, became susceptible to short-sighted and often clientelist practices, as political expediency and lack of consensus among those in power often led to mismanagement and misuse of funds (Mouzelis 1990: A6). As a result, the ascendance of capitalism as a dominant mode of production occurred without an economically dominant industrial middle-class exercising control over the state apparatus, which explains both the dependence of Greek businesses on state capital and confirms the state's relatively "autonomous economic role." The Greek state's "ideological function" refers to the fact that, without the control of an industrial middle-class, the Greek state became an ideological instrument for the parties in power. However, the ideologies of these parties did not correspond to beliefs and interests of specific social classes; rather they often cynically served the pursuit of party power.

The above is particularly relevant to a discussion of the Greek media industries environment, especially with regard to broadcast media. Both radio and television were established by the state, and in particular, by authoritarian regimes – the former during the Metaxas fascist dictatorship in 1935 and the latter during the *junta* of the Colonels in 1967 (although introduced a year earlier). After democracy was restored in 1974, radio and television remained under the direct control of the state (Katsoudas 1986: 142). This provided ample evidence that both media functioned as "arms of the state" (Papathanassopoulos 1997: 352), and that clientelist practices abounded. It was only in the 1990s and after the deregulation of Greek broadcast media that the state monopolies were dissolved as private radio and television stations entered the media market. However, clientelist practices persisted, enabling the new media entrepreneurs to benefit from a political culture based on the exchange of political favors (Iosifidis and Papathanassopoulos 2019: 14–15).

The process of European integration and the gradual adoption of digital technologies in many spheres of public life increased processes of technocratic transparency and accountability, especially in the post-2008 economic crisis years. However, the legacy of clientelism has not as yet been erased, while the (seemingly contradictory) attitudes of both reliance on and suspicion of the state are, arguably, still present. Under these circumstances, it is not surprising that research in the field has focused on analyzing news and public affairs programs with the aim of questioning the relationship of media with national politics, while developing arguments about their impact on democratic processes via political economy and mass communication approaches.

The relationship between the Greek film industry and the Greek state, however, has been markedly different. Until the last quarter of the twentieth century, cinema was left to the realm of free – albeit state-censored – enterprise and prioritized "harmless entertainment." Cinema was not perceived by the state as an industry worth investing in. Rather, its popularity rendered it a valuable source of taxation to support other arts, such as theater (Sotiropoulou 1989). This changed in the 1980s, as the collapse of the commercially driven film industry and the introduction of state models of film financing (as elsewhere in Europe) led Greek filmmakers to become dependent on the state. However, the films thus produced were predominantly of the "art cinema" category and failed to attract significant audiences, while investment in infrastructure was nonexistent. The introduction of private capital in broadcasting in the 1990s led to an increasingly converged media landscape that saw television companies investing in film. The reemergence of film as a commercial proposition reinvigorated discourses of cinema as an industry and whetted the appetite for industry-oriented studies (Kokonis 2012). The advent of the 2008 global financial crisis and its powerful impact on the Greek economy deeply affected Greek cinema, leading to a reconsideration of, among other things, its mode of production. This refers, on the one hand, to a more artisanal approach, consisting of informal means of mutual support and "solidarity" among filmmakers (Tsangari 2016: 238, 242–243) as well as communal film financing methods, such as crowdfunding (Papadimitriou 2017a); and, on the other, a more European and "extrovert" orientation, in other words, an increasing embrace of European co-productions and the desire for films to appeal to audiences beyond the Greek borders (Papadimitriou 2018a, 2018b). The role of the state in supporting Greek cinema was yet again weakened.

The advent of digital technologies has played a major role in transforming the Greek media landscape (Papadimitriou 2020). It has also contributed toward disrupting, though not erasing, the role of the state as regulator and supporter. Beyond the impact on legacy media, digitization and new technologies have opened up new creative and business opportunities, while the increasingly globalized Greek economy and culture invites continuous redefinition of Greek media and its industries. Just as MIS more broadly challenges the hegemony of political economy and political communication approaches in the field, the same can be also argued for Greek Media Industry Studies. The main difference is that the small size, global peripherality, and (to a large degree) state-dependent status of the Greek media industries make it important not only to scale the claims, but to ensure that the circumstances of a particular industry's functioning are explored in all their political, economic, and cultural specificity. In what follows, we will point to some key research in and about Greek media industries, outlining some of the distinctive questions raised in this context, and tracing the extent and ways in which the scholarly agenda has recently expanded to embrace greater methodological plurality.

## Greek Media Industries Studies: from political economy to Media Industry Studies

As already suggested above, the MIS agenda has been to expand the topics, approaches, and methodologies concerning research on media industries beyond the domain of the social sciences, quantitative methods, and the dominance of political economy and mass communications. In Greece, until recently, such work has been prominent, and it developed in social sciences-defined university departments that had very little – if any – dialogue with the arts and humanities.[2]

Representative of this tradition is the work of Stylianos Papathanassopoulos, whose books and articles in communication-focused journals in Greece and internationally have often explored the historic relationship of the Greek press and broadcasting with the country's political parties and politics.[3] His most highly cited work is a co-authored (with Daniel C. Hallin) article that compares political clientelism and the media in Southern Europe (Greece, Spain, Italy, and Portugal) and Latin America (Mexico, Brazil, and Colombia) (Hallin and Papathanassopoulos 2002). The article identifies many similarities across these countries' media systems, including: the low level of newspaper circulation, presence of advocacy reporting, control of the media "by private interests with political alliances and ambitions which seek to use their media properties for political ends" (p. 177), politicization of public broadcasting and broadcast regulation, and the limited development of journalism as an autonomous profession. Such issues are typical of the concerns of social sciences-orientated Greek media industries research.[4]

In this context, the deregulation of Greek broadcast media in the late 1980s was seen as a defining moment in the operation of national media industries. The introduction of new technologies and the emergence of media convergence were also regularly addressed, often situated within Western (and Southern) European contexts. While these issues continue to concern political economy-informed media industries research,[5] some have also expanded their focus on ownership patterns and business models.[6] Furthermore, political economy approaches have showcased a more hybrid character, such as Masouras's (2015) study of television programming under the lens of content diversity, that includes policy perspectives, content analysis and production insights.

Until recently, media (industry) studies in Greece were represented almost entirely by work such as the above, while research on film, music, games, and other media was not considered part of "media studies" or "media industries." Film studies entered Greek universities gradually since the 1990s, but film industry-related research was initially very scarce, and such studies were conducted outside an academic context.[7] Also, in television studies, with the exception of Koukoutsaki's (2003) study on production trends in entertainment programming and Paschalidis's (2005) overview of broader institutional (including regulatory and financial) logics defining Greek television, there has been little interest in activating industrial approaches and methodologies.

However, since the 2010s, a number of factors pertaining both to the media landscape and to the academic environment in Greece led to the embrace of a more wide-reaching research agenda that reflects the pluralistic and interdisciplinary aims of MIS. Triggered by the combination of the 2008 financial crisis and the widespread implementation of digital technologies, such factors include: the establishment of informal networks of media production and dissemination, the emergence of a variety of independent and/or alternative media organizations, the appearance of a video game sector following its recognition as a legitimate industry by Greek law (Roinioti 2020), the introduction of on-demand television, and efforts to regulate broadcasting after almost 30 years of private television stations operating on a temporary license. They also include the evolving role of the Greek state in more actively supporting the production of television drama, an aspect of Greek television programming that had been particularly hit by the financial crisis. The economic support provided by the newly established National Centre of Audiovisual Media and Communication (EKOME) has enabled private broadcasters (such as SKAI, Alpha, ANT1) and pay TV channels (Cosmote TV) to finance some productions, while ERT, the public broadcaster, has also reset the production of original TV dramas after an almost ten-year long hiatus. Such developments, combined with the establishment of new, more interdisciplinary, university departments in Greece and the contributions of scholars based outside Greece who have been working within the parameters established by MIS, have led to a significant expansion of the scope of Greek media industries research.

In film, relevant work has focused on "tendencies of independence" in 2000s Greek cinema (Chalkou 2012), European co-productions and their impact on Greek cinema (Gourgoulianni 2015) and marketing and promotion in 1990s Greek cinema (Nikolaidou 2017). Based in a university outside Greece, Lydia Papadimitriou has systematically explored a range of distinct but inter-related Greek film industry-related topics, mostly with reference to the 2010s, including independent filmmaking (2015), funding (2017a), co-productions (2018a, 2018b), and distribution (2018c). Papadimitriou has also analyzed the effects of the 2008 financial crisis on the overall ecosystem of film production, circulation, and reception (2017b), while her more recent work (2020) has focused on the challenges and opportunities presented by the rapid expansion of digital distribution for the film and television sectors in Greece. Together with Tzioumakis (2015), she has examined matters regarding the localization of film marketing with reference to US independent films depicting Greek (and Greek diasporic) culture. Papadimitriou (2016) has also engaged with Film Festival Studies, an area of research very much covered by the broad disciplinary "tent" of MIS.

Television studies has seen a significant turn to questions of industry away from politics, news, and public affairs. Indicatively, Vovou (2010) offered a historical reading of the development of television genres in Greece with an emphasis on how different production models translate into specific cultural/ideological agendas; she addresses politics, but also ownership, sponsorship/advertising, and technology. Koukoutsaki-Monnier (2010) provided a diachronic analysis of the pre- and post-deregulation production context of television fiction, focusing on production patterns and their ideological implications. More recently, Thessaloniki-based Paschalidis (2018) and Vamvakas (2018) have been very vocal about how, historically, media studies in Greece and especially political economic approaches have discouraged engagement in grounded empirical research, including questions pertaining to industry research. However, an increasing number of Greek scholars based at universities both inside and outside the country have started providing these kinds of studies, utilizing production cultures and other theoretical frameworks, and focusing on issues such as creative agency, format localization, casting, and scheduling, among others.

For instance, in Greece, Betty Kaklamanidou has examined issues of scheduling, casting, and localization of foreign formats, such as a Colombian telenovela (2013), and highlighted the role of specific individuals in introducing the genre of sitcom to Greek audiences (2017). Based in Cyprus, Photiou, Charalambous, and Maniou (2019) have illustrated how creative decision-making was affected by cultural and linguistic factors in the context of Σ' αγαπώ μ' αγαπάς (*S' agapo m' agapas*) (2000–2002), the Greek remake of the Canadian comedy series *Un gars, une fille* (1997–2003). Based in Sweden, Georgia Aitaki has explored authorial synergies and production processes in private television (2020a, 2020b). Finally, Jo Frangou (2019), currently based in the United States, applied an auto-ethnographic approach in her analysis of how affective relationships, creative visions, and commercial pressures informed a particular channel's production logics.

## Conclusion

With Greek media industries research having also recently welcomed studies of media labor (Spyridakis 2017) and work dealing with the media under the banner of "creative and culture industries" (Avdikos 2014), it is clear that the field is undergoing rapid transformation. While traditional social science and political economy-driven research continues to dominate media departments in the country's universities, media industries research associated primarily (but not exclusively) with the arts and humanities has been making significant strides. Such studies have provided empirically grounded descriptions of the production and dissemination of Greek media, theorized the specificities of the Greek case, and related it to other – both globally dominant and peripheral – media industries often by engaging with questions of politics indirectly. They have also explored past practices, identified continuities and changes, and overall illuminated the workings of these industries at both the micro and macro levels. In doing this, they have been gradually challenging the hegemony of mass communication/political economic approaches.

Given the above, Greek Media Industry Studies seems to have become integrated into research agendas and methodological practices visible elsewhere, especially in the United States and other Western countries. Indeed, Greek MIS increasingly showcases research from arts and humanities scholars, highlights the importance of cultural processes in the organization and operation of media industries, and invites dialogue with dominant research paradigms while challenging the currency of some. In this regard, MIS seems to be highly transferable and applicable to variable political, social, or economic contexts.

However, on a closer look, the specific research questions and topics that researchers choose to examine are highly dependent on these contexts. In the Greek case, the role of the state, for example, remains an important parameter in media industries research even if it is not always the main focus. Issues concerning independence in film and media, regulation of new digital technologies, subsidies for film and television production, licensing television channels, facilitating particular production contexts, accommodating format localizing practices, and many others often involve the state as a key player – whether directly or indirectly. The impact of specific political, social, and economic contexts can also explain why certain issues – such as those related to race, gender, equality, and inclusivity – have received little attention in Greek media industries research (while in the United States and elsewhere they are prominent).[8] It also explains why studies rarely focus on private media companies and their business strategies. Furthermore, it is worth reflecting on how research is shaped by the availability of resources, for it should also be noted that unlike in the United States and other large media producing countries, Greece does not have a strong trade press covering the media industries, nor archives dedicated to the history of particular media. These factors impact on the possible methodologies used and on the specific kind of questions that can be explored.

One can therefore argue that, despite the overall transferability of the goals and agenda of MIS, the specific research questions and agenda that media industry scholars examining the Greek case address are highly dependent on both the broader context in which media industries operate and specific factors related to their operations. In seeking to locate and localize Media Industry Studies, it is important to call not only for an increased and meaningful dialogue between humanities and social sciences in the Greek context, but also for an understanding of the media landscape that invites this type of the work as well as the institutional contexts within which it takes place.

# Notes

1 A characteristic example is Veneti and Karatzogianni (2020), which, despite being about "Digital Media in Greece" does not address cinema, video games, or television fiction in any of its 26 chapters and considers internet, streaming platforms, and social media only as carriers of "information" rather than "entertainment."
2 Such as the Department of Mass Communications at the National and Kapodistrian University of Athens, or Journalism at the Aristotle University of Thessaloniki. For more on the institutional context of media studies in Greek universities, see Aitaki, Papadimitriou, and Tzioumakis (2020).
3 See, for instance, Papathanassopoulos (1990, 1997, 2001).
4 Even before Papathanassopopoulos's studies, one could see such focus in other work, such as Katsoudas (1986).
5 See, in particular, Iosifidis (2007, 2008), Papathanassopoulos (2017), and Iosifidis and Papathanassopoulos (2019).
6 See, for instance, Leandros (2008, 2010).
7 For the film studies institutional context in Greece, see Aitaki, Papadimitriou, and Tzioumakis (2020). For early Greek film industry studies, see Sotiropoulou (1989) and Kouanis (2001).
8 For an example that does takes into consideration gender questions, see Tsaliki and Chronaki (2016).

# References

Aitaki, G. (2020a) "In Search of the Greek Television Author: The Social Dramas of Manousos Manousakis," *Screen*, 61 (3): 403–422.

Aitaki, G. (2020b) "Making Television Fiction in a Commercial Context: Commercialization, Ideology and Entertainment in a Production Study of Greek Private Television," *Journal of Greek Media and Culture*, 6 (2): 219–240.

Aitaki, G., Papadimitriou, L., and Tzioumakis, Y. (2020) "Greek Screen Industries: From Political Economy to Media Industry Studies," *Journal of Greek Media and Culture*, 6 (2): 155–178.

Avdikos, V. (2014) *Oi Politistikes kai Dimiourgikes Viomihanies stin Ellada*, Athens: Epikentro.

Chalkou, M. (2012) "A New Cinema of 'Emancipation': Tendencies of Independence in Greek Cinema of the 2000s," *Interactions: Studies in Communication and Culture*, 3 (2): 243–261.

Frangou, J. (2019) "MEGA mou: An Insider Perspective on Working for Greece's First Private Television Channel," *Filmicon: Journal of Greek Film Studies*, (6): 138–152.

Gourgoulianni, S. (2015) "Greek European Film Co-Productions in the Three Major European Film Festivals from 2001 to 2013," *Journal of Arts and Humanities*, 4 (5): 68–73.

Hallin, D. C. and Papathanassopoulos S. (2002) "Political Clientelism and the Media: Southern Europe and Latin America in Comparative Perspective," *Media, Culture and Society*, 24 (2): 175–195.

Havens, T., Lotz, A., and Tinic, S. (2009) "Critical Media Industry Studies: A Research Approach," *Communication, Culture and Critique*, 2 (2): 234–253.

Herbert, D., Lotz, A., and Punathambekar, A. (2020) *Media Industry Studies*, Cambridge: Polity.

Holt, J. and Perren, A. (2009) "Introduction: Does the World Really Need One More Field of Study?" in J. Holt and A. Perren (eds), *Media Industries: History, Theory, and Method*, Chichester: Wiley-Blackwell, 1–16.

Holt, J. and Perren, A. (eds) (2009) *Media Industries: History, Theory, and Method*, Chichester: Wiley-Blackwell.

Iosifidis, P. (2007) "Public Television in Small European Countries: Challenges and Strategies," *International Journal of Media and Cultural Politics*, 3 (1): 65–87.

Iosifidis, P. (2008) "Public Television Policies in Europe: The Case of France and Greece," *International Journal of Media and Cultural Politics*, 4 (3): 349–367.

Iosifidis, P. and Papathanassopoulos, S. (2019) "Media, Politics and State Broadcasting in Greece," *European Journal of Communication*, 34 (4): 345–359.

Kaklamanidou, B. (2013) "The Greek *Maria i Aschimi*: The Never-Ending Journey of a Myth," in J. McCabe and K. Akass (eds), *TV's Betty Goes Global: From Telenovela to International Brand*, London: I. B. Tauris, 175–188.

Kaklamanidou, B. (2017) "Introduction to the Greek Sitcom: The Case of *I Tris Charites/The Three Graces*," *Filmicon: Journal of Greek Film Studies*, (4): 138–154.

Katsoudas, D. (1986) "Greece: A Politically Controlled State Monopoly Broadcasting System," in R. Kuhn (ed), *Broadcasting and Politics in Europe*, London: Frank Kass, 137–151.

Kokonis, M. (2012) "Is There such a Thing as a Greek Blockbuster? The Revival of Contemporary Greek Cinema," in L. Papadimitriou and Y. Tzioumakis (eds), *Greek Cinema: Texts, Histories, Identities*, Bristol: Intellect, 37–54.

Kouanis, P. (2001) *I Kinimatografiki Agora stin Ellada 1944–1999*, Athens: Finatec.

Koukoutsaki, A. (2003) "Greek Television Drama: Production Policies and Genre Diversification," *Media, Culture and Society*, 25 (6): 715–735.

Koukoutsaki-Monnier, A. (2010) "Ellinika Programmata Mythoplasias: Diachroniki Exelixi kai Taseis Paragogis," in I. Vovou (ed.), *O Kosmos tis Tileorasis: Theoritikes Proseggiseis, Analysi Programmaton kai Elliniki Pragmatikotita*, Athens: Irodotos, 417–451.

Leandros, N. (2008) *Epiheirimatikes Stratigikes kai Viomihania ton Meson*, Athens: Politeia.

Leandros, N. (2010) "Structural Media Pluralism. Media Concentration and Systemic Failures in Greece," *International Journal of Communication*, (4): 886–905.

Masouras, A. (2015) *Understanding Competition and Diversity in Television Programming*, Hamburg: Anchor Academic Publishing.

Mouzelis, N. (1980) "Capitalism and the Development of the Greek State," in R. Scase (ed.), *The State in Western Europe*, London: Croom Helm, 241–273.

Mouzelis, N. (1990) "I Ellada sto Perithorio: Poios Ftaiei?" *To Vima*, December 30: A6–7.

Nikolaidou, A. (2017) "Marketing Communications in the Greek Film Industry: Rethinking Contemporary Greek Cinema," in T. Kazakopoulou and M. Fotiou (eds), *Contemporary Greek Film Cultures from 1990 to the Present*, Bern: Peter Lang, 291–318.

Papadimitriou, L. (2015) "In the Shadow of the Studios, the State and the Multiplexes: Independent Filmmaking in Greece," in M. Erickson and D. Baltruschat (eds), *The Meaning of Independence: Independent Filmmaking Around the Globe*, Toronto: Toronto University Press, 113–130.

Papadimitriou, L. (2016) "The Hindered Drive Towards Internationalisation: Thessaloniki (International) Film Festival," *New Review of Film and Television Studies*, 14 (1): 93–111.

Papadimitriou, L. (2017a) "Transitions in the Periphery: Funding Film Production in Greece Since the Financial Crisis," *International Journal on Media Management*, 19 (2): 164–181.

Papadimitriou, L. (2017b) "The Economy and Ecology of Greek Cinema Since the Crisis: Production, Circulation, Reception," in D. Tziovas (ed.), *Greece in Crisis: The Cultural Politics of Austerity*, London: I. B. Tauris, 135–157.

Papadimitriou, L. (2018a) "Greek Cinema as European Cinema: Co-Productions, Eurimages and the Europeanisation of Greek Cinema," *Studies in European Cinema*, 15 (2–3): 215–234.

Papadimitriou, L. (2018b) "European Co-Productions and Greek Cinema Since the Crisis: 'Extroversion' as Survival," in J. Hammett-Jamart, P. Mitric, and E. N. Redvall (eds), *European Film and Television Co-Production: Policy and Practice*, London: Palgrave, 207–222.

Papadimitriou, L. (2018c) "Film Distribution in Greece: Formal and Informal Networks of Circulation Since the Financial Crisis," *Screen*, 59 (4): 484–505.

Papadimitriou, L. (2020) "Digital Film and Television Distribution in Greece: Between Crisis and Opportunity," in P. Szczepanik, P. Zahrádka , J. Macek, and P . Stepan (eds), *Digital Peripheries: The Online Circulation of Audiovisual Content from the Small Market Perspective*, Cham: Springer, 181–197.

Papadimitriou, L. and Tzioumakis, Y. (2015) "My Big Fat Life in Ruins: Marketing 'Greekness' and the Contemporary US Independent Film," in N. Mingant, C. Tirtaine, and J. Augros (eds), *Film Marketing in a Global Era*, London: British Film Institute, 36–46.

Papathanassopoulos, S. (1990) "Broadcasting, Politics and the State in Socialist Greece," *Media, Culture and Society*, 12 (3): 387–397.

Papathanassopoulos, S. (1997) "The Politics and the Effects of the Deregulation of Greek Television," *European Journal of Communication*, 12 (3): 351–368.

Papathanassopoulos, S. (2001) "The Decline of Newspapers: The Case of the Greek Press," *Journalism Studies*, 2 (1): 109–123.

Papathanassopoulos, S. (2017) "Greece: A Continuous Interplay Between Media and Politicians," in P. Bajomi-Lázár (ed.), *Media in Third-Wave Democracies: Southern and Central/Eastern Europe in a Comparative Perspective*, Budapest: L'Harmattan, 75–89.

Paschalidis, G. (2005) "I Elliniki Tileorasi," in N. Vernikos, S. Daskalopoulou, P. Bantimaroudis, N. Boubaris, and D. Papageorgiou (eds), *Politistikes Viomihanies: Diadikasies, Ypiresies kai Agatha*, Athens: Kritiki, 173–200.

Paschalidis, G. (2018) "To Chameno Paradeigma tis Ellinikis Tileorasis," in V. Vamvakas and G. Paschalidis (eds), *50 Chronia Elliniki Tileorasi*, Athens: Epikentro, 9–41.

Photiou, I., Charalambous, P., and Maniou, T. (2019) "'Battle of the Sexes' on Television: The Cases of the Greek-Cypriot and Greek Adaptations of *Un Gars, Une Fille*," *Filmicon: Journal of Greek Film Studies*, (6): 90–111.

Puppis, M. (2009) "Media Regulation in Small States," *International Communication Gazzette*, 71 (1–2): 7–17.

Roinioti, E. (2020) "Caught in the War Against Gambling: A Critical Analysis of Law History and Policy Making in Video Games in Greece," *Journal of Greek Media and Culture*, 6 (2): 261–278.

Sotiropoulou, C. (1989) *Elliniki Kinimatografia: 1965–1975. Thesmiko Plaisio, Oikonomiki Katastasi*, Athens: Themelio.

Spyridakis, M. (2017) "Coping with Uncertainty: Precarious Workers in the Greek Media Sector," in E. Armano, A. Bove, and A. Murgia (eds), *Mapping Precariousness, Labour Insecurity and Uncertain Livelihoods: Subjectivities and Resistance*, London: Routledge, 98–109.

Tsaliki, L. and Chronaki, D. (2016) "Producing the Porn Self: An Introspection of the Mainstream Greek Porn Industry," *Journal of Porn Studies*, 3 (2): 1–13.

Tsangari, A. R. (2016) "On Solidarity, Collaboration and Independence: Athena Rachel Tsangari Discusses Her Films and Greek Cinema with Vangelis Calotychos, Lydia Papadimitriou and Yannis Tzioumakis," *Journal of Greek Media and Culture*, 2 (2): 237–253.

Vamvakas, V. (2018) "I Ysteri Metapolitefsi me ti Matia ton Tiletheaton stis Ellinikes Seires," in V. Vamvakas and G. Paschalidis (eds), *50 Chronia Elliniki Tileorasi*, Athens: Epikentro, 213–231.

Veneti, A. and Karatzogianni, A. (eds) (2020) *The Emerald Handbook of Digital Media in Greece: Journalism and Political Communication in Times of Crisis*, Bingley: Emerald Publishing.

Vovou I. (2010) "Stoiheia gia Mia Meta-istoria tis Ellinikis Tileorasis: To Meso, i Politiki, kai o Thesmos," in I. Vovou (ed.), *O Kosmos tis Tileorasis: Theoritikes Proseggiseis, Analysi Programmaton kai Elliniki Pragmatikotita*, Athens: Irodotos, 93–140.

Ziemann W. and Lanzendorfer, M. (1977) "The State in Peripheral Societies," in R. Miliband and J. Saville (eds), *The Socialist Register 1977: A Survey of Movements and Ideas*, New York: Monthly Review Press, 143–177.

# PART II

# Interventions

## Rethinking the field

Chapters in the previous part outlined how certain perspectives have predominated in media industries research. Yet we cannot regard this field as settled ground: the vibrancy of media industries scholarship is sustained by ongoing efforts to innovate the conceptual and methodological landscape, while at the same time constructively attending to lacunae found in the existing body of scholarship. In this part, chapters therefore present a series of interventions that positively challenge the scope or range of media industries analysis while offering fresh routes into thinking about the purposes and objectives of this work.

Media industries research would appear to commence from a self-evident understanding of its object, yet the following four chapters productively challenge the contours of media industries and in so doing the scope of the research field. Conventionally, the "media" in "media industries" means creative content (e.g., books, music recordings, digital games), yet as Lee McGuigan points out, the workings of those industries – and indeed all industries – depend on various administrative, communicative, and informational resources (e.g., documents, databases, spreadsheets, algorithms), the media through which the workings of industry are conducted, or what McGuigan terms "industrial media." Taking as his case study audience commodification in advertising and marketing, McGuigan highlights the multiple bureaucratic, calculative, and logistical inputs involved with observing and measuring human attention and turning this into actionable and tradeable information. For McGuigan, therefore, analyzing the industrial production of culture necessitates engaging with a larger realm of media to disclose the otherwise concealed inputs that are necessary to conducting commercial relationships.

In recent media research, studies of "infrastructure" have sought to make visible the otherwise overlooked material substructures that make communication possible. Evaluating the "infrastructural turn" in media and internet research, David Hesmondhalgh identifies the benefits of, but also the blind spots in, this work. Countering bold and occasionally hyperbolic claims made about the potentials of networks, attention to infrastructure can offer useful reminders of the physical and quotidian fabric anchoring such systems. Furthermore, infrastructure draws attention to the distribution rather than the contents of communication. At the same time, Hesmondhalgh suggests these benefits become compromised wherever definitional and conceptual vagueness obscure the meaning and material existence of infrastructures. Still,

DOI: 10.4324/9780429275340-11

Hesmondhalgh concludes a focus on infrastructure can valuably reconcile and synthesize otherwise distinct research perspectives.

Where McGuigan looks to expand media industries research by problematizing the meanings of "media," Ramon Lobato questions the determinacy of "industry." While perspectives in media industries research can differ in their conceptual and methodological approaches, implicitly they coalesce in taking as their object of study highly organized, regulated, and professionalized sectors of creative and commercial activity. Yet, as Lobato notes, this "formal" sphere of media forever coexists with, and is also permeated by, forms of employment and industry activity that remain "informalized" by their loose organization and lack of regulatory monitoring. Placing both formal and informal aspects within the research purview can therefore constructively introduce a degree of indeterminacy into how we imagine the constitution of media industries.

Prompting rich ground for interrogating how we might conceptualize any industrial formation, Gregory Steirer and Alisa Perren recommend three ways into perceiving and defining the comics industry. Viewing comics as an industry in their own right emphasizes the comic book as the primary product category, distributed through the "direct market" system of specialized comics publishers, wholesalers, and retailers. At the same time, newsstand and bookstores sales place comics in the same context as book publishing, an association particularly pronounced with the graphic novel. Licensing comic characters for films and programmes also extends comics into the screen media industries, where intellectual property becomes the key source of value. Rather than privilege any one perspective, Steirer and Perren argue the validity of each encourages thinking about intra- and inter-industrial relationships.

For the remainder of this part, chapters address ways of enlarging and enriching the critical agenda of media industries research. Critiquing the relative absence of race in media industries scholarship, Anamik Saha proposes studies of race and industry can be mutually reinforcing by combining analyses of diversity in media work with how cultures of media production influence the depiction, and therefore the commodification, of racially marginalized groups. Saha argues recognizing complexity, contradiction, and contestation in relations between production and representation necessitates equal attention to structural/macro and agency/micro dimensions. Taking inspiration from work on racial capitalism, which foregrounds the racial character of capitalism, Saha advises media industries research can most productively engage with race by addressing racism as a structuring force upon, rather than an epiphenomenon of, capitalist cultural production.

Recent controversies regarding cases of sexual misconduct and abuse experienced by women working in US film and television demonstrated how gendered power relations can take form in media industries. Beyond these high-profile cases, however, there is the need to recognize how gender inequity and marginalization retain a wider systemic presence in these industries. On this note, Courtney Brannon Donoghue identifies three approaches to understanding women's work in Hollywood. Countering how the work of women has gone undocumented in many histories of Hollywood, archival research not only recovers the historical presence of women in the industry but also serves to reevaluate the types of work they undertook. Quantitative data-gathering evince structural employment disparities in the number of women working in Hollywood and the types of role they occupy. Beyond such macro-level analyses, Brannon Donoghue advocates for using qualitative methods to capture how women negotiate gendered power on-the-ground in their work and careers, illuminating how the industry works for women, and how women work in the industry.

This focus on the micro workings of media labor is echoed by Kevin Sanson. Accounts of "Global Hollywood" commonly note how the historical shift toward a flexibly specialized mode of production combined with the geographic extension of production activity across international territories. Suspending analysis at the level of broad contextual trends results, however, in an abstracted account of how media industries operate globally. To grasp the complexities of how the socio-spatial transformation of production is operationalized in practice therefore, Sanson argues for a mode of analysis that attends to how the ordinary, everyday realities of media workers actually sustain a mobile production regime.

When seeking to understand the most significant dynamics driving globalization and digitalization, media industries research can revert to only focusing on the world's largest media producing nations or richest media markets. Consequently, this partial purview gives a skewed account, overlooking how the media industries of smaller (in terms of size and resources) and peripheral (marked by dependence on the economic or cultural power of a "core") nations are positioned in the global digital economy. To theorize that position, Petr Szczepanik outlines how the audiovisual industries of smaller nations are vulnerable to external forces, being disadvantaged by their relative lack of resources, difficulties achieving economies of scale, reduced domestic audiences, and limited export potential. Peripherality should not be equated with smallness, although it similarly describes how, regardless of size, nations can be marginalized by imbalances in economic and cultural power. Examining how smallness and peripherality are actually experienced and inhabited by media professionals, Szczepanik offers a case study of independent producers in the Czech Republic to demonstrate the ways in which they articulate and act upon their positionality.

Michael Keane questions the explanatory value of terms like "soft power" or "flows" for conceptualizing East Asian media industries. Reflecting on the prominence of China's media industries, Keane argues claims of soft power – a concept used to describe how nations practice image management when seeking to exercise their influence globally by promoting the attractiveness of their political values or cultural beliefs – ignore the empirical actuality and complexity of media reception practices. Equally, describing transnational movements of media products, the flow metaphor misrepresents the Chinese context where quotas, censorship, and protectionism impede trade, and obscure processes actioned through exchanges of policies, people, and industry relationships.

Linking media industries to the built environment, Elizabeth Evans advances a new analytic direction focused on investigating the functions and meanings of media buildings. While these can include sites used as locational backdrops in media outputs or the structures supporting communication infrastructures, Evans is primarily interested in spaces regularly occupied in the quotidian workings of the media – offices, production facilities, and sites of consumption. For Evans, analyzing the purpose, design, location, and context of buildings delivers insights into the spaces of media work, the physicalization of managerial structures, organizational branding, and relationships between media industries and local communities.

While media production is always a fundamentally collective enterprise, interest, and belief in the primacy of individualized creative agency – sometimes conceptualized as "authorship" – persist. Eva Novrup Redvall highlights how tensions between authorship and collaboration, or the individual and industry, play out in the media industries. As she notes, the collective and institutionalized characteristics of media work challenge romantic ideas of solitary authorial autonomy, yet isolating individual contributions is a practical and financial consideration in matters such as the ownership of intellectual property, attribution of production credits, or the disbursement of royalty payments. Equally, issues of agency resonate in tales of creative or decision-making control versus organizational constraint, or the vulnerabilities of precarious employment. Rather than celebrate or dismiss authorship and agency, therefore, we might hold onto these foci as ways to unpack interfaces between individual and institutional power.

# 9

# INDUSTRIAL MEDIA STUDIES

## Considering infrastructures for audience manufacture

*Lee McGuigan*

What are the "media" in "media industries studies"? Without hesitation, we might list television, books, magazines, newspapers, sound recordings, video games, and more. At a general level, we could say that media are discernible constellations of apparatus, organizations, rules, and conventions involved in producing, circulating, and consuming uniquely meaningful representations or texts – namely, news and entertainment. The boundaries of a medium and its industry derive from technical features, business models, laws and regulations, aesthetic formats, cultural habits, loyalties to craft groups and career paths, and historical accidents. Put simply, this subfield concerns itself with the distinctive systems that provision *creative content* for *personal consumption*.

These traditional definitions can be useful. They provide bright-line parameters for highly detailed research, including both concrete and formalistic studies of markets, corporations, public policies, labor and professional cultures, textual patterns, technologies, and social welfare. They lend a sense of stability and coherence to the otherwise motley assemblages implied by a word like "television." But our taken-for-granted standbys also posit units of analysis and assumptions about society and history that delimit consideration of profound, critical questions; they gloss over the messiness of these sociotechnical assemblages; and they may even blunt the sorts of inquiry that could help us imagine and pursue radical possibilities. Referring to the investments in artificial intelligence and other machinic systems mustered by companies like Google and Microsoft, Graham Murdock (2018: 365) advocates a reappraisal: "Communications research needs to match the scope and ambition of these companies and expand the range of areas and applications it addresses."

Endorsing this prescription in full, I suggest that one way to follow it involves attending not only to fanciful and futuristic consumer products and experiences. We should also delve into more mundane territory – the bureaucratic, calculative, and logistical elements and activities that hold together media systems. Perhaps we need a new "administrative" research – not instrumental work serving corporate and/or state prerogatives, but critical and materialist research on the infrastructures that traffic information, coordinate and conduct relationships within and across firms, and configure forms of knowledge and power (see Parks and Starosielski 2015; Plantin and Punathambekar 2019). Our familiar creative texts constitute but one stream in the massive flows of capital, commerce, and data channeled by countless media of administration.

DOI: 10.4324/9780429275340-12

## Industrial media: Dirt research for digital capitalism

In asking how media industries are "made up," Nitin Govil (2013: 176) urges scholars "to broaden the range of practices that count as industrial." This chapter argues that we should also broaden the range of materials and practices that count as media, and that this will contribute to a fuller understanding of how industries are "made up." We should think not only of *media industries* (print, film, radio, TV, internet, etc.), but also of *industrial media* (wires, documents, databases, spreadsheets, algorithms, etc.). This pivot in emphasis jars us from fixating fully on media industries' visible, "textual" outputs, and instead invites us to consider the unseen inputs and infrastructures that make commercial relationships durable (or not).

I use the term industrial media for rhetorical effect. Much of what I refer to here is not categorically different from other aspects of bureaucracy and organization (Yates 1989). In fact, I am arguing precisely for what Beverungen, Beyes, and Conrad (2019) call a "medial" perspective, which sees organizing, in general, as constituted by media and forms of mediation. I have chosen to speak of industrial media because the term forces us to confront questions about the boundaries of our subfield. It calls into question our preoccupation with certain symbolic creations and symbol creators. It brings into focus a range of sociotechnical systems and forms of labor that don't factor into considerations of the creative and managerial work that contributes directly to consumer-facing texts and technologies. And it may permit a fuller inventory of participants in the production and commodification of culture.

So, what exactly count as industrial media? As a provocation, this chapter skews more toward being generative than discriminating. I would include things that media industries scholars have already considered: technologies of data extraction and analysis (Turow and Couldry, 2018); formats, protocols, and software for encoding and transporting messages (Braun 2013; Lobato 2019; Sterne 2012); hardware and interfaces for accessing content or services (Hesmondhalgh and Lotz 2020); legal instruments, like privacy policies and terms-of-service contracts, that secure corporate privileges to exploit personal data (Draper and Turow 2019); algorithms and "infomediaries" (Morris, 2015; Napoli 2014; Caplan and boyd 2018); and also technical support and workplace communications (Hughes 2014; Patterson 2020). In another thoughtful example, Johnson, Kompare, and Santo (2014) describe management in cultural production as a type of "discourse" – a productive force that assembles and enacts social arrangements, in part by categorizing and organizing knowledge. By emphasizing industrial media, I want to add a complementary focus on the sociomateriality of discourses – including ways of seeing and knowing. Of special interest here are technologies and procedures for measuring audiences (Bermejo 2007; Bourdon and Méadel 2011; Hessler 2019; Mattelart 1991; Meehan 2005; Napoli 2003; Petrie 2018).

More particularly, then, I have in mind various means for generating, processing, and circulating information, for configuring relationships and knowledge practices, and for facilitating communication and exchange. This includes all sorts of information technologies and (meta)data work that animate corporate spaces, as well as components embedded in homes, personal devices, and privatized public spaces. Think of sensors that participate in the creation of data about consumers (Andrejevic and Burdon 2015; Brodemerkel and Carah 2016); or tracking, profiling, and identification systems in retail environments (Elmer 2003; Gandy 1993; Turow 2017). Consider, also, the vast epistemological backend, where companies use artificial intelligence and other decision-support technologies to fabricate predictions and judgments (Goldenfein 2020). Out-of-home advertising, for example, fits the traditional ambit of media industries studies and calls to mind a set of interests, actors, and artifacts. But how do we accommodate digital billboards as components within the logistical designs we call "smart cities," wherein dynamically adaptive advertising is one financial and consumer-management strategy taking advantage of internet-connected devices (Gandy and Nemorin 2019; Shapiro 2020)? What new interests, actors, and artifacts enter our purview when billboards are detecting and responding to our movements, biometrics, and perceived emotions or cognitive capacities (McStay 2018)?

Perhaps a way to further clarify what I am getting at is to ask: how do media industries deal with information? How do organizations and individuals use media to record, analyze, count, classify – to know and order the realities in which they operate and to decide on and evaluate courses of action? These questions will require us to go down unusual paths and to cross our trusted borders. Even our understanding of any specific industry is incomplete without accounting for its means of moving information – not to mention cultural industries' entanglements with theories and policies of an "information society" (Garnham 2005; Schiller 2007). Computerization, to take a dramatic example, is inseparable from how companies have thought about and constructed audiences and consumer populations (Turow 2011). Decades before news and entertainment were encoded as binary digits, digital technologies were part of the knowledge infrastructures and information regimes that constituted layers of administration in "legacy" media (McGuigan 2019).

I suggest the value of shifting from media industries studies to industrial media studies through a discussion of advertising and audience commodification, which today must be recognized to implicate a wide range of "data-driven" marketing activities, including behavioral tracking and profiling. These activities are substantially oriented around the production (and automation) of strategic predictions and judgments, around information processing and decision-making. They mobilize industrial media for capturing elements of reality, formatting and storing that data in particular ways, and circulating and analyzing the data to generate a whole range of resources and claims – such as estimates of a consumer's lifetime value to a firm, or the probability that a user will click on an ad. These are bedrock features of media industries, and sites for observing interconnections with broader systems of discrimination, accumulation, and control. Industrial media are important sinews and circulatory systems for a data- and surveillance-intensive form of capitalism (Sadowski 2019; West 2019).

Inspired by Charles Acland's (2014) call for "dirt research" in media industries studies, I want us to dig deeper into the production of culture, beneath operations for handling "creative" content, to sift out the vital operations necessary for turning human attention and behavior into commodities. Acland is referring to the methodological approach encouraged by historian and political economist Harold Innis, who excavated nitty-gritty details about the many materials, techniques, and institutions that configure knowledge, culture, commerce, and power, and how these broadly defined media relate to the durability of social arrangements. This involved retracing trading routes and collecting receipts and other market ephemera. Our account of "media" is incomplete if it misses these often-invisible means for orienting industrial thought and action.

Media industries studies would benefit from a serious effort to theorize media. Acland lights a useful path for beginning this excursion, since Innis (1950) located media at the heart of economic history, social organization, and cultural continuity and change. Drawing on this tradition, John Durham Peters (2015: 19) pushes us to look beyond the "message-bearing institutions" that dominated twentieth-century thinking, to recognize that media "have always been in the business of recording, transmitting, and processing culture; of managing subjects, objects, and data; of organizing time, space, and power." Media, Peters argues, "are fundamental constituents of organization."

Like the "transparent intermediaries" (Braun 2013) that support content distribution by translating file formats, negotiating interchange across junctions, and handling other logistics that end-users don't see, industrial media are *infrastructural*. Infrastructures are not just big, physical constructions, like broadcast towers or cable plant; more generally, they are pervasive, enabling (or disabling) resources and relationships, and they include small components and administrative protocols (Star 1999). Referring again to Innis, Edward Comor (2017) regards media similarly as "means of organizing and sustaining power-laden relations" (p. 183). Media "imply the structuring of capacities – the parameters of what is possible or impossible, imaginable or unimaginable" (p. 188). They are "developed, applied, or modified to mediate capacities concerning power and knowledge" (p. 189). Media, Peters (2015: 2) says, are "infrastructures of data and control."

The ambitions of this essay are far more modest than Innis's approach to media theory, in that they still focus on those industries the twentieth century regarded uniquely as "*the media.*" But we might bring new insights to this subfield by admitting a broader appreciation of media as ordering infrastructures for knowledge, power, and the many relationships among actors and artifacts that "make up" industrial systems. Thinking in this way helps bring to light essential coordinating functions that hold together critical parts of traditional media industries, where documents and data register more than sounds and images. This might give us cause for considering how media industries share important affinities with other information-intensive forms of capital, like finance and insurance. Historian Dan Bouk (2015: xxi) draws our attention to the industrial media of contracts and invoices when he points out that the process for turning a resource like grain into a commodity "set[s] quite a bit of paper in motion." So it is with commodifying human attention.

## Audience commodification

Historically, and still today, revenue from advertisers has been a financial engine across print, broadcasting, and electronic media. A well-established tradition in critical media studies has analyzed how these businesses sell audiences to advertisers. Perhaps the most forceful statement on the audience-as-commodity originates with Dallas Smythe (1977). Smythe argues that as people attend to advertisements and the news and entertainment those ads help finance, they learn habits of consumption and consequently work at reproducing themselves, their labor power, and capitalist social relations. Smythe's thesis has been critiqued and adapted extensively. Sut Jhally and Bill Livant (1986) suggest that it is not advertisers but the owners of the means of communication and/or intellectual property who profit from the "work of watching." Eileen Meehan (1984) introduces an important insight by distinguishing actual audiences (or publics) from the commodity audiences represented as "ratings" – information products assembled through market-focused metrological procedures. Where Smythe, Jhally, and Livant sketch, with different emphases, the relationships linking advertisers, corporate media, and consumers, Meehan points out the importance of information service providers, particularly in rendering certain consumption-related activities and attributes as "knowable" and exchangeable.

Research following from this "blindspot debate" – so-called because of Smythe's claim that media industries were a blind spot in Marxian political economy – is too vast to summarize here (see McGuigan and Manzerolle 2014). Suffice it to say that many critical media scholars are probably familiar with some variation of the argument that media users, their attention, and/or their data are the products of ad-supported industries. The argument has also travelled beyond academia. For example, Tim Wu's 2017 book *The Attention Merchants* packaged some of these ideas for a broader readership, giving the press and the public a vocabulary to talk critically about the business models powering Google, YouTube, Facebook, Instagram, and many more websites and mobile apps.

The title of Wu's book makes plain that when advertisers buy audiences, they are really paying to access the *attention* of potentially valuable customers or voters. In most cases, of course, advertisers want to go further still. They pursue what Oscar Gandy (1993) calls the production of sales, or more generally, the production of influence. But influence is a difficult thing to guarantee; and although a close look at the evolution of marketing communications reveals dogged efforts to institute the sorts of industrial media that could better predict and confirm returns on marketing investments (Mattelart 1991), advertisers mostly have had to settle short of buying sales or influence. And, so, we say they buy "audiences," or "eyeballs," or "attention." But can these "things" be bought? We hope no company is plucking eyeballs from their sockets – though eye-tracking has a past and, most likely, a future in audience manufacture. Terms like "attention economy" are usefully provocative and suggest the vital social importance of human cognition and collective energy. Yet we don't often consider how attention is packaged as a discrete product.

Borrowing a term from Karl Polanyi, political economist Zoe Sherman (2014) argues that audience attention is a "fictitious commodity." Polanyi (1944) famously claimed that resources like land and labor do not exist in nature as commodities, and to compel them to behave as commodities that conform to market dynamics requires an intensive effort, often coordinated by government. This helps illuminate the powerful role occupied by companies like Nielsen, which provide authoritative measurements of audiences (Meehan 2005; Napoli 2003). Of course, we need to be careful when speaking of audience attention as a natural resource. As Meehan and others have taught us, commodity audiences are not naturally occurring phenomena waiting to be observed; they are constructed and manifested by particular ways of defining, measuring, and packaging consumer activities and attributes. A media audience is, in the perceptive words of Marcel Rosa-Salas, "a commodity invented by and through the knowledge practices of media industry professionals invested in understanding people *as* consumers" (original emphasis 2019: 26). Likewise, the forms of attention that are eligible for observation are at least partly determined by elements of the media environment. For example, Taina Bucher (2018) shows how the algorithmic and commercial logics designed into Facebook enact certain modes of sociality; some forms of connection and expression count more than others – both in that they are considered more important and in that they are carefully enumerated. As Joseph Turow (1984: 75) concluded decades ago, audience research "does not provide a more accurate image of the true audience" so much as it "elaborates upon and makes explicit the categories of the target population" that most interest the corporations involved. Jérôme Bourdon and Cécile Méadel (2011: 799) lay bare the issue: "The audience can never be considered independently of the instruments used to 'measure' it."

The point is that the process of audience commodification *operationalizes* attention – as well as consumer identities and behaviors – in particular ways. Attention is not just measured, it is produced and formatted within a discernable set of institutions and infrastructures. When we speak of a marketplace for audiences or attention, then, we are talking about the trade in *evidence of attention*, however it might be packaged. That marketplace is a site of contest and compromise, as the interests of buyers and sellers are negotiated in the construction and stabilization of a product whose tangible existence is defined precisely through those exchange relations. Ratings, or other operationalized evidence of attention, can be considered a "medium" of exchange – a currency that facilitates thought and transactions within a market (Napoli 2003). Audience ratings are an example of a "socially constructed information regime," through which actors perceive and relate to their organizational field (Anand and Peterson 2000). "Within media industries," as Joshua Braun (2013: 135) puts it, "audiences constitute an essential but complex unknown whose wants, needs, opinions, and interests must be selectively measured and simplified to produce an actionable market."

## Information, knowledge, and power

The concept of market or audience information regimes helps us recognize larger questions about the production of knowledge, rationality, or decision-making capacities within firms and industries. What can be known and how knowledge can be mobilized depends, both materially and in terms of affordances (or perceived possibility), on the architectures through which actors in cultural industries record, interpret, and tame the realities in which they operate. Even something as simple as how information about advertising inventory is communicated can affect the orientations of buyers and sellers in a market (McGuigan 2019).

To talk about information and knowledge infrastructures might seem a grand vocabulary for describing decision-making practices often characterized as instinctive and unsystematic. But decisions that seem like "gut feeling" still typically involve some ensemble of devices for apprehending aspects of reality, however unsophisticated by contemporary standards, as well as repertoires of sensemaking that enjoy legitimacy in a time and a place. For all the limitations of Nielsen ratings, for example, decision-makers can appeal to "the numbers" as a legible and authoritative justification for choices that are inherently risky. As Todd Gitlin (2000: 42–43) observes in his classic study of the US television networks' organizational cultures, "the people who specialize in gathering and evaluating the numbers have climbed high in the hierarchies ... These executives were able to convert the hard currency of numbers into a reputation for the right decisions, or at least the right way of going about decisions." The "language of numbers," Gitlin reports, "has become the language of first and last resort, the prime language in which the networks carry out their business."

This discussion points to the relevance of another concept from Innis's toolkit. Innis (1950) used the term "monopoly of knowledge" to indicate how well-positioned experts leverage claims to mastery over means of communication/information. Influence within social organizations can be mediated and concentrated through the prism of the conceptual systems and craft skills enacted (and protected) by "a cadre of specialists" (Peters 2015: 21). Audience ratings provide a straightforward example of how a cadre of specialists, invested with authority to define reality, produce a form of "truth" that mediates relationships, procedures, and assessments of value. It is a monopoly both with respect to the concentrated market power of technical experts and in that cognitive capacities, organizational structures, and allocations of resources are mediated through a relatively singular way of seeing and knowing. The construction of information regimes, so central to media industries, is a bottleneck for the exercise of power, raising important questions about legitimacy, expertise, and authority.

Over at least the last half century, quantitative technicians have harnessed their interests and authority to means of generating, sorting, circulating, and making sense of information, both responding to and advancing certain ways of thinking about individuals and social segments (Arvidsson 2004). It will surprise almost no one to read that "data-driven" decision-making rules in many areas of cultural industries. Data scientists are heralded (and hired) as high priests in media and marketing firms – and companies with core competencies in "tech" or "analytics" manage an expanding portfolio of functions in media industries, while traditional media and advertising companies maneuver to accentuate their calculative capacities. Experts in big data, artificial intelligence, and other computational and statistical ways of seeing, knowing, and managing social worlds have laid authoritative claims to "truth" within these organizational fields.

While we're prone to considering this a new and disruptive arrangement, the quantitative evolution in marketing and audience manufacture is an *extension* of longstanding priorities – toward efficiency, optimization, personalization. At least since a theory of market segmentation gained traction in the mid-twentieth century, pressures toward precision targeting have motivated investments in, and consequently empowered, the information and analytics services that advertising agencies and others have provided to help identify and profile consumers, buy access to the right people at the right moments, and generally to isolate finer profit opportunities in marketing and media buying (Turow 2011). A social and economic logic of discrimination has been built into and enacted through the sociotechnical systems and monopolies of knowledge that structure many parts of ad-supported cultural production (Gandy 1993).

Whatever the ethical valence of discrimination in any situation, it is an exercise in recognizing and distinguishing the imputed value of different people. Discrimination in marketing and audience manufacture is not just a disposition (i.e., the perception that some people are worth more than others), but a *process* that is executed and reproduced. That process enlists many industrial media for purposes of observation, identification, evaluation, prediction, and intervention. A very quick survey of just some of the industrial media involved in advertising today offers a window on an infrastructure for administering discrimination – what is now called "ad tech."

## Ad tech: discrimination by design

Just putting ads in front of media users is an involved affair. Digital video ad insertion, for example, makes use of server and decision-making technologies, including the set-top boxes (STBs) used for subscription television and app-based internet streaming services. These networked systems execute instructions that, given variable inputs, trigger the delivery of certain ads. Accounting for details about the inventory (e.g., the presumed recipient) and campaign parameters, ad servers will make decisions to satisfy publishers' obligations to buyers or to regulate buyers' spending. These devices also record logs of ads served, and so they can perform detailed measurement functions. STBs, for example, now belong to the list of components for assembling television ratings, which historically has included telephones, paper diaries, audimeters that record the tuning of a TV set, and portable people meters that detect an audio signature encoded into a broadcast (that audio signature is itself an example of the industrial media we should take seriously [see Hessler 2019: 14–15]). Increasingly with internet-connected TV sets, viewing behaviors are observed with automated content recognition (ACR) technologies, which can track the pixels rendered on a screen and recognize metadata that identify a piece of content. This "glass-level" measurement enables ACR services to collect a complete history of viewing, regardless of distribution source (e.g., cable provider, streaming app, etc.). And it is now well documented that "over-the-top" (OTT) video service apps and devices are collecting user information and sending it to dozens or hundreds of third-party trackers. Importantly, server logs and platform-specific tracking often involve different dynamics than third-party, sample-based audience ratings. An OTT service, for example, can promise granular and exhaustive records of user activities, but its insights are specific to that population of users (not generalizable to people not directly observed), and the market actors relying on these measurements often complain that the platform company, in reporting on audiences and ad impressions, is "grading its own homework."

Web browsers and mobile devices factor crucially into audience manufacture today, supported by a dizzying variety of familiar and obscure industrial media. Web cookies, beacons, and pixels are examples of data collection and storage formats used to assign persistent identifiers to browsers and their users, so that advertisers and publishers may recognize individuals across sites or sessions, build profiles of behaviors, and distinguish one profile from another. While behavioral targeting often draws critics' focus, surveillance and identification are also important for "attribution" services, which try to determine or make data-based guesses about causality between advertising and business outcomes. Identifying and tracking users *across devices* is thus a top priority for marketers and attention merchants today, and so we see various schemes for trying to determine who is using specific devices. Mobile phone operating systems generate a numerical code to identify a device for ad targeting and measurement – AdID for Google's Android, and Identifier for Advertisers (IDFA) on Apple iPhones. Other marketing trackers, exploiting permissions granted to a downloaded app, for example, can "fingerprint" a smartphone or browser by taking stock of its unique collection of apps, software versions, fonts, and so on. This inventory of elements is distinctive for virtually every device, providing an extremely personal identifier without divulging "personally identifiable information" (one of the slyest euphemisms in advertising). A few companies also attach universal IDs to individuals so that publishers, advertisers, and intermediaries can reconcile the discrete profiles associated with devices, social media accounts, IP addresses, or other data sets.

The hope for marketers is to tell the difference between users, to make bets about their worth and their responses to specific stimuli with competitively high probability, and to verify outcomes with greater confidence because those target consumers can be followed across the entire "path to purchase."

These elements feed into a complex ecosystem of automated auctions for buying and selling audience impressions. Here, in "programmatic advertising," we find supply-side platforms (SSPs), demand-side platforms (DSPs), ad exchanges, and data management platforms (DMPs) – often all lumped together as forms of "ad tech." SSPs began as decision-support systems that predicted which advertising sales network was likely to return the best price for the inventory supplied by a publisher. Today SSPs have been largely absorbed as part of the ad exchanges that execute auctions. DSPs started by helping ad-buyers allocate budgets and manage workflows, and then began to bid directly into the auctions on behalf of clients. DMPs sell data services both to SSPs that want to package audiences more rationally, and to DSPs that want to make smarter bids on impressions – largely based on cookie matching to identify users across contexts, but also including the brokerage of data from various sources. This is currently the infrastructure for most online advertising, though regulatory and policy changes, and the gradual crumbling of a cookie-based ecosystem, raise serious questions about its future.

Information, impressions, and investments speed through this system by way of countless industrial media and various types of engineering, administrative, and marketing labor – including the often-overlooked work required just to prepare datasets for even basic usage and to manually facilitate "automation." While ad tech wears a glossy digital sheen, a properly historical perspective should apply the term to any and all information and communication technologies involved in advertising transactions and audience commodification. The lifeblood of advertising and media organizations, especially as pertaining to the commodification of audience attention, circulates through networked computers and databases, paper work and filing methods, modes of statistical inference and prediction, traffic and billing systems, and identification schemes that not only classify consumer targets, but also facilitate documentation and management of types of inventory, specific ad units, the participants in exchanges, and so on. And that's to say nothing of the tactics for perpetrating and defending against the billion-dollar business of ad-fraud.

The production and exchange of media audiences (and, of course, the broader and scientifically managed sales effort of which advertising is one part) mobilizes an array of instruments, knowledge practices, and data infrastructures – it depends on and urges development of institutions and infrastructures far beyond those that populate studies centered on content and consumer experiences. Studying these processes reveals that research into media industries – like other industries affected by the computerization and actuarialism characteristic of informational or digital capitalism – needs to engage with science and technology studies and traditions of media theory that cast media as the connective tissues of social organization and all the power-laden relationships that come with it.

## Conclusion

What media contribute to the production of culture? Is culture produced only through expressive texts that represent ideas and ways of being? What about the media that format information about, and practices in, the world? For good reasons, scholars have emphasized that media industries are uniquely important because their products depict and potentially influence human thought and action – though the population deserving this unique status is hardly obvious. But we should also consider how the industries typically understood as producing consciousness and culture are among a group of sectors directly involved in observing, quantifying, commodifying, and managing human life. Sensitivity to certain boundaries of technology, policy, or cultural practice is crucial; but to have these definitions delimit the field of inquiry narrows our focus and denies critical media researchers our full participation in analyzing the political economy of capitalism and the institutional and infrastructural bases of social and commercial organization across a range of domains. When we start from consideration of the industrial media involved in shaping, ordering, and circulating knowledge, materials, bodies, and other matter in a range of formats, we have a warrant to assert our place in conversations at the heart of all social sciences and humanities. Newspapers, film, broadcasting, and streaming – these are important, even epoch-shaping categories; but media are at the crux of social formation, of making human and material relationships concrete and durable. It is important to study media industries, but we should keep our eye on a larger unit of analysis – the *mediation* of cultural and political-economic relationships.

None of this is to deny the importance of the stories people tell, but instead to further examine the circuitry affecting who gets to tell what stories and how those stories travel. It also puts a spotlight on organizational discourses – like ratings, metrics, and predictions – that might not seem like "stories" at all from a different perspective. I have tried to show that industrial media are levers of power; they are resources, situations, and sites for negotiating and enacting authoritative ways of seeing, knowing, and managing social worlds. Industrial media draw our attention to questions about what counts: What people and phenomena are considered important? What actors, arts, and artifacts are involved in counting those people and phenomena, or making these or other parts of reality visible and manageable? In the end, we must ask ourselves, what do we really want to know and how do we hope to intervene? I worry that "media industries studies" implies a mandate that is fatally limited. For this subfield to account for the industrial production of culture and to have force and relevance in conversations about technology, information, communication, and power in today's societies, we need to ask much more of our "media."

## References

Acland, C. R. (2014) "Dirt Research for Media Industries," *Media Industries*, 1 (1): 6–10.

Anand, N. and Peterson, R. A. (2000) "When Marketing Information Constitutes Fields: Sensemaking of Markets in the Commercial Music Industry," *Organization Science*, 11 (3): 270–284.

Andrejevic, M. and Burdon, M. (2015) "Defining the Sensor Society," *Television and New Media*, 16 (1): 19–36.

Arvidsson, A. (2004) "On the 'Pre-History of the Panoptic Sort': Mobility in Market Research," *Surveillance & Society*, 1 (4): 456–474.

Bermejo, F. (2007) *The Internet Audience: Measurement and Constitution*, New York: Peter Lang.

Beverungen, A., Beyes, T., and Conrad, L. (2019) "The Organizational Powers of (Digital) Media," *Organization*, 26 (5): 621–635.

Bouk, D. (2015) *How Our Days Became Numbered: Risk and the Rise of the Statistical Individual*, Chicago, IL: University of Chicago Press.

Bourdon, J. and Méadel, C. (2011) "Inside Television Audience Measurement: Deconstructing the Ratings Machine," *Media, Culture and Society*, 33 (5): 791–800.

Braun, J. (2013) "Transparent Intermediaries: Building the Infrastructure of Connected Viewing," in K. Sansom and J. Holt (eds), *Connected Viewing: Selling, Streaming & Sharing in the Digital Era*, New York: Routledge, 124–143.

Brodmerkel, S. and Carah, N. (2016) *Brand Machines, Sensory Media and Calculative Culture*, London: Palgrave Macmillan.

Bucher, T. (2018) *If…Then: Algorithmic Power and Politics*, New York: Oxford University Press.

Caplan, R. and boyd, D. (2018) "Isomorphism Through Algorithms: Institutional Dependencies in the Case of Facebook," *Big Data & Society*, available at https://journals.sagepub.com/doi/full/10.1177/2053951718757253 (accessed December 2, 2020).

Comor, E. (2017) "Ubiquitous Media and Monopolies of Knowledge: The Approach of Harold Innis," in M. S. Daubs and V. R. Manzerolle (eds), *Mobile and Ubiquitous Media: Critical and International Perspectives*, New York: Peter Lang, 183–200.

Draper, N. and Turow, J. (2019) "The Corporate Cultivation of Digital Resignation," *New Media and Society*, 21 (8): 1824–1839.

Elmer, G. (2003.) *Profiling Machines: Mapping the Personal Information Economy*, Cambridge, MA: MIT Press.

Gandy, O. H., Jr. (1993) *The Panoptic Sort: A Political Economy of Personal Information*, Boulder, CO: Westview Press.

Gandy, O. H., Jr. and Nemorin, S. (2019) "Toward a Political Economy of Nudge: Smart City Variations," *Information, Communication and Society*, 22 (14): 2112–2126.

Garnham, N. (2005) "From Cultural to Creative Industries," *International Journal of Cultural Policy*, 11 (1): 15–29.

Gitlin, T. (2000) *Inside Prime Time*, Berkley, CA: University of California Press.

Goldenfein, J. (2020) *Monitoring Laws: Profiling and Identity in the World State*, Cambridge: Cambridge University Press.

Govil, N. (2013) "Recognizing 'Industry,'" *Cinema Journal*, 52 (3): 172–176.

Hesmondhalgh, D. and Lotz, A. D. (2020) "Video Screen Interfaces as New Sites of Media Circulation Power," *International Journal of Communication*, 14: 386–409.

Hessler, J. (2019) "Peoplemeter Technologies and the Biometric Turn in Audience Measurement," *Television and New Media*, available at https://journals.sagepub.com/doi/abs/10.1177/1527476419879415 (accessed December 2, 2020).

Hughes, K. (2014) "'Work/Place Media: Locating Laboring Audiences," *Media, Culture and Society*, 36 (5): 644–660.

Innis, H. A. (1950) *Empire and Communications*, Toronto: University of Toronto Press.

Jhally, S. and Livant, B. (1986) "Watching as Working: The Valorization of Audience Consciousness," *Journal of Communication*, 36 (3): 124–143.

Johnson, D., Kompare, D., and Santo, A. (2014) "Introduction: Discourses, Dispositions, Tactics: Reconceiving Management in Critical Media Industry Studies," in *Making Media Work: Cultures of Management in the Entertainment Industries*, New York: New York University Press, 1–21.

Lobato, R. (2019) *Netflix Nations: The Geography of Digital Distribution*, New York: New York University Press.

Mattelart, A. (1991) *Advertising International: The Privatisation of Public Space*, New York: Routledge.

McGuigan, L. (2019) "Automating the Audience Commodity: The Unacknowledged Ancestry of Programmatic Advertising," *New Media and Society*, 21 (11/12): 2366–2385.

McGuigan, L. and Manzerolle, V. (eds) (2014) *The Audience Commodity in a Digital Age*, New York: Peter Lang.

McStay, A. (2018) *Emotional AI: The Rise of Empathic Media*, Los Angeles, CA: Sage.

Meehan, E. R. (1984) "Ratings and the Institutional Approach: A Third Answer to the Commodity Question," *Critical Studies in Mass Communication*, 1 (2): 216–225.

Meehan, E. R. (2005) *Why TV is not Our Fault: Television Programming, Viewers, and Who's Really in Control*, Lanham, MD: Rowman & Littlefield.

Morris, J. W. (2015) "Curation by Code: Infomediaries and the Data Mining of Taste," *European Journal of Cultural Studies*, 18 (4–5): 446–463.

Murdock, G. (2018) "Media Materialities: For a Moral Economy of Machines," *Journal of Communication*, 68 (2): 359–368.

Napoli, P. M. (2003) *Audience Economics: Media Institutions and the Audience Marketplace*, New York: Columbia University Press.

Napoli, P. M. (2014) "Automated Media: An Institutional Theory Perspective on Algorithmic Media Production and Consumption," *Communication Theory*, 24 (3): 340–360.

Parks, L. and Starosielski, N. (eds) (2015) *Signal Traffic: Critical Studies of Media Infrastructures*, Urbana, IL: University of Illinois Press.

Patterson, E. (2020) "Maintaining Transmission: DirecTV's Work-at-home Technical Support, Virtual Surveillance, and the Gendered Domestication of Distributive Labor," *Television and New Media*, available at https://journals.sagepub.com/doi/abs/10.1177/1527476420928552?ai=1gvoi&mi=3ricys&af=R (accessed December 2, 2020).

Peters, J. D. (2015) *The Marvelous Clouds: Toward a Philosophy of Elemental Media*, Chicago, IL: University of Chicago Press.

Petre, C. (2018) "Engineering Consent: How the Design and Marketing of Newsroom Analytics Tools Rationalize Journalists' Labor," *Digital Journalism*, 6 (4): 509–527.

Plantin, J. and Punathambekar, A. (2019) "Digital Media Infrastructures: Pipes, Platforms, and Politics," *Media, Culture and Society*, 41 (2): 163–174.

Polanyi, K. (1944) *The Great Transformation*, Boston, MA: Beacon Press.

Rosa-Salas, M. (2019) "Making the Mass White: How Racial Segregation Shaped Consumer Segmentation," in G. D. Johnson, K. D. Thomas, A. K. Harrison, and S. A. Grier (eds), *Race in the Marketplace: Crossing Critical Boundaries*, Basingstoke: Palgrave Macmillan, 21–38.

Sadowski, J. (2019) "When Data is Capital: Datafication, Accumulation, and Extraction," *Big Data and Society*, available at https://journals.sagepub.com/doi/full/10.1177/2053951718820549 (accessed December 2, 2020).

Schiller, D. (2007) *How to Think About Information*, Urbana, IL: University of Illinois Press.

Shaprio, A. (2020) *Design, Control, Predict: Logistical Governance in the Smart City*, Minneapolis, MN: University of Minnesota Press.

Sherman, Z. (2014) "Pricing the Eyes of Passersby: The Commodification of Audience Attention in U.S. Public Spaces, 1890–1920," *Review of Radical Political Economics*, 46 (4): 502–508.

Smythe, D. W. (1977) "Communications: Blindspot of Western Marxism," *Canadian Journal of Political and Social Theory*, 1 (3): 1–27.

Star, S. L. (1999) "The Ethnography of Infrastructure," *American Behavioral Scientist*, 43 (3): 377–391.

Sterne, J. (2012) *MP3: The Meaning of a Format*, Durham, NC: Duke University Press.

Turow, J. (1984) *Media Industries: The Production of News and Entertainment*, New York: Longman.

Turow, J. (2011) *The Daily You: How the New Advertising Industry Is Defining Your Identity and Your Worth*, New Haven, CT: Yale University Press.

Turow, J. (2017) *The Aisles Have Eyes: How Retailers Track Your Shopping, Strip Your Privacy, and Define Your Power*, New Haven, CT: Yale University Press.

Turow, J. and Couldry, N. (2018) "Media as Data Extraction: Towards a New Map of a Transformed Communications Field," *Journal of Communication*, 68 (2): 415–423.

West, S. M. (2019) "Data Capitalism: Redefining the Logics of Surveillance and Privacy," *Business and Society*, 58 (1): 20–41.

Wu, T. (2017) *The Attention Merchants: The Epic Scramble to Get Inside Our Heads*, New York: Vintage.

Yates, J. (1989) *Control Through Communication: The Rise of System in American Management*, Baltimore, MD: Johns Hopkins University Press.

# 10

# THE INFRASTRUCTURAL TURN IN MEDIA AND INTERNET RESEARCH[1]

*David Hesmondhalgh*

In recent years, media studies (including "screen studies" and television studies, among other sub-fields) and internet studies have paid increasing attention to the concept of *infrastructure*, and to the related concept of *distribution*. In everyday usage, the term infrastructure refers to "the basic systems and services that are necessary for a country or an organization to run smoothly, for example buildings, transport and water and power supplies" (*Oxford English Dictionary*, n.d.). There could hardly be a more timely concept in an era where the COVID-19 pandemic has made clear how dependent more or less everyone is on such systems and services. As we shall see, however, the term has come to be used in a diffuse range of ways in media and internet research.

Interest in infrastructure within media and internet studies has often built upon earlier research on infrastructures in social science and humanities, especially sociology of science and technology, anthropology, and geography (see Larkin 2013 for a fine survey that covers these fields). The recent revival of distribution as a key concept in media studies is closely related to the growth of interest in infrastructure, and the growing concern with both concepts can ultimately be attributed to the challenges to existing models of communication thrown up by the internet and the web from the 1990s onward.

In this chapter, I discuss some of the benefits for media and internet research generated by the "infrastructural turn" and the associated turn to distribution. These advantages include a welcome concern with the mundanity and ordinariness of existing systems rather than optimistic speculation about future impacts, and an invigorating interest in questions of representation and meaning in relation to often taken-for-granted technologies. But when terms and concepts become fashionable in academia, problems often arise, and so I also want to discuss some of the problems surrounding these turns: a tendency in media and internet studies to use the term "infrastructure" in such a variety of ways that the term risks losing its analytical value; an uncertain engagement with ideas of materiality and "relationality"; and a tendency toward banality and vagueness (including dubious defenses of vagueness itself). I close by reflecting on how the problems identified seem to have led to a neglect of other traditions of research, such as political economy of media, that might provide insights into the workings of media infrastructures as traditionally understood, but in a call for synthesis, I also point to how those other traditions have often failed to pay due attention to the best contributions of recent media infrastructural studies.

DOI: 10.4324/9780429275340-13

## Studies of media and information infrastructures: Development and contributions

Underlying a great deal of recent work on media infrastructures has been a desire to puncture inflated and generalized claims about networked information systems by emphasizing the *mundane* combinations of technological and social factors that allow such systems to function. Many discussions of infrastructure in media and internet studies refer to the work of the sociologist Susan Leigh Star. In a much-cited piece on "The Ethnography of Infrastructure", Star (1999) pointed to the potential benefits of studying the most ordinary, everyday aspects of the information systems that, at the time she was writing, were emerging from the commercialization of digital networks. "Information infrastructure" had become a popular term in public and media debate about the future of computing in the 1990s, as policymakers pondered the construction of a new "national information infrastructure." Seeking to challenge technicist understandings of infrastructure in such debates, Star and her collaborators provocatively used the term to refer as much to social and organizational factors, most notably classifications and standards (Bowker and Star 1999), as to technical, material ones. In doing so, Star borrowed from her colleague and husband Geoffrey Bowker, another sociologist of science and technology, who had previously called for what he termed *infrastructural inversion* (Bowker 1994: 10), importing a metaphor from psychology to argue that "ground" or background infrastructural elements should be treated as "figure" or foreground. Picking up on this, Star (1999: 377) advocated the study of "boring things," such as wires, settings, and engineering standards. The version of media and information infrastructural studies propagated by Star, Bowker, and others in the 1990s and 2000s, focused on mundanity, helped to counter prevalent discourses, which saw the internet as imbued with rebellion and adventure (Streeter 2011: 119–137).

Star and her colleagues, in other words, sought to de-romanticize and demystify information, and the focus on the ordinary and taken-for-granted in studies of "information infrastructures" was to prove appealing to many social science and humanities researchers. The most eloquent advocate of such boringness has been the communication scholar John Durham Peters, for whom a focus on infrastructures helps counter a habit, shared by academics and many others, of "isolating the bright, shiny, new or scary parts of our made environment and calling them 'technology' to the neglect of the older, seemingly duller parts" (2015: 36). In this respect, infrastructural studies fit with a long-standing desire in media and cultural studies to question what is taken for granted, and to make obscured processes, systems, and values more visible.

Infrastructural studies, in the mode shaped by Star, Bowker and others, was one of a number of strands of social science research, especially in sociology, that paid close attention to the social and cultural factors influencing the form and use of technologies in ways that challenged mainstream understandings of technology within science, engineering and public policy. There was a body of research that, from the 1980s onward, had focused on "the social construction of technical systems" (Bijker, Hughes, and Pinch 1987) or the "social shaping of technology" (MacKenzie and Wajcman 1999), challenging science, engineering and public policy's often excessive focus on the agency of technology itself. Sometimes intersecting with these strands, though in some ways at odds with it, was actor network theory (ANT), focused (at least initially, before it expanded into other domains) on how scientific and technological knowledge was produced out of relations and associations between "actors," used in a very particular way to refer to objects and practices, as much as humans (Michael 2017). A term widely used for these sociologically oriented ways of studying science and technology, often focused on their most mundane aspects, is science and technology studies (STS). Very little STS research had paid attention to the concept of infrastructure until Star, Bowker, and their associates published their influential research, so the information infrastructuralists deserve credit for expanding the range of STS.[2] They also paid much greater attention to the communicative dimensions of science and technology communities and organizations than previous STS work.

It is important to realize, however, that the sense of infrastructure invoked by Star, Bowker, and their colleagues was in many ways quite at odds with how the term is generally used – for example, the *Oxford English Dictionary* definition quoted at the beginning of this chapter. Instead, the new infrastructural theorists derived their understandings of infrastructure from public policy debates of their time. In seeking to develop a "national information infrastructure" in the early 1990s, US policymakers had begun to use the term to refer not to networks of computer hardware and connecting cables, as in everyday understandings of infrastructure, but rather to a whole set of services and standards that could be developed and distributed using the internet. These services and standards included those pertaining to apps and software, but now infrastructure was extended to cover the people who "create the information, develop the apps and services, construct the facilities, and train others" (IITF, cited in Frederiksen and Schmidt 2018: 184), and even "the information itself" that would be carried over the internet, such as video programming, images, scientific databases, and archives. As Frederiksen and Schmidt (2018: 184) point out, "information superstructure" would actually be a more accurate term for such people and services than information infrastructure.

Nevertheless, even though the new information infrastructural studies took up this strange definition, to include not only people but also services that were centered on media *content*, neither this new strand of research, nor the STS tradition it was aligned with, paid much attention at all to media and communication research. And it took some time after the publication of Star and her colleagues' influential writings for the concept of infrastructure to become fashionable in media and communication studies. One of the earliest works that is regularly cited as part of the infrastructural turn in humanities and social sciences, and that actually addresses communication media, is Brian Larkin's 2008 book on Nigeria. Larkin traced a historical shift, from the installation of media infrastructure as part of imperialist projects that sought to impose Western modernity on colonial subjects, for example via mobile cinema and radio, to the development of new infrastructures based on informal "pirate" economies, in the form of Nigeria's booming video industry in the 2000s (Larkin 2008). His focus was still on the mundane, the ordinary and the overlooked, as in the earlier research on information infrastructures, but now with much greater attention to questions of culture and representation, and to the Global South and historical legacies of colonialism. In these respects, Larkin's interest in infrastructure was inspired by developing critical research on the subject in anthropology and urban geography (Larkin 2013).

The real surge in media infrastructural studies came somewhat later, however, in a series of publications from around 2012 onward. A key figure has been Lisa Parks, who developed further Larkin's interest in questions of *representation*, emphasizing "the multiple ways that [media] infrastructures have become intelligible to citizen-consumers and intersect with cultures of everyday life" (2013: 288), and focusing on the "infrastructural imaginaries" (Parks 2015: 355) that develop around media. By this term, Parks meant "ways of thinking about what infrastructures are, where they are located, who controls them, and what they do" (p. 355). In the compelling essay where she introduced this concept, Parks (2015) analyzed three contrasting examples of the representation of infrastructure: a 1903 documentary about mail sorters, a contemporary art project about telephone "linemen" (who work on the poles carrying telephone wires), and a series of photographs and videos of the destruction by police of satellite dishes in Iran. Each case demonstrated a different case of the human work involved in enabling or disabling the distribution of communication messages – and this focus on labor was to be another positive feature of the infrastructural turn in media. In another contribution, Parks (2013) examined changing modes of the representation of communication infrastructure in maps and diagrams, and in particular how one particular layer incorporated within Google Earth, "FCC Info," a radio and television search engine, offered a degree of transparent public information about media infrastructure in the United States, in contrast with the proprietary information created by mapping companies that sell their services to infrastructure industries themselves.

Parks also emphasized the potential methodological value of visiting infrastructure sites, a challenge taken up by, among others, Nicole Starosielski (2015), in her book on the historical development and contemporary configurations of undersea cables, which carry most of the world's digital traffic. Starosielski visited some of the cable stations and coastal cable landing points through which digital networks pass. Her visits provided insights into how "human labor and embodied experience remain integral to the maintenance of global information exchange" (p. 98). The combination of such fieldwork with historical research and visual analysis in the work of writers such as Parks and Starosielski challenges everyday understandings of digital systems as wireless, decentralized, resilient and urban, instead showing their wired, semi-centralized, precarious, rural, and aquatic nature. Such work also valuably makes visible the materiality of media infrastructures, challenging the way in which some treatments of digital media downplay the substantial and physical nature of the systems undergirding contemporary communication.

As already indicated, an interest in the distribution or circulation of media messages is apparent in these studies. Starosielski (p. 6) comments on how media studies have tended to focus on the content, messages, and reception of digital media, paying less attention to "the infrastructures that support its distribution." An admirable example of the contributions of infrastructure and distribution concerns to media industry studies is Ramon Lobato's research on Netflix. As Lobato (2019: 75) points out, earlier infrastructural studies invited engagement with topics that were previously considered out of bounds by humanists, such as electrical engineering or information systems. Lobato shows that, while Netflix frequently claims to be available across the world, low bandwidth speeds mean a very much diminished Netflix experience for users in many countries, not just in the "emerging world," but in wealthier countries such as Australia and Taiwan as well. In general, equipment and subscription costs make Netflix a service primarily for the world's wealthier middle classes (pp. 82–85).

Lobato's research also demonstrates how some media infrastructural studies are playing a role in pushing environmental issues belatedly up the agenda of media studies (e.g., Miller 2015). He shows how Netflix's global lobbying for the provision of higher bandwidth shows little regard for the material and ecological consequences of the push to high-definition (HD) and Super HD. A growing body of research on data centers also pursues environmental questions (Velkova 2016), and some of it addresses the questions of representation and discourse explored by Parks in her work (Jakobsson and Stiernstedt 2012; Holt and Vonderau 2015). The role of communication infrastructures in contributing to the global climate emergency certainly needs to be even higher on the media studies agenda, but it is not the fault of infrastructural studies that more work needs to be done.

Lobato also illuminates some of the *complexity* of Netflix's infrastructures, and the challenges for media scholars of understanding not only the telecommunications and internet governance systems on which the video streaming service relies, but also more obscure technologies such as video and audio encoding standards, metadata formatting, and user interface design standards, not to mention credit card and banking systems. A wave of media research has begun to take seriously this wider set of technologies, such as Jonathan Sterne's (2012) work on engineering standards and audio compression in his book on the MP3 audio format, and Jeremy Morris's (2015) history of the development of audio formats. In more recent work, the interest in "infrastructure studies" has been combined with another fashionable concept, that of platforms, as powerful tech companies increasingly invest in infrastructure, strengthening their control over global communication (Plantin, Lagoze, Edwards, and Sandvig 2018).[3]

## Problems and limitations

The above developments are welcome, for reasons just outlined, but the infrastructural turn has been hindered by definitional and conceptual problems. Over the last year, my email inbox has regularly contained messages advertising events, symposia, and seminars featuring "infrastructures" in their titles. To read these messages is disorienting. A call for papers for a conference at Humboldt University, Berlin, on *Digital Truth-making: Ethnographic Perspectives on Practices, Infrastructures and Affordances of Truth-making in Digital Societies*, for example, observes that "the ubiquity of digital infrastructures has brought about numerous drastic changes to a globalized world," but the text that follows suggests that infrastructure is being used essentially to refer to what not so long ago would have been called "digital networks" or "the internet."[4] Another call for papers, this time for an event addressing "feminist approaches to digital infrastructures, cultures and economies" refers to "algorithmic processes of selection, identification and discrimination" – but it is not at all clear in what way the organizers understand algorithms to be "infrastructural."[5] A three-day workshop *Knowledge Infrastructures and Digital Governance. History, Challenges, Practices* at the University of Luxembourg promises exploration of how "digital knowledge infrastructures … frame themselves, evolve and adapt," and of their role in fostering "innovative models of governance."[6] However, the only example the organizers provide of such a digital knowledge infrastructure is Wikipedia, and it seems bizarre to conceptualize Wikipedia in this way, rather than as a website (some might describe Wikipedia as a "platform," but it isn't really one of those either). Even the most accomplished published work shows the definitional strain. Davis, Fenton, Freedman, and Khiabany (2020) argue for the need to discuss infrastructures of political communication, but they seem to be using the term metaphorically to refer to the importance of understanding underlying social relations. The term "infrastructure" is now used in media studies, internet studies, and related fields in such a variety of ways – as a synonym for the internet, for algorithms, for websites and for "structural" social arrangements and much else besides (see Johnson 2021) – that it is hard not to wonder whether the term is still analytically useful – see Shipwright (2017). Moreover, the confusing and inconsistent usage obscures many of the issues to which the concept might helpfully draw our attention, as evident in the work cited earlier: the mundane and often invisible, or unnoticed, materialities upon which our communication depends.

The above confusions about the meaning of the concept appear to have been inherited by contemporary media and internet research from STS-style information infrastructure studies in the Susan Leigh Star mode, and I now want to home in on some of the elisions and uncertainties that commonly occur in recent research using the term, making reference to their seeming origins in this STS work.

### *Materiality, hardness, and softness*

The first set of confusions concern materiality, and related discussions of "hardness" and "softness." Those advocating the "infrastructural turn" regularly claim or imply, following Star and her colleagues, that infrastructure used to refer only or primarily to hard things (pipes, cables etc.) but now refers to "soft" things too (people, protocols, organizational norms). One of the most accomplished researchers working in media and internet studies, Christian Sandvig (2013: 100), for example, observes that "the average person" would expect infrastructure to refer to "roads, power systems, and communications networks", but that many analysts following Star and her colleagues use infrastructure analytically "as a way to materialize the ephemera of norms and organizations". In what sense is "materialize" being used here though? It seems to be a metaphor for "making visible" organizational ephemera rather than a reference to materiality per se, that is, the quality of being composed of *matter*. And if the analytical interest is actually in the "ephemera of norms and organizations," why not highlight concepts, rather than fetishize infrastructure?

There is surprisingly little actual theoretical engagement with materiality as such, as opposed to non-material things such as ideas, processes, flows, discourses and so on (although of course things sometimes take material forms). In media infrastructure studies, terms such as hard, soft, and material are bandied around so freely that infrastructure could potentially cover any kind of system at all. Again, the earlier STS sociologists of infrastructure regularly provide theoretical legitimation for this vagueness. Shannon Mattern for example, cites Star and Bowker to support her view that "intellectual and institutional structures and operations – measurement standards, technical protocols, naming conventions, bureaucratic forms, etc. – are *also* infrastructures" (original emphasis; 2018: 325). Anyone expecting some kind of *explanation* of how media infrastructure in the everyday sense of the term, or even in the extended sense regularly invoked by analysts, actually works, or what effects it might have on the communication media is likely to be frustrated.[7] This lack of interest in causality and explanation seems to be a feature of both the original STS work and the more recent media and internet studies work. In much "infrastructure studies," the word infrastructure seems mainly to operate as a way of merely saying that entities such as norms or organizations are *fundamental*, that they metaphorically provide a *basis* for things that happen, that they *underlie* certain elements, processes, and things. But whether this fundamental or basic nature actually has causal consequences is not really explored much.

## *"Relationality"*

Even more troubling is the constant refrain in media and information infrastructural studies that the meaning of infrastructure is, in Star and Ruhleder (1996)'s framing, "relational." Regularly cited as an authoritative source in recent research, the piece claims that we need to ask "*when* – not *what* – is an infrastructure?" Star and Ruhleder expand on this claim by observing that infrastructure only "becomes infrastructure in relation to organized practices" (p. 113), and they give examples of different distinct practices: cooks consider the household water supply connected to the city supply as infrastructure because it helps them make dinner, but city planners and plumbers do not – for the former, it is just a variable in a complex equation, for the latter it's something to be fixed (p. 113).

As Frederiksen and Schmidt (2018: 188–193) show, however, the argument about infrastructure being a "relational concept" is confused and confusing. What do Star and Ruhleder mean by "relational"? It is indisputable but obvious that infrastructure is relational in a very narrow sense, in that an infrastructure is always an infrastructure *of* something; otherwise it would not be an infrastructure at all. Presumably, Star and Ruhleder must mean more than this. They seem at times to intend "relational" to refer to an idea that an infrastructure is only an infrastructure when it is being used as one. But as Frederiksen and Schmidt (p. 191) remark, that would be like saying a chair is only a chair when it is being sat on, which is nonsense: unused or paused infrastructure is surely still infrastructure. Perhaps, Frederiksen and Schmidt ask, referring to the examples above, Star and Ruhleder mean that infrastructure is only an infrastructure for people who *use* it as an infrastructure – in the example above, for users such as the cook. But Frederiksen and Schmidt are surely right that the cook, the plumber and the planner all presumably understand that they are drawing upon some kind of unified system that delivers water. Given this, why would Star and Ruhleder claim that the water supply infrastructure is infrastructure *only* for the cook and not for city planners and plumbers? Their interpretation seems completely arbitrary.

Yet, in spite of the fundamental incoherence of Star and Ruhleder's notion of relationality, their discussion is regularly invoked as authoritative even by insightful scholars. Plantin and Punathambekar (2019: 168), for example, cite them to remark that "what an infrastructure is quite simply depends on the status of the person looking (e.g. a user, or a designer)."[8] Frederiksen and Schmidt (2018: 193) point out, referring to Star and Ruhleder, that this is not really a *relational* understanding, it is an uncomfortably *relativist* one.

## Banality and vagueness

In spite of these problems, Star and Ruhleder used their sketchily "relational" conception of infrastructure as the basis for a list of properties or "dimensions" supposedly characteristic of systems they deemed infrastructural, a list that has been very widely cited in infrastructural studies. They write that infrastructures are embedded in "other structures, social arrangements and technologies," that "infrastructure has reach beyond a single event or one-site practice," and that infrastructures are learned as part of a community of practice (Star and Ruhleder 1996: 113). But these observations are rather *banal*: they are statements of the obvious that lead on to very little substantial insight into why infrastructures matter for our understanding of social or technical systems. They are also extremely vague. In each case, the word "infrastructure" might be replaced with other fundamental sociological concepts such as "organization" or "culture." If this is so, the concept surely lacks specificity. Perhaps as a result of this vagueness, Star and Ruhleder make dubious claims, such as that infrastructures only become visible once they break down (p. 113) but as Larkin points out, some infrastructures are spectacularly present, from dams to pylons to bridges, so this element of Star and Ruhleder's definition is "flatly untenable" (Larkin 2013: 336).

## Does vagueness matter?

It is little wonder that with widely cited sources for the infrastructural turn offering such a thin and inconsistent conceptual foundation that the term is being used to mean so many different things. But does it matter that infrastructure is being used in varied and confusing ways, and in ways that goes beyond its everyday usage? Those who advocate infrastructure studies, within media studies and beyond, often imply that this variation in usage *doesn't* matter, and indeed that such definitional vagueness might actually be attractive, on the grounds that such vagueness might be generative of enquiry. Sandvig (2013: 89), for example, comments that

> although infrastructure is at times inchoate as a concept and it holds many, sometimes inconsistent meanings for different researchers, nevertheless the term is now galvanizing a newly vibrant pool of Internet-related scholarship in the same way that equally diffuse and inconsistently applied concepts like "network" have in the past.

As I've indicated above, I think Sandvig is right about the vibrancy of some of the research on media infrastructure. And it is part of any area of intellectual enquiry that the meanings of words become extended beyond their widely used meaning into new terrains. Some humanities scholars in particular are rightly attuned to the fluidity and blurred boundaries around definitions. But the dangers of inchoateness are often underestimated by academics as they move on busily from topic to fashionable topic. There are benefits to considering, in a more measured way, questions of conceptual robustness, even if this sometimes risks slowing down "vibrant" enquiry.

## Intellectual disjuncture

It is good that a new generation of media and internet researchers is showing interest in the concept of infrastructure. Attention to the concept of infrastructure offers, as I have already indicated above, the chance to analyze the ways in which communication depends on mundane but crucial material systems in order to function. It focuses attention on processes and practices of distribution, often marginalized in the production-text-consumption triangle that still haunts media research. Some of the research undertaken in the infrastructural turn is creative and innovative in bringing issues of representation and culture to bear on such systems. However, the definitional looseness I've been discussing may also have reinforced another unfortunate feature of media infrastructure research: disjuncture between different traditions of research.

As I have explained, the information infrastructure research of Star and her colleagues was not concerned with infrastructure as traditionally understood, so it is perhaps not surprising that they also overlooked areas of media research that had addressed media infrastructures (at least implicitly, if not always using that term) in the original sense of the term, such as researchers concerned with the importance of telecommunications as a basis for mediated communication and information (e.g., Schiller 1981; Garnham 1990).[9] It is strange, though, how little attention recent media infrastructural studies have paid to the large body of research on the historical development of communication networks (Mattelart 2000; Hills 2007) and their regulation (Noam 2001). Perhaps this is because such work has often been carried out in sub-fields such as political economy of media, or media policy and regulation studies, sometimes regarded with disdain by some media scholars drawn to the humanities.[10] This neglect is unfortunate, because such research has cast light on important developments. Winseck (2017) for example, shows that while internet infrastructure, based on fiber optic cable, shares a basic geography with the copper that supported telegraphy and telephony, it is utterly different in terms of capacity, ownership, and regulation. The tech giants have invested in infrastructure, but they exist alongside a diverse array of other powerful players, including governments in the Global South (complicating simplistic notions of "platform imperialism") and huge telecom companies that are hardly mentioned in the excessive focus on the famous Google, Apple, Facebook, Amazon, and Microsoft (GAFAM) tech oligopoly, such as Level 3, Global Cloud Xchange, and Tata.

Equally, recent political economy and media regulation research has paid little attention to STS-influenced work on infrastructures. Graham Murdock's otherwise fine essay on "media and materiality" (Murdock 2018) ignores the infrastructural studies discussed earlier, for example. This means lost opportunities to understand relationships between dynamics of investment, ownership, and control, on the one hand, and the role of infrastructure in everyday life (including how "infrastructural imaginaries" shape that role), on the other. That failure of dialogue echoes the long-standing divide between political economy and cultural studies, which persists even after decades of researchers calling for greater synthesis (Hesmondhalgh 2019: 73–77). Another factor here is the preference of some humanities scholars for values of exploration, innovation and the opening up of new areas of enquiry or modes of understanding, whereas political economy and regulation analysts often seek to identify mechanisms of causation, in order to provide explanation and evaluation. Both of these forms of academic knowledge have benefits and shortcomings – and infrastructure is surely a concept that would be better understood if these different strands were brought together.

It is certainly not unusual for academics to use modish words and phrases without really defining or explaining (and sometimes without really understanding) what they mean: infrastructure is not the first, and it definitely won't be the last term to suffer from this problem. But to close, it is worth asking why the concept of infrastructure is so seemingly fashionable *now*. Part of its currency undoubtedly derives from the high quality of some of the scholarship discussed above. It also derives however from the increasing dominance in recent media studies and internet studies of "sociotechnical" as opposed to "sociocultural" research. STS was fashionable in the 2010s in a way that cultural studies was in the 1990s. Writers familiar with technology have the wind behind them compared with those who analyze video or audio content and textuality. Discussions of infrastructure regularly invoke the way that a concern with infrastructure moves "beyond" long-standing media studies concerns with production, texts, and reception. There tends to be an assumption that engagement with sociocultural and textual concerns can simply be added, as a supplement or complement, to concerns with fundamentally sociotechnical issues such as infrastructures, platforms, and distribution. The really significant and difficult question, raised by infrastructure studies but by no means resolved, is how to reconcile and synthesize those projects.

## Notes

1 My thanks to Des Freedman, Paul McDonald and Lisa Parks for their comments on drafts, and Julia Velkova, Anne Kaun and Sander de Ridder for inviting me to the *Infrastructures and Inequalities* conference they organized at the University of Helsinki in October 2019, where I first tried out some of the ideas developed here – and where I had a brilliant laugh with a lovely group of people (special thanks to the other D. McQuail, and to Todd Johnson).

2 While Star's own empirical studies were elegant and stimulating, in retrospect they seem somewhat limited or unsurprising in their findings: Star and Ruhleder (1996), for example, conclude that scientists preferred web-based systems of collaboration to other early forms based on closed networks.

3 Some would claim that the idea of "platforms" suffers from the same problems of vague and loose usage as "infrastructures" in contemporary media studies (and beyond), and there is certainly some truth in such assertions. But I think there have been greater efforts among researchers to define what platforms might mean in analytical terms (e.g., van Dijck, Poell, and de Waal 2018).

4 www.carmah.berlin/events/conference-digital-truth-making-ethnographic-perspectives-on-practices-infrastructures-and-affordances-of-truth-making-in-digital-societies/.

5 www.kcl.ac.uk/events/algorithms-for-her.

6 https://operas.hypotheses.org/3850.

7 There are notable exceptions to this lack of explanation, including Starosielski (2015) and Sterne (2012), referred to above, and Paul Dourish (2015), whose essay on internet routing protocols is an unusual example in media and information infrastructural studies in explicitly conceptualizing relations between materiality and immateriality.

8 Sandvig (2015) distinguishes this concern with relationality from the approach of "materialists" such as Parks, who for him are guided by something like an opposite impulse: finding the material dimensions "behind" cultural phenomena.

9 An exception is that there tends to be some reference in infrastructural studies to the work of Harold Innis, especially Innis (1951).

10 Parks and Starosielksi (2015: 6) are unusual in recognizing the existence of such work.

## References

Bijker, W. E., Hughes, T. P., and Pinch, T. J. (1987) *The Social Construction of Technological Systems, New Directions in the Sociology and History of Technology*, Cambridge, MA: MIT Press.

Bowker, G. C. (1994) *Science on the Run: Information Management and Industrial Geophysics at Schlumberger, 1920–1940*, Cambridge, MA: MIT Press.

Bowker, G. C. and Star, S. L. (1999) *Sorting Things Out: Classification and Its Consequences*, Cambridge, MA: MIT Press.

Davis, A., Fenton, N., Freedman, D., and Khiabany, G. (2020) *Media, Democracy and Social Change*, London: SAGE.

Dourish, P. (2015) "Protocols, Packets, and Proximity: the Materiality of Internet Routing," in L. Parks and N. Starosielski (eds), *Signal Traffic: Critical Studies of Media Infrastructures*, Urbana, IL: University of Illinois Press, 183–204.

Frederiksen, C. L. and Schmidt, K. (2018) "A Bridge Too Far? Critical Remarks on the Concept of 'Infrastructure' in Computer-supported Cooperative Work and Information Systems", in V. Wulf, V. Pipek, D. Randall, M. Rohde, K. Schmidt, and G. Stevens (eds), *Socio-informatics: A Practice-based Perspective on the Design and Use of IT Artifacts*, Oxford: Oxford University Press: 177–217.

Garnham, N. (1990) *Capitalism and Communication: Global Culture and the Economics of Information*, London: Sage.

Hills, J. (2007) *Telecommunications and Empire*, Urbana, IL: University of Illinois Press.

Holt, J. and Vonderau, P. (2015) "'Where the Internet Lives': Data Centers as Cloud Infrastructure', in L. Parks and N. Starosielski (eds), *Signal Traffic: Critical Studies Of Media Infrastructures*. Urbana: University of Illinois Press, 71–93.

Jakobsson, P. and Stiernstedt, F. (2012) "Time, Space and Clouds of Information: Data Center Discourse and the Meaning of Durability," in G. Bolin (ed.), *Cultural Technologies: The Shaping of Culture in Media and Society*. New York: Routledge, 103–118.

Johnson, T. (2021) *Last Night an Infrastructure Saved My Life: Pipes, Sewers, Sex and Music*, Bedford Falls, NY: Jargon Press.

Larkin, B. (2008) *Signal and Noise: Media, Infrastructure, and Urban Culture in Nigeria*, Chapel Hill, NC: Duke University Press.

Larkin, B. (2013) "The Politics and Poetics of Infrastructure," *Annual Review of Anthropology*, 42: 327–343.

Lobato, R. (2019) *Netflix Nations: The Geography of Digital Distribution*, New York: New York University Press.

MacKenzie, D. A. and Wajcman, J. (1999) *The Social Shaping of Technology*, Buckingham: Open University Press.

Mattelart, A. (2000) *Networking the World, 1794-2000*, Minneapolis, MI: University of Minnesota Press.

Mattern, S. (2018) "Scaffolding, Hard and Soft: Critical and Generative Infrastructures," in J. Sayers (ed.), *The Routledge Companion to Media Studies and Digital Humanities*, New York: Routledge, 318–326.

Michael, M. (2017) *Actor Network Theory: Trials, Trails and Translations*, London: SAGE.

Miller, T. (2015) "The Art of Waste: Contemporary Culture and Unsustainable Energy Use," in L. Parks and N. Starosielski (eds), *Signal Traffic: Critical Studies of Media Infrastructures*, Urbana, IL: University of Illinois Press, 137–156.

Morris, J. W. (2015) *Selling Digital Music, Formatting Culture*, Berkeley, CA: University of California Press.

Murdock, G. (2018) "Media Materialities: For a Moral Economy of Machines," *Journal of Communication*, 68 (2): 359–368.

Noam, E. M. (2001) *Interconnecting the Network of Networks*, Cambridge, MA: MIT Press.

*Oxford English Dictionary*. (n.d.). Database.

Parks, L. (2013) "Earth Observation and Signal Territories: Studying U.S. Broadcast Infrastructure Through Historical Network Maps, Google Earth, and Fieldwork," *Canadian Journal of Communication*, 38 (3): 285–307.

Parks, L. (2015). "'Stuff You Can Kick': Toward a Theory of Media Infrastructures," in P. Svensson and D. T. Goldberg (eds), *Between Humanities and the Digital*, Cambridge, MA: MIT Press, 355–373.

Plantin, J.-C., Lagoze, C. Edwards, P. N., and Sandvig, C. (2018) "Infrastructure Studies Meet Platform Studies in the Age of Google and Facebook," *New Media and Society*, 20 (1): 293–310.

Plantin, J.-C. and Punathambekar, A. (2019). "Digital Media Infrastructures: Pipes, Platforms, and Politics," *Media, Culture and Society*, 41 (2): 163–174.

Sandvig, C. (2013) "The Internet as Infrastructure," in W. H. Dutton (ed.), *The Oxford Handbook of Internet Studies*, Oxford: Oxford University Press, 86–108.

Schiller, H. I. (1981) *Who Knows: Information in the Age of the Fortune 500*, Norwood, NJ: Ablex.

Shipwright, F. (2017) "Turtles All the Way Down – Or, Escape from Infrastructure," *Transmediale*, available at https://transmediale.de/content/turtles-all-the-way-down-or-escape-from-infrastructure (accessed December 4, 2020).

Star, S. L. (1999) "The Ethnography of Infrastructure," *American Behavioral Scientist*, 43 (3): 377–391.

Star, S. L. and Ruhleder, K. (1996) "Steps Towards an Ecology of Infrastructure: Design and Access for Large Information Spaces," *Information Systems Research*, 7 (1): 111–34.

Starosielski, N. (2015) *The Undersea Network*, Chapel Hill, NC: Duke University Press.

Sterne, J. (2012) *MP3: The Meaning of a Format,* Chapel Hill, NC: Duke University Press.

Streeter, T. (2011) *The Net Effect: Romanticism, Capitalism, and the Internet*, New York: New York University Press.

Velkova, J. (2016) "Data that Warms: Waste Heat, Infrastructural Convergence and the Computation Traffic Commodity", *Big Data & Society*. doi:10.1177/2053951716684144

Winseck, D. (2017) "The Geopolitical Economy of the Global Internet Infrastructure," *Journal of Information Policy*, 7: 228–267.

# 11

# INFORMALITY AND INDETERMINACY IN MEDIA INDUSTRIES RESEARCH

*Ramon Lobato*

In a thought-provoking essay published in 2013, Nitin Govil poses a series of questions about how media industry research understands its central analytical category – industry. As Govil notes, much research into media industries is guided by a definition of industry as something "pre-given and stable," reflecting "a general understanding of what an industry comprises, with a tacit sense of its boundaries and capacities" (2013: 173). We can think here of the expansive literature on twentieth-century mass media – including broadcast television, radio, and newspapers – with their routinized production and distribution practices, publicly listed firms or state-run providers, and codified regulation. However, Govil goes on to suggest that the question of what constitutes an industry is not always straightforward, and that researchers in the field may need to "broaden the range of practices that count as industrial" (p. 176) in their analyses if they wish to account for the diversity of actually existing media industries.

The category of industry, as Govil argues, should not be taken for granted. Industries only exist to the extent that they are made visible through measurement, certification, and authorization. Govil uses the case of Indian cinema to interrogate some common assumptions about what constitutes a media industry. A vast and multifaceted ecology of production, distribution, exhibition, promotion, and merchandising, the Indian film industry spans multiple regional sub-industries and caters to a billion-plus passionate viewers at home and abroad. Historically, much of India's film output has been unmeasured, its revenues untaxed, and its finance murky. Cinema only attained official industry status in India in 1998, and a great deal of film spectatorship and production and distribution labor in India occurs off-the-books. "In the Indian film trade," Govil writes

> various practices produced disparate sets of numbers that only occasionally combined to convey an overall sense of "an industry" … as if the diversity and informality of film practice could not be aggregated into an industry in the modern sense.
>
> *p. 175*

A key question for Govil is how industries *become* industries, and what is at stake in this category. He concludes by asking questions that our field might address in order to "introduce indeterminacy into the study of industry" (p. 176):

DOI: 10.4324/9780429275340-14

What are the provisional forms, sites, and practices that constitute media industries? What are the social, textual, political, and cultural infrastructures and interactions assembled under the sign of "industry"? What are these formal and informal processes of assembly, and how do exchange practices move in and out of industry status? In other words, how are industries "made up"?

*p. 173*

These provocations provide a basis for the present chapter, which explores how informal media industries and workers surface as a topic in media industry research. It considers various challenges for research in this area, and surveys recent studies that ask generative questions about how to conceptualize media industries. After some framing comments, the essay proceeds in three parts by considering research in the following areas: (i) informal media industries (including media piracy); (ii) informal employment in otherwise formal media industries; and (iii) the formalizing and deformalizing effects of digital platforms.

## What is a media industry?

Govil's intervention highlights what is both a defining feature and an inherent limitation of the media industry research paradigm: the category of "industry" itself. Of course, the industrial status of the established, consolidated, and regulated sectors characteristic of mass media is not in question here. Television, radio, advertising, and publishing are all clearly industries in the sense that they have large and visible workforces, their own technical standards, metrics, and industry associations, and are formally (albeit unevenly) regulated in most nations. The centrality of these industries to how the field conceptualizes its object can be seen plainly in the chapter structure of key textbooks, such as *Media Today* (Turow 2019), which features dedicated chapters on book publishing, news, magazines, recorded music, radio, cinema, television, games, and the Internet industries. Likewise, the evergreen collection *Media and Communications in Australia* (Cunningham and Turnbull 2020) deals with the press, telecommunications, radio, video, television, magazines, advertising and marketing, popular music, Internet and mobile communication, and games. Certainly, some of these industries are more identifiably "industrial" than others: for example, commercial radio, with its limited number of licensed operators competing within circumscribed geographic markets, is a more organized sector than videogame development, where a vast number of independent developers (and a few giant firms) compete, and where freelance, outsourced, and offshored labor are common. Our knowledge of videogame development is usually more provisional than of radio, not only because of the emergent nature of digital media but also because research approaches, concepts, and empirical techniques for studying fragmented and globally dispersed media workforces are still evolving. Hence it is often necessary to ask different questions of different media industries, rather than employing a standardized analytical toolkit. It may also be necessary to modify sources, given that institutional archives, regulatory documents, case law, and official statistics may be unavailable for many media industries.

In *The Informal Media Economy* (Lobato and Thomas 2015), Julian Thomas and I explore the history of research into informal media and develop a framework for analyzing how informal and formal aspects of media industries interact. Informal media have distinctive organizational features that are not only worthy of study in their own right, but which can also enrich and expand our understanding of *all* media. A key research challenge is distinguishing between different *kinds* of formality and informality. Some media industries have unpredictable combinations of formal and informal elements, with the effect that they defy easy categorization (this is often the case with digital media). We propose the concept of a "spectrum of formality" in which key characteristics of media firms, sectors, and entire industries – such as taxation, capital intensity, centralization, state oversight, labor practices, ease of entry, quality control, and so on – may occupy different positions along a continuum from formal to informal. This approach seeks to productively de-center the most common objects of media industry studies while at the same time opening a space for understanding a wider variety of organizational forms.

Informality has a long history in social science, economic, and policy research, and the term has been subject to sustained debate. We see informality as a productive concept for media industry research, as it evokes a number of interlinked phenomena, including informal labor, informalization, and the informal economy, which together draw attention to diverse forms of quasi-industrial activity not easily captured by conventional industry measurement. Jobbing scriptwriters, freelance designers, itinerant newspaper vendors, YouTube creators, and unregistered workers in device assembly plants can all be described as informal in the sense that their work occurs outside the boundaries of formal industry, while providing essential inputs into such industry. Over time, different activities are formalized or deformalized due to changes in technology, regulation, or social structure. Such diversity reflects the ever-changing boundaries – the "variable geometry" (Castells and Portes 1989: 26) – of the informal economy, and its shifting relationship to the formal economy.

## Informal industries

A key consideration for research into informal media industries is the question of scale. Informal media industries may be very small, but they may also conversely be large, organized and highly productive. Examples of small-scale informal media include minority-language and ethnic media systems that address small or scattered audiences, and which have developed their own unique ways of producing for and distributing to these audiences. Jason Pine's (2012) study of Neapolitan pop music in Italy and Simeon Floyd's (2008) work on Quichua video in Ecuador document two memorable examples of such systems, which cater to defined markets within specific national contexts. Many diasporic media industries – which distribute goods across rather than within national borders – have also developed distinctive informal modes of organization, as documented in classic studies of Iranian (Naficy 1993) and Vietnamese diaspora video (Cunningham and Sinclair 2001).

Other informal industries are larger in scale. As Govil (2013) observes, Indian cinemas retain significant informal characteristics, including unconventional financing, partly undocumented workforces, and a dispersed theatrical exhibition network. A second example is Nollywood – Nigeria's enormous video industry – which is likewise unmeasured in its output, informal in its financing, and lacking the institutions characteristic of most national film industries, such as major studios, formal training, and accreditation systems. Nollywood has instead an exuberant and productive ecology of entrepreneurs, funders, and performers that work together to produce hundreds of feature-length movies per year, exporting them worldwide (Krings and Okome 2013; Miller 2016).

Media piracy too has long been of interest to scholars of informal media industries. Pirate markets for DVDs, books, and other media goods are by nature illicit, yet in many cases these markets are also highly organized and exhibit many of the same characteristics and rationalities of formal markets. Shujen Wang (2003), Joe Karaganis (2011), Ravi Sundaram (2009) and John Cross (1998) have studied the dynamics of pirate street vending in Asia and Latin America, using field methods including observation and interviews. Karaganis (2011) and Paul McDonald (2020) have analyzed the international organization of copyright enforcement by government agencies, industry groups, and private actors. Collectively, this work challenges common assumptions about piracy as a disorganized sector of the media industries, revealing instead a more complex set of interactions between the formal and the informal.

Research into informal media industries can be found across multiple disciplines including anthropology, ethnomusicology, and business studies as well as media studies. Such research is instructive for a number of reasons. First, it prompts us to think creatively about what constitutes an industry and how industries may be described, investigated, and critiqued in a research context. By broadening our understanding of industry, it reveals connections between different kinds of institutions and markets. For example, Karaganis' analysis of legal and pirate DVD pricing showed deep interconnection between formal and informal markets, leading him to argue that piracy cannot be understood in isolation from "[t]he structure of the licit media economy" (2011: iii). Such research highlights structures, patterns, and innovations in the production and distribution of media content that can both parallel, or diverge from, equivalents in the formal media economy. Second, the nature of informal media industries requires scholars to be adventurous with methods, and to look beyond official metrics and other sources of empirical "truth" when studying a particular industry. In the absence of official records and national statistics, qualitative field methods including site visits, observations, interviews, and case studies are often used to study informal media industries because they can capture business practices, routines, and labor dynamics in a fine-grained way. This provides opportunities to link social-scientific and humanistic, quantitative, and qualitative, and critical and empirical modes of inquiry into media industries.

## Informal labor practices

A second, related body of research investigates informal labor within otherwise formal media industries. Unlike the examples discussed above, which involve whole media institutions and markets outside the formal realm, the focus here is instead on informality within certain *parts* of an industry, rather than the whole. This brings into focus particular features of a media industries – such as employment practices – that exist in the "gray zone."

For example, research in media production studies and media labor studies has documented the project-based, freelance, and precarious nature of media production work. While some of this work is well-paid, much of it is unglamorous, low-wage labor where informality often has exploitative characteristics: unpaid internships are widespread, unionization is limited or absent, and an oversupply of aspiring workers suppresses wages. As Rosalind Gill observes,

> informality is the structuring principle in which many small and medium-sized new media companies seem to operate: finding work, recruiting staff, getting clients are all seemingly removed from the formal sphere governed by established procedures, equal opportunities legislation, or union agreements, and located in an arena based on informality, sociality, and "who you know".
>
> *2011, p. 256*

This characteristic of media production work has been documented in other studies. Leung, Gill, and Randle (2015: 56) note that for freelance film and television professionals in the UK, "recruitment in the film and television industries is deregulated, informal and often ad hoc." Curtin and Sanson (2017), through their extended interviews with Hollywood screen professionals, document widespread informality of employment practices. Hesmondhalgh and Baker (2011) use interviews and participant observation in three industries – magazines, television, and recorded music – to investigate the pleasures and challenges of working in these notoriously nepotistic sectors, where personal relationships, "who you know" networks and intangible qualities such as passion and style are inordinately important. As Hesmondhalgh and Baker explain, the tendency of these industries to attract "creative people … who value informality" (p. 88) allows employers to exploit the blurry boundaries between work and pleasure. Here, the twin faces of informality become visible: the relaxed informality of a "no collar" (Ross 2003) workplace, and ultra-flexible employment practices that lack the labor protections associated with formalized employment.

Informal labor practices within what are otherwise organized and regulated media industries remind us that informal employment can be found – indeed, is even widespread – among high-wage professionals in the cultural industries of major cities in the Global North as well as in industries such as Bollywood and Nollywood. This provides an important corrective to accounts that associate formality with development and informality with underdevelopment, underlining instead the fact that informality is "a fundamental politico-economic process at the core of many societies" (Castells and Portes 1989, p. 15).

Media labor research has been enormously valuable because it reminds us that professionalized, regulated, formal industries are also fields in which many workers operate at the margins of salaried labor, outside of scrutiny and regulation. Such research foregrounds the heterogenous nature of media production, which involves both skilled and unskilled labor and paid and unpaid work. Keeping these informal aspects of media industries in the frame introduces that important element of indeterminacy – in Govil's words – into our analyses, and reminds us that even the most established media professions have aspects that are irregular, extra-legal, non-professional or artisanal.

One challenge for media labor research is how to account for and normatively evaluate profound variations in the organization of media work across different countries. At times, research on media labor has tended toward theoretical generalization about precarity, extrapolated from the experiences of a specific fraction of media workers in the United States, United Kingdom, and Europe. As Alacovska and Gill (2019, p. 197) argue, "the informality of creative work is multifarious, ambivalent and, above all, relational – embedded in local informal economies, neighborhoods and localized webs of collegiality, care and reciprocity." Hence, research into informal employment in media industries should be careful not to default to a universalized mode of critique but should instead attend to specific conditions of media work in the locations under study.

## Informality in the age of platforms

We now consider a third strand of research that is asking important questions about informality in digital media industries. In recent years, scholars have increasingly turned their attention to the formalizing and deformalizing effects of platforms, including social media platforms, on-demand service platforms, and business-to-business platforms. Such research explores how distinct processes of "platformization" – or "the penetration of the infrastructures, economic processes, and governmental frameworks of platforms in different economic sectors and spheres of life" (Poell, Nieborg, and van Dijck 2019, pp. 5–6) – are differentially impacting media industries,, workers, and institutional structures.

Consider the video platform YouTube and its vast global army of creators. Cunningham and Craig (2019) have documented the diverse motivations, revenues, and working conditions of YouTubers in several countries. From their analysis, it is clear that a great deal of YouTube video production remains informal in nature. Yet YouTube has strong formalizing tendencies as well, bringing nonprofessional and do-it-yourself (DIY) media production into the sphere of private regulation, advertising, and automated measurement. Consequently, YouTube creator communities are increasingly characterized by disputes over monetization, revenue shares, advertiser fraud, and takedowns – an unusual combination of amateur and professional concerns.

Sophie Bishop (2020) has explored new kinds of media professions and services appearing in the interstices of the YouTube economy. Bishop's study describes how a new breed of entrepreneurial "algorithmic experts" – intermediaries who advise YouTube creators on how to increase visibility on the platform – are seeking to bring a more structured character to the wild west of user-generated content by making platforms amenable to the established measurement, attribution, and promotional techniques used in marketing, while also peddling their own, sometimes questionable services. This example shows the subtle formalization that has been occurring throughout social video platforms, as those platforms have shifted from the margins to the center of contemporary marketing, while also pointing to the informal ways of working that characterize many service providers around the edges of the YouTube economy. In this way, Bishop's research provides a fresh perspective on a tradition of media industry research concerned with understanding the intermediaries that "proliferate in the space between production and consumption" (Negus 2002, p. 502).

These examples show the paradoxical effects of platformization on video culture. On one hand, YouTube has clearly expanded the terrain of video production and distribution by providing a space for amateur content to circulate freely, and has also been accused by major rights-holders of deformalizing video industries by allowing rampant copyright violation. On the other hand, YouTube and its growing number of ancillary service providers seek to professionalize content and creators by raising standards, removing problematic uploads, automating copyright enforcement, and instilling an entrepreneurial sensibility attuned to the needs of YouTube's advertiser market. Unquestionably, the YouTube platform has had both formalizing and deformalizing effects on video production.

Alongside this literature on video platforms, other research is investigating the hidden low-wage labor that sustains major social media platforms. In a major study of content moderators, Sarah T. Roberts (2019) documents the vast yet invisible workforce of "cleaners" that assess potentially offensive posts on social media platforms. These workers are spread all over the world, from Silicon Valley to the Philippines, and frequently work under highly irregular and informal conditions. Some are employed directly by platforms, others by intermediaries. Most are lowly paid and all are regularly exposed to extreme and upsetting material.

Other research concerned with documenting hidden online labor looks beyond media platforms to consider the many different labor-hire platforms that enable users to hire others to complete small tasks. Gray and Suri (2019) and Tubaro and Cassili (2019) analyze the hidden manual "microwork" (repetitive testing, labelling and tagging work) integral to the development of machine learning and other artificial intelligence applications. This microwork is often organized through on-demand labor platforms, such as Amazon's Mechanical Turk (a crowdsourcing marketplace through which businesses can outsource jobs, processes, or project to be conducted virtually by a globally distributed workforce) and is undertaken from workers' homes on a piecework basis for a few cents or dollars per task. Gray and Suri offer a strong critique of these practices, noting "on-demand labor can quickly become alienating, debasing, precarious, and isolating ghost work" (2019, xxvi).

Sociologist Juliet Schor and her research team interviewed more than 300 platform workers and service-providers in the US, including Uber drivers, AirBnB hosts, and TaskRabbit tradespeople. Schor's research emphasizes the divergent experiences of these individuals – from well-off urban professionals renting out their apartment on Airbnb through to lowly paid workers for whom on-demand gig work replaces traditional salaried roles in industries such as security and transport (Schor and Attwood-Charles 2017; Schor 2020). In contrast to critiques of platform labor that directly equate platformization with exploitation (Scholz 2017), Schor and her collaborators offer a more nuanced account, emphasizing the wide variance in the conditions and affordances of platform labor and the lack of a uniform "platform effect":

> the question of whether platforms are empowering or immiserating workers depends to a significant [extent] on the specific platform being examined, as well as its temporal trajectory. Platforms not only change policies and procedures but also confront an evolving institutional ecology. Furthermore, platform workers are differentially positioned in terms of the assets they bring to the work and their dependency on these income streams. These dimensions are important for understanding why some workers praise platform work, whereas others are extremely critical of it.
>
> *Schor and Attwood-Charles 2017, p. 7*

As Schor and Attwood-Charles argue, attention must be paid to the specificities of each platform, its workforce, and its socioeconomic context. A microwork task remunerated at a few dollars may be more or less appealing to workers depending on a range of factors including average wages in their countries (noting that such work is often globally distributed). We need to calibrate our normative assumptions about what constitutes "good work" to the specific contexts, histories, and norms of particular platforms and their diverse workforces. At the same time, the question of *who* extracts most value from the labor transaction – the employer, employee, or platform – is also a vital consideration. The politics of informal platform work, like the politics of informal media production discussed earlier, resist simplistic diagnosis.

Most of the published English-language literature on platform labor has focused on American and European experiences, or on the global dispersion of taskwork mediated through US-based platforms. However, recent work on platform labor in Asia offers a timely reminder that Silicon Valley is not the only crucible in which futures of informal work are being invented. A growing literature documents the experiences and impacts of platforms, platformization, and platform labor in China (van Dijck, Poell, and de Waal 2018; Sun 2019; Chen and Qiu 2019), India (Kumar 2019; Athique and Parthasarathi 2020), and the Philippines (Soriano and Cabañes 2020), among other nations.

A major contribution to this literature is Elaine Zhao's book *Digital China's Informal Circuits: Platforms, Labor and Governance* (2019), which explores the platform dynamics of Chinese app, mobile, video, and transport services. Drawing on interviews with taxi drivers, electronics salespeople and software developers, Zhao explores how Chinese digital platforms have evolved over time, amid evolving state policies for telecommunications, information, and data industries. Her analysis foregrounds ongoing interactions between markets, the state, and China's informal economies, with the effect that Chinese digital media industries emerge as hybrid formations spanning the formal–informal divide.

A key focus for Zhao is how current working practices in Chinese tech firms utilize informal labor for cost reduction, speed, and talent recruitment. Zhao describes a patchwork of elite and indentured workers, fans, and entrepreneurs all contributing diversely to China's mature platform economy. Zhao stresses that informal workers do not benefit equally or participate for the same reasons:

> Indeed, multiple publics participate in these informal circuits, including profit-motivated entrepreneurs, enthusiastic fans, creative users and necessity-driven,

on-demand laborers. Some are pressured into the informal economy with little option otherwise, while others venture there to seek entrepreneurial gains. Some step into the informal zones for fun while others are subject to precarious conditions. Some are located in the illegal zone while others are in the grey area, which can be more innovative than is generally assumed. Indeed, between black and white are many shades of grey.

*2019, p. 131*

Zhao's remarkable analysis is grounded within the social histories and political economy of contemporary China: its rapid marketization following accession to the World Trade Organization, its vast rural–urban migration, and the state's ongoing policy interventions in technology, information, and creative industries. As Zhao explains, the specificity of these conditions means that analysis of formal–informal interactions in China cannot uncritically apply drag-and-drop frameworks designed for other countries. Zhao pays close attention to how the boundaries between the formal and the informal manifest in different parts of China and how these boundaries are shaped by patterns of local, regional, and national governance. Describing how the state variously organizes, regulates, invests in, and also withdraws from media industries, Zhao argues against a "simplistic state-market dichotomy in approaching informal circuits in China's digital media economy," instead urging attention to "both converging and diverging interests between the state and market" (p. 13).

## Conclusion

This brief journey through the research landscape has shown that the category of "industry", so fundamental to the field of media industry studies, requires constant interrogation. As we have seen, industries come in many different shapes, sizes, and degrees of formality and informality. While the history of media industries is often narrated through the prism of formal institutions, informality remains a constant feature – and informal labor practices are widespread even in the most regulated and institutionalized sectors.

Research in the field can therefore benefit from retaining an open-minded view of what constitutes a media industry. This creates a productive indeterminacy – in Govil's words – that allows scholars to appreciate connections between diverse practices, systems, and institutions, and to interrogate commonsense thinking about how industries operate and evolve. Despite the obvious challenges of empirical research in this area, a rich body of literature now considers these questions, often using qualitative methods such as interviews, observations, and case studies to capture the texture of informality from the point of view of those involved.

As I write this in late 2020, the effects of the COVID-19 pandemic are rippling through media industries across the world, causing widespread disruption while also unleashing new innovations in media production and distribution. While the long-term implications of COVID-19 for media industries cannot be currently predicted, the events of 2020 suggest a range of uncertain futures that may include mass unemployment and under-employment, reduced consumer spending, increased tele-working, and deepening platformization of service industries. One possible lesson that media industry scholars may like to take away from these disruptions is that institutions, business models, and commercial practices that once seemed solid and durable may in fact be more vulnerable than we realized, and that formal structures sometimes rapidly give way to more informal and ad-hoc ways of doing things. Seen from this perspective, the traditions of informal media research surveyed in this chapter remind us that the industrial forms central to twentieth-century media are products of historical formalization but also that these long-term trajectories of formalization are not guaranteed. Media industries research must therefore be prepared for a range of possible futures, including those involving deformalization of media work and institutions.

# References

Akshaya K. (2019) "Informality in the Time of Platformization," *Media Industries*, 6 (2): 117–132.

Alacovska, A. and Gill, R. (2019) "De-Westernizing Creative Labor Studies: The Informality of Creative Work from an Ex-Centric Perspective," *International Journal of Cultural Studies*, 22 (2): 195–212.

Athique, A. and Parthasarathi, V. (eds) (2020) *Platform Capitalism in India*, Basingstoke: Palgrave.

Bishop, S. (2020) "Algorithmic Experts: Selling Algorithmic Lore on YouTube," *Social Media and Society*, 6 (1): 1–11.

Castells, M. and Portes, A. (1989) "World Underneath: The Origins, Dynamics, and Effects of the Informal Economy," in A. Portes, M. Castells, and L. A. Benton (eds), *The Informal Economy: Studies in Advanced and Less Developed Countries*, Baltimore, MD: Johns Hopkins University Press, 11–40.

Chen, J. Y. and Qiu, J. L. (2019) "Digital Utility: Datafication, Regulation, Labor, and DiDi's Platformization of Urban Transport in China," *Chinese Journal of Communication*, 12 (3): 274–289.

Cross, J. (1998) *Informal Politics: Street Vendors and the State in Mexico City*, Stanford, CA: Stanford University Press.

Cunningham, S. and Craig, D. (2019) *Social Media Entertainment: The New Intersection of Hollywood and Silicon Valley*, New York: New York University Press.

Cunningham, S. and Sinclair, J. (eds) (2001) *Floating Lives: The Media and Asian Diasporas*, St. Lucia: University of Queensland Press.

Cunningham, S. and Turnbull, S. (2020) *The Media and Communications in Australia*, 4th ed., Abingdon: Routledge.

Curtin, M. and Sanson, K. (2017) *Voices of Labor: Creativity, Craft, and Conflict in Global Hollywood*, Oakland, CA: University of California Press.

Floyd, S. (2008) "The Pirate Media Economy and the Emergence of Quichua Language Media Spaces in Ecuador," *Anthropology of Work Review*, 29 (2): 34–41.

Gill, R. (2011) " 'Life Is a Pitch': Managing the Self in New Media Work," in M. Deuze (ed.), *Managing Media Work*, Thousand Oaks CA: Sage, 249–262.

Govil, N. (2013) "Recognizing 'Industry'," *Cinema Journal*, 52 (3): 172–176.

Gray, M. L. and Suri, S. (2019) *Ghost Work: How to Stop Silicon Valley from Building a New Global Underclass*, New York: Houghton Mifflin Harcourt.

Hesmondhalgh, D. and Baker, S. (2011) *Creative Labour: Media Work in Three Cultural Industries*, Abingdon: Routledge.

Karaganis, J. (2011) "Rethinking Piracy," in J. Karaganis (ed.), *Media Piracy in Emerging Economies*, New York: Social Science Research Council, 1–12.

Krings, M. and Okome, O. (2013) *Global Nollywood: The Transnational Dimensions of an African Video Film Industry*, Indianapolis, IN: Indiana University Press.

Kumar, A. (2019) "Informality in the Time of Platformization," *Media Industries*, 6 (2): 117–132.

Leung, W.-F., Gill, R. and Randle, K. (2015) "Getting In, Getting On, Getting Out? Women as Career Scramblers in the UK Film and Television Industries," *The Sociological Review*, 63 (1): 50–65.

Lobato, R. and Thomas, J. (2015) *The Informal Media Economy*, Cambridge: Polity.

Mbaye, J. and Dinardi, C. (2019) "Ins and Outs of the Cultural Polis: Informality, Culture and Governance in the Global South," *Urban Studies*, 56 (3): 578–593.

Miller, J. (2016) *Nollywood Central*, London: British Film Institute.

McDonald, P. (2020) "Pirate-states: Imagining the Geography of Media Piracy," *International Journal of Cultural Studies*, available at https://journals.sagepub.com/doi/full/10.1177/1367877919850828 (accessed December 2, 2020).

Naficy, H. (1993) *The Making of Exile Cultures: Iranian Television in Los Angeles*, Minneapolis, MN: University of Minnesota Press.

Negus, K. (2002) "The Work of Cultural Intermediaries and the Enduring Distance between Production and Consumption," *Cultural Studies*, 16 (4): 501–515.

Pine, J. (2012) *The Art of Making Do in Naples*, Minneapolis, MN: University of Minnesota Press.

Poell, T., Nieborg, D., and van Dijck, J. (2019) "Platfomisation," *Internet Policy Review*, 8 (4): 1–13.

Roberts, S. T. (2019) *Behind the Screen: Content Moderation in the Shadows of Social Media*, New Haven, CT: Yale University Press.

Ross, A. (2003) *No-collar: The Humane Workplace and Its Hidden Costs*, Philadelphia, PA: Temple University Press.

Scholz, T. (2017) *Uberworked and Underpaid: How Workers Are Disrupting the Digital Economy*, Cambridge: Polity.

Schor, J. B. (2020) *After the Gig: How the Sharing Economy Got Hijacked and How to Win It Back*, Berkeley, CA: University of California Press.

Schor, J. B. and Attwood-Charles, W. (2017) "The 'Sharing' Economy: Labor, Inequality, and Social Connection on For-profit Platforms," *Sociology Compass*, 11 (8): 1–16.

Serenella, M. (2015) *Audiovisual Translation in the Digital Age: The Italian Fansubbing Phenomenon*, Basingstoke: Palgrave.

Soriano, C. R. R. and Cabañes, J. V. A. (2020) "Entrepreneurial Solidarities: Social Media Collectives and Filipino Digital Platform Workers," *Social Media + Society*, 6 (2), available at https://journals.sagepub.com/doi/full/10.1177/2056305120926484 (accessed December 2, 2020).

Sun, P. (2019) "Your Order, Their Labor: An Exploration of Algorithms and Laboring on Food Delivery Platforms in China," *Chinese Journal of Communication*, 12 (3): 308–323.

Sundaram, R. (2009) *Pirate Modernity: Delhi's Media Urbanism*, Abingdon: Routledge.

Tubaro, P. and Casilli, A. A. (2019) "Micro-work, Artificial Intelligence and the Automotive Industry," *Journal of Industrial and Business Economics*, 46 (3): 333–345.

Turow, J. (2019) *Media Today: Mass Communication in a Converging World*, 7th ed., Abingdon: Routledge.

van Dijck, J., Poell, T., and de Waal, M. (2018) *The Platform Society: Public Values in a Connected World*, Oxford: Oxford University Press.

Wang, S. (2003) *Framing Piracy: Globalization and Film Distribution in Greater China*, Lanham, MA: Rowman & Littlefield.

Zhao, E. J. (2019) *Digital China's Informal Circuits: Platforms, Labor and Governance*, Abingdon: Routledge.

# 12

# AN INDUSTRY OF ITS OWN?

## Approaching the American comic book industry

*Gregory Steirer and Alisa Perren*

Comics, which we will define here provisionally as non-animated series of hand-drawn sequential images, are one of the oldest modern media forms. Predating broadcasting, motion pictures, and sound recordings, comics emerged as a recognizable cultural form at roughly the same time that mass markets for printed work developed in the nineteenth century. Although comics have thus existed for well over a century, only recently have media and communication scholars begun to take the medium seriously as an object of study. In the field of media industry studies in particular, comics remain surprisingly under-researched, with little consensus having yet developed among scholars as to how the industry should be defined, how it should be studied, and why its study matters. In the only article on comics yet to appear in the journal *Media Industries*, Benjamin Woo (2018) even goes so far as to argue provocatively *against* the study of the comics industry, asserting that such a thing does not in fact exist.

Although we find Woo's argument extreme, it helpfully demonstrates the difficulty scholars face in situating the comics industry within preexisting frameworks of media industries scholarship. Does the comics industry require the development of its own research field or sub-field? Or should it be approached as part of some other industry and thus folded into an already established field of research? Our purpose in this chapter is not to provide a definitive answer to these questions, but rather to clarify their stakes, and in doing so, we hope, prompt future industry scholars to take up the study of comics from *multiple* positions – perhaps even within the same work of scholarship. Accordingly, we present below three different ways of construing the twenty-first-century North American comics industry: as its own industry, as part of the book industry, and as part of the filmed entertainment industry. None is intrinsically superior to any other, nor do these three ways exhaust the possible perspectives scholars might take. Each does, however, encourage different approaches to research, with respect to both (1) how one conceptualizes the industry's primary output and mode of distribution and (2) what methodologies appear most productive.

## Comic books on their own: the American direct market

Although comic books debuted on newsstands in the 1930s and continued to be sold this way, alongside other periodicals, through the end of the twentieth century, if we were to ascribe to American comics their own distinct industrial formation, its boundaries would be roughly

DOI: 10.4324/9780429275340-15

coterminous with the specialized comic book distribution system begun in the 1970s and named the "direct market." In this system, privately owned specialty stores (which are usually small businesses or a part of small, regional chains) purchase inventory from specialized comics wholesalers, which are the sole distributors for much, or in many cases all, of American comic book publishers' products. Despite the growing importance of the graphic novel as a product category (which we define at length in the next section), the primary product category here is the comic *book*, a 32-page full-color periodical, typically issued monthly, and usually containing a single segment of an ongoing story along with a small number of advertisements. Prices are set by retailers, but compared to other media, the manufacturer's suggested retail price has been high for decades: $2.99–$4.99 during the twenty-first century. In contrast to most other periodical distribution systems, comics are usually sold to retailers on a non-returnable basis, placing most of the burden of sales and promotion on the retailer. Although sell-through data to consumers is not tracked, the number of copies collectively purchased by retailers has been relatively modest in recent years: for most titles, it is less than 30,000 an issue; for a select few titles each month, the number can be as high as 150,000.

Construed in this fashion, the American comics industry is at the time of this writing in 2020 a monopoly with respect to distribution and an oligopoly with respect to production. Since the late 1990s, Diamond Comics Distributors has been the only wholesaler, and three publishing companies – DC, Marvel, and Image – have together accounted for a hefty majority of direct-market sales (around 75 percent in recent years) (*Comichron* n.d.). Although the range of ownership models with regards to characters, stories, and other intellectual property (IP) has broadened considerably this century, with more opportunities for creator ownership having emerged, the industry is still heavily organized around publisher ownership of IP, a model that positions most artists and writers as independent contractors. At the retail level, the industry is highly competitive, with no one company having any significant market share, except in localities where only one direct-market retailer exists. The result has been a tremendous diversity of retail forms, which are often highly idiosyncratic with respect to store or website aesthetic, profit strategy, and inventory range.

As for consumers, although the market has long been more diverse than scholarly and journalistic accounts have acknowledged, it has often been perceived as heavily straight, male, and white. Usually imagined in terms of highly committed adult *fans* and *collectors*, who are sometimes cast as excessively insular and often politically retrogressive, the consumer market has in reality been considerably more complex, especially in recent years, as publishers and retailers have invested heavily in attracting a diverse audience that includes women, people of color, and parents and children, as well as occasional or impulse shoppers. That said, until fairly recently the vast majority of writers, artists, and editors have been straight, male, and white. The monthly product cycles and limited number of retail outlets would also seem to encourage the kind of intense, sustained commitment that is characteristic of fan cultures. Perhaps for this reason, the consumer market is small in comparison to other media markets and currently appears largely self-contained with respect to demand. Sales data, for example, reveals no substantive bump to comics sales from the debut of high-profile film or television shows that utilize comic-book IP (Steirer 2021).

As this brief overview of the US direct market demonstrates, conceptualizing comics as their own industry privileges the comic periodical as the industry's core output and retailing as its primary distribution form. Given such privileging, what kinds of scholarship would we most expect to see from scholars who adopt this conceptualization? For starters, and perhaps most obviously, we would expect studies of production focusing on the multiple labor inputs – most of them creative and some highly collaborative – that the comic periodical can require: writer, scripter, penciler, inker, colorist, letterer, editor, etc. Interviews and ethnographic fieldwork seem particularly well-suited for such studies, as they are for studies of comics consumption – which we would also expect to see in some quantity, with both the practices of fans and non-fans as research objects. Perhaps less obviously, bracketing off of the comics industry from other media industries would also seem to lend itself to studies of the business of retailing, ideally from both an ethnographic and a microeconomic perspective. These studies might explore such concepts as inventory management, customer maintenance and acquisition, tax planning, and revenue modeling. Beyond its value for understanding how the comics industry functions, such research also strikes us as having much to offer the broader field of media industry studies, which has only just begun to take retailing seriously as a research object. Lastly, we would expect the kind of economic, organizational, and historical studies that have been produced by scholars focusing on other "self-contained" industries, such as the film, radio, or video game industries: corporate histories, examinations of distribution structures, analyses of basic business practices and core institutions, work on the effects of law and regulation, etc.

Given how recently the comics industry has emerged as a scholarly research area, it should not be surprising that very few of the kinds of studies just outlined have yet been published. Although there exists a large body of work on comics fans and a few studies of comics retailing, most of these have adopted the research paradigm of cultural sociology and have thus paid more attention to questions of cultural capital than they have capital itself or the industrial practices and institutions expressly concerned with it. Bourdieusian perspectives have similarly governed a good deal of the work on creative labor (which has focused, for the direct market, almost exclusively on writers and pencilers), although more diverse approaches have recently begun to emerge, such as Actor Network Theory (e.g., Perren and Steirer, 2021). Basic economic, organizational, and historical studies remain rare, especially those that examine companies other than Marvel and DC or genres other than that of the superhero. Much more common are cultural histories of the comic book as a popular (or sub-cultural) media form. Although such histories have been especially valuable in demonstrating how the comics industry has been shaped by broader historical processes, the processes that have drawn the most attention are typically (admitting the reductiveness of such labels) those associated with political, social, or technological change; by contrast, little work has traced the effects of economic, organizational, and managerial forces on the industry.

## Comics as part of the American book industry

For most of the twentieth century, American comic book periodicals were distributed to newsstands, bookstores, and other retailers that carried periodicals via the same distribution systems that handled magazines and other periodicals. Under this "newsstand" system, comic books were, like other periodicals, returnable goods with short shelf-lives, and thus received little to no in-store marketing or dedicated sales efforts. The aforementioned emergence of the direct market as an alternate distribution venue in the 1970s – and with it the option of non-returnable distribution – led comic book publishers to gradually abandon the newsstand model and with it the bookstore as a sales venue. Although newsstand distribution technically still exists, most bookstores carry no comic book periodicals at all and those that do (such as Barnes & Noble, one of the last remaining national chains) stock fewer than 20 titles. If we take comic book periodicals as the primary product of the comics industry – as we did in the previous section – bookstores would appear at best a vestigial part of that industry.

If we were to take instead, however, graphic novels as the comics industry's primary product, bookstores emerge as so key to comics publishers' business models that the comics industry might be more accurately characterized as a part of the book industry. In industrial parlance, the term *graphic novel* describes a square-bound comic book that is (in most cases) assigned an International Standard Book Number (ISBN). Formally speaking, graphic novels come in a tremendous variety, from pocket size to coffee-table size, black and white to color, 20 to 1,500 pages. Some are original works, containing material that has never been printed elsewhere; others are reprint collections of previously published comic books. As a product category, the graphic novel developed in the 1970s and early 1980s as an experiment by comic book publishers aimed primarily at the direct market. By the early 1990s, DC Comics and Pantheon Books (a book publisher) both had considerable sales success with some of these products in bookstores. Not until the early 2000s, however, did graphic novels become a major product category for these stores. Today, most graphic novels are distributed through both the direct market and bookstores, but the vast majority of sales – especially by book publishers, some of which forgo the direct market – occur in bookstores.

Compared to the direct market, US bookstore distribution is highly competitive, with multiple distributors competing to carry publishers' products. As a result, different distributors currently represent different comics publishers. Penguin Random House, for example, distributes DC Comics and Dark Horse; Hachette distributes Marvel Comics; and Simon & Schuster distributes BOOM! Studios books. All book distributors, however, are alike in selling products to bookstores on a returnable basis. Because books are returnable, the bookstore sales system is qualitatively different from that of the direct market; sales comparisons between the two, although common, thus often obscure as much as they reveal. In the bookstore market, for example, advertising to consumers is a key cost for publishers, who – through such things as sales promotions and bookstore end caps – must work hard to mitigate returns. In the direct market, by contrast, the plethora of titles, low profit margins, and lack of returnability have made advertising a comparatively small element of the industry. As for the bookstore retail market itself, although dominated by Amazon, it is extremely diverse, with both highly capitalized corporations and small, single-store businesses.

Publishing itself is also highly competitive in the book market. Although Marvel, DC, and Image are major players, so too are comics publishers Drawn & Quarterly and Fantagraphic Books, manga publishers Viz and Kodansha Comics, and traditional book publishers Scholastic, Penguin Random House, and Macmillan. The number of competitive publishers reflects the broad consumer market captured by bookstores: both male and female (though more heavily female) and all ages – including, importantly, children and young adults. The importance of the youth demographic is reflected in the book market's top-selling graphic novels, which for many years have been works expressly designed for young adults. Unlike most direct-market comics, these works tend to be single-author productions, with the same creative worker responsible for both the art and the story. These authors include Raina Telgemeier and *Dog-Man* author Dav Pilkey, both published by Scholastic, the leader in non-manga bookstore sales. Despite outselling by multiple orders of degree any title from DC or Marvel, such authors are virtually unknown among traditional direct-market comics "fans."

Although bookstores function as the keystone of the book industry, they are not the only means through which consumers gain access to books. Non-profit institutions, such as libraries, schools, and museums, also play a major role in distributing and marketing books in the United States, especially for young readers. The effect such institutions have on the industry is complex, simultaneously (for example) boosting sales through the purchases they make while also dampening sales via the alternate circulation pathways they provide. Without a doubt, however, these institutions have contributed significantly over the past two decades to the growth of the graphic novel as a product category and have likely been responsible for many young readers' first encounters with the medium.

As this brief introduction to the place of comics within the book industry suggests, when we conceptualize the comics industry as part of the book industry instead of its own industry, the product with which we are most concerned shifts from the comic book to the graphic novel. Retailing remains the primary distribution form as before (albeit possessing a very different structure), but other non-retail, non-profit forms of distribution also appear important. Given the shared emphasis on retailing, as well as the relatively similar production processes required for both comic books and graphic novels, we would expect to see many of the same basic approaches to research by scholars adopting a book-industry framework to the comics industry that we would from those utilizing a direct-market framework. Studies of labor inputs, the role of agents, retail approaches, and consumption practices all seem called for, particularly those that employ interviews, ethnographic fieldwork, and micro-economics. We would also expect economic, organizational, and historical studies focusing on the graphic novel's changing function both within the industry as a whole and on the businesses of specific industrial actors. In contrast to the direct-market framework, the book-industry framework should also encourage research into the role that non-profit institutions have played in shaping the graphic novel market. Certainly, this would include research into the involvement of public educational institutions, but we would also expect to see work on private organizations such as the Comic Book Legal Defense Fund, which has emerged this century as an important anti-censorship campaigner and advocate for inclusive library practices.

Perhaps not surprisingly, however, at the time we are writing this there exists virtually no scholarship, other than work on manga in the United States, that treats the American comics industry as part of the book industry (e.g., Brienza 2016). To be sure, comics are a relatively new research area for media scholars, but we suspect that the absence of scholarship adopting a book-industry approach has more to do with the way that media studies as a discipline has been constructed than the novelty of the research area. In most university systems, "the book" belongs, as a field of study, to language and literature programs. Although this has begun to fray with the growth of young-adult literature, most communication and media studies programs have long accepted this division. As a result, courses and faculty lines focusing on books and book culture are almost nonexistent in these programs. The absence of the book as a research object in media studies programs is not, however, simply the result of a turf war, for the book would also seem to gel poorly with the collectively oriented approaches to mass media and reception on which communication and media programs traditionally have been built. The history of the book stretches long before the advent of mass media, and the medium's reception, at least in the discursive formulation that has grown out of literary studies, has been more commonly understood in non-collective – and often personal or familial – terms. Unless literary studies is wrong about its primary research object (and there seems little evidence to us that it is), a turn to books by media scholars would require those scholars simultaneously to turn away from or significantly reimagine some of the most productive research areas of the last two decades: fandom, on-demand culture, and transmedia – all of which are heavily rooted in collective models of reception. Treating comics as part of the book industry thus strikes us as a particularly challenging research direction at the moment, albeit one that is likely to result in valuable and potentially groundbreaking work.

## Comics as part of the filmed entertainment industry

Throughout much of the twentieth century, comic book characters, especially superheroes, appeared consistently on daytime radio, prime-time live-action television series, daytime animated children's programs, and in theatrical motion pictures. Despite their regular presence across these media forms, it was not until the early 2000s, with the launch of the X-Men (in 2000) and Spider-Man (in 2002) film franchises along with television's *Smallville* (aired on The WB [2001–2006] and The CW [2006–2011] networks), that comic book characters and story worlds began to dominate screens large and small. By the late 2010s, comics-based IP was omnipresent, reliably generating substantial box office returns and widespread critical acclaim (*Black Panther* [2018], *Joker* [2019]), launching expansive televisual and cinematic universes (the Marvel Cinematic Universe, The CW's Arrowverse), helping jump-start the move by streaming services into original programming (Marvel/Netflix's Defenders series), and fostering dedicated cult followings (*Scott Pilgrim vs. The World* [2010]). While disproportionate scholarly and jour-nalistic attention has been dedicated to big-screen superhero characters targeted to a global moviegoing audience, comics-based IP film and TV adaptations actually have been far more varied both in terms of generic affiliations and demographic appeals. Even as non-superhero fare such as horror film *30 Days of Night* (2007) and action comedy *Red* (2010) appealed to young men and older audiences respectively, *Teen Titans Go!* (2013–) targeted children, *iZombie* (2015–2019) aimed for twenty-to-thirtysomething women, *Black Lightning* (2018–) hailed adult African Americans, and *The Boys* (2019–) pursued adult men.

As comics IP has become more attractive to Hollywood, so too has interest grown in the publishers involved in acquiring such content. While most media attention has been directed toward Marvel and DC, a number of smaller publishers including BOOM! Studios (*2 Guns* [2013]), Dark Horse (*Umbrella Academy* [2019–]), and IDW (*Wynonna Earp* [2016–2021]), also have successfully developed and licensed properties to Hollywood. In addition, several comic book writers including Mark Millar (*Kick-Ass* [2010]) and Robert Kirkman (*The Walking Dead* [2010–]) have signed lucrative licensing deals with Hollywood studios and streaming ser-vices. Meanwhile, a number of figures who first gained prominence for their comics-related work – including writers Warren Ellis and Jeph Loeb, as well as artist Jim Lee – have procured high-profile positions writing for television series, producing motion pictures, or working as executives at major media conglomerates. Whereas before the 2000s, comics professionals often struggled to gain a foothold working in film and television, by the late 2010s, many were sought after to work on TV writing staffs or to serve as art directors on animated series and storyboard artists on motion pictures. The heightened interest by Hollywood in working with comics IP and hiring comics creatives has in turn contributed to a growing number of agents, managers, and attorneys specializing in these areas of representation.

There are a number of reasons why comics are desirable sources of IP for filmed enter-tainment today. Shawna Kidman (2019) cites as key factors the ascent of comics fans into positions of power as executives and creatives, the improvement of digital technologies capable of depicting comics-related stories effectively, and the accessibility of these visually dynamic stories to a global market. In the course of our interviews (Perren and Steirer 2021), we often heard mentioned how comic books could be pitched in Hollywood with relative ease – instead of reading through a script, executives have the stories and characters depicted accessibly in visual form. Not only does the comic book represent "proof of concept," we were told, it also comes with sales data as well as evidence of a built-in fanbase.

Importantly, even though comics are an attractive source of IP for film and television produ-cers, that does not mean that comic book publishers should be perceived solely as "IP farms."

The use of such a label by many popular commentators dramatically oversimplifies the relationship between the comic book industry and Hollywood. Such a depiction of comic book publishers stems in part from a conflation of the comics industry as a whole with the two major publishers of superhero books, Marvel and DC, which are both relatively small divisions in terms of revenue and staff size within massive media conglomerates (AT&T/WarnerMedia and Disney, respectively). When framed as underperforming divisions of conglomerates, these publishers appear to have little function other than to provide character and story-world IP for their parent companies' other, more profitable business divisions – not only those of film and television, but also gaming, merchandise, and theme parks. Although some high-level conglomerate executives no doubt see publishers this way, the relationship between the publishing divisions and the divisions of these conglomerates is in practice more complex and dynamic. Comics divisions often function as sites of innovation and experimentation – places where ideas are tested out before they are translated into other media, often with the same creative figures shepherding these ideas across media forms and business divisions. What is more, as indicated above, there are other publishers beyond Marvel and DC, and each has a different relationship to Hollywood. For example, Image functions solely as a comics publisher; the creators of books published by Image retain all rights to license their content for other media forms. BOOM!, meanwhile, has a sister production company that develops and produces its comics content for film and television. This does not mean, however, that BOOM! strives to develop all its comics properties for film or TV; rather, the company assesses each property on a case-by-case basis to determine its suitability for development in other media. Beyond these varied models for IP development, it is also worth noting that the relationship between comics and the filmed entertainment industry is not unidirectional: film and television IP are regularly licensed to comics publishers as well. The resulting comics series either continue stories that have been completed in other media (e.g., *Buffy the Vampire Slayer* [1997–2003]), flesh out characters and story details provided only limited attention on the screen (e.g., *Star Wars: Captain Phasma*), or experiment – sometimes quite wildly – with the core assets of the original IP (e.g., *Adventure Time*).

Given the varied kinds of companies, organizational forms, markets, and products that must be taken into account when we conceptualize the comics industry as part of the filmed entertainment industry, identifying a core industry "output" and primary mode of distribution might seem more difficult here than when treating comics as their own industry or as part of the book industry. If we adopt a fan studies or narratological approach, we would likely identify the *character* or *story world* as the output and *adaptation* or *transmedia* as the distribution form (e.g., Jenkins 2006). Despite the importance these terms play in those fields, however, such concepts appear less helpful (and have thus been much less common) in media industry studies approaches. We thus propose, in contrast, that *intellectual property* – that is, copyrights and trademarks (including creative workers' rights to their own names), in distinction from characters and story worlds – be taken as the core product of the comics industry when framed as part of the filmed entertainment industry. This means that the primary mode of distribution should, in this framework, be seen as the *license*, that is, the legal and organizational infrastructure though which rights to use IP get made, marketed, and managed. Focusing on the production, exchange, and exploitation of copyrights and trademarks would also provide a clarifying – and we think highly productive – approach to understanding creative labor, firm structure, and profit models. Instead of focusing on comics artists, for example, as creative individuals hired to tell visual stories about characters, we might also see them as vendors selling to a publisher the copyrights to their completed drawings, which may or may not be based upon intellectual property that the publisher itself owns or has licensed from another firm. Although such an approach to creative labor might appear at first unnatural (not to mention unromantic), most of the comics creators – and nearly all of the business executives – we have interviewed sometimes explicitly characterized creative labor with respect to the comics industry in this manner.

In part, we suspect, because of the theoretical and methodological appeal of fan and transmedia studies to young media scholars, scholarship on IP management and licensing, either taking a comics-based or broader media industry studies approach, has remained relatively rare this century. Derek Johnson's *Media Franchising* (2013) and M. J. Clarke's *Transmedia Television* (2013) both significantly advance the examination of licensing, with comics featuring as some of their prime examples, but they are sui generis. Much work in this area remains to done. Organizational and managerial studies that address both inter-firm and intra-firm dealings over IP rights strike us as especially needed right now. More expansive studies of corporate structures and business strategies might also be undertaken, perhaps through a micro-economics lens or a theory of the firm. This could involve examining accounting strategies, financing practices, and mergers and acquisitions, both past and present. Though such objects of study might prove challenging to undertake due to issues of access, creative approaches to analyzing materials such as filings from publicly held companies, trade and journalistic publications, policy documents, third-party market reports, and court filings might be employed. Relatedly, scholars might turn to statutes, case law, lawsuits, and corporate legal strategies to explore developments in the theory and practice of trademark, copyright, and unfair competition law. Along with these forms of document analysis, interviews with industry stakeholders can point to new ways of understanding evolving managerial practices, brand management strategies, and labor conditions. For example, in the course of interviewing comics artists and writers (Perren and Steirer 2021), we learned of a growing number of intermediaries (literary agents, managers, and attorneys) focused on facilitating these professionals' transition into film and television. These talent representatives also increasingly represented smaller publishers as well; in this role, they focused on formulating new deal structures and contractual relationships (often involving innovative approaches to IP rights) between publishers, studios, networks, and other key Hollywood stakeholders. As such an example indicates, a turn to organizational, micro-economic, and legal approaches can expand the ways in which we understand the comics–Hollywood relationship.

## Conclusion

Though scholars from a variety of disciplinary perspectives – including communication and media studies, sociology, cultural geography, and cultural studies – have examined the comics industry, it is notable how much still remains to be studied. The origins of comics studies in fields such as art history and literary studies served to limit the extent to which topics ranging from business models to distribution strategies, marketing practices to labor conditions were examined in relation to comics. It is likely that the modest revenues earned by comics relative to other media industries, as well as the perception that the medium functions only or primarily as a source of characters and story worlds for other industries, have contributed to reductive approaches to both comics-as-industry and comics in relation to other industries. However, as our above analyses indicate, the comic book industry's distinctive status as an industry in its own right, as well as a component of both the book and filmed entertainment industries, makes it a potentially rich site of analysis. We see the comic book industry's straddling of multiple fields of study and diverse industry sectors as offering the possibility of imagining new ways of thinking about intra- and inter-industrial relationships and posing fresh ways of approaching familiar – and not so familiar – research objects.

# References

Brienza, C. (2016) *Manga in America: Transnational Book Publishing and the Domestication of Japanese Comics*, London: Bloomsbury.

Clarke, M. J. (2013) *Transmedia Television: New Trends in Network Serial Production*, New York: Bloomsbury Academic.

*Comichron* (n.d.) "Comic Publisher Market Shares by Year," available at www.comichron.com/vitalstatistics/marketsharesyearly.html (accessed March 7, 2020).

Jenkins, H. (2006) *Convergence Culture: Where Old and New Media Collide*, New York: New York University Press.

Johnson, D. (2103) *Media Franchising: Creative License and Collaboration in the Culture Industries*, New York: New York University Press.

Kidman, S. (2019) *Comic Books Incorporated: How the Business of Comics Became the Business of Hollywood*, Berkeley, CA: University of California Press.

Perren, A. and Steirer, G. (2021) *The American Comic Book Industry and Hollywood*, London: British Film Institute.

Steirer, G. (2021) "Industry," in R. Fawaz, D. Whaley, and S. Streeby (eds), *Keywords for Comic Studies*, New York: New York University Press, 127–130.

Woo, B. (2018) "Is There a Comic Book Industry?" *Media Industries*, 5 (1): 27–46.

# 13

# APPROACHING RACE IN MEDIA INDUSTRIES RESEARCH

*Anamik Saha*

In recent times we have seen the ascendency of diversity discourse in Western media industries. Across both commercial and public service media, there is a consensus that media industries lack racial and ethnic diversity. While diversity discourse also speaks to the lack of working class representation, gender inequalities, and the marginalization of lesbian, gay, bisexual, transgender, and intersex (LGBTI) communities and the disabled, the overwhelming *whiteness* of UK media industries in particular feels stark. But as diversity remains high on the policy agenda for media organizations with various initiatives put in place to try and increase participation from racialized groups (pre-COVID-19 at least), media industries remain overwhelmingly white, as well as middle-class (O'Brien, Laurison, Miles, and Friedman 2016).

Alongside diversity talk inside media, we have seen a growing interest in race and production in critical media industries research. This is a relatively new development in a field that, like its subject, denounces racism but has so far paid insufficient attention to the specific character of racial inequalities in media. Researchers exploring race and production have situated themselves within media industries research in order to contextualize the textual accounts that generally dominate race and media research. While they come from a range of different perspectives, they share an interest in how representations of race are shaped by the industrial processes of cultural production. Race and production studies then are broadly engaged – whether explicitly or implicitly – in the question of cultural commodification, and the implications when race is transformed into a commodity to be bought and sold.

In this chapter I draw from this research to outline an approach for studying race in the context of media industries. This entails a close focus on the production process that captures the complex dynamics of cultural commodification, but I also argue for greater consideration of structure and agency, the macro and micro (I'll suggest that structural issues and the question of political economy gets neglected in race and production research) in order to better understand how the material shapes the symbolic. The purpose of the chapter is to demonstrate the value of a media industries-centered approach to the topic of race and media. But in addition, I want to think through what research into race brings to media industries research as a whole.

DOI: 10.4324/9780429275340-16

## Research context

As stated, race and production studies is a relatively new field. Early examples come from Kristal Brent Zook (1999) and Herman Gray (1995) who both explore the rise and fall of black-cast sitcoms in US network television during the 1990s (driven by the Fox Network's strategy of "narrowcasting"). Other key texts include Vicki Mayer's (2001) analysis of the political economy of Latino media in San Antonio, Texas, and Sarita Malik's influential book *Representing Black Britain* (2002), which, as the title suggests, is mostly concerned with the depiction of black and Asian people in British television and film but provides some insights into the production contexts of making onscreen representations of racialized minorities (based on Malik's own experience working in media). But in recent years we have seen the expansion of this field through the work of a new generation of scholars sitting more squarely in critical media industry studies. Research in this field examines race in a number of media contexts including television (Martin 2015; Warner 2015), film (Nwonka 2019), music (Saha 2011), journalism (Nothias 2020), web series (Christian 2018), podcasting (Florini 2015; Vrikki and Malik 2019), and video games (Srauy 2019). These studies inject the issue of race into media industries research – a topic that has been generally neglected. But they make an important contribution to race and media studies more generally, adding much needed context to the studies of representations of racialized minorities that dominate, deepening our understanding of why representations of race take the shape that they do.

Running alongside and at times overlapping with race and production studies research are studies of creative labor – another field that has seen a relative boom in the broad context of media industries research. This work is more sociological in character and directly interested in inequalities in creative and cultural industries (CCIs). With a greater interest in cultural policy, it speaks more directly to the issue of "diversity" in CCIs, especially in the UK. Much of this research is interested in dismantling the myths of meritocracy that define CCI's sense of self. While the lack of concerted research on race is a big gap in the field (class and gender inequalities are the predominant interest), the subject of racial inequities inevitably features in an area explicitly framed by issues of social justice (Banks 2018).

While creative labor studies expose the rampant forms of inequality that characterize media industries, there is less concern with how this translates into how marginalized groups are represented in media (see De Benedictis, Allen, and Jensen (2017) for a notable exception). Why is this important? Put simply, how minorities are represented in media matters. Time and time again, race and media research demonstrates how minorities are represented according to the same narrow range of racialized tropes. Media discourses of race contribute to a "hegemonic field of meaning" (Alsultany 2012: 7) that structure the experience of racialized minorities, from government policy to everyday racisms. In this way, how minorities are represented in media is what Iris Marion Young (2011: 23) calls a "nondistributive" form of social justice, relating to "the symbols, images, meanings, habitual comportments, stories and so on through which people express their experience and communicate with each other."

As stated, race and production studies are focused on cultural production but have the question of how media *represents* race as their foundation. Put another way, this work is not just interested in the structural challenges encountered by racial minorities who work in media, but with how the cultures of production within media industries affect how particular groups are represented in the goods produced. Indeed, a concern with the symbolic nature of cultural commodities (the production of which is precisely what makes media industries distinct from other industries) can sometimes go missing in media industries research. Race and production studies can make an important contribution in this regard. However, we need to be careful not to invoke simplistic ideas of representation. The approach to race and media industries that I outline in this chapter is not about how we can represent minorities more "accurately." Rather, it is based upon Stuart Hall's (1988) notion of the politics of representation, founded on the idea that meanings around race are contingent and always ongoing and are never as simple as *biased/truthful, stereotypical/authentic, negative/positive*. In this regard my normative frame is *how to open up representational practices*. This shifts us from the question of representation back to the question of production. Thus, an approach to race in media industries is based upon a close (preferably empirical) examination of the production process. This entails unpacking the nature of industrial cultural production itself – in what Hesmondhalgh (2013: 11) (drawing on Raymond Williams) calls the "complex professional era" of cultural production – by examining the broader structural forces that shape it but also observing how production activity unfolds *on the ground*. In what follows, I flesh out an approach to race and media industries that as we shall see takes equally seriously structure and agency, the macro and the micro.

## How media industries make race

Studying race explicitly in the context of media industries deepens our understanding of the relations between race and media more generally. Without such an analysis, there is a danger of slipping into reductive arguments that claim that the media industries are nothing more than an apparatus for the dominant culture to spread racial ideology, or that sees racism as an outcome of a profit-driven media. While I am not totally dissuaded by the first of these perspectives outlined, I argue that the picture is much more complex. An approach to race and media industries recognizes complexity and contestation while nonetheless exposing the discursive forces that ensures the relative consistency in which racialized minorities have been represented in media. In what follows, I flesh out a broad approach to race in the context of media industries that as stated in the previous section is equally attentive to structural/macro and agency/micro dimensions.

There are two ways that we can address the issue of structure. The first follows a fairly traditional political economy approach. I am referring specially to critical political economy research that has mapped the shift toward neoliberalism and explored the impact this is having on media industries. The ascendency of neoliberal doctrine has seen media industries across the world become more marketized and commercialized. This has even had an impact upon public service media, ordinarily buffered from market forces, which are being forced to act more commercially. Neoliberal policies have led to the further expansion of already huge media conglomerates who have been allowed to expand across and within markets. This in turn has intensified media concentration, with some industries dominated by just a handful of media corporations (the music industry is now dominated by just three major groups that make up almost 80 percent of the global music market). While we should acknowledge the significance of smaller media companies that continue to play a significant role in CCIs, the means of cultural production remains firmly in the hands of the dominant elite who, needless to say, share a very particular ethnic and class makeup.

An approach to race and media industries as an initial step needs to situate its analysis against this backdrop of increasing marketization and commercialization. Very basically, representations of race made in the context of mainstream media industries at least, need to show economic value. This to an extent explains the prevalence of particular tropes of race that have proven popular with mainstream audiences. According to Oscar Gandy (1998), who provides a rare structural analysis of race and communication, the reproduction of racial stereotypes is fundamentally profitable for media industries. Crucially though Gandy also stresses complexity, recognizing the "changes in technology, media ownership, and finance, as well as market demographics and audience preferences" that have changed or even broadened the representation of racial minorities (p. 4). Indeed, the strongest political economy accounts are the ones that stress contradiction (Hesmondhalgh 2013). Either way, changes in the political economy of media shape how race is *commodified* and exploited by media industries. But while this speaks to market-based forces, what about the discursive?

One approach that thinks through the material and ideological/discursive dimensions is from a growing body of literature exploring the idea of "racial capitalism." This literature emerges from a number of theoretical perspectives and disciplinary foundations but it, broadly speaking, explores the *racial* character of capitalism (Robinson 2000; Melamed 2015; Bhattacharyya 2018). Theorists working with the idea of racial capitalism fundamentally challenge the idea that racism is an epiphenomenon of capitalism. Instead, they shed light on how the very idea of race was central to the Western project of modernity both economically (in terms of the economic exploitation of the Other) and ideologically (giving the West a sense of its own innate superiority, which in turn justified colonial conquest). In the context of media industries research, reframing our analysis of structure in terms of racial capitalism helps us challenge the idea that racism is a mere by-product of media's profit-driven orientation. It suggests instead that media industries are structured by racism, an idea that I shall return to in the next section. Rather than saying that racism is *intrinsic* to capitalism however, racial capitalism, in the context of media industries at least, entails an understanding of racial and capitalist ideologies as separate but inextricably intertwined, coming together to shape racism in particular ways in particular moments. Thus, racial capitalism needs to be understood conjuncturally, that is, specific interrelations between racial ideology and capitalism need to be placed in their historical contexts.

How does this apply to race and media? In the current conjuncture we are experiencing the neoliberalism era of racial capitalism, which has seen the emergence of the discourse of "postrace": the idea that racism has been surmounted and is no longer a structural force. Postrace plays out in media in two ways. First is through the notion of what Jo Littler (2017: 153) calls "postracial neoliberal meritocracy" and the idea that society is a level-playing field in which racialized minorities can achieve if they work hard enough. Second is through the way that race has been subsumed into a discourse of "diversity" that sidelines the question of racism and turns racial identity into a value that distinguishes a particular lifestyle, brand, or a niche audience (Gray 2013). For Sarita Malik (2014), there has been a rise in lifestyle programming, reality television, and self-improvement shows that rely on having a diverse range of social types, resulting in a "hypervisibility of multicultural societies" (p. 34), but one that is devoid of any reference to social inequality let alone racism. (In fact such depictions, before the 2020 Black Lives Matter protests at least, fed a narrative that such societies were *postrace*.) Thus, in contemporary media culture, narratives of race are made according to a discourse of diversity, where race is no longer invisible but *hypervisible*. But as much as we see more black and brown faces on our screens, to what extent do we learn about black and brown lives (Saha 2018)?

These are the macro forces – both economic and ideological/discursive – that shape the making of race in media. But this is only one half of the picture. An approach to race and media industries needs to also explore the micro level of production and the question of agency in particular. Some of the most nuanced accounts of cultural production as it unfolds in the everyday has comes from scholars working in the cultural studies tradition (e.g., see contributors to Mayer, Banks, and Caldwell 2009). Cultural studies of production broadly seek to challenge the fatalism and pessimism of Frankfurt School-style theorizations of cultural commodification. Instead, they highlight the complexity of cultural production in media industries, deconstructing simplistic, monolithic conceptions of the very idea of a singular "culture industry." The concern here is with the "cultures of production" (Negus 1997) through which culture is made, entailing a close examination of the practices, rituals, and understandings that shape symbol creation. A major insight derived from cultural studies of production is how production choices, rather than being entirely economically determined, are equally shaped by the cultural values of creative managers and producers. Cultural studies of production in this way stress the messy, human nature of cultural production.

Cultural studies of production specifically focused on race are an emerging field. One of the key examples of this approach, and which happens to be one of the earliest examples of cultural studies of production, comes from Keith Negus (1999) in his study of corporate production in the music industry. Interestingly Negus is not interested in race directly, but by conducting case studies on rap and Latin music he provides a fascinating (and rare) empirical study of how race is commodified in the products of media industries. His examination of the making of Latin music and rap are part of a broader study of "genre cultures" (p. 3) that shape the production, circulation, and consumption of popular music. Exemplifying the cultural studies approach to these issues, Negus emphasizes the "interplay and uneasy interaction between economics (music as commodity, various business strategies, and organizational structures) and culture (the practices, interpretations, and ways of life of musicians, fans, and industry workers) and the ways in which the two often blur and fuse" (p. 3).

Negus' aim is to smudge the distinctions between economy and culture upon which political economy approaches to culture rest. Moreover, in his analysis of rap and Latin music in particular, he wants to challenge the mass culture argument about the co-option of those genres in terms of the commodification or homogenization of culture. In doing so Negus calls for a shift from a top-down production of culture perspective (which characterizes the mass culture argument he is critical of), to thinking through instead, as stated earlier, a more discursive notion of the cultures of production that exist within media industries. How does such an approach illuminate the production of rap and Latin? First, Negus demonstrates how these genres are marginalized in relation to "white" genres like rock. But with his focus on cultures of production Negus argues that this, on the surface at least, is a product of how record executives manage uncertainty, rather than a straightforward case of racism (though this of course comes into play). For instance, Negus finds that the genre of rap, despite its profitability, is still considered a "wild cat" enterprise by music executives

> uncertain about its future aesthetic changes and nervous when trying to predict potential market growth, and by business personnel who are uncomfortable with the politics of black representation foregrounded by the genre and anxious about confronting political pressure from the moral opponents of rap.
>
> *p. 87*

Thus, Negus aims to provide a more nuanced analysis of the commodification of race as embodied in the production of rap by stressing (a) the fundamental unpredictability of cultural production and (b) the way that cultural values shape production choices. Though he does not address this explicitly, what is noteworthy about the above quote is how these cultural values are clearly racialized.

Negus' argument is captured in Tim Havens (2013) notion of "industry lore," which refers to the knowledge that creative managers use – whether drawing from professional experience, market research or gut feeling – to make decisions on black cultural production. For Havens, industry lore amounts to a form of power/knowledge (considering that the upper echelons of media industries are dominated by white men) that shape the production of, to use Havens' example, black television, in particular ways that constrain (though at times open up) its production, distribution, and syndication, especially in international markets. Though he was writing much earlier than Havens, Negus effectively describes lore in his analysis of rap music, specifically the understanding among executive that the genre does not travel well, that it is "too black" for international promotion, and that rap lyrics are too parochial for mainstream music audiences. As Negus puts it, this latter argument he finds in the industry effectively reducing "the genre's aesthetic complexity and rhythmic, harmonic and melodic cosmopolitanism to rap lyrics" (1999: 95). Negus' main concern is the economic impact of such an understanding of rap, with less resources spent on racialized genres/texts, but the previous quote also speaks to the aesthetic implications of industry lore. Thus, cultural studies of race and media industries shed light on the assumptions about race that inform the production of certain genres. Or put another way, they demonstrate how creative choices are racialized. But such studies at the same time stress messiness and uncertainty. As a consequence, this is a more nuanced understanding of the commodification of race in the context of racial capitalism. Such insights are important for race and media industries research.

One more perspective that should feed into the study of race and media industries comes from a cultural industries perspective – a tradition of critical political economy also concerned with the nature of commodification (Hesmondhalgh 2013). Cultural industries research addresses historical shifts in the political economy of media industries – not just in terms of policy but the very organization of production. Like cultural studies of production, it recognizes that cultural production is a site of struggle and contestation but draws specific attention to the distinctiveness of cultural industries, specifically the symbolic nature of the cultural commodity that contains the very particular use value of novelty and difference (Garnham 1990: 160). In other words, as much as audiences may turn to the same cultural products, they also demand originality, which explains those moments where a cultural text emerges as if from out of nowhere to huge commercial and critical acclaim but also the spectacular flops that seemingly tick all the right commercial and aesthetic boxes. This is an underrated but hugely significant point for race and media industries scholars as it helps account for the contradictory tendencies of media industries that rely on racial stereotype, but can also produce rich, alternative, enlightening depictions of race (Saha 2018). This contradiction is prized open by audience demands or the creativity of symbol creators. Earlier, I cited Oscar Gandy who describes how racial stereotypes are immensely profitable for media industries, but also admits that audience demands can lead to the broadening of representations of race. David Hesmondhalgh (2013) highlights the persistence of the romantic conception of the artist in Western societies, which explains why symbol creators are afforded relatively autonomy, or "loose control" that in turn has opened a space for black, brown, and Asian cultural producers to shift the regime of representation of those groups.

## What an analysis of race brings to media industries research

This chapter has outlined an approach to studying race and media industries. The intention was to offer a broad framework rather than a prescriptive program. The main concern was to convey the importance of focusing on both the macro and the micro, structure and agency, as well as to think through how production is related to representation. Production studies of race produce valuable insights into the dynamics of cultural production at the micro level and how this affects the making of representations of race, but in this literature there is less emphasis on the structural, by which I mean the broader political economic forces that impact upon the labor of creative workers, especially those from racialized backgrounds. In other words, researchers of race and production would benefit from greater engagement with political economy approaches to media industries. An approach to race and media industries needs to have as its foundation an historical understanding of the development of media industries and the changes in their organization, as well as the ways that legacies of empire shape modern formations of race. I suggest that the concept of racial capitalism offers us a route toward thinking together the relations between racial and capitalist ideology/political economy within the given social formation, and how these affect the production of race in the media industries.

Conceptualizing commodification as a historical process, racial capitalism helps us understand how economic forces and racial ideology come together to shape the commodification of race in a specific moment. In this neoliberal stage of racial capitalism, we have seen the ascendency of diversity discourse, which this chapter has argued results in the proliferation of images of race, albeit radically decontextualized, unbound from racism.

This chapter has been framed in terms of demonstrating the value of media industries research for the study of race and media. But to conclude this chapter I want to briefly demonstrate what a focus on race brings to the field of media industries. As stated earlier, the topic of race has been of marginal interest in media industries research, yet such a focus helps deepen our understanding of media industries. In the previous section I stated that Keith Negus is not so much interested in race but rather the nature of corporate production and cultural commodification. But the genres of rap and Latin music provide rich sites through which Negus can explore the complexity and contestation – and lack of certainty – that characterizes cultural production. Negus demonstrates empirically how cultural production is unpredictable, and how creative managers strive to manage this unpredictability, or at least, try to *appear to* look in control. His main argument is that corporate production is essentially based on what creative managers *think* will be successful, rather than what will be successful, and that such judgment contains values about culture, and in turn, race. More broadly, Negus' case studies on two racialized genres allow him to complicate reductive arguments he sees in media/cultural studies, whether those be in the form of Frankfurt School-style despair over the commodification of culture on the one hand, or celebratory postmodern accounts of the creativity of consumption on the other. What a focus on race brings to the table for media industries research is therefore how cultural production is a fundamentally cultural process, highlighting how industrial processes, far from being neutral, contain within them values about culture, including whose culture matters and whose does not.

Moreover, a focus on race brings attention to a neglected issue within media industries: the textual. The main concern of research into media industries is the distinctive nature of a production, including its institutional arrangements and the particular experience of creative work. But as suggested earlier, it can leave out precisely what makes media industries distinct: the symbolic quality of its goods. Yet media industries studies as a whole – even the subfield of creative labor research most explicitly concerned with the question of inequality – seem to dodge the question of the textual. Maybe it is because media studies researchers do not have the methodological tools to conduct such analysis, being more comfortable with social scientific methods rather than the techniques of deconstruction found in literary studies. Or maybe the reason is more political, and the fear there is too much focus on ideology and not enough on the actual exploitation of the worker (for a famous articulation of this argument see Garnham 1990: 61–62). I argue that research on media industries surely has to center the primary symbolic nature of the textual commodities it makes, and which in turn contribute to inequalities in society. And this is precisely what race and production studies brings to media industries research, taking seriously the politics of representation as well as labor issues. A key concern for media industries research should be thinking through the relation between the material and symbolic, and this is precisely what a focus on race can bring.

Finally, centering race in media industries research challenges assumptions that reduce racism to a mere outcome of a capitalistic media system. Rather, an approach to race and media industries demonstrates how racism is a determining force upon cultural production. Within media industries research and beyond, the question of race gets siloed, which Gray (2016: 249) explains as the "the result of the analytic confinement and discursive linkages of race to people of color (and not the operation of whiteness)." Very basically the issue of racism in media industries is seen as only relevant when the subject matter is explicitly about race – whether a portrayal of a racial minority group in a documentary, or the experience of racism in the creative workplace. But what Gray alludes to in this quote is how media industries (and dare I say, media industries research itself) are structured by whiteness. Even when race is absent racism is at play. As such focusing on media industries' racializing dynamics is a significant part of unpacking how power operates and inequalities reproduce in media at large. I argue that media industries researchers, particularly those working in the tradition of political economy, would benefit from a stronger engagement with the concept of racial capitalism/racial neoliberalism. Doing so highlights how the dominant culture maintains control of media industries precisely through the economic exploitation and racial subjugation of the Other. To repeat, racism is not a tragic side-effect of profit-driven media industries but rather central to the security of the dominant culture that owns them.

## Conclusion

In this chapter I have outlined an approach to researching race in media industries research. A media industries approach to the broader subject of race and media has much to bring in terms of deepening our understanding of why particular representations of race recur over time. In this regard, it brings much needed context to the studies of texts that dominate media studies of race. Moreover, a media industries approach points us to how interventions can challenge the reductive ways that minorities are represented in the media, broadening the regime of representation. In this way, media industries research not only speaks directly to – but can steer toward new directions in – ongoing debates on diversity in media/cultural policy. Namely, media industries research shows that solving racial inequalities is not just about increasing the numbers of minorities in the creative workforce, which is the current way that diversity is conceptualized, but subverting/undermining/transforming the cultural values (which appear neutral/objective yet are anything but) that shape the production of representations of race.

In this chapter I also argued that a focus on race can enhance media industries research as a whole. While production studies are a growing field, the topic of race remains marginal. I suggested that media industries researchers mistakenly see the problem of racism as a mere by-product of a capitalistic media system. Instead, I argue that racism is a determining force upon cultural production, that shapes media industries and is a central facet to the operation of power. Tackling racism head-on in the context of media will immediately destabilize the authority of the dominant culture that own the means of cultural production. Studying race in media industries does not just shed light on instances of racism, but the very (racial) character of media industries themselves.

# References

Alsultany, E. (2012) *Arabs and Muslims in the Media: Race and Representation After 9/11*, New York: New York University Press.

Banks, M. (2018) "Creative Economies of Tomorrow? Limits to Growth and the Uncertain Future," *Cultural Trends*, 27 (5): 367–380.

Bhattacharyya, G. (2018) *Rethinking Racial Capitalism: Questions of Reproduction and Survival*, London: Rowman and Littlefield International.

Christian, A. J. (2018) *Open TV: Innovation Beyond Hollywood and the Rise of Web Television*, New York: New York Press.

De Benedictis, S., Allen, K., and Jensen, T. (2017) "Portraying Poverty: The Economics and Ethics of Factual Welfare Television," *Cultural Sociology*, 11 (3): 337–358.

Florini, S. (2015) "The Podcast 'Chitlin' Circuit': Black Podcasters, Alternative Media, and Audio Enclaves," *Journal of Radio and Audio Media*, 22 (2): 209–219.

Gandy, O. H. (1998) *Communication and Race: A Structural Perspective*, London: Arnold.

Garnham, N. (1990) *Capitalism and Communication: Global Culture and the Economics of Information*, London: Sage.

Gray, H. (2013) "Subject (ed) to Recognition," *American Quarterly*, 65(4): 771–798.

Gray, H. (2016) "Precarious Diversity: Representation and Demography," in M. Curtin and K. Sanson (eds), *Precarious Creativity: Global Media, Local Labor*, Oakland, CA: University of California Press, 241–253.

Gray, H. (1995) *Watching Race: Television and the Struggle for Blackness*, Minneapolis, MN: University of Minnesota Press.

Hall, S. (1988) "New Ethnicities," in K. Mercer (ed.), *Black Film, British Cinema*, London: Institute of Contemporary Art, 27–31.

Havens, T. (2013) *Black Television Travels: African American Media around the Globe*. New York: New York University Press.

Hesmondhalgh, D. (2013) *The Cultural Industries*, 3rd ed. London: Sage.

Littler, J. (2017) *Against Meritocracy: Culture, Power and Myths of Mobility*, Abingdon: Routledge.

Malik, S. (2014) "Diversity, Broadcasting and the Politics of Representation," in G. Titley, K. Horsti, and G. Hultén (eds), *National Conversations: Public Service Media and Cultural Diversity in Europe*. Bristol: Intellect, 21–42.

Malik, S. (2002) *Representing Black Britain: A History of Black and Asian Images on British Television*, London: Sage.

Martin Jr., A. L. (2015) "Scripting Black Gayness: Television Authorship in Black-Cast Sitcoms," *Television and New Media*, 16 (7): 648–663.

Mayer, V. (2001) "From Segmented to Fragmented: Latino Media in San Antonio, Texas," *Journalism and Mass Communication Quarterly*, 78 (2): 291–306.

Mayer, V., Banks, M. J., and Caldwell, J. T. (eds) (2009) *Production Studies: Cultural Studies of Media Industries*, New York: Routledge.

Melamed, J. (2015) "Racial Capitalism," *Critical Ethnic Studies*, 1 (1): 76–85.

Negus, K. (1999) *Music Genres and Corporate Cultures*, Abingdon: Routledge.

Negus, K. (1997) "The Production of Culture," in P. Du Gay (ed.), *Production of Culture/Cultures of Production*, Milton Keynes/London: Open University/Sage, 67–118.

Nothias, T. (2020) "Postcolonial Reflexivity in the News Industry: The Case of Foreign Correspondents in Kenya and South Africa," *Journal of Communication*, 70 (2): 245–273.

Nwonka, C. J. (2019) "The New Babel: The Language and Practice of Institutionalised Diversity in the UK Film Industry," *Journal of British Cinema and Television*, 17 (1): 24–46.

O'Brien, D., Laurison, D., Miles, A., and Friedman, S. (2016) "Are the Creative Industries Meritocratic? An Analysis of the 2014 British Labour Force Survey," *Cultural Trends*, 25 (2): 116–131.

Robinson, C. J. (2000) *Black Marxism: The Making of the Black Radical Tradition*, Chapel Hill, NC: University of North Carolina Press.

Saha, A. (2011) "Negotiating the Third Space: British Asian Independent Record Labels and the Cultural Politics of Difference," *Popular Music and Society*, 34 (4): 437–454.

Saha, A. (2018) *Race and the Cultural Industries*, Cambridge: Polity Press.

Srauy, S. (2019) "Precarity and Why Indie Game Developers Can't Save Us from Racism," *Television and New Media*, 20 (8): 802–812.

Vrikki, P. and Malik, S. (2019) "Voicing Lived-experience and Anti-racism: Podcasting as a Space at the Margins for Subaltern Counterpublics," *Popular Communication*, 17 (4): 273–287.

Warner, K. J. (2015) *The Cultural Politics of Colorblind TV Casting*, New York: Routledge.

Young, I. M. (2011) *Justice and the Politics of Difference*, Princeton, NJ: Princeton University Press.

Zook, K. B. (1999) *Color by Fox: The Fox Network and the Revolution in Black Television*, New York: Oxford University Press.

# 14

# METHODOLOGICAL APPROACHES TO WOMEN'S WORK IN HOLLYWOOD

*Courtney Brannon Donoghue*

The year 2017 proved a particularly tumultuous year for women in the American political and popular landscape. From battling inequity and sexual misconduct in the workplace, to fighting for reproductive rights in Capitol Hill, familiar feminist issues emerged front and center in the national conversation with Hollywood as a key player. Three particular moments dominating the news cycle during that year stand out as part of evolving conversations around inclusion, equity, and access. First, in January, social media reaction to the 2016 US presidential election mobilized individuals into an active community organizing a series of Women's Marches in cities across the United States. This pro-feminist movement emerged largely in response to Hillary Clinton losing the November presidential election to the newly sworn in Donald Trump. Breaking demonstration attendance records, marches took place in New York, Los Angeles, Dallas, and many other US cities as well as expanding worldwide. Popular and trade press widely covered Hollywood's star-studded participation during these events. For example, the DC march included speeches by America Ferrera and Janelle Monáe, while Jane Fonda and Natalie Portman spoke in Los Angeles. During the Sundance Film Festival, Chelsea Handler and producer Mary McCormack organized and led women on a march down Park City's Main Street in parallel to the usual premieres and parties (Miller 2017; Chenoweth and Pressman 2017).

Another battle was taking place along different lines by summer. Warner Bros. released the studio's first female-directed (Patty Jenkins) and led (Gal Gadot) superhero movie *Wonder Woman* in June. Weighed down by long-held industry lore that "female superhero movies don't make money" and "women don't like comic book movies," the much-anticipated film reportedly was underestimated by the studio and industry at large as a box office "gamble" and "risk" (Brannon Donoghue 2019). In a turn of events, *Wonder Woman* performed beyond expectations globally, smashing box office numbers set by Warner Bros./DC Comics films to become one of the top-grossing movies of the year (Cavna 2017; Siegel 2017).

By October, the publication of two investigative reports resulted in a third seismic wave. Articles by Jodi Kantor and Megan Twohey (2017) in *The New York Times*, and Ronan Farrow (2017) in *The New Yorker*, exposed decades of sexual misconduct and abuse by former Miramax and Weinstein Company executive Harvey Weinstein. First-hand accounts revealed a powerful executive who intimated, coerced, and abused female film professionals from A-list actresses to assistants, which had been covered up for decades. Women in the entertainment industries

DOI: 10.4324/9780429275340-17

collectively began to organize across social media. Founded by activist Tarana Burke in 2006 for sexual assault survivors to share their stories, #MeToo re-emerged as a hashtag movement and rallying cry in fall 2017. Contradictory conversations, cancellations, and calls for action followed. As a result, a series of high-profile men from on-screen talent to executives were called out and pushed out of positions of power for predatory and abusive behavior at TV networks, film studios, tech companies, and more (Garcia 2017). By the end of 2017, a group of Hollywood A-list women formed the Time's Up movement to further push against gendered employment disparities and questioning industry power dynamics (Time's Up 2018).

These highly publicized events highlight systemic gender inequity at the root of American life and work. The film industry may merely represent one particular pressure point in a larger push for equity and access in the US workforce. For Hollywood, a growing wave of political, economic, and cultural backlash swelled by the late-2010s that increasingly called male-dominant studio systems and structures into question. This transformative moment offers an unprecedented opportunity for media industries scholars to examine the complex gender and labor dynamics for media workers unfolding in real time. The purpose of this chapter is to consider different methodological approaches for examining gender in the media industries. Two questions frame my thinking: (1) what methodological approaches to women's work in Hollywood have media industry scholars employed in the past and (2) what approach can we develop moving forward? I first look at the rich cycle of recent archival work that complicates long-held assumptions about women's exclusion for most of the twentieth-century Hollywood studio system. From there I consider the data-driven trend for mapping gender inequity through quantitative employment studies. The remainder of the chapter explores interview-based research methods that help to map the limited mobility for female creatives in the contemporary studio environment.

Grounded in industry interviews and trade coverage, the chapter offers a different approach to understanding how women navigate work conditions and culture in twenty-first-century Hollywood. I encourage media industry scholars to rethink the field's earlier investment in measuring gender parity by tracking employment data or more specifically who is in the director's chair. Instead, by focusing on precarious employment, intersectional disparities, and the global pandemic, I highlight the value of on-the-ground methodological work for examining how women navigate working conditions and struggle with career mobility in this transformative industrial moment. This chapter is an exercise in considering the available frameworks for studying women's place in Hollywood, from the emergence of the #MeToo and Time's Up movements, to the unfolding and open-ended implications for what a post-pandemic Hollywood may look like.

## Historical, archival approaches to women's work

A robust series of recent studies reconsider women's work in Hollywood across three key periods – silent film, the classical era, and New Hollywood. Extensive historical accounts utilize archival research not only to complicate popular narratives about the lack of women behind the camera and on the studio lot, but also uncover their contributions in various roles across the major studios. Feminist film scholars, most notably the Women Film Pioneers Project founded by Jane Gaines, pushes back against earlier narratives about female filmmakers in the silent period. By 1909, women actively worked in almost all sectors of the American film industry, with their numbers peaking between 1918 and 1922. For example, as a contemporary of D. W. Griffith and Cecil B. DeMille, Lois Weber was one of the most prolific writers and directors of the silent period. Shelley Stamp describes Weber's career as a "notorious blind spot" of Hollywood film historians (2015: 4). Even as early Hollywood appealed directly to the sensibilities and aspirations of a generation of modern "woman-made women" flocking to the West Coast, they arrived to find increasingly limited access and opportunities for employment by the 1920s (Hallett 2013: 219). The film studios strategically sought what Karen Ward Mahar describes as "financial legitimacy" and Gaines calls "finance capital" through consolidation and concentration of ownership (Mahar 2006: 2–3, 7; Gaines 2018: 28). As a result, the number of women working in the production sector declined drastically.

Female studio creatives – Dorothy Arzner, Joan Harrison, Virginia Van Upp, Anita Loos – during the 1930s and 1940s were the exception and not the rule. In contrast, most women working for the major studios reflected a traditional "feminization of labor." Erin Hill contends that

> women were never absent from film history; they often simply weren't documented as part of it because they did 'women's work', which was – by definition – insignifcant, tedious, low status, and noncreative. In the golden age of Hollywood, women could be found in nearly every department of every studio, minding the details that might otherwise get in the way of more important, prestigious, or creative work (a.k.a. men's work). If film historians consider the classical Hollywood era's mode of production a system, we ought to consider women this system's mainstay, because studios were built on their low-cost backs and scaled through their brush and keystrokes.
>
> *2016: 5*

Women's film jobs largely reflected the gendered division shaping the US workforce. They held a variety of roles including food and janitorial departments, teaching, nursing, clerical, and administrative positions (pp. 4–6).

By the 1960s and 1970s, the studio system transformed as a new generation of executives and filmmakers took the helm. Women climbed the ranks to entry level, assistant positions increasingly working in creative, albeit still feminized and clerical, roles in development, scripts, and casting (Hill 2016). Maya Montañez Smukler (2019: 2) describes the 1970s as a "crucial decade" for women filmmakers including Elaine May and Barbara Loden. Between 1967 and 1980, 16 women directed studio projects, averaging around one film per year. Even as 20th Century-Fox appointed Sherry Lansing as the first female president of production in 1980, followed by Columbia hiring Dawn Steel as their first female studio president in 1987, the gains for women in powerful financial and creative decision-making roles were slow and minimal (pp. 279–280).

The acceleration of the American independent sector from the 1980s and 1990s into the following decade opened the door to a new generation of female filmmakers. Yet, Christina Lane (2004: 195) argues, as the indie scene commercialized in the Sundance-Miramax era, the careers of emerging female filmmakers often stalled after their first studio feature. Despite the increasing commercialization of film festivals, and studio investment in acquisition and distribution of independent films, women's careers did not benefit to the same degree as their male peers as a result of the 1990s boom driven by the emergence of studio boutique divisions like Sony Pictures Classics and Fox Searchlight.

If telling the story of Hollywood in the twentieth century is based on who is directing studio features, then yes, it would appear very few or no women were present at all. Despite the intervention of recent media industries historical work, the legacy of auteur theory that has shaped decades of film history's director-driven Hollywood narratives still places an unprecedented value on a role historically dominated by white men. J. E. Smyth questions the long-lasting implications:

how appropriate is it to reconstruct a woman's filmmaking "canon" using the same exclusionary language that erased women from active participation in the earlier eras of US history? … film historians schooled in conventional auteurism are committed to a hierarchy of work emphasizing directors as the definitive creative force in film-making, a position that masks women's wider presence in the industry during the studio era.

*2018: 16*

Even as a limited number of women occupied the studio director's chair in the past century, accounts of lone genius directors, boy wonder producers, and larger-than-life studio moguls have dominated film industry studies. Normalized images of the director as a masculine pos-ition, and of filmmaking as a fantasy space for men, have broadly shaped decades of scholarship and syllabi, leaving women's contributions in other areas largely overlooked until recently.

## Structural, data-driven approach to employment

A second approach, grounded in industrywide quantitative studies, highlights structural employ-ment disparities in the 2000s and 2010s. The Geena Davis Institute on Gender in Media, University of Southern California's (USC) Media, Diversity, and Social Change Initiative, and University of California, San Diego's (UCSD) Center for the Study of Women in Film and Television publish annual industry reports mapping employment numbers for women working behind the camera. As these macro-level studies illustrate, into the twenty-first century women did not fare much better in securing above-the-line positions or financing for studio features. In her 2019 "Celluloid Ceiling" report, UCSD's Martha D. Lauzen highlights "recent his-toric highs" for the top-grossing 100 domestic studio films. On the one hand, female directors proportionally helmed more bigger budget, wide release projects, jumping from 2 percent in 2010 to 12 percent in 2019 (p. 5). There were slight increases also for writers, producers, and editors, although on the other hand, taking a wider sample with the 500 highest grossing films domestically, the overall percentage of women working above-the-line and as department heads fluctuated, with different job roles showing far smaller or no gains (p. 7).

Industrywide pressure may have led to some strategic hiring efforts by a minority of the Hollywood studios. From 2016 to 2019, Universal and Sony reportedly employed 20 female directors more than any other peer studios, while Disney and Fox's numbers declined, and Paramount remained at zero (Smith, Choueiti, Yao, Clark, and Pieper 2020). Even as the numbers of women directing, writing, and producing studio films slowly crept up by the 2000s, the types of projects women helmed were often limited in size and scale. Until Patty Jenkins in 2017 with Warner Bros.' *Wonder Woman* and Ava DuVernay in 2018 with Disney's *A Wrinkle in Time*, Kathryn Bigelow was the only woman to direct a Hollywood movie – *K-19: Widowmaker* (2002) – budgeted over $100 million (Ford 2017). Despite publicized gains moving toward more equitable hiring practices at the start of the 2020s, the levels of women working in above-the-line and below-the-line roles compared to their male peers remain stun-ningly disproportionate.

Broad industry studies have contributed significantly toward gathering quantitative data that shed light on how deeply rooted these structural inequities are. Macro-level data serves more as a starting point for identifying systemic gender discrimination and disparities and applying public pressure using trade publications, social media, and industry events. Yet, this approach has a number of limitations. First, while the director may be the most visible and historically lauded production position, as noted by historians in the previous section, digging beyond the director's chair and further into employment data is necessary. Second, because these data studies offer such a broad look at the industry, further context is necessary to look beyond industrywide employment trends into the nuances of comparing vastly different production companies, distributors, budgets, geographical locations, etc.

Hiring women offers one perspective on gendered employment trends, but what about the specificity of women's labor and working experiences? What can women's contributions and struggles on individual projects and inside institutions reveal about developing sustainable career paths? Broadening the approach and line of questioning for the current industrial moment has the potential to open up new lines of enquiry for understanding the complexity of the gender gap.

## Mapping gendered precarity and mobility

Archival accounts offer a striking industrywide snapshot of gender disparities over a historical period, while recent quantitative employment data present a fixed data point of where women are employed, or more often are not, in a given year. Building upon macro-level views of industry dynamics, business models, and institutional cultures, a micro-level analysis is necessary to understand how power is gained, leveraged, and negotiated by individuals and collaborators over time in ways that are not linear and often fluid. Interviews, oral histories, participant observation, and industrial ethnography are crucial for understanding how a creative career path is built in Hollywood through relationships, networks, mentoring, and other formal and informal industry practices (Caldwell 2008; Banks 2014, 2016). Specifically, I am interested in ways contemporary scholarship can integrate micro-level approaches to trace the complexities of women's lived experiences in the midst of navigating working conditions and sustainable career trajectories in an industry characterized by precarity and freelance conditions.

In an effort to map the emergence and evolution of women's film work in parallel to the #MeToo and Time's Up movements, media industry scholars need to move beyond the question that still dominates industry and popular discourse – *why aren't more women hired, present, valued?* In contrast, reframing our research questions around *how* – *how does the industry work for women? how do women work in the industry?* – will offer new lines of inquiry. Media industry scholars have the opportunity to reframe and reimagine the questions we are asking that locate not only sites of tension and conflict but also potential sites for change. Understanding the complex power dynamics and stakes at work in the media industries comes when simultaneously embracing the contradictions and tensions between personal individual experiences, and systemic structural inequities. Future directions for media industry research to take must address fissures and connections between structural disparities and individual experiences.

With this approach in mind, one of the ways I'm increasingly thinking about the current moment is through the lens of mobility. Specifically, the dynamics or conditions that encourage, ease, constrict, or prohibit movement for creative workers in the media industries – precarious employment, intersectional disparities, and the global pandemic. Before, during, and after the emergence of #MeToo and Time's Up, as part of a larger book project about gender inequities across the phases of filmmaking, I interviewed over 30 women living and working in the Los Angeles entertainment industries. Ranging from established screenwriters and producers, to editors, line producers and assistants to studio executives, female film professionals at various stages of their careers readily expressed the precarity of their jobs fairly early in our conversations. In many ways, the price of experience and entry is a steep one. Years of unpaid internships, underpaid apprenticeships, and low-wage assistant jobs represent for many working in the film industry an entry into more stable and fulfilling film work. This is an industry built on narratives of paying your dues, networking with the right people, and investing one's unpaid sweat equity by developing projects in your "free" time with hopes of future compensation. In their work on precarity and media work, Michael Curtin and Kevin Sanson describe how "workdays are growing longer, productivity pressures are more intense, and creative autonomy is diminishing," and this leads to "severe financial, physical, and emotional strain on workers and their families" (2016: 2). For those who secure freelance, short-term production gigs, this work requires long, strenuous hours for weeks and months at a time. Twelve- to 16-hour daily schedules are not conducive for relationships, families, care work, or much of a healthy work/life balance.

Aged primarily in their twenties to forties, the women I spoke to worried about paying monthly bills, student loans, and high rents, and enduring long commutes in LA. Some talked about struggling to afford childcare while others debated whether they can realistically become a parent at all. One freelance crew member who completed her Master of Fine Arts (MFA) in a prestigious program at the University of California at Los Angeles (UCLA) seven years earlier recalled how maintaining steady work on a television series required her moving between Atlanta, Austin, and Los Angeles. She described how despite a well-developed professional network, and having mentors and production experience, she had struggled to ascend the below-the-line ladder toward her goal of becoming a line producer. Meanwhile, fellow male crew members were routinely promoted above her: "I watched the men around me and thought: 'I'm just as competent and talented. Why not me?'" Due to the high cost of living in Los Angeles, mounting student loan debt, and the stress of living from freelance paycheck to paycheck, she decided to leave Southern California in hopes of finding production work and affordable healthcare in a lower cost production hubs like New Orleans or Atlanta (Crew Member 2018).

After her move from New York to Los Angeles, a female producer of color faced the difficult choice of leaving the studio management track for a non-profit institution in the independent film sector (Producer 2018). She recounted struggling with expectations for networking, meetings over drinks, and attending industry events, all commitments necessary to building connections and achieving successful at her film studio. Company culture was still the "typical Hollywood boy's club." She pointed to business meetings her male peers and supervisors left her out of that took place on the golf course or at a private club. She also recalled the alienation and pressure she felt working during her first pregnancy and her decision to eventually step off the studio ladder: "I didn't want to lose steam or my identity as a professional … but I [just] could not do it anymore." This account echoes the experiences of a number of well-connected, experienced, hardworking, and ambitious women who shared the physical, mental, and economic realities of precarious employment, and who were living with long-term uncertainty and the anxiety of "waiting for your big break."

The precarity of film work is pervasive and impacts women in dramatically different ways than their male peers. As I have written elsewhere, female creatives are too often caught in a bind where they cannot direct or write a studio feature because they don't have the requisite experience, and then because they cannot get experience, they are not given the directing or writing opportunities (Brannon Donoghue 2019). Journalist Scott Mendelson (2016) describes the experience trap for female filmmakers: "men are offered the presumption of competence regardless of experience. Women are considered a risk regardless of experience." Framing access to employment around "experience" and "the best person for the job" obfuscates historical and systemic marginalization of white women, and more so women of color, from opportunities with the promise that one studio open door may lead to more work (Warner 2016: 173).

Significantly, Kristen J. Warner calls attention to how conversations about gender disparities often assume whiteness and largely discount "precarity as a historical state of being for marginalized men and women of color in the entertainment industries" (2016: 172). As Warner argues:

> Women do not all experience precariousness and contingent labor in the same way. Some women have more access to opportunities than other women simply by virtue of their racial identity, and while all women certainly suffer under patriarchal labor regimes, some suffer less and some suffer more.
>
> *p. 172*

Women of color do not experience access to opportunities and employment in the same ways as white women. This is dramatically clear if you look beyond macro-level data that too often reduces statistics on employment and pay rates by measuring either all women *or* all minorities. The day-to-day impact of microaggressions, unconscious biases, and blatant exclusionary work cultures are missed if only tracking rates of employment.

One woman of color working in creative development I interviewed, who asked not to be identified, described working in a "toxic culture" at a media franchise-building studio division known widely as a prized jewel of the parent conglomerate. She discussed being the only person of color in the room and one of only two women on her team. She explained:

> It was a weird situation, not what women would hope for in the creative environment…. a troublesome culture [created by mostly male executives]. They treat people poorly on a general level but [particularly] if you are a woman or person of color. I would hope not to work for them again if I don't have to. I don't have the bandwidth or patience every day to deal with the misogyny and racism again.
>
> *Creative Professional 2018*

She described at length the stress and fear around precarious employment and being made to feel like a replaceable diversity hire who was brought in to write for the Black characters. Despite the toxic work environment, this creative worker planned to stay at her job long enough to springboard to a better opportunity. But what does better look like and what is the cost of staying in a toxic work environment? Just because a woman of color is hired or promoted, is she able to contribute, affect change, or successfully collaborate in these creative spaces? How do Black, Latinx, Asian, or Native American women gain access to and experience industry spaces differently? Women of color are granted less opportunities for access to sustainable career paths and even fewer chances for failure.

As we grapple with how best to address shifting industry conversations and varied responses to the realities of gender disparities in Hollywood, media industry studies has the opportunity to complicate the often uncritical and celebratory discourse around progress and equity. There is immense methodological value for contributing insights through extensive interviewing where women's voices are centered and experiences made visible. Micro-level methods produce thick descriptions that foreground an intersectional perspective have the opportunity to center marginalized voices largely missing from broader macro-level studies.

## Moving forward in a pandemic

Whether *The New York Times*' "More Women Than Ever Are Directing Major Films, Study Says," *Variety*'s "Women Will Direct Four Major Superhero Movies in 2020, and Hollywood

May Never Be the Same," or *The Atlantic*'s "The Most Exciting Films at Sundance Were Made by Women," 2020 began with a string of hopeful headlines promising a strong year for female-driven films in Hollywood (Buckley 2020; Vary 2019; Lee 2020). A handful of big budget projects – Disney's *Mulan*, Disney/Marvel's *Eternals* – promised a modest increase of women directors helming studio franchises. The Sundance Film Festival featured a program line-up where women directed 44 percent of the films (Lee 2020). Hollywood was moving toward a promising summer theatrical season until the industry was hit by an unexpected series of events that changed the state of film production, distribution, and exhibition seemingly overnight. Hollywood could not anticipate the global COVID-19 pandemic would not only halt their theatrical release schedule but upend the entire global business.

Many individuals across the United States, and worldwide, left their offices, classrooms, film sets, labs, and more to begin sheltering at home in the spring of 2020. Local and state governments began to place restrictions on public gatherings, business operations, and essential versus non-essential workplaces. Because I wrote most of this chapter while isolating at home and watching as news of the virus changed by the hour, my thinking shifted quickly from understanding the evolution of women's work in the handful of years since the #MeToo and Time's Up movements emerged, to the implications of the pandemic for female media workers in this moment and their well-being and livelihoods in the future. While this chapter considers how film and media studies scholars have approached gender inequity, I kept wondering one simple question: where do we go next? I conclude this discussion not just by considering the work we have in moving forward but in asking what does moving forward look like for women in the film industry on the other side of this pandemic?

Widespread unemployment and economic insecurity followed the global health crisis, as 2020 rapidly transformed into a period of isolated uncertainty. On a wide scale, job loss reports peaked at record numbers with nearly 15 percent of Americans out of work by May that year. What quickly became clear early during quarantining was how unemployment numbers disproportionately fell along gender lines: in the first few months, women made up 55 percent of jobs lost (Gupta 2020; Kurtzleben 2020). Furthermore, with schools and daycare centers closed, and with many parents working from home, childcare, home schooling, and domestic labor responsibilities largely fell on working women (McCarthy, Gibson, Andrews-Dyer, and Joyce 2020). As discussed above, for many female media workers, even in economically robust times precarious employment is fraught. With the devastation wrought be a global pandemic, however, a path toward job security and economic stability feels like a distant dream. The uncertainty and devastating changes brought on by the pandemic will have implications for years to come and bring to the forefront questions about where industrywide momentum for gender equity and inclusion will fall?

Through using on-the-ground, interview, and fieldwork-driven analyses of media workers experiences and institutional cultures, media industry studies has a unique challenge to trace a path forward for female filmmakers in this devastating moment. Rethinking how to develop a qualitative, empirically driven methodological approach for the current transformative moment is vital. For an industrywide perspective, a series of pointed questions may be a place to start. What does social distancing and quarantine mean for film production characterized by weeks and months of intense and collaborative close working conditions? What protections will be put in place and will these ease or exacerbate precarious employment and working conditions for freelance creatives? How will these conditions impact the uneven demands of childcare, family care, and domestic work for female creatives based at home? Media industry studies has the opportunity to parse not only the evolving conditions of women's work in the film industry but also what "film work" might look like during and beyond the pandemic.

# References

Banks, M. J. (2014) "Oral History and Media Industries: Theorizing the Personal in Production History," *Cultural Studies,* 28 (4): 545–560.

Banks, M. J. (2016) *The Writers: A History of American Screenwriters and Their Guild,* New Brunswick, NJ: Rutgers University Press.

Brannon Donoghue, C. (2019) "Gendered Expectations for Female-driven Films: Risk and Rescue Narratives Around Warner Bros.' *Wonder Woman,*" *Feminist Media Studies,* available at www.tandfonline. com/doi/abs/10.1080/14680777.2019.1636111?journalCode=rfms20 (accessed December 15, 2020).

Buckley, C. (2020) "More Women Than Ever Are Directing Major Films, Study Says," *The New York Times,* January 2, available at www.nytimes.com/2020/01/02/movies/women-directors-hollywood.html (accessed March 17, 2020).

Caldwell, J. T. (2008) *Production Culture: Industrial Reflexivity and Critical Practice in Film and Television,* Durham, NC: Duke University Press.

Cavna, M. (2017) "How *Wonder Woman* Director Patty Jenkins Cracked the Superhero-movie Glass Ceiling," *The Washington Post,* May 31, available at www.washingtonpost.com/news/comic-riffs/ wp/2017/05/31/how-wonder-woman-director-patty-jenkins-cracked-the-superhero-movie-glass-ceiling/?utm_term=.ef25289fbaf9 (accessed June 3, 2017).

Chenoweth, E. and Pressman, J. (2017) "This is What We Learned by Counting the Women's Marches," *The Washington Post,* February 7, available at www.washingtonpost.com/news/monkey-cage/wp/ 2017/02/07/this-is-what-we-learned-by-counting-the-womens-marches/?noredirect=on&utm_ term=.72f55631f3fc (accessed February 1, 2020).

Creative professional (2018) major studio, Interview with the Author, February 15, phone.

Crew member (2018) Interview with the Author, July 18, Los Angeles.

Curtin, M. and K. Sanson (2016) "Precarious Creativity: Global Media, Local Labor," in M. Curtin and K. Sanson (eds), *Precarious Creativity: Global Media, Local Labor,* Oakland, CA: University of California Press, 1–18.

Ford, R. (2017) "Disney's New $100M Club of Female Directors Pose for Group Photo," *The Hollywood Reporter,* December 6, available at www.hollywoodreporter.com/news/disneys-new-100m-club-female-directors-pose-group-photo-1063697 (accessed January 15, 2018).

Gaines, J. (2018) *Pink-slipped: What Happened to Women in the Silent Film Industries,* Urbana, IL: University of Illinois Press.

Garcia, S. E. (2017) "The Woman Who Created #MeToo Long Before Hashtags," *The New York Times,* October 20, available at www.nytimes.com/2017/10/20/us/me-too-movement-tarana-burke.html (accessed November 1, 2017).

Gupta, A. H. (2020) "Why Some Women Call This Recession a 'Shecession'," *The New York Times,* May 9, available at www.nytimes.com/2020/05/09/us/unemployment-coronavirus-women.html (accessed May 20, 2020).

Hallett, H. (2013) *Go West, Young Women!: The Rise of Early Hollywood,* Berkeley, CA: University of California Press.

Hill, E. (2016) *Never Done: A History of Women's Work in Media Production,* New Brunswick, NJ: Rutgers University Press.

Hunt, D. M. (2016) "Renaissance in Reverse?" Writers Guild of America, 2016 Hollywood Writers Report, available at www.wga.org/uploadedFiles/who_we_are/HWR16.pdf (accessed May 1, 2020).

Kantor, J. and Twohey, M. (2017) "Harvey Weinstein Paid Off Sexual Harassment Accusers for Decades," *The New York Times,* October 5, available at www.nytimes.com/2017/10/05/us/harvey-weinstein-harassment-allegations.html (accessed November 1, 2017).

Kurtzleben, D. (2020) "Women Bear the Brunt of Coronavirus Job Losses," *NPR,* May 9, available at www.npr.org/2020/05/09/853073274/women-bear-the-brunt-of-coronavirus-job-losses (accessed May 20, 2020).

Lane, C. (2004) "Just Another Girl Outside the Neo-indie," in C. Holmlund and J. Wyatt (eds), *Contemporary American Independent Film: From the Margins to the Mainstream,* New York: Routledge: 193–209.

Lauzen, M. D. (2020) "The Celluloid Ceiling: Behind-the-Scenes Employment of Women on the Top 100, 250, and 500 Films of 2019," available at https://womenintvfilm.sdsu.edu/wp-content/uploads/ 2020/01/2019_Celluloid_Ceiling_Report.pdf (accessed March 1, 2020).

Lee, B. (2020) "Will 2020 Be a Turning Point for Female Film-makers?" *The Guardian,* February 4, available at www.theguardian.com/film/2020/feb/04/2020-turning-point-female-film-makers-sundance-festival (accessed March 17, 2020).

Mahar, K. W. (2006) *Women Filmmakers in Early Hollywood*, Baltimore, MD: Johns Hopkins University Press.

McCarthy, E., Gibson, C., Andrews-Dyer, H., and Joyce, A. (2020) "A Working Mom's Quarantine life," *The Washington Post*, May 6, available at www.washingtonpost.com/lifestyle/2020/05/06/coronavirus-pandemic-working-moms-quarantine-life/?arc404=true (accessed May 20, 2020).

McNary, D. (2017) "Facts on Pacts," *Variety*, October 25, available at https://variety.com/2017/biz/news/studios-first-look-deals-women-1202598087/ (accessed June 1, 2019).

Mendelson, S. (2016) "Female Directors Don't Need 'Experience' – They Just Need to Get Hired," *Forbes*, November 28, available at www.forbes.com/sites/scottmendelson/2016/11/28/female-directors-dont-need-experience-they-just-need-to-get-hired/#562e191050e8 (accessed June 15, 2017).

Miller, J. (2017) "Sundance," *Vanity Fair*, January 21, available at www.vanityfair.com/hollywood/2017/01/sundance-womens-march-donald-trump (accessed February 1, 2020).

Producer (2018) Interview with the Author, July 24, Los Angeles.

Screenwriter (2017) Interview with the Author, April 24, Los Angeles.

Siegel, T. (2017) "The Complex Gender Politics of the Wonder Woman Movie," *The Hollywood Reporter*, May 31, available at www.hollywoodreporter.com/features/complex-gender-politics-wonder-woman-movie-1008259 (accessed June 3, 2017).

Sims, D. (2020) "The Most Exciting Films at Sundance Were Made by Women," *The Atlantic*, January 28, available at www.theatlantic.com/culture/archive/2020/01/standout-films-2020-sundance-festival/605626/ (accessed March 17, 2020).

Smith S. L., Choueiti, M., Yao, K., Clark, H., and Pieper, K. (2020) *Inclusion in the Director's Chair: Analysis of Director Gender and Race/Ethnicity Across 1,300 Top Films from 2007 to 2019*, January, available at http://assets.uscannenberg.org/docs/aii-inclusion-directors-chair-20200102.pdf (accessed March 2, 2020).

Smukler, M. M. (2019) *Liberating Hollywood: Women Directors and the Feminist Reform of 1970s American Cinema*, New Brunswick, NJ: Rutgers University Press.

Smyth, J. E. (2018) *Nobody's Girl Friday: The Women Who Ran Hollywood*, Oxford: Oxford University Press.

Sperling, N. (2019) "Why Hollywood is 'Shocked and Devastated' Over Fox 2000's Imminent Death," *Vanity Fair*, March 2, available at www.vanityfair.com/hollywood/2019/03/disney-fox-2000-elizabeth-gabler (accessed June 15, 2019).

Stamp, S. (2015) *Lois Weber in Early Hollywood*, Oakland, CA: University of California Press.

Sun, R. (2018) "Why Hollywood's Pay Gap for Women of Color is Wider: Infrequent 'Golden Opportunities'," *The Hollywood Reporter*, January 17, available at www.hollywoodreporter.com/news/why-hollywoods-pay-gap-women-color-is-wider-infrequent-golden-opportunities-1075057 (accessed April 1, 2020).

Sun, R. (2019) "*Crazy Rich Asians* Co-Writer Exits Sequel Amid Pay Disparity Dispute," *The Hollywood Reporter*, September 4, available at www.hollywoodreporter.com/news/crazy-rich-asians-screenwriter-adele-lim-exits-sequel-pay-disparity-dispute-1236431 (accessed September 15, 2019).

Time's Up (2018) "Open Letter from Time's Up," *The New York Times*, January 1, available at www.nytimes.com/interactive/2018/01/01/arts/02women-letter.html (accessed February 1, 2018).

Vary, A. D. (2019) "Women Will Direct Four Major Superhero Movies in 2020, and Hollywood May Never Be the Same," *Variety*, December 10, available at https://variety.com/2019/film/news/superhero-movies-female-directors-wonder-woman-birds-of-prey-black-widow-1203430914/ (accessed March 17, 2020).

Warner, K. J. (2016) "Strategies for Success? Navigating Hollywood's 'Postracial' Labor Practices," in M. Curtin and K. Sanson (eds), *Precarious Creativity: Global Media, Local Labor*, Oakland, CA: University of California Press: 172–185.

Wong, J. C. (2018) "TV Writers Circulate Anonymous Spreadsheet to Fight Gender Pay Gap," *The Guardian*, January 25, available at www.theguardian.com/tv-and-radio/2018/jan/24/tv-writers-women-men-pay-gap-anonymous-spreadsheet (accessed May 12, 2020).

# 15

# GLOBAL CONFIGURATIONS

## Re-spatializing labor in contemporary film and television production

### *Kevin Sanson*

I have spent a great deal of time over the past ten years talking to a number of film and television workers, especially craft workers and location managers in particular, who have been involved in the making of large-scale Hollywood productions. I interviewed people where I could find them, and the results logically corresponded to the locations where Hollywood has been dispersing its production activities since the late 1990s and early 2000s. Following the hyper-mobile nature of contemporary film- and TV-making, I spoke to creative professionals who have worked "for Hollywood" in places as disparate as Atlanta, Dublin, Budapest, Glasgow, the Gold Coast in Australia, London, Los Angeles, and Prague. A secondary list broadens the geography of production to include Iceland, Romania, South Africa, Korea, Slovakia, and Thailand, among others. Sometimes these individuals lived *and* worked in the most prominent hubs (i.e., "local hires"), though they were just as likely to be part of a growing class of itinerant craft workers who move from place to place as opportunities arise. This latter group of workers are often invoked in the persistent debates about "runaway production" in Southern California, serving as evidence of the perilous impact the loss of production to other territories has had on employment numbers in the state's entertainment industries. According to this narrative, LA-based workers are forced to leave the medium's "rightful home" to find meaningful employment elsewhere; staying put threatens livelihoods or prompts career changes. Yet, I also have spoken to workers from Glasgow, London, Prague, and even Los Angeles, among other locations, who welcome the mobility as an exciting benefit of a jet-set career that takes them to different foreign locations for a new project every six to eight months.

Of course, a shift in the socio-spatial relations of production is more complex and contradictory than what the binary between "mobile career" or "no career" suggests. Accordingly, the emergence of a mobile production regime over the past 20 years has animated interdisciplinary debates about a range of issues: urban infrastructure and cultural renewal, economic development and jobs growth, policymaking and (de)regulation, and global tourism, to name but a few. For film and television scholars, a common heuristic for these concerns has been the contentious disputes over the value of production incentives, the economic subsidies and tax rebates that public authorities use to attract attention and foreign investment from international producers. Often explored on a location-by-location basis (e.g., Vancouver or New Orleans) or as a case study of a particular job category (e.g., visual effects), the focus often interrogates

DOI: 10.4324/9780429275340-18

the logics behind and consequences of regional competition for international capital, what appears to many observers as a "race to the bottom" with deleterious impact on long-standing cultural and economic safeguards, from public service media to local investment priorities. Less research, however, has attempted to engage with mobile production as a new global configuration of capital, territory, and resources, explicitly linking socio-spatial transformations in the mode of production to the workaday experiences of screen media workers. This requires a more multi-valent perspective that can weave the macro-level complexities of flexible capitalism into the quotidian, even mundane, realities of how a vast global network of screen media labor *actually works* to sustain mobile production. Based on the interviews referenced earlier, for example, I learned early in the research process that making film and television is not all craft and creativity. Someone has to coordinate (with equal commitment and professional pride) rubbish removal in order for the whole endeavor to function, or the production can, quite literally, turn into a pile of garbage.

On the one hand, then, I am suggesting attention be paid to the socio-spatial relations of production, making explicit how the division of labor is structured across geography and how power operates within and across those divisions, even when it involves dealing with entities not normally associated with film and television work. On the other hand, I am suggesting attention be paid to work routines and working conditions that now constitute the workplace for film and television workers. These are not discrete tasks but constitute an integrated frame through which media industry scholars can interrogate the operations of global capital without resorting to a level of abstraction when discussing the consequences of structural change on the personal and professional livelihoods of screen media workers, or what actually constitutes "work" in the film and television industries in the first place. Further, this isn't just a shift with relevance to Southern California. We know the French production *#jesuislá* (2019) filmed in Seoul. US premium television network Showtime decided to move the production of its series *Penny Dreadful* (2014–16) from Dublin to Los Angeles for its fourth season reboot. More than 20 Bollywood productions have exploited the lush highland landscape in Scotland in as many years, while Prague continues to attract a significant share of large-scale film and television productions from the United States, UK, and elsewhere in the world, including the recent Hong Kong action film *Xia dao lian meng* (*The Adventurers*) (2017). For an entirely different geo-political agenda, China welcomes a number of Hollywood productions to film within its borders. By disrupting the assumption that the space and place of production is uniformly mapped onto national origin or a singular territory, these global configurations point to screen media production as more protean entity with significant impact on workers in Hollywood and beyond (Curtin and Sanson 2017). Consequently, screen media labor is being re-spatialized and re-socialized across a range of geographic scales, engendering new forms of craft work, collaboration, and competition that don't easily map onto assumptions about global capital and control within flexible regimes of accumulation.

In what follows, I start with a brief and necessarily simplified sketch of the concept of the mode of production before outlining how it has been employed to study historical change in the film and television industries, particularly at key moments when there has been an organizational shift in the processes of capital accumulation. I'll weave into this discussion some of the consequences such changes posed for workers based on a curated selection of existing literature. I'll conclude with some indication of how critical media industry studies can chart a distinctive engagement with the socio-spatial transformations in the division of labor, embracing the contradictions of global capital without losing sight of the material conditions on the ground that shape both the precariousness and process of screen media work. While my own focus is on the film and television industries, I hope the provocation I provide here inspires industry scholars studying the relationships between capital and labor in music, gaming, news media, and other media industries to pursue similar lines of inquiry.

## How Hollywood works

As conceived by Karl Marx, the capitalist mode of production is constituted by a particular constellation of social relations, productive forces, and capital. According to David Harvey, "By 'productive force' Marx means the sheer power to transform nature. By 'social relations' he means the social organization and social implications of the what, how and why of production" (1984: 99). Productive forces include the machinery, knowledge, and techniques used by labor to transform raw materials into commodities for sale. These are always enmeshed within broader social and cultural relations, defined in Marxist terms as a matter of social class: those who own the means of production and the wage laborers whose toil under their control. Capital is the means to purchase both human labor power and the mechanical or digital tools necessary to extract surplus value and drive wealth accumulation. Further, the "mode" is a historical classification system, conceived as a way to distinguish economic systems over time and the different social structures they produced. As an iterative and historically contingent construct, then, the capitalist mode of production is not only distinct from other modes of production (e.g., feudalism), but also marked by its own internal transformations, changing and incorporating differences overtime to continue its dominance. Capital, after all, is a process that functions to keep money in circulation, and "when it encounters limits it works assiduously to convert them into barriers that can be transcended or by-passed" (Harvey 2010: 90). The question of space in relation to the mode of production, especially among geographers, has made it known that space and place matter, usually as a geographic structure that reflects and reproduces class relations: where you are determines what you do and your position within a broader geography of power and subordination. Yet, I frame the question about spatial relations differently in this essay, one that depends less on theories of uneven development and instead queries the specific socio-spatial complexities of capital operations: how does the temporary and transient gathering of screen media workers into iterative configurations actually operationalize the circulation of capital on the ground?

Janet Staiger's early work on the mode of the production in Hollywood is one of the few academic exercises to explicitly adopt the concept of the mode of production as an analytical framework to "ground the film practices of Hollywood in the particular historical situation of their making" (Bordwell, Staiger, and Thompson 1985: 87; see also Staiger 1979). While most often discussed in the context of what the study tells us about the coherence of a "group style" among Hollywood films through the collapse of the integrated studio era, Staiger's individual contributions are an incredibly valuable (if somewhat overlooked) precursor for industry scholars interested in wrangling with the industrialization of creativity and social relations of screen media production. There are three points with particular value to contemporary debates. First is the recognition of a highly detailed division of labor that continued to subdivide over time into ever more specific work functions. Second is a concern with changes in management structures (à la Harry Braverman) and the tools of cost containment, control, and efficiency that enabled a split between those responsible for "conception" and those responsible for "execution." For Staiger, the ongoing subdivision of production work and the evolving management systems allowed her to establish specific organizational systems at particular points in time and identify change within the mode of production without ever calling into question the capitalist orientation of Hollywood. Lastly is the acknowledgment of the social dimension of screen media production. Critically, screen media's division of labor "never reached the assembly-line degree of rigidity that it did in other industries" (Bordwell, Staiger, and Thompson 1985: 93). Production was (and remains) a highly collaborative endeavor among an assemblage of craftworkers with well-honed and distinctive skillsets whose individual creative decisions were never made in isolation. They are inseparable from the broader social relations within which those creative flourishes are embedded and upon which they have impact. A costume designer's decision to dress the protagonist in a lush, velvety red dress, for instance, must be made in coordination with their counterparts in hair and makeup, production and art design, and camera operations, among others, who must coordinate their own activities to ensure the film's style does not distract from, but supports, the narrative.

The historical circumstances that underscore the mode of production during the studio era do not, for the most part, complicate the spatial relations of production. Once the industry relocated to California, soundstages and backlots offered tools to manage efficiency and contain costs across the simultaneous production of multiple films, including a full suite of *permanent* and *internal* services able to supply productions with everything from costumes to camera equipment. While productions did shoot on location, decisions to do so were understood as a deviation from normal industrial practice, a choice motivated by distinct factors at different historical junctures as a supplemental or alternative activity to studio-based production, a decision to "accept the *unpredictability of actual places* over the hermetic environment of studio production facilities" (emphasis added; Gleich and Webb 2019: 5). Perhaps the biggest exception took place in the 1950s when the studio system disintegrated, giving rise to a "package-unit" division of labor in which the relations and forces of production were drawn from a number of (now) *external* service providers that producers utilized on a *temporary*, project-by-project basis, while the studios retained control of capital. The post–World War II period, in particular, witnessed a significant increase in the number of Hollywood productions that relocated to European countries with notable impact on the socio-spatial relations of production and the processes, practices, and technologies necessarily to pull off an early incarnation of mobile production (Steinhardt, 2019).

For her part, Staiger does not explicitly engage in questions of appropriation or class struggle but does periodically reference the recurring conflict between management and organized labor that started in the American film industry from the 1910s (Bordwell, Staiger, and Thompson 1985: 311). Turning to histories of organized labor in Hollywood, however, we find a detailed chronicle of jurisdictional disputes, bargaining strategies, leadership struggles, and conflict with management that characterized the unions' early efforts to close shop in Southern California (cf. Harsough 1992; Horne 2001; Nielsen and Mailes 1995; Prindle 1988; Ross 1941). Battling for recognition and benefits on behalf of workers often played out against a colorful backdrop somewhat befitting for the dream-makers in Hollywood. Physical conflict, red-baiting, and blacklisting all proffered plot points as a cast of greedy studio moguls, union thugs, mobsters, committed organizers, and New Deal crusaders grappled with the effort to establish collective representation for craft and technical workers. By the late 1940s, Murray Ross (1947: 58) argues, the unions had "sank their roots into the studios" and completely transformed Hollywood from an open shop into a union town, "with painters and electricians hobnobbing with writers and actors at union conclaves." Notwithstanding the significant inroads that the unions made into the entertainment industry during the studio era, taken together, these histories more effectively chart the ebbs and flows of early union politics, framing the fight for democratic representation and collective action as an always ongoing, iterative, and open-ended conflict between management and labor. Indeed, contemporary Hollywood may very well remain a union town, especially compared to the plight of organized labor in other industries, but organized labor in show business also operates under a near-constant specter of vulnerability. These histories are important reminders that the conditions of craft and technical work have never existed within stable employment relations but emerge from a continuous cycle of power struggle and negotiation that, at times, flares up in intensity before returning to a period of dormancy.

I single these characteristics out because they illustrate how our historical understanding of labor relations in Hollywood depends upon quite *localized* accounts of power struggles that center the action around the soundstages and backlots in Los Angeles. The histories pit clearly defined protagonists (union leaders and labor activists) against antagonists (studio producers and even other union leaders) alongside an array of (sometimes nefarious) supporting characters, all struggling to establish the autonomy and value of craft and technical workers in the eyes of management and, at times, in the eyes of other workers. However, the circumstances within which craft workers now operate, and indeed the very nature of craft work in the division of film and television labor, has changed, prompting a critical need to re-evaluate our assumptions about the contours of craft work and the socio-spatial boundaries within which it takes place. While the transnational exchange of skills and knowledge is not an inherently "new" phenomenon given the postwar relocation of production activities to Europe, the emergence of a project-based division of labor after the end of the studio system is an important conduit (or, in Harvey's terms, "conversion") within the mode of production. The shift from factory-like "mass production" to "flexible specialization" externalized the social relations and forces of production, transforming long-term or permanent employment relations within a single studio into a series of temporary contractual arrangements between management and highly specialized but external firms and individuals (from catering services to camera operators). Such flexible arrangements helped accommodate broader economic shifts in the 1970s and 1980s, structural transformations within global capitalism that proffered more pronounced and permanent impacts on the socio-spatial division of labor, in the entertainment industries and the economy more generally.

First described by economists seeking to explain a spatial adjustment in manufacturing operations, the concept of the New International Division of Labor (NIDL) captures a shift in which production activities (and later, service work) are largely outsourced to developing countries as a way to contain costs vis-à-vis cheaper labor and infrastructural costs; advances in transportation and communication technologies further ensured oversight remained in the hands of global elites (Harvey 1990). Miller, Govil, McMurria, Maxwell, and Wang (2005) extend this concept to the media and entertainment industries, attributing the ongoing dominance of Hollywood to the emergence of a New International Division of *Cultural* Labor (NICL) whereby the major studios collude with overseas firms and individuals, national governments and policymakers, labor organizations, educational institutions, and others to engender competition among regions eager to host international productions. Competition, in other words, begets concessions, largely by exploiting wage labor across international territories. Competitive pressures enable Hollywood to hopscotch from one location to the next in the interests of containing costs. This is a persuasive and robust critique that effectively links a threat to wage labor and working conditions in the media and entertainment industries to the emergence of a global regime of accumulation in Hollywood, one that continues to serve the interests of the major studies (now part of much larger corporate conglomerates) and depends on (among other mechanisms) the exploitation of a global network of screen media workers.

As a counterpoint to the top-down meta-theory that underpins the critical political economy in Miller et al.'s argument, production studies research has provided more localized, empirically rich accounts of how media workers themselves contend with some of the changes upending their workplace, tackling concerns about everything from technological change and productivity pressures, to collaboration, power relations, and gender or diversity (Caldwell

2008; Mayer, Banks, and Caldwell 2009; Banks, Conor, and Mayer 2016). Beyond Hollywood, researchers who take up questions about the creative industries as mechanisms for economic and cultural development tend to privilege more complex assessments of global integration, largely wrangling with the *agency* rather than subordination of local institutions that "have acted as junior partners, collaborators and investors, innovators and supporters in the very transformation and creation of this system of globally dispersed production" (Goldsmith, Ward, and O'Regan 2010: 29; see also Tinic 2005). This work provides insightful accounts of the complex power dynamics and controversial policy contexts shaping a locale's global ambitions, and is especially attuned to the economic and cultural contradictions inherent in local agents' efforts to attract the attention of Hollywood capital.

Of course, Hollywood isn't the only global conduit despite the disproportionate attention it has received in media studies. Indeed, recent efforts to extend conventional analytic frameworks have proffered lucid accounts of the dynamics that shape the socio-spatial relations of alternative production hubs, including China (Curtin 2007), India (Ganti 2012; Punathambekar 2013), and Hong Kong (Martin 2017). Here we learn how central players in other contexts navigate the intersecting, though not always aligned, economic and cultural logics involved in scaling up their own production activities. Collectively, these contributions, while not always directly concerned with work and working conditions, nevertheless underscore the need to think more globally about the transformations upending the geographies of screen media work, implicitly indicating a need for more detailed and multi-valent considerations of global capital's peculiar operations and the various ways they extend and complicate assumptions about what such logics demand from screen media workers.

## Complicating capital

I started this chapter with a call for media industry scholars to engage more explicitly with the shifting socio-spatial relations of production as well as the routines and rituals that constitute the experience of work for media laborers. The first prompt directs attention to some of the more macro-level and abstract adjustments upending media production today, like globalization, while the second prompt urges a turn to the day-to-day machinations of labor that not only operationalize those changes, but also give them meaning. By tracing these adjacent concerns through a certain intellectual lineage, I hoped to have made a case for their recurring, if somewhat never fully convergent, value to industry studies and planted the seeds for reassessing capital–labor relations today.

Whereas Staiger's early work provides a model for a rich and nuanced understanding of particular changes to the organization of production, for example, its historical focus pre-dates the socio-spatial disruptions of the 1990s and 2000s and precludes the experience of workers as a central concern. We find an important corrective from the histories of organized labor, detailing the contentious disputes between management and workers, as well as between and within the unions themselves. These richly textured narratives privilege archival analysis, political intrigue, and prominent historical figures to which can be attributed agency over grounded consideration of the structuring role capital plays in the relations of production. Miller, Govil, McMurria, Maxwell, and Wang (2005) is an important addendum in the political economy of the media, reinserting questions of class, exploitation, and appropriation into a *global* exploration of the shifting socio-*spatial* relations of production. Yet, because the authors too easily conflate the operations of the media and entertainment industries with the operations of industry more generally, the analysis lacks attention to the idiosyncrasies of creative production, and certainly doesn't engage with the quotidian experiences of screen media workers on the ground (see also Curtin and Sanson 2016, 2017). It also relies on a monolithic model of power at odds with the complex socio-spatial dynamics of contemporary production. Economic development arguments similarly abstract labor from their assessment of global integration, while production studies often limit their analytical framework to discrete communities of practice without linking their arguments to the wider structuring dynamics of global capital.

I am drawn to the anthropological work of Anna Lowenhaupt Tsing as one way to work through the contemporary conditions of global capital. Central to her argument is the recognition that our explanations of capital need to abandon tales of industrial progress and ruin, the analytical tendency to link industrial transformation and expansion to the human and environmental destruction it leaves in its wake. This is the story of Global Hollywood and the precarious livelihoods it propagates. She cautions, "neither tales of progress nor of ruin tell us how to think about collaborative survival," by which she means the temporary, patched-together, and sometimes unpredictable encounters across time and place that not only engender livable conditions in precarious times, but also shape and sustain global capitalism (Tsing 2015: 19). She clarifies further:

> The economic system is presented to us as a set of abstractions requiring assumptions about participants (investors, workers, raw materials) that take us right into twentieth-century notions of scalability and expansion as progress. Seduced by the elegance of these abstractions, few think it important to take a closer look at the world the economic system supposedly organizes. [...] Livelihoods are various, cobbled together, and often temporary. People come to them for diverse reasons and only rarely because they offer the stable wages-and-benefits packages of twentieth-century dreams. I have suggested we watch patches of livelihood come into being as assemblages. Participants come with varied agendas, which do their small part in guiding world-making projects.
>
> *Tsing 2015: 132*

Ultimately, this closer look at the global configurations that form as a consequence of and response to a more geographically expansive mode of production in the media industries is what my opening argument suggests for industry scholars with investments in labor, taking seriously the socio-spatial dynamics of media labor not as a foregone conclusion to the story of globalization but as an organizational shift in the mode of production that helps operationalize it. Further, this is an account of labor that attends to workers' own stories of precariousness, pleasure, and process, as a way to make sense of screen media production not as a rational procedure but one marked by the complexities and contradictions of global capital.

Some of these complexities and contradictions are most acute in my conversations with location experts. Filming in public or private spaces, for example, requires an immense amount of bureaucratic maneuvering, positioning location experts as primary conduits for smoothing over contradiction and complexity as they negotiate permits and permissions with a range of external parties: business owners, local residents, municipal authorities, state authorities, public transport officials, rubbish bin collectors, port-o-loo providers, private security firms, police and fire squads, among many others. They need permission to redecorate storefronts, fire semiautomatic weapons in residential neighborhoods, reroute public foot traffic through the inner city, and facilitate road closures on major interstate thoroughfares. Oftentimes, they are negotiating such objectives near major historical sites, like the Charles Bridge in Prague, or in heavily populated areas, like a major intersection in Brisbane's Central Business District or an inner-city subway stop in Budapest. Moreover, these processes are not uniform around the world, meaning location experts face a learning curve every time they venture into a new region for the very first time, often relying on local counterparts to help translate, assemble, or convert local obstacles – bureaucratic or material – to fit the requirements of production and pave the way for global capital.

This is a client-focused mode of labor in which location experts work to unite disparate agendas around a common goal: a professional standard that has been repeatedly described to me as a "seamlessness of experience." The emphasis here is to ensure the production remains a minimally disruptive experience for everyone potentially impacted by its presence. Of course, the client-service metaphor extends to internal managerial agents as well, like executive producers, directors, production designers, and others who hold key positions within the overall power dynamics of a production. The singularity of their creative visions – and often, their whatever-it-takes mentality – can strain the financial and human resources of the locations department. It also often jeopardizes the logistical capacity of any given location, which can threaten the safety of the crew, harmonious relations with local communities, and the overall sustainability of the location itself by simply destroying it or creating political, social, or environmental circumstances that prohibit its ongoing use by future productions. The goal, remember, is to ensure productions have a seamless experience when they setup in places like Budapest or the Gold Coast in Australia. Impediments, like contending with a disgruntled bureaucrat that disrupts production, limit prospects in the region for returning business and can tarnish the professional reputations of the individuals who are caught between the often-conflicting demands of producers, fellow crew members, municipal authorities, business owners, and residents.

These experiences point to the expansive socio-spatial relations that define locations work within screen media's mobile mode of production, a division of labor that stretches beyond the normal boundaries of a film or television crew to include a range of agents whose contributions and coordination are necessary to fix global capital to a particular place or places. Of course, the consequences of this re-spatialization and re-socialization are not exclusive to locations experts, nor unique to workers caught up in the production of marquee titles. Michael Curtin and I previously have argued (2017: 6; see also 2016) that screen media labor more broadly

> operates within a complex matrix of social relations that are iterative, mutable, and contingent. Static conceptions of class relations between management and labor—or even between producer, talent, and crew—simply fail to appreciate these elaborate social ties or the ways in which they are changing in the current era of corporate conglomeration and globalization.

Mobile production, and the (im)mobility of different creative and craft workers, is both cause and effect, expanding the geography of production while transforming work routines and conditions in the process.

While preoccupied with slightly different theoretical concerns or frameworks, other media scholars, too, have started to grapple with more complex arrangements within screen media's division of labor. Pawanpreet Kaur (2020), for example, links the influx of foreign stunt workers from North America, Europe, and Russia into the Bollywood film industry not only to the ongoing concessions producers can extract from their local counterparts, but also to a racialized division of labor that undermines the value of indigenous workers. Slightly further afield, Vicki Mayer (2011) traces the division of labor in the new television economy to places and people otherwise ignored in the production of screen texts, including television assembly-line workers in Manaus, Brazil, and soft-core videographers in New Orleans. Collectively, the account of location experts, stunt workers, assembly-line workers, and soft-core videographers all underscore in their own ways the more complex and paradoxical socio-spatial relations of production, weaving together the experiences and at times mundane realities of screen media workers into a tapestry of interconnection and difference that results from the operations of global capital.

# References

Bordwell, D., Staiger, J., and Thompson, K. (1985) *The Classical Hollywood Cinema: Film Style and Mode of Production to 1960*. New York: Columbia University Press.

Banks, M., Conor, B., and Mayer, V. (eds) (2016) *Production Studies, the Sequel!: Cultural Studies of Global Media Industries*, London: Routledge.

Caldwell, J. (2008) *Production Culture; Industrial Reflexivity and Critical Practice in Film and Television*, Durham: Duke University Press.

Curtin, M. and Sanson, K. (eds) (2016) *Precarious Creativity: Global Media, Local Labor*, Berkeley, CA: University of California Press.

Curtin, M. and Sanson, K. (eds) (2017) *Voices of Labor: Craft, Creativity, and Collaboration in Global Hollywood*, Berkeley, CA: University of California Press.

Curtin, M. (2007) *Playing to the World's Biggest Audience: The Globalization of Chinese Film and TV*, Berkeley, CA: University of California Press.

Ganti, T. (2012) *Producing Bollywood: Inside the Contemporary Hindi Film Industry*, Durham, NC: Duke University Press.

Gleich, J. and Webb, L. (2019) "Introduction," in J. Gleich and L. Webb (eds), *Hollywood on Location: An Industry History*, News Brunswick, NJ: Rutgers University Press, 1–15.

Goldsmith, B., Ward, S., and O'Regan, T. (2010) *Local Hollywood: Global Film Production and the Gold Coast*, St. Lucia: University of Queensland Press.

Hartsough, D. (1992) "Film Union Meets Television: IA Organizing Efforts, 1947–1952," *Labor History*, 33 (3): 357–371.

Harvey, D. (1984) *The Limits to Capital*, Oxford: Basil Blackwell.

Harvey, D. (1990) *The Condition of Postmodernity: An Enquiry into the Origins of Cultural Change*, Malden, MA: Blackwell.

Harvey, D. (2010) "The Limits to Capital and the Crisis this Time," in C. Calhoun and G. Derluguian (eds), *Business as Usual: The Roots of the Global Financial Meltdown*, New York: New York University Press, 89–112.

Horne, G. (2001) *Class Struggle in Hollywood: Moguls, Mobsters, Stars, Reds, and Trade Unionists, 1930–1950*. Austin: University of Texas Press.

Kaur, P. (2020) "'If Globalization is Happening, It Should Work Both Ways': Race, Labor, and Resistance Among Bollywood's Stunt Workers," *Media Industries* 7 (1): 111–125.

Martin, S. J. (2017) *Haunted: An Ethnography of the Hollywood and Hong Kong Media Industries*. Oxford: Oxford University Press.

Mayer, V., Banks, M., and Caldwell, J. (eds) (2009) *Production Studies: Cultural Studies of Media Industries*. New York: Routledge.

Mayer, V. (2011) *Below the Line: Producers and Production Studies in the New Television Economy*, Durham, NC: Duke University Press.

Miller, T., Govil, N., McMurria, J., Maxwell, R., and Wang, T. (2005) *Global Hollywood 2*, London: British Film Institute.

Nielsen, M. and Mailes, G. (1995) *Hollywood's Other Blacklist: Union Struggles in the Studio System*. London: British Film Institute.

Punathambekar, A. (2013) *From Bombay to Bollywood: The Making of a Global Media Industry*. New York: New York University Press.

Ross, M. (1941) *Stars and Strikes: The Unionization of Hollywood*. New York: Columbia University Press.

Ross, M. (1947) "Labor Relations in Hollywood," *Annals of American Academy of Political and Social Science*, 254 (1): 58–64.

Prindle, D. (1988) *The Politics of Glamour: Ideology and Democracy in the Screen Actors Guild*, Madison, WI: University of Wisconsin Press.

Staiger, J. (1979) "Dividing Labor for Production Control: Thomas Ince and the Rise of the Studio System," *Cinema Journal*, 18 (2): 16–25.

Steinhardt, D. (2019) *Runaway Hollywood: Internationalizing Postwar Production and Location Shooting*, Berkeley, CA: University of California Press.

Tinic, S. (2005) *On Location: Canada's Television Industry in a Global Market*, Toronto: University of Toronto Press.

Tsing, A. L. (2015) *The Mushroom at the End of the World: On the Possibility of Life in Capitalists Ruins*, Princeton, NJ: Princeton University Press.

# 16

# PRODUCING FOR SMALL AUDIENCES

## Smallness and peripherality in the global media industries

*Petr Szczepanik*

Media globalization and digitalization, recently epitomized by online services such as YouTube and Netflix, have been making more visible than ever how the vast majority of media markets in the world are both relatively small and peripheral. These peripheries and semi-peripheries don't interact with each other as much as they receive media flows from the "core" media powers, mainly Hollywood and other "media capitals" (Curtin 2009). It is impossible to understand media globalization without paying close attention to these small peripheries, to the ways transnational media flows are facilitated, acted upon, transformed, and even limited by local agents on the ground. Since transnational video-on-demand services (VOD) have increasingly embedded in local markets, they have opened a unique opportunity for comparative studies of smallness and peripherality from a media industries perspective.

Smallness and peripherality should not be confused with each other because they are defined by different parameters: size and resources in the first case, distance from the centers of economic or cultural power in the second. Small countries (such as Denmark) might achieve a more central position in transnational flows than larger peripheral cases (such as Poland). Small media economies have recently enjoyed increased attention in several subfields of media and communication studies, namely in studies of media policy, public service broadcasting, and world cinema and its cross-border circulation. A longer research tradition of studying peripheral media markets developed after core–periphery models explaining inequalities and dependencies in the world system of global capitalism were adopted in studies of global cultural flows. So far, however, smallness and peripherality have not been systematically linked together to propose an analytical model for studying the position and behavior of media markets in the global digital media system.

In the first section, this chapter provides an overview of key theoretical frameworks for studying smallness and peripherality in media markets and industries. It then suggests how small-market research could employ theories of peripherality to better understand unevenness in global digital media industries. In the final section, the chapter moves to issues specific for critical media industry studies, asking how market smallness and peripherality play out in the mezzo level of industry analysis: the level of hands-on agents, their everyday practices, self-conceptions, and contradictory power relations (Havens, Lotz and Tinic 2009). The chapter

DOI: 10.4324/9780429275340-19

uses Czech independent producers as a case study to illustrate how media practitioners reflexively relate their experiences of producing for very small audiences, articulated through what might be termed "small or peripheral market industry lore."

## Small scale and peripherality: two perspectives on unevenness of media markets

Rather than understanding markets in purely economic terms, media industry research, influenced by political economy and economic sociology, approaches them as socially and culturally embedded institutions co-constructed by nation-states as well as supranational regulators (Cunningham, Flew, and Swift 2015: 67–99). Social and cultural embeddedness is especially important in the case of small and peripheral markets where media are integral parts of nation-building endeavors.

Although various measures can be used to distinguish small markets, population size and economic size (GDP) are the basic and most widely used variables. This is because they determine the magnitude of domestic audiences and advertising markets, infrastructures, financial resources, relative production costs, available talent pools, dependence on imports, and vulnerability to external takeovers or disruptions. Since the late 1990s, three parallel strands of research on small media markets have developed: European media policy literature looking at the impacts of national and supranational regulation on small markets; political-economic research examining public service broadcasters (PSBs) and the impacts of economic liberalization on broadcasting in small countries; and transnational film studies of small-nation cinemas.

Researchers looking at media policies in small countries investigate size-specific national regulatory tendencies as well as the uneven impacts of supranational regulation on small states. They tend to presume that supranational regulations such as the European Commission's Digital Single Market (DSM) strategy are usually tailored to the needs of large and powerful countries, despite the fact that small countries are over-represented in the European Union (EU) institutions (Burgelman and Pauwels 1992; Puppis, d'Haenens, Steinmaurer, and Künzler 2009; Trappel 2014). Small states are thus expected to implement reactive and ad-hoc policies responding to liberalization and globalization processes initiated in large countries. Conscious of their economic and cultural volatility, and their competitive disadvantages, some incline toward protectionist regulations supporting domestic production and defending national culture and industry from foreign competition (especially countries sharing a language with larger neighbors), even if these measures limit media diversity in domestic markets (Puppis 2009). Others, such as Central and Eastern European countries (CEE), have combined interventionism with liberalization, even at the cost of weakening their national production, including public service media. Either way, authorities in small-market territories lack the leverage to regulate big media multinationals, especially those of US origin. Consequently, small countries must rely on supranational regulation such as the European Union's Audiovisual Media Services directive (AVMSD 2018), which introduced higher quotas on European content and instruments for national regulators in order to demand financial contributions from transnational VOD services. This approach locks small markets into a paradoxical situation, whereby EU media regulation empowers them to protect their markets from American giants, while at the same time limiting their culturally based protectionist tendencies (through competition law and state aid rules), pushing them to liberalize and thus subjecting them to a marginal position within a European single market (Michalis 2014).

A second body of small market literature investigates how globalization, commercialization, and the economic liberalization of European broadcasting markets have taken their toll on small–country PSBs, traditionally the cornerstones of local audiovisual industries, who extensively support domestic production with low international appeal. The legitimacy of small market PSBs has been questioned after governments imposed quantitative commercial criteria for measuring their performance. Economic justifications for public subsidies based on "market failure" have become challenged by the growing abundance and diversity of commercial content supply, including transnational online services. European media regulation has been relying on competition law and state aid rules rather than actively supporting the role of public service media in sustaining democracies and media diversity. This economic approach proved dangerous for small-country PSBs, for they lack the financial resources (mostly license fee revenues) to be competitive in the commercialized broadcasting market while still fulfilling their core public mission (Lowe Berg, and Nissen 2011). At the same time, PSBs in small countries with lower GDP per capita surprisingly tend to produce proportionately more domestic content (Picard 2011). This might indicate efforts to mitigate the vulnerability of local audiovisual industries and sustain their own legitimacy regardless of the free market logic promoted by national governments and the EU.

The third area of research on small audiovisual industries emerged in the late 1990s and 2000s from transnational film studies. It was largely inspired by the work of Mette Hjort, who concentrated on the tremendous international successes of Danish arthouse cinema and the Danish film policy. In a series of articles, chapters, and edited volumes, Hjort proposed a typology of challenges, risks, and opportunities she identified in small-nation cinemas (Hjort and Petrie 2007; Hjort 2015). While Hjort and her followers mostly use the same basic criteria as the media economists and policy scholars mentioned above (i.e., population, GDP), they are more interested in creative practices and cultural representations. By focusing on opportunities rather than the limits of small nationhood (sustainable production methods, collaborative practices, solidarity movements), Hjort developed her model to serve progressive cultural-political agendas and knowledge transfer between various small-nation cinemas. Her writings have helped attract international academic attention to various small film industries in Europe, Asia, and Africa. It also seems that different forms of innovative, internationally oriented collaborative film practice, which turn small market limitations into creative opportunities, have since flourished across the continent, including what Constantin Parvulescu termed the "New Romanian Cinema radical auteurism" (Parvulescu and Hanzlík 2020: 7). When confronted with actual data on the commercial performance of CEE film production in terms of the proportional contribution to the international revenues, however, Hjort's model of small-nation opportunities proves overly optimistic. The export performance of small-nation film productions lags far behind the big-five European producing countries, with CEE being the least successful EU region (Grece 2017; Higson 2018).

These three areas of research all agree on the basic presumption that small-country markets, industries, and public institutions are affected by globalization, Europeanization, and economic liberalization in different ways from their larger counterparts. They tend to focus on patterns of behavior that occur across different geopolitical contexts. Small countries appear to be more vulnerable and reactive toward these external forces, finding it difficult to compete with imported content and transnational media services while struggling to preserve national audiovisual culture, a democratic public sphere with independent PSBs, and media diversity. Audiovisual industries of small nations are characterized by their relative lack of resources, inability to achieve economies of scale, and production values comparable with larger markets, and even in the era of online distribution the export performance of their media products remains low due to limits imposed by cultural specificity and linguistic barriers. However, their limited audiences, financial resources, and talent pools don't prevent them from heavily subsidizing film and television production aimed at domestic markets, and in some cases from developing strategies for innovative low-budget production aimed at specialized transnational distribution circuits. The bodies of literature outlined above offer useful frameworks for size-sensitive comparative analyses but have not gone far enough in considering different political and cultural traditions, as well as different positions in the global digital media system. Consider for example Poland and Romania, which by some measures would qualify as larger EU countries, but which nevertheless fit many criteria of small media markets, especially in terms of their limited resources and the restricted exportability of their audiovisual cultures.

Small market research has not yet sufficiently benefited from the tradition of studying imbalances and peripherality in transnational media flows that started in the mid-1970s and which recently seems to be re-emerging as a response to the boom of transnational VOD services and platforms driven by the FAANG companies (Facebook, Amazon, Apple, Netflix, and Google) (Iordache, Van Audenhove, and Loisen 2018). Peripherality is not measured by absolute market size but by the distance from and dependency on the "core" or center; it is caused by external forces rather than the inherent features of a market. Most theories of dependency and unevenness that work with center–periphery or core/semi-periphery/periphery hierarchies draw on Immanuel Wallerstein's (1979) world-systems theory, which was designed to explain historical patterns of inequalities in the world economy. Paradigms of cultural or media imperialism and their successors (e.g., Schiller 1976; Mirrlees 2013; Jin 2019) criticized power imbalances between hegemonic media powers (mostly the United States and Western Europe) and the "receiving" cultures. Neo-Marxist critiques of the new international division of cultural labor study exploitative relationships between Hollywood's center of command and control, and the overseas destinations of runaway productions (Miller, Govil, McMurria, Maxwell, and Wang 2005). To sum up, global media studies drawing on these traditions investigate, among other issues, the directions, ratios, and uneven impacts of transnational flows of capital, content, or labor to study the position of markets in the core–periphery hierarchy of the global media industries. Core–periphery thinking and models of one-way flow have been criticized as simplistic and revised many times, including by the proponents of cultural globalization and hybridization (Kraidy 2005), "cultural discount" or "cultural proximity" as ways of explaining audience preferences for local television programs (Straubhaar 2007), audiovisual "counter-flows" (Thussu 2007), or "polycentric" world cinema paradigms (Nagib, Perriam, and Dudrah 2012). However, studies of flows also seem to be regaining validity when confronted with the current treatment of small and/or peripheral markets by global VOD services and platforms (Lobato 2018; Jin 2019).

In the era of global online platforms and EU regulatory attempts to control their impact on the European single market and national cultures, media industries of small nations are positioned in tensions between globalizing and nationalizing tendencies. New measures of scale and hierarchies of centrality and peripherality are suggested, for example, by the country catalogs of transnational VOD services, their differing composition, and uneven levels of investments in localization and local content production (Szczepanik, Zahrádka, and Macek 2020). These developments thus reawaken debates over media concentration, unequal cultural power, and one-way flows. The long-distance approach of "programming from afar" as well as the focus on global cosmopolitan class as exemplified by Netflix and HBO potentially clash with the illiberal trends of populist nationalisms spreading across Europe (Imre 2018). The "return of the state" (Flew, Iosifidis, and Steemers 2016) as a powerful regulator in the era of so-called "post-globalization" (Flew 2018) signals that the seemingly smooth expansion of transnational media services might inspire a regulatory backlash coming in the form of quotas, financial obligations, platform liability, or even soft censorship. The new AVMSD, approved in 2018 and implemented by most EU member states in 2020, provides a legal framework for stricter national regulation of global platforms and VOD services. In European audiovisual policy, anti-American protectionism has been a well-documented common thread, from the 1989 "Television without Frontiers" Directive to the AVMSD. The anxieties of "peripheral" nations facing the power of FAANG and the revival of "cultural imperialism" debates reach beyond Europe as illustrated by the widely criticized claim of the president of the Canadian public service broadcaster CBC who likened Netflix to the British Empire (Houpt and Robertson 2019).

## Taking research of smallness and peripherality to the mezzo level: the small/peripheral market producer habitus

Most existing literature on small scale and peripherality in the audiovisual field focuses either on the macro-structure characteristics of national markets and industries, or on individual auteurs and cultural representations. The explanatory power of media industry research, however, lies in its ability to explain agency and power relationships in the industry operations on the middle level of hands-on industry actors, examining their everyday practices and lived realities (Caldwell 2008; Havens, Lotz, and Tinic 2009). If we want to approach smallness and peripherality from an industry studies perspective, the key question should be: how do media workers situated up and down professional hierarchies act upon the small scale and peripheral position of their markets and what are their strategies and tactics for dealing with smallness and peripherality? How do their professional self-conceptions represent and perform smallness and peripherality? How is smallness and peripherality put to work when they assess potential market demand and rationalize their decisions about shaping, greenlighting, or acquiring audiovisual content, that is, how do smallness and peripherality feature in their "industry lore" (Havens 2014)?

Little has been done in academic research to tackle these questions so far. Hjort addressed them in her studies of "creativity under constraints," mostly centering on Danish directors, whose experience may be illustrated with Thomas Vinterberg's telling words: "The claustrophobic feeling that accompanies the thought of being financed by the state, of being guaranteed only a tiny audience, and of being part of a small industry is compensated for by the circus that those directors are able to generate" (cited in Hjort and Bondebjerg 2001: 271). Ruth McElroy and Caitriona Noonan (2018: 174) perhaps came closest to applying a critical media industry studies approach to a small-nation production culture facing digital disruption when they set the objective of studying

> shared understandings of what it means to work within small nations where issues of power are lived and negotiated daily, where the scale, geographic location, and cultural characteristics of one's nation are factors that commonly need to be explained before one can speak to interlocutors from larger dominant global nations. This everyday reality – and the tacit grasp of power it entails – engenders a certain disposition to navigate translation across cultural, national, and linguistic borders. Indeed, this translational imperative may itself be a normative condition of small nationhood.

Hjort's "creativity under constraints" and McElroy and Noonan's "translational imperative" may serve as useful concepts for further comparative research in small market production cultures, but they definitely don't apply to all small markets, or not to the same extent.

As a way of proposing possible routes for further, more inclusive research along these lines, the last section of this chapter draws on a qualitative analysis of interviews with Czech producers,[1] tracing whether and how their self-conceptions and industry lore are embedded in the small scale and peripherality of the Czech audiovisual market. In a previous article, I have described the self-conceptions of Czech producers – conditioned by the lack of resources to develop a sustainable, market-oriented and internationally competitive business model, and by their deep dependence on public subsidies – as feeling disempowered, precarized, stripped of entrepreneurial autonomy (Szczepanik 2018). Here I propose several related tropes that might serve as a starting point for comparative research in small and/or peripheral market agency.

The first, most general size-relevant trope relates to small culture specificity: the supposed lack of internationally appealing themes, talent, and cultural barriers for transnational circulation:

> It is the unattractive place we live in. Nothing is happening here apart from corruption. There are no big themes, we are atheists [...] The South of Europe is much more interesting, people believe in God and are not afraid of tackling metaphysical dimensions. We are just earthbound mockers, to exaggerate a bit. There are simply no themes here.
>
> *mainstream-arthouse film producer, October 1, 2014*

The second trope is the lack of high industry standards, mainly in script development and marketing. Due to the undercapitalization of the small independent production houses, and the absence of mechanisms for funding script development, producers can't afford a diversified slate of projects, with only the best of them greenlighted. They feel constantly under pressure to rush all projects into production so as to pocket the so-called production fee, which is the cornerstone of their business model rather than box office and licensing. Producers perceive themselves as struggling from one project to the another, without a sense of a long-term strategy and continuity. Small market size (a domestic population of 10 million) is also seen as strongly limiting producers' marketing options, preventing the targeting of specific groups, because anything below the whole national audience is too small for a serious marketing campaign:

> I don't do any target groups. [...] To achieve a broad audience appeal, you need to create a social phenomenon, click with the audiences, and that's not something you can calculate. [...] There is no marketing approach that could help you achieve high attendance numbers across all the age groups and the whole social spectrum, and to get near the goal of 500,000 [a benchmark for a national box office hit]. You could commission some marketing and define a target group, but this way you can make maximum 150,000 or 200,000. But an audience of a million or 800,000 is not a target group.
>
> *mainstream-commercial film producer, November 5, 2014*

Third, producers reflect on the limitations these small-market features impose on the scope of projects produced. While the number of films per capita is higher in small countries because of the relative intensity of public funding (Poort, Hugenholtz, Lindhout, and Van Til 2019: 62–63), the diversity of content tends to be lower (in terms of genre and budget categories). Factors contributing to the homogenization of audiovisual content include the limited scope and scale of financing options, tiny size of niche audience groups, and structural fragmentation of the production system, composed of dozens of micro companies producing one or two features a year, in contrast with the highly concentrated distribution and broadcasting sector. Consequently, certain production types (e.g., high-budget spectacles), minority themes, genres, and styles remain under-represented or entirely absent from the market, while production values are kept down by low budgets averaging just €1 million. Rather than conceptualizing audience preferences, producers anticipate the expectations of industry gatekeepers who decide about the funding and circulation of their projects. Independent producers often see the committee-based decision-making of public institutions (e.g., the boards of the Czech Film Fund or the national PSB) as impersonal, opaque, unpredictable, and arbitrary. They construct different, often contradictory theories, to rationalize what they perceive as an institutional black-box limiting their opportunities:

> The Fund supports many films just a little bit, so we end up with 40 supported films a year that have not enough money and they all look as DIY. [...] All the films are based on similar themes, because we can't do a historical spectacle, we can't do sci-fi or new kinds of films, because we don't have money, because everybody wants just 20 or 30 million CZK. And then all the films look dull.
>
> *mainstream-arthouse film producer, November 10, 2014*

Finally, market size affects producer responses to digitalization and globalization. While in the national market, VOD is smoothly integrated into the business models and practices of traditional distributors, producers have yet to find efficient ways and the right intermediaries for using online distribution to enhance their foreign sales. Currently, the only way out of the digital periphery seems to be co-producing with HBO or Netflix, or otherwise finding an established international sales agent with business links to powerful foreign distributors and VODs. Examples of recent HBO Europe originals such as *Hořící keř* (*The Burning Bush*, 2013), widely sold to international buyers and distributed via HBO's multiple territorial catalogs including the United States, show that transnational subscription VOD (SVOD) services have the potential for giving locally produced content unprecedented exposure and marketing support.

Facing these new challenges and opportunities, many producers defensively reassert their hyperlocal orientation and ties with traditional buyers (distributors, broadcasters, sales agents), while others speculate about HBO and Netflix's criteria for co-producing or buying local content, and possibilities for moving into higher-budget or niche genre production:

> For me and my screenwriter, HBO Europe's approach to genre was the new experience, the real change. In a climax scene of our project, the main bad guy is shot from a distance [...] and his head explodes. We knew from the past that everybody in the Czech PSB tends to reject or treat with a lot of suspicion genre elements like that, which however make our project what it is. [...] We didn't manage to persuade the responsible PSB executive to get involved, because he thought it is a B-movie ending. When we came to HBO and told them about the ending, that a guy's head explodes, they really liked it. Suddenly the perception of genre was entirely different. It was such a contrast, for the first time somebody told us we can shoot through a character's head.
>
> *mainstream TV and film producer, February 7, 2018*

Producers have mostly internalized small market limitations, taking them for granted, and articulating them when criticizing their conditions when compared to their counterparts in larger markets. When doing so, they tend to construct significantly different tropes from those foregrounded by Hjort in her optimistic accounts of small-nation constraints turned into opportunities, clever cultural policies, or solidarity and sharing among filmmakers. In the Czech market, perceptions of provincialism, limited resources, and disadvantageous conditions do not inspire any shared discourse of emancipation, innovation, and nation branding. These sentiments also do not lead to coordinated efforts for breaking through into the international arthouse film or quality television scenes in the way that Denmark may have done so. Solidarity among Czech producers is not absent, and small-nation proximity between the production community, policymakers, and the public indeed creates a sense of trust and sharing, but the prevailing producer mindset is based on a pragmatic and even opportunistic acceptance of small market and small culture limitations. Producers have adapted their business models to the few available resources and developed survival strategies based on careful risk reduction, accepting rather predictable rules of the game for financing projects.

## Conclusion

From the literature overview and the case study, there are at least three lessons that might be derived as starting points for further comparative research into the smallness and peripherality of certain media markets in the digital era:

1 Small and/or peripheral media markets are social and cultural constructions, and they need to be studied as internally diversified ensembles, with some segments strongly embedded in small nationhood (such as PSB production), and others connected to transnational flows of capital, labor and content (such as foreign production services).
2 Different combinations of market size and of positioning in center/periphery hierarchies need to be distinguished and approached as dynamic: small peripheries, small semi-peripheries, small semi-centers, large peripheries, etc. From the outside, distinctions and groupings among small and peripheral markets are co-constructed by supranational regulators such as the European Commission, and continuously reconfigured by the ever-changing multinational corporations such as the FAANG group.
3 Small-nation "claustrophobia," "creativity under constraint," and the "translational imperative" are significant features of the more liberal, open, and outward-looking production cultures. But there are also examples, especially among the CEE countries, of centripetal (inward-looking) markets where smallness and peripherality are deeply internalized and – with more or less bitterness – pragmatically accepted by most industry agents and policymakers.

If it is indeed the case that the increasingly competitive transnational SVOD market is going to be changed by a "trend toward volume" or "anything goes," there might be much higher demand for cheaper local content around the world (Weiner 2019). How will small market producers react? Will they merely facilitate the "glocalization" strategies of global brands by producing localized versions of their branded product? Or, will they try "delocalizing" their stories (Straubhaar 2007: 169–171), adapting them to the "grammar of transnationalism" (Jenner 2018: 229)? Or, will they attempt to strategically use their distribution and marketing power for a wider circulation of local voices and stories? Growth of transnational VOD services certainly presents a threat to small-nation audiovisual production in terms of creative autonomy and authenticity, as well as copyright control, and might lead to decreasing media diversity in individual small markets. But current developments in European high-end TV drama production open opportunities for more equal and sustainable co-production and joint venture arrangements, bringing together multiple public service media, independent production houses from smaller and larger countries, and regional as well as global streamers. Due to the increasing importance of original local serial drama for global SVODs, these kinds of collaborations might open better chances for wider cross-border circulation than "treaty" film co-productions previously, which typically took the form of arthouse films targeting festivals rather than the commercial box office (Bondebjerg, Redvall, Helles, Lai, Søndergaard, and Astrupgaard 2017: 79–98). Small media market researchers should be able to critically and comparatively study all these trends and industry modes: from successful examples of "affinitive transnationalism" (Hjort 2010: 49–51), to the stubborn provincialism and illiberalism of more nationally oriented media markets.

## Acknowledgment

This work was supported by the European Regional Development Fund project "Creativity and Adaptability as Conditions of the Success of Europe in an Interrelated World" (reg. no.: CZ.02.1.01/0.0/0.0/16_019/0000734).

## Note

1  The analysis worked with two pre-existent sets of semi-structured interviews: 23 interviews with Czech independent film producers from 2014 to 2015 for an industry report on practices of script development (Szczepanik, Kotišová, Macek, Motal, and Pjajčíková 2015); 14 interviews with Czech producers and commissioning editors from 2018 to 2019 conducted by myself and Johana Kotišová for research assessing the impacts of transnational online distribution and the DSM strategy on creative, production, and distribution practices.

## References

Bondebjerg, I., Redvall, E. N., Helles, R., Lai S. S., Søndergaard, H., and Astrupgaard, C. (2017) *Transnational European Television Drama Production: Genres and Audiences*, Basingstoke: Palgrave Macmillan.

Burgelman, J-C. and Pauwels C. (1992) "Audiovisual Policy and Cultural Identity in Small European States: The Challenge of a Unified Market," *Media, Culture and Society*, 14 (2): 169–183.

Caldwell, J. T. (2008) *Production Culture: Industrial Reflexivity and Critical Practice in Film and Television*, Durham, NC: Duke University Press.

Cunningham, C., Flew, T., and Swift, A. (2015) *Media Economics*, Basingstoke: Palgrave Macmillan.

Curtin, M. (2009) "Thinking Globally: From Media Imperialism to Media Capital," in J. Holt and A. Perren (eds), *Media Industries: History, Theory, and Method*, Boston: Wiley-Blackwell, 108–119.

Flew, T. (2018) "Post-Globalisation," *Javnost – The Public*, 25 (1–2): 102–109.

Flew, T., Iosifidis, P., and Steemers, J. (eds) (2016) *Global Media and National Policies: The Return of the State*, Basingstoke: Palgrave Macmillan.

Grece, Ch. (2017) *The Circulation of EU Non-national Films*, Strasbourg: European Audiovisual Observatory.

Havens, T. (2014) "Towards a Structuration Theory of Media Intermediaries," in D. Johnson, D. Kompare, and A. Santo (eds), *Making Media Work: Cultures of Management in the Entertainment Industries*, New York: New York University Press, 39–63.

Havens, T., Lotz, A. D., and Tinic, S. (2009) "Critical Media Industry Studies: A Research Approach," *Communication, Culture and Critique*, 2 (2): 234–253.

Higson, A. (2018) "The Circulation of European Films Within Europe," *Comunicazioni sociali* (3): 306–323.

Hjort, M. (2010) "Affinitive and Milieu-Building Transnationalism: The 'Advance Party' Initiative," in D. Iordanova, D. Martin-Jones, and B. Vidal (eds), *Cinema at the Periphery*, Detroit, MI: Wayne State University Press, 46–66.

Hjort, M. (2015) "The Risk Environment of Small-Nation Filmmaking," in J. Blankenship and T. Nagl (eds), *European Visions: Small Cinemas in Transition*, Bielefeld: Transcript: 49–64.

Hjort, M. and Bondebjerg, I. (2001) *The Danish Directors: Dialogues on a Contemporary National Cinema*, Bristol: Intellect.

Hjort, M. and Petrie, D. (2007) "Introduction," in M. Hjort and D. Petrie (eds), *The Cinema of Small Nations*, Edinburgh: Edinburgh University Press, 1–23.

Houpt, S., and Robertson, S. (2019) "CBC Head Under Fire After Comparing Netflix to the British Raj, Warns of 'Cultural Imperialism'," *Globe and Mail*, January 31, available at www.theglobeandmail.com/arts/article-cbc-head-warns-netflix-poses-cultural-threat-to-canada (accessed December 20, 2019).

Imre, A. (2018) "HBO's e-EUtopia," *Media Industries Journal*, 5 (2), available at 10.3998/mij.15031809.0005.204 (accessed March 24, 2020).

Iordache, C., Van Audenhove, L., and Loisen, J. (2018) "Global Media Flows: A Qualitative Review of Research Methods in Audio-visual Flow Studies," *Communication Gazette* 81 (6–8): 748–767.

Jenner, M. (2018) *Netflix and the Re-invention of Television*, Basingstoke: Palgrave Macmillan.

Jin, D. Y. (2019) *Globalization and Media in the Digital Platform Age*, New York: Routledge.

Kraidy, M. M. (2005) *Hybridity, or the Cultural Logic of Globalization*, Philadelphia, PA: Temple University Press.

Lobato, R. (2018) *Netflix Nations: The Geography of Digital Distribution*, New York: New York University Press.

Lowe, G. F., Berg, C. E., and Nissen, C. S. (2011) "Size Matters for TV Broadcasting Policy," in G. F. Lowe and C. S. Nissen (eds), *Small Among Giants: Television Broadcasting in Smaller Countries*, Göteborg: Nordicom, 21–42.

McElroy, R. and Noonan, C. (2018) "Public Service Media and Digital Innovation: The Small Nation Experience," in G. F. Lowe, H. van Den Bulk, and K. Donders (eds), *Public Service Media in the Networked Society*, Göteborg: Nordicom, 159–174.

Michalis, M. (2014) "Focal Points of European Media Policy from Inception till Present: Plus ça Change?" in K. Donders, C. Pauwels, and J. Loisen (eds), *Palgrave Handbook on European Media Policy*, Basingstoke: Palgrave Macmillan, 128–142.

Miller, T., Govil, N., McMurria, J., Maxwell, R., and Wang, T. (2005) *Global Hollywood 2*, London: British Film Institute.

Mirrlees, T. (2013) *Global Entertainment Media: Between Cultural Imperialism and Cultural Globalization*, New York: Routledge.

Nagib, L., Perriam, C., and Dudrah, R. (2012) "Introduction," in L. Nagib, C. Perriam, and R. Dudrah (eds), *Theorizing World Cinema*, London: I. B. Tauris, xvii–xxxii.

Parvulescu, C. and Hanzlík, H. (2020) "Beyond Postsocialist and Small: Recent Film Production Practices and State Support for Cinema in Czechia and Romania," *Studies in European Cinema*, available at www.tandfonline.com/doi/full/10.1080/17411548.2020.1736794?needAccess=true (accessed December 7, 2020).

Picard, R. G. (2011) "Broadcast Economics, Challenges of Scale, and Country Size," in G. F. Lowe and C. S. Nissen (eds), *Small Among Giants: Television Broadcasting in Smaller Countries*, Göteborg: Nordicom, 43–56.

Poort, J., Hugenholtz, P. B., Lindhout, P., and Van Til, G. (2019) *Research for CULT Committee – Film Financing and the Digital Single Market: Its Future, the Role of Territoriality and New Models of Financing*, Brussels: European Parliament, Policy Department for Structural and Cohesion Policies.

Puppis, M. (2009) "Introduction: Media Regulation in Small States," *The International Communication Gazette*, 71 (1–2): 7–17.

Puppis, M., d'Haenens, L., Steinmaurer, T., and Künzler, M. (2009) "The European and Global Dimension: Taking Small Media Systems Research to the Next Level," *The International Communication Gazette*, 71 (1-2): 105–112.

Schiller, H. I. (1976) *Communication and Cultural Domination*, White Plains, NY: M. E. Sharpe.

Straubhaar, J. (2007) *World Television: From Global to Local*, Thousand Oaks, CA: Sage.

Szczepanik, P. (2018) "Post-socialist Producer: The Production Culture of a Small-Nation Media Industry," *Critical Studies in Television*, 13 (2): 207–226.

Szczepanik, P., Kotišová J., Macek, J., Motal, J., and Pjajčíková, E. (2015) *A Study of Feature Film Development in the Czech Republic*, Prague: Czech Film Fund, available at fondkinematografie.cz/assets/media/files/H/EN/Study_development.pdf (accessed March 24, 2020).

Szczepanik, P., Zahrádka, P., and Macek, J. (2020) "Introduction: Theorizing Digital Peripheries," in P. Szczepanik, P. Zahrádka, J. Macek, and P. Stepan (eds), *Digital Peripheries: The Online Circulation of Audiovisual Content from the Small Market Perspective*, Cham: Springer, 1–31.

Thussu, D. K. (2007) "Mapping Global Media Flow and Contra-flow," in D. K. Thussu (eds), *Media on the Move: Global Flow and Contra-flow*, Abingdon: Routledge, 10–29.

Trappel, J. (2014) "Small States and European Media Policy," in K. Donders, C. Pauwels, and J. Loisen (eds), *The Palgrave Handbook of European Media Policy*, Basingstoke: Palgrave Macmillan, 239–253.

Wallerstein, I. (1979) *The Capitalist World-Economy*, Cambridge: Cambridge University Press.

Weiner, J. (2019) "The Great Race to Rule Streaming TV," *The New York Times Magazine*, July 10, available at nyti.ms/2xCP7eN (accessed March 24, 2020).

# 17

# CURRENTS OF CHANGE

## The unstoppable momentum of the Chinese media industrial complex

### *Michael Keane*

Over the past five decades, the East Asian region has undergone intensive industrialization. Economic revitalization in the region has resulted in a major shift from labor-intensive industries to service economies. The knowledge economy has delivered tangible and intangible benefits and has been responsible for connecting populations to the global public sphere. Media workers, formerly employees of the state, or even "engineers of the soul" in the People's Republic of China (PRC), now have considerable creative autonomy. Many are celebrities in their own right; many are actively seeking out inter-regional collaboration. Even in the PRC, where the state retains its visible hand, there is unprecedented dynamism and diversity in media offerings.

In this chapter, I want to question some accepted approaches to conceptualizing media industries in East Asia. The chapter does not attempt to summarize the field or catalog the variety of excellent work that is representative. My aim is quite modest: to illustrate academic trends. I correlate some of these trends with what the urban sociologist Ann Markusen has called "fuzzy concepts." Markusen says: "A fuzzy concept is one that means different things to different people, but flourishes precisely because of its imprecision" (2013: 293). Markusen was writing about the practice of using "imprecise" indicators such as "livability" and "vibrancy" in urban policy. With respect to media industries scholarship, two of the most used terminologies are "soft power" and "flows. While I am not advocating abandoning these "fuzzy" terms, I would argue for more criticality when using them. In particular, the rapid rise of the Chinese media industrial complex requires us to rethink our approaches.

Soft power is generally situated within the field of international relations (Nye 1990), but increasingly media scholars have refitted it to the task of adjudicating cultural influence. States maintain a strong interest in managing soft power, akin to keeping up the appearances of being a good global citizen. States can gain advantage by deploying media to promote a positive image as we saw with China's "mask diplomacy" efforts in the wake of COVID-19 pandemic (Yu and Keane 2020). In April 2020, sensing the need to refurbish China's tarnished image, Xi Jinping (2020) exhorted Chinese media outlets to raise the level of "discursive power when telling China's stories well."

Flows (similar terms include waves, currents, and tides) imply a lack of state intervention, a consumer-led model of natural forces in which users and markets adjudicate value. The term

DOI: 10.4324/9780429275340-20

"wave" has a stronger connotation, implying change, novelty, and variation, a ripple effect, or even a *zeitgeist*; for instance, the term "new wave" is often used critically to designate film and music, or the avant-garde, or in relation to feminism (e.g., the "third wave"). The wave metaphor often gestures toward a peak, and a wave may gain in momentum with the help of government; for instance, the Korean Wave, which I will discuss later in this chapter, has become a focus of South Korean national identity.

Naturalistic metaphors are deployed to explain the rapid expansion of East Asian media industries. As most people would be aware, the field of media and communication studies has diversified over the past few decades. This diversification is largely due to the internationalization of scholarship, which has moved from observing Western industrial hegemons, for example, Hollywood players and transnational companies such as News Corporation, to acknowledging the rise of "peripheral" territories, to use the depiction of Sinclair, Jacka and Cunningham (1996). In this chapter, I focus my attention primarily on East Asian media industries, which by most accounts, rose to prominence in the early 1990s, at least in the sense that media studies academics deemed them to be worthy of attention. This is a somewhat belated recognition considering the numbers of East Asian graduate students in the west, as well as the excellence of scholarship already emerging from Hong Kong, Japan, Taiwan, and South Korea. In fact, by the end of the 1990s, the East Asian periphery had captured a great deal of attention: Japanese cool, Hong Kong action cinema, and the Korean Wave soon entered the lexicon of scholars and media pundits (e.g., McGray 2009; Shim 2006; Jin 2016; Chua and Iwabuchi 2008). Media industries were "de-westernized," although as Colin Sparks (2017) remarks, the critical mass of media studies research remains Western.

The legacy of the 1980s and 1990s was a macro view of a developing region. With respect to China, research lacked in-depth analysis. Political economy, often combined with insights from political science, offered a useful but sometimes blunt lens to frame China's media: the propaganda state model, the media as the mouthpiece of the Chinese Communist Party, the struggling tellers of truth shacked by censorship. These images reflected the theoretical perspectives of much of the research community, echoing Francis Fukuyama's (1989) belief in the end of history. Researchers looked inward, applying Western models and Western theories. Because the vantage point from which to examine Chinese media was generally from the outside, textual interpretation (content analysis, discourse analysis, policy analysis) prevailed. Cultural studies looked at texts, and the field of research was largely represented by case studies of ground-breaking TV drama serials and Chinese Fifth generation cinema. Of course, while it was possible to do textual analysis, the ideological divide that prevailed between liberal democratic and socialist media systems made research into production cultures difficult. Researchers struggled to get close to the subject, often because they (the author included) were regarded as outsiders. Many of us were denied access to informants; this distancing is symptomatic of research in PR China and has increased rather than loosened with the commercialization of media sectors. In the past, the fear was that Chinese media workers might talk to foreigners about censorship although in many instances, an astute researcher could read the environmental conditions and draw conclusions. Nowadays one of the key issues is commercial confidentiality.

## Regional convergence

The impact of East Asian media industries beyond their national borders is undeniable, encapsulated in Michael Curtin's (2007) aptly titled book *Playing to the World's Biggest Audience*. Consumption of East Asian media can perhaps be best characterized as a diverse constellation of socio-linguistic communities paralleling the global dissemination of English-language, Spanish,

Arab, and Indian media. These East Asian communities are far from homogeneous entities; for instance, Chua Beng-huat (2012) points out that overseas Chinese groups consider cultural differences between them to be greater than similarities. Production meanwhile has diversified. Hong Kong, once renowned as a "media capital" (Curtin 2007), has lost significant talent and investment to Mainland China. Indeed, with the rise of the PRC and the extension of its online media platforms into the Mandarin-speaking diaspora, it is possible to countenance an Asian media industrial complex (Wang and de Kloet 2016), which now looks toward a shared future in Greater China. By virtue of this relocation China's new internet industry companies and platforms such as iQiyi, Tencent, TikTok, Bilibili, and Youku-Tudou are reaching even deeper into the Asia-Pacific (Keane, Yu, Zhao, and Leong 2020). How then do we conceptualize the rapid developments that have taken place in the region since the 1970s, a time when the very concept of a media industry in PR China was considered bourgeois?

As I will discuss below, the default metaphor in East Asia, at least for the past two decades, has been the "wave." The PRC missed the first, but it is now riding, financing, and generating the next wave. The reason China missed the 1990s wave was that ideological correctness reigned supreme in the minds of China's leaders. In fact, the term media industry (and cultural industry) did not gain acceptance within China until the late 1990s, a time when the nation was preparing to enter the World Trade Organization (WTO). From the perspective of international scholarship, China's media were deemed to be too state-owned to be industrial and too ideological to be considered in the same vein as the free-spirited media of Japan, Hong Kong, South Korea, and even Taiwan, a view that prevailed until Deng Xiaoping released the entrepreneurial spirit of writers, directors, and producers in the early 1990s.

The rise of China's media industries took some time, however, largely due to excessive state management and fears that commercialization would erode the moral legitimacy of the Chinese Communist Party. Eventually, even public institutions (*shiye*) like China Central Television (CCTV) adopted a more commercial outlook, banking on talking head celebrities and game shows (Zhu 2012). Today, while still heavily constrained by censorship, the Chinese media industrial complex is an unstoppable force, drawing investment and talent from its region (Keane, Yecies, and Flew 2018), although it is sometimes hard to know just how influential it is outside the PRC.

Before I explore the applicability of soft power and flow metaphors to these developments, it's worth accounting for the change in focus. Two related concepts are relevant to our discussion: "Sinophone" and "Greater China." The Sinophone, according to Shih (2007: 4), refers "to a network of places of cultural production outside China and on the margins of China and Chineseness, where a historical process of heterogenizing and localizing of continued Chinese culture has been taking place for several centuries." Sinophone does not denote a person, as in Anglophone or Francophone, or specific places such as the Anglosphere, but rather "a network of places" where Chinese dialects are spoken. These dialects include Mandarin, Cantonese, Minnan, Shanghainese, and Hakka. Scholars have used Sinophone to reinforce the distinctiveness, and criticality, of Chinese cultural production outside the Chinese mainland. However, with the mainland cultural production apparatus now drawing talent and investment from the region, and with regional talent now energizing Chinese production, the concept becomes elastic. Where are these networks of cultural production now centered? Increasingly, they are in the Chinese mainland.

A similar reframing applies to the geographical term "Greater China" (Harding 1993), which in many accounts implied the "outside of China," its extension into the world through Chinese-speaking communities. Some scholars have chosen to use these terms to privilege Chinese-speaking cultures or subcultures in Hong Kong, Taiwan, and Singapore, a portrayal that has accommodated the addition of Japan and South Korea, similarly modern democratic states with respect to the kind of media produced. Chua Beng-Huat (2012), for example, has conceptualized a matrix to explain what he called the "trans-regional media order." The Sinophone (Hong Kong, Taiwan, Singapore), plus Japan and South Korea, were more technically advanced, a fact reflected in the quality of media products offered for consumption. Because of technical advantages, Chua maintained that there was "a greater tendency for production and export to dominate over import and consumption" (p. 14). At the time of writing his book in 2012, Chua had said: "China with its huge market, is still primarily a location of import and consumption due to the weak production quality of its still nascent media industry" (p. 14).

The outside of China, however, has been reactivated due to China's economic rise. I have described the reimagining of the Sinophone and Greater China as "reconnecting" (Keane 2016). While the media of the PRC has long been adjudged by media scholars – and many viewing communities – to be unimaginative, formulaic, and propaganda-riven, it is now rejuvenated. China and East Asia are more integrated in media industry collaboration, allowing the former to learn directly from the successes of the talent pool that is migrating to China. Observing these changes, Anthony Fung (2013: 2) refers to new forms of structure and operation in the East Asian region, which illustrate "how Asia is being connected and reconnected to the world." A similar process of reconnecting with the world is occurring in China, as the nation uses its digital power to reconnect with the diaspora.

Scholarship was initially slow to pick up on this transformation. Analysis of Chinese media outside China has increased but it is now associated with the negative concept of a China threat, for instance encroachments of Chinese state media into liberal democratic territories. Overseas territories have Chinese communities that are more aligned with liberal democratic values than socialist authoritarianism, and for this reason perceptions of the value of made-in-China media content has taken longer to change. But the efforts of China's media to internationalize has paid dividends. If China's industry was "nascent" in 2012, according to Chua (2012), things have turned around. The changes are a result of several factors. First was recognition of the concept of cultural industries in China in 2001. Following this designation, media was officially accorded an industrial status, leading to an acceleration in the amount of internal research, mostly promulgated in state-sponsored Blue Books. Second, the Chinese leadership sought to incentivize its commercial media and cultural industries, as well as official media, to "go out," a term referring to the mission of going global. Chua's point about exports is therefore pertinent here. Third, China absorbed a great deal of expertise from the region (Keane, Yecies, and Flew 2018).

## Soft power

In the late 1980s, US political scientist Joseph Nye Jr. developed a heuristic that he termed "soft power" to explain why some nations' ideas are more attractive globally. The concept was popularized in Nye's 1990 book about the "changing nature of American power" (Nye 1990). Within a decade, his work led to a league table model of normative attributes. The most cited global soft power ranking is Soft Power 30, a joint initiative between Portland, a strategic communications consultancy, and the University of Southern California's Center on Public Diplomacy. The Soft Power 30 evaluation currently covers 60 countries although the polling data is drawn from only 25 countries. The data assess "impressions" of a nation's appeal in various categories including cuisine, tech products, friendliness, culture, luxury goods, foreign policy, and livability (Yecies, Keane, Yu, Zhao, Zhong, Leong, and Wu 2019).

The culture sub-category of the Soft Power 30 index, which includes numbers of international tourists and even national sporting prowess, avoids the tricky question of counting actual media reception. Soft power is thus "fuzzy," subjective and largely based on impressions. If soft power is adjudicated by people outside the nation in question, there is the ever-present problem of cultural stereotyping; for instance, a person situated outside the PRC might be predisposed to think PRC media content is excessively controlled by the government, and therefore inclined to "read" it as propaganda (see Chu 2014). Soft power, moreover, waxes and wanes. Although liberal democratic nations fill the top rankings in the international metrics, perceptions change. For instance, the US's global rankings on the Soft Power 30 have fallen, from position one in 2016 to five in 2019.

Evaluations of mediated soft power are therefore hard to substantiate. Nick Couldry (2012) argues that it is difficult to calculate the behavioral effects of media texts, an argument that has been put to the test with audience research. I am reluctant to revisit debates about active audiences versus the behavioral sender–receiver model, or even cultivation and uses and gratifications theory, although it's necessary to note that tangible effects exist. The success of the Korean Wave has led to a surge in tourism to South Korea and a greater sense of Korean cultural confidence on the world stage, something that the Chinese government evidently views with envy.

While the terminology of soft power is borrowed from international relations and adapted to describe media content, it goes hand in glove with other readymade aquatic metaphors. Before dismissing that happy collusion, however, it is worthwhile considering the efficacy of the concept as it pertains to media industries. By the early 2000s, soft power captured the vitality of East Asian media industries. A quick search on Amazon.com, for instance, reveals that books on soft power have increased over the past decade, albeit with variations in scholarly rigor. Many publications listed on Amazon featuring "soft power" in the title emanate from within China, offering government-endorsed accounts of China's so-called "great rejuvenation." This desire to make use of this Western concept features in academic publishing. A recent study of Chinese soft power by Kingsley Edney, Stanley Rosen, and Ying Zhu reveals that "The number of Chinese articles in social science journals that reference soft power in their title jumped to 826 in 2008 and continued to rise steadily in subsequent years, reaching a peak of 1,134 articles in 2012" (2019: 2–3).

The key questions therefore are: why has the concept achieved global credibility, and more specifically, why has it been taken up in the East Asian region? The answer to the first question is that governments take it seriously. It's ultimately about image management. National tourism agencies and local tourism operators use their country's soft power positioning as a means of attraction; a high indicator is good news. When it comes to media and its relative attractiveness within East Asia, soft power is highly subjective, for instance the aforementioned trans-regional matrix proposed by Chua (2012). Some might disagree with evaluations, depending on what one is evaluating. For manga and anima, Japan is the regional power; but for dynastical costume dramas, it's hard to go past the PRC.

Movies, TV serials and anime have a larger "net effect" than just tangible box office returns. Instead of just thinking about conventional metrics then, another way to proceed is to observe what Couldry calls "media as practice." He says: "A practice approach starts not with media texts or media institutions but from media-related practice in all its looseness and openness" (2012: 37). The varieties of media-related practice include browsing and searching online; making content available to others by sharing (i.e., showing); circulating representations of oneself and others; and commenting on media and media celebrities. In addition to these various mediated practices are the practices of using second screens, for instance people watch on mobile devices or tablets, or using catch-up TV to binge watch. Industry metrics companies are only now coming to terms with the various ways of consuming media in the digital age.

Capturing the value of online media is problematic and the practice of applying results to soft power sometimes strains the limits of credibility. Billions of views evidently take place on streaming websites and platforms; for instance, a 2015 Chinese historical drama serial, *Langya bang* (*Nirvana in Fire*) reportedly achieved over 13 billion views globally (de Burgh 2017: 11). Other reports claimed 3.3 billion views on iQiyi, China's version of Netflix, by the end of the serial. Another dynastic serial *Yanxi gonglüe* (*Yanxi Palace*) is reported to have garnered 15 billion streams in 2018 on iQiyi alone, an interesting and timely release of industry data when one considers that the Western streaming platform Netflix does not release such figures (BBC 2018). Even so, as researchers we need to be constantly aware of the unreliability of data released by online platforms. For example, in 2019 Facebook agreed to pay $40 million to settle lawsuits from advertisers who alleged the company inflated its video views – in some cases, by as much as 900 percent (Spangler 2019). Aside from the issue of inflation, what does a view entail: does it mean a person watched an episode, or did they just click on the service? The point of this example is that misinformation prevails but may be taken as fact. More problematic is that these kinds of fanciful statements are recirculated, adding to the potency of the wave metaphor.

## Waves, flows, currents

It has become a common practice among communication scholars to describe the trade in media content in metaphorical terms as waves, traffic, flows, or currents. *Hallyu*, the Korean Wave, has precipitated a steady and diversified flow of commentary. A Google Ngram search reveals over 20 books in English published between 2002 and 2017 featuring the Korean Wave somewhere in the title. In addition, myriad book chapters, journal articles, and symposia reference the Korean Wave, and countless books, articles, and dissertations are published on this topic in Korea. In fact, these terms have directed a great deal of research and framed the opportunities for papers submitted for review in the field of communications and media studies.

Flows appears in numerous book titles, chapters, journal articles, and international reports and has been the subject of fora, conference panels, and symposia. But the term is rarely used by industry journalists or actual media practitioners, so why do media scholars resolutely subscribe to it? Does media content really flow? Where did this metaphor come from, and why has it remained largely uncontested? Of course, in the age of streaming, and user-generated content, one could argue with some conviction that flows have increased both in intensity and volume. Should "streams" now be the default metaphor?

Like all influential concepts, there are originating landmarks. In 1980, the United Nations' McBride Report fueled anxiety about the homogenizing effects of Western media, advocating for a New World Information and Communication Order (NWICO), although at the time these concerns were more focused on news information channels than audiovisual content. By the late 1990s, UNESCO had followed up the initial McBride Report with a *World Culture Report*, which suggested the traffic was not all one way, and that media diversity was in fact multiplying in the age of globalization. Prior to this, Manuel Castells (1999: 295) had coined the term "space of flows," referring to "the technological infrastructure of information systems, telecommunications and transportation lines." The anthropologist Arjun Appadurai (1990) famously referred to five "scapes" of cultural flow (mediascapes, technoscapes, ethnoscapes, financescapes, and ideoscapes) that show how cultures influence each other. Flows, meanwhile, found adherents in the political economy of the media, and among Marxist media scholars. Concepts of "cultural imperialism," in particular, which had informed the NWICO, implied an uneven flow of media products and ideas, mostly Western, moving from the Global North to the South. The harms alleged to arise from these imbalances were presumed rather than identified through actual audience research; that would come much later. In-flows of foreign stuff were viewed as more likely to arouse the interest of youth audiences and it is here where the term acquired a kind of laissez-faire status. Many scholars and political elites in the receiving nations saw the potential of a rising tide that would erode domestic culture and cultural values. This was certainly the case in the PRC. Political elites argued for the erection of quotas, which along with strong censorship, functioned as a kind of restraining dam. Uncontrolled flows needed to be stopped or slowed down. Fortunately for the regulators, the metaphor of the dam resonated with narratives in Chinese culture. In the 1990s, the Chinese government created what it called the Green Dam project, installing filtering software on computers, to stop the flow of unhealthy content, a forerunner of the Great Firewall (of China).

Usage of the term "flow" consolidated with the recognition of East and South Asia as media production centers. The visual metaphor of a "wave" captured attention with the popularity of manga and anime in East and Southeast Asia, and later the "Korean Wave." In 1993, Thomas Gold (1993) drew attention to the influence of *gangtai* (Hong Kong and Taiwanese) pop music and television serials on the Chinese mainland. In 1996, Sinclair, Jacka, and Cunningham had identified "new patterns" in global television, coinciding with the recognition of diasporic communities. Non-Anglophone content flowed in different directions and with different degrees of effectiveness because communities resided overseas. In 2004, Iwabuchi, Muecke, and Thomas (2004: 1) suggested the variation "rogue flows," to emphasize "the ways in which accelerating movement of goods, ideas, cultural products and finance in West-dominated globalization processes have affected the framing of the transnational cultural traffic and encounters among Asian societies." Berry, Liscutin, and Macintosh (2009) have noted "transborder cultural flows" in the Northeast Asian region, while other commentators (Black, Epstein, and Tokita 2010) have spoken of "complicated currents, media flows and soft power." Concepts of flow have utility when applied well and some of the best analysts have used the term effectively to theorize movements of cultural product. Daya Thussu (2007), for instance, has proposed a useful typology, apportioning media flows into three categories: "global, transnational and geo-cultural," with a secondary triad of "dominant, contra and subaltern" flows. As he puts it: "The global media landscape in the first decade of the twenty-first century represents a complex terrain of multi-vocal, multimedia and multi-directional flows" (p. 12).

## Conclusion: processes not soft power, or flows

Soft power and flows are fuzzy concepts. I believe they are overused and often lack explanatory value. The problems with soft power go beyond media reception, the core concern of this chapter. Many of the surveys that purport to measure it, such as the Soft Power 30, reinforce the assumption that it is little more than a national popularity contest. Findings are inconsistent because they are based on comparative data that can be conveniently pulled together. The Soft Power 30 index, moreover, is biased toward Western democracies. In 2018, the addition of Michelin restaurants to the performance indicators gave a significant boost to France, while not helping China where the concept has not been used (Zhang and Wu 2019). In addition, much of the indexing is de-contextualized from actual lived experience. Most measurements reveal little about the emotional or subjective response of audiences to cultural products or their engagement with the political institutions that shape national image. Whereas global soft power surveys attend to a heterogeneous mix of indicators, largely informed by Joseph Nye's initial concept, use of the term in East Asian media industries scholarship is mostly applied to consumption. Export sales figures and industry ratings are offered as evidence, and in a more qualitative sense, so is the enthusiasm of fan communities.

Despite the prevalence of the flow metaphor within scholarship, it is also a fuzzy concept when used to account for cross-border or transnational media. This fuzziness is apparent when we examine China. Flows generally refer to finished products (e.g., films, TV series, and animations) conceived and produced in one nation, which are then circulated and traded across boundaries. However, how might co-productions be positioned in these dynamics? As China has opened its media industries, the government has encouraged co-productions and media collaborations. Chris Berry writes of film production, "the cast and crew might hold passports of different countries; and elements of the final product, such as the music, the editing, special effects, and so forth may be outsourced across national borders" (2014: 454). These can even be characterized as "assemblages." For example, when writing about television formats, Cho and Zhu (2017: 2337) argue "cultural assemblages … enables us to expand the scope of television format studies beyond its industrial and technical dimensions … underscore[ing] diverse, recurring, and reciprocal flows and ensuing social discourses."

Applying the concept of flows is problematic in China where barriers – including quotas, censorship, protectionism, and market distortions – impede the normal trade of media seen in neighboring territories. In contrast to liberal democracies, movements of media and personnel in China are heavily monitored. Increasingly, the Chinese government under Xi Jinping is moving to restrict the free flow of ideas. A case in point is Hong Kong where restrictions on civil society are being enforced, including residents' access to the short video site TikTok. While the Sinophone and Greater China served as symbols of the free flow of creative content a decade ago, this no longer holds true. The China media industrial complex has spread its tentacles. Processes, technology, and specialist know-how, rather than flows, are gradually changing the balance of cultural power in East Asia and beyond. An emphasis on policies, people, and industry relationships that allow producers, writers, actors, investors, and technicians to engage in collaborative efforts calls for an explanation more akin to technology transfer, albeit one that takes more account of political realities.

# References

Appadurai, A. (1990) "Disjuncture and Difference in the Global Cultural Economy," *Theory, Culture and Society*, 7 (203): 295–310.

BBC (2018) "Yanxi Palace: The Most Googled Show on Earth," *BBC News*, December 23, available at www.bbc.co.uk/news/world-asia-china-46630781 (accessed October 21, 2020).

Berry, C. (2014) "Transnational Culture in East Asia and the Logic of Assemblage," *Asian Journal of Social Science*, 41 (5): 453–470.

Berry, C., Liscutin, N., and Macintosh, J. (eds) (2009) *Cultural Studies and Cultural Industries in Northeast Asia*, Hong Kong: Hong Kong University Press.

Black, D., Epstein, S. and Tokita, A. (eds) (2010) *Complicated Currents, Media Flows, Soft Power and East Asia*, Melbourne: Monash University Publishing.

Castells, M. (1999) "Grassrooting the Space of Flows," *Urban Geography*, 20 (4): 294–302.

Cho, Y. and Zhu, H. (2017) "Interpreting the Television Format Phenomenon Between South Korea and China Through Inter-Asian Frameworks," *International Journal of* Communication, 11: 2332–2349.

Chu, Y. (2014) "The Politics of Reception. Made in China and Western Critique," *International Journal of Cultural Studies*, 17 (2): 159–173.

Chua, B-H. (2012) *Structure, Audience and Soft Power in East Asian Pop Culture*, Hong Kong: Hong Kong University Press.

Chua, B-H. and Iwabuchi K. (eds) (2008) *East Asian Pop Culture: Analyzing the Korean Wave*, Hong Kong: Hong Kong University Press.

Couldry, N. (2012) *Media, Society, World: Social Theory and Digital Media Practice*, London: Polity.

De Burgh, H. (2017) *China's Media in the Emerging World Order*, Buckingham: University of Buckingham Press.

Curtin, M. (2007) *Playing to the World's Biggest Audience: The Globalization of Chinese Film and TV*, Berkeley, CA: University of California Press.

Edney, K. Rosen, S. and Zhu, Y. (2019) "Introduction," in K. Edney, S. Rosen, and Y. Zhu (eds), *Soft Power with Chinese Characteristics*, Abingdon: Routledge.

Fukuyama, F. (1989) "The End of History?" *The National Interest* (16): 3–18.

Fung, A. (ed.) (2013) *Asian Popular Culture: The Global (Dis)Continuity*, Abingdon: Routledge.

Gold, T. B. (1993) "Go with Your Feelings: Hong Kong and Taiwan Popular Culture in Greater China," *The China Quarterly*, 1 (36): 907–925.

Harding, H. (1993) "'The Concept of 'Greater China': Themes, Variations and Reservations," *The China Quarterly*, 136: 660–686.

Iwabuchi, K., Muecke, S., and Thomas, M. (2004) *Rogue Flows: Trans-Asian Cultural Traffic*, Hong Kong: Hong Kong University Press.

Jin, D. Y. (2016) *New Korean Wave: Transnational Cultural Power in the Age of Social Media*, Urbana, IL: University of Illinois Press.

Keane, M. (2016). "Disconnecting, Connecting, Reconnecting: How Chinese Television Got Out of the Box," *International Journal of Communication*, 10: 5426–5443.

Keane, M., Yecies, B., and Flew, T. (eds) (2018) *Willing Collaborators: Foreign Partners in China's Media*, London: Rowman & Littlefield International.

Keane, M., Yu, H., Zhao, E. J., and Leong, S. (2020) *China's Digital Presence in the Asia-Pacific: Culture, Technology, Platforms*, London: Anthem Press.

McGray, D. (2009) "Japan's Gross National Cool," *Foreign Policy Journal*, November 11, available at https://foreignpolicy.com/2009/11/11/japans-gross-national-cool/ (accessed April 30, 2012).

Markusen, A. (2013) "Fuzzy Concepts, Proxy Data: Why Indicators Would Not Track Creative Placemaking Success," *International Journal of Urban Sciences*, 17 (3) 291–303.

Nye, J. S. (1990) *Bound to Lead: The Changing Nature of American* Power, New York: Basic Books.

Shih, S-M. (2007) *Visual and Identity: Sinophone Articulations Across the Pacific*, Berkeley, CA: University of California Press.

Shim, D. (2006) "Hybridity and the Rise of Korean Popular Culture in Asia," *Media Culture and Society*, 28 (1): 25–44.

Sinclair, J., Jacka, E and Cunningham. S. (1996) *New Patterns in Global Television: Peripheral Vision*, Oxford: Oxford University Press.

Spangler, T. (2019) "Facebook to Pay $40 Million to Settle Claims that It Inflated Video Viewing Data," *Variety*, October 7, available at https://variety.com/2019/digital/news/facebook-settlement-video-advertising-lawsuit-40-million-1203361133/ (accessed November 18, 2020).

Sparks, C. (2017) "Hegemonic Shadows: USA, China and Dewesternising Media Studies," *Westminster Paper in Communications and Culture*, 12 (1): 19–20.

Thussu, D. (2007) "Mapping Global Media Flow and Contra-flow," in D. Thussu (ed.), *Media on the Move: Global Flow and Contra Flow*, Abingdon: Routledge, 11–32.

Wang, Q. and de Kloet, J. (2016) "'From Nothing to My Name'," Market, Capital and Politics in the Chinese Music Industry," in M. Keane (ed.), *The Handbook of the Cultural and Creative Industries in China*, Cheltenham, Edward Elgar, 293–310.

Xi, J. P. (2020) "renmin yaolun: zai jianghao zhongguo gushi zhong tisheng huayuquan" ("People's Important Discussion: When Telling China's Stories Well, Raise the Level of Discursive power"), *Chinese Communist Party Online News*, April 3, available at http://theory.people.com.cn/n1/2020/0402/c40531-31658343.html (accessed November 18, 2020).

Yecies, B., Keane, M., Yu, H., Zhao, E. J., Zhong, P., Leong, S., and Wu, H. (2019) "The Cultural Power Metric: Towards a Reputational Analysis of China's Soft Power in the Asia-Pacific," *Global Media and China*, 4 (2): 203–219.

Yu, H. and Keane, M. (2020) "Masking Power in the Age of Contagion: The Two Faces of China in the Wake of Coronavirus.' *The Conversation*, April 1, available at https://theconversation.com/masking-power-in-the-age-of-contagion-the-two-faces-of-china-in-the-wake-of-coronavirus-135035 (accessed November 18, 2020).

Zhang, C. and Wu, R. Q. (2019) "Battlefield of Global Ranking: How do Power Rivalries Shape Soft Power Index Building?" *Global Media and China*, 4 (2): 179–202.

Zhu, Y. (2012) *Two Billion Eyes: The Story of China Central Television*, New York: The New Press.

# 18

# BRICKS, MORTAR, AND MEDIA

## Understanding the media industries through their buildings

*Elizabeth Evans*

The media industries rely on buildings. They are a key resource and component of the media industries' work throughout the production, distribution, and exhibition cycle. However, media buildings are not simply functional constructions. As Anthony D. King (1980: 1) argues:

> buildings, indeed, the entire built environment, are essentially social and cultural products. Buildings result from social needs and accommodate a variety of functions – economic, social, political, religious and cultural. Their size, appearance, location and form are governed not simply by physical factors (climate, materials or topography) but by a society's ideas, its forms of economic and social organization, its distribution of resources and authority, its activities, and the beliefs and values which prevail at any one period of time.

Examining buildings as socially, culturally, and politically informed spaces offers insight into the both visible and hidden structures of the media industries, illuminating practices and relationships within individual organizations, between organizations, and between the industry and the wider structures in which media sit.

Interrogating media buildings opens up numerous valuable avenues of enquiry. The spaces and locations in which media work happens structure the practices and hierarchies of media workers (who gets access to which floor, for instance). The design and architecture of media buildings can carry cultural meanings or associations, with some becoming iconic symbols of the organizations they housed, such as the circular Capitol Records building in Los Angeles, the neo-gothic Tribune Tower in Chicago, the newspaper buildings of London's Fleet Street, or Shanghai's Oriental Pearl Radio and Television Tower. Media buildings are also embedded in local communities, acting as examples of industrial and urban change and tied to economic and political factors such as regeneration projects, changing business rates in city centers, or tax incentive programs. Media buildings therefore act as a nexus of multiple concerns for media industry scholars including working practices, organizational hierarchies, branding, the position of media organizations in local communities and national or local media policy.

This chapter will explore the various ways that media scholars have interrogated buildings to present a framework for critically evaluating how buildings not only facilitate and shape the operation of the media industries but also, in some cases, take on symbolic meanings in wider

DOI: 10.4324/9780429275340-21

cultural contexts. Scholarship on media buildings is often highly focused on a particular *type* of building, for example the studio lot or cinema. This chapter will therefore firstly offer a way of classifying media buildings. It will particularly focus on the screen industries (film, television, gaming, and promotional content) but will also point to other media-related buildings where relevant. Through this taxonomy it will draw out key questions that can be used to frame an interrogation of media buildings. It will end with a case study of Television Centre, the BBC's main headquarters from 1960 until 2013, in order to explore the multifaceted role that buildings can play and how they can illuminate the structures and operations of the media industries.

## Classifying media buildings

What counts as a "media building"? Buildings of all varieties obviously appear *within* media products, especially those with screen-based content, with houses, offices, shops, and factories regularly featuring as *location buildings* in films, television programs, adverts, and music videos. The role of buildings within a location shoot raises questions around the importance of architecture or design features to buildings' narrative function (see, for example, Lamster, 2013) or the economic and practical imperatives behind filming on location rather than in a studio (see, for example, Stringer 2017; Gleich and Webb 2019). Equally, *infrastructural buildings* such as the BT and CN Towers or Google's data centers act as physical markers of the hidden backbone that makes the media industry work. Here, however, I will focus on the media buildings owned or permanently occupied by front-line media industry organizations, rather than those that are temporarily borrowed to fulfil a narrative purpose or that equally serve the broader communications industry. While location and infrastructure buildings are used by the media industries, they are not integrated into the everyday workings of the media industries in the way that other production, distribution, and exhibition related buildings are. The following taxonomy is based primarily on function – what are the buildings used for? There are other ways that they could be classified, for instance whether the building is purpose-built or renovated, the type of building (office vs warehouse), or its location. However, focusing on function allows for a clearer connection between a building's structure and appearance and its role within the media industries. This then leads to three primary categories of media building: production management and support offices, production facilities, and sites of exhibition.

## *Production management and support offices*

Despite the veneer of glamour that gets associated with media or entertainment products in the popular press, many of the buildings owned and used by the media industries consist of rather unexciting office complexes. Office space most commonly functions to house the large amount of development and support work that surrounds the creation of media products (whether that is the shooting of a film, television episode or advert, the recording of an album or the creation of a videogame). This work takes place in offices with desks and computers, meetings rooms, and other communal spaces that barely differ in appearance or function from office spaces in other, less "glamourous" sectors. These administrative offices, and the buildings that contain them, however, can frame and shape the work that goes on inside them and in turn offer insight into the structures of media work.

Paul Grainge and Catherine Johnson's work on the promotional screen industries provides an explicit example of how an office building inflects and shapes media practice. They describe how the layout of digital agency Red Bee Media's offices in the White City area of London facilitates certain kinds of working practices. Red Bee is responsible for creative strategy around content promotion and audience development but also acts as the transmission hub for much of the UK's television broadcasts. Originally created as a commercial spin-off of the BBC (Grainge and Johnson 2015: 68), Red Bee's offices sit within a BBC-owned building, just down the road from the former BBC Television Centre (discussed in more detail below). The location of these offices therefore speaks to the company's legacy as well as placing Red Bee in a geographical location steeped in UK television history (p. 71).

In a lengthy quote that is worth reproducing given its detail and insight, Grainge and Johnson describe how differences in the company's office space reflect the different kinds of work they do:

> Behind secure glass rooms in a bomb-proof building, banks of monitors play out the BBC's terrestrial and digital channels (alongside other major networks) with continuity announcers ready to voice links within the linear flow. Red Bee Creative uses three atria around these playout suites and occupies the entire floor above. The atria have been designed to facilitate different kinds of activity, self-described as "making", "meeting" and "working". The "making" atrium has thirty-two desks with pens and tablets for creatives to produce and edit in groups or with their creative heads, "meeting" provides a space with soft seating and desks for discussion of projects, and "working" is for quiet work such as scriptwriting. The main office floor has additional meeting and presentation rooms, a kitchen (with table football for staff breaks) and a floor layout where management and production support coordinators have fixed desks, and where teams of account managers, planners and creatives hot-desk to maximize their flexibility within and between projects.
>
> *p. 74*

Grainge and Johnson highlight a number of factors linking the architecture and design of Red Bee's building to the nature of the company as an organization and the work its employees do. There is a clear distinction between the creative team who work in shared open-plan spaces, and those responsible for broadcast transmission working in "secure glass rooms" that display and protect their work while also separating them from their colleagues. Different spaces are named according to different kinds of work involved in planning or writing. Some workers have personal desks while others hot desk, reflecting varying flexibility in working styles but also creating a physical distinction between the two groups – some can "own" their workspace while others cannot. Recreational spaces show a recognition of the necessity for breaks while also keeping those breaks close to workspaces and so spatially (and in turn temporally) limited. The structure of the building and its internal design help to reflect and shape the practices of those working in it.

While seemingly non-descript, the media industry's production management and support offices are evidence of how media labor and practice is shaped in often semi-visible or invisible ways. The layout (what goes where), facilities (what is and isn't available), and fabric (what materials are walls and furnishings made of) of office spaces reinforce working practices and organizational structures while also acting as evidence of those practices and structures. Equally, where media organizations choose to operate from, and the spaces they place their employees in, act as evidence for how they understand and present themselves to their employees, clients, and partners. Office buildings such as the one that houses Red Bee are a, if not the, most common type of media building and present a rich site for analysis in terms of how media work is organized. Examining such everyday spaces reveals the often overlooked mundane elements of media practice and how the structures shaping that practice manifest not only in the people and work that make up media companies, but are also physically embedded in the structures they are housed in.

## Production facilities

If office space forms the majority of media buildings, the type most readily associated with the media industries, especially the screen industries, are the sites where production takes place. *Production facilities* refers to custom-built or renovated spaces in which media products are created. At one end of the scale, media production can happen in relatively standard office spaces much like those described above. The creation of visual effects (VFX) or videogame production, for instance, rely predominantly on practitioners working on banks of computers. For example, major VFX houses like Industrial Light and Magic or videogame developers such as Rockstar operate out of outwardly generic office complexes. Even more unusual, sector-specific production tools can be housed in small, inconspicuous buildings. In the music industry, for example, the famous Abbey Road Studios occupy a rather non-descript building in among shops, homes, and a school on a quiet street in suburban London.

At the opposite end of the scale lies large production spaces that house the filming of sets and actors or presenters in studios and sound stages. Such facilities may be accompanied by "backlots" with a mix of functional buildings and facades, that act as controllable outdoor filming locations. The purpose of studios, sound stages, and backlots is to house the narrative (fictional and non-fictional) worlds of film and television content. This normally results in spaces that are utilitarian and anonymous, capable of transforming into anywhere or anything with the addition of specific sets. The Pinewood Group Ltd.'s site just west of London, for example, offers buildings ranging from 2,640 square feet television studios equipped with fixed lighting rigs and support offices, to its famous 007 Stage, an essentially empty warehouse-style structure of 59,062 square feet. The Group's website[1] displays its range of production facilities through photos of empty sound stages that highlight their generic architecture and subsequent transformative potential. Production buildings such as studios and sound stages are therefore designed to be deliberately "undesigned" and easily transform into anywhere or anything. Backlots are equally designed to stand in for a variety of real-world locations, and as such either offer large empty spaces for temporary sets to be built on or imitate generic categories such as "city street" or "suburban neighborhood."

Production facilities are enmeshed within local and national media policy and planning procedures. As Ben Goldsmith and Tom O'Regan (2005: 31–33) argue, the sheer amount of land needed for major production facilities means they are often located on the outskirts of major cities, with their development actively encouraged or facilitated by local and national governments (p. 45). Incentive schemes based on tax credits act as key factors, which determine where the media industries, and its buildings, settle (see Kerr 2014; McNutt 2015). Considerations of production buildings therefore cannot be limited to their functions, architecture, or structure but must also position those buildings within the wider political and economic contexts that determine whether, and where, they exist.

## Sites of consumption

Media industry buildings can also be the space where media products meet their audience. One of the most prominent trends of scholarship on media buildings emerges out of film studies and work on cinemas as exhibition sites. Most media consumption happens in the home, and so does not happen in a "media building." However, spaces such as cinemas, television studios that cater for on-screen audiences, or even theme parks and retail spaces such as the Disney Store are controlled by branches of the media industries and as such can also be considered as buildings that connect the production of media products and the audiences they are made for. Here we shall focus on the cinema as an example of perhaps the most publicly visible of all media buildings.

Cinemas demonstrate the importance of location and context to understanding the media industries through their buildings. A significant body of work on cinemas merges the analysis of cinema buildings, and their changing fortunes over time, with wider cultural, political, and economic changes in specific regions, towns, or cities (Jancovich, Faire and Stubbings 2003; Jones 2003; Abel 2007; Grainge 2008; Allen 2010, 2011; Gomery 2013; Hanson 2013). The importance of seeing cinemas as buildings within a specific locational context, rather than as mere conduits to film content, is typified though Jeffrey Klenotic's analysis of debates around the building and opening of the Paramount Theatre in Springfield, Massachusetts. Klenotic (2013: 191–192) argues that "the reception of the Paramount [cinema] had as much to do with property values, taxes, job-creation, debates over the built environment and problems coping with urban modernization as it did with the attractions of famous players in famous plays." The importance of a cinema's hyperlocal context has not diminished, and sites of consumption remain closely intertwined with the political, social, cultural, and economic character of their region and/or city (see Singer 1995; Grainge 2008: 156–160).

In addition to placing cinemas within their historical and hyperlocal contexts, studying cinemas as media buildings also reiterates the importance of architecture, design, and the fabric of buildings themselves. On the one hand, cinema architecture can encourage or limit certain kinds of behavior or social relations (see, for example, Doherty 2007; Shail 2007). On the other hand, the materials used to build and decorate cinemas work to assign meanings to both the buildings and the experiences they offer. The ornate movie palaces of the early twentieth century echoed their namesakes with extravagant architectural and design features that made the cinema building more important than what was on screen (Kracauer 1987; Jones 2003: 234–235; Jancovich, Faire and Stubbings 2013: 214–215). More recent cinema architecture takes the opposite approach, with more generic, simplistic design approaches that work to focus audience attention on the film itself (Recuber 2007: 317). The interior design of cinema buildings plays a key part of the framing of cinema-going experiences and these debates echo Grainge and Johnson's (2015) examination of Red Bee's offices in exploring how the bricks and mortar (and glass, wood and fabric) of media buildings are a site ripe for critical evaluation.

## A framework for interrogating media buildings

We can study the buildings occupied and used by the media industries for insight into how these buildings shape the various forms of professional or social relations that go on inside them and the wider meanings that can become attached to them. The above discussion has outlined the different functions that media buildings can have within administrative, pre-production, production, distribution, marketing, and exhibition processes. These must not be seen as impermeable distinctions, however. Multiple buildings may be brought together into a single coherent media industry site such as a studio lot (see Goldsmith and O'Regan 2005: xi). In contrast, a single building may have multiple functions. Tour guides taking tourists around studio lots in Los Angeles, for example, often make a point of identifying administrative buildings that have also appeared on-screen in various films and television episodes. Distinguishing media buildings by type and function therefore serves only as a first step toward interrogating how buildings

*Table 18.1* Framework for analyzing media buildings

| Purpose | • What is the building for?<br>  • Who uses it and what do they do there?<br>  • Is it internal to the industry or audience facing? | |
|---|---|---|
| Architecture and design | • What does the building look like?<br>  • Which architectural style(s) does it call on?<br>  • How do these connect to its purpose or historical context? | • How is it organized in terms of layout, access points?<br>  • How does its layout facilitate or shape intra-organizational relationships and hierarchies?<br>  • How does its structure and design encourage or inhibit working practices or media experiences? |
| Location | • Where is the building?<br>  • Is it urban, suburban, or rural?<br>  • Is it one of a collection of media buildings (e.g., part of a studio lot) or is it isolated?<br>  • What surrounds it in terms of commercial, civic, or residential areas? | • Why is it there?<br>  • Does the location have specific historical and/or cultural meanings or connotations?<br>  • What national, regional, or local urban planning, cultural, or economic policy shape its location? |
| Context | • What is the building's history?<br>  • Is it purpose built or repurposed?<br>  • What connotations come with any previous ownership or use? | • Who owns the building?<br>  • How does ownership relate to use?<br>  • How does ownership relate to issues around the global and/or local? |

shape and are shaped by media industries practice. Thinking across these different functions allows us to develop a set of questions that can be used to interrogate media buildings through purpose, architecture, design, and location (Table 18.1).

This chapter will now take this framework and apply it to a case study of BBC Television Centre. Doing so allows for a greater examination of how the function and fabric of media buildings reveal the structures of the media industries and also collect symbolic cultural meanings.

## Case study: BBC Television Centre

BBC Television Centre opened in 1960 to meet the BBC's desire to "have a building adequate for the expanding television service" (IEE 1962a: 197). The building would eventually replace Alexandra Palace in north London, which had been the Corporation's main site for television production since the launch of its television service in 1936. Television Centre was therefore specifically designed to meet the needs of television production as perceived in the 1950s. This was an era when television production was still predominantly – though not exclusively – live, but new production technologies, such as videotape and pre-recorded content or color television, were being experimented with and were soon to become industry staples. A presentation made to the Institution of Electrical Engineers (IEE) shortly after the building opened repeatedly referred to a desire for it to evolve and accommodate to the changing demands of a relatively new but rapidly developing media industry and the building's capacity to handle technological innovation (IEE 1962b). The BBC continued to occupy other buildings, most notably Broadcasting House and Bush House in central London, which housed its radio and World Service units, respectively. However, Television Centre became the Corporation's head-quarters and most widely visible building, housing sound stages, production facilities as well as production management and support offices.

Television Centre was designed by architect Graham Dawbarn (Coomes 2012). Its key physical feature was a circular courtyard, surrounded by the main sound stages and produc-tion offices. Subsequent extensions then added additional production support offices until the building resembled a question mark (and Dawbarn's original design). The IEE discussion framed the circular design as a necessary compromise between function and available space, with BBC Chief Engineer Sir Harold Bishop commenting that:

> Of course there were criticisms of the design. The installation, it was said, would be more expensive and it would be difficult to fit equipment into rooms which had not parallel walls ... In other counties a rectangular type of design has been successfully adopted, but the space required is much more than is available at Television Centre.
>
> *IEE 1962b: 219*

The location of the building had a number of historical associations. The site in west London had earned the name "White City" from the white buildings erected for the 1908 Olympic Games and Franco-British Exhibition of Science (Littlefield 2012). Construction of Television Centre therefore literally built upon and erased part of London's cultural past (p. 75), acting as a symbol of the emergent media industries staking a claim over UK cultural life and reinforcing the BBC's role at the center of the UK media industries.

Beyond the building's origins, its layout also offered insight into the Corporation as a media organization. Georgina Born's ethnographic study of the BBC in the early 2000s hints at how the structure of Television Centre reflected the corporation's internal hierarchies. Born describes everyday programming and strategy decisions as happening in anonymous spaces such as "a large room in the basement" (2004: 95) with senior management sitting higher in the building, in offices on "the sixth floor" (p. 295). Her interviews with BBC personnel also reveal how power relations between different divisions emerged through whether they were located in Television Centre or in one of the Corporation's other buildings. One Broadcasting Research execu-tive is quoted as saying that "When David Docherty [Deputy Director of BBC Television] came in '91 or '92 ... he immediately argued that ... if research is going to make an impact, it needs to be here, in TV Centre" (p. 271). Presence inside Television Centre was seen as being at the heart of the Corporation and so something that would be taken seriously. Conversely, a television news editor expressed concern over radio news moving into the same building from Broadcasting House, arguing that bringing radio and television news into the same phys-ical building risked losing each service's distinctive character (pp. 390–391). For a multi-sited media organization such as the BBC, which departments and personnel sit in which building, and which got the "privilege" of being in Television Centre, shaped the internal relationships between those departments.

Television Centre's value as a case study of a media building stretches beyond the relation-ship between its architecture or design and issues of labor and practice. More so than any other media-related building in the UK, Television Centre became a visible and public representation of the BBC's work and position within UK culture. The building regularly appeared on screen, with its circular courtyard and the dotted outside wall of Studio 1 featuring most prominently. Presenters would frequently self-reflexively refer to programs being filmed in Television Centre, with its address repeatedly mentioned as somewhere audiences could write to, and the canteen becoming the punchline for recurring jokes. The Centre also acted as the staging point for protests over what the Corporation should or should not do. Programs such as charity telethons *Comic Relief* (1985–) or *Children in Need* (1980–) featured segments filmed in the Centre's car park. Long-running children's magazine program *Blue Peter* (1958–) made a key feature of a small garden behind the main building, even using it as a cemetery and memorial for the program's pets. The Centre also functioned simultaneously as a site of production and con-sumption, for some members of the general public, as studio audiences were invited inside the building to watch certain productions being recorded. The visibility of Television Centre made the processes of television production more visible to the television audience by foregrounding the physical spaces in which it happens.

Television Centre therefore became a physical and locational representation of the BBC and was far more prominent on screen than other BBC-owned buildings. Ultimately, the building also came to represent the BBC's economic and political fragility in the 2010s. The Conservative–Liberal Democrat coalition government, elected in 2010 shortly after the 2008 financial crash, ushered in an era of "austerity" politics to the UK. Part of this included increasing economic pressure on publicly funded UK institutions, including the BBC. Owning a large plot of West London real estate became both a financial burden to the Corporation and a way for it to address political pressure. Faced with an explicit directive to cut costs and more clearly address the needs of non-London based audiences, the BBC sold Television Centre for redevelopment in 2012 for £200 million (Plunkett, 2012), moving its headquarters to Broadcasting House, and also relocating certain departments outside of London to the MediaCityUK development in Salford. Portions of the building remain active television studios, while other sections have been converted into high-end residential apartments.

The wider cultural value and meaning associated with Television Centre has extended into its post-BBC life. In 2018, commercial broadcaster (and BBC rival) ITV's *This Morning* (1988–) began broadcasting from the redeveloped Television Centre studio complex. The first episode broadcast from the new studios brought significant attention to both the location and its media heritage (ITV1, tx. April 16, 2018). The program's opening credit sequence featured helicopter shots of the building, highlighting the architectural features of the circular courtyard and dotted outside wall (still labelled "Television Centre" but now missing the "BBC" logo). The episode opened with hosts Holly Willoughby and Philip Schofield standing at the center of the court-yard. Schofield, who had previously worked in Television Centre as a children's presenter for the BBC, proceeded to speak about "the old days," describing his memories of working in the building and pointing out where his old studio was. Despite no longer being owned by the BBC, the building retained its connection to the Corporation and its history. This connection was not restricted to its continuing role in media production. In an interview with *The Wall Street Journal*, Paul Monaghan of Allford Hall Monaghan Morris, lead architect of the redevel-opment project, said:

> Everyone in the country has grown up looking at this building because of all the tele-vision shows that were filmed there, and because it was so often used as a backdrop for live broadcasts … When people come in, they stop and take a selfie – there are not many buildings that have that effect.
>
> *Bloomfield 2016*

The architects behind the site's redevelopment equally sold its residential section on its media-related cultural heritage. Television Centre became the physical embodiment of not only the BBC's organizational practices, but also its wider position within the UK media industries.

This case study discussion is necessarily brief, and in many ways Television Centre is unique in its public profile, but it does offer an example for how the practices of the media industries and the ways in which cultural meaning becomes attached to media practice and media organizations can be interrogated through their buildings.

## Conclusion

As the physical structures that house media industry organizations, media buildings may seem to be merely functional. Indeed, function offers a useful method for classifying different media buildings. Determining whether buildings accommodate administrative production support, serve as sites for the production of media texts, or act as spaces for industry-controlled media consumption allows us to categorize the variety of spaces in which the media industries operate. However, the value of analyzing media buildings extends far beyond identifying what each building is used for. The way buildings are structured and designed reveals the myriad of visible and invisible ways in which they shape media practice and engagement. Locating media buildings within local and national contexts offers ways of interrogating how the media industries become embedded in wider cultural and political structures. While it may be tempting to assume that media buildings are secondary to the content produced in them, they are in fact vital conduits to a greater understanding of how the work and cultural status of the media industries are organized and facilitated.

This chapter has offered a framework for analyzing media buildings in terms of a building's purpose, architecture and design, location, and context. These four categories not only account for the physical spaces that buildings create, but also how those spaces acquire additional meanings for those within the industry as well as for audiences and other stakeholders such as local or national governments. Applying this framework to the BBC's Television Centre, possibly the most well-known media building in the UK, demonstrates how the building, its location, layout, and fabric are intertwined with the Corporation's history and position within UK cultural life. The changes that BBC Television Centre has undergone offer a physical manifestation of the Corporation's own internal hierarchies as well as a microcosm of its shifting relationships with stakeholders ranging from the government to other industry organizations and audiences. Its presence on UK television screens grounded what for much of the general population could otherwise be an abstract, mysterious process – the production of television programs – in a real, visible space that audiences became familiar with. The attention that the Centre's redevelopment garnered revealed that the building had meaning beyond simply being where the BBC makes programs. Just as media products are made by real people they are also made in real spaces, and those spaces are much more than simply bricks and mortar.

## Note

1 www.pinewoodgroup.com

# References

Abel, R. (2007) "Patchwork Maps of Moviegoing, 1911–1913," in R. Maltby and M. Stokes (eds), *Going to the Movies: Hollywood and the Social Experience of Film*, Exeter: University of Exeter Press, 94–112.

Allen, R. C. (2010) "Getting to *Going to the Show*," *New Review of Film and Television Studies*, 8 (3): 264–276.

Allen, R. C. (2011) "Reimagining the History of the Experience of Cinema in a Post-Movie-Going Age," *Media International Australia*, 139 (1): 80–87.

Bloomfield, R. (2016) "From 'Monty Python' to Luxury Condos: The $1.5 Billion Redesign of the BBC's Television Centre," *The Wall Street Journal*, May 26, available at www.wsj.com/articles/from-monty-python-to-luxury-condos-the-1-5-billion-redesign-of-the-bbcs-television-centre-1464272596 (accessed January 30, 2020).

Coomes, P. (2012) "Goodbye Television Centre," *BBC News*, July 6, available at www.bbc.co.uk/news/in-pictures-18627051 (accessed January 20, 2020).

Doherty, T. (2007) "Race Houses, Jim Crow Roosts, and Lily White Palaces: Desegregating the Motion Picture Theater," in R. Maltby and M. Stokes (eds), *Going to the Movies: Hollywood and the Social Experience of Film*, Exeter: University of Exeter Press, 196–-216.

Goldsmith, B. and O'Regan, T. (2005) *The Film Studio: Film Production in the Global Economy*, Oxford: Rowman & Littlefield.

Gomery, D. (2013) "Movie-Going in the Shenandoah Valley of Virginia: A Case Study of Place, Transportation, Audiences, Racism, Censorship and Sunday Showings," in K. Aveyard and A. Moran (eds), *Watching Films: New Perspectives on Movie-Going, Exhibition and Reception*, Bristol: Intellect Books, 171–188.

Gleich, J. and Webb, L. (2019) *Hollywood on Location: An Industry History*, New Brunswick, NJ: Rutgers University Press.

Grainge, P. (2008) *Brand Hollywood: Selling Entertainment in a Global Media Age*, Abingdon: Routledge.

Grainge, P. and Johnson, C. (2015) *Promotional Screen Industries*, Abingdon: Routledge.

Hanson, S. (2013) "From Out-of-town to the Edge and Back to the Centre: Multiplexes in Britain from the 1990s," in K. Aveyard and A. Moran (eds), *Watching Films: New Perspectives on Movie-Going, Exhibition and Reception*, Bristol: Intellect Books: 245–260.

IEE (1962a) "B.B.C. Television Centre and its Technical Facilities," *Proceedings of the IEE – Part B: Electronic and Communication Engineering*, 109 (45): 197–219.

IEE (1962b) "Discussion on 'The B.B.C. Television Centre and its Technical Facilities' before the Institution, November 23, 1961," *Proceedings of the IEE – Part B: Electronic and Communication Engineering*, 109 (45): 219–221.

Jancovich, M., Fair, L. and Stubbings, S. (2003) *The Place of the Audience: Cultural Geographies of Film Consumption*, London: British Film Institute.

Jancovich, M., Faire, L. and Stubbings, S. (2013) "A Progressive City and its Cinemas: Technology, Modernity and the Spectacle of Abundance," in K. Aveyard and A. Moran (eds), *Watching Films: New Perspectives on Movie-Going, Exhibition and Reception*, Bristol: Intellect Books, 209–222.

Jones, J. (2003) *The Southern Movie Palace: Rise, Fall and Resurrection*, Gainesville, FL: University of Florida Press.

Kerr, A. (2014) "Placing International Media Production," *Media Industries*, 1 (1): 27–32.

King, A. D. (1980) *Buildings and Society: Essays on the Social Development of the Built Environment*, London: Routledge & Kegan Paul.

Klenotic, J. (2013) "From Mom-and-Pop to Paramount-Publix: Selling the Benefits of National Theatre Chains," in K. Aveyard and A. Moran (eds), *Watching Films: New Perspectives on Movie-Going, Exhibition and Reception*, Bristol: Intellect Books, 189–208.

Kracauer, S. (1987) "Cult of Distraction: On Berlin's Picture Palaces," *New German Critique* 40: 91–96.

Lamster, M. (2013) *Architecture and Film*, New York: Princeton Architectural Press.

Littlefield, D. (2012) "White City: The Art of Erasure and Forgetting the Olympic Games," *Architectural Design*, 81 (1): 71–77.

McNutt, M. (2015) "Mobile Production: Spatialized Labor, Location Professionals, and the Expanding Geography of Television Production," *Media Industries* 2 (1): 60–77.

Plunkett, J. (2012) "BBC Sells Television Centre for £200," *The Guardian*, July 16, available at www.theguardian.com/media/2012/jul/16/bbc-sells-television-centre (accessed January 30, 2020).

Recuber, T. (2007) "Immersion Cinema: The Rationalization and Reenchantment of Cinematic Space," *Space and Culture* 10 (3): 315–330.

Shail, A. (2007) "Penny Gaffs and Picture Theatres: Popular Perceptions of Britain's First Cinemas," in J. Lyons and J. Plunkett (eds), *Multimedia Histories: From the Magic Lantern to the Internet,* Exeter: University of Exeter Press, 132–147.

Singer, B. (1995) "Manhattan Nickelodeons: New Data on Audiences and Exhibitors," *Cinema Journal,* 34 (3): 5–35.

Stringer, J. (2017) "Location Filmmaking and the Hong Kong Crime Film: Anatomy of a Scene," in E. Yau and T. Williams (eds), *Hong Kong Neo-Noir,* Edinburgh: Edinburgh University Press, 159–177.

# 19

# AUTHORSHIP AND AGENCY IN THE MEDIA INDUSTRIES

*Eva Novrup Redvall*

As long as there has been cultural production, there has been fascination with the people making cultural products. Where did this product/artwork come from? What were the intentions behind its making? How can we understand a particular product in relation to those by others or by the same maker/makers?

Much has been written about authorship and agency in the humanities, in many different disciplines, from art history and music studies, to film and media studies. Discussions of authorship and agency have always been an issue while scholars have tried to pinpoint what defines an author and creative agency. In some disciplines this task is fundamentally easier than in others, due to a tradition of practitioners working primarily alone and being able to make their visions come alive at a relatively low cost. In the media industries, these processes are most often much more complex and marked by a number of commissioners, collaborators, and contributors who have an impact on the final product at hand.

Rather than offering a comprehensive outline of the many overall discussions and theories about authorship and agency across disciplines, this chapter focuses on the particularities of thinking about authorial voice and agency in relation to media industry studies, based on writings from this specific scholarly field. While many media industry scholars build on theories and frameworks from other traditions, for example, from literature studies or creativity theory, thinking about authorship in the media industries is marked by focusing not only on art and individual expression, but also on "social and institutional structures that govern cultural production, enabling and compelling, and authorizing some forms while constraining others" (Gray and Johnson 2013: 6). Analyses of authorship and agency in the media industries take the industrial context into account, insisting that different cultures of production not only influence *what* is made, and *how* and *why* it is made, but also *who* gets to make things in the first place.

Studying authorship has always been "a contested terrain rather than a stable designation" (Chris and Gerstner 2013: 11), and this is definitely still the case in the digital media industries where notions of authorship can take on many forms. Broadcasters or studios can be understood as having "institutional authorship" or "corporate authorship," with the authorial function augmenting productions that are part of a company's primary brand identity (e.g., Thompson and Burns 1990; Johnson 2013; Hogan 2013). Co-creation and fan fiction challenge the relationship between producers and audiences (e.g., D. Johnson 2013), for instance by elaborating

DOI: 10.4324/9780429275340-22

on or inventing new storylines in different fan outputs, or by giving a cult series such as *Twin Peaks* (1990–91 and 2017) a "social media afterlife" (Williams 2016). While there is still what Jonathan Gray and Derek Johnson describe as a cultural fascination with authors "and with the super powers ascribed to them" (2013: 2), the romantic view of the individual author has long been challenged in media industry studies where most scholars agree that one needs to think about authorship as collaborative, marked by creative contributions from a number of different people as well as the industrial constraints shaping different production frameworks. With the rise of production studies since the late 2000s (e.g., Caldwell 2008; Mayer, Banks, and Caldwell 2009), many media industry scholars became more focused on how exploring the actual production processes behind new works can nuance understandings of authorship and agency, allowing for more detailed and explicit analysis of "makers and making" in specific circumstances (Banks 2014).

There are many excellent examples of what can be learned about the complexity of authorship in the media industries when thinking more carefully about production processes. For example, Jason Mittell's study of "complex TV" discusses authorship from the perspectives of "origination" and "responsibility" as well as "management," analyzing a move from how television has traditionally been viewed as "produced" rather than "authored," to a fanbase needing for an "imagined authorial power to account for narrative complexity and provide ongoing serial assurance that somebody is actually in control" (2015: 117). Matt Hills (2013) has explored "marginalized authors" and discourses of "counter-authorship" in a study focusing on how influential contributors can be written out or opt out during challenging production processes or because of disagreements, but should still be considered when assessing media authorship. Studies such as these have scholarly value, but attributing authorship is also a crucial issue in the media industries themselves where ownership of IP, obtaining credits/royalties, and being paid according to your professional role and contribution, remain recurrent sources of conflict. Discussions of who contributed what, and so who should be acknowledged accordingly, are continuing practical and financial concerns.

While there is no definite answer as to how to define authorship and agency in the media industries, focusing on these concerns are still "a key entry point into examining much of how media culture works" (Gray and Johnson 2013: 4). Writing about "methodological gateways" to media industry studies, Matthew Freeman agrees that despite many transformations in the digital media industries, a defining element in media industry studies still involves trying to identify and understand "media industry operations as modes of authorship across multiple sites of macro and micro perspectives" (2016: 65). Freeman proposes the need for understanding "socialised authorship" by acknowledging the larger social structures in which individual practitioners and particular media industries operate (p. 66). In the following discussion, the focus will be on the film and television industries, but authorship and agency discussions are of course also part of many other studies of the media industries, such as the comic industry (e.g., Meskin and Cook 2012; Gordon 2013) or the gaming industry (e.g., Bernardi and Hoxter 2017).

## Issues of authorship: the artistic genius vs. the genius of the system

As the art historian Ernest Gombrich originally noted in 1950, art is not some mysterious activity, but is made for human beings by human beings (2006: 28). The same goes for productions in the media industries where issues of authorship are always an issue. Much has been written about cinema and authorship (e.g., Gerstner and Staiger 2003), and even though everyone acknowledges that filmmaking is a collaborative enterprise, film scholars have tended to focus on theories about individual authorship and film directors as "auteurs" (e.g., Caughie 2008). Specific theories on collaborative authorship only started to emerge in the late 1990s (e.g., Gaut 1997; Livingston 1997) where scholars began writing about "multiple authorship" (Gaut 1997), "collaboration analysis" (Carringer 2001), "joint authorship" (Livingston 2009), or "collective authorship" (Sellors 2007).

In contrast to film studies, television studies positioned itself against the auteurist discussions from the outset (see e.g., Hadas 2019), and for many years television production has been discussed as "collective action" (e.g., Sandeen and Compesi 1990). In a similar vein, media industry studies have always challenged the notion of individual authorship, insisting that media production is a group effort where one needs to take many factors into account when exploring the making of media productions (e.g., Holt and Perren 2009). To capture this complexity, Timothy Havens and Amanda Lotz argue in favor of building on an "industrialization of culture framework" that not only focuses on individuals and practices, but also on the mandates and conditions of particular media institutions and production cultures (2017: 23). As argued by Michele Hilmes, there can be many advantages to singling out one person as the creator (not the least for promotional and press purposes), but from a scholarly perspective it is more honest and conducive to bring the struggles behind the scenes into productive analyses and foreground the many complexities and interdependencies of production processes rather than reducing them to the work of one person (2009: 26).

The insistence on including contextual factors and industrial concerns into an analysis of media authorship can be seen in discussions about the tensions between "the artistic genius" trying to make his or her vision come alive, and "the genius of the system" (Schatz 1996) where a certain production framework shapes what is produced, allows some people access rather than others, or privileges certain themes, storytelling strategies and aesthetic choices. The classical Hollywood system (as analyzed by Bordwell, Staiger, and Thompson 1985) has long been perceived as a particular mode of production where authorship can be regarded as a negotiation between filmmakers, strong producers, and studios granting certain people a voice and a way to make their films within a well-defined industrial structure. Even in the silent film era, the financial issues related to producing ambitious films entailed fierce fights for creative freedom and adequate budgets between filmmakers and studios. For example, archived correspondence between Danish filmmaker Carl Theodor Dreyer and the studio Nordisk Film document how Dreyer gradually moved from high-strung writings about his grand vision and toward accepting the fact that he would have to remarkably downscale his ambitions and settle with small budgets (Thorsen and Redvall 2018). Consequently, we must see the work of "authors" in the media industries as always and inevitably linked to financial, logistical, and practical concerns.

While directors have traditionally been regarded as the main authors in film studies, with individual careers carefully scrutinized and assessed, screenwriters have gradually also risen to attention. In part this is due to new research initiatives such as the Screenwriting Research Network (SRN, established 2008) and the emergence of a particular strand of scholarly screenwriting research (e.g., Maras 2009; Price 2010; Macdonald 2013; Millard 2014; Ganz and Price 2020 interestingly exploring the relationship between screenplays and screen performance through a case study of Robert De Niro's authorial influence on the storytelling and characters in his films). In media industry studies, filmmaking has also been understood as clearly marked by the decision-making of commissioners and producers at specific studios and distributors (e.g., Perren 2013; Meir 2019) aiming for a specific content profile. This is even more common in television studies, where broadcasters have always fought to brand their channels (Johnson 2012), and television has traditionally been understood as "the producer's medium" (e.g., Newcomb and Alley 1993) before attention to the professional role of the "showrunner" complicated matters by highlighting the importance of the hyphenate writer-producer role (e.g., Banks 2015).

As discussed by David Hesmondhalgh and Sarah Baker, in the cultural industries the question of authorship is central to the politics of creative labor "because it creates hierarchies and inequalities among cultural producers" (2010: 84). The division of labor in most media productions raises questions about power and who is regarded as having significant creative control. Historically, most discussions of authorship in media industry studies have focused on above-the-line talent (such as producers, directors, and writers), but more recently research has also emphasized the value of including attention to the contributions made by below-the-line talent and work (e.g., Mayer 2011; Caldwell 2013). This has led to explorations of the work done by those in previously invisible roles, for example, production designers (Brisbin 2013) and prop-makers (Vonderau 2015), as well as analysis of how to think of issues such as ownership when several authors are, for instance, creating serial narratives for comic books together (Gordon 2013).

## Issues of agency: autonomy, power, and questions of "final cut"

Media industry studies thus have many different notions of and approaches to thinking about and studying authors and the authorial voice. Part of the explanation for this is related to issues of agency, focusing on who actually has the power and creative freedom to make final decisions about what is to be produced and how to go about it. The relation between structure and agency is a common topic among social theorists as well as in studies of contemporary culture (e.g., Hartley et al. 2013). The notion of agency traditionally refers to an individual's capacity to act independently and to make free choices (Barker 2005), although agency takes place in certain structures that can be conducive to, or limiting for, the individual's decision-making. In media industry studies, the focus on agency is normally tied to issues of creative agency, that is whether a person is able to make free creative/artistic choices, or whether these are limited by certain constraints and industrial demands. In creativity studies, constraints are often regarded as intrinsic (inherent in the material), imposed (by external structures) or self-imposed (such as working with creative constraints like the Dogma 95 Manifesto) (e.g., Elster 2000). Media industry studies most often focus on the tensions between creative agency and the imposing external structures that create particular frameworks for the emergence, development, financing, and production of new works.

Media industry scholars recognize how agency always has to be understood based on the context in which one's agency is practiced. This can be understood as practitioners working in different kinds of "Screen Idea Systems" (Redvall 2016) where individual choices are always marked and shaped by what already exists in the particular domain for which one intends to create something new, and by the complex social field of decision-makers who select what to produce or not to produce. Timothy Havens and Amanda Lotz suggest thinking of agency in the media industries as different forms of "circumscribed agency" where practitioners are perceived as "agents with some degree of individual autonomy, even though their autonomy is delimited by a range of forces including the cultures from which they come, the conventions of the media in which they work, and the priorities of their organizations and superiors" (2017: 11). This agency can be hard to analyze and assess, not least since one can study what is being done and said, but – as qualitative researchers agree – people do not always transparently state things as they are, or maybe are unaware of their own biases and blind spots. There is a lot of "corporate storytelling" in the media industries (Caldwell 2008). Moreover, to find success practitioners have often internalized certain notions of quality or best practices (Havens and

Lotz 2017: 10). An example of this can be found in Jimmy Draper's (2014) study of how magazine editors use "discerned savvy" to narrow their ideas down to what will appeal to superiors in what Draper regards as an example of "subtly circumscribed" agency in the media industries.

Most scholars studying creative labor in the media industries emphasize how media professionals regard autonomy as a feature of "good work" (Hesmondhalgh and Baker 2010: 39–43), no matter whether you are at the top of the food chain as A-list talent or working as a more regular crew member or practitioner. However, it can be hard to obtain autonomy in industries that are most often marked by precarious work conditions going from one project-based "semi-permanent work group" (Blair 2003) to the other in a field with many "complimentary and often competing pressures and forces" (Deuze and Prenger 2019). The notion of "self-authorship" has emerged as a way to describe how people employ their sense of self to make meaning of their experiences and careers in the highly competitive media job market (Bennett and Hennekam 2018) where a commonly held perception is that, in the words of Helen Blair, "you're only as good as your last job" (2001).

Studying "practitioners' agency" in the media industries is a way to not only understand media products, but also the conditions of their making. One strand of media industry scholarship uses interviews to directly document practitioners' perceptions of agency and of their possibilities of building sustainable careers (e.g., Hjort, Jørholt, and Redvall 2014 interviewing documentary filmmakers). The COVID-19 lockdown of much of the world in 2020 pointed to the fragility of employment in the media industries with almost no job security and challenges for both above-the-line and below-the-line practitioners when many productions suddenly stalled. The pandemic clearly illustrated how unions have an important part to play in relation to overall questions of authorship and rights in specific contracts as well as to the general conditions for exercising one's agency, maintaining an acceptable work life balance, and building a career in the media industries.

When studying how new media products are shaped, the interest has traditionally been on professions with a direct impact on the outcome, based on theories of whether certain individuals have "sufficient control" to shape productions as they would like to while using and absorbing the work of others (Gaut 2010: 112). Taking directors as an example, issues related to agency, autonomy, and creative control can look very different depending on whether the project being produced is a major Hollywood feature, a smaller independent film, or public service television series for a license fee-financed broadcaster. Who has "final cut" is linked to holding agency and executive decision-making powers. As an example, in the US studio system this power is invested in the studio and the producer of a film accepts the Oscar if a film wins an Academy Award. In many European film cultures, directors are granted final cut and are the ones accepting any prizes since they are regarded as the main author with the agency to create and shape a production based on his or her vision.

Questions of agency, power, and control are also linked to who is able to create something in the first place, raising issues concerning structural inequalities based on gendered, class, and racial divisions (e.g., Milestones 2015; Randle 2015; Saha 2017). Who gets to tell their stories? Who can enter the media industries, and whose voices are heard? Media content is always marked by certain ideologies. While textual analysis can explore how these ideologies come across in the final product, media industry research is interested in "the processes whereby various ideologies become embedded into media content, how they are framed, and how they are organized, silenced, privileged, or dismissed vis-à-vis other ideologies" (Havens and Lotz 2017: 10). Understanding notions of and approaches to authorship and agency during the making of media products can shed light on precisely *why* and *how* a product ended up as it did, for artistic/creative reasons but also due to financial, corporate, or ideological concerns.

## Authorship and agency in the digital era

Media studies have always highlighted how "the embodied practices of authorship" are mobile sites "that are by necessity malleable and whose contours shift, given the cultural and techno-logical circumstances in which these practices emerge" (Chris and Gerstner 2013: 11). This is not least the case when researching the media industries where change can happen rapidly and new technologies and ways of producing can quickly challenge traditional professional roles and established routines, particularly in the digital era marked by media convergence and more complex interplays between producers, users, and "produsers" (Bruns 2008).

While there has always been the possibility to include "regular people" in the making of new products, the advent of digital media platforms and of social and participatory media has fundamentally changed the relationship between creators and audiences and the possibilities for interactivity and feedback. This has naturally led to new lines of discussion, including how to define authors in user-generated content (e.g., van Dijck 2009; Sarikakis et al. 2017), the rise of "trans-texts" (Kurtz and Bourdaa 2017), and the implications for how to think of authorship and agency in "legacy media." Fan studies have long acknowledged how dedicated followers can have an impact on the way in which media franchises evolve, including attention to how fans create different kinds of "fan fiction" to continue or revive a cancelled series (Williams 2016), or by exercising "online cult television authorship" through "paratexts" such as podcasts or commentary tracks (Kompare 2011). Scholars have analyzed these relationships between makers and fans in terms of "decentered authorship" (Stein 2013), exploring how the producers of long-running serial narratives can be influenced by the input and opinions of dedicated viewers when deciding where to take a story and its characters from season to season (Mittell 2015).

Listening to and building on the input of audiences can happen from the very outset, as was the case with the Norwegian hit web series *SKAM* (2015–2017). Showrunner Julie Andem built on the NABC model (i.e., analyzing the Need, Approach, Benefit, and Competition when developing new ideas, products, or processes) to conduct extensive research into the needs and desires of 16-year-old girls before writing a series targeting them and aiming to involve their inputs through social media during the telling of the story (Redvall 2018; Sundet 2019). While this manner of working can be regarded as just another way of doing more detailed research into one's imagined target audience, it is also an example of giving the audi-ence agency, particularly if one continues to respect their input in social media as the story-telling evolves. However, co-creating in this way can be exhausting, as Andem experienced when it became too much for one person to keep up with the ambitious real-time publishing strategy of *SKAM* and the continuous interaction with enthusiastic fans.

Traditionally, the stages of production and reception have been conceptually regarded as sep-arate, but digital media have brought these closer together by giving global audiences a distinct and immediate voice. As a consequence, the late 2010s saw what can be regarded as "an audi-ence turn" in production studies of the media industries with more focus on how authors try to engage viewers during the early stages of development, writing, and production, and how audiences are thus invited to co-create by being given a sense of agency (e.g., Hill 2018). This is, for instance, a major concern when trying to target children and young audiences, an audi-ence segment that is still harder to reach for legacy media when competing with social media, gaming, video-sharing platforms, and social network services such as YouTube or TikTok. As an example, in the 2010s the Danish Broadcasting Corporation's children's channel DR Ultra worked with a wide range of initiatives to involve children already during the idea development and writing of new fictional content for them, for instance by using (and crediting) "junior editors" who read screenplays to make sure that the action and dialogue was true to what children presently do and say (Christensen and Redvall 2019).

Another aspect of authorship that is not new but is now more prevalent in the digital media industries is the use of authorship discourses in the promotion and marketing of media content with the focus on a singular "star" author as a common strategy within the logic of media branding and publicity to mainstream audiences, for example, in relation to trying to create the sense of one author around blockbuster franchises, television showrunners, or video games. Media industry scholars are interested in exploring this kind of "promotional authorship" (e.g., Hadas 2017, 2020) and the ways in which the construction of certain author figures as celebrities can help sell products to audiences.

## Conclusions and cliffhangers

Assessing the state of media industry studies going into the 2020s, Jennifer Holt and Alisa Perren describe the contemporary digital media industries as a "moving target of study" (2019: 34). This chapter has outlined how this is definitely the case when specifically focusing on issues of authorship and agency from both micro and macro perspectives. It makes sense to keep investigating these complex and contested notions and the many different ways in which authorship and agency works in the media industries of today and tomorrow.

While much research has already been conducted in this field, there is still plenty to explore that should be of value to media industry scholarship, as well as to practitioners in the media industries. This is particularly the case if media researchers move beyond primarily focusing on the traditionally dominant media industries of the United States and Europe to explore notions of authorship and agency from other parts of the world and production frameworks that tend to receive less scholarly attention. Another interesting strand of research to pursue would be to focus less on "best practice" and major success stories, toward also carefully studying what can be learned from the many examples where things did not go as planned and discussions of authorship and agency were a site of conflict. While media practitioners rarely want to talk about failure, since they work in industries where you get hired based on a successful track record, scholars can offer valuable insights on what can be learned from tensions and conflict.

In a similar vein, much can be learned from studying the many instances where productions did *not* happen, and issues of authorship and agency related to practitioners who are finding it hard to find acceptance in the media industries. Questions of authorship and agency are not only related to what is produced, but also to what is *not* produced. Hopefully future studies will offer fruitful analysis in this regard, while also taking the traditional field of research further.

## References

Banks, M. (2014) "How to Study Makers and Making," in M. Alvarado, M. Buonanno, H. Gray, and T. Miller (eds), *The SAGE Handbook of Television Studies*, Los Angeles, CA: Sage, 117–132.

Banks, M. (2015) *The Writers: A History of American Screenwriters and their Guild*, New Brunswick, NJ: Rutgers University Press.

Barker, C. (2005) *Cultural Studies: Theory and Practice*, London: Sage.

Bennett, D. and Hennekam, S. (2018) "Self-authorship and Creative Industries Workers' Career Decision-making," *Human Relations*, 71 (11): 1454–1477.

Bernardi, D. and Hoxter, J. (2017) *Off the Page: Screenwriting in an Era of Media Convergence*, Oakland, CA: University of California Press.

Blair, H. (2001) "'You're Only as Good as Your Last Job': The Labour Process and Labour Market in the British Film Industry," *Work, Employment and Society*, 15 (1): 149–169.

Blair, H. (2003) "Winning and Losing in Flexible Labour Markets: The Formation and Operation of Networks of Interdependence in the UK Film Industry," *Sociology*, 37 (4): 677–694.

Bordwell, D., Staiger, J., and Thompson, K. (1985) *The Classical Hollywood Cinema: Film Style and Mode of Production to 1960*, New York: Columbia University Press.

Brisbin, D. (2013) "Production Design and the Invisible Arts of Seeing," in J. Gray and D. Johnson (eds), *A Companion to Media Authorship*, Oxford: Wiley-Blackwell, 370–390.

Bruns, A. (2008) *Blogs, Wikipedia, Second Life, and Beyond: From Production to Produsage*, New York: Peter Lang.

Caldwell, J. T. (2008) *Production Culture: Industrial Reflexivity and Critical Practice in Film and Television*, Durham, NC: Duke University Press.

Caldwell, J. T. (2013) "Authorship Below-the-Line," in J. Gray and D. Johnson (eds), *A Companion to Media Authorship*. Oxford: Wiley-Blackwell, 347–369.

Carringer, R. L. (2001) "Collaboration and Authorship," *PMLA*, 116 (2): 370–379.

Caughie, J. (2008) "Authors and Auteurs: The Uses of Theory," in J. Donald and M. Renov (eds), *The SAGE Handbook of Film Studies*, London: Sage.

Chris, C. and Gerstner, D. A. (eds) (2013) *Media Authorship*, New York: Routledge.

Christensen, K. B. and Redvall, E. N. (2019) "Producing Public Service Serial Drama Children and Young Audiences," *CST Online*, December 13, available at https://cstonline.net/producing-public-service-serial-drama-for-children-and-young-audiences-towards-a-new-future-for-the-danish-broadcasting-corporations-tween-channel-dr-ultra/ (accessed March 15. 2020).

Deuze, M. and Prenger, M. (eds) (2019) *Making Media: Production, Practices and Professions*, Amsterdam: Amsterdam University Press.

Draper, J. (2014) "Theorizing Creative Agency Through 'Discerned Savvy': A Tool for the Critical Study of Media Industries," *Media, Culture and Society*, 36 (8): 1118–1133.

Elster, J. (2000) *Ulysses Unbound: Studies in Rationality, Commitment, and Constraints*, Cambridge: Cambridge University Press.

Freeman, M. (2016) *Industrial Approaches to Media: A Methodological Gateway to Media Industry Studies*, Basingstoke: Palgrave Macmillan.

Ganz, A. and Price, S. (2020) *Robert De Niro at Work: From Screenplay to Screen Performance*, Cham: Palgrave Macmillan.

Gaut, B. (1997) "Film Authorship and Collaboration," in R. Allen and M. Smith (eds), *Film Theory and Philosophy*, Oxford: Clarendon Press.

Gaut, B. (2010) *A Philosophy of Cinematic Art*, Cambridge: Cambridge University Press.

Gaut, B. and Livingston, P. (eds) (2003) *The Creation of Art: New Essays in Philosophical Aesthetics*, Cambridge: Cambridge University Press.

Gerstner, D. A. and Staiger, J. (2003) *Authorship and Film*, New York: Routledge.

Gombrich, E. H. (2006) *The Story of Art*, London: Phaidon.

Gordon, I. (2013) "Comics, Creators and Copyright: On the Ownership of Serial Narratives by Multiple Authors," in J. Gray and D. Johnson (eds), *A Companion to Media Authorship*. Oxford: Wiley-Blackwell, 221–236.

Gray, J, and Johnson, D. (2013) *A Companion to Media Authorship*, Oxford: Wiley-Blackwell.

Hadas, L. (2017) "A New Vision: J. J. Abrams, *Star Trek*, and Promotional Authorship," *Cinema Journal*, 56 (2): 46–66.

Hadas, L. (2019) "Television Authorship," *Oxford Bibliographies*, available at www.oxfordbibliographies.com/view/document/obo-9780199791286/obo-9780199791286-0323.xml (accessed March 15, 2020).

Hadas, L. (2020) *Authorship as Promotional Discourse in the Screen Industries: Selling Genius*, New York: Routledge.

Hartley, J., Potts, J., Cunningham, S., Flew, T., Keane, M., and Banks, J. (2013) *Key Concepts in Creative Industries*, London: Sage.

Havens, T. and Lotz, A. (2017) *Understanding Media Industries*, 2nd ed., New York: Oxford University Press.

Hesmondhalgh, D. and Baker S. (2010) *Creative Labour: Media Work in the Cultural Industries*, Abingdon: Routledge.

Hill, A. (2018) *Media Experiences: Engaging with Drama and Reality Television*, Abingdon: Routledge.

Hills, M. (2013) "From Chris Chibnall to Fox: *Torchwood*'s Marginalized Authors and Counter-Discourses in Television Authorship," in J. Gray and D. Johnson (eds), *A Companion to Media Authorship*, Oxford: Wiley-Blackwell, 200–220.

Hjort, M., Jørholt, E., and Redvall, E. N. (2014) *Danish Directors 2: Dialogues on the New Danish Fiction Cinema*, Bristol: Intellect Press.

Hogan, L. (2013) "The Mouse House of Cards: Disney Tween Stars and Questions of Institutional Authorship," in J. Gray and D. Johnson (eds), *A Companion to Media Authorship*, Oxford: Wiley-Blackwell, 296–313.

Holt, J. and Perren, A. (eds) (2009) *Media Industries. History, Theory, and Method*, Malden, MA: Wiley-Blackwell.

Holt, J. and Perren, A. (2019) "Media Industries: A Decade in Review," in M. Deuze and M. Prenger (eds), *Making Media: Production, Practices and Professions*, Amsterdam: Amsterdam University Press, 31–44.

Johnson, C. (2012) *Branding Television*, Abingdon: Routledge.

Johnson, C. (2013) "The Authorial Function of the Television Channel: Augmentation and Identity," in J. Gray and D. Johnson (eds), *A Companion to Media Authorship*, Oxford: Wiley-Blackwell, 275–295.

Johnson, D. (2013) "Participation is Magic: Collaboration, Authorial Legitimacy, and the Audience Function," in J. Gray and D. Johnson (eds), *A Companion to Media Authorship*. Oxford: Wiley-Blackwell, 133–157.

Kurtz, B. W. L. D. and Bourdaa, M. (2017) *The Rise of Transtexts: Challenges and Opportunities*, New York: Routledge.

Kompare, D. (2011) "More Moments of 'Television': Online Cult Television Authorship," in M. Kackman, M. Binfield, M. T. Payne, A. Perlman, and B. Sebok (eds), *Flow TV: Television in the Age of Media Convergence*, New York: Routledge, 95–113.

Livingston, P. (1997) "Cinematic Authorship," in M. Smith and R. Allen (eds), *Film Theory and Philosophy*, Oxford: Oxford University Press.

Livingston, P. (2009) *Cinema, Philosophy, Bergman: On Film as Philosophy*, Oxford: Clarendon.

Livingston, P. and Plantinga, C. (eds) (2009) *The Routledge Companion to Philosophy and Film*, London: Routledge.

Macdonald, I. W. (2013) *Screenwriting Poetics and the Screen Idea*, Basingstoke: Palgrave Macmillan.

Maras, S. (2009) *Screenwriting: History, Theory and Practice*, London: Wallflower Press.

Mayer, V., Banks, M. J., and Caldwell, J. T. (eds) (2009) *Production Studies: Cultural Studies of Media Industries*, New York: Routledge.

Mayer, V. (2011) *Below the Line: Producers and Production Studies in the New Television Economy*, Durham, NC: Duke University Press.

Meir, C. (2019) *Mass Producing European Cinema: Studiocanal and Its Works*, New York: Bloomsbury Academic.

Meskin, A. and Cook, R. T. (2012) *The Art of Comics: A Philosophical Approach*, Malden, MA: Wiley-Blackwell.

Milestone, K. (2015) "Gender and the Cultural Industries," in K. Oakley and J. O'Connor (eds), *The Routledge Companion to Cultural Industries*, Abingdon: Routledge, 501–511.

Millard, K. (2014) *Screenwriting in a Digital Era*, Basingstoke: Palgrave Macmillan.

Mittell, J. (2015) *Complex TV: The Poetics of Contemporary Television*, New York: New York University Press.

Newcomb, H. M. and Alley, R. S. (1993) *The Producer's Medium: Conversations with Creators of American TV*, New York: Oxford University Press.

Perren, A. (2013) *Indie Inc.: Miramax and the Transformation of Hollywood in the 1990s*, Austin, TX: University of Texas Press.

Price, S. (2010). *The Screenplay: Authorship, Theory and Criticism*, Basingstoke: Palgrave Macmillan.

Randle, K. (2015) "Class and Exclusion at Work: The Case of UK Film and Television," in K. Oakley and J. O'Connor (eds), *The Routledge Companion to Cultural Industries*, Abingdon: Routledge, 330–344.

Redvall, E. N. (2018) "Reaching Young Audiences Through Research: Using the NABC Method to Create the Norwegian Web Teenage Drama SKAM," in D. Thornley (ed.), *True Event Adaptation: Scripting Real Lives*, Basingstoke: Palgrave Macmillan, 143–161.

Redvall, E. N. (2016) "Film and Media Production as a Screen Idea System," in P. Macintyre, J. Fulton and E. Paton (eds), *The Creative System in Action: Understanding Cultural Production and Practice*, Basingstoke: Palgrave Macmillan, 134–154.

Saha, A. (2017) *Race and the Cultural Industries*, Cambridge: Polity Press.

Sandeen, C. A. and Compesi, R. J. (1990) "Television Production as Collective Action," in R. J. Thompson and G. Burns (eds), *Making Television: Authorship and the Production Process*, New York: Praeger Publishers, 161–74.

Sarikakis, K., Krug, C., and Rodriguez-Amat, J. R. (2017) "Defining Authorship in User-generated Content: Copyright Struggles in *The Game of Thrones*," *New Media and Society*, 19 (4): 542–559.

Schatz, T. (1996) *The Genius of the System: Hollywood Filmmaking in the Studio Era*, New York: Henry Holt.

Sellors, P. C. (2007) "Collective Authorship in Film," *Journal of Aesthetics and Art Criticism,* 65 (3): 263–271.

Stein, L. E. (2013) "#Bowdown to Your New God: Misha Colling and Centered Authorship in the Digital Age," in J. Gray and D. Johnson (eds), *A Companion to Media Authorship.* Oxford: Wiley-Blackwell, 403–425.

Sundet, V. S. (2019) "From 'Secret' Online Drama to International Cult Phenomenon: The Global Expansion of SKAM and Its Public Service Mission," *Critical Studies in Television,* 15 (1): 69–90.

Thompson, R. J. and Burns, G. (eds) (1990) *Making Television: Authorship and the Production Process,* New York: Praeger Publishers.

Thorsen, I. and Redvall, E. N. (2018) "When Grand Ambitions Meet the Harsh Realities of Filmmaking," *Journal of Scandinavian Cinema,* 9 (2): 143–156.

van Dijck, J. (2009) "Users Like You? Theorizing Agency in User-generated Content," *Media, Culture and Society,* 31 (1): 41–58.

Vonderau, P. (2015) "How Global is Hollywood: Division of Labor from a Prop-Making Perspective," in M. Banks, B. Conor, and V. Mayer (eds), *Production Studies: The Sequel!* New York: Routledge, 23–26.

Williams, R. (2016) "Ontological Security, Authorship and Resurrection: Exploring Twin Peaks' Social Media Afterlife," *Cinema Journal,* 55 (3): 143–147.

# PART III

# Transformations
## Digitalization and industry change

Chapters in this part offer a series of studies looking at how different industries have encountered digitalization, the modifying of business processes through the application of digital technologies. In this context, it is important to avoid teleological accounts of "digital disruption," which portray, and often implicitly promote, technology as a singular driver for bringing about comprehensive, unidirectional, and monocausal change. While embedded in technological innovation, digitalization is not reducible to purely technological determinist explanations of industry change. Instead, as the chapters here show, whatever the impacts are of digital technologies on the workings of the media industries, these always co-exist with, and are conditioned by, multifarious economic, social, and cultural dynamics. Chapters address digitalization in the context of separate industries, yet when read together, cumulatively they offer a heterogenous and sometimes contradictory account of how digitality weaves into the media sector.

Catherine Johnson addresses digitalization by providing a framework for mapping the multiple sectors inputting to the online television industry. Conceptualizing this industry necessitates looking beyond those elements concerned with television production, sales, and marketing, to recognize how companies active in consumer electronics, software development, and technological infrastructure are essential to the provision of online entertainment. While accounts of this new landscape may frequently focus on the types of video service now offered, Johnson emphasizes the lines of power relationship to emerge as the industry has consolidated around a few power players.

Continuing the focus on online television, with child audiences habituated to watching paid video-on-demand services or open video sharing platforms, Anna Potter and Jeanette Steemers evaluate the consequences for the business of children's television. Where services or platforms reach children internationally, pressures are placed on the traditional national providers of children's entertainment: production output maybe weakened if global reach is not reciprocated with investment in original homegrown content; competition from rich global services, combined with fragmentation of the child audience, threaten underfunded public service broadcasters; and if national systems for content or advertising regulation are not applied in equal degree to online sources, then ethical questions arise concerning protection of the vulnerable child.

DOI: 10.4324/9780429275340-23

At least in Western markets, Netflix has aggressively asserted its branded presence in online screen entertainment. Examining how this online giant influences the production and availability of content, Geoff King evaluates the impact of Netflix on the American indie film sector. Balancing benefits and threats, King views Netflix as a contradictory force. On the one hand, Netflix is boosting indie production by massively enhancing production finance and providing niche films with an outlet for potential global visibility. On the other, the company inflates acquisition prices, absorbs any film into an overall catalog of content, undermines theatrical exhibition, and prevents producers profiting from possible commercial hits.

Andrew Leyshon and Allan Watson note how music streaming services contributed to stabilizing the recorded music market, remedying declining revenues from sales of physical formats, while at the same time attracting criticisms for how low payment rates per stream inadequately remunerate artists. For Leyshon and Watson, these criticisms articulate moral economy arguments that misunderstand the economics of platforms. They contend that the issues over artist compensation must be viewed in the context of how streaming services balance assets and liabilities in a risky and volatile market, and the arrangements applied when disbursing revenues among artists.

On the digital news industry, Henrik Bødker sees social media users, platforms, and algorithms as reshaping the audience and news commodities. Traditionally, the economics of news publishing relied in part on bringing readers or audiences to advertisers, but pressure has been placed on this system as search engines or social media platforms intervene in news circulation, diverting ad revenues from news organizations and towards outlets better placed to generate the rich audience data prized by advertisers. Equally, online circulation changes the news commodity as it becomes just one form of (often free) content, augmented by likes, comments, and shares.

New technologies are ushering in multiple transformations, yet it is important to avoid presuming there has been a wholesale digital makeover of the media industries. Surveying the current state of the book publishing, Angus Phillips sees evidence of change and continuity. Online retailers – most obviously Amazon – have threatened but not eradicated bricks-and-mortar bookshops, and the physical printed book has remained remarkably resilient against ebook sales. Industry consolidation has strengthened the power of leading publishing groups, but with opportunities for posting writings online or releasing ebooks, self-publishing has achieved new popularity and legitimacy, bypassing the gatekeeping functions of literary agents or editors to go some way toward arguably democratizing the publishing sphere. Furthermore, open access challenges the industry's foundational logical of exploiting copyright.

Since the late 1990s, the most significant expansion of the media industries has come with the launch of social media companies founded in the United States and China. Pieter Verdegem sees social media industries as characterized by their dependence on user-generated content, operating multi-sided markets mediating between various categories of user, where value increases for the service and its users through network effects. Performing the function of platforms, social media industries selectively organize interpersonal interactions to capture human behavior and identities as digital information, using this data to improve their own services while also packaging it as a tradeable commodity.

Regionalizing the impacts of digitalization, Anthony Fung and Georgia Chik compare how media industries have negotiated digital transformations between East Asian territories. Taking China, Japan, and South Korea as case studies, Fung and Chik see the countries' respective political and economic systems as shaping the conditions in which media companies enter, adapt, survive, or compete in the digital realm. State controls variously materialize in China, while Japan's commercially driven market has shielded legacy media conglomerates from foreign competitors, and in South Korea the government's promotion of the internet as an engine for national economic recovery provided the infrastructural support for the online media economy.

# 20

# THE ONLINE TELEVISION INDUSTRY

## Fragmentation, consolidation, and power

*Catherine Johnson*

In 2015 Andrew Wallenstein published a map of the US television industry in the trade paper *Variety*, which he titled "The OTT-Viewniverse." A far cry from the "Big 3" networks that dominated the US television industry over the 1960s and 1970s (NBC, CBS, and ABC), or even the six media conglomerates (General Electric, Disney, Viacom, Time Warner, CBS, and News Corporation) that *Business Insider* claimed controlled 90 percent of US media in 2011 (Lutz 2012), the map painted a striking picture of the increased complexity of the television industry in the age of streaming. Wallenstein divided the US television industry into three large categories. The first of these, "The Pay-TV Powerhouses," broadly mapped on to the major US media conglomerates and referred to the multichannel video programming distributors (MVPD) that provide packages of internet, television, and phone services, such as Comcast, Verizon, Dish, and AT&T, and their related content services, like 21st Century Fox, ABC Networks, and NBC Universal. Wallenstein's map expands beyond these traditional stalwarts of the US television industry to include a second category, "The Big Three" of Amazon Prime, Netflix, and Hulu. These were, in 2015, the main providers of over-the-top (OTT) television services offered direct to consumers without the need for a cable subscription.[1] This category also includes niche subscription video-on-demand (SVOD) services focused around specific genres, such as Sesame Street Go and NFL Mobile. The third and largest category in Wallenstein's map, however, referred to the transformation of social media sites into video hubs and was named "The Big Kahuna" in reference to the company that dominates this sector: YouTube. Here Wallenstein included multichannel networks (MCNs) and other video services, such as Vevo (music) and Twitch (gaming), that are the backbone of what Cunningham and Craig (2019) refer to as "social media entertainment."

I start with Wallenstein's map because it articulates a key problem facing scholars of the television (and other media) industries. Over the first decades of the twenty-first century, the television industry has fragmented, its boundaries blurring with other industrial sectors. There has been significant growth in the number of television providers. In the UK, for example, Sky (the primary pay-TV provider) offers more than 600 channels[2] and Ofcom regulates 326 on-demand program service (ODPS) providers, covering "TV catch-up, online film services and those providing a library of archive content" (Ofcom 2020). Ofcom's regulatory purview only covers on-demand services under the jurisdiction of the UK whose principal purpose is the

DOI: 10.4324/9780429275340-24

provision of an editorial catalog of TV-like programs. Beyond this are a range of other online video services, from YouTube channels focused on user-generated content, to gaming services like Twitch, and news websites that include video.

The organizations that provide these services come from a number of different industrial contexts and could be understood to include:

- established television corporations: from major global media conglomerates, such as Disney, to national public service broadcasters, like the BBC;
- organizations from other media sectors: from cinema chains, such as Curzon Cinemas which provides the on-demand service Curzon Home Cinema, to newspapers like *The Guardian*, which includes video content in its online offering;
- non-media companies: from sporting organizations, such as the Premier League football team Arsenal with its online video service Arsenal Player, to charities such as the British Sign Language Broadcasting Trust who operate an online service for signed programming;
- platforms and technology companies: such as Apple, Facebook, Google, and Amazon, which have become central players in the provision of online video services;[3]
- digital startups: such as Azoomee, a company offering subscription video-on-demand (SVOD) access to ad-free and age-appropriate content for children.

These online video services are delivered to consumers across an expanded and transformed set of technologies. No longer confined to the television set in the living room (or the big cinema screen), audiovisual content can now be watched on a laptop, tablet, or mobile, or through a games console or internet-connected smart TV that also provides access to text, audio, and interactive services.[4] Users can move relatively seamlessly from watching a video, to interacting on social media, to reading the news and calling a friend, all on the same device. How do we conceptualize the television industry in a context in which video has expanded and fragmented beyond the traditional industries, technologies, and textual forms historically associated with television? This chapter addresses this problem by mapping what it refers to as the "online TV industries." Although it uses UK and United States examples as illustration, the model set out here is designed to be adaptable to other contexts where the nature and development of online TV varies. The chapter argues that such mapping is essential, not only to understand the new parameters of the contemporary television industry, but also to interrogate the shifting power dynamics at play in a period of rapid change.

Although Wallenstein's map of the OTT Viewniverse is helpful for revealing the complexity of the contemporary television industry, by categorizing the industry in terms of the kinds of services offered (OTT, MVPD, social media), it risks obscuring rather than revealing the relationships of power between the organizations operating within and across these sectors. Indeed, in the twenty-first century, the significant expansion and fragmentation of television, and video more broadly, has led to an industry rhetoric of increased user choice and control. In a *Forbes* article, Kevin Harrington (2014) argued that the internet enables us to "watch what we want to watch … when we want to watch it." This language was reiterated in a 2016 report by international media measurement company, Nielsen, which claimed that the "growth of video-on-demand (VOD) programming options (via download or stream) gives consumers greater control over what they watch, when they watch and how they watch." This is what Mark Stewart (2016: 692) refers to as the "myth of televisual ubiquity," which he describes as the "touted ability to watch any television content we want, anywhere, anytime." Stewart argues that this myth obscures geographical constraints (through intellectual property (IP) rights and geo-blocking), perpetuates assumptions about taste and quality, and fails to account for the ongoing industrial strategies that work to constrain access to television. The rhetoric of increased choice and control also works to obscure the presence and effects of industrial consolidation. Wallenstein's map can be understood as part of this wider industry rhetoric. By organizing the TV landscape according to type of service it fails to register the ways in which large companies are involved in offering online video services across the categories of OTT, MVPD, and social media. In doing so, it paints a picture of rapidly expanded viewer choice in which the major media conglomerates have ceded power to a multitude of large and small companies from a range of sectors. This would seem to make redundant questions of ownership and consolidation and the ways in which they work to limit diversity and choice. But to what extent has the emergence of new forms of online and streaming video, and the resulting fragmentation of the television industry, challenged the consolidation of power within a small number of large conglomerates that characterized the television industry in the twentieth century?

## Conceptualizing the contemporary television industry

To answer this question, we need to be able to map out not just the different kinds of video services that make up the contemporary television industry (as Wallenstein does), but also the organizations that provide these services and the relationships between them. However, the fragmentation of television as a medium makes this a challenging proposition because before we can lay out the power relations at work, we need to be able to define the parameters of what counts as the television industry itself. Amanda D. Lotz, Ramon Lobato and Julian Thomas (2018: 36) in a recent "provocation" on research into internet-distributed television argue that

> there is no singular internet-distributed television "industry" distinct from established film and television industries. [...] Nor can we easily designate a separate streaming industry comprising only internet-distributed services, as most established television players now utilize internet distribution as well as broadcast and cable/satellite.

In doing so, they are arguing that we need to understand the television industry as being comprised of broadcast, cable/satellite, *and* streaming services. However, conceptualizing the television industry as comprising *all* broadcast, cable/satellite, and video streaming services would cast a wide net. In the world of online video, as we have seen, corporations from multiple sectors cooperate and compete in the provision of a wide range of audiovisual services offering access to different types of content (sometimes combined within one service) provided across technologies that allow users to switch easily from one form of content/activity to another.

It could be argued that in the wake of such convergence, defining the television industry as separate from other media industries is a redundant exercise. A broader "media industries" approach, for example, might be better able to accommodate the relationships between organizations from a range of media sectors that now provide video services. Yet such an approach would fail to capture the significant role of non-media organizations (from sports teams and theaters to tech companies and platforms) in the provision of contemporary online video. Furthermore, conflating different media industries (such as news, music, film, and television) as the "media industries" threatens to flatten out the historical, sociocultural, economic, and industrial factors that continue to shape distinct industry and audience practices. In doing so, there is a danger of overlooking the specificities that make the production and distribution of, for example, cinema, different from newspapers and/or television.

At the same time, however, the convergence that threatens previously stable concepts of distinct industries (e.g., the television industry vs the film industry) provides a useful opportunity to challenge historically dominant common-sense assumptions about the media industries more generally. Convergence draws into relief the constructed nature of well-established and often entrenched notions of distinct media industries. Benjamin Woo (2018: 40) reminds us that "What we perceive as an industry is itself the result of boundary-drawing practices imposed on a fluid, complex field of social practices." The television industry, for example, has historically intersected in important ways with the consumer electronics industry (that manufactures the devices required to watch TV),[5] the sports industry (which has played a significant role in driving the business models and uptake of pay-TV), and the film industry (which has produced television content and services and been involved in the distribution of films created by TV companies).[6] The blurred boundaries that seem to threaten stable theorizations of the television industry in the contemporary internet era (Johnson 2019) merely reveal the inadequacy of established conceptualizations of the television industry as a distinct entity.

What is at stake in asking what might constitute the contemporary television industry, therefore, is less the definition of a distinct and coherent industrial sector, but rather the identification of what Jonathan Sterne (2014: 53) refers to in relation to the music industry as "a polymorphous set of relations among radically different industries and concerns." Woo (2018) concurs, drawing on Pierre Bourdieu to argue that the role of the social scientist is not to draw dividing lines between different industry sectors, but to describe the state of the struggles between competing agents. Such an approach requires the researcher to map the kinds of agents, industries, and concerns at stake within different fields of cultural production and distribution. Lotz, Lobato, and Thomas (2018: 36), for example, argue that the industry responsible for internet-distributed television "is composed of a series of complex, interlocking submarkets that integrate legacy and new players who provide different kinds of content to different audiences. Each submarket has its own idiosyncratic geography, regulatory conditions, and industrial practices." As a consequence, they argue that the starting point for any industrial study of internet-distributed television should be to disaggregate the wide range of different services according to geography, business model, non/linearity (whether the services offer access to linear or non-linear content, or both), ownership and library structure. Rather than talking about the television industry, we might be advised to refer to a set of industries that co-exist and intersect with each other and other sub-sectors in polymorphous ways.

One benefit of this approach is that it offers a more nuanced picture of a complex market structure made up of different kinds of internet-distributed television services that, as Lotz, Lobato and Thomas (2018: 39) argue, are not all competing with each other: some are complementary, others compete for ad or subscription revenue but not for content. Assuming that these different kinds of services are operating in the same way in the same market could lead to false assumptions about the levels of competition and diversity within a given sector or industry. Therefore, to understand the ways in which power is enacted in the contemporary television industries, we need to differentiate the kinds of "television" at play and pay particular attention to the intersections, relations, and blurred boundaries between organizations, sectors, and industries involved in its provision.

## Mapping the power dynamics of the online TV industry

It is this approach that I took in my book *Online TV*, which focuses on a specific subset of online video services, referred to as "online TV," that facilitate the viewing of editorially selected audiovisual content through internet-connected devices and infrastructure. This definition would include both linear television channels and video-on-demand (VOD) services but exclude social media platforms like YouTube and Facebook that depend on users uploading content. This is helpful because, although YouTube and Facebook may compete with online TV services for people's attention, they face quite different regulatory and industrial challenges. For example, at the time of writing, Facebook and YouTube are under pressure to accept editorial responsibility for the content on their sites, which they have to balance against a business model based on creating the conditions for third parties (primarily non-professionals) to share content. By contrast, online TV services such as Netflix, the BBC, or Sky operate within a regulatory and industrial context in which they provide closed services where users can watch (but not upload) content that has been acquired and editorially selected for them.

Industrially, we can think of online TV as a "field of action" that depends on a number of intersecting sectors that operate along what we might term an "online TV value chain":

1 Film and TV production: companies responsible for making the content distributed through online TV services. These are either studios that operate as part of media conglomerates, networks, or broadcasters, or independent production companies.
2 Sales and licensing: organizations selling rights to films and TV programs on national and international markets. In addition, this would include the licensing of films and TV programs to third parties for the production of transmedia content, merchandise, and other forms of consumer product. These are often sub-divisions of the studios that produce films and TV programs.
3 Marketing: the sector that produces the campaigns and adverts that promote online TV services and content. This work is largely undertaken by in-house divisions within broadcasters, networks, and studios but would also include the agencies that produce the advertising and other promotional interstitials that form part of the content distributed through advertiser-funded online TV services.[7]
4 Delivery: television providers that own and operate the online TV services that deliver content to viewers, from broadcasters to OTT providers such as Netflix.
5 Consumer electronics: companies creating the devices through which online TV can be viewed, from smartphones and tablets, to smart TVs and set-top boxes.
6 Software development: companies creating the software upon which the delivery of online TV increasingly relies, from the organizations that construct the operating systems for internet-connected devices, to the app designers who produce TV and TV-related apps.
7 Technological infrastructure: the companies that create and manage the transmission, cable, satellite, broadband, Wi-Fi, playout, and online infrastructure (such as content delivery networks, data servers, and cloud computing) upon which online TV delivery depends.

The online TV industry, therefore, can be understood as a field of action made up of seven different (if not distinct) sectors that are essential to the production, distribution, and delivery of online TV. Power can be exerted within this industry through horizontal consolidation, in which a corporation attempts to control core sectors upon which third parties rely in the provision of online TV (Evens 2013: 489), vertical consolidation, in which a corporation seeks to have a presence across multiple stages of the supply chain, and the formation of strategic partnerships. These strategies are not new to the television industry, however as we shall go on to see, the expansion and fragmentation of television services has increased, rather than decreased, the imperative toward consolidation.

## Consolidation in the production and distribution of online TV content

The first four sectors above are broadly concerned with the production and distribution of content. The rise of online TV has been accompanied by accelerated competition for content as an increased number of TV providers seek the rights to programming to fill the catalogs of their streaming services. VOD services demand more content because they have greater capacity than the schedules of linear television channels (Lotz 2017: 24). Lotz (2017) argues that on-demand streaming services operate through "economies of aggregation," whereby a bundle of goods (in this instance TV programs and films) are collected together to enable one service to appeal to the heterogeneous tastes of different consumers.[8] Larger bundles of content make it easier "to extract more value from goods than smaller bundles" (p. 38) because they offer greater opportunities to analyze and predict consumer tastes. The economics of aggregation upon which online TV operates, therefore, increases the demand for, and value of, content.

The industrial consequences of this have been to heighten the benefits of both vertical and horizontal integration, as can be illustrated by Disney's strategy in the lead-up to the launch of its OTT streaming service, Disney+, in 2019.[9] In 2018, Disney completed the purchase of 21st Century Fox's film and TV studios, FX and National Geographic channels, satellite and cable network Star India, and stakes in the North American streaming service Hulu. Bob Iger (CEO of Disney, cited in Franck 2019) claimed that the Fox deal was designed to increase the volume of content that Disney could make available on Disney+. Disney valued 21st Century Fox less as a collection of studios and networks and more as a library of content that could be used to shore up the corporation's move into SVOD. While Disney has expanded the number of production companies, channels, and networks that it owns, other corporations have moved into content production for the first time, from national companies, such as BT in the UK, to global operators like Amazon, Apple, and Netflix. Indeed, most organizations that provide online TV services to viewers also produce content (Johnson 2019: 67–68).

The horizontal and vertical integration within and across the sectors responsible for the production and distribution of online TV content emerges not only because there is greater need to access large catalogs of content, but also because of the increased value of owning and controlling content rights. Control over IP proffers two potentially competing advantages that rights holders are having to negotiate. On the one hand, it gives control over where content can be accessed, enabling rights holders to use IP to drive users to their online TV services. For example, Disney announced in 2017 that in preparation for the launch of Disney+, it would be removing Disney content from rival service Netflix by not renewing existing licensing deals (Katz 2019). Disney has also made high-profile content, such as *Mulan* (2020) and *The Mandalorian* (2019-), available exclusively on Disney+. By controlling where people can access its content, Disney uses IP as a way of increasing demand for Disney+. On the other hand, however, ownership of IP rights is also a valuable source of income (Given, Brealey, and Gray 2015: 31). It has been reported that Disney will lose around $150 million in annual revenues from terminating its licensing deal with Netflix (Whitten 2019). It is, therefore, perhaps unsurprising that Disney announced in 2019 that every Disney movie released between January 2016 and December 2018 that was available on Netflix will return to the SVOD service around 2026 (Katz 2019). Such deals enable Disney to balance the benefits of retaining a level of exclusive access on Disney+, particularly during its first years of operation, while continuing to benefit from licensing income from Netflix.

The value of IP has also led to increased consolidation in the production sector (Doyle 2018: 286), given that acquisition of independent production companies enables greater control over the rights to content. For production companies, integrating vertically with TV providers, particularly those with international distribution arms, facilitates access to vital revenues from domestic and overseas sales. Gillian Doyle argues that the potential "for improved access to *international* markets and funding is now a significant incentive for vertical and horizontal mergers" (original emphasis, 2018: 291). The move of Netflix and Amazon into original production has led to high-end drama and documentary emerging as a key site of competition, particularly for VOD services (Doyle 2016: 639), and a resulting escalation in production costs. Where it is estimated that Netflix and Amazon Prime spent a combined £12.7 billion on content globally in 2018, the total network program spend of the UK's public service broadcasters (PSBs) was just under £2.9 billion (Ofcom 2019a: 54). To compete, UK PSBs are turning to co-production agreements and international finance. Ofcom (p. 54) notes that

> as the UK marketplace becomes increasingly driven by global players such as SVOD and the multichannels, PSBs are seeking to partner with other producers to increase investment in programming and to produce content whose quality matches that of global players.

Mergers and acquisitions, such as UK commercial broadcaster ITV's acquisition since 2010 of a number of US independent television production companies (Doyle 2018: 286), enhances access to international markets and finance.

## The power dynamics of technology and content

The push toward horizontal and vertical integration is in evidence not just in the sectors responsible for the production and distribution of content, but also at the other end of the value chain with the sectors responsible for the technological devices, software, and infrastructures required to deliver and access online TV (sectors 5–7 in the list above). Again, consolidation is not a new feature for these segments of the industry. Internet service provision and control over the cables and satellites that deliver the internet to the home has long been integrated with content production and distribution through pay-TV companies, such as Sky and AT&T. Over the 2010s, new global platforms have expanded across the online TV value chain. Amazon, for example, produces and delivers content (through Amazon Studios and Amazon Prime Video, respectively) and also provides the devices (Amazon Fire TV Stick), software and the online infrastructure (Amazon Web Services offers cloud storage, software, web and app hosting) necessary to access and deliver online TV.[10] It is notable that a number of businesses at the technological end of the value chain (consumer electronics, software, and technological infrastructure) have made aggressive moves into content production and delivery, from pay-TV providers like Sky and BT, to the major platforms such as Amazon and Apple. By contrast, the high barriers to entry mean that the content businesses at the other end of the value chain (such as Disney, the BBC, and Netflix) have not been able to move into the provision of technological infrastructures and devices (Johnson 2019: 68).

However, the larger transnational content businesses can use their market power to make strategic partnerships with those organizations responsible for technological devices, software, and/or infrastructure. Netflix, for example, has entered into deals with international device manufacturers to add a "Netflix button" to their smart-TV remote controls. Device manufacturers can also generate income by selling the opportunity for online TV services to be pre-loaded or occupy a prime position within their user interfaces (UIs) (Hesmondhalgh and Lobato 2019: 966–967), and to increase the visibility of specific programs and movies in text/voice search results and recommendations (Ofcom 2019b: 23; Johnson 2020). In this economics of prominence, international online TV providers (such as Netflix and Amazon Prime Video) have an advantage because device manufacturers are reluctant to make changes to hardware and software on a country-by-country basis.[11] As a consequence, national and more niche online TV services could find that the most prominent positions within the UIs of smart TVs, set-top boxes and digital media devices are already taken by transnational online TV services (MTM 2019: 22).

Across both content and technology, the online TV industry favors economies of scale. Large and transnational vertically integrated corporations, such as Amazon, Sky, Netflix, and Disney, have greater negotiating power and are also able to be more resilient in a media ecology characterized by rapid change. As Tom Evens and Karen Donders (2018: 253–254) point out, capital is a core controlling point of the contemporary television industry. In this market, access to credit is both crucial and more available to larger international and/or integrated businesses. Netflix, for example, is able to leverage its international market dominance across content production and distribution to access cheap debt and raise capital in financial markets. Large integrated conglomerates further benefit from cross-subsidization, whereby they can offset losses in one sector against the wide range of other businesses that they operate. In this market, this kind of financial capitalization and cross-subsidization is far harder for smaller organizations, such as national broadcasters. Far from the fragmented and expanded industry illustrated in Wallenstein's OTT Viewniverse, the online TV industry is, as Evens and Donders note, a "winner-take-all" market characterized by significant consolidation, power asymmetries, and financial inequalities (p. 244).

## Conclusion

This chapter began by asking how we conceptualize the television industry in a context in which television has fragmented and blurred with other industry sectors. Such moments of industrial disruption offer valuable opportunities to reconsider what we might mean by the "television industry," reminding us that industries are, first and foremost, conceptual categories that impose order on polymorphous sets of relationships between organizations and sectors. However, this does not mean that we should give up conceptualizing specific industries. This chapter has argued that mapping the online TV industry is essential to understand the power dynamics at play in the production and distribution of contemporary television. This is particularly important at a time when the apparent fragmentation of television has led to an industry rhetoric of increased user choice, belying the consolidation at work at an industrial level.

The approach proposed in this chapter has been to start by identifying online TV as a subset of the wider online video market. It is then possible to map out the online TV industry as a field of action made up of different industrial sectors involved in the production and distribution of online TV and examine the relationships within and between these sectors. Through this analysis, the chapter has revealed significant levels of consolidation in the online TV industry, despite the fragmentation of television and the entrance of new players from different industrial backgrounds. This is a market that favors economies of scale in which global platforms and larger transnational conglomerates (that operate across multiple points of the value chain) are able to exert significant competitive advantage. In this chapter, it has only been possible to sketch out the power dynamics at play across the online TV value chain, drawing only from examples in the UK and the United States. What is needed is more work that maps out these relationships in different geographic contexts and in different areas of the broader online video industry (such as social media entertainment or online news). Such an approach retains a recognition of the fundamentally constructed and polymorphous nature of the media industries, while also enabling analysis of the relations and power dynamics at work in an industrial sector still characterized by significant power inequalities.

## Notes

1 Since 2015, when Wallenstein was writing, the picture has become more complicated as the major US networks have launched OTT services, with Disney+ in 2019, and HBO Max (from Warner Media) and Peacock (from NBC Universal) following in 2020.

2 It is difficult to calculate the precise number of television channels because of duplications arising from offering both standard and high-definition channels, as well as regional variations, part-time channels and radio stations delivered as television channels.

3 Thomas Poell (2019) has argued that to characterize companies such as Apple and Google as media organizations overlooks the wide range of other sectors within which they operate.

4 There is a longer history of interactive services provided through the television set, from the teletext services developed in the UK in the 1970s (Gazzard 2015), to the interactive "Red Button" services offered by the BBC from the late 1990s (Bennett 2008).

5 David Hesmondhalgh and Leslie Meier (2018) make a similar argument about the historical intersection of the music industry with the consumer electronics industry.

6 For example, Hannah Andrews (2014) documents the central role that UK public service broadcaster, Channel 4, has played as a major producer (as well as distributor) of movies in the UK.

7 There is little space in this chapter to interrogate this sector in more detail, but it is notable that the advertising sector has become more directly involved in the production of television programs and films over the 2000s in response to a fragmented media ecology in which audiences are more able to avoid traditional advertising (Grainge and Johnson, 2015; and see Chapter 31 by Grainge in this collection).

8 Although Lotz argues that this is a characteristic of what she terms "portals" (defined as internet-delivered SVOD services provided on the open web that distribute long-form television content), bundling is also a feature of ad-funded and free-to-air VOD services.

9 Disney+ launched in the United States, Canada and the Netherlands in November 2019 and was rolled out to multiple countries in Australasia and Western Europe over 2019 and the first half of 2020.

10 In 2019 Amazon announced a partnership with TV set manufacturer JVC for the production of "Fire TV" sets powered by Amazon's smart TV software.

11 Amazon has an additional advantage in that it also manufactures its own devices.

## References

Andrews, H. (2014) *Television and British Cinema: Convergence and Divergence Since 1990*, Basingstoke: Palgrave Macmillan.

Bennett, J. (2008) "'Your Window-On-the-World': The Emergence of Red-Button Interactive Television in the UK," *Convergence*, 14 (2): 161–182.

Cunningham, S. and Craig, D. (2019) *Social Media Entertainment: The New Intersection of Hollywood and Silicon Valley*, New York: New York University Press.

Doyle, G. (2016) "Digitization and Changing Windowing Strategies in the Television Industry: Negotiating New Windows on the World," *Television and New Media*, 17 (7): 629–645.

Doyle, G. (2018) "Television Production: Configuring for Sustainability in the Digital Era," *Media, Culture and Society*, 40 (2): 285–295.

Evens, T. (2013) "Platform Leadership in Online Broadcasting Markets" in M. Friedrichsen and W. Mühl-Benninghaus (eds), *Handbook of Social Media Management: Value Chain and Business Models in Changing Media Markets*, Heidelberg: Springer, 477–491.

Evens, T. and Donders, K. (2018) *Platform Power and Policy in Transforming Television Markets*, Cham: Palgrave Macmillan.

Franck, T. (2019) "Iger Says Disney Bought Fox Because of Value It Adds to Streaming Service: 'The Light Bulb Went Off'," *CNBC*, April 12, available at: www.cnbc.com/2019/04/12/disney-wouldnt-have-bought-fox-assets-without-streaming-plans-iger-says.html (accessed April 6, 2020).

Gazzard, A. (2015) "Extending the Aerial: Uncovering Histories of Teletext and Telesoftware in Britain," *VIEW Journal of European Television History and Culture*, 4 (7): 90–98.

Given, J., Brealey, M., and Gray, C. (2015) *Television 2025: Rethinking Small-Screen Media in Australia*, Hawthorn: Swinburne Institute for Social Research.

Grainge, P. and Johnson, C. (2015) *Promotional Screen Industries*, Abingdon: Routledge.

Harrington, K. (2014) "Changing the Way We Watch TV," *Forbes*, March 6, available at: www.forbes.com/sites/kevinharrington/2014/03/06/changing-the-way-we-watch-tv/#5117dd455eeb (accessed April 6, 2020).

Hesmondhalgh D. and Lobato R. (2019) "Television Device Ecologies, Prominence and Datafication: The Neglected Importance of the Set-Top Box," *Media, Culture and Society*, 41 (7): 958–974.

Hesmondhalgh, D. and Meier, L. M. (2018) "What the Digitalisation of Music Tells Us About Capitalism, Culture and the Power of the Information Technology Sector," *Information, Communication and Society*, 21 (11): 1555–1570.

Johnson, C. (2020) "The Appisation of Television: TV Apps, Discoverability and the Software, Device and Platform Ecologies of the Internet Era," *Critical Studies in Television*, 15 (3): 165–182.

Johnson, C. (2019) *Online TV*, Abingdon: Routledge.

Katz, B. (2019) "Don't Bury Netflix Just Yet: New Deals Will Return Disney Content to the Streamer," *Observer*, June 3, available at: https://observer.com/2019/06/netflix-disney-warnermedia-nbcu-shows-movies/ (accessed November 13, 2020).

Lotz, A. D. (2017) *Portals: A Treatise on Internet-Distributed Television*, Ann Arbor, MI: Maize Books.

Lotz, A. D., Lobato, R., and Thomas, J. (2018) "Internet-Distributed Television Research: A Provocation," *Media Industries Journal*, 5 (2): 35–47.

Lutz, A. (2012) "These Corporations Control 90% of the Media in America," *Business Insider*, June 14, available at: www.businessinsider.com/these-6-corporations-control-90-of-the-media-in-america-2012-6?r=US&IR=T (accessed November 13, 2020).

MTM (2019) *Review of TV User Interfaces in the UK Market: Current Offerings and Future Developments*, May, available at: www.ofcom.org.uk/__data/assets/pdf_file/0022/154390/mtm-review-tv-user-interfaces-uk-market-full-report.pdf (accessed April 6, 2020).

Nielsen (2016) "Remote Control: VOD Puts Global Consumers in the Viewing Driver's Seat," *Nielsen Insights*, March 16, available at: www.nielsen.com/eu/en/insights/news/2016/remote-control-vod-puts-global-consumers-in-the-viewing-drivers-seat.html (accessed April 6, 2020).

Ofcom (2020) "On-demand Programme Service (ODPS) Providers," available at: www.ofcom.org.uk/tv-radio-and-on-demand/information-for-industry/on-demand (accessed November 13, 2020).

Ofcom (2019a) *Media Nations: UK 2019*, August 7, available at: www.ofcom.org.uk/__data/assets/pdf_file/0019/160714/media-nations-2019-uk-report.pdf (accessed April 6, 2020).

Ofcom (2019b) *Review of Prominence for Public Service Broadcasting*, July 4, available at: www.ofcom.org.uk/__data/assets/pdf_file/0021/154461/recommendations-for-new-legislative-framework-for-psb-prominence.pdf (accessed April 6, 2020).

Poell, T. (2019) "Platforms, Values and Public Service Media," conference paper presented at *Screen Industries in East-Central Europe Conference VIII – Public Service Media's Online Strategies: Industry Concepts and Critical Investigations*, November 23, National Film Archive, Prague.

Sterne, J. (2014) "There Is No Music Industry," *Media Industries Journal*, 1 (1): 50–55.

Stewart, M. (2016) "The Myth of Televisual Ubiquity," *Television and New Media*, 17 (8): 691–705.

Wallenstein, A. (2015) "The OTT View-niverse: A Map of the New Video Ecosystem," *Variety*, April 29, available at https://variety.com/2015/digital/news/ott-map-video-ecosystem-1201480930/ (accessed April 6, 2020).

Whitten, S. (2019) "Disney Expects to Take a $150 million Hit as it Cuts Ties with Netflix – and That's OK," *CNBC*, February 5, available at: www.cnbc.com/2019/02/05/disney-expects-to-take-a-150-million-hit-as-it-cuts-ties-with-netflix.html (accessed April 6, 2020).

Woo, B. (2018) "Is There a Comic Book Industry?" *Media Industries Journal*, 5 (1): 27–46.

# 21

# CHILDREN AND THE MEDIA INDUSTRIES

## An overlooked but very special "television" audience

*Anna Potter and Jeanette Steemers*

Children in multiple territories, including Europe, North America, Australia, and China, are deserting linear, scheduled television channels in favor of internet-distributed, video-on-demand services offered by providers such as YouTube, Netflix, Amazon Prime Video, and Hulu (Bisson and Deane 2018; Woodgate 2018). For example, according to a 2020 report by UK broadcasting and telecommunication regulator Ofcom, 45 percent of UK children aged 5–15 years would pick YouTube as their favorite platform ahead of TV channels offered by broadcasters such as the BBC, which are the first-choice platform of a mere 17 percent of UK children (Ofcom 2020: 10). The evidence suggests that children are exercising their choice from a wide array of advertiser- and subscriber-supported options, with offerings that include television-like content but extend to games and social media as well.

The fragmentation of young audiences across multiple platforms and services is so far-reaching that it poses an existential threat to public service broadcasters (PSBs). The UK's BBC, for example, was warned at the end of 2019 by Ofcom (2019a: 13) that its future was in doubt from the "risk that as children and young people age, they do not come to engage with the BBC as previous generations once did." Denmark's DR is pondering similar dilemmas about declining engagement by young people. A key question for PSBs is the extent to which production and distribution need to be shifted to higher volumes of short "snackable" content better suited to online distribution and coordinated with social media, rather than traditional, long-form broadcast formats (Sakr and Steemers 2019: 113). Changes in children's media consumption are far from uniform, however. Many children around the world, even in so-called developed countries, have limited access to digital media, because of a lack of financial resources or digital infrastructure (Steemers 2019). Even in wealthy countries like the UK, an estimated 12 percent of schoolchildren do not have internet access, while up to a third are without access to a device for educational or entertainment purposes (Cullinane 2020).

Although significant variations exist in children's access to technology and gadgets, industry narratives frequently frame children and families as the catalysts for change within screen media industries. Certainly, children have always been early adopters. They were just as keen to embrace newly arrived TV sets in the 1950s as they were video recorders in the 1970s and DVDs in the 1980s, exercising their "choice" and even self-curating their selections from

DOI: 10.4324/9780429275340-25

an early age (Mitroff and Stephenson 2007). Not surprisingly then screen media industries have always been keen to attract and target child consumers. They recognize that while children do not have financial independence themselves, they exert significant influence on family purchases, including spending on entertainment and licensed merchandise like toys.

Since the earliest years of television during the 1940s and 1950s, children's television and cartoons were used to entice families into buying television sets (Melody 1973). Children's importance to screen industries continues in the multiplatform age, with family and children's content promoted to push pay-TV subscriptions, initially to satellite and cable services, and now more recently to internet-distributed subscription video-on-demand (SVOD) family packages. While SVOD services share the common characteristic of online, on-demand distribution, their business models vary considerably. Netflix, for example, only sells content to subscribers, while Amazon Prime Video and Disney use their online television services to support other parts of their revenue streams: retail in Amazon's case, and the further monetization of its own film, television, and video libraries for Disney. Developing brand loyalty in children is important to SVODs, who are keen to attract audiences at every stage of their life cycles (Potter 2018).

Despite the importance of children and family audiences to the success of television and video streaming services, surprisingly little work has been undertaken about media industries and children's screen content in the post network era (see Jenner 2018; Lobato 2019; Lotz 2017), with a few exceptions (Johnson 2019: 63; Potter 2020). With this absence in mind, this chapter focuses on media industries that produce and distribute screen content for children in a rapidly transforming landscape, where children are discovering and consuming content on demand across multiple platforms and devices. We ask what these changes might mean for media industries, in terms of how they define the child audience and "television" for children, and how they conceive, fund, and distribute content in these new circumstances. We also consider how these industries manage ethical issues linked to addressing a "vulnerable" sector of the population, which require policy interventions that balance children's right to protection as well as their right to participation (Livingstone and Third 2017).

This contribution starts by looking at what we mean by children's "television" in the on-demand age, before focusing on the changes that shape screen content for children in the twenty-first century. The final section reminds us of the continuities in provision that continue to make children a "special" audience. The examples we cite in this chapter are confined to Europe, North America, and Australia as parts of the world with which we are familiar, and we draw on relevant industry reports, news coverage, and policy documents in our analysis.

## Changing definitions of television for children

The first question to answer is what is meant by children's television or children's screen content in the post-network era, given many children no longer watch a television set but use mobile phones, tablets, and games consoles to access content on demand. The abundance of options available to children due to digitization stands in stark contrast to the earliest days of broadcast television. Then children had to be satisfied with perhaps an hour of dedicated programming from linear broadcasters scheduled for after they got home from school or on Saturday mornings (Buckingham, Davies, Jones, and Kelley 1999). Introduction of subscriber-supported cable and satellite channels in Europe from the 1970s resulted in greater scheduled options and saw dozens of specialized children's channels established from the 1980s onward. This proliferation in dedicated children's channels led to a boom in the production of US teen sitcoms, and especially animation sourced from North America, Asia, and later from Europe and Australia.

These animated series in turn fueled a transnational market in licensed merchandise based largely around toys (Westcott 2002).

However, the real game changer for children's screen industries has been internet distribution and the introduction of new services – including YouTube – since the mid-2000s. As an advertiser-supported, global video-sharing platform, YouTube gives children free access to vast amounts of screen content, both user-generated and professionally produced, in short and long form, and including content produced and presented by young people or children themselves (Dredge 2015; Craig and Cunningham 2017). YouTube is forcing a rethink of what children's television means, as it exists alongside SVOD services like Netflix and Amazon Prime Video, as well as some specialist local children's VOD providers such as the UK-based companies Hopster and Azoomee. Despite their shared means of distribution, online television and video streaming services vary considerably in their efforts to monetize their young audiences. Subscriber revenues may (Amazon Prime, Disney+) or may not (Netflix) exist in tandem with efforts to market children licensed products on curated services while YouTube's advertising revenues depend on children accessing minimally regulated content.

These technological developments and the new business models they engendered for television funding and distribution raise questions that are pertinent to how different parts of the industry decide to cater to the child audience. First, is YouTube really television – or online TV – by any other name? For some commentators (Johnson 2019: 19; Lotz 2017), this is doubtful. YouTube is not curated, is an open platform, and those who upload content do not control the interfaces or "environment where the content sits" (Johnson 2019: 39). YouTube also has complete control over the algorithms that determine how data is collected and used, for the purposes of targeting content and advertising. YouTube is therefore quite unlike an SVOD such as Netflix, which is subscriber supported, operating a closed system "portal" (Lotz 2017) to offer audiences licensed professionally produced, curated content. In contrast, YouTube sees itself as a "platform" with responsibility placed squarely on those who can freely upload material to its servers, be they children, their parents, or professional companies (Burroughs 2017). This position whereby YouTube takes far less responsibility than linear and SVOD services for what is carried on its platform has not been universally accepted, particularly after scandals about the use of children's characters in disturbing or violent videos (Bridle 2017). Another cause for disquiet is how the targeting of children within YouTube's "hyper-commercialised media environment" (Kunkel 2015) uses algorithms to push advertising in ways that are not permitted on regulated television services for children, blurring the boundaries between entertainment and advertising.

YouTube is morphing however, changing how it engages with children in ways that suggest a move toward a more curated model. In 2015, the YouTube Kids app was launched, designed to safeguard children from encountering unfiltered and inappropriate content on the standard YouTube platform. But YouTube Kids has not always been entirely successful at shielding children, with reports of failures in filtering and targeted advertising (Bridle 2017). In 2019, in the wake of a $170 million fine from the US Federal Trade Commission (FTC) for breaching the Children's Online Privacy Protection Act (COPPA), YouTube took steps to protect itself, promising to invest $100 million into original children's content over three years (Wojcicki 2019). The company's investment is a small sum compared to the annual expenditure of approximately $96 million a year by UK public service broadcasters (Franks 2019a; Ofcom 2019b: 56). According to the 2019 FTC ruling, YouTube, owned by Google, violated the COPPA because it allowed children's personal data to be collected; COPPA rules stipulate that internet services must obtain parental permission for those aged 13 and under. Retreating back to its position as a mere platform and intermediary, YouTube stated in 2019 that producers and creators of videos targeting children must now label these as such, so that personalized advertising, data collection, and comments can be blocked (Wojcicki 2019; Alexander 2019). For producers, content owners, and creators who turned to YouTube to generate advertising revenues in the wake of declining broadcast commissions for children's content, the change was a financial blow. Some predicted a decline in low-cost children's content and a shift by companies like Moonbug Entertainment, which owns the *Little Baby Bum* YouTube channel, to a "more premium model" (John Robson, COO of Moonbug, quoted in Alexander 2019). This move suggests that in future YouTube may become the preserve of large conglomerates rather than smaller companies. Regardless, YouTube is likely to remain a highly commercialized and popular platform for children, where their access, even if they are under 13, is unlikely to be restricted to children's content alone.

What these developments underline is the difficulty of looking at children's content purely through a television studies perspective. Such an approach usually foregrounds regulatory and policy interventions on national organizations/institutions to protect children or promote content that is deemed culturally valuable to children, usually on a national basis (Lustyik 2013; Steemers 2017a). Platforms like YouTube, which are US-owned entities, do not operate at this level. They act transnationally and shift the accountability to producers, including the threat of fines. Writing about television generally, Lobato (2019: 30–34) argues for a new paradigm that while recognizing many similarities with the past – in this case in the type of content viewed by children and certain production norms – acknowledges emerging differences in industry infrastructure and goals. These are closer to a platform perspective that centers on user interaction with particular interfaces and software, rather than the curated operations of broadcasters or broadcasting hybrids like Netflix. A television perspective (p. 34) reminds us of the continuities of children's "television" (e.g., around professional production norms, trusted brands, and quality). In contrast, a platform perspective allows us to view children's "television" in new ways, acknowledging children's agency and their interactions with social media platforms. It can also accommodate the increasing possibility for some children of becoming the "vlogger next door," an online influencer who is local rather than national or transnational, and to whom children and young people are attracted by a particular shared interest (Ofcom 2020: 13).

In many ways, YouTube does offer a television experience because children watch programs on a screen, but they are watching on-demand. It would be remiss therefore to exclude YouTube from any overview of screen media industries targeted at children. It is seen by many children in numerous but not all countries around the world (especially China) as their preferred alternative to subscription and linear broadcasting services. It is also important to include YouTube among the spectrum of services/platforms available to children, as its stance on children's content is constantly changing. YouTube challenges traditional models of funding, distributing, curating, and commissioning children's content. Yet it also shows some degree of alignment to previous models, based increasingly on concerns about the welfare of children and an implicit acknowledgment that they are a "special" audience. This is true even for YouTube which is keen to restrict reputational damage and counter any initiatives by governments to impose statutory controls. While content for adults can be passed off as lying outside regulatory rules, children's content has become a site of tension between YouTube, regulators, governments, producers, and advocacy groups, all of whom claim to represent children's interests, although children as an invisible stakeholder are rarely consulted (Steemers 2019).

In contrast, subscriber-supported online television services such as Netflix explicitly draw on the curation of children's content. Netflix is even able in some instances to deliver on certain types of public service credentials that "super-serve" youth and minority audiences more effectively (House of Lords 2019: 24). US-owned SVODs Netflix, Amazon Prime Video and

Disney+, benefit from public recognition and perceptions that their children's offerings are curated and high quality. Consequently, they are seen to provide safe spaces for families and children to access transnational television, at a price. This approach is not however consistent. In 2019, for example, Amazon Prime announced that it would no longer be commissioning its own preschool and children's content, preferring instead to concentrate on family shows (that will attract children in co-viewing arrangements with parents), and content for young adults (Franks 2019b). Children are an important audience for SVODs, as content watched by children adds value to family subscription packages. For providers like Disney+ and Amazon Prime, their SVOD services contribute to broader strategies of monetization, including through the sale of licensed products and toys.

Set against the rising number of SVOD and advertising-supported video-on-demand (AVOD) offerings for children, legacy national broadcasters, both public service and state-owned, claim to curate and distribute high-quality content for children. Yet broadcasters increasingly struggle to compete with better resourced transnational SVOD providers, and the loss of child audiences to online platforms such as YouTube. For those which are publicly funded, including PSBs in Europe, North America, and Australia, lack of funding combined with declining audiences presents a perfect storm (Potter and Steemers 2017).

## Changes in the development, production, and distribution of screen content for children

Rather than adopt an either/or perspective, seeing the landscape of children's screen entertainment as either just television presented in new ways or something entirely new, it is much more useful to think holistically about the practical changes that are occurring within the children's screen content sector. These include how the industry is dealing immediately with new situations such as the impact of COVID-19. Such an approach allows for an assessment of implications and trends, and how unforeseen consequences from COVID-19 have accelerated pre-existing problems and issues. These include declining advertising avenues for linear channels and video-sharing sites alike, alongside a slump in licensed merchandise. At the same time, viewing of SVODs, YouTube, and some public service providers has been boosted. PSBs like the BBC and Australia's ABC have responded to lockdown by reinforcing their educational provision for children and capitalizing on renewed public support (ABC 2020; BBC 2020). One survey in April 2020 of 4,322 children in 42 countries saw 47 percent aged 9–13 saying they used television more, with 28 percent watching more YouTube, and 15 percent more Netflix (Götz et al. 2020). Similarly, an April 2020 survey of 1,117 UK children showed a 5 percent uplift in viewing of linear TV and a 4 percent lift in non-subscription streaming, including broadcaster streaming services. YouTube remains a favored service nonetheless (Woodgate 2020).

Taking one step back to the period before COVID-19, the arrival of SVODs opened up what had been a relatively closed market of commissioners for children's programming that comprised national broadcasters, some cable and satellite channels, and large transnational operators (Disney, TimeWarner, Viacom). They were joined in the late 2010s by the transnational SVOD commissioners, including Netflix and Amazon Prime, and some local and national providers in other parts of the world such as China. Internet distribution thus allowed new sources of funding and new gatekeepers to enter the market. For producers of children's content, who have traditionally struggled to find funding (Steemers 2017b), this was a welcome development, and also brought the additional advantage of distributing their content on a global service through a single contractual arrangement (Potter 2018). The arrival of SVODs has led to changes in funding models for children's content, including where financial benefits accrue.

The new opportunities they present, particularly for funding children's animation and international children's drama, must be weighed against what might be lost. Many children's content producers have tended to rely on broadcaster commissions and deficit funding, bringing together investors from multiple territories and hoping to make profits from their intellectual property through ancillary rights such as licensed merchandise. But dealing with transnational SVODs often means a return to the old cost-plus system (Doyle 2016). Under this system, production companies more or less become companies for hire, without the ability to build their own IP, a key route to company growth (Richard Bradley, Managing Director of Lion TV, quoted in Brown 2020.) As transnational operators, SVODs also place greater emphasis on transnational appeal: shows must be attractive to many markets but prioritize the largest and/or wealthiest. For animation, this does not represent a significant change from the past, as transnational players like Disney and Nickelodeon also operated a cost-plus system. Yet many are concerned about the sustainability of local industries and the future of specifically local content such as drama, news, and factual programming for children. These forms of television are not always well-suited for international distribution but are felt to enhance children's sense of civic engagement and affiliation to their local communities (ACTF 2017; Children's Media Foundation 2019).

The arrival of YouTube may not have created much space for new commissioners, but it has become a platform for lucrative "channels" aimed at children, commissioning some material, albeit usually at low cost. Some of the most successful professionally produced YouTube channels are targeted at very young children, and preschoolers. They usually show nursery rhymes and simple animation. Examples include *Little Baby Bum*, now owned by UK-based Moonbug, Indian-owned ChuChu TV, and US-based Cocomelon, the top-rating YouTube channel during May 11–17, 2020, with more than 1 billion weekly views (Gutelle 2020). Other popular offerings within the top 50 of all YouTube channels suggest an opening up of what had previously been US dominance of transnational distribution with the most popular children's channels in 2020 emanating from Argentina (El Reino Infantil), Romania (LooLoo Kids), Russia (Eva Bravo Play; Little Nastya Show), South Korea (Pinkfong: Kids Songs and Stories), Canada (Super Simple Songs; Little Angel), Brazil (Maria Clara and JP), India (Wow Kidz), and Vietnam (Pop Kids) (Gutelle 2020). For these providers, YouTube has been the main source of income, and they may now be challenged by the stricter parameters on children's data exploitation and targeting enforced by YouTube in late 2019.

Challenges to the regulatory parameters of children's content expose global variations in protection for children across the full range of online services (HM Government 2019). National regulatory interventions over broadcasting, cable, and satellite systems in many countries promote domestically produced content through transmission, production, or investment quotas, as well as tax incentives that invite investment (Steemers and Awan 2016). For transnational providers, these types of positive interventions are virtually non-existent, meaning little or no guarantees of investment in local content for children. National systems of regulation also operate interventions designed to protect children from content deemed inappropriate, including advertising bans and restrictions on content that is violent or deemed obscene.

A final challenge is trying to understand and predict the behavior of the child audience whose interaction and engagement with media are changing so rapidly, with profound implications for screen media industries. For traditional broadcasters, transformations in children's consumption habits represent a major challenge at a time of decreasing budgets and audiences overall (Steemers 2017b). This declining ability to engage young audiences poses an existential challenge for broadcasters as legacy players with aging audiences (Enli, Raats, Syvertsen, and Donders 2019). Indeed, the challenge of holding onto child and young audiences has prompted some broadcasters in Denmark, Finland, Switzerland, and France to move or start to move children's services to online distribution only. They recognize that YouTube represents both an opportunity for promoting their own content and a challenge in shaping children's content for new modes of consumption (Sakr and Steemers 2019: 120). For some commercial broadcasters, the difficulty of monetizing children's content from advertising has spelled the end of engagement with that audience completely, while for subscription services, child and family audiences remain sought after. Netflix's refusal to release program ratings and lack of interest (at this stage) in licensing opportunities hampers producers' efforts to monetize their IP (Potter 2020). Producers also face the ongoing challenge of attracting child audiences with discoverable content within a declining linear broadcasting universe. And they are encountering growing difficulties distributing content on their own account on YouTube, where options for generating income from advertising are limited by YouTube's new stance on the collection of children's data. All this is taking place within a wider economy of attractions for children that includes gaming and social media, seeing children engaging less with licensed products like toys.

## Continuities: inclusion, equality, regulation, and curation

Among all these disruptive changes in children's screen industries, several continuities remain. Indeed, the challenges posed by the COVID-19 pandemic have made these more marked. First is the continued lack of equality in children's access to screen content, particularly their access to digital technology. This divide was brought into sharp relief during lockdown, when children's use of free-to-air television and free video-on-demand services grew globally (Woodgate 2020). Free-to-air television became a particularly important source of news and information for children (Götz et al. 2020; Woodgate 2020). Far from being uniformly connected, not all children have access to Wi-Fi, mobile phones, or tablets, a fact reinforced by many families' experiences of lockdown, and the shift of schooling to home learning.

A further continuity is ongoing concern about the regulation of children's content, in tandem with the ethical implications of personalization of children's content and the use of algorithms to construct their viewing options (Livingstone and Local 2017). While sharp divisions between the approaches of different countries have always existed, newer divisions are emerging between national and transnational providers. In some instances, transnational providers are simply excluded from a market, notably China. The regulation of offerings differs between transnational providers as well. Subscriber-supported online television services, whose success depends on parental trust, are more inclined to self-regulate than advertiser-supported video streaming platform. As national regulators turn their focus to YouTube and demonstrate their willingness to intervene in its operations, the adoption of a more curated approach by video-sharing sites seems likely. Notions of curated content and the provision of safe spaces for children are also becoming greater points of emphasis that underline distinctiveness. For PSBs, this is part of their remit: COVID-19 saw some public service broadcasters – the BBC and ABC included – rise to the challenge of providing different types of content, including educational content for children. The uptake in Disney+ subscriptions and the continued growth of audiences for Netflix and Amazon Prime Video suggest that SVODs are also benefiting from COVID-19, unlike advertiser-supported television, which is more vulnerable to economic downturns.

Despite increasing acceptance of children's offerings on multiple on-demand services, the precarity of smaller producers continues, a situation exacerbated by COVID-19 when commissioning and productions were halted and companies had to abandon projects (Steemers and Götz 2020). In some countries, government interventions continue to support domestic screen industries. In the UK, the launch of the Young Audience Content Fund in 2019 – a three-year pilot project run by the British Film Institute – established an alternative source of funding for children's public service content distributed by free-to-air broadcasters. In France, a series of investment and transmission quotas supported by tax breaks continue to underpin French animation. In Australia, long-standing transmission quotas for children's content on commercial broadcasters were suspended in April 2020 during the COVID-19 crisis. Their absence (which may be permanent) leaves the onus of children's content provision on the ABC, an under-funded public service broadcaster operating without any formalized local content obligations. At a pan-European level, European Broadcasting Union initiatives for drama, pre-school content, and factual programming continue to support initiatives by smaller countries. But without a brand that goes on to be global hit, like *Peppa Pig* (2004–), these supports cannot shield producers from uncertain futures.

The screen industries sector for children has always had a strong international presence, but existing processes of globalization have been accelerated and compounded since the mid-2010s by the online distribution of television and video. Dominated by animation, a genre that is easily dubbed and infinitely repeatable, children's screen media industries have always been characterized by global properties; brands that are recognized by children around the world and supported by lucrative ancillary rights (Sakr and Steemers, 2019). What has been much harder to sustain in the post-network era is programming for domestic audiences where contextual factors play a role – including culture and language, size of market, the role and status of national broadcasters, and policy dynamics. As this chapter has demonstrated, children's screen industries, the veritable canary in the media industries' coal mine, can tell us a great deal about how distribution and financing models are evolving in the on-demand age and shed light on some of the complex interactions between the national and the global in the spaces of regulation, production, and consumption.

# References

ABC (2020) "ABC Expands Education Schedule to Support Students at Home Suring COVID-19 Crisis," April 1, available at https://about.abc.net.au/press-releases/abc-expands-education-schedule-to-support-students-at-home-during-covid-19-crisis/ (accessed May 25, 2020).

Alexander, I. (2019) "YouTube Fine to Impact Kids' Producers," *C21 Media*, December 9, available at www.c21media.net/youtube-fine-to-impact-kids-producers/?ss=Coppa (accessed October 27, 2020).

ACTF (2017) *Australian and Children's Content Review Submission*, September 21, available at https://actf.com.au/assets/submissions/actf_submissions_australian_childrens_content_review.PDF (accessed May 25, 2020).

BBC (2020) "BBC Sets Out Plan to Inform, Educate and Entertain During Unprecedented Times," *BBC Media Centre*, March 18, available at www.bbc.co.uk/mediacentre/latestnews/2020/bbc-keeping-nation-informed-educated-entertained (accessed May 25, 2020).

Bisson, G. and Deane, O. (2018) "Where Next for Kids' TV: Predicting the Future of Children's Content," *MIPTrends*, April 24, available at www.miptrends.com/tv-business/where-next-for-kids-tv-predicting-the-future-of-childrens-content-exclusive-white-paper/ (accessed May 25, 2020).

Bridle, J. (2017) "Something Is Wrong on the Internet," November 6, available at https://medium.com/@jamesbridle/something-is-wrong-on-the-internet-c39c471271d2 (accessed May 23, 2020).

Brown, M. (2020) "Are the Kids Alright?" Royal Television Society, February 26, available at https://rts.org.uk/article/are-kids-alright (accessed October 27, 2020).

Buckingham, D., Davies, H., Jones, K., and Kelley, P. (1999) *Children's Television in Britain*, London: British Film Institute.

Burroughs, B. (2017) "YouTube Kids: The App Economy and Mobile Parenting," *Social Media + Society*, 3 (2): 1–8.

Children's Media Foundation (2019) *Response to the House of Lords Communications Committee Consultation on Public Service Broadcasting in the Age of Video on Demand*, April 25, available at www.thechildrensmediafoundation.org/wp-content/uploads/2019/04/Response-to-House-of-Lords-Communication-Committee-Inquiry-on-PSB-Apr2019.pdf (accessed November 26, 2020)

Cullinane, C. (2020) "COVID-19 and Home-schooling: The Crisis Has Exacerbated and Highlighted Existing Educational Inequalities," April 27, available at https://blogs.lse.ac.uk/politicsandpolicy/home-schooling-covid-19/ (accessed October 27, 2020).

Craig D. and Cunningham, S. (2017) "Toy Unboxing: Living in a(n Unregulated) Material World," *Media International Australia*, 163 (1): 77–86.

Doyle, G. (2016) "Digitization and Changing Windowing Strategies in the Television Industry: Negotiating New Windows on the World," *Television and New Media*, 17 (7): 1–17.

Dredge, S. (2015) "Little Baby Bum: How UK Couple Built World's Fifth-biggest YouTube Channel," *The Guardian*, March 19, available at www.theguardian.com/technology/2015/mar/19/little-baby-bum-worlds-fifth-biggest-youtube-channel (accessed May 25, 2020).

Enli, G., Raats, T., Syvertsen, T., and Donders, K. (2019) "Media Policy for Private Media in the Age of Digital Intermediaries," *European Journal of Communication*, 34 (4): 395–409.

Franks, N. (2019a) "YouTube Pledges $100m Kids Fund," *C21 Media*, September 9, available at www.c21media.net/youtube-pledges-100m-kids-fund/?ss=YouTube (accessed October 27, 2020).

Franks, N. (2019b) "Amazon Explains Kids' Originals Shift," *C21 Media*, October 23, available at www.c21media.net/amazon-explains-kids-originals-shift/?ss=Amazon (accessed November 26, 2020).

Götz, M. et al. (2020) "Children, Covid-19 and the Media: A Study on Challenges Children are Facing in the 2020 Coronavirus Crisis," *Televizion*, (33): 4–9, available at www.br-online.de/jugend/izi/english/publication/televizion/33_2020_E/Goetz_Mendel_Lemish-Children_COVID-19_and_the_media.pdf (accessed November 26, 2020).

Gutelle, S. (2020) "Top 50 Most Viewed YouTube Channels Worldwide: Week Of 5/18/2020," *Tubefilter*, May 18, available at www.tubefilter.com/2020/05/18/top-50-most-viewed-youtube-channels-worldwide-2020-05-18/ (accessed October 27, 2020).

HM Government (2019) *Online Harms White Paper*, April, available at https://assets.publishing.service.gov.uk/government/uploads/system/uploads/attachment_data/file/793360/Online_Harms_White_Paper.pdf (accessed October 27, 2020).

House of Lords (2019) *Public Service Broadcasting: As Vital as Ever*, Select Committee on Communications and Digital, November 5. available at https://publications.parliament.uk/pa/ld201919/ldselect/ldcomuni/16/16.pdf (accessed October 27, 2020).

Jenner, M. (2018) *Netflix and the Re-invention of Television*, Cham: Palgrave Macmillan.

Johnson, C. (2019) *Online TV*, Abingdon: Routledge.

Kunkel, D. (2015) "Digital Deception: Legal Questions Surround New 'YouTube Kids' App," November 30, available at https://blogs.lse.ac.uk/parenting4digitalfuture/2015/11/30/digital-deception-legal-questions-surround-new-youtube-kids-app/ (accessed October 27, 2020).

Livingstone, S. and Third, A. (2017) "Children and Young People's Rights in the Digital Age: An Emerging Agenda," *New Media and Society*, 19 (5): 657–670.

Livingstone, S. and Local, C. (2017) "Measurement Matters: Difficulties in Defining and Measuring Children's Television Viewing in a Changing Media Landscape," *Media International Australia*, 161 (1): 67–76.

Lobato, R. (2019) *Netflix Nations: The Geography of Digital Distribution*, New York: New York University Press.

Lotz, A. D. (2017) *Portals: A Treatise on Internet-Distributed Television*, Ann Arbor, MI: Maize Publishing.

Lustyik, K. (2013) "Media Regulation: The Protection and Promotion of Home-grown Children's Television," in D. Lemish (ed.), *The Routledge International Handbook of Children, Adolescents and Media*, Abingdon: Routledge, 386–394.

Melody, W. (1973) *Children's Television: The Economics of Exploitation*, New York: Yale University Press.

Mitroff, D. and Herr Stephenson, R. (2007) "The Television Tug-of-War: A Brief History of Children's Television Programming in the United States," in J. A. Bryant (ed.), *The Children's Television Community*, Mahwah, NJ: Lawrence Erlbaum, 3–34.

Ofcom (2019a) *Ofcom's Annual Report on the BBC*, London: Ofcom, available at www.ofcom.org.uk/__data/assets/pdf_file/0026/173735/second-bbc-annual-report.pdf (accessed November 26, 2020).

Ofcom (2019b) *Media Nations: UK 2019*, London: Ofcom, available at ofcom.org.uk/__data/assets/pdf_file/0019/160714/media-nations-2019-uk-report.pdf (accessed November 26, 2020).

Ofcom (2020) *Children and Parents: Media Use and Attitudes Report 2019*, London: Ofcom. available at www.ofcom.org.uk/__data/assets/pdf_file/0023/190616/children-media-use-attitudes-2019-report. pdf (accessed November 26, 2020).

Potter, A. (2018) "Creating Children's Television for SVODs: The Alignment of Global Production Practices with National Screen Policies in the Netflix Original *Bottersnikes and Gumbles*," *Media Industries Journal*, 5 (2): 111–127.

Potter, A. (2020) *Producing Children's Television in the On Demand Age*, Bristol: Intellect.

Potter, A. and Steemers, J. (2017) "Children's Television in Transition: Policies, Platforms and Production," *Media International Australia*, 163 (1): 6–12.

Sakr, N. and Steemers, S. (2019) *Screen Media for Arab and European Children. Policy and Production Encounters in the Multiplatform Era*, Cham: Palgrave Macmillan.

Steemers, J. (2017a) "Public Service Broadcasting, Children's Television and Market Failure: The Case of the United Kingdom," *International Journal of Media Management*, 19 (4): 298–314.

Steemers, J. (2017b) "International Perspectives on the Funding of Public Service Media Content for Children," *Media International Australia*, 163 (1): 42–55.

Steemers, J. (2019) "Invisible Children: Inequalities in the Provision of Screen Content for Children," in J. Trappel (ed.), *Digital Media Inequalities: Policies Against Divides, Distrust and Discrimination*, Göteborg: Nordicom, 179–192.

Steemers, J. and Awan, F. (2016) *Policy Solutions and International Perspectives on the Funding of Public Service Media Content for Children: A Report for Stakeholders*, Communications and Media Research Institute, May, available at https://westminsterresearch.westminster.ac.uk/download/ 76b369e2f3c7969f50666facdd3e79664e17bbb26584ae12cbeede85345bbcad/1478454/1.%20 UoW%20final%2014%20June.pdf (accessed October 27, 2020).

Steemers, J. and Götz, M. (2020) "'Keep the Energy': The Children's Screen Industry in the Time of Lockdown," *Televizion*, (33): 42–44, available at www.br-online.de/jugend/izi/english/publication/ televizion/33_2020_E/Steemers_Goetz-Keep_the_energy.pdf (accessed November 26, 2020).

Westcott, T. (2002) "Globalisation of Children's TV and Strategies of the 'Big Three'," in C. von Feilitzen and U. Carlsson (eds), *Children, Young People and Media Globalisation*, Göteborg: Nordicom, 69–76.

Wojcicki, S. (2019) "An Update on Kids and Data Protection on YouTube," *YouTube*, September 4, available at https://youtube.googleblog.com/2019/09/an-update-on-kids.html (accessed October 27, 2020).

Woodgate, J. (2018) "Is Kids' Preferred TV Content Changing? – Exclusive White Paper" *MIPTV Trends*, November 13, available at www.miptrends.com/tv-business/kids-preferred-tv-content-changing/ (accessed October 27, 2020).

Woodgate, J. (2020) "CMC Webinar – Kids and Media in the Time of Corona," *The Children's Media Conference*, April 27, available at www.thechildrensmediaconference.com/blog/2020/04/27/blog-kids-in-the-time-of-corona/ (accessed October 27, 2020).

# 22

# GAME-CHANGER OR A NEW SHAPE TO FAMILIAR DYNAMICS?

## Netflix and the American indie film sector

*Geoff King*

The subscription-based streaming platform Netflix became a dominant force in the online distribution of film (as well as television) during the 2010s. Along with Amazon Prime, Apple's iTunes and the potential of other web giants such as Google/YouTube and Facebook, it represented one of the most serious challenges ever made to the hegemony of the Hollywood studios and their corporate parents (Cunningham and Silver 2013). Its status as a major player was confirmed by its admittance in 2019 to the powerful lobbying group, the Motion Picture Association (MPA), the first online or non-studio company to achieve such status. Netflix posed a competitive threat most obviously in the realm of the post-(or non-) theatrical distribution of films, in a period when this market moved increasingly from hard-copy sales and rentals into the online sphere, but also by making moves into the production of features as well as original television programming. If this was a major issue facing the established studio film business during the period, Netflix also gained a distinctive presence within the sphere of American indie film, the focus of this chapter. Netflix's move into this arena was welcomed by some and condemned by others. Whether as potential savior or threat, Netflix has widely been seen as a game-changer for the indie economy, alongside Amazon. This chapter seeks to identify the impact of Netflix and to emphasize not just what was new about its role but also to identify the extent to which the company's involvement reproduced past or existing tendencies in the indie scene.

The involvement of Netflix in the indie sector came to particular prominence in the second half of the 2010s, but it includes an earlier phase, in both the acquisition and production of films. Netflix was founded in 1997, as an online operation through which subscribers could order DVDs sent by post. Its "Watch Instantly" streaming facility began in 2006, as a free extra service, followed by a move to a monthly subscription for unlimited viewing from 2010 (Cunningham and Silver 2013: 25). In 2006, when it remained primarily a hard-copy operation, Netflix established a small unit, Red Envelope Entertainment, to acquire and in some cases to finance independent films, the distribution of which tended to mix theatrical and DVD release. This unit was closed in 2008, at which point a spokesman said the company did not want to be competing at festivals with studios with which it partnered in its main business, for

DOI: 10.4324/9780429275340-26

both DVD and online release (Jesdanun 2008). Notably, the early excursion into indie production led a contributor to *Wired* magazine to draw a parallel with the previous operations of Miramax (Biba 2006). A key phase in the development of Miramax was a move into production as well as distribution, one of the sources of its domination of the indie sector after the company's takeover by Disney in 1993. If the early era of Netflix-funded indies was short-lived and curtailed by a desire not to upset its studio partners, its subsequent involvement in both acquisitions and production seemed reminiscent of the operations of Miramax more generally, suggesting the activities of a larger player competing more directly with its studio rivals or their speciality divisions.

Netflix first became a significant buying presence at the Sundance Film Festival, the signature event in the American indie calendar, in 2015. That year saw Netflix purchase the African-war drama *Beasts of No Nation* for the headline-grabbing sum of $12 million, outbidding the two strongest studio speciality divisions at the time, Fox Searchlight and Focus Features (McClintock 2015b). Netflix and Amazon were reported to be the biggest buyers at Sundance in 2016, acquisitions of the former including *The Fundamentals of Caring* for $7 million (Desta, 2017). The following Sundance brought more high-profile acquisitions, including *Mudbound* ($12.5 million), *To the Bone* ($8 million), and *Fun Mom Dinner* ($5 million) (Donnelly 2017). Some commentators interpreted a lack of purchases at Sundance 2018 as part of a move by Netflix away from the sector (e.g., Lopez 2018), although the company had by this time developed and expanded a new generation of indie production, through the establishment of the Netflix Indie Content (NIC) division. As *Indiewire* reported: "Netflix acquisition czar Matt Brodlie did not end up buying anything at Sundance 2018, partly because he didn't have to" (Thompson 2018). Moving from buying into production for some of its product, as Miramax had done before, was a way of securing early access to attractive properties while also avoiding the potential problem posed by increasing acquisition costs (on the latter point, see Cunningham and Silver 2013: 89).

Sundance had, before this point, become a venue both for acquisitions and for the showing of Netflix's own new generation of in-house productions. The latter tended to achieve less high profile, largely because they lacked the attention gained by the reporting of the more prominent acquisitions. In some cases, Sundance featured at both ends of the life cycle for an individual title – pre-production and screening – in a process that could be unusually accelerated for any kind of film development and circulation. *I Don't Feel at Home in This World Anymore*, for example, was pitched to the Netflix Indie Content (NIC) division at Sundance 2016, reportedly going into production the following month. It won the Grand Jury prize at the festival in 2017 and was streaming less than a month later (Thompson 2018). Another three NIC films showed at Sundance the same year, with an additional four Netflix films following in 2018, one developed by NIC and three acquisitions (Thompson 2018).

That Netflix had at this stage become a substantial new force in the indie economy is without doubt. Netflix was viewed by some commentators as a game-changer – along with Amazon – although closer examination shows that what it offered to the sector was a combination of the novel and the more familiar, both in its operations and the responses they generated from others. One part of the familiar was the tone and language of much of the reaction. Netflix was, for many, a large force with "deep pockets" or "financial muscle" that represented a "threat" to more traditional ways of doing business (see, e.g., Lyttelton 2016, Donnelly 2017; Dreier 2017). It offered larger payments for acquisitions than the norm for the sector and was thus perceived as effectively a disruptive and bullying presence, "swooping" in to buy up many of the most desirable products at excessive rates unaffordable by anyone else; to "nab" such films, as it was characteristically put in one piece in *The Hollywood Reporter* (McClintock 2015b), or acting like an "alpha predator," for *IndieWire*, "robbing indigenous animals of their food sources" (Lyttelton 2016). Another concern was that inflated acquisition payments were forcing others to pay more than they would otherwise, notably the record-breaking $7.5 million paid by Fox Searchlight for *Birth of a Nation* in 2016; or, in the case of smaller distributors, more than they could afford (Lyttelton 2016). To anyone familiar with indie history, this sounded strikingly similar to attitudes expressed toward Miramax in its heyday during the 1990s. The same impression was created by responses to its increasing move into production, as identified at the earlier stage by *Wired* (Biba 2006). Netflix and Amazon were ideal candidates to play the role of the overly large and/or bullying forces that often appear as negative others in the discourse around indie film, forces against which the distinctive and more virtuous qualities of independence are regularly established (King 2014).

There was a key difference in Neflix's approach, however, with implications for another core issue in discourse on the state of the indie economy. In most cases, production or purchase by Netflix meant no theatrical distribution, or occasional limited openings, usually combined with simultaneous availability online. If an expansion into production as well as distribution had marked a move toward vertical integration, this was more encompassing than past examples, such as Miramax or other indies that followed the Miramax lead from the 1990s, given the effective collapse of exhibition into streaming-distribution for films that received no theatrical release. As well as representing a more consolidated form of business in general, this was seen as a threat to the importance vested in theatrical release as a marker of "proper film" status – as opposed to categories such as "straight to video" that are accorded lower cultural standing. A central ambition for the majority of indie filmmakers has been to achieve theatrical distribution, as a key marker of achieving fully "cinematic" status, even where this might not result in financial gain. A related issue is the ability of films streamed without theatrical release, or a period of exclusive screening in cinemas, to quality for major awards such as Oscars, an issue on which Netflix was notably challenged by Steven Spielberg after the success of *Roma* (2018) at the Academy Awards in 2019 (see, e.g., Gleiberman 2019). Most indie filmmakers considering a sale to, or production by, Netflix were faced with the likelihood of abandoning theatrical status, even if in return for a larger payment up front. Some have been happy to accept this as the price for getting any payment at all, something that can rarely be taken for granted in the lower-budget indie world (e.g., Adam Leon in relation to *Tramps* [2016], which sold to Netflix for $2 million, in Kenny 2017), while others have mourned the loss of theatrical screenings (e.g., Noah Baumbach and *The Meyerowitz Stories* [2017] in Kuchera 2018). Where Netflix had at this point offered theatrical release, as in the case of *Beasts of No Nation*, its potential scale was hampered by opposition from major cinema chains to the strategy of simultaneous release in theaters and online (McClintock 2015a).

For many of those commenting on the state of the indie sector, this was an occasion for familiar rhetoric. To *Indiewire* columnist David Ehrlich, the sale of *Tramps* to Netflix condemned the film to "a graveyard with unlimited viewing hours" (Ehrlich 2017); the company did not release films but "inters them." Such rhetoric included questioning whether or not a film that premiered on Netflix was "still even a movie." Netflix is characterized here as "a volatile sea of content that likes to measure itself in terms of dimension rather than depth." This is negatively inflected language characteristic of that applied to large-scale media entities seen as threatening notions of more distinctive quality. For another commentator, Netflix was "stealing" the theatrical experience from such films, denying viewers the power they might have when viewed on the big screen, even if this was combined – as in many such accounts – with a recognition of the boost the streaming service had given to indie film (Kuchera 2018). It was probably in response to such criticism, particularly the unhappiness of some established filmmakers, that

Netflix moved to a strategy of offering advance theatrical opening to a select few titles in 2019, beneficiaries of which included Martin Scorsese's *The Irishman*, Baumbach's *Marriage Story*, and Steven Soderbergh's *The Laundromat*. Each was given a three- or four-week run before streaming (Sharf 2019), considerably less than the three-month window considered likely to be sought by figures such as Spielberg (Gleiberman 2019). A further complication of the "Netflix vs theatrical" opposition came with the company's takeover of the lease for the historical arthouse, the Paris Theatre, in New York.

The sense that Netflix offered a combination of threat and promise was widely shared and another characteristic familiar from responses to Miramax. A law firm partner who had advised filmmakers on distribution deals was quoted in *Variety* as saying: "Netflix and other streaming services have been a boon to the indie space in terms of pricing, but it feels like the companies under them are getting squeezed" (Lang 2018a). Difficulties faced by some other indie operations were viewed in some reporting of the activities of Netflix and Amazon at Sundance 2017 as "fallout" from the impact of the new players. This included, for example, the closure of the production division of Broad Green Pictures, founded in 2014 by hedge-fund billionaire brothers Gabriel and Daniel Hammond (Donnelly 2017). Such closures are commonplace in the indie economy, however, and cannot be attributed to the impact of new entrants such as the streaming giants.

Other indie players were reported to have "overhauled" some of their strategies in an attempt to remain competitive in the face of the high payments offered by Netflix. In this context, the acquisition of *I Tonya* (2017) by the newly created distributor Neon was interpreted in one *Variety* article as highlighting how the company had "snatched" the film from Netflix "by promising a robust theatrical release," a deal that proved more attractive than a larger sum offered by the latter (Lang 2018b). Strong emphasis was placed on the theatrical experience and the detailed needs of individual films (Lang 2018b). A similarly individualized approach to releases was stressed by Good Deed Entertainment and again interpreted as a way for a small indie operation to differentiate itself from larger-scale operators such as Netflix (Lang 2018a). Rather than bringing anything new to the sector, the deal reaffirmed a very traditional model of indie operations, even if such continuity was not usually acknowledged in the press coverage.

If lack of theatrical distribution was a feature of Netflix's approach, even in comparison with Amazon (Kuchera 2018), it might be argued that this could be of limited concern to producers of the great majority of indie films, which never achieved this goal anyway. If a theatrical release has always been beyond the reach of most, why should this be such a big issue? The answer is that theatrical retains a significant symbolic and cultural value, as at least an aspiration. One of the reasons for the level of concern expressed by Ehrlich was that the films bought or funded by Netflix were considered to be "getting better," thus seeming to threaten the special status of theatrical screening for what are seen as higher quality indies (Ehrlich 2017). Often brushed aside within this discourse was the fact that most indie productions are never shown in cinemas and that a significant number of these might achieve sales and a streaming release through Netflix. A dismissive tone was also used here for the manner of streaming release. In the case of *I Don't Feel at Home in this World Anymore*, Netflix was characterized as having "quietly uploaded the movie onto their platform in the middle of the night like it was a new episode of [the sitcom] 'Fuller House.'" This phrasing draws on the implicitly negative associations of a popular television genre while also suggesting there was something underhand about the whole operation (as if it made any significant difference at what time of day or night a film was uploaded).

Another distinctive feature of the model adopted by Netflix was the structure of actual or potential payments made to filmmakers. Netflix made its initial impact on the indie sector primarily through the large sums paid for acquisitions, funds gratefully received by many filmmakers where this entailed the abandonment of any dream of theatrical release. Larger than usual upfront payments came at a price, however, usually being all a filmmaker could expect to receive. Sale to, or development by, Netflix would often be for global rights more or less in perpetuity. One of the advantages of going with Netflix was that it involved "presenting their movies simultaneously around the world in 190 countries, with subtitled and dubbed versions in 30 languages" (Thompson 2018). Aggregating what could be many small audiences was a major plus, far more easily achieved by Netflix than through a web of separate deals that might be negotiated through a sales agency (Thompson 2018). Given its ability to sweep up some films that would otherwise not have found a traditional distributor, Netflix also had potential to save filmmakers the time-consuming labor of self-distribution, one factor cited as a positive by the director Adam Leon (quoted in Kenny 2017).

A potential downside was the loss of any prospect of filmmakers benefiting from the "back end" that might result from theatrical box-office success. More conventional sales deals have often involved small payments in advance and much larger ones if a film becomes a hit. Netflix, however, offered more at the start and usually nothing afterward. This, for *The Hollywood Reporter*, was one of the reasons for Netflix's controversial status among filmmakers: "striking a deal with the streaming giant means giving up on the fantasy lurking in the psyche of every producer, director and star: that your movie will become a box-office phenomenon and make you rich" (McClintock 2015b). Large upfront payments also made Netflix unpopular with more traditional rivals, given the likelihood that many indie filmmakers, often struggling financially, would prefer the guarantee of a solid figure now over the promise of future rewards that will usually be unfulfilled, even if some might be prepared to forgo this in favor of theatrical release and the closer individual attention promised by some indie distributors. In some cases, however, this meant the loss of what could potentially be huge dividends, such as those involved in an exceptional case such as Steven Soderbergh's *Magic Mike* (2012), where the $167 million global box office earned the star Channing Tatum payments reportedly totaling $40 million (Pomerantz 2015).

Other sources of complaint relate to what happens to films once they are on the streaming site. Netflix notoriously refuses to divulge viewing figures for individual products, leaving filmmakers with little way of gauging the reach of their work. This was a new situation for the indie scene, as with other sectors of the film market entered by Netflix, although more general worries about reach or promotional spending (and the possibility of "creative" or less than transparent accounting on the part of distributors) were a familiar part of the business. Being available on Netflix made a small indie film potentially available to a far larger audience than it would ever be likely to reach in theaters or through physical video formats, other than in exceptional circumstances. Concerns were often expressed about the risk of individual films disappearing into the huge Netflix catalog, however, as in the "graveyard" characterization provided by Ehrlich. While some films gain attention by their notable acquisition prices, appearances at leading festivals, or limited theatrical releases, many more are destined to have only a low profile. Netflix gives more marketing to some titles than to others, particularly favoring films branded as "Netflix originals" (Dreier 2017).

A key issue is the extent to which Netflix might be seen as offering an illustration of the contentious "long tail" principle advocated by Chris Anderson (2006). The long tail is the term given to what is seen as an extended version of the lower end of a typical product-sales curve, one that falls off from a small number of top sellers at one end to larger numbers of products with very limited sales at the other. The general distinction maps neatly onto the contrast between the Hollywood blockbuster and the smaller indie film, the idea being that sales or distribution online can potentially aggregate the demand for small-niche products to a point that it becomes profitable and a business worth pursuing, for some participants, at least. An important dimension of the long tail concept is the existence of online consumer feedback and recommendations, as I have argued elsewhere, what Anderson terms "an amplified word of mouth" that can offer a form of unpaid-for marketing to products for which paid promotion is not viable (Anderson 2006: 107; King 2014: 118).

One of the most debated features of Netflix is precisely such a system, a recommendations algorithm that provides viewers with suggestions for products identified as similar to those they have previously watched. For advocates, this can benefit less well-known products, drawing attention to films that otherwise would receive little exposure and also leading to recommendations identifying other productions that would struggle to gain any headway within the huge volume of Netflix content, or more generally. How such recommendations actually function was tested, against the thesis of Anderson, in a study by Henry Zhu Tang (2014), using film ratings data released by Netflix (a rare occurrence) as part of a competition held in 2006 to seek to improve its existing system, a collaborative filtering algorithm. Measuring the difference in the responsiveness of demand to ratings (that is, how far viewers take up recommendations), Tang concludes that a distinct "indie" effect is identifiable: that a rating for a niche film appears to be considered more informative and valuable than one for a Hollywood blockbuster, with Netflix serving "to match indie films to users who otherwise could not discover them" (2014: 3). According to Tang's findings, however, Netflix recommendations have limited value in extending the take up of indie films. Recommendations are found to be of greater value to "heavy" users or frequent viewers than in helping to bring together a wider range of different viewing "communities" (2014: 3). Even if it helps consolidate the kind of audience that already exists for small indie films, the recommendation system might not spread the uptake more broadly for films of this kind.

Tang's findings still suggest something of value to the indie community, as opposed to the claim by Ehrlich (2017) that "Netflix doesn't help movies find an audience any more than it helps audiences to find a movie." Indie films available on Netflix can benefit from third-party promotional showcasing, in the form of websites running features with titles such as "The Best Indie Movies on Netflix Right Now" (Toomer 2018). Many such examples exist, along with other "Best [add category] on Netflix" lists (others include Aquino, Eidelstein, Foucault, and Herrera, 2018; Bradshaw, Radford, and Fletcher, 2019). Secondary forums such as these can potentially draw attention to indie films, although they are likely to favor those which are already relatively better known.

However effective its recommendation system might be in widening audiences for indies, Netflix has been praised by some for what *Indiewire* terms "leaning into under-served audience segments," its production pipeline for 2018 including five features from women filmmakers, among them Nicole Holofcener's *The Land of Steady Habits* (Thompson 2018). That might be a small proportion overall, but was deemed to be notable, in a context in which women have struggled disproportionately to be able to sustain ongoing careers. Ashok Amritraj, chairman and chief executive of Hyde Park Entertainment Group, has viewed Netflix as enhancing racial diversity and gender equality in the film business (Chmielewski 2018). This sentiment was echoed by Charles King, head of the company behind *Mudbound*, the focus of which includes struggles against racism in rural Mississippi after the Second World War. After acquiring the film at Sundance, Netflix committed to an Academy Awards campaign – a key promotional investment – that resulted in four nominations. *Mudbound* was subsequently included in a "Black Lives Matter" themed collection on Netflix, created two weeks after the company became one of the first major media players to declare its support for the anti-racist movement during protests that followed the killing of George Floyd in May 2020 (Spangler 2020; Low and Yap 2020). This joined other collections related to black creators or subjects, including "Black Behind the Camera" and "Black & Queer" (Spangler 2020). The company has also received praise for playing a leading role in increased inclusivity more broadly, a perceived value it shares with the indie film sector, including from LGBTQ+ sources (see, e.g., Damshenas 2020).

If we consider Netflix's own specific benefits from investing in the indie sector, beyond the general aim to offer a wide range of material, these seem likely to lie in the potential some indies can offer for "quality" branding. On the one hand, picking up or funding a substantial number of smaller films provides an inexpensive way of filling out the company's roster, a key feature of which is to offer breadth of choice. On the other, the attention gained by higher-profile releases, often those branded as "Netflix Originals, sees the company marking a claim to offer distinctive, more artistic material. Highlighting "quality" work, even if representing only a minority of the overall output, had been established at the time as an effective way of promoting television channels (e.g., AMC with series including *Mad Men* [2007–2015] and *Breaking Bad* [2008–2013]), a role that might be performed by certain indie releases or productions from Netflix (examples including *Beasts of No Nation, Mudbound, Roma,* and others with quality/indie cachet such as *The Laundromat, The Irishman,* and *The Two Popes* [Fernando Meirelles, 2019]).

For some commentators, any Netflix indie "bubble" was set to burst by the late 2010s. One "prominent film agent" involved in the indie sector was quoted as suggesting that the streaming giant was shifting away from such films to focus on larger-scale productions that were more likely to make a bigger splash on release (Chmielewski 2018). A similar conclusion was reached by others and seen as marked by the absence of acquisitions at Sundance 2018. It was suggested that Netflix was no longer prepared to pay higher prices for indie films that it could obtain at a later stage through the ongoing library deals it had with studios or other distributors (Lopez, 2018, citing a report in *Business Insider*). On the other hand, embarking on what was described as "Netflix's biggest commitment to theatrical exhibition in a single movie season" (Sharf 2019) in the fall of 2019, including the examples cited above, could be interpreted as an attempt to answer some of the company's indie-sector critics.

Overall, assessing what Netflix, or other such operations, contribute to the American indie sector – whether as opportunity or threat, game-changer, or source of continuity – remains open to debate and is subject to future developments. The threat posed by such companies to the dominance of the Hollywood majors is significant, particularly in online distribution. Writing before the concerted moves into the indie sector detailed above, Stuart Cunningham and Jon Silver saw evidence that developments up to that point had presaged "real change" (2013: 5). Despite historical precursors suggesting emergent large-scale online corporations would be likely to follow the tendencies of established entities – that is, use their market power to limit competition – Cunningham and Silver argued that the challenge to existing players presented by the new video-on-demand services "may be good news for independents around the world" because of the widening numbers of available distribution platforms (p. 5). The accession of Netflix to the MPA might suggest otherwise, or at least that the company had by 2019 come to share some broad interests in common with the Hollywood studios, if still as competitors – as the latter start to launch their own streaming services and as Netflix and other online enterprises that have moved into production join existing anti-piracy campaigns (Johnson 2019).

It is not easy to come to a single conclusion on how this might be judged in the wake of the role Netflix came to play in the following years. Potentially the company might be seen as a "bullying" presence but one that helped many filmmakers by either providing distribution that might otherwise be unavailable or by paying high acquisition fees. The verdict is likely to differ across varying positions within the sector: for example, between filmmakers happy to accept the benefits that Netflix can offer and smaller rival distributors or filmmakers worried about lost opportunities for theatrical distribution. As Cunningham and Silver argue, critics often over- or under-read change of the kind represented by the move of online giants into film (p. 5). More useful, as they suggest, is a "middle way" between alternative rhetorics, one I adopt here (as in King 2014) in trying to balance notions of change and continuity. A much-debated issue following from the question of the impact of Netflix on the indie sector has been what potential might exist for the creation of an alternative "indie Netflix," dedicated to the speciality realm of indie or international art cinema. A number of potential candidates have been identified (see, e.g., Schoenbrun 2016) but at the time of writing no single, clear occupier of such a position was in place. One prominent but corporate-owned contender, FilmStruck, closed in 2018. Any enterprise involved in this arena is likely to find itself in a position broadly similar to that taken by smaller distributors in the past: promising greater individual and special attention to individual films, but facing very familiar pressures from bigger corporate rivals such as Netflix and others; or, as with FilmStruck, owned by a larger entity (in that case Warner Media) but vulnerable to the tendencies of big corporations to favor mass over niche market initiatives.

# References

Aquino, T., Eidelstein, E., Foucault, M., and Herrera, A. (2018) "The Best Independent Movies on Netflix Right Now," *Complex*, April 30, available at www.complex.com/pop-culture/the-25-best-independent-movies-streaming-on-netflix-right-now/i-dont-feel-at-home-in-this-world-anymore (accessed November 1, 2018)

Anderson, C. (2006) *The Long Tail: How Endless Choice is Creating Unlimited Demand*, London: Random House.

Biba, E. (2006) "Netflix Presents," *Wired*, September 1, available at www.wired.com/2006/09/netflix-5/ (accessed November 1, 2018)

Bradshaw, P., Radford, I., and Fletcher, R. (2019) "17 Underappreciated Films to Watch on Netflix UK," *Den of Greek*, October 8, available at www.denofgeek.com/uk/movies/netflix-uk/34709/underappreciated-netflix-movies-hidden-gems-uk (accessed November 1,2018)

Chmielewski, D. (2018) "Netflix Accused of Favoring Tentpoles Over Indies," *Deadline Hollywood*, June 9, available at https://deadline.com/2018/06/netflix-tentpoles-over-indies-produced-by-1202407107/ (accessed November 1, 2018)

Cunningham, S. and Silver, J. (2013) *Screen Distribution and the New King Kongs of the Online World*, Basingstoke: Palgrave Macmillan.

Damshenas, S. (2020) "42 of the Best LGBTQ+ Shows You Can Watch Right Now on Netflix: Representation for the LGBTQ+ Community Has 'Never' Been Better," *Gay Times*, July 21, available at www.gaytimes.co.uk/culture/the-best-lgbtq-inclusive-shows-you-can-watch-right-now-on-netflix/ (accessed August 10, 2020)

Desta, Y. (2017) "Amazon and Netflix Race to Outspend Each Other at Sundance," *Vanity Fair*, January 25, available at www.vanityfair.com/hollywood/2017/01/sundance-netflix-amazon (accessed November 1, 2018)

Donnelly, M. (2017) "Toronto Film Market: Indie Distributors Struggle as Netflix, Amazon Look to Dominate (Again)," *The Wrap*, September 7, available at www.thewrap.com/toronto-film-market-indie-distributors-struggle-netflix-amazon/ (accessed November 1, 2018)

Dreier, T. (2017) "How Netflix and Amazon are Changing the Indie Movie Business," *Streaming Media*, July 28, available at www.streamingmedia.com/Articles/ReadArticle.aspx?ArticleID=119614&PageNum=2 (accessed November 1, 2018)

Ehrlich, D. (2017) "Netflix Keeps Buying Great Movies, So It's a Shame They're Getting Buried," *IndieWire*, April 17, available at www.indiewire.com/2017/04/netflix-bad-for-movies-theaters-okja-tramps-1201806272/ (accessed November 1, 2018)

Gleiberman, O. (2019) "Steven Spielberg vs. Netflix: A Preview of the War for Cinema's Future," *Variety*, March 10, available at https://variety.com/2019/film/columns/steven-spielberg-vs-netflix-a-preview-of-the-war-for-cinemas-future-1203159522/ (accessed November 1, 2018)

Jesdanun, A. (2008) "Netflix Shuts Movie Financing Arm to Focus on Core," Associated Press, July 23, available at https://web.archive.org/web/20080726232337/http://ap.google.com/article/ALeqM5iKwZUPaTeYqpyM5ombXf-AXxTVoAD923Q2G01 (accessed November 1, 2018)

Johnson, T. (2019) "Netflix Joins the Motion Picture Association of America," *Variety*, January 22, available at https://variety.com/2019/biz/news/netflix-mpaa-1203114133/ (accessed August 11, 2020)

Kenny, G. (2017) "With 'Tramps', Netflix Digs Deeper for Original Films," *The New York Times*, April 14, available at www.nytimes.com/2017/04/14/movies/tramps-netflix-adam-leon.html (accessed November 1, 2018)

King, G. (2014) *Indie 2.0: Change and Continuity in Contemporary American Indie Film*. London: I.B. Tauris.

Kuchera, B. (2018) "Netflix and the 'Stolen' indies," *Polygon*, January 1, available at www.polygon.com/2018/1/1/16829714/netflix-movies-independent-film-theater-amazon (accessed November 1, 2018)

Lang, B. (2018a) "Sundance: Changing of the Guard Opens Door for Forward-Thinking Players," *Variety*, January 17, available at https://variety.com/2018/biz/news/sundance-changing-landscape-1202665638/ (accessed November 1, 2018)

Lang, B. (2018b) "Tom Quinn on How Neon Nailed the Landing With 'I Tonya'," *Variety*, February 22, available at https://variety.com/2018/film/features/neon-margot-robbie-i-tonya-1202706572/ (accessed November 1, 2018)

Lopez, M. (2018) "Netflix and Amazon Leave Sundance with Zero Films for the First Time in Two Years," *The Wrap*, January 29, available at www.thevideoink.com/2018/01/29/netflix-amazon-leave-sundance-zero-films-first-time-two-years/ (accessed November 1, 2018)

Low, E. and Yap, A.C. (2020) "Netflix, Hulu, Amazon, HBO and Other Hollywood Players Take a Stand in Support of Black Lives Matter Movement Amid George Floyd Protests," *Variety*, May 30, available at https://variety.com/2020/tv/news/netflix-hulu-amazon-hbo-black-lives-matter-george-floyd-protests-1234621292/ (accessed August 10, 2020).

Lyttelton, O. (2016) "Disruptors: How Netflix and Amazon Are Creating Greater Tumult in the American Independent Film Industry," *IndieWire*, February 9, available at www.indiewire.com/2016/02/disruptors-how-netflix-amazon-are-creating-greater-tumult-in-the-independent-film-industry-272596/ (accessed November 1, 2018).

McClintock, P. (2015a) "Most Theater Circuits Won't Screen Netflix's War Drama 'Beasts of No Nation'," *The Hollywood Reporter*, March 3, available at www.hollywoodreporter.com/news/theater-circuits-wont-screen-netflixs-778993 (accessed November 1, 2018).

McClintock, P. (2015b) "Netflix Movies: Producers Weigh Hidden Downsides," *The Hollywood Reporter*, March 19, available at www.hollywoodreporter.com/news/netflix-movies-producers-weigh-hidden-782403 (accessed November 1, 2018).

Pomerantz, D. (2015) "How the Netflix Model Can Screw Filmmakers," *Forbes*, March 19, available at www.forbes.com/sites/dorothypomerantz/2015/03/19/how-the-netflix-model-could-screw-filmmakers/#4cf5f43d3c47 (accessed November 1, 2018).

Schoenbrun, D. (2016) "Can There be an 'Indie Netflix'?" *Filmmaker*, November 7, available at https://filmmakermagazine.com/100514-can-there-be-an-indie-netflix/ (accessed November 1, 2018).

Sharf, Z. (2019) "Netflix Commits to Exclusive Theatrical Releases for 'Marriage Story', 'The King', and 8 More Fall Films," *IndieWire*, August 27, available at www.indiewire.com/2019/08/netflix-theatrical-releases-marriage-story-the-king-fall-films-1202168980/ (accessed November 1, 2018).

Spangler, T. (2020) "Netflix Launches 'Black Lives Matter' Collection of Movies, TV Shows and Documentaries," *Variety*, June 10, available at https://variety.com/2020/digital/news/netflix-black-lives-matter-collection-1234630160/ (accessed August 10, 2020).

Tang, H. Z. (2014) "The Collaborative Filtering Effect of Netflix Ratings for Indie Films versus Blockbusters and Heavy Users versus Casual Users," thesis for Department of Economics, Stanford University, available at https://economics.stanford.edu/sites/default/files/publications/henrytanghonorsthesismay2014.pdf (accessed November 1, 2018).

Thompson, A. (2017) "Broad Green: How Wall Street Wealth, A-List Talent, and Brash Decisions Made an Indie Player Implode," *IndieWire*, August 2, available at www.indiewire.com/2017/08/broad-green-shuts-down-production-lays-off-staff-1201862906/ (accessed November 1, 2018).

Thompson, A. (2018) "Meet Netflix's Indie Content Team, at Sundance and Beyond," *IndieWire*, January 28, available at www.indiewire.com/2018/01/netflix-indie-content-production-sundance-2018-private-life-1201921906/ (accessed November 1, 2018).

Toomer, J. (2018) "The Best Indie Movies on Netflix Right Now," *Uproxx*, October 4, available at https://uproxx.com/movies/best-indie-movies-on-netflix-right-now/ (accessed November 1, 2018).

# 23

# USER AS ASSET, MUSIC AS LIABILITY

## The moral economy of the "value gap" in a platform musical economy

*Andrew Leyshon and Allan Watson*

The rise of streaming platforms such as Spotify and Apple Music has stabilized the market for recorded music after nearly 20 years of revenue decline. But they have also transformed the bases of competition as they relentlessly pursue a winner-takes-all dynamic that forces out less successful firms (Kenney and Zysman 2018). Streaming platforms have quelled anxieties about the long-term survival of the market for recorded music but have brought to the surface new concerns about the equity implications of this development. Fairness, or rather a sense that structural changes in the musical economy have brought about an inequity that is manifestly unfair to economic agents that have traditionally been most invested in the music industry, has emerged as a recurring theme among many commentators and musical economy practitioners (Arditi 2013, 2015). In criticizing the rise of digital platforms, and their unerring ability to capture markets and revenue, market participants and commentators have implicitly drawn on *moral economy* arguments to make the case for some kind of restitution in favor of those who have lost out, appealing to public policy to seek redress or supporting further rounds of innovation and disruption that might unseat the new incumbents from their dominant positions.

Arguments about the fairness of a new digital settlement within the musical economy have circulated not only within the corporate suites of the large record labels but also among musicians. Numerous leading artists have boycotted, withdrawn catalog from, or engaged only reluctantly with Spotify and other streaming services in opposition to the low rates of return they receive from the playing of their music on such platforms (Hesmondhalgh 2020). Very few artists spoke out in support of streaming platforms. Those that did adopted a stance that might be described as "market realist" in tone. For example, Dave Allen (2013), former member of Gang of Four, argued that while the internet certainly brought fundamental change to the musical economy, there is little place for nostalgia given the music industry's tradition of exploiting artists. Moreover, the industry has no special case for market protection given the ways in which a wide range of other industries were radically transformed through the advent of e-commence at first and then digital platforms like Spotify. Musicians, like it or not, Allen argued, simply must make the best of the transformations unfolding in front of them.

This chapter seeks to explore the disjuncture in the musical economy brought about by the emergence of digital platforms that have revealed highly contested understandings about

DOI: 10.4324/9780429275340-27

the place of musicians within a market economy, the role of technological change, and the extent to which a lay understanding of moral economy has been mobilized to understand the implications of these changes. Initially, the discussion provides a brief account of the recovery of the musical economy following the crisis of the early twenty-first century, before the second part looks at the rise of platforms in the musical economy through the emergence of music streaming services. The third part critically evaluates moral economy claims of structural unfairness within the contemporary musical economy, made both by industry practitioners and sympathetic academics.

## The post-crisis musical economy

The causes of the decline and fall of the recorded music industry from the late 1990s onward are well known (e.g., Arditi 2015; Leyshon 2014; Morris 2015). In short, the rise of MP3 disrupted the ways in which such format changes in the musical economy had previously been managed. In the past, the music industry organized to first resist and then negotiate with large technology companies to ensure that new formats would not undermine returns on intellectual property rights in sound recordings (Knopper, 2009). However, MP3 was an "accidental format," escaping from the emerging online worlds of software programmers and hackers, so there were no large companies to engage, and the format was eagerly seized on by a growing wave of peer-to-peer (P2P) networks, many initially supported by venture capital funding (Leyshon 2014). These networks operated as illegal digital intermediaries using the promise of free access to music catalogs to attract users to the networks, which then sold advertising and, in some cases, malware, generating revenues for network owners.

Some compensation for the decline in income from recorded music sales came from live performance, inverting the traditional music industry business model. Whereas previously, artists would tour to promote album sales, the decline in revenue from recorded music meant that most artists – save for those with a large and storied "back catalog" – were required to record new music to generate interest in live performance. According to Krueger (2019: loc 638), the leading 48 touring acts of 2017 made on average 80 percent of total income from performances, with only 15 percent from recorded music and just 5 percent from publishing fees. As the cost of purchasing recorded music per capita fell, consuming became something akin to a metered utility as streaming platforms made a vast repertoire of recorded music available, either for a set monthly fee or free subject to exposure to advertising. In turn, the experience of consuming live music was more highly valued (Behr, Brennan, and Cloonan 2016; Naveed, Watanabe, and Neittaanmäaki 2017; Simon 2019), with ticket prices increasing as sales of record music fell (Krueger 2005, 2019). Revenues from live performance first overtook recorded music in the UK as early as 2008, and by 2010 in the rest of the world (Leyshon 2014). In the UK context, by 2018, live music doubled revenues from recorded music, and employed six times as many workers (Table 23.1).

While welcome, revenues for live only tempered and did not reverse the overall decline. It was not until 2016 when, after nearly 20 years of decline, revenues across the music industry finally began to increase again. By 2019, total global revenues had returned to levels last seen in the mid-2000s (IFPI 2020). This recovery was driven overwhelmingly by the income generated by streaming services, which in less than 10 years emerged to become the dominant mode of music distribution. Between 2016 and 2019, music revenue growth averaged 8 percent per annum, with streaming revenues accounting for over 56 percent of total industry revenues (Table 23.2).

Table 23.1 Revenue and employment by UK music industry sector (2018)

| Music industry sectors | Gross value added that is, grand total of all revenues, from final sales and (net) subsidies, which are incomes into businesses | | Exports that is, total export revenue equals the total receipts generated from music within all sectors from outside the UK | | Employment that is, full-time equivalent | |
|---|---|---|---|---|---|---|
| | (£bn) | % | (£bn) | % | Total | % |
| Music creators (musicians, singers, composers, songwriters, lyricists, producers, and engineers) | 2.5 | 48.1 | 1.1 | 40.7 | 139,352 | 24.3 |
| Live music | 1.1 | 22.2 | 0.8 | 29.6 | 30,529 | 16.0 |
| Recorded music | 0.6 | 11.5 | 0.5 | 18.5 | 5,379 | 2.8 |
| Music publishing | 0.5 | 9.6 | 0.6 | 22.2 | 1,363 | 0.7 |
| Music retail | 0.4 | 7.6 | 0.2 | 7.4 | 11,688 | 6.1 |
| Music representatives | 0.2 | 3.8 | 0.4 | 14.8 | 2,624 | 1.3 |
| **Total** | **5.2** | **100** | **2.7** | **100** | **190,935** | **100** |

Source: UK Music (2019).

Table 23.2 Global music revenue growth per annum (2016–2019)

| | 2016 | 2017 | 2018 | 2019 |
|---|---|---|---|---|
| Total global revenue growth | 5.9 | 8.1 | 9.7 | 8.2 |
| Digital/streaming share of total revenues★ | 50.0 | 54.0 | 46.8 | 56.1 |
| Streaming revenue growth | 60.4 | 41.0 | 32.9 | 22.9 |

Note:

★ In 2016 and 2107 streaming revenue was included with wider digital revenues.

Sources: IFPI (2017, 2018, 2019, 2020).

Therefore, the rise of digital platforms in the music industry would seem to have helped first stem the losses of the early twenty-first century and then began to drive growth for the first time in almost two decades. While this recovery quelled fears that the industry might be in terminal decline, new concerns emerged about the equity implications of the reconfigured music industry. We return to this subject in the third section of the chapter, but we next examine the logics of the platform economy of which music streaming services are a constituent part.

## The rise of the platform economy

The dot.com boom of the late 1990s consolidated the rise of web-based and e-commerce business and laid the foundation for the rise of P2P networks that went on to destabilize the musical economy. Indeed, P2P networks were prototypes for the emergent platform businesses that became dominant across a range of economic sectors. P2P networks acted as intermediaries, using music files to link users to advertisers and, on occasion, also to malware coders.

Intermediation is a key part of the platform mode of business organization (Kenney and Zysman 2020; Langley and Leyshon 2017; van Dijck, Poell, and De Waal 2019). The internet solved the problem of two-sided or multi-sided markets in new ways, where economic agents connect with each other to transact. Exemplars of intermediation within two- or multi-sided markets include entities such as physical place-based exchanges, such as stock or commodities markets, which host buyers and sellers (for a fee). Other examples include transaction systems, such as credit and debit cards (e.g., Visa), that act as a form of payment between buyer and vendor to the mutual benefit of both (with an interchange fee charged to vendors). The underlying intermediary logic of platforms is that they solve coordination problems in market exchange by extending the networking capacities of the internet first identified in its growing use and application during the mid-1990s.

The rise of the platform organization has been accelerated through processes of capitalization and assetization (Muniesa, Doganova, Ortiz, Pina-Stranger, Paterson, Bourgoin, Ehrenstein, Juven, Pontille, Saraç-Lesavre, and Yon 2017; Birch and Muniesa 2020). Waves of new technology companies have been fueled by venture capital and other forms of investment driving the companies to grow quickly and to "scale" to levels where they may become public companies, offering large financial windfalls to their founders and investors. A key part of building this value is "turning things into assets" that can generate both income and value into the future (Birch and Muniesa 2020: 4). These assets are used to extract rents, usually in one of two ways (Langley and Leyshon 2017). First, through direct rent on "constrained" or "closed" platforms, which earn income from the circulations that they intermediate by charging users (vendors, borrowers, those with assets to share, etc.) directly for transacting via their infrastructures. Second, through income generated from automated targeted advertising, data harvesting, and analytics where users make payments to platforms through giving attention, providing information, or expressing affiliation, "which … can be sold to advertising companies and market researchers who require access to users, their content, and their networks" (O'Dwyer 2015: 234–235).

Streaming and social media platforms can generate significant revenues through intermediating performers and audiences (*The Economist* 2016). For example, the website Sheepstat. com estimates the revenues of YouTube performers based on channel subscriptions and views, indicating the value of their audiences to advertisers. One of the most consistently followed YouTube performers is Felix Kjellberg, better known by his onscreen nickname, "PewDiePie." Mainly posting comedic vlogs and commentaries on video games, by October 2020 Kjellberg's channel had over 100 million subscribers with over 26 billion views. Statsheep.com estimates the potential advertising revenue that social media influencers can earn based on subscription and viewing numbers for two-week windows. Between September 28 and October 11, 2020, Kjellberg's earnings from advertising were estimated at between $50,763 and $253,817 (*StatSheep* 2020). At the lowest end this works out at $1.3 million per annum, and at the upper end $6.6 million per annum. YouTube, which is part of Google, earns its income by charging commissions at a rate of around 45 percent of these revenues (based on the above, either $585,000 or $3.0 million per annum). In this regard, social media platforms resemble record companies in building diverse rosters of performers who might appeal to different audiences and taking their share as tastes change and develop.

However, the stakes for music streaming platforms are higher, as they are working with an existing industry that has a tradition of established legal rights and intellectual property protection, which necessitates balancing assets with liabilities. This dilemma is explored in more detail with the next section, which also addresses the moral economy of the platform musical economy.

## The platform music industry as a moral economy

As the survivors of the MP3 crisis of the early twenty-first century surveyed the new terrain of a streaming dominated musical economy, they became agitated about the terms of exchange with streaming platforms. Practitioners and commentators alike developed criticisms that implicitly evoked normative arguments about fairness and equity associated with the concept of *moral economy*. This idea reveals a concern with "the moral norms and sentiments that structure and influence economic practices, both formal and informal, and the way in which these are reinforced, compromised or overridden by economic pressures" (Sayer 2007: 262).

It is an approach particularly associated with academic work that has sought to question the ways in which mainstream neoclassical economics narrowed the focus of how an economy is understood. As Buck-Morss (1995: 460) has argued, the discipline of economics has successfully reduced understandings of what an economy should be through a narrow identification of " 'laws' that account for regularities of market behavior as a self-interested rationality of means, while ... remain[ing] totally indifferent to the normative questions about the reasonableness of individual motives or the substantive rationality of social end." While normative issues of rights and responsibilities were key concerns of the classical economists that preceded the neoclassical "marginal revolution," these ideas were quickly discarded through a new focus on utility, where the cold logic of self-interest and the dynamics of markets were identified as the processes that would bring the best possible outcomes. These outcomes, by their very nature, would be amoral. A focus on moral economy faded in economics and was confined to cognate disciplines such as economic history, sociology, and anthropology, but even here interest ebbed and flowed over time (Götz 2015; Jessop and Sum 2019).

One place where one might not expect to see a revival of interest in the moral economy would be in the main professional body for global music, the International Federation of the Photographic Industry (IFPI). Since at least 2016 – coinciding both with platforms assuming a position of dominance within the musical economy and the recovery of global music industry revenues – the IFPI and major record companies have been critical of what they describe as a "value gap" in the industry; that is, a structural underpayment of royalties to artists (Arditi 2019). In 2017, the IFPI's annual *Global Music Report* even included a dedicated section titled "Rewarding Creativity: Fixing the Value Gap," setting out its understanding of the problem:

> significant challenges need to be overcome if the industry is going to move to sustainable growth. The whole music sector has united in its effort to fix the fundamental flaw in today's music market, known as "the value gap," where fair revenues are not being returned to those who are now creating and investing in music. The value gap is now the single highest legislative priority as it seeks to create a level playing field for the digital market and secure the future of the industry.
>
> *IFPI 2017: 24*

From the perspective of the IFPI and its supporters, the cause of the value gap was initially the decline of revenues arising from the disruption of the record music industry by P2P networks in the early twentieth century, and the failures of direct download and streaming services to restore the rates of return previously delivered by physical formats despite their later contributions to income recovery. Jonathan Taplin, previously manager of critically acclaimed and commercially successful act The Band, described how the advent of free downloading in the late 1990s dramatically undermined the standard of living enjoyed by his former employers:

groups like The Band had some assurance that, if their music was of lasting quality, they could continue to reap financial rewards long after they'd stopped writing new music. When the CD format was introduced in the early 1980s, their record royalties jumped as old fans bought The Band's classic albums on disc. That royalty stream continued right up until the introduction of Napster in 2000. And then it ended. It was horrifying to see The Band members go from a decent royalty income of around $100,000 per year to almost nothing.

*Taplin 2017: 41–42*

Taplin was particularly aggrieved at the fate that befell The Band's drummer and vocalist, Levon Helm. He was diagnosed with throat cancer in 1998, just as P2P networks began to erode royalty income, and faced the dilemma of paying his medical bills as his royalty income withered away:

he couldn't go on the road because he could hardly sing. Eventually he figured out how to do something by having shows at his house, getting a bunch of friends to come and play and calling it the Midnight Rambles. He made a little money, but not enough, just barely paid his bills. It just seemed incredibly *unfair* to me.

*emphasis added, Taplin quoted in Schechter 2017*

Taplin's (2017) entanglement within this personal tragedy motivated him to develop a critique of Silicon Valley as a whole, which he blamed for enabling free downloading sites he described as "bloodsuckers who made millions off the hard work of musicians" (Taplin 2012). The initial target of Taplin's ire was the first wave of P2P networks such as Napster, the Pirate Bay, and other companies that developed business models based on a flagrant disregard of copyright law so that no incomes flowed directly to owners of the intellectual property rights in recorded music. But from the late 2000s onward, both his and the wider music industry's criticism moved to authorized streaming platforms as they introduced business models that combined the demand for instant online music created by P2P networks with provision of a regular income stream to copyright holders.

One of the issues for this criticism was the rate at which rights holders were paid per stream, which at only fractions of a cent were also known as "penny streams" (Hesmondhalgh 2020). The small rates were considered by artists and their representatives as derisory, particularly when compared to the rates per unit for physical products such as CDs. Beginning in 2014, *The Trichordist* website – "a community blog for those interested in contributing to the advancement of a Sustainable and Ethical Internet for the protection of Artists Rights in the Digital Age," which declares itself to be "work[ing] towards defining and setting a fair per stream rate" (*The Trichordist* n.d.) – began posting details on royalty rates per stream for different music platforms. This data was released to them by one independent record label, with a 150-album catalog that generated well over 100 million streams from 30 platforms. Table 23.3 compares streaming rates for this label between 2016 and 2019. The fact that each play, or stream, of a song generates at best only a tenth of a cent and at worst a thousand of a cent helped fuel arguments about a value gap and failure to pay "just" returns. Publishing this information in aggregate form provided some heft to reports emanating from numerous musicians over several years aggrieved about how little income they received from the streaming of their repertoire, especially when compared to CD sales. For example, cellist Zoe Keating publicly revealed that in 2018 that she earned just $21,000 from over 4.6 million streams across 11 platforms (Hesmondhalgh 2020: 6).

On the face of it, it does seem remarkable that millions of streams can produce such relatively modest revenues. However, there are at least three related reasons that help explain this. First, once a revenue rate is set at a fraction of a monetary unit, then simple arithmetic calculation means that a very large number of plays are needed to generate significant monetary returns. For example, one figure that has been used by advocates of the value gap is the number of individual streams required to generate the United States monthly minimum wage from streaming alone. With the US rate set at $7.25 per hour, many accounts use a monthly gross minimum wage of around $1,400 as a benchmark, or about 200 hours per month. In 2018, even streaming on Akazoo, the most generous platform (paying $0.37847 per stream), according to the data presented in Table 23.3, would have required 19 steams per hour to generate $7.25, and 3,700 streams to generate a monthly wage of $1,400. But Akazoo was a relatively obscure platform and accounted for a very small percentage of total streams for the label's catalog, making it an unreliable source of regular income at scale. By 2019, Akazoo was no longer among the top 30 streaming platforms, and the most generous rate was now offered by Peloton, an exercise and equipment platform. At $0.03107 per stream, Peloton offered less than a tenth of what Akazoo had returned in 2016, and required 233 streams per hour to reach $7.25. Given that Spotify accounted for the largest share of the label's total stream revenue in both 2016 and 2019, this platform is a better reference point. At $0.00348 per stream in 2019, it would require over 2,000 streams per hour to generate the minimum wage and over 400,000 streams per month. This is clearly possible, as some superstar artists record tens of millions of streams per month and the most listened to song on Spotify has generated nearly 2.5 billion steams.[1] But, most artists are not superstars, and so are unable to generate streams on such a scale. Moreover, as Table 23.3 suggests, streaming rates per song are in decline, falling from an average of $0.00395 in 2016, to $0.00173 in 2019.

Second, stream rates are a product of the music platform business model. Streaming platforms were only able to replace P2P platforms as the main intermediary in the consumer market for digital music by ensuring the barriers to entry for consumers were low and would encourage users to move from systems that appeared free at the point of use to another system that would at least commit to providing revenues streams to rights holders. For example, a key part of Spotify's strategy and attempt to enroll the record industry into its project was to present itself as *"the* solution to illicit downloading" (original emphasis Eriksson, Fleischer, Johansson, Snickars, and Vonderau 2019: 7). To do so, Spotify also had to enroll users who had previously been using P2P networks, which were ostensibly free at the point of use, exposure to advertising and malware notwithstanding. Weaning users off such networks meant that Spotify and other streaming platforms rolled out dual use membership modes with an advertising-supported "freemium" model on the one hand, and a subscription-based model on the other. A key objective was to move P2P users from the free-advertising model to becoming feepayers in an advertising-free premium tier of membership, but with an understanding that fees needed to be low enough to represent value to users habituated to obtaining such services for free, subject to the inconveniences and disruption of advertising content (Eriksson, Fleischer, Johansson, Snickars, and Vonderau 2019).

However, the recruitment of these *assets* – advertising consuming users or fee-paying subscribers – needed to be reconciled on the platform balance sheet with *liabilities* – the payments for each stream made to rights owners. Such payments were never a consideration for illegal P2P networks. Ideally, platforms would have an all-subscription service, facilitating better management of assets and liabilities, with an effective process of capitalization through direct revenue. Some platforms, such as Apple Music for example, have achieved this. Apple was, however, already a large technology company and so had the advantage of having a wider

*Table 23.3* Music streaming platforms, revenues, and users for one independent record label (2016 and 2019)

| Rank by revenue share (2019) | Music streaming platform | Average $ per stream | | Total streams of label roster (%) | | Total stream revenue of label roster (%) | | Streams per song | | Streams per album | |
|---|---|---|---|---|---|---|---|---|---|---|---|
| | | 2016 | 2019 | 2016 | 2019 | 2016 | 2019 | 2016 | 2019 | 2016 | 2019 |
| 1 | Spotify | 0.00437 | 0.00348 | 62.97 | 22.09 | 69.57 | 44.33 | 139 | 175 | 1,394 | 1,752 |
| 2 | Apple Music | 0.00735 | 0.00675 | 7.18 | 6.36 | 13.35 | 24.79 | 83 | 90 | 828 | 902 |
| 3 | You Tube Content ID | N/A | 0.00022 | — | 51.00 | — | 6.42 | — | 2,794 | — | 27,940 |
| 4 | Amazon Unlimited | — | 0.01123 | — | 0.83 | — | 5.35 | — | 542 | — | 542 |
| 5 | Deezer | 0.00640 | 0.00562 | 2.19 | 0.80 | 3.54 | 2.58 | 95 | 108 | 952 | 1,048 |
| 6 | Google Play | 0.00676 | 0.00554 | 2.36 | 0.79 | 4.03 | 2.54 | 90 | 110 | 901 | 1,099 |
| 7 | Pandora | 0.00133 | 0.00203 | 0.07 | 1.91 | 0.02 | 2.24 | 456 | 299 | 4,565 | 2,993 |
| 8 | YouTube | 0.00069 | 0.00154 | 21.70 | 1.90 | 3.81 | 1.70 | 876 | 395 | 8,764 | 3,947 |
| 9 | Amazon Music | 0.00402 | 0.01123 | 0.63 | 0.65 | 0.64 | 1.60 | 151 | 143 | 1,515 | 1,431 |
| 10 | Facebook | — | 0.05705 | — | 0.05 | — | 1.56 | — | 11 | — | 107 |
| 11 | YouTube Red | — | 0.01009 | — | 0.23 | — | 1.37 | — | 60 | — | 604 |
| 12 | Peloton | — | 0.03107 | — | 0.07 | — | 1.28 | — | 20 | — | 196 |
| 13 | TaiHe Music Group | — | 0.00044 | — | 4.92 | — | 1.25 | — | 1,386 | — | 13,862 |
| 14 | Yandex LLC | 0.00016 | 0.00109 | 0.77 | 0.93 | 0.03 | 0.58 | 3,744 | 559 | 37,444 | 5,585 |
| 15 | Tidal | 0.01250 | 0.00876 | 0.10 | 0.11 | 0.33 | 0.58 | 49 | 70 | 487 | 695 |
| 16 | Rhapsody/Napster | 0.01900 | 0.00916 | 0.52 | 0.07 | 2.52 | 0.37 | 32 | 66 | 321 | 665 |
| 17 | TDC Play | — | 0.00994 | — | 0.06 | — | 0.37 | — | 61 | — | 612 |
| 18 | LOEN | — | 0.00235 | — | 0.13 | — | 0.18 | — | 259 | — | 2,594 |
| 19 | UMA | — | 0.00022 | — | 1.17 | — | 0.15 | — | 2,779 | — | 27,794 |
| 20 | PlayNetwork | 0.00065 | 0.00032 | 0.07 | 0.67 | 0.12 | 0.12 | 943 | 1,916 | 9,429 | 19.157 |
| 21 | Telecom Italia | 0.02189 | 0.01693 | 0.04 | 0.01 | 0.25 | 0.09 | 28 | 36 | 278 | 360 |

| | | | | | | | | | | | |
|---|---|---|---|---|---|---|---|---|---|---|---|
| 22 | KKBOX | 0.00358 | 0.00408 | 0.74 | 0.04 | 0.12 | 0.09 | 170 | 149 | 1,701 | 1,492 |
| 23 | VEVO | — | 0.00083 | — | 0.13 | — | 0.06 | — | 737 | — | 7,374 |
| 24 | Slacker | 0.00442 | 0.00713 | 0.02 | 0.01 | 0.03 | 0.06 | 138 | 85 | 1,379 | 854 |
| 25 | iHeartRadio | — | 0.01798 | — | 0.01 | — | 0.05 | — | 34 | — | 339 |
| 26 | LINE | — | 0.00970 | — | 0.01 | — | 0.05 | — | 63 | — | 628 |
| 27 | iMusica | — | 0.02247 | — | 0.00 | — | 0.05 | — | 27 | — | 271 |
| 28 | Bugs Corporation | — | 0.00427 | — | 0.01 | — | 0.03 | — | 143 | — | 1,426 |
| 29 | Reliance Jio | — | 0.00133 | — | 0.02 | — | 0.02 | — | 346 | — | 3,463 |
| 30 | Gaana | — | 0.00133 | — | 0.02 | — | 0.01 | — | 457 | — | 4,575 |
| | **Total** | **0.00395★** | **0.00173** | | | | | **154★** | **352** | **1,540★** | **3,516** |

★ Average includes data from MSPs in leading 30 platforms for 2016 but that did not rank in in 2019

*Source: The Trichordist* (2017, 2020).

portfolio of revenues that could cross subsidize the new service as it became established. Such breathing room was unavailable to startup platforms that, while cosseted by large volumes of venture capital funds (Srnicek 2016), were nevertheless on relatively tight deadlines to grow their business and scale to a size that it could be "cashed out" through an IPO providing returns to investors (Langley and Leyshon 2017).

For this reason, platforms such as Spotify have exerted considerable effort in attempting to monetize the large number of users that pay no subscription. By 2019, Spotify had recruited 100 million paid *subscribers* (compared to Apple Music's 50 million), but the total number of Spotify *users* was 217 million (Apple only has subscribers), so that more than 50 percent of Spotify's users might be generating liabilities through streams not covered by subscription assets. Indeed, the process of converting users to subscribers has been a central aim of Spotify's business model since its inception:

> Spotify was founded with the stated aim to mediate between the interests of two conflicting economic actors, the music industry on the one hand, and non-authorized file-sharers on the other ... To do so, they had first to transform the meaning of online music listening, shifting focus from ownership to access, and then "from access to context" so that a business model based on advertising revenue could take hold.
>
> *Vonderau 2019: 8*

Despite the considerable efforts made in this regard, such as developing personalized playlists that create listener demographics to categorize users, or running sophisticated online competitions among advertisers to get appropriate advertisements in front of potentially receptive users, still there is considerable risk in this form of revenue generation as it might not cover the liabilities generated by the streams of unsubscribed users. Seeking to balance assets and liabilities in a new, risky, and volatile market offers some explanation for the low income per stream rates.

Finally, revenues per stream appear low due to historical power imbalances between artists and corporate rights holders in the music industry, which have been amplified by the platform economy. As Hesmondhalgh (2020: 7) points out, streaming platforms do not in reality pay according to a pre-determined per stream rate; rather, the rate is better understood as "an analytical construct, an average produced by taking the income generated by an individual recording, by an artist, or by a label, and dividing that income by [the] number of streams achieved by that recording." This, like much else in the platform economy, is a winner-takes-all model. The higher the share of total streams generated by subscribers, and the higher the volume of advertising revenue generated by non-subscribers, the higher the rate per stream. Although the (variable) per stream rate will determine artist income from streaming, Hesmondhalgh (2020) and Arditi (2019) emphasize the importance of recognizing these revenues are actually paid to rights holders (record companies and publishers) with only a portion then passed on to the artists:

> The value gap is pure ideology. By arguing streaming services underpay recording artists, the IFPI ... and major record labels turn the process of exploiting artists on its head. Streaming services do not pay recording artists, record labels pay recording artists.
>
> *Arditi 2019: 20*

Therefore, representatives of the music industry are correct in claiming that the rates of return per stream offered by digital platforms are symbolic of a power inequity, with artists on one side and intermediaries on the other. However, record companies and other holders of intellectual property rights holders are themselves powerful intermediaries, with significant financial stakes in many streaming platforms, illustrating how the industry has successfully coopted digital platforms.

## Conclusions

This chapter has explored the emerging musical platform economy with a particular focus on moral economy arguments about equity and normative expectations. Digital platforms have their own dynamics of economic transformation, encouraging capital concentration and centralization. They also reflect existing structural inequalities and amplify them in new ways. Platforms have served to reinforce the power structures of the traditional musical economy but have added new dynamics based on a winner-takes-all sensibility. These new markets offer significant returns to winners but little to those unable to quickly become successful and self-sustaining. The traditional record company model, which signed artists to multi-record deals to provide time to for audience development, became unaffordable as P2P networks undermined revenues, and appears now to be an historical example of corporate welfarism in a very different economic conjuncture.

The chapter has argued that the moral economy arguments developed by the music industry in the face of the growing dominance of platforms are flawed. They fail to recognize the agency of music corporations in the platform economy, particularly given their extensive stakes in music streaming platforms such as Spotify (Vonderau 2019). Moreover, such arguments disregard the nature of the platform business model and the need to balance assets with liabilities. Moral economy arguments circulate, we argue, because there remains sufficient institutional memory within the music industry that remembers all too well the damage done by P2Ps in the early twentieth century. While platforms are the new corporate titans, they were formed in the libertarian furnace of Silicon Valley, and music streaming platforms share the DNA – and indeed, in some cases, the same code – as P2P networks (Eriksson, Fleischer, Johansson, Snickars, and Vonderau 2019). Moreover, it may also be that senior figures in the music industry can see that platforms are coming to colonize all aspects of the diverse "value ecology" of the musical economy. Having reached an already dominant position within the recorded music industry ecology, they are pushing this even further with the growing use of crowdfunding platforms to replicate the funding of creative activity that used to be the preserve of record companies (Gamble, Brennan, and McAdam 2017). Moreover, platforms play an ever more critical role in the mobilization of affect, or the conversion of fan enthusiasm into income (Dewan and Ramaprasad 2014; Leyshon, Thrift, Crewe, French, and Webb 2016).

Finally, streaming services are now even making inroads into the final preserve of the musical value economy once considered to be immune to the reach of platforms, live performance. Public policy responses to the COVID-19 pandemic restricted face-to-face activity across a range of industries, but one of the worst effected was live music. In response, artists turned to platforms such as Twitch, previously the territory of live gaming streaming, to stream live performances for fans. Such platforms provide affordances that artists can use to enhance their streams and provide an experience that is both enticing for viewers and generates revenue for the streamer, many of which are based around social interaction with the audience (Sjöblom, Törhönen, Hamari, and Macey 2019). Users support artists by subscribing to their channel, with subscriptions providing a recurring income to streamers, and the money collected is split 50/50 between platforms and streamers. Artists generate additional income from fan donations, sponsorships, brand deals, and affiliate links. Live streaming platforms offer the opportunity to offset some of the loss in earnings from the closure of live music venues. In the pandemic, the live streaming of performances was celebrated as a critical resource for artists to replace lost income, but at the same time threatens the future livelihoods of performance venues post-pandemic.

In response both to the MP3 crisis of the early twentieth century and the COVID-19 crisis of 2020, digital platforms have demonstrated a capacity to reconfigure business models, stemming overall losses, and developing new sources of revenue. But in so doing, they also fractured taken for granted ways of doing business and created new sets of winners and losers, prompting concerns over fair returns derived from normative expectations forged in an earlier conjuncture. As streaming platforms sink into the background of the music business, new moral economies based on new taken for granted ways of working will be formed.

# Note

1  "Shape of You," by Ed Sheeran. Based on the figures in Table 23.3, this would equate to nearly $11 million in revenue. Generating at least 10 million streams per month on Spotify would generate a gross monthly income of almost $44,000, or $524,000 per annum. See, for example, Iqbal (2020).

# References

Allen, D. (2013) "Why David Byrne Is Wrong About Spotify," *The Guardian*, October 16, available at www.theguardian.com/commentisfree/2013/oct/16/why-david-byrne-wrong-spotify-thom-yorke (accessed November 11, 2020).

Arditi, D. (2013) "iTunes: Breaking Barriers and Building Walls," *Popular Music and Society*, 37 (4): 408–424.

Arditi, D. (2015) *iTake-Over: The Recording Industry in the Digital Era*, Lanham, MD: Rowman & Littlefield.

Arditi, D. (2019) "Digital Hegemony: Net Neutrality, the Value Gap, and Corporate Interests," in D. Arditi and J. Miller (eds), *The Dialectic of Digital Culture*, Lanham, MD: Lexington Books, 13–28.

Behr, A., Brennan, M., and M. Cloonan, M. (2016) "Cultural Value and Cultural Policy: Some Evidence from the World of Live Music," *International Journal of Cultural Policy*, 22 (3): 403–418.

Birch, K. and Muniesa, F. (eds) (2020) *Assetization: Turning Things into Assets in Technoscientific Capitalism*, Cambridge, MA: MIT Press.

Buck-Morss, S. (1995) "Envisioning Capital: Political Economy on Display," *Critical Inquiry* 21 (2): 434–467.

Dewan, S. and Ramaprasad, J. (2014) "Social Media, Traditional Media, and Music Sales," *MIS Quarterly*, 38 (1): 101–122.

*The Economist* (2016) "Celebrities' Endorsement Earnings on Social Media," October 17, available at www.economist.com/graphic-detail/2016/10/17/celebrities-endorsement-earnings-on-social-media (accessed November 11, 2020).

Eriksson, M., Fleischer, R. Johansson, A. Snickars, P. and Vonderau, P. (2019) *Spotify Teardown: Inside the Black Box of Streaming Music*, Cambridge, MA: MIT Press.

Gamble, J. R., Brennan, M. and McAdam, R. (2017) "A Rewarding Experience? Exploring How Crowdfunding is Affecting Music Industry Business Models," *Journal of Business Research*, 70: 25–36.

Götz, N. (2015) "'Moral Economy': Its Conceptual History and Analytical Prospects," *Journal of Global Ethics*, 11 (2): 147–162.

Hesmondhalgh, D. (2020) "Is Music Streaming Bad for Musicians? Problems of Evidence and Argument," *New Media and Society*, OnlineFirst, available at https://journals.sagepub.com/doi/full/10.1177/1461444820953541 (accessed November 11, 2020).

IFPI (2017) *Global Music Report 2017: Annual State of the Industry*, London: International Federation of the Phonographic Industry.

IFPI (2018) *Global Music Report 2018: Annual State of the Industry*, London: International Federation of the Phonographic Industry

IFPI (2019) *Global Music Report 2019: State of the Industry*, London: International Federation of the Phonographic Industry

IFPI (2020) *Global Music Report: The Industry in 2019*, London: International Federation of the Phonographic Industry, available at www.ifpi.org/wp-content/uploads/2020/07/Global_Music_Report-the_Industry_in_2019-en.pdf (accessed December 3, 2020).

Iqbal, M. (2020) "Spotify Usage and Revenue Statistics (2020)," *Business of Apps*, October 30, available at www.businessofapps.com/data/spotify-statistics/ (accessed November 11, 2020).

Jessop, B. and Sum, N-L. (2019) "Polanyi: Classical Moral Economist or Pioneer Cultural Political Economist?," *Österreichische Zeitschrift für Soziologie*, 44 (2): 153–167.

Kenney, M. and Zysman, J. (2018) "Unicorns, Cheshire Cats, and the New Dilemmas of Entrepreneurial Finance?" *SSRN*, available at https://papers.ssrn.com/sol3/papers.cfm?abstract_id=3220780 (accessed November 11, 2020).

Kenney, M. and Zysman, J. (2020) "The Platform Economy: Restructuring the Space of Capitalist Accumulation," *Cambridge Journal of Regions, Economy and Society*, 13 (1): 55–76.

Knopper, S. (2009) *Appetite for Self-Destruction: The Spectacular Crash of the Record Industry in the Digital Age*, New York: The Free Press.

Krueger, A. B. (2005) "The Economics of Real Superstars: The Market for Rock Concerts in the Material World," *Journal of Labor Economics*, 23 (1): 1–30.

Krueger, A. B. (2019) *Rockonomics: What the Music Industry Can Teach Us About Economics (and Our Future)*, Kindle edition, London: John Murray.

Langley, P. and Leyshon, A. (2017) "Platform Capitalism: The Intermediation and Capitalisation of Digital Economic Circulation," *Finance and Society*, 3 (1): 11–31.

Leyshon, A. (2014) *Reformatted: Code, Networks and the Transformation of the Music Industry*, Oxford: Oxford University Press.

Leyshon, A., Thrift, N., Crewe, L., French, S., and Webb, P. 2016) "Leveraging Affect: Mobilizing Enthusiasm and the Co-production of the Musical Economy," in B. J. Hracs, M. Seman, and T. Virani (eds), *The Production and Consumption of Music in the Digital Age*, London: Routledge, 24–62.

Morris, J. W. (2015) *Selling Digital Music, Formatting Culture*, Berkeley, CA: University of California Press.

Muniesa, F., Doganova, L., Ortiz, H., Pina-Stranger, Á., Paterson, F., Bourgoin, A., Ehrenstein, V., Juven, P-A., Pontille, D., Saraç-Lesavre, B., and Yon, G. (2017) *Capitalization: A Cultural Guide*, Paris: Presse des Mines.

Naveed, K., Watanabe, C., and Neittaanmäaki, P. (2017) "Co-evolution between Streaming and Live Music Leads a Way to the Sustainable Growth of Music Industry: Lessons from the US Experiences," *Technology in Society*, 50: 1–19.

O'Dwyer, R. (2015) "Money Talks: The Enclosure of Mobile Payments," in G. Lovink, N. Tkacz, and P. de Vries (eds), *MoneyLab Reader: An Intervention in Digital Economy*, Amsterdam: Institute of Network Cultures, 230–44.

Sayer, A. (2007) "Moral Economy as Critique," *New Political Economy*, 12 (2): 261–270.

Schechter, A. (2017) "'Google is as Close to a Natural Monopoly as the Bell System Was in 1956'," *ProMarket*, May 9, available at https://promarket.org/2017/05/09/google-close-natural-monopoly-bell-system-1956/ (accessed November 11, 2020).

Simon, J. P. (2019) "New Players in the Music Industry: Lifeboats or Killer Whales? The Role of Streaming Platforms," *Digital Policy, Regulation and Governance*, 21 (6): 525–—.

Sjöblom, M., Törhönen, M., Hamari, J., and Macey, J. (2019) "The Ingredients of Twitch Streaming: Affordances of Game Streams," *Computers in Human Behavior*, 92: 20–28.

Srnicek, N. (2016) *Platform Capitalism*, Cambridge: Polity.

StatSheep (2020) "PewDiePie," available at www.statsheep.com/PewDiePie (accessed November 11, 2020).

Taplin, J. (2012) "The Band's Ex-tour Manager Blasts Reddit Founder Alexi Ohanian, Kim Dotcom, The Kickstarter 'Begging Bowl'," *Fast Company*, April 23, available at www.fastcompany.com/1834866/bands-ex-tour-manager-blasts-reddit-founder-alexis-ohanian-kim-dotcom-kickstarter-begging-bo (accessed November 11, 2020).

Taplin, J. (2017) *Move Fast and Break Things: How Facebook, Google and Amazon Have Cornered Culture and What it Means for All of Us*, New York: Little, Brown and Company.

*The Trichordist* (n.d.) " About," available at https://thetrichordist.com/about-2/ (accessed December 4, 2020).

*The Trichordist* (2014) "The Streaming Price Bible – Spotify, YouTube and What 1 Million Plays Means to You!," November 14, available at https://thetrichordist.com/2014/11/12/the-streaming-price-bible-spotify-youtube-and-what-1-million-plays-means-to-you/ (accessed November 16, 2020).

*The Trichordist* (2017) "Updated! Streaming Price Bible w/ 2016 Rates: Spotify, Apple Music, YouTube, Tidal, Amazon, Pandora, Etc.," January 16, available at https://thetrichordist.com/2017/01/16/updated-streaming-price-bible-w-2016-rates-spotify-apple-music-youtube-tidal-amazon-pandora-etc/ (accessed November 11, 2020).

*The Trichordist* (2020) "2019–2020 Streaming Price Bible: YouTube is STILL The #1 Problem to Solve," March 5, available at https://thetrichordist.com/2020/03/05/2019-2020-streaming-price-bible-youtube-is-still-the-1-problem-to-solve/ (accessed December 4, 2020).

UK Music (2019) *Music by Num8ers*, London: UK Music.

van Dijck, J., Poell, T., and de Waal, M. (2019) *The Platform Society*, New York: Oxford University Press.

Vonderau, P. (2019) "The Spotify Effect: Digital Distribution and Financial Growth," *Television and New Media*, 20 (1): 3–19.

# 24

# THE DIGITAL NEWS INDUSTRY

## The intertwining digital commodities of audiences and news

*Henrik Bødker*

A central and persevering issue in relation to the institution of journalism and, relatedly, to the news industry, is the role of the market. This is so since the institution of journalism is seen to deliver a key service to democratic societies through what Sjøvaag (2010) terms a reciprocal social contract between the state and civil society or, in a liberal model, the marketplace (of ideas). Such a connection naturally raises questions about interests, power and money, questions often tackled within the framework of the political economy of news, which seeks to understand and reveal how, for instance, business concentration, finance from advertising, and audience data relate to the processes through which news are produced and circulated. An important consequence of digital technologies is that processes of production and circulation are becoming increasingly intertwined as when, for instance, the logics of social media (may) influence the selection and production of news and thus ultimately the autonomy of journalism (van Dijck, Poell, and de Wall 2018). While this concerns the functioning of the institution of journalism, it is deeply related to changes in the processes constituting the primary products of the news industry, namely content and audiences. This chapter consequently addresses the contemporary and largely digital news industry by focusing on the digital constitution of the audience and news commodities.

An important and long-standing issue related to the communications industries, not least that of journalism, is the complex relations between commodity forms and meaning. By approaching the changes from the perspective of the commodity form, I am not attempting to shy away from questions of meaning but rather wishing to point out, as will become clear below, that it is increasingly difficult to separate commodity forms and their circulation from processes of meaning making. In doing so, I am following recurrent calls for combining elements of what Hardy (2017: 3) calls "culturalist media studies" with insights from critical political economy. At issue in such a combination is the old but persistently relevant discussion of how economic structures and flows of money are interlinked with culture and thus processes of meaning making; and, of course, whether digital developments should cause us to rethink such relations. By structuring my discussion around two important concepts from political economy, namely the audience commodity and the news commodity, I precisely wish to forefront how the processes of meaning making and economic processes are intertwined in novel ways, which – in relation to the commodity – can be seen as new and complex ways in which "the circulation of meaning" is related to the "meaning of circulation" (Bødker 2015).

DOI: 10.4324/9780429275340-28

The relations between journalism and the market are, of course, about balance and ethics – that is, the old discussion of whether you "make a newspaper to make money" or "make money to make a newspaper" – and the related perspective of seeing the editorial and commercial sections of a newspaper organization as church and state. Perhaps there have been times where all the counterveiling forces were perfectly balancing out each other so that the market delivered something untainted by commercialism. In popular music, this has often been linked to the creative outburst at the peak of the counterculture in the late 1960s. At approximately the same time, in journalism this was (at least in America) seen as what Hallin (1992) called the moment of "high modernism of American journalism" in which "journalists felt they had overcome all the basic contradictions that historically have troubled the practice of journalism" (p. 14), which, in relation to the market, meant "that journalists could think of themselves more as public servants or as keepers of the sacred flame of journalism itself than as employees of a profit-making enterprise" (p. 15).

Yet, despite Hallin talking about a specific historical conjecture, thoughts about existing in relative isolation from the market are still alive among journalists, a condition that Meijer and Kormelink (2019: 1) describe as "[a]udiences and journalism [being] an uneasy match. Although ultimately dependent on their viewers, listeners, readers, and users, historically newsrooms and journalists have wanted little to do with audiences." It might be that (some) journalists (have) perceive(d) themselves in relative isolation from the market and/or audiences, but this is arguably increasingly difficult to do as the news industry is undergoing important changes through which commercial processes and, relatedly, audience activities, are becoming simultaneously both much more important and visible (e.g., through audience metrics) but also more complex and less transparent (e.g., through digital intermediaries). Legacy news organizations and digital natives are obviously positioned somewhat differently in relation to such processes, for example, the integration of "online audience metrics into their day-to-day operations" (van Dijck, Poell, and de Wall 2018: 59); yet, as a whole it is fair to say that the news industry is changing with regard to its boundaries and relations to (other) commercial and/or social practices. Below I discuss some important aspects of such changes from two interrelated perspectives, namely that of the *audience commodity* and the *news commodity*, after which I return to the issue of money and meaning before finally suggesting some directions for future research.

## The digital audience commodity

In a broad sense, the major reasons for journalism becoming differently aligned to the market are twofold: a sifting away of advertising income from publishers and, relatedly, an expectation among audiences to be able to access information without having to pay directly for it. The dual market model that sustained journalism in pre-digital times – that is, selling content to audiences, on the one hand, and audiences to advertisers, on the other – was based on different kinds of measurements and sampling as the "agreed currency of exchange" (Andrew 2019: 79). A key explanation with regard to the advertising side is that search engines and social media platforms account for an increasing amount of online traffic. First, this means that many users meet news in settings away from publishers' own websites, where they could have been exposed to advertising. A more important explanation is, however, that social media can sell more finely demarcated audiences to advertisers. The sifting away of advertising toward organizations not involved in content production but which are experts in using (aggregated) digital footprints of online users for arguably more precise targeting of consumers is thus directly linked to the broad aim of much journalism: namely to address a relatively loosely conceived (politically) interested citizen. One way to address such disconnections might be through "recommender algorithms" that strive to balance fit, diversity, and "long term journalistic goals" (see Bodó, Helberger, Eskens, and Möller 2019) and which then can be coupled with advertising linked to specific target groups, something which also can be done for automatically produced news targetting specific, smaller audiences (e.g., news about small, local sports clubs).

What is ultimately at stake here is how audience activity or engagement is turned into value and, related to that, to what extent we should talk about such activities as labor. I concur with Hesmondhalgh (2010) that, at least from one perspective, this is a somewhat crude perception through which most social activities, even sleep, can be seen as adding value to capitalistic structures and that it might be problematic to "see individual audience members as undertaking unpaid work when they watch television programmes" (p. 280). Yet, one could also argue that audience members enter into an exchange through which attention to advertisements is "paid" with content and that, if we follow Caraway (2011), "the typical audience member is, in fact, aware of and party to the transaction. He or she understands that the transaction actually involves the barter of entertainment products in exchange for the service of watching advertisements" (p. 697). In a strict sense, this can be seen as exploitation as the audience spend more time watching advertisements than is necessary for the production of content, which is why (some) media industries make a profit. Having said that, it is also important to point out that there is no direct line between such processes and audience power and pleasure, and I thus fully agree with van Dijck (2013) when she argues that: "Obviously, social media services can be both intensely empowering and disturbingly exploitative; sociality is enjoyed and exercised through precisely the commercial platforms that also exploit online social activities for monetary gains" (p. 18). "[D]isturbingly exploitative" may here refer to audience desires rather than actual work and, as Hesmondhalgh (2015) points out, there might be "less exploitation here because there is, other things being equal, likely to be less suffering involved on the part of such workers" (p. 36) in comparison with certain other industries, for example, mining. Thus, while acknowledging some of the deeper implications of seeing audience activities as labor, such a view does arguably help to put into perspective some of the changes that have come with digital media.

In the pre-digital media system, for both print and broadcasting, the audience mainly "labored" by seeing adverts as part of the exchange for content. The audience have thus been asked to work increasingly harder, in both "extensive" (i.e., more time) and "intensive" (i.e., becoming more intimately engaged in the viewing of commercial content as this is more closely targeted through market segmentation) terms. As Fisher (2015) says, however, there were limits to how far analog media could extend and intensify their audiences: it was difficult to expand the time given to viewing, listening, and reading much beyond what already happened, while the costs of segmentation – both in terms of content and delivery and in relation to more precise measurement – prohibited developing closer fits between audience characteristics and (commercial) content. Digital media pushes those limits by, on the one hand, integrating media use into daily life, creating a situation where many users are almost "always on," and more importantly, users continuously segmenting themselves in ways that allow for the presentation of tailored commercial content, thereby reducing the costs of measurement or tracking. In addition, the audience as labor is here also involved in the actual production of content, "the construction and maintenance of networks or media channels through which ads are disseminated" (p. 51) and, of course, data (p. 52), which in many ways is the most important (by-)product of audience labor on social media.

For the news industry, the irony of this perspective is that (news) consumers labor as hard as ever but in ways that do not directly benefit the publishers of news. A related irony is that while many are not willing to pay for news, they are willing to invest large amounts of time and energy in media activities that produce huge profits for big tech companies. This situation is at the center of discussions concerning free labor in the cultural industries, and is somewhat beyond the concerns of this chapter, although it can be added that audience labor and free labor in some instances overlap in the sense that audience activities also add value to the news commodity by aiding its circulation, and/or adding layers of interaction that raise the value of the original commodity (something I will return to below). The news business has always been focused on their products occupying an important position in the sociality of the relevant markets to which publishers cater, and this is in a sense no different with social media, which has become an increasingly important mediated layer around a vast amount of digital content. Thus, while social media platforms profit from audience labor on their platforms, the question is if and how news publishers can extract value from the sociality produced around news on social media.

This question is addressed by Kleis and Ganter (2018) when interviewing both management and journalists from a major British news organization about the relations between publishers and platforms which they call "digital intermediaries." What the interviews reveal is a constant tension between short- and longer-term goals linked to, on the one hand, visibility and reach, and on the other, control and monetization. In relation to the audience commodity the most immediate concerns are related to maximizing referrals, which send users to a publisher's website where they can be exposed to advertisements and, ideally, turned into subscribers. An important issue in relation to this, and more generally concerning the platform–publisher relationship, is a lack of clarity and conformity in terms of metrics; what precisely do news publishers gain in their understanding of the audience commodity through social media? While various new types of measurement are available for news publishers to gauge "how users engage with and share their content across the platform ecosystem" (e.g., "CrowdTangle" obtained by Facebook in "late 2016" (van Dijck, Poell, and de Wall 2018: 56)), the processes remain non-transparent "in part because of limited data on performance, lack of benchmarks, and problems of comparing various metrics across channels" (Kleis and Ganter 2018: 1610). Following this, the platform–publisher relationship also remains very "asymmetrical" both in terms of size and power, and in relation to who is most in need of the other (1612–1613). A similar issue of transparency is related to the shift from "manual to automated" trading of the digital audience commodity, which can be seen, write Ohlsson and Facht (2017), as a kind of "automated" auctioning through which the target groups that media can deliver are matched and priced in relation to the demands of those wishing to place ads. Through this mechanism, prices and placements are determined by supply and demand. Regarding the spread of this practice, Andrew (2019: 74) writes:

> While globally programmatic trading only accounted for 17% of digital advertising spends in 2016–17 ..., it was predicted to become the dominant method for trading online advertising, accounting for up to 67% of all digital advertising expenditure by 2019.

This kind of "Real Time Bidding for advertising placement," which grew out of "ad exchange networks" (Andrew 2019: 82), arises as it has become "impossible for advertisers to have knowledge of, let alone consider, every single online media provider that would possibly be of interest to their target audience" (p. 81). At the same time, it has become possible to log and process large amounts of audience activity data instead of looking only at a respresentative sample. This is "significantly more complicated in the transaction of audiences" (p. 82), adding to the lack of transparency between publishers and social media platforms described above. Fully understanding such processes from the outside is indeed difficult as it both requires access to data and relevant mixtures of methodologies for investigating such processes. We are thus, as Myllylahti (2020) writes (based on a call from van Dijck, Poell, and de Wall (2018: 71)), in need of a better "academic understanding of 'monetization of news through the platform ecosystem'." Myllylahti argues closer scrutiny is needed of attention as "a scarce and fluid commodity," "a unit for measurement," and a "source of monetisation" (568–569). Yet, such a perspective also requires a closer examination of changes in the desired object of attention, in this case the digital news commodity, which, although it is becoming less important from an advertiser's perspective, by its circulation on social media platforms is being redefined by processes similar to those affecting the audience commodity.

## The digital news commodity

While some media industries may see the audience commodity as primary, the news commodity has for the most part been central to the news industry. Here the audience commodity is, at least ideally, a secondary concern and thus simply an avenue for income that allows for the continued production and distribution of the primary commodity, news content. Thus, the news, and its status as a commercial product, has most often been discussed in terms of content, and how meaning and commercial or political relations mold processes of content production. A significant part of this work has involved critiques of how dominant ideologies permeate news, but some of these discussions have also focused on the commodity status of news content (e.g., Hall (2005 [1980]). In general, however, it is fair to say that increasingly the production of journalism takes place at a shorter distance from the demand side, being influenced by audience metrics and/or measurements of sharing on social media. Such diminishing distances are related to the evermore differentiated ways in which the news commodity reaches its audiences or users – as this term points at processes of interactivity distinct from the activities related to the consumption of analog content. While the news commodity remains central, there are a number of ways in which its circulation affects its commodity status in terms of both money flows and meaning.

A central part of these changes is the fact that news commodities – or parts of them – circulate on social media in ways that are often not linked directly to an immediate exchange or relation between news organizations and their audiences. Circulation through what Kleis and Ganter (2018) call "digital intermediaries" thus inserts a intervening layer that affects the nature of the commodity. From one perspective, we may say that this new layer strips the news commodity of its original commodity status as it now simply appears as another piece of free content on social media. Another way to see this is to regard news content as a free sample, and thus as a marketing device, in order to turn some users into customers, that is, by directing them to the online site of the publisher where they can subscribe to the outlet. Yet, if we follow Hall (2005 [1980]) and see news as a discursive product whose commodity status is fulfilled through its reading, the news product – even if freely available – remains a commodity through its many subsequent readings. The point is here that news becomes a commodity through its circulation and that in order to fulfil the commodity chain it must (again following Hall) be decoded "within the limit of dominant definitions in which it has been connotatively signified" (p. 124). On this note, Bødker (2016: 415) states:

> The specific form and extent of [such new reading practices] is obviously an empirical question but one might assume that such processes are invoked simply by reading

headlines, lead paragraphs and/or seeing news photographs in the sense that such short forms arguably often rely on connotation.

Yet, an important point is here that such connotations are deciphered through a layer of user interaction. While the news commodity always has been surrounded by both informal news talk, letters to the editor, editorials, and columns, it appears on social media within a differently constituted "filter of commentary" (Bødker 2013) consisting of the digital traces of other people's decodings. This "mediated form of consumption on social media [thus] creates and circulates an augmented commodity that contains additional value by bearing traces of social interaction" (Bødker 2016: 415). The argument is here that the orginal news commodity, that is, the text emanating from the publisher gains addional (or a different) value by accumulating likes, comments, and shares that become attached to the original commodity as an edge or metadata.

This augmented commodity is linked to both the news industry responsible for its production and the social media industry through which it is circulated. While the news industry is related both to the primary content of the commodity (i.e., the discursively circulated news event) and to embedded social contexts, social media platforms are only interested in the traces of social interaction generated by news content. As discussed above, circulation of the content creates an audience commodity of interest to both social media platforms and the news industry, with the issue being how to monetize this interaction. In relation to these processes, Martin and Dwyer (2019: 71) write:

> In social media news sharing, we also see the metadata about the way we communicate and organize our social relations being used to restructure those social connections and contexts, and to shape our exposure to news on social media. This third level of meaning making creates a "triple articulation" of commodification, which urgently requires scholarly investigation into its impacts on our cultural landscape and social relations.

Following on from this, they describe the "augmented commodity" discussed above as a "*metadata commodity* [which] refers to the value of information about our social relations in time and space, which can only be collated and interpreted as part of a 'machinic assemblage' or 'the platform'" (original emphasis, p. 71). What emerges from this embeddedness in social media is that the news commodity exists within complexly intertwined commodity layers in terms of both money flows and meaning making. In relation to this, Langlois (2014: 17) writes that one of the paradoxes of

> semiotechnological software is the predominantly corporate context within which it is deployed problematically links the economic, cultural, and psychological values of meaning: the attribution of meaningful value serves to create markets as much as it is an essential human activity.

On social media we are, she argues, thus seeing a "new governance of meaning" (p. 41). Thus, while it has always been necessary to look beyond the signification of texts, this is increasingly so in order to understand the complex ways in which algorithmic connectivity helps us make sense (or makes sense for us) at a fundamental level. Thus, while the deeper meaning, the resonance of the news commodity, relied to a large extent on the ability of journalists to insert the news into some of the fundamental and ongoing stories of the community to which they communicated, resonance may now (also) be the result of computational processing of the connective layers of the "metadata commodity."

## Money, meaning, and future directions

When Smythe (1977) initiated the discussion of the audience commodity it was, as the subtitle of his article suggests – "Blindspot of Western Marxism" – to turn very much against the preoccupation with meaning and/or ideology. For Smythe, the "threshold question" was, rather: "What is the commodity form of mass-produced advertiser-supported communications?" (p. 2) and his answer to this question was the audience commodity. It is indeed interesting to note Smythe's intervention was written almost simultaneously with Hall's (2005 [1980]) move in the opposite direction by transposing Marxist thinking on the commodity form to the communicative commodity and thus processes of meaning making in the encoding/decoding model.

While the two perspectives, the audience commodity and the news commodity (and its meanings), are not exclusive and do not necessarily contradict each other, the discussion has hopefully made it clear that it is more important than ever to approach the commodity relations of the news industry from both perspectives. As meaning and value are partly constituted through digital circulation, and as circulation is created through mediated consumption and algorithmic connectivity, it is as important to untangle the different and complexly intertwined and overlapping commodity layers in terms of both money flows and meaning. In relation to this, it is interesting to note that in a review of articles in the journal *Digital Journalism* (which started in 2013), Steensen, Larsen, Hågvar, and Fonn (2019) point out there has been a "social science bias, both methodologically and theoretically, which leads to several blinds [sic] spots especially related to journalism as a producer of meaning and knowledge in the digital age" (p. 336). They continue, the

> future reader who consults *Digital Journalism* to find out how ideas and discourses were constructed in journalistic texts in the 2010s, how journalism created meaning of and for societies and cultures it served, how journalism functioned as a system of knowledge creation, and how such questions were connected to historic developments, is likely to be disappointed. To provide answers to such questions, digital journalism studies should to a greater extent embrace the disciplinary perspectives and qualitative methods of the humanities.
>
> *p. 336*

Although not within a Marxist frame, this call echoes but reverses Smythe's argument for abandoning messages and meaning – "concepts … [that] all deal with superficial appearances" (1977: 2) – and turn toward the real "commodity form of mass-produced, advertiser-supported communications under monopoly capitalism," namely "audiences and readerships," which – contrary to meaning – constitute a part of the "material reality under monopoly capitalism" (p. 3).

It is, however, as pointed out in this chapter, increasingly difficult to separate the news commodity form (the "material reality") from processes of meaning making; another way of saying this is that circulation and consumption partly have coalesced. Circulation thus happens increasingly *through* the consumption of and/or interaction with news. This was and is, of course, also partly true for the newspaper, which – as a mobile object – may be passed around among family members, neighbors, and colleagues. A really significant distinction is, however, that post-publication circulation in the analog landscape was fully social, that is, not directly influenced by institutional interest (apart perhaps from the availability of newspapers in cafes and library reading rooms), whereas the processes in digital circulation are also programmed and thus based on commercial logics that transcend the social.

On such processes, Raetzsch and Bødker (2016) argue for seeing the news commodity as a "communicative object" that is defined both through "its digital materiality and its epistemic function in social interaction[s]" (p. 131). The "meta-data commodity" and/or "augmented commodity" are thus unstable and increasingly complex objects that accumulate traces telling a story of the news commodity's social life and partly determine some of its future trajectories and values. Additionally, the audience commodity has also acquired a new materiality in the sense that it increasingly consists of digital traces of the behaviors of "actual" audiences rather than sampled data. Fisher and Mehozay (2019) describes this transition in audience knowledge as a shift from a "scientific episteme" to an "algorithmic episteme" (p. 1176). In the former, during "the mass media era," "members of the audience ha[d] no individual existence" but were rather "conceptualized as part of 'institutionally effective audiences that ha[d] social meaning and/or economic value within the system'" (p. 1182). With the latter, audience members are seen as "individuals based on the behavioral data they produce …, bypassing their self-understanding, and identifying patterns from which a predictive behavioural analysis can be deduced" (p. 1188). While Fisher and Mehozay are interested in the broader epistemic implications of this shift, the important point for the present discussion is that each (potential) audience member is digitally manifested in new ways, which hold the potential of new commodifications. The audience commodity and news commodity temporarily overlap in the sense that social interaction attached to the news commodity simultaneously make up parts of the audience commodity. Rather than constituting two distinct entities, the two commodity forms become perspectives on intertwined processes, which each in their related ways produce both economic value and meaning.

Untangling these entwinements in both empirical and theoretical detail is indeed no easy task as this necessitates thorough knowledge of digital technology, commercial relations, and the hermeneutics of digital news consumption. In an overall fashion both Hermida (2020 and Carlson (2020: 231) point in that direction by building on the notion of "journalism as a cultures of circulation" (Bødker 2015) and/or the idea of "communicative objects" (Raetzsch and Bødker 2016). Carlson (2020: 231) argues for applying "digital news circulation to journalistic epistemology," which "turns attention to how news as a form of knowledge is shared, transformed, contested, and controverted, by a variety of actors deploying a range of practices across digital media platforms." Hermida (2020: 14) turns his attention "to post-publication" as an "overarching theme to unpack the complex, contextual, and contested processes through which the Four Ps – publics, platforms, paraphernalia [devices/materiality], and [audience] practices – interact to assign prominence and profile to the news." While commercial aspects are not foregrounded here, the framework is helpful for focusing on some of the complex processes outlined above. Finally, and moving closer to the target by building on Bødker (2016), Palmer (2020) in her work on "Hyper-Decoding News Posts" focuses on how the decoding process is divided into pre- and post-decoding moments each of which – including their articulations – are influenced by algorithmically aided processes and interactions, and as such help us understand how commercial and meaning-making processes are increasingly intertwined. Indeed, as Hardy (2017) and Larsen, Hågvar, and Fonn (2019) ask for, we need more studies combining insights from critical political economy and technology studies with key questions in media studies and the humanities.

## Acknowledgments

I wish to thank David Hesmondhalgh and Chris Anderson (both from the University of Leeds) for insightful, constructive and encouraging comments on a draft of this chapter; I also sincerely wish to thank the editor of this volume Paul McDonald for a detailed and close reading as well as thoughtful editing and comments.

## References

Andrew, D. (2019) "Programmatic Trading: The Future of Audience Economics," *Communication Research and Practice*, 5 (1): 73–87

Bodó, B., Helberger, N., Eskens, S. and Möller, J. (2019) "Interested in Diversity," *Digital Journalism*, 7 (2): 206–229.

Bødker, H. (2013) "Social medier som journalistisk kommentarfilter," in J. Linaa and J. Tække (eds), *Facebook i den danske hverdag*, Copenhagen: Samfundslitteratur, 211–227.

Bødker, H. (2015) "Journalism as Cultures of Circulation," *Digital Journalism*, 3 (1): 101–115.

Bødker, H. (2016) "Stuart Hall's Encoding/Decoding Model and the Circulation of Journalism in the Digital Landscape," *Critical Studies in Media Communication*, 33 (5): 409–423.

Caraway, B. (2011) "Audience Labor in the New Media Environment: A Marxian Revisiting of the Audience Commodity," *Media, Culture and Society*, 33 (5): 693–708.

Carlson, M. (2020) "Journalistic Epistemology and Digital News Circulation: Infrastructure, Circulation Practices, and Epistemic Contests," *New Media and Society*, 22 (2): 230–246.

Fisher, E. (2015) "'You Media': Audiencing as Marketing in Social Media," *Media, Culture and Society*, 37 (1): 50–67.

Fisher, E and Mehozay, Y (2019) "How Algorithms See Their Audience: Media Epistemes and the Changing Conception of the Individual," *Media, Culture and Society*, 41 (8): 1176–1191.

Hall, S. (2005 [1980]) "Encoding/Decoding," in S. Hall, D. Hobson, A. Lowe, and P. Willis (eds), *Culture, Media, Language: Working Papers in Cultural Studies, 1972–79*, London: Routledge, 117–127.

Hallin, D. C. (1992) "The Passing of the 'High Modernism' of American Journalism," *Journal of Communication*, 42 (3): 14–25.

Hardy, J. (2017) "Money, (Co)Production and Power," *Digital Journalism*, 5 (1): 1–25.

Hermida, A. (2020) "Post-Publication Gatekeeping: The Interplay of Publics, Platforms, Paraphernalia, and Practices in the Circulation of News," *Journalism and Mass Communication Quarterly*, Online first.

Hesmondhalgh, D. (2010) "User-generated Content, Free Labor and the Cultural Industries," *Ephemera: Theory and Politics in Organization*, 10 (3/4): 267–284.

Hesmondhalgh, D. (2015) "Exploitation and Media Labor," in R. Maxwell (ed.), *The Routledge Companion to Labor and Media*, New York: Routledge, 30–39.

Kleis R. S. and Ganter, S. A. (2018) "Dealing with Digital Intermediaries: A Case Study of the Relations between Publishers and Platforms," *New Media and Society*, 20 (4): 1600–1617

Langlois, G. (2014). *Meaning in the Age of Social Media*, New York: Palgrave Macmillan.

Martin, F. and Dwyer, T. (2019) *Sharing News Online: Commendary Cultures and Social Media News Ecologies*, London: Palgrave Macmillan.

Meijer, I. C. and Kormelink, T. G. (2019) "Audiences for Journalism," in T. P. Vos and F. Hanusch (eds), *The International Encyclopedia of Journalism Studies*, Hoboken, NJ: John Wiley & Sons, 1–7.

Myllylahti, M. (2020) "Paying Attention to Attention: A Conceptual Framework for Studying News Reader Revenue Models Related to Platforms," *Digital Journalism*, 8 (5): 567–575.

Ohlsson, J. and Facht, U. (2017) *Kampen om reklamen*, Gothenborg: Nordicom.

Palmer, M. (2020) *Hyper-Decoding News Posts: A Qualitative Study of Meaning-Making on Facebook*, unpublished PhD, University of Technology Sydney.

Raetzsch, C. and Bødker, H. (2016) "Journalism and the Circulation of Communicative Objects," *TECNOSCIENZA: Italian Journal of Science and Technology Studies*, 7 (1): 129–148.

Sjøvaag, H. (2010) "The Reciprocity of Journalism's Social Contract," *Journalism Studies*, 11 (6): 874–888.

Smythe, D. W. (1977) "Communications: Blindspot of Western Marxism," *Canadian Journal of Political and Social Theory/Revue canadienne de theorie politique etsociale*, 1 (3): 1–28.

Steensen, S., Grøndahl Larsen, A.M., Benestad Hågvar, Y., and Kjos Fonn, B. (2019) "What Does Digital Journalism Studies Look Like?" *Digital Journalism*, 7 (3): 320–342.

van Dijck, J. V. (2013) *The Culture of Connectivity: A Critical History of Social Media*, Oxford: Oxford University Press.

van Dijck, J. V., Poell, T. and de Wall, M. (2018) *The Platform Society: Public Values in a Connective World*, Oxford: Oxford University Press.

# 25

# THE DYNAMICS OF THE BOOK PUBLISHING INDUSTRY

*Angus Phillips*

As a creative industry, book publishing is notable for both its economic impact and its wider influence. Book publishing covers a range of types of books from the academic monograph to the latest international bestselling work of fiction. Notable trends within the industry are digitization, globalization, and the democratization of authorship. While illustrative examples in this chapter are mainly taken from the UK and United States, as the business is international, analysis of the industry requires attention to trends across borders. The level of risk varies by sector, but overall the industry has faced challenges from other media, user-generated content, and the rise of digital access.

Digital access to books means that they have a ready global market, and some genres such as romance have shifted from print to the ebook. Yet the printed book demonstrates resilience while offering a reliable business model for publishers. In contrast to the world of self-publishing, commercial publishers offer authors validation of their work, editorial and marketing support, and retail exposure. Whether read on holiday or for study, or adapted for TV and film, books continue to play an important role in our society and culture.

## Industry structure

The total value of the UK book industry was £3.6 billion in 2018, reaching around £6 billion with the inclusion of journals, and over 50 percent of revenues came from exports. The gross value added was over £10 billion, 0.5 percent of the total value added in the UK economy (DCMS 2020). The importance of English as a global language reinforces the strength of the industry, and there are countries in Europe where the penetration of sales of English language books is as high as 20 percent.

Consolidation has been a key trend in the structure of the publishing industry (Clark and Phillips 2019). There are large publishing groups evident across sectors from academic publishing to trade (or consumer publishing). In the area of journals, efficiencies have been found by creating large libraries of content for digital distribution. In consumer publishing, international publishing groups operate across many different markets. The top four publishers in the UK had in 2017 a total share approaching 50 percent of the market. The merger in 2013 of Penguin and Random House created the largest publishing group in the UK, with a market

DOI: 10.4324/9780429275340-29

share in 2017 of 23 percent. The second largest group, Hachette, is French-owned and has significant operations in France, Spain, the United States, and the UK. HarperCollins, the next largest player, is headquartered in New York with operations in 17 countries. Pan Macmillan, part of the Macmillan Group, operates in over 70 countries worldwide.

That consolidation works can be seen in rising profitability – the combined Penguin Random House recorded a profit margin of 16 percent in 2016, double the level achieved by the individual parties before the merger. The large publishing groups have greater negotiating power with brand authors, suppliers, and retailers. At the same time, barriers to entry in the publishing industry are low, enabling both self-publishing and startups to flourish. With the arrival of ebooks and digital printing of physical stock in low numbers, there is less need to invest capital in a warehouse of books. Amazon offers a level-playing field for all the players, whether authors, small and medium enterprises (SMEs), or large publishers, as consumers do not purchase by publisher when buying online. By contrast, it is much harder for the smaller players to place their books in high-street bookshops.

Digitization opens debates about technology and determinism. The technology is there for print to disappear completely, and indeed print is in severe decline in the world of newspapers and magazines. Yet the rapid growth of ebooks in consumer publishing stalled and print has staged a limited revival. There remains an attraction to the physical, and print is much easier to gift and pass around friends and family. We do not own an ebook – it is only acquired under a license and is not owned by the user. With other media, this perhaps does not matter to those who have become accustomed to streaming music or video, but ownership of the printed book is still valued, with the attraction of the smell of the paper or the building of a physical library.

Rather than technology, was it economics that drove the initial burst of enthusiasm for ebooks? Amazon offered both an electronic reading device and ebooks at low prices – the Kindle was first released in November 2007 and there were 90,000 ebooks available to purchase and download. Electronics giant Sony first sold an e-reader in 2004, discontinuing sales ten years later. At one stage, to encourage take-up of the device, it was pricing ebooks as low as 20p. Today users of ebooks can read them across devices, not simply on a dedicated reader, for example by using Amazon's Kindle app. Amazon has the dominant market share in the ebook market, strengthened by the sales of self-published titles in this format.

The subsequent plateauing of ebook sales made the headlines, but this coincided with the attempt by publishers to raise the level of prices. There is continued demand for ebooks in fiction genres such as romance or fantasy, published by mainstream companies but also from self-published authors at competitive prices. In academic markets, shrinking demand for research monographs has pushed prices up above the reach of the average user, and it is to be anticipated that digital access will become the norm as institutions purchase online libraries, or works are made available through open access routes, leaving printed copies only made to order.

It is remarkable the attention paid to book publishing by the large technology companies. This has coincided with a shift in value away from content producers toward those companies that own the channels into the markets. Amazon started in 1994 with sales of books, as the company founder Jeff Bezos saw the potential for an online operation in a business with so many different product lines, many more than could be stocked in a physical shop. Consequently, bricks and mortar shops have had a torrid time, with only Waterstones in the UK and Barnes & Noble in the United States left as significant chains dedicated to books. Amazon, meanwhile, has made a foray into the US market with its own physical stores. Internet sales now account for over half of the volume sales of print books in the UK. Reflecting on the US context, Shatzkin (2019) comments:

The movement of book sales from physical stores to online has been unabated since Amazon began. There is no reason for it to stop. Books have a ton of characteristics that make them perfect for online shopping. You want to shop from a full selection no store has. It is very seldom when you must have a book right now. And books are heavy, so you don't really want to carry them around if you can avoid it.

To survive, bookstores have needed to be flexible in their approach, offering author events, coffee, and a variety of non-book merchandise (stationery, games, and book-related gifts). Having seen their numbers cut in half in both the UK and United States, independent bookstores are staging a comeback. The concept of independence is attractive to consumers in a globalized world where high streets all look the same.

> A core segment of book-buying consumers who drive sales in independent bookstores is attached to the bookstores' communal identity. When a consumer shops at an independent bookstore, they are reinforcing a set of beliefs that they have about themselves and their ability to contribute to the economic welfare of their local community.
>
> *Raffaelli 2020: 12*

In the UK, Waterstones has experimented by opening its own small branches that look like independents:

> But what the company has done in Southwold, Rye and Harpenden is naughty. And it's more than just a storm in an overpriced Emma Bridgewater teacup. Waterstones has opened up shops that purport to be both local and independent, when they are neither. In Southwold, the branch is called Southwold Books, in Rye it's The Rye Bookshop and in Harpenden, Harpenden Books.
>
> *Wallop 2017*

Google could see many dimensions to working with books, yet its business model – to make as much content freely available and derive income from advertising – has remained at odds with the model of book publishers, keen to sell their content. Google saw books as high-value content to have in its databases, helping to feed its artificial intelligence (AI) development and algorithms. Digitizing the collections of major research libraries was a prestigious and high-profile project. Problems arose when the company started digitizing so-called "orphan works" – those still in copyright but where the copyright holder is difficult to trace. Google took the line that this should be viewed as "fair use," the doctrine in US law permitting certain limited uses of copyrighted works without authorization from the rights holder. However, this approach became mired for years in the US courts following legal action by the Authors Guild, before being finally settled in Google's favor in 2016.

> In its youth, Google Books inspired the world with a vision of a "library of utopia" that would extend online convenience to offline wisdom. At the time it seemed like a singularity for the written word: We'd upload all those pages into the ether, and they would somehow produce a phase-shift in human awareness. Instead, Google Books has settled into a quiet middle age of sourcing quotes and serving up snippets of text from the 25 million-plus tomes in its database.
>
> *Rosenberg 2017*

Publishers recognize the value of having their content visible to the Google search engine, and selected pages searchable in Google Books, and their hope is that browsers will go on to purchase the book.

The democratization of authorship is another key trend (Phillips 2014). Previously gatekeepers such as literary agents or editors controlled access to the publishing process (Phillips, 2020). Authors might have been discovered in the slushpile of unsolicited manuscripts, but those authors who funded their own print runs were branded with the stigma of vanity publishing. Today self-publishing is seen as perfectly acceptable and there are many routes to an audience, from social media and blogs to podcasting. Self-published authors can have a few print copies produced or reach a global audience with an ebook published on Amazon. "Self-publishing on Amazon's platforms benefits authors in some genres – including romance and mystery, where readers tear through books and writing them might not take a long time – over those who spend years writing novels, or who do deeply researched nonfiction books" (Semuels 2018). The number of self-published titles is huge with over a million print and ebooks published each year in the United States. Evidence indicates self-published authors are more likely to be female and "educated and busy, and not self-publishing in retirement, bitter from a lifetime's disappointment from the traditional industry" (Baverstock 2014). Few indie authors reach a wider audience, but there are notable successes such as romcom author Nicola May and the thriller writer Rachel Abbott. Hybrid authors will carry on self-publishing while doing deals with mainstream publishing houses who offer editorial and marketing support plus access to physical bookstores. Abbott has sold over 3 million copies of her self-published books (Clark and Phillips, 2019), and in 2020, signed a deal with the publisher Boukouture to publish her new psychological thriller in the United States and Canada. Community platforms attract writers and readers: for example, Wattpad is home to a community of more than 90 million people who spend over 23 billion minutes a month engaged in original stories. The company is using AI to analyze content and predict the most successful stories.

There is a global market for books and around 50 percent of UK production goes to overseas markets. The success of English globally as a language of business and culture ensures healthy markets around the world. With the arrival of ebooks and the digital printing of small numbers or even single copies to order, the book is global, able to reach all parts of the world. At the same time, in the face of globalization (Phillips 2014), many countries are keen to preserve their own cultural and literary distinctiveness. Often this means the availability of grants for authors and translations into other languages, as well as subsidies for booksellers and publishers, and funding for libraries. For example, in Norway,

> The Norwegian Arts Council purchases up to 1,500 copies of about 600 new titles every year. These books are distributed to local libraries throughout the country. The scheme was established in the 1960s and is still extremely important for both publishers, writers and, eventually, the readers.
>
> *NPA 2020*

## The business of books

The business of book publishing depends on the fundamental framework of copyright. Publishers license content from authors and then have the freedom to exploit the rights in the work, from selling print copies or ebooks, to licensing translations to publishers in other countries. In trade publishing, authors have their interests managed by literary agents, who may keep back from publishers the translation rights, or film or TV rights (Phillips 2020). Breaking up the rights by territory (separately selling rights in different markets) has proved to be a successful strategy, although the larger publishers remain keen to acquire as many rights as possible. They are able to publish in many different parts of the world simultaneously and increasingly in other languages through local offices (HarperCollins offers the ability to reach 15 translation markets). As the quality of automatic language translation improves, this option will become more attractive for books.

Challenges to the established ways of exploiting copyright arise from a number of directions. The movement toward open content often comes from authors in the first place. If they are earning little by way of income from their writing, they would prefer to be read more widely through open methods of distribution. As Sundara Rajan (2019: 78) comments:

> Every writer wants to be read – every author's goal, fundamentally, is communication with the public. Extreme restrictions on the communication of works, including extreme reactions to copying and piracy, make little sense for authors, who typically have every interest in maintaining a constructive relationship with their public, rather than allowing their audiences to be antagonized.

In academic publishing, there is now considerable pressure from policymakers for research outputs to be immediately available on publication through open access. The international initiative Plan S, backed by major research funders, has accelerated this change and publishers are moving toward Read and Publish agreements, often by country, whereby payments to them cover both authorship and access on publication. For example, in 2020 Leiden-based publisher Brill announced an agreement with a consortium of Dutch university libraries to provide reading access to Dutch researchers and allowing unlimited open access publishing in all Brill journals (Brill 2020).

Piracy continues to be an issue, facilitated by digital publication and distribution. In countries such as Spain and Russia, the problem is so large across all sectors of publishing that there is little financial incentive for authors to continue their work. Some see a ray of hope with the new business models popularized for film and TV, where viewers pay a monthly subscription for streaming services, extending into the book business. Javier Celaya, an expert on the Spanish-speaking markets, says:

> As with Netflix, subscription platforms with unlimited access to thousands of audiobooks and podcasts create new consumption habits, create new audiences, and create new markets. Subscription platforms prevail in Spain and Latin America's markets as the main channels for audiobooks, accounting for an aggregate 83 percent of sales in the audiobook format.
>
> *(Anderson, 2020)*

Few would support piracy as a way of enabling open access to academic literature, yet this has occurred. The publisher Elsevier sued the site Sci-Hub, which hosts millions of scientific papers, but the site is still in operation under the leadership of the Kazakhstani computer programmer Alexandra Elbakyan.

> That 2015 lawsuit would, however, place a spotlight on Elbakyan and her homegrown operation. The publicity made Sci-Hub bigger, transforming it into the largest Open Access academic resource in the world. In just six years of existence, Sci-Hub had

become a juggernaut: the 64.5 million papers it hosted represented two-thirds of all published research, and it was available to anyone.

*Graber-Stiehl 2018*

Risk is an essential element of the publishing business. As Bhaskar (2013: 160) argues,

> bearing risk is part of what a publisher does. They advance funds to the author, create the product, pay for it to be produced, hold the stock, invest in the marketing and promotion of the book. Everything a publisher does requires investment without certainty of return. Publishing without cash is impossible.

The level of risk varies by publishing sector, with the highest stakes to be found in trade or general publishing. Authors receive large advances for high-profile projects, and investments made in printed stock, marketing campaigns, and author tours. The risk for authors comes if sales are poor and the investment does not pay off – they may be dropped by their publishers and possibly their literary agents. The gambling culture moves on to the next project with editors keen to highlight their successes and bury their mistakes. Thompson (2012: 211) writes of this culture:

> It's a gamble, a roll of the dice, which pays off in some cases and fails in others, and the challenge for the publisher is to try to ensure that you win enough times to compensate for the books that fail, and that, when you do win, you are able to turn it into a success on a scale that will make up for all those failures and make a serious difference to your top and bottom lines.

Bright spots in commercial publishing include non-fiction (which has grown in contrast to the decline in literary fiction), children's publishing, and audio. As genre fiction has experienced increasing ebook sales, bookshops have given more prominence to non-fiction. Since the days of Harry Potter, children's books have seen healthy growth, encouraged by the success of Young Adult fiction like Stephanie Meyer's *Twilight Saga* (2005–2008) and Suzanne Collins' *The Hunger Games* trilogy (2008–2010), followed by the more recent growth in middle grade fiction. With younger children, parents are keen to buy books in print as a release for their offspring from time on screens, for while the web has kept the facility for reading a key skill, the popularity of YouTube among younger audiences is just one sign of a definite shift toward a visual culture.

Publishers are in constant search of the next trend, whether coloring books, psychological fiction, or serious non-fiction. One hit may generate a new genre or a short-lived bubble. Cycles of sales are observable over time in particular categories, such as puzzle books or celebrity autobiographies (Bunyard, 2020). There is constant experimentation around business models, whether digital or audio first, or crowdfunding to guarantee a market for the book. Targeted at young readers, the publishing hit *Good Night Stories for Rebel Girls* (2017) first achieved prominence through a tremendously successful campaign on the crowdfunding site Kickstarter, while "the second-most funded Kickstarter book [is] *Chassepot to FAMAS*, a detailed history of French military rifles, which started with a $25,000 goal and ended up raising over $800,000" (Nicolas, 2020).

A prominent area of growth is that of audio sales (doubling in the UK between 2014 and 2018), and audio is particularly popular among younger readers. In 2019, half of all American consumers said they had listened to an audiobook; the rise is attributed to an increasing reliance on the technologies that can play digital audio, from smartphones to smart speakers to in-dash car entertainment systems. The simultaneous rise of podcasting may also have spurred interest in audiobooks, given that 55% of audiobook listeners had also listened to a podcast within the last month.

*Rowe 2019*

Again, Amazon is a prominent player, with big budget productions available through their Audible platform, and there are new players arriving from outside the traditional publishing industry. Consumers choose on the book and the author, but also on the name of the narrator. In the UK for example, anything read by writer and actor Stephen Fry is likely to command a large audience. There is growing interest in audio first projects, with authors writing for the medium. Alice Lutyens of literary agency Curtis Brown foresees more innovation on the way:

I've been encouraging agents to consider which of their authors is ready for something a bit different and fun … Writing something just for audio, or doing a series of podcasts that go beyond the book, or getting in people who are not authors, such as screenwriters.

*quoted in Tapper 2018*

With academic book publishing, research monographs continue to survive despite falling print runs and high pricing from publishers. There will surely come a point where the book goes digital with a few physical copies only created for the author through digital printing. Already the larger academic publishers often fold new books into their online libraries. The environment for textbooks is difficult with increased competition from rental sites and sluggish demand from students who expect their universities to provide free access in print or online. Educational and academic publishers have moved from selling discrete products to the sale of services, such as testing materials for schools or a comprehensive database of book and journal content accessible anywhere on a range of devices. The pandemic of 2020 accelerated a shift to digital in educational and academic markets, with the growth of learning online.

## Society and culture

Books compete for our time and attention, and there is acceptance that they have diminished in importance with the arrival of other media.

Whether radio, television, or digital media, among others, books are no longer the only or even the most powerful mechanisms of communicating to wider audiences. Other media companies and entities, and other media forms, whether the BBC or Netflix, talk radio or the massively-multiplayer online game, have arisen to occupy spaces once inhabited by the book.

*Phillips and Bhaskar 2019: 5*

Yet the reading culture in the UK remains strong and books continue to enjoy the societal benefit that there is no Value Added Tax on books and ebooks. During the global pandemic of 2020, many people retreated to the comfort of books as other forms of entertainment such as theater and cinema disappeared.

Books play a lesser part in our water cooler culture than say 30 years ago, but there is no doubt that Harry Potter and *Fifty Shades of Grey* have been widely popular and much discussed.

Over the period 2010–2019, installments in E. L. James' erotic romance trilogy (2011–12) were the top-selling books in the UK market selling over 11 million copies. Originally posted by the author as fan fiction online (in the vein of the *Twilight* series), the first book was published as an ebook and through print on demand by a small Australian publisher, Writer's Coffee Shop, before the rights were bought by Random House. In the United States, *50 Shades of Grey* stayed on *The New York Times*' Bestseller List for 133 consecutive weeks.

Seeking sales from new directions, publishers have commissioned books from influencers and new authors with large followings on social media. In a world of soundbites and short attention spans, books represent long-form content, but as Caroline Harris (2020: 201) reflects: "The bound-ness of books has been contrasted in negative terms to the supposed freedom of digital forms. However, in an era of in-finite information and scrolling without end, the finiteness of a book becomes a point of difference." Many politicians, journalists, and policymakers still feel the need to have a published work as a calling card and part of their personal branding. Books contain important ideas and thought-through arguments, and their continuing importance in society is reflected in the need for censorship in authoritarian regimes such as in China and Iran. Their intellectual currency remains high and reactions to the 2008 financial crisis, Brexit, and the election of Donald Trump have been prominent in book form. Examples include Thomas Piketty's *Capital in the Twenty-First Century* (2013), Robert Peston's *WTF?* (2017), and Michael Wolff's *Fire and Fury* (2018).

There are strong links between books and other creative industries. Featured among the top five most valuable film franchises are Harry Potter, James Bond, and *The Lord of the Rings*, and film adaptations of the *50 Shades of Grey* titles grossed more than a billion dollars at the global box office. There are many connections between books and theater, TV, and other creative productions. Classic authors such as Charles Dickens and Jane Austen continue to inspire TV and film adaptations, alongside contemporary writers such as Philip Pullman and Sally Rooney. The TV adaptation of Rooney's *Normal People* (2018) was a big hit for the BBC in 2020. Adaptations feed back into the sales of books: when the TV series of John Le Carré's *The Night Manager* (1993) was shown in 2016, there was renewed interest in the book, and 80 percent of its total sales occurred in 2016 and 2017 (PA 2018).

Debates continue about diversity in the industry and the book market across different axes. The UK and US markets have been less open to works in translation, although some progress has been made with the growth of genres such as Scandi noir and manga. Attempts have been made to redress gender imbalances across the awarding of literary prizes, book reviewing, and occupancy of senior roles within the publishing industry. In the UK, lack of geographical diversity is highlighted with most publishing companies and literary agencies being based in London and the South-East, although the large publishing groups are opening new operations in the north of England, and the publishing scene in Scotland is lively.

Ethnic diversity is also a live topic with industry efforts focused on the commissioning of books from authors from a range of communities, together with blind recruitment processes for jobs and special schemes to attract diverse talent. In 2020, Barnes & Noble created a furor by re-covering classic novels such as *The Secret Garden*, *Frankenstein*, and *Moby Dick* with images of people of color.

> But the project quickly encountered criticism from writers who questioned why these books were promoted instead of ones written by or featuring African-Americans. The writer Rod T. Faulkner called the project "literary blackface" ... On Twitter, Angie Thomas, the author of the young-adult novel *The Hate U Give*, wrote that the company should instead: "Promote books by authors of color. Just a thought."
>
> *de León 2020*

The project was swiftly suspended. In the United States, research commissioned by the New York–based multicultural children's publisher Lee & Low into race, gender and sexual orientation in the publishing workforce found that employment was about 74 percent cis women and 23 percent cis men (Lee & Low Books 2020). Of those working in publishing, 76 percent self-reported as white, compared to 79 percent from a similar 2015 study. Progress is being made but a particular problem lies around progression once successful candidates from diverse backgrounds have made it into publishing. Lee & Low's report noted that in 2019 "efforts to make the book community a more inclusive one is an ongoing – oftentimes herculean – struggle, conducted predominantly by people of color," and while data may suggest some progress has been made with expanding the reach of internship opportunities,

> keeping diverse employees engaged and believing they have a home in this industry is another matter. Without a clear career path and the promise of opportunities for a bright future, retention will continue to be a serious problem, and the needle will not move.

## The future

The book industry has weathered a number of storms over the years, from the financial crisis of 2008, the arrival of ebooks, and ever-increasing competition from other media. The pandemic of 2020 saw the temporary closure of bookstores and stimulated online shopping habits, while heightening institutional demand from libraries and schools for digital resources. The crisis also highlighted the need for reliable and authoritative content, as provided by publishers. Where it was once TV and film, the present challengers for consumer attention include social media and gaming. Authors are having their heads turned by the money on offer from services such as Netflix and Amazon, and some are self-publishing rather than seeking a mainstream publisher. The survival of bookstores remains uncertain and they have to sell a range of non-book stock to make a profit.

In a world of content abundance, the publisher still performs the important role of curating the best works and ensuring they reach a wider audience. Books retain an authority when viewed alongside competing, commoditized content. Many authors would prefer to concentrate on writing rather than having to market and promote their own work, and publishers bear the risk of publication in print while giving access to high-street retail. Audio offers a new revenue stream and the opportunity to reach younger audiences. We should expect to see the growth of digital first and audio first models of publication.

While the death of the book has been much predicted, to the surprise of many observers, the physical book remains with us. It offers a respite from screens, the opportunity to enter the world of the imagination, and is the home of long-form writing as this disappears from newspapers and magazines. Ebooks do not furnish a room; neither do they provide a backdrop for a Zoom call. Ultimately, though, the future of the book industry depends on new generations of readers and the creativity of authors.

## References

Anderson, P. (2020), "Audiobook Subscriptions: Audible and Podimo Join Storytel in Spain," *Publishing Perspectives*, September 21, available at https://publishingperspectives.com/2020/09/audible-and-podimo-join-storytel-in-unlimited-streaming-in-spain-covid19/ (accessed October 4, 2020)

Baverstock, A. (2014) "Self-publishing's Vices and Virtues," *The Guardian*, November 20, available at www.theguardian.com/books/booksblog/2014/nov/20/self-publishing-vices-virtues-alison-baverstock (accessed February 20, 2020).

Bhaskar, M. (2013) *The Content Machine: Towards a Theory of Publishing from the Printing Press to the Digital Network*, London: Anthem.

Brill (2020) "Dutch Universities and Brill Reach Transformative Agreement," brill.com, February 6 (accessed February 21, 2020).

Bunyard, D. (2020), "Why We Buy Books," *Logos*, 31 (2): 28–51.

Clark, G. and Phillips, A. (2019) *Inside Book Publishing*, 6th ed., Abingdon: Routledge.

DCMS (2020) *Sector Economic Estimates 2018*, Department for Digital, Culture, Media and Sport, released February 5.

Graber-Stiehl, I. (2018) "Science's Pirate Queen," *The Verge*, February 8, available at www.theverge.com/2018/2/8/16985666/alexandra-elbakyan-sci-hub-open-access-science-papers-lawsuit (accessed 19 February 2020).

Harris, C. (2020) "The Real New Publishing", in A. Baverstock, R. Bradford, and M. Gonzalez (ed.), *Contemporary Publishing and the Culture of Books*, Abingdon: Routledge, 185–205.

de León, C. (2020) "Barnes & Noble, Criticized for Book Covers, Pulls Plug on Diverse Editions Project," *The New York Times*, February 5, available at www.nytimes.com/2020/02/05/books/barnes-and-noble-fifth-avenue.html (accessed February 10, 2020).

Lee & Low Books (2020) "Where Is the Diversity in Publishing? The 2019 Diversity Baseline Survey Results," released January 28, available at blog.leeandlow.com/2020/01/28/2019diversitybaselinesurvey (accessed March 1, 2020).

Nicolas, S (2020) "Why Do People Choose to Publish Their Books Via Kickstarter?" *Book Riot*, February 7, available at https://bookriot.com/publishing-via-kickstarter/#:~:text=For%20Greg%20Stolze%E2%80%94an%20author,motive%20to%20act%20right%20away.%E2%80%9D (accessed March 1, 2020).

NPA (2020) "The Norwegian Literary System," available at https://forleggerforeningen.no/the-norwegian-literary-system/ (accessed January 22, 2020).

PA (2018) *Publishing's Contribution to the Wider Creative Industries*, London: Publishers Association.

Phillips, A. (2014) *Turning the Page: The Evolution of the Book*, Abingdon: Routledge.

Phillips, A. (2020) "The Modern Literary Agent," in A. Baverstock, R. Bradford, and M. Gonzalez (eds), *Contemporary Culture and the Publishing of Books*, Abingdon: Routledge, 170–184.

Phillips, A. and Bhaskar, M. (eds) (2019) *The Oxford Handbook of Publishing*, Oxford: Oxford University Press.

Raffaelli, R. L. (2020) *Reinventing Retail: The Novel Resurgence of Independent Bookstores*, Working Paper 20-068, Boston, MA: Harvard Business School.

Rosenberg, S. (2017) "How Google Book Search Got Lost," *Wired*, April 11, available at www.wired.com/2017/04/how-google-book-search-got-lost/ (accessed February 22, 2020).

Rowe, A. (2019) "US Audiobook Sales Neared $1 Billion in 2018, Growing 25% Year-Over-Year," *Forbes*, July 16, available at www.forbes.com/sites/adamrowe1/2019/07/16/us-audiobook-sales-neared-1-billion-in-2018-growing-25-year-over-year/#2587c3d96050 (accessed February 27, 2020).

Semuels, A. (2018) "The Authors Who Love Amazon," *The Atlantic*, July 20; available at www.theatlantic.com/technology/archive/2018/07/amazon-kindle-unlimited-self-publishing/565664/ (accessed January 16, 2020)

Shatzkin, M. (2019) "7 Ways Book Publishing Will Change Over the Next Few Years," *The Idea Logical Company*, October 8, available at www.idealog.com/blog/7-ways-book-publishing-will-change-over-the-next-few-years/ (accessed February 20, 2020).

Sundara Rajan, M. T. (2019) "Copyright and Publishing," in A. Phillips and M. Bhaskar (eds), *The Oxford Handbook of Publishing*, Oxford: Oxford University Press, 71–83.

Tapper, J. (2018), "Audio is Publishing's New Star as Sales Soar Across Genres", *The Guardian*, June 9, available at www.theguardian.com/uk-news/2018/jun/09/audiobooks-audible-publishing-sales-boost (accessed December 3, 2020).

Thompson, J. (2012) *Merchants of Culture: The Publishing Business in the Twenty-first Century*, Cambridge: Polity.

Wallop, H. (2017) "Waterstones Deserves to be Judged by its Bookshop Cover-up," *The Spectator*, February 27, available at www.spectator.co.uk/article/waterstones-deserves-to-be-judged-by-its-bookshop-cover-up (accessed February 6, 2020).

# 26

# SOCIAL MEDIA INDUSTRIES AND THE RISE OF THE PLATFORM

*Pieter Verdegem*

A handful of companies founded around the 2000s have quickly risen to the top ten of the most valuable companies in the world (*Forbes* 2020). What unites them is that they are all engaging in social media, advertising, big data, cloud computing, and Artificial Intelligence (AI). I am talking here about platforms such as Google, Amazon, Alibaba, Facebook, and Tencent.

If we want to understand the rapid development of these companies, we need to investigate how they are organized and what dynamics exist within the markets in which they operate (Smyrnaios 2018). Social media have rewritten the rules about media production, distribution, and consumption: they are defining how businesses interact with their customers; and they seem to have disrupted political communication and campaigning with far-reaching impact on our democracies (van Dijck, Poell, and de Waal 2018). A thorough understanding of social media industries is not only important for how traditional media deal with them, but for society at large.

What distinguishes social media industries from traditional media industries? The purpose of this chapter is to look into key aspects such as platformization and datafication. The combination of these dynamics leads to a social media landscape characterized by a tendency to monopolization, driven by network effects (Moazed and Johnson 2016). To fully understand this as well as its impact, I argue that our analysis of social media industries benefits from a combination of insights and approaches originating from media economics and critical political economy. These frameworks combined allow us to comprehend the behavior of individual firms but also to evaluate the consequences of concentrations in ownership.

This chapter begins with defining social media industries and explains their specific characteristics. After this, I briefly introduce what frameworks can be used for analyzing social media industries. I continue with conceptualizing platformization and datafication. Thereafter, I provide an overview of the global social media landscape and examine how we have ended up with social media giants dominating and controlling the market. I conclude with pointing at some of the challenges this brings about and how we should move forward.

## Conceptualizing social media industries

In order to define *social media industries* (SMIs), we first of all need to come up with a working definition of social media. Some scholars contribute to this conceptualization by pointing at the opportunities for business and users to collaborate, share content, and engage in creative

DOI: 10.4324/9780429275340-30

production (Fuchs 2014; Hinton and Hjorth 2013). But this still seems relatively general and vague. Meikle (2016: 6) provides with a more comprehensive definition that manages to grasp the complexity of the term: "Social media are networked database platforms that combine public with personal communication." This definition puts the role of platforms central, which rely on networks and infrastructures in order to deal with large amounts of data. Platforms function as the intermediator between different types of users, thereby mixing public and private communication.

Following this, we can shift the attention to SMIs. In addition to pushing the boundaries between the public and the private, they have some other defining characteristics (Albarran 2013). First, social media platforms depend on *user-generated content*. Content on social media platforms is produced and distributed – by the users – at a near-zero marginal cost. Consequently, social media platforms are seen as price efficient because they operate with fixed and variable costs that are lower in comparison to traditional media. Second, social media platforms operate in *multi-sided markets*, unlike traditional media firms that merely produce commodities for two well-defined groups: audiences and advertisers. Platforms, however, position themselves as middlemen, creating value by matching stakeholders with complementary needs: different user groups, advertisers but also app developers, and other businesses (Gillespie 2010; Srnicek 2017). Third, social media platforms are heavily dependent on *network effects*. In simple terms, this refers to the fact that the value of the network is determined by its size (Katz and Shapiro 1985): more users make it more interesting to be active on a certain platform, which will also result in more content being shared and more data produced. Network effects contribute to intense competition, and even monopolization (Moazed and Johnson 2016).

We are now in the third decade of social media. SixDegrees.com is considered one of the first social network sites and operated between 1997 and 2001 (boyd and Ellison 2007). Major social media platforms emerged in the early 2000s: MySpace (2003), Facebook (2004), YouTube (2005), Twitter (2006), WhatsApp (2009), Instagram (2010), and Snapchat (2012). What unites these platforms is that they are all US-owned, founded in or around Silicon Valley. In the same period, the first Chinese social media platforms also started: QQ (1999), Qzone (2005), and Sina Weibo (2009). WeChat (2011) and more recently Douyin/TikTok (2016) also became increasingly popular platforms.

Given the importance of network effects, major social media companies started to purchase new and younger competitors. Facebook, for example, acquired Instagram in 2012 for $1 billion, and WhatsApp in 2014 for $19 billion. Similar developments happened in China too, where especially Tencent established itself as a social media giant. The worldwide tech landscape is now dominated by "GAFAM" (Google/Alphabet, Apple, Facebook, Amazon, and Microsoft) in the United States and "BAT" (Baidu, Alibaba, and Tencent) in China. This concentration of corporate power deserves further scrutiny; it is also why we need to revisit our frameworks and perspectives to look at these developments and their impact.

## Frameworks for analyzing SMIs

When analyzing (social) media industries, there seems to be a division between scholars who adhere to mainstream economics on the one hand, and political economy on the other. This has led to the emergence of academic fields such as media economics (ME) and critical political economy (CPE). It adds to the confusion that classical economics, with founding fathers Adam Smith, David Ricardo, and Karl Marx, originally was called *political economy*. It is, however, important to understand what the two traditions respectively contribute.

Albarran (2002: 5) defines ME as "the study of how media industries use scarce resources to produce content that is distributed among consumers in a society to satisfy various wants and needs." According to Doyle (2013), ME it is a discipline that applies economics to the study of media and, as such, is concerned with the changing economic forces that constrain choices of stakeholders involved across the media. ME thus analyses how media commodities are being produced and how the structure of the markets producing them looks like. The focus is very much on aspects such as competition, consumption, cost structures, decision making, and efficiencies.

While CPE is also interested in how commercial entities organize the production of commodities, it pays particular attention to "the nature of the relationship between media and communication systems on the one hand and the broader societal structure of society on the other" (McChesney 2004: 43). CPE is particularly concerned with who has power to make decisions about media and communication systems and who benefits from these decisions (Hardy 2014). It focuses on issues relating to the growing concentration of media industries, as well as the impact of commodification and globalization. The attention of CPE is specifically targeted toward the social, political, and cultural effects on communication systems and policies.

In this contribution, I argue we need a combination of ideas originating from ME and CPE to fully grasp SMIs and their impact on society. It is important to simultaneously look at how individual firms are organized, how they operate within specific markets, and how they are competing over the attention of users. In addition, it is vital to critically analyze ownership structures and concentration, plus investigating what the social, cultural, and political effects are on society at large. If one decides to solely use a ME or CPE lens to look at recent developments in social media industries, there is a risk of missing opportunities that are being offered by combining them. Especially with the growing impact of platformization and datafication on society, we need to have theoretical and empirical tools at hand to grasp the underlying dynamics so that we can better understand what is at stake and what can/should be done about this.

## Platformization, datafication, and SMIs

The global social media landscape is increasingly characterized by *platformization*. What does this mean? First of all, we need to explain what *platforms* are. Srnicek (2017: 43) defines them as: "digital infrastructures that serve as the in-between connecting two or more groups." Platforms bring demand and supply together, becoming the driver for a new type of commercial organization that connects consumers and producers in exchanges of goods, services, and information (Gillespie 2010). Srnicek (2017) distinguishes different types of platforms: advertising, cloud, industrial, product, and lean platforms. Social media companies are examples of advertising platforms, where users produce goods (content and data) that can be sold to advertisers.

Why do we talk about platformization? Helmond (2015: 5) uses this term to refer to the "rise of the platform as the dominant infrastructural and economic model of the social web and the consequences of the expansion of social media platforms into other spaces online." One of the key aspects of platformization is that third parties increasingly invest in making their data platform-ready. Platforms function as digital technologies that are cheaper, more competitive and dynamic in comparison to (quasi-) governmental infrastructures, but do this "in exchange for a transfer of wealth and responsibility to private enterprises" (Plantin, Lagoze, Edwards, and Sandvig 2018: 306). As a result, public values (e.g., social connectivity) have become increasingly the subject of private interests. This is why we need to question whose interests the platforms' activities serve, which values are at stake and who benefits from this.

For now, let us look closer how platforms are organized. In essence, they make use of three key mechanisms: datafication, commodification, and selection (van Dijck, Poell, and de Waal 2018). *Datafication* refers to the ability of platforms to render into data many aspects of the world that have never been quantified before. Our social relationships, communication patterns, shopping behavior, etc. are transformed into digital data. Central within datafication are processes of capturing and circulating. The former refers to the ability of platforms to intensify data collection practices, while the latter means that platforms function as an ecosystem as data are constantly exchanged between a wide variety of online (platform) services. *Commodification* is a central concept in CPE and refers to the processes whereby online and offline objects, activities, ideas, and emotions are transformed into tradable commodities (Hardy 2014). Social relationships, communication patterns, and shopping behavior are not only datafied; they also have become valuable commodities (Sadowski 2019). Last, *selection* refers to the ways platforms organize and regulate user interaction in order to facilitate datafication and commodification. They offer personalized services, curated to serve specific interests, and needs, but also increase the value of trends and reputation. Platforms are under pressure to develop moderation activities, and not just let algorithms be in charge of selection (van Dijck, Poell, and de Waal 2018).

Platformization and datafication, alongside commodification and selection, are closely intertwined: data-driven network effects entail that more users active on a certain platform means more possibilities for data collection and analysis (Srnicek 2017). As a result, the platform has better opportunities to use that data for improving features and services offered on the platform and this will strengthen its position (Moazed and Johnson 2016). Now it is time to apply these concepts to practice and offer an overview of how the SMI landscape is organized globally.

## The global SMI landscape

In this section, I briefly introduce the dominant players in the global social media landscape. I discuss them here separately while the next section looks at the strategies behind the evolution toward their dominance and asks the question about their impact. While there are more acronyms for referring to the leading companies, I use GAFAM and BAT (Kaplan and Haenlein 2020; Smyrnaios 2018).

Technology companies dominate the top ten of most valuable companies in the world (*Forbes* 2020), with Microsoft #2 ($1,359.0 billion), Apple #3 ($1,285.5 billion), Amazon #4 ($1,233.4 billion), Alphabet #5 ($919.3 billion), Facebook #6 ($583,7 billion), Alibaba #7 ($545.4 billion), and Tencent #8 ($509.7 billion). In 2020, their combined market value was more than $6.4 trillion (Table 26.1). While Apple and Microsoft have existed for more than 40 years, most of the other companies in these groups were founded in the 1990s or early 2000s.

Google was launched in 1998 by Larry Page and Sergey Brin and its main product was a search engine. Where its original mission was "to organize the world's information and make it universally accessible and useful," the company has since diversified its activities. In 2015, Alphabet was set up as a holding company. Its main segment is Google, which includes internet products such as search, advertising, maps, YouTube (acquired in 2006), apps, cloud, the mobile platform Android, Chrome, Google Play, but also hardware products such as Chromecast, Chrome/Pixel laptops, tablets, and phones. Other segments of Alphabet are X Development, Fiber, Nest, CapitalG, DeepMind, etc. As Table 26.1 shows, Google is extremely profitable.

Steve Jobs and Stephen Wozniak started Apple in 1976. They began as a hardware company, but since have engaged in the design, manufacture, and marketing of personal computers, media devices, mobile communication, and portable digital music players. In addition to hardware,

Table 26.1 The world's leading technology companies

| Name | Founded | Country | Ranking ★ | Industry | Sales ($billion) | Profits ($billion) | Assets ($billion) | Market value ($billion) |
|---|---|---|---|---|---|---|---|---|
| Apple | 1976 | United States | 9 | Computer Hardware | 267.7 | 57.2 | 320.4 | 1,285.5 |
| Google/Alphabet | 1998/2015 | United States | =13 | Computer Services | 166.3 | 34.5 | 273.4 | 919.3 |
| Microsoft | 1975 | United States | =13 | Software and Programming | 138.6 | 46.3 | 285.4 | 1,359.0 |
| Amazon | 1994 | United States | 22 | Internet and E-Commerce | 296.3 | 10.6 | 221.2 | 1,233.4 |
| Alibaba (Group) | 1999 | China | 31 | Internet and E-Commerce | 70.6 | 24.7 | 189.4 | 545.4 |
| Facebook | 2004 | United States | 39 | Computer Services | 73.4 | 21.0 | 138.4 | 583.7 |
| Tencent (Holdings) | 1998 | China | 50 | Computer Services | 54.6 | 13.5 | 137.0 | 509.7 |
| Baidu | 2000 | China | 705 | Computer Services | 15.5 | 0.3 | 43.3 | 27.6 |

Source: Forbes (2020).

★This (overall) ranking of global 2000 companies is based on a composite score for each company based on their rankings for sales, profits, assets, and market value (Forbes 2020).

they also launched iTunes and later AppStore, which helped Apple to develop an ecosystem that brings together consumers and app developers but also allows Apple to control its brand and the products and features being offered. Apple has revolutionized the communication industry with eye-catching products such as the iPod, iPhone, and iPad. While still dominant in the market of mobile devices, the company is under pressure from other hardware producers and has increasingly shifted its attention to services to drive profits, which has made Apple one of the wealthiest companies in the world.

Mark Zuckerberg founded Facebook in 2004 with a couple of fellow students and roommates. Since then, Facebook has become the most important social media company in the world. Originally a social network site, Facebook has evolved into a giant communication platform and one of the world's largest advertising agencies. It has used an aggressive acquisition strategy to either take over potential competitors or to increase control over its platform, services, and users. Platforms such as Instagram (acquired in 2012 for $1 billion), WhatsApp (2014, $19 billion) but also other companies such as Oculus VR (2014, $2 billion), facial recognition company Face.com (2012, $100 million), or advertising technology company Atlas (2013, $100 million) have come under control of Facebook.

Amazon was founded by Jeff Bezos in 1994 as an online book retail company. Since then, it has expanded its activities into overall e-commerce providing services to four primary sets of customers: consumers, sellers, enterprises, and content creators. In addition, it provides marketing and promotional services, content production, and other digital services. Amazon's strategy has been to develop a dominant brand and market share, driving competitors out of the market and re-investing to optimize the customer experience and keeping them within the Amazon ecosystem. While still growing its user base and control, Amazon is now most profitable through its activities in cloud computing. Amazon Web Services (AWS) was launched in 2006 to offer IT infrastructure services to other businesses. AWS enables businesses to rely on Amazon's global network of servers to store and process data rather than having to invest in their own server infrastructure, and consequently Amazon is now the leading supplier of cloud services. In addition to being highly profitable, AWS gives Amazon a strategic competitive advantage by having access to and control over immense datasets. With business models becoming increasingly data-driven, this requires a performant computing infrastructure and Amazon has become a world leader in this market.

Microsoft is the oldest company among GAFAM, founded in 1975 by Bill Gates and Paul Allen. Microsoft has developed its business around personal computing (PC) operating systems (MS-DOS and Windows) and other software products of which the Office package is the most famous. From this initial focus on PC software, Microsoft has since diversified its activities, engaging in the provision of multiple hardware and software services. In addition to operating systems for PC, Microsoft also offers systems for servers, phones, game consoles, and intelligent devices. Microsoft increasingly invested in distributed computing environments, productivity applications, business solutions, video games, and online advertising. In this context, it has acquired other companies such as Skype (2011, $8.5 billion) and LinkedIn (2016, $26.2 billion), to name just a few.

Baidu is a technology company specializing in internet-related services and AI. It was set up in 2000 by Robin Li and Eric Xu. Initially, its main service was internet search using an algorithm that ranked results based on the number of incoming links. In the early 2000s, the Chinese internet was dominated by portals such as Sina and Sohu. Baidu's services rapidly gained in importance as they allowed users to search for text, images, and news in Mandarin. Similar to Google, its increased popularity and resulting dominance as a search engine allowed Baidu to let advertisers compete and pay maximally to get exposure for ads in the top of search results. Baidu also collaborated with the Chinese government to censor sensitive information, unlike Google, which had to leave mainland China after refusing to do so. Baidu invested heavily in establishing additional services, including transaction services, maps, Baidu Baike (an online encyclopedia), human resource (HR)-related services, and more recently AI.

Alibaba is a Chinese conglomerate holding company specializing in internet infrastructure, e-commerce, and online financial and content services. Founded in 1999 by Jack Ma, Alibaba's main activities initially were in online retail, operating three main platforms: Alibaba.com as the largest business-to-business (B2B) platform, Taobao as China's biggest consumer-to-consumer (C2C) platform, and Tmall being one of the most powerful business-to-consumer (B2C) sites in China. These platforms together offer Alibaba an extremely powerful network of (third party) providers for packaging, logistics, delivery, and customer service. Alibaba is also known for Alipay, an online payment service facilitating digital transactions. Alipay is similar to PayPal but only finalizes the payment once products have been delivered as advertised, helping to boost trust in purchasing goods online in China. Similar to Amazon, Alibaba has developed and diversified its services to make both corporate and residential customers dependent on its infrastructure, which gives it a competitive advantage over other platforms. Alibaba has also pursued a strategy for global development, investing in developing markets such as Brazil and Russia.

Tencent is an investment holding company, founded in 1998 by Ma Huateng and Zhang Zhidong. Through its subsidiaries, Tencent provides internet and mobile services, online advertising, and e-commerce transactions. Its most popular digital products are QQ (instant messaging client), Qzone (social network), QQ Games (gaming platform), WeChat (mobile IM service), and Tenpay, an online payment competitor to Alipay. QQ was launched in 1999 and one of the most popular instant messenger (IM) services, and it userbase contributed to the successful launch of Qzone in 2005. While often compared to Facebook, Tencent differentiates itself by having online gaming as its largest source of revenue. WeChat, nowadays the largest Chinese social network service, was launched in 2011. Monetization on WeChat happens via advertising but much more via other services, such as animated *stickers* used in text messages, in-game upgrades, and online payments through Tenpay.

## Analyzing SMIs: characteristics and challenges

Having introduced the leading players, we now need to move onto what is behind their evolution toward dominance. Most of the GAFAM and BAT players were founded at the end of the twentieth or the beginning of the twenty-first century. After the experience of the dotcom-bubble, these companies realized that in order to be sustainable, they needed to develop value-added services for a large and growing userbase. Two main events played a crucial role in how they achieved sustenance: the mobile revolution and the social network revolution (Rainie and Wellman 2012).

First, the mobile revolution refers to the spectacular uptake of mobile devices in the first decades of the twenty-first century. Ownership of, but also time and money spent on, mobile devices has increased rapidly (Goggin 2010). In the early 2000s, tech companies had already developed strategies to compete for the attention of their online users and to sell this to advertisers. The next step, however, was to come up with a successful mobile strategy, including mobile advertising. Especially Apple, until then mainly active in hardware, played a crucial role in this transition: the launch of iPod/iTunes (2001) and later iPhone/iOS (2007) contributed to a rapid uptake of mobile devices and services. Apple, together with Google's Android, also became the winner of the mobile operating systems war, where others – such as Microsoft with Windows Mobile – failed. Second, the mobile revolution meant that users suddenly became hyperconnected: they could use internet and social media services everywhere and anytime. Due to the social network revolution, distance was no longer an obstacle to staying connected and this also contributed to the blurring of boundaries between public and private spaces (Rainie and Wellman 2012). Of course, tech companies saw the potential of keeping users on their platforms by offering them new services with innovative affordances. This combination of mobile and social network revolutions allowed platforms to build complete (eco)systems, which were difficult to leave. Network effects established *lock-in* effects, meaning users became dependent on a platform for products and services, and making it difficult to switch to another platform without considerable *switching costs* (Doyle 2013).

Network effects play a central role in the multi-sided social media markets, and they constitute an important dynamic in linking platformization and datafication. Earlier I explained network effects occur where the wider usage of certain products or services results in greater value for all users. Katz and Shapiro (1985) distinguish between direct and indirect network effects. The former refers to the positive effect of another user joining a network or platform. The latter means that more users joining a certain platform also creates extra benefits because that platform becomes the standard for a certain activity (e.g., online commerce, instant messaging, images, or video sharing), which then also result in a more popular network. Indirect network effects thus exist when increased usage of a certain platform also increases the value of complementary services. The intense battle between Alibaba (Alipay) and Tencent (Tenpay) to become the standard for mobile payments in China is an example of this. Another example is the very high price Facebook paid to acquire WhatsApp, even though the latter had not generated any profit. A common pattern we see behind the strategy of digital platforms is to pursue growth rather than (immediate) monetization.

In addition to network effects and the high switching costs arising from lock-in, there is a third mechanism that platforms use to become bigger: *economies of scale*. In general terms, this refers to the cost advantages obtained by an increased scale of operation (Doyle 2013). For platforms, the fixed development costs are high, but the marginal costs for distribution are low to close to zero. This also means that dominant platforms have an important competitive advantage. Economies of scale can take different forms. Let us take the online search market as an example. Google, Baidu, and Bing (a search engine owned and operated by Microsoft) use similar search algorithms, but their market share is quite different. In January 2020, Google's global market share was 92.51 percent, while Baidu's was 1.1 percent, and Bing's 2.45 percent (*StatCounter* 2020). The impact of this is that Google's higher volume of searches produces more data about what internet users are looking for, meaning the company is able to write more effective algorithms. Economies of scale, in interaction with network effects and lock-in, result in a *winner-take-all economy* (Moazed and Johnson 2016; Smyrnaios 2018). One platform becomes dominant over a certain market and new entrants to that market are faced with the difficulty of competing against the strong user base of the existing platform. The winner-take-all character of platform markets creates a tendency of monopolization (Srnicek 2017) and this becomes a concern when the dominance of one player in a market, but also one – extremely powerful – company over society, becomes critical. And yet, this tendency is likely to only increase because of datafication.

The network effect-driven data feedback loop (more users > more data > better algorithms > better services) becomes even more important in the context of AI, which is currently the engine behind a lot of innovation in the digital economy. The GAFAM and BAT companies are not only leading social media platforms, they control the cloud computing market and are also frontrunners in the AI race (Dyer-Witheford, Kjøsen, and Steinhoff 2019; Kaplan and Haenlein 2020). Amazon Web Services and Microsoft's Azure have been dominant in the cloud computing market, but Alibaba (Aliyun), Baidu (Wangpan), Google (Google Cloud), and Tencent (Tencent Cloud) have also invested massively with the goal to increase their market shares. They do so because of the demands of dealing with large-scale data (collection, analysis, and extraction) but also for future possibilities in terms of monetization (algorithms and machine learning as tools for developing profitable AI services).

AI services depend on having access to large datasets but also the necessary computing power to train advanced machine learning and deep learning models. To make AI applications – such as the self-driving car – a reality, an upgraded technical infrastructure is crucial. This infrastructure facilitates techniques such as edge computing, a distributed computing paradigm that allows computation to move away from data centers and toward the edge of the network, enabling the performance of tasks and provision of services on behalf of the cloud. Edge computing offers new, essential, possibilities when it comes to security, reliability, and speed. The latter is crucial, for the slightest delay in response time can have severe consequences for self-driving cars (e.g., crashes). This example illustrates the growing importance of data (alongside computing infrastructure) as not only a commodity in itself but also a resource for developing new (AI) products and services, intensifying capital accumulation and value extraction in the realm of data (Sadowski 2019). GAFAM and BAT are currently not only controlling the social media market but are also strengthening their position on the markets of cloud computing and AI too, leading to even more power and control on behalf of these companies.

## Concluding remarks

This chapter looked into the landscape of the global social media industries. One of the main observations is that the combination of platformization and datafication, supported by network effects, lock-in, and economies of scale, has led to a situation where a small number of social media giants dominate the market. Two important groupings – GAFAM in the United States and BAT in China – effectively control social media platforms and have become the leading players in the winner-take-all economy. This domination brings about all kind of economic and societal concerns. The economic power of these groups raises the question whether new players will be able to enter this market. Additionally, we have to ask what impact will increasing and omnipresent datafication and commodification have on the social, cultural and political realms of the corporate giants (Smyrnaios 2018).

In order to fully understand how social media industries are organized and what their impact on society is, this chapter adopts the view that it is beneficial to combine insights from media economics (ME) and critical political economy (CPE). Whereas ME offers a number of useful approaches to understand how individual firms operate as platforms, and what decisions they take to increase their competitive advantage, CPE looks into the social and political consequences of concentrating power among a small number of extremely wealthy companies.

Then we are left with the question of how to address this. It is clear that social media giants are very hard to regulate, partly because their economic and political power exceeds that of quite some countries in the world. We seem to have evolved into a situation where there exist three different ways of how to deal with the social media landscape: first, the US model positions itself as giving the market as much freedom as it needs; second, the Chinese model characterized by a strong overlap between economic and state power, with government control over the industry; third, a European model of interventionism, whereby the European Union has effectively stood up against social media platforms with regulatory initiatives. These include the General Data Protection Regulation (GDPR), introduced in 2018, which is a regulation in EU law on privacy and data protection, but also empowering the European Commission to fine social media giants for breaking antitrust rules, or for not taking measures against the circulation of disinformation.

It seems we also need to think about new ways of how to deal with the power of digital platforms, and especially how and what role regulation can play in the winner-take-all economy. This includes scrutinizing platform power (Van Dijck, Nieborg, and Poell 2019) and thinking about what responsibilities these platforms bear in terms of their impact on society (Helberger, Pierson, and Poell 2018). This becomes only more important now we are at a turning point where these platforms not only control the social media market but will also dominate the data and AI economy (Dyer-Witheford, Kjøsen, and Steinhoff 2019). Indeed, social media platforms have access to large-scale possibilities for data collection, analysis, and extraction, which together with their investments in computing infrastructure and unlimited financial resources, allows them to hire the brightest computer and data scientists in the world. These advantages put them in a position where their impact over our lives will only intensify and their prominence in the digital economy seemingly becomes increasingly unchallengeable for potential competitors or governments.

# References

Albarran, A. B. (2002) *Media Economics: Understanding Markets, Industries and Concepts*, Ames, IO: Iowa State University Press.

Albarran, A. B. (2013) "Introduction," in A. B. Albarran (ed.), *The Social Media Industries*, New York: Routledge, 1–15.

boyd, d. and Ellison, N. B. (2007) "Social Network Sites: Definition, History, and Scholarship," *Journal of Computer-Mediated Communication*, 13 (1): 21–230.

Doyle, G. (2013) *Understanding Media Economics*, 2nd ed., London: Sage.

Dyer-Witheford, N., Kjøsen, A. M., and Steinhoff, J. (2019) *Inhuman Power*, London: Pluto Press.

*Forbes* (2020) "Global 2000: The World's Largest Public Companies," available at www.forbes.com/global2000/#37459221335d (accessed October 19, 2020).

Fuchs, C. (2014) *Social Media: A Critical Introduction*, London: SAGE.

Gillespie, T. (2010) "The Politics of 'Platforms'," *New Media and Society*, 12 (3): 347–364.

Goggin, G. (2010) *Global Mobile Media*, New York: Routledge.

Hardy, J. (2014) *Critical Political Economy of the Media*, New York: Routledge.

Helberger, N., Pierson, J. and Poell, T. (2018) "Governing Online Platforms: From Contested to Cooperative Responsibility," *The Information Society*, 34 (1): 1–14.

Helmond, A. (2015) "The Platformization of the Web: Making Web Data Platform Ready," *Social Media + Society*, 1 (2): 1–11.

Hinton, S. and Hjorth, L. (2013) *Understanding Social Media*, London: SAGE.

Kaplan, A. and Haenlein, M. (2020) "Rulers of the World, Unite! The Challenges and Opportunities of Artificial Intelligence," *Business Horizons*, 63 (1): 37–50.

Katz, M. L. and Shapiro, C. (1985) "Network Externalities, Competition and Compatibility," *The American Economic Review*, 75 (3): 424–440.

McChesney, R. (2004) "Making a Molehill out of a Mountain: The Sad State of Political Economy in U.S. Media Studies," in A. Calabrese and C. Sparks (eds), *Toward a Political Economy of Culture. Capitalism and Communication in the Twenty-First Century*, Lanham, MA: Rowman & Littlefield Publishers, 41–64.

Meikle, G. (2016) *Social Media: Communication, Sharing, and Visibility*, New York: Routledge.

Moazed, A. and Johnson, N. L. (2016) *Modern Monopolies*, New York: St. Martin's Press.

Plantin, J-C., Lagoze, C., Edwards, P. N., and Sandvig, C. (2018) "Infrastructure Studies Meet Platform Studies in the Age of Google and Facebook," *New Media and Society*, 20 (1): 293–310.

Rainie, L. and Wellman, B. (2012) *Networked: The New Social Operating System*, Cambridge, MA: MIT Press.

Sadowski, J. (2019). "When Data Is Capital: Datafication, Accumulation, and Extraction," *Big Data and Society*, 6 (1): 1–12.

Smyrnaios, N. (2018) *Internet Oligopoly*, Bingley: Emerald Publishing Limited.

Srnicek, N. (2017) *Platform Capitalism*, Cambridge: Polity.

*StatCounter* (2020) "Search Engine Market Share Worldwide," available at https://gs.statcounter.com/search-engine-market-share (accessed February 6, 2020).

Van Dijck, J., Poell, T., and de Waal, M. (2018) *The Platform Society. Public Values in a Connective World*, Oxford: Oxford University Press.

Van Dijck, J., Nieborg, D., and Poell, T. (2019) "Reframing Platform Power," *Internet Policy Review*, 8 (2): 1–18.

# 27

# WHEN EAST ASIAN MEDIA INDUSTRIES ARE FACED WITH DIGITALIZATION

## Transformation and survival strategies

*Anthony Y. H. Fung and Georgia H. N. Chik*

Digital media are presenting challenges to traditional media industries, bringing fundamental changes to the ways in which information is created, disseminated, and consumed. By traditional, we refer to the two major media of newspaper and television. On the other hand, digital media refer to prominently internet media outlets, such as video platforms and online news platforms. To name a few, the emergence of social media platforms and video service providers have encouraged the production and consumption of user-generated content. New media consumption methods have appeared, such as viewing programming on tablet computers via video-on-demand services and live streaming instead of the television box (Keane 2016: 5426). These change the practices of journalism as well as how we entertain ourselves. Exciting as it may be to us as an audience, such creative disruptions urge traditional media industries to transform. Newspaper circulation, paid television subscriptions, and advertising income for both newspaper and television were reportedly declining as audience attention floods to the digital space. At its extreme, the digital wave may threaten the long-term survival of traditional broadcasters.

In this chapter, we have collected data about the traditional and digital media industries in three Asian countries: China, Japan, and South Korea (hereafter Korea). In particular, we investigate newspaper publishing and television broadcasting as representative examples of the traditional media industries. In the three countries, these industries have chosen different strategies: some digitalize and migrate in slow and piecemeal manner, while others attempt to maintain dominance through conglomeration. They attempt not only to survive, but to thrive in the digital age.

We propose to understand the current state of the Asian media industry by applying a matrix across two axes: state-supported/commercially driven and political control/economic control (Figure 27.1). Positioning an industry in the matrix interrogates the origin and form of power shaping the transformation of that industry. To locate the origin of the forces behind an industry, the horizontal axis examines whether the industry is supported by state finance or driven by market dynamics. The vertical axis concerns whether control is exerted through political or economic means. This is significant as media industries create not only economic

DOI: 10.4324/9780429275340-31

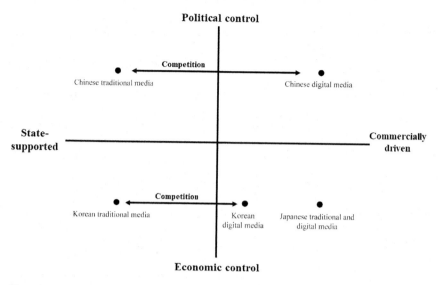

*Figure 27.1* Ecology of digital and traditional media.

value but also convey certain ideological values that can shape social culture, challenge the status quo, and thereby create the future ahead. With these axes in mind, we are able to deduce and reason the survival strategies adopted by the three selected countries in the hope of identifying insights applicable worldwide.

## China

China has always been in the spotlight of Asian media studies, given its massive population and market opportunity. In 2018, television broadcasting covered 99.25 percent of China's population according to national statistics (National Radio and Television Administration 2018). Since the Maoist era, media were considered tools to enforce the party's ideological hegemony (Lynch 1999). Traditionally, mass media in China were designed and structured as a state propaganda vehicle and mouthpiece for the government and the Chinese Communist Party (Keane and Fung 2018). China's opening-up policies in 1978 prompted reform of the media's role and practices (Kalathil 2002). While control is still exerted from the state, we've witnessed commercialization of the media industries (Kalathil 2003: 491). That said, traditional media industries in China remain under state support and political control, sheltering them from the competition of the digital media industry.

On the other hand, despite visible political control, economic drivers are shaping China's digital media industries. Internet video platforms mushroomed in the dot-com era. Many were peer-to-peer (P2P) platforms that facilitated file-sharing via BitTorrent. The content available was often unauthorized copies of foreign films and television series, which attracted high demand in China due to quota restrictions placed on the import of foreign films. Furthermore, users of P2P networks, especially young audiences, desired more diversified content than was available from the state-approved broadcaster, and so developed the habit of consuming media entertainment online. As other platforms supporting user-generated content emerged, amateur producers found their voice online, while professional creators also launched commercial video-on-demand services (Zhao and Keane 2013). Digital media served as an alternative to traditional media. Among the most well-known sites were Tudou, Youku, and 56.com (Keane 2016: 5432).

As of today, China's digital media industry has acquired a remarkable size. The online video industry benefits from the state's ambition to develop an internet economy and its potential contribution to "cultural system reform" (Li 2017: 395). According to Chinese big data analytics firm QuestMobile (2019), in 2019 the three largest video service platforms Tencent Video, iQiyi, and Youku (the latter following the merger with Tudou in 2012) all possessed a monthly active base of over 40 million users each. These three platforms are owned by China's three digital titans, respectively Tencent, Baidu, and Alibaba. Effectively, a "Chinese-style oligopoly with close connections to the government" had taken form (Keane 2016: 5436). User-generated content platform Bilibili, resembling the Japanese counterpart Niconico discussed later, was also catering for over 9 million active users per month according to its annual report.

Nonetheless, traditional broadcasters in China do not stand still when facing evolving technologies and methods in the production, dissemination, and consumption of information. While the Hu-Wen administration (2003–2013) had attempted integration of traditional and digital media platforms (Repnikova and Fang 2019: 2), a watershed moment came with the "Guiding Opinions for the Converged Development of Traditional Media and New Media" released in 2014 by the Central Leading Group for Overall Reform led by Xi Jinping himself, outlining a vision for building a diverse, modern, and competitive new media system (Yin and Xiang 2017: 99).

Responding to the changing media landscape, newspapers and broadcasters have transplanted their content online to digital platforms for convenient access. A reasonable guess is that these media believe an online presence can retain or attract younger audiences. *People.cn* (2019), the online outlet for China's largest national newspaper *People's Daily*, has identified 97.1 percent of all central and municipal television channels as having a website, while establishing their own platforms and participating in conglomerate video-service platforms. State-owned media are no exception. For example, *People.cn* itself uses a relatively modern interface and includes an online chatroom, as does the web presence of China Central Television (CCTV), the country's largest official channel.

Transplanting content and services online respond to the new consumption behaviors of accessing media through tablets and other mobile devices. By establishing an online presence, broadcasters cater to an audience who may otherwise be lost to pirate sites at the same time as earning income through advertising and subscription revenues. Development of digital media has also encouraged innovative programming and distribution via social media. For instance, Hunan Satellite Television created its digital extension Mango TV (2014–) to act as the official database for the channel's programs. On top of this, the platform utilizes a price differentiation strategy to provide premium services to paid members. While most content is free to watch with advertisements, the premium package offers exclusive behind-the-scenes videos and early access to content.

At the same time, political control hovers over the digital media industry in China. To comply with the obligations for entering the World Trade Organization in 2001, the state had to open the domestic market while at the same time exercising a stronger grip on the new digital media. To combat unauthorized media distribution, many video service platforms were shut down to enforce international standards of copyright. In 2007, regulations were implemented to regulate internet service platforms: for instance, the licensing regime required online video platforms to have an element of state ownership or participation. As a result, most private platforms with unauthorized contents disappeared, for only those with substantial assets and good connections with the government could remain standing. Political control is also exerted over program content. In part, the "Guiding Opinion" stresses the development of "influential and credible" media conglomerates. Liu Qibao, the Head of the Propaganda Department for the Central Committee, explains that the Guiding Opinion serves the purpose of reinforcing ideological promotion and strengthening of the majority opinion (*People.cn* 2014).

Censoring sensitive material by taking-down online postings or deactivating accounts has been discussed in a great wealth of literature. Top-down political pressure and censorship are "unavoidable" in many cases (Zeng and Sparks 2019), but in practice, political control is often manifested indirectly. Video-service platforms avoid political sensitivity by opting for soft uncontentious entertainment and sports content, justifying such choices on the basis of alleged consumer appetite. In news reporting, platforms usually do not attempt to differ from the official perspective. Independent and objective investigative journalism is rare. Nonetheless, despite these limitations, digital outlets can contribute to the liberalization of Chinese media. For instance, by aggregating local news from across China, platforms can bring to national attention issues that may otherwise be left unnoticed.

While video platforms became pioneers in digital media over the past decade, today they are perhaps seen as the status quo. Now they face newfound competition from "self-media" (Repnikova and Fang 2019), in particular micro-video platforms led by companies such as Douyin and Kuaishou. On these platforms, independent creators earn more flexibly than through the conventional advertising and subscription revenues sources, which have previously financed video platforms. Using various business models – such as sponsorship, product placement in videos, and commissioned sales on integrated e-commerce platforms – they are experimenting with far more opportunities than their Western counterparts (Cunningham, Craig, and Lv 2019). These challengers cannot be underestimated.

## Japan

Japan is a unique case in Asia, in which traditional media industries, such as newspaper and television, have survived well in a changing media ecology. This can be explained by economic control of the market, which has inherently favored the traditional media. Established media conglomerates have formed a prevailing oligopoly, which gives them an overwhelming advantage over newcomers. Slow adaptation does not acutely threaten Japan's position, unlike the case of South Korea discussed later.

As Hayashi and Kopper (2014: 1136) explain, since the country's modernization, Japanese society has conceived the primary task of journalism to be the dissemination of "practical, everyday-life information." While notions of liberal journalism have been imported, journalism has not served the purposes of motivating political activities or commenting on social affairs. Over decades, legacy broadcasters in Japan established networks across industries, from newspapers and television to radio and publishing houses. These companies have rooted their dominance in newspaper publishing and gradually expanded into other media industries. Structurally, they have diversified to participate in various areas of media production, post-production, advertising, and public relations. Consequently, Japan's media are largely controlled by an oligopoly of five major conglomerates, namely Nikkei, Fuji, the Tokyo Broadcasting System (TBS), Yomiuri, and Asahi.

Previously, digitalization has presented opportunities for established media industries in Japan. In the 1960s, for instance, Japan led Asia in computerizing the newsroom (Lent 1989: 22). In comparison to other Asian countries, however, traditional media such as newspaper and television in Japan has taken a relatively resilient attitude toward the digital revolution (Zhu 2019).

The development of digital media in Japan is mostly commercially driven and caters to the audience's viewing habits. Most television channels in Japan are free-to-air. Viewers have habitually recorded programs, rented physical copies, or watched from pirated sites. Consequently, established consumption practices have prevented audiences from proactively demanding alternative solutions.

Still, as Japanese consumers became early adopters of accessing digital content and communication via smartphones, the mobile ecosystem supported growth in mechanisms for purchasing content online (Steinberg 2019: 166). Audiences have grown more accustomed to watching audio-visual content on personal computers and tablet devices. Streaming technology and the rise of video-on-demand services have therefore posed challenges to traditional television channels. At the outset, changes took place at a slow pace and with low magnitude. Nonetheless, in Japan the digital media industry – defined by consultancy firm MarketLine (2019) as the sector generating revenues from legally downloaded or streamed of music, audio-visual and books content – has experienced continuous growth in recent years. In 2018, the sector reached a total value of $2,455 million, with e-books and video being the leading contributors, respectively accounting for 42.9 and 34.8 percent of the total.

The five major conglomerates (Nikkei, Fuji, TBS, Yomiuri, and Asahi) have their own online presence and provide video-on-demand services for free access to recent television programming, usually from the previous week. These platforms adopt a freemium model, although viewers can purchase a premium, supplementary subscription for unlimited access to older, archival program content. Like the digital media industry in China, some of these platforms also create and disseminate exclusive online content to attract users. For example, Abema TV (2015–), a digital platform launched by Asahi TV, airs some of Asahi's programs before their broadcast premiere, while also offering platform-exclusive content such as interactive variety shows. Most importantly, in October 2015, the five major broadcasters joined forces with four major advertising agencies Dentsu Group, Hakuhodo DY Group, ADK Group, and Tokyu Agency to launch TVer, an advertising-supported streaming video-on-demand service allowing viewers to catch-up on the previous week of programming from the partner networks. Collaborations such as this between the conglomerates effectively raises the entry barrier for any similar services, maintaining their preexisting dominance, a position strengthened by involvement of the advertising agencies. Additionally, the legacy broadcasters also tend to be copyright holders for large libraries of television programs, awarding them enormous bargaining power by holding control over popular content. However, significant competition is presented by the subscription video-on-demand (SVOD) services dTV, owned by telecom giant DoCoMo, and Japanese versions of US services Netflix and Hulu. Nonetheless, the dominance of the five major networks is maintained, and TVer has been described as a "pre-emptive measure" against Netflix and Amazon Prime Video (Sanson and Steirer 2019: 1223). Notably, in Japan, Hulu operates as a separate company from its US mother company, after the Japanese business was sold in 2014 to Nippon TV, the country's oldest broadcaster. These factors all indicate how the dominance of the established oligopoly appears shatterproof.

Apart from accessing video-on-demand services, Japanese netizens also participate in the production and consumption of user-generated content. Aside from YouTube, the key international counterpart, Japan-based Niconico is popular among the youth and ACG (anime, comic, and games) subculture. A distinct feature of Niconico is how rolling comments fly across the screen as videos play, encouraging interactivity amongst viewers. Following merger in 2014, Niconico's mother company – the telecommunication and media firm Dwango – became a direct subsidiary of media conglomerate the Kadokawa Group, which operates across multiple business segments, principally book and manga publishing, and film and anime.

The Japanese case illustrates the enduring and spectacular dominance of legacy media conglomerates. Collaboration between the major players has created a fortress against external competitors, especially foreign ones, maintaining a buffer zone that allows these giants to gradually experiment, grow, and transform through digitalization. Looking forward, it is undoubtedly worthy of our attention to see whether the dominance of the conglomerates will be perpetuated.

## South Korea

As with China and Japan, media in South Korea are dominated by a handful of powerful players, namely the four major newspapers (*Chosun Ilbo, JoongAng Ilbo, Dong-A Ilbo*, and *Munhwa Ilbo*) and four television broadcasters (MBC, SBS, KBS, and EBS). Like their Japanese counterparts, South Korea's media industries are propelled by market dynamics, although we can observe traces of active government initiatives, especially in developing digital media industries as a national strategy.

It may perhaps be surprising to note that the new media industries in South Korea developed relatively late, starting in the 1990s, after the government promoted media literacy in the late 1980s. Development of the internet industry was encouraged and supported as a reparative measure following the 1997 Asian financial crisis and the country's governance has emphasized the sociopolitical importance of information and communication technology (Ok 2011: 321). Korean authorities saw opportunities for promoting the internet industries as an engine for economic recovery, thus leading and facilitating technological infrastructure and human resource development. Today, South Korea is acclaimed as "a strong internet nation" (Kim 2006), becoming the most developed information and communication technology (ICT) country with the highest level of household internet penetration (99 percent) in the world (*Forbes* 2018). It also tops the world in smartphone ownership: 94 percent of the country's population (*The Korean Herald* 2019). Attachment to technology has created a population of fast adaptors with a daily habit of viewing digital media content (Dwyer, Shim, Lee, and Hutchinson 2018: 4556), placing tremendous pressure on traditional media industries to transform.

Conventionally, the press in South Korea have received revenues from newspaper subscriptions and advertising. Major newspapers, especially the original "Chojoongdong" oligopoly, were known to be conservative voices and maintained a close relationship with the governing body (Lee 1997, 2017). Critics have long questioned whether freedom of the press was effectively exercised, given the adherence to the government's political point of view. The emergence of independent online news sites therefore threw down the gauntlet to these giants, including the ideological values they embraced. One example of these new outlets is *OhmyNews*, a citizen-based participatory journalism platform that many Korean citizens regard as a more credible source than the established press (Kim and Johnson 2009).

Apart from the newspapers' content and attitude towards public issues, the method of distribution has also changed materially. Today, news content is circulated via print, the online platforms of the papers, and other internet portals such as Naver and Daum. About 70 percent of Korean people access news via internet portals at least once a week (Reuters Institute 2016: 74), creating a new power relationship derived from the business model of the portals. To explain this phenomenon, we explore the case of Naver, Korea's favorite search engine. Established in 1999 by Naver Corporation, the portal also acts as a news aggregator, so that on its landing page, Naver presents users with news reports collected from multiple media sources. Naver formats the news reports into the site's standard templates while offering auxiliary functions such as comments and sharing via social media (Im, Kim, Kim, and Kim 2011). Assistive functions, such as audio versions of the news articles and adjustable font sizing, improve the user experience. A reader can complete their daily news update without ever leaving the Naver portal, although links to the websites of the source newspapers are also provided. Featuring on Naver is therefore crucial to a newspaper's exposure, and in some cases also its survival.

When a piece of content is read on an external portal, the newspaper company responsible for the original story only earns a "content fee," a standard charge for the piece of content that does not account for advertising income (Hong, Nam, and Kim 2018: 1721). When a viewer only reads articles on Naver, their intention to purchase a paper copy of the newspaper or visit a newspaper's website decreases. As a result, internet portals have brought a devastating blow on the subscription and advertising revenues of newspaper corporations. According to one estimate, newspaper subscriptions halved from 2011 to 2016, and only a quarter of the Korean population remained newspaper readers (Reuters Institute 2016).

The growth of digital media industries has also encouraged the transformation of broadcasting in South Korea. Broadcasters in Korea have depended on three income sources: TV license fees or public funds, subscriptions, and advertising. Among these, the former account for around 40.5 percent of income (MarketLine 2015a). Due to political and policy support, the networks are partially shielded from fierce competition, contributing to the quasi-monopoly formed by the legacy broadcasters.

South Korea is one of the earliest markets to experience competition in online video services (Park 2018: 4647). One interesting feature of the Korean digital media industry is the large number of participants, including telecommunication companies, IPTV providers, traditional broadcasters, and independent web-based over-the-top (OTT) service providers. South Korea is home to Pandora.tv, created in 2004 and allegedly the world's first user-generated video portal platform (Dwyer, Shim, Lee and Hutchinson 2018). Pandora's competitor, Afreeca.tv, entered the market in 2005, three years earlier than YouTube's launch in South Korea. A similar pattern is observed for commercial OTT services. Video portal Naver TV was launched in 2013. Similarly, Kakao TV (a subsidiary of the internet company Kakao, and offered as a feature of KakaoTalk, Korea's most popular instant messaging app) was launched in 2015 and later merged with an even earlier competitor Daum TV Pot, launched in 2007. These developments therefore preceded Netflix's entry in 2016. Launch of these services was encouraged by the relatively looser regulations and greater flexibility applied to OTT providers than regular broadcasting channels (Hsu, Liu, and Chen 2016: 5).

Despite their early entrance, OTT services fought a tough, though not impossible, battle to secure an audience base as legacy broadcasters defended their market cautiously and proactively (Dwyer, Shim, Lee, and Hutchinson 2018). Korea has one of the highest pay-TV penetration levels (172.9 percent)[1] in the Asia–Pacific region (MarketLine 2015b), and adding a digital platform is a natural extension for existing customers (Park 2017). Utilizing a vertical integration strategy, these broadcasters develop their respective platforms to provide video-on-demand and online streaming services. Similar to Japan's TVer, South Korea's four major terrestrial broadcasters (KBS, MBC, SBS, and EBS) formed an alliance to launch the video-on-demand platform POOQ. Audiences do not therefore leave a broadcaster's embrace when switching devices, which Park (2018) denotes as their "N-Screen Strategy": providing services across multiple screens. This model competes well with other services such as Netflix due to the competitive pricing strategies of broadcasters and audience preferences for national or local content (Dwyer, Shim, Lee, and Hutchinson 2018: 4561). In late 2019, POOQ sealed it's dominance by merging with the existing market leader OKSUSU to form WAVVE. Together, they represent 46 percent of subscriptions amongst the top five paid OTT services in Korea (KCC 2019).

As in Japan, South Korea's legacy broadcasters have leveraged their existing leadership to establish dominance in the digital media environment. Still, there remain more competitors for viewers than in the Japanese context. Some experience first-mover advantages, while others derive strength from powerful mother companies such as the electronics manufacturer LG or leading telecom companies. As a nation of technological pioneers, it is exciting to see what will be next for Korea's media industries.

## The digital challenge: cooperation and absorption

Worldwide, digital newcomers are presenting a potentially disruptive challenge to traditional media industries. Faced with changing audience behavior and advancements in information technology, media industries cannot remain static. In this chapter, we suggest that by focusing on two dimensions, namely the origin and nature of control, it is possible to understand holistically how East Asia's traditional media industries have negotiated digital transformation and adaptation.

Despite differences in these dimensions, similar strategies have been identified among the three countries studied. Common to successful transformation is an active strategy of vertical integration to establish the presence of a media companies across platforms and devices, with expansion into other platforms necessary to capturing changes in readership and audience viewing preferences. At the same time, experiences have varied between countries in light of their differing circumstances. For instance, the launch of digital platforms by Japan's legacy broadcasters has proved successful in excluding competition and maintaining their long-established dominance, and yet the same strategy has been less effective in Korea because of the early appearance and relative strength of new entrants. China's government supports state-run broadcasters and a handful of selected others, enabling these to flourish while restraining media coverage of sensitive topics and encouraging adherence to the Party's perspective. The flipside is perhaps the Korean newspaper industry, which has experienced huge crisis in the changing mediascape despite attempts to embrace digitalization.

Conglomeration is also a crucial factor in preserving existing patterns of dominance when transitioning into the digital era. Media conglomerates bind together precious resources while excluding smaller competitors. Japan serves as a prime example for such a mechanism, where the dominance of the leading networks has created a buffer, mitigating the relatively slower pace of digital transformation among Japanese broadcasters. Similarly, in the case of South Korea, we witness how mergers and alliances between conglomerates has allowed traditional broadcasters to establish a major online presence despite launching online video-on-demand services later than independent, third-party service providers. In China, state-support has enabled broadcasters to assert their dominance, and now in the digital scene, the BAT (Baidu, Alibaba, and Tencent) technology giants stand side by side with the broadcasters, developing their strength from the massive capital resources and customer bases of their mother companies. Market dynamics have had a stronger influence online than offline, although political control should not be brushed off lightly and is especially apparent in the selection of who remains in the digital arena.

Strategies adopted by the East Asian media industries are certainly not unique but are incidental to technology trends and so can offer insights relevant to other contexts. Many of the developments we've observed root themselves in infrastructural conditions, such as high broadband penetration and widespread mobile usage. Equally, where audiences acquire online viewing habits and familiarity with the necessary technology, it is easier for traditional broadcasters to construct an online presence. In contrast, audience tastes in favor of local content increase the bargaining power of traditional broadcasters. Owning copyrights for popular content exerts a prevailing advantage over third-party platforms, especially foreign players.

What could be next for East Asia's media industries? Consultancy companies such as Reuters and MarketLine expect continuous moderate growth (Reuters Institute 2016; MarketLine 2019), and we are thrilled to witness a vibrant and diverse digital mediascape, particularly as fresh forms – such as user-generated content and social media entertainment – compete for audience eyeballs. Catering to markets and audiences, digital media have to a certain extent eroded the legitimacy and influence of traditional media in East Asia, at least in the cases of China and South Korea. In theory, therefore, those who are slow to innovate and insensitive to developing trends risk being swallowed by the everchanging tides. Yet in practice, a quite contrary picture emerges, with existing power players continuing their dominance protected by state influence, or by effectively employing strategies to expand and diversify in the digital economy.

## Acknowledgment

This research project is funded by a grant from the Research Grant Council of HKSAR (Project no. GRF 14600618) and Key Fund of the National Social Science Foundation of China: Arts category (18ZD12).

## Appendix

*Table 27.1* Major media outlets in China, Japan, and South Korea

| Country | Name | Established |
| --- | --- | --- |
| **Traditional television broadcasters** | | |
| **China** | Beijing Television | 1958 |
| | China Central Television | 1958 |
| | Zhejiang Television | 1960 |
| | Hunan Television | 1997 |
| | Jiangsu Television | 1997 |
| | Dragon Television (Shanghai) | 1998 |
| **Japan** | NHK (Japan Broadcasting Corporation) | 1950 |
| | TBS TV (under Japan News Network) | 1951 |
| | TV Tokyo (under the TXN Network) | 1951 |
| | Nippon TV (under the Nippon News Network) | 1952 |
| | Fuji TV (under the Fuji News Network) | 1957 |
| | TV Asahi (under the All-Nippon News Network) | 1957 |
| **South Korea** | Korean Broadcasting System | 1927 |
| | Munhwa Broadcasting Corporation | 1961 |
| | Educational Broadcasting System | 1980 |
| | Seoul Broadcasting System | 1990 |
| **Digital broadcasters** | | |
| **China** | Le.com (previously LeTV) | 2004 |
| | PPTV | 2004 |
| | Sina Video | 2004 |
| | TV.Sohu (acquired 56.com in 2014) | 2004 |
| | 56.com | 2005 |
| | Mango TV | 2006 |
| | Youku | 2006 |
| | Tudou | 2005 |
| | AcFun | 2007 |
| | CNTV | 2009 |

*Table 27.1* Cont.

| Country | Name | Established |
|---------|------|-------------|
| | Bilibili | 2010 |
| | iQiyi | 2010 |
| | Tencent Video | 2011 |
| **Japan** | NicoNico | 2006 |
| | NHK On Demand | 2008 |
| | テレ朝キャッチアップ (TV Asahi Catch App) | 2009 |
| | テレ朝動画プレイヤー (TV Asahi Video Player) | 2009 |
| | ★日テレオンデマンド (Nippon TV On Demand) | 2010 |
| | Business On Demand | 2013 |
| | 日テレ無料 (TADA) | 2014 |
| | dTV (previously dVideo powered by BeeTV) | 2015 |
| | Fuji On Demand | 2015 |
| | TBS Free | 2015 |
| | Tver | 2015 |
| | テレ東動画 (TV Tokyo Video) | 2015 |
| | Abema TV | 2016 |
| | Paravi | 2018 |
| **South Korea** | Pandora TV | 2004 |
| | Afreeca TV | 2005 |
| | B TV Mobile | 2006 |
| | Gom TV | 2006 |
| | Daum TV Pot★ | 2007 |
| | Kakao TV (Integrated with Daum TV Pot in 2018) | 2015 |
| | U+ HDTV | 2007 |
| | Everyon TV★ | 2011 |
| | Hoppin | 2011 |
| | POOQ★ | 2011 |
| | Olleh TV | 2011 |
| | Tving | 2011 |
| | Naver TV | 2013 |
| | Hyundai HCN Mobile TV (Replaces Everyon TV) | 2019 |
| | WAVVE (previously POOQ) | 2019 |

★ Discontinued as of February 2020.

*Source*: Authors' compilation from multiple sources.

# Note

1 This exceeds 100 percent as subscriptions to multiple channels are counted.

# References

Bilibili (2019), *Annual Report 2019*, available at https://ir.bilibili.com/static-files/86aadb81-263c-4162-9433-285994bd0f16 (accessed January 31, 2020).

Cunningham, S., Craig, D., and Lv, J. (2019) "China's Livestreaming Industry: Platforms, Politics, and Precarity," *International Journal of Cultural Studies*, 22 (6): 719–736.

Dwyer, T., Lee, H., and Hutchinson, J. (2018) "Comparing Digital Media Industries in South Korea and Australia: The Case of Netflix Take-Up," *International Journal of Communication*, 12: 4553–4572.

Hayashi, K. and Kopper, G. G. (2014) "Multi-layer Research Design for Analyses of Journalism and Media Systems in the Global Age: Test Case Japan," *Media, Culture and Society*, 36 (8): 1134–1150.

Hong, A., Nam, C., and Kim, S. (2018) "A Customer-Based Indirect Approach to Determine the Value of News Provided to Internet Portals in Korea," *Telematics and Informatics*, 35 (6): 1718–1732.

Hsu, W. I., Liu, Y. L., and Chen, Y. L. (2016), "The Impact of Newly-Emerging Media on the Cable TV Industry," *Taiwan Communication Society*, available at https://www.ncc.gov.tw/chinese/files/16010/3359_32658_160107_2.pdf (accessed June 14, 2021).

Im, Y. H., Kim, E, Kim, K., and Kim, Y. (2011) "The Emerging Mediascape, Same Old Theories? A Case Study of Online News Diffusion in Korea," *New Media and Society*, 13 (4): 605–625.

Kalathil, S. (2002) "Chinese Media and the Information Revolution," *Harvard Asia Quarterly*, 6 (1): 41–47.

Kalathil, S. (2003) "China's New Media Sector: Keeping the State In," *Pacific Review*, 16 (4): 489–501.

Keane, M. (2016) "Disconnecting, Connecting, and Reconnecting: How Chinese Television Found its Way out of the Box," *International Journal of Communication*, 10: 5426–5443.

Keane, M. and Fung, A. (2018) "Digital Platforms: Exerting China's New Cultural Power in the Asia-Pacific," *Media Industries Journal*, 5 (1): 47–50.

Kim, D. and Johnson, T. J. (2009) "A Shift in Media Credibility: Comparing Internet and Traditional News Sources in South Korea," *International Communication Gazette*, 71 (4): 283–302.

Kim, P. (2006) "Is Korea a Strong Internet Nation?" *Information Society*, 22 (1): 41–44.

Korea Communications Commission (2019) *Annual Report 2018*, available at https://eng.kcc.go.kr/user.do?boardId=1053&page=E02020000&dc=E02020000 (accessed January 31, 2020).

Lee, J. (1997) "Press Freedom and Democratization: South Korea's Experience and Some Lessons," *Gazette*, 59 (2): 135–149.

Lee, K. (2017) "Looking Back at the Candlelight Protests of 2008, South Korea: Reflection on its Multiple Implications and Lessons," *International Journal of Cultural Studies*, 20 (2): 193–208.

Lent, J. A. (1989) "Mass Communication in Asia and the Pacific: Recent Trends and Developments," *Media Asia*, 16 (1): 16–24.

Li, L. N. (2017) "Rethinking the Chinese Internet: Social History, Cultural Forms, and Industrial Formation," *Television and New Media*, 18 (5): 393–409.

Lynch, D. (1999) *After the Propaganda State: Media, Politics and Thought Work in Reformed China*, Redwood City, CA: Stanford University Press.

MarketLine (2015a) *Broadcasting & Cable TV in South Korea*, June, available at https://store.marketline.com/report/ohme3862--broadcasting-cable-tv-in-south-korea-4/ (accessed January 31, 2020).

MarketLine (2015b) *Music & Video in South Korea*, May, available at https://store.marketline.com/report/ohip3009--music-video-in-south-korea/ (accessed January 31, 2020).

MarketLine (2019) *Digital Media in Japan*, December, available at https://store.marketline.com/report/ohmf8011--media-in-japan-5/ (accessed January 31, 2020).

National Radio and Television Administration (2019) *2018 National Television Broadcasting Industry Report*, available at www.nrta.gov.cn/art/2019/4/23/art_2555_43207.html (accessed January 31, 2020).

Organisation for Economic Co-operation and Development (2019) *Broadband Portal*, available at www.oecd.org/sti/broadband/broadband-statistics/ (accessed January 31, 2020).

Ok, H. (2011) "New Media Practices in Ghana," *International Journal of Communication*, 5: 320–348.

Park, E. A. (2017) "Why the Networks Can't Beat Netflix: Speculations on the US OTT Services Market," *Digital Policy, Regulation and Governance*, 19 (1): 21–39.

Park, E. (2018) "Business Strategies of Korean TV Players in the Age of Over-The-Top (OTT) Video Service," *International Journal of Communication*, 12: 4646–4667.

People.cn (2014) "Towards the Integrated Development of Traditional and New Media," available at www.media.people.com.cn/BIG5/22114/387950/index.html (accessed January 31, 2020).

People.cn (2019) "Press Release of the Report on 2018 Chinese Media Integration and Distribution Index," available at http://media.people.com.cn/n1/2019/0326/c120837-30994743.html (accessed January 31, 2020).

QuestMobile (2019) *QuestMobile Half-Yearly Report 2019 on Chinese Mobile Internet*, available at www.cioall.com/uploads/f2019082719214979767.pdf (accessed January 31, 2020).

Ramirez, E. (2017) "Nearly 100% of Households in South Korea Now Have Internet Access, Thanks to Seniors," *Forbes*, January 31, available at www.forbes.com/sites/elaineramirez/2017/01/31/nearly-100-of-households-in-south-korea-now-have-internet-access-thanks-to-seniors/#1f9547605572 (accessed January 31, 2020).

Repnikova, M. and Fang, K. (2019) "Digital Media Experiments in China: 'Revolutionizing' Persuasion Under Xi Jinping," *China Quarterly*, 239: 679–701.

Reuters Institute for the Study of Journalism (2016) *Reuters Institute Digital News Report 2016*, available at https://reutersinstitute.politics.ox.ac.uk/sites/default/files/research/files/Digital%2520News%2520 Report%25202016.pdf (accessed January 31, 2020).

Sanson, K. and Steirer, G. (2019) "Hulu, Streaming, and the Contemporary Television Ecosystem," *Media, Culture and Society*, 41 (8): 1210–1227.

Sohn, J. (2018). "Korea No. 1 Worldwide in Smartphone Ownership, Internet Penetration," *The Korea Herald*, June 24, available at www.koreaherald.com/view.php?ud=20180624000197 (accessed January 31, 2020).

Steinberg, M. (2019) *The Platform Economy*, Minneapolis, MN: University of Minnesota Press.

Yin, L. and Xiang, J. (2017) "Report on China's Television Industry Convergence and Transformation in 2014," In X. Tang, X. Wu, C. Huang, and R. Liu (eds) *Development Report on China's New Media*, New York: Springer, 99–110.

Zeng, W. and Sparks, C. (2019) Production and Politics in Chinese Television. *Media, Culture and Society*, 41 (1): 54–69.

Zhao, E. J. and Keane, M. (2013) "Between Formal and Informal: The Shakeout in China's Online Video Industry," *Media, Culture and Society*, 35 (6): 724–741.

Zhu, Z. (2019) "Mass Media Industry of Japan: Is 'Decline but Not in Recession' or 'Trap of Mature Market'?" *Contemporary Economy of Japan*, 223 (1): 33–44.

# PART IV

# Intersections

## Transnational exchanges and industry traversings

In analyses of media industries, it is commonplace to find industries labelled by specific media: for example, "the publishing industry," "music industry," or "social media industries." This labelling of industries assumes another level of meaning when classifications are interpenetrated by territorial or geographic constructs: for example, the "American film industry," "Polish games industry," or "sub-Saharan television market." Segmenting the media landscape in these ways certainly serves the practical purpose of acknowledging industries as distinct sectors of productive and commercial activity located in particular contexts. At the same time, however, the resulting vision can unintentionally mislead by presuming boundaries between industries or territories that obscure multidirectional interactions enacted between media industries or between the media and other industries; how such interactions may form hybrid subsidiary sectors represented by their own specialized categories of firm, labor, and working practice; or the endemic transnationality, which in routine ways permeates media activity. Problematizing media-specific and nation- or regional-based ways of thinking, the first three chapters in this part address intersections formed through transnational exchanges, before the remaining chapters turn to connections formed between industries.

Dubbing is crucial to the trade in audiovisual products, with the recording of new dialogue tracks enabling film and television programming to cross language markets. Through original fieldwork examining the dubbing of Hollywood films into Hindi for the Indian market, Tejaswini Ganti challenges perceptions that dubbing simply involves literal "translation." Instead, dubbing operates as a specialized area of media production, in which interpretative and performative actions are made to creatively negotiate linguistic and cultural specificities. As such, the work of "transcreation" partially remakes the audiovisual text, disrupting nation-bounded understandings of film industries.

Wendy Su characterizes relations between Hollywood and China as locked into mutual dependence. Focusing on the years 2015 to 2020, Su discusses how despite US foreign policy antagonizing US–China relations, Hollywood and "Chinawood" pursued joint interests. For a period, China became the leading investor in Hollywood, and regardless of quotas restricting film imports or revenue-sharing arrangements reducing returns to Hollywood distributors, growth made China's box office vital to Hollywood's international market. At the same time,

DOI: 10.4324/9780429275340-32

downturns in Chinese film production, company closures and tighter censorship of domestic movies created market opportunities for Hollywood to fill.

In the international television marketplace, formats have provided an effective mechanism for balancing global flows with localized distinctiveness. For Andrea Esser, several factors signal the expansion and intensification of the format business. Transnationalization of production structures has been marked by format distributors moving toward self-producing international versions, accompanied by the export of expertise through the emergence of globe-trotting "flying producers," and the creation of dedicated facilities as hubs for producing multiple versions. Diversification in the range of territories originating exportable formats has also multiplied and dispersed the direction of format flows.

Paul Grainge describes promotional screen industries as a hybrid formed at the intersection of media and marketing. Largely ignored in most accounts of media industries, the outcomes of this sector are visible in the generation of film trailers, television channel idents, title sequences, and commercials, gifs, or memes circulated through social media. Populated by production companies and advertising and media agencies, the promotional screen industries produce audiovisual marketing content for clients inside and outside the media industries. With multiple parties competing intensely to capture public attention, producers of promotional media are significant for their mediating role in "connecting viewers to content."

The merging of media and promotion is maybe most clearly exemplified by branded entertainment. Product placement, the paid insertion of commercial artifacts into the storyworlds of narrative audiovisual content, has long exploited films or television programming as shop windows. For Katharina Stolley, Finola Kerrigan, and Cagri Yalkin, the ground shifts with brand placements, where promotion of a brand becomes the actual starting point for storytelling. In branded entertainment, media producers and brands collaborate to form "creative partnerships," so that the meaning of brands is enhanced by association with attractive entertainment at the same time as producers gain from expanding their financial resources. Criticisms of this practice, however, address the potential negative impacts on creative decision-making and also the ethics of promoting by stealth.

Examining a further area of promotional media – music video – Emily Caston identifies another industry hybrid, in this case positioned at the intersection of recorded music, film and video production, and television outlets or outline platforms. Music labels commission and own videos, hiring the services of independent production companies. Originally created to widely promote artists on broadcast television, music video attained new visibility during the 1980s with the global expansion of MTV, but more recently popularization of video-sharing through the likes of YouTube and TikTok has integrated the circulation of music video into the arena of social media and digital marketing.

Outlining what they describe as the immersive cinema experience economy (ICEEc), Sarah Atkinson and Helen W. Kennedy identify an emergent area of entertainment production. Staging live events based on particular film or television properties, immersive cinema remains anchored in the products of the screen industries while operating to the side of those industries, utilizing inputs from other creative and service industries but also expertise in augmented and virtual reality, experiential branding, and film tourism. Through their case study of Secret Cinema, the UK's leading immersive cinema provider, Atkinson and Kennedy see the ICEEc as characterized by a distinctive combination of places, practices, and participants.

Producing connections between media is explicitly the purpose of transmedia storytelling. Media industries engage in transmedia production when coordinating the dispersal of a narrative or experience across multiple media. In this respect, transmediality implicates the building of story worlds into the building or extension of media brands. To theorize the industrial form of transmediality, Matthew Freeman proposes two related concepts. Participatory brand extension describes creative strategies directed toward enhancing emotional engagements amongst audiences by constructing layered experiences across and within media forms and devices. Producing personalized immersive experiences then involves the synchronized use of multiple digital media to engage audiences in subjective and sometimes immersive ways.

Closing this part, Paul Smith examines the relationship between the media and sports industries. In the pay-TV market, live sports continue to be prized as premium content for attracting subscribers, while for sport organizations, sale of media rights provides a lucrative – and in many cases essential – revenue stream. In this context, the impacts of the internet as an entertainment outlet are visible through the unauthorized streaming of sporting events, plus the entrance of powerful new buyers represented by specialized over-the-top (OTT) sport services or the digital titans such as Amazon and Facebook. Regulatory issues arise over the effect on competition of leading sports leagues collectively selling rights and calls to preserve coverage of certain sporting events for free-to-air television.

# 28

# CREATING THAT "LOCAL CONNECT"

## The dubbing of Hollywood into Hindi

*Tejaswini Ganti*

In 2019, *The Hollywood Reporter, The Economist, The New York Times*, and the *Los Angeles Times* ran stories about Netflix's increased attention to and investment in dubbing (*The Economist* 2019; Goldsmith 2019; Lee 2019; Roxborough 2019). According to these media outlets, Netflix was sparking a "dubbing revolution" (Roxborough 2019) by trying to make foreign shows "less dubby" (Goldsmith 2019). While these stories focused specifically on Netflix's motivations and interventions, what they remind us is that a significant proportion, perhaps even a majority, of the entertainment media in the world – from Hollywood films to Bollywood films, from Brazilian telenovelas to Turkish soap operas, from Japanese anime to Korean dramas – is consumed in a form of translation either through subtitling or dubbing. The latter is the more common mode of audiovisual translation since it is cheaper than remaking the same film into several languages or hiring multilingual casts to make a film simultaneously in multiple languages. Furthermore, by not requiring literacy, dubbing is more accessible to mass audiences. Even if dubbing is the prevalent mode of translating media texts globally, it is frequently treated with derision in the Anglo-American world, a point that all the previously mentioned articles emphasized. For example, the subtitle of *The Economist's* (2019) story, "Dubbing Is Coming to a Small Screen Near You," is "Once Associated with Poor Quality and Foreigners too Lazy for Subtitles, the Art Form is Having a Comeback." *The Hollywood Reporter's* story begins with " 'localized' content has traditionally been sneered at..." and then states, "Dubbing ... is more often derided or ignored than celebrated. In the US 'localization' is still mainly associated with cheap and schlocky overdubs of martial arts movies and spaghetti Westerns" (Roxborough 2019).

This chapter aims to counter mainstream Anglo-American perspectives on dubbing, as well as expand the scholarship on audiovisual translation beyond its current European emphasis, by focusing on the dubbing of Hollywood films into Hindi for the vast Indian market.[1] Since 1994, when *Jurassic Park* was dubbed into Hindi and enjoyed unparalleled commercial success for a Hollywood film in India, the number of Hollywood films dubbed into Hindi and released in the Indian market has been steadily increasing. Most major action, horror, and superhero franchises are now released theatrically in India in dubbed Hindi versions. According to a 2017 report, nearly 40 percent of English-language releases have been dubbed into at least one Indian language (KPMG 2017: 125). In addition to Hindi, Hollywood's large franchise or tent-pole

DOI: 10.4324/9780429275340-33

films are dubbed into Tamil and Telugu as well. A 2018 report pointed out that the box-office revenues of Hollywood films comprised 13 percent of the total theatrical box-office in India whereas in the past these had only accounted for about 4–5 percent (Ernst & Young 2018: 79).

When Disney's *The Jungle Book*, released on April 8, 2016, in India, became the highest grossing Hollywood film ever in India, it generated a great deal of Indian and international media attention. *The Jungle Book* earned an estimated \$38.2 million across 1,640 screens, with 58 percent of these revenues being generated from the versions dubbed in Hindi, Telugu, and Tamil (Bhushan 2016; Busch 2016; Cain 2016; Jha 2016; KPMG 2017; Ramachandran 2016; Rapoza 2016). While initially more English than Hindi prints were released theatrically in India, by the third week, the ratio of Hindi to English had flipped, with more Hindi versions playing in theatres. Several other high-profile Hollywood films released in India have also received a significant proportion of their revenues from dubbed versions: *Captain America: Civil War* (2016) where 41 percent of revenues were from its dubbed versions, and *Avengers: Age of Ultron* (2015) where the proportion was 45 percent (KPMG 2017: 125). Dubbing allows Hollywood studios to broaden their audience base in India, which leads to increased overall revenues from the Indian market.

While dubbed Hollywood films are often characterized by the Indian and international press as threats to the Mumbai-based Hindi language film industry, better known as "Bollywood" (Bhushan 2017; Chatterjee 1999; Gupta 2015; Sehgal 2010), examining the production process of dubbing, however, reveals a much more complex picture that disrupts simple binaries such as "foreign/domestic" or "global/local." The decision to dub a particular film for theatrical release is taken in India by the Indian executives of the Hollywood majors headquartered in Mumbai, who then hire a local dubbing studio to carry out the scripting, dubbing, and sound mixing of the film. All of the personnel doing the labor – scriptwriters, dubbing directors, voice-over artists, and recording engineers – are located in Mumbai and many frequently work in the mainstream Bollywood industry. Not only do Hollywood majors rely on local companies in India to carry out the translation and dubbing of their films, but increasingly for their Hindi versions, are eager to utilize Bollywood stars for the dubbing and employ established screenwriters from the Hindi film industry to write the dub scripts.

Furthermore, the same distributors and exhibitors who distribute mainstream Mumbai produced/Bollywood films also distribute and exhibit the Hindi-dubbed Hollywood films. In fact, since dubbed films are part of the same distribution and exhibition apparatus as mainstream Bollywood films, the release schedule of dubbed Hollywood films is now calibrated with the release schedule of Bollywood films and vice versa. High-profile Bollywood producers avoid releasing their films on the same date as a heavily anticipated Hollywood film, which would be dubbed into Hindi, and Hollywood studios avoid releasing their high-profile projects opposite a heavily anticipated Bollywood film.[2] When taking the dubbing industry into account, the boundaries between Hollywood and Bollywood appear blurred and porous (Ganti 2021).[3]

Based on fieldwork in a dubbing studio in Mumbai in 2016 and 2018, observing the dubbing of Hollywood films and Netflix series into Hindi, as well as interviews with voice artists, script writers, dubbing directors, and local executives of Hollywood studios in India, this chapter illustrates how the production of dubbed films involves much more than translating dialogues from one language to another. Dubbing a Hollywood film into Hindi involves the deployment of linguistic, cultural, technical, performative, and marketing expertise on the part of a wide array of dubbing professionals. Simply dubbing a Hollywood film, however, is not sufficient for its successful circulation in India. Bollywood stars, social media, and digital platforms play a crucial role in the increased visibility and viability of dubbed Hollywood films in India. What becomes apparent is that a focus on audiovisual translation, such as dubbing, challenges conventional understandings of media industries and cultural imperialism, and disrupts nation-bounded understandings of film industries.

## Cultural, creative, and performative expertise

While dubbed films are often ridiculed by members of the mainstream Hindi film industry for being substandard or laughable translations of the English originals, examining the production process of dubbing challenges such assertions. Dubbing professionals go to great lengths to make Hollywood films seem as familiar as possible through the use of local idioms and cultural references, even if this entails radically departing from the original script. Just as filmmakers in the Hindi film industry are constantly making and evaluating their choices when creating film dialogue, dubbing professionals also evaluate the intelligibility, suitability, and register of the Hindi they employ during the dubbing process. In this section, I focus on two types of expertise – cultural-linguistic and technical-performative – deployed by dubbing professionals to emphasize the varied skills necessary to transform an English-language Hollywood film into a Hindi-language one, with the primary objective being that the film does not "sound dubbed." In other words, the language should sound conversational, and there should not be a disconnect between the onscreen actor and the offscreen voice.

A neologism that dubbing professionals use to describe their work is "transcreation" rather than "translation," as script writers assert that a literal translation can never be successful, either linguistically or culturally.[4] Scholars of audiovisual translation have argued that dubbing films or television shows always involves more than an inter-lingual transfer (Ascheid 1997; Bernabo 2017; Ferrari 2011). Dubbing "transforms the original into a blueprint, which shifts its status from that of a finished and culturally specific text to that of a transcultural denationalized raw material, which is to be reinscribed into a new cultural context via the dubbing process" (Ascheid 1997: 33). This point was echoed by Kalpesh Parekh, a dubbing director at Sound & Vision India – a studio that spearheaded the dubbing of Hollywood films into Hindi – who had overseen numerous Hollywood superhero franchises such as the *Avengers*, *X-men*, *Deadpool* films, and many others: "Once you dub a Hollywood film into Hindi, it's not the same. You're almost creating a new film. It's as if you're directing a new film because you have to think about everything from scratch" (Parekh 2016). When Indian dubbing professionals describe their process as "transcreation," they are referring primarily to their efforts to make Hollywood films appear less alien and more familiar to Indian audiences. However, unlike the European contexts where Hollywood circulates, Indian dubbing professionals speculate that white faces speaking in Hindi is inherently alienating and constantly calls attention to the foreignness of Hollywood films. Dubbing professionals attempt to reduce this disjuncture as much as possible, so while the faces may remain foreign, the slang, dialect, stereotypes, and pop culture references, are resolutely local and familiar. Transcreation, therefore, is a process of domesticating and erasing difference in the audio track, even as difference remains in the image track.

Mayank Jain, who has written the dub scripts for numerous Hollywood films like *Independence Day* (1996), *The Martian* (2015), *Deadpool* (2016), *The BFG* (2016), all three *Kung Fu Panda* (2008, 2011, and 2016) films, all of the *Ice-Age* films, *Avengers*, *X-Men*, and many, many more, stated bluntly during our interview, "I always believe and I still believe, two languages cannot be translated literally. They never can be ... . At a point you have to adapt, you have to go regional" (Jain 2016). Jain then proceeded to describe how in his adaptation of the Steven Spielberg directed feature *The BFG* (2016), he created a language for the giant that was a hybrid of Hindi and Bhojpuri since in the English, the giant speaks in a peculiar dialect. He also listed the ways that he adapted the giant's unique terminology for animals and vegetables into Hindi:

The giant who is the main lead in that movie, speaks a very different language, like he calls hippopotamus, "hippo dumplings"; he calls giraffe "garage" or something like that; and crocodile "croco-dial-a," something weird like that. For us if we had written the same words in Hindi it would have sounded very stupid. So, the giraffe became "*jeera-saunf*" [cumin-fennel] – very Hindi context. The hippo-dumplings became "*hippo-motalo*" – *hippo mota hota hai*, [hippos are fat] and the crocodile became "*agar-magar-much*" – *agar-magar hum boltein ha na*? [Don't we say if and but?] "*Jaise unki sabzi thi*" [Like his vegetable] – snooze-cumber – again, it was a made-up vegetable. I made a combination of *kakdi* [cucumber] and *kharbooja* [cantaloupe] – I made it "*kakad-bhooja*," because I also had to be creative.

*Jain 2016*

Jain's neologisms were part of his effort to generate humor by playing with the language. He maintained throughout our interview that translating the English dialogue literally would never produce an enjoyable viewing experience.

Another strategy for producing an enjoyable viewing experience and to make a dubbed film appear more familiar is to cite and make references to popular Hindi films. Divya Acharya of Sound & Vision India, who had supervised the dubbing of *Ice Age 5: Collision Course* (2016), discussed how older Hindi movies are an important resource for dubbed films. She said, "We go back to our movies and use their dialogues, which are very popular," and related an example from *Ice Age 5*:

Shangri-Lama is very upset with Sid and he calls him "Nincompoop," and a few more expletives, so to match that we went back to an old Hindi movie, *Jaane bhi do Yaaron* – and used the dialogue, "*durachari, brashtachari, bol* sorry!" ["You dirty, corrupt jerk, say you're sorry!"] It fit perfectly on his expressions. We used that Hindi movie line because it is such a famous movie, it's a cult movie, people know that particular scene, so it is relatable and it is funny in its own right, so we used that instead of what was being said originally.

*Acharya 2016*

Such examples of mining older Hindi films for material points to the relative freedom that dubbing professionals have in terms of creative decision-making.

Acharya's comments also reveal how the task of translating and adapting a film does not solely rest with the scriptwriter, but also critically involves the dubbing director and voice artist as well. In fact, what I observed during fieldwork was how much the dubbing director and voice artist improvised dialogues to fit the lip sync and length of sentences on screen so that the script served more as a skeletal outline than a definitive and authoritative text. This is partly because writers do not have unfettered access to the original film. In order to safeguard against piracy, films that have to be dubbed are delivered electronically on a secure server to the dubbing studio, and scriptwriters – who are freelancers – are only allowed to see films there. After the writer views the film in the studio, he or she is given the original English script as the source text from which to write the dubbing script, so decisions about word choice and dialogue length are in relation to the written text (English script) rather than the performed text.

Translating the dialogues and localizing the content are not the only challenges faced by dubbing professionals. There are a host of other constraints that they have to contend with during the actual dubbing process. Mona Ghosh Shetty, head of Sound & Vision India and a voice artist herself, listed all of the constraints:

You can't ignore what you have on screen; you have to follow that. At the same time, you have to localize it enough for somebody to understand. You're limited by the visual; you're limited by body language; you're limited by performance, by length, timing, meter, spoken meter; very often we can't say the same things as short as English, which is a very precise language. There're so many words [in English], there are so many words for specific things, and at the same time, some words can have double meaning so easily; we can't always tread that line in a local language.

*Shetty 2014*

Anju Jamwal, a voice artist, dubbing director, and the co-director of Mayukhi In-sync, which focuses primarily on dubbing American television content, explained how important it was for the voice artist to match her vocal expression with the facial expressions of the character on screen. Jamwal (2014) stated:

The audience will see the image, and if they don't hear its equivalent in the voice, then it will be jarring. Then you are not doing justice to this work. If the facial expressions are of an angry sort, then we can't say the line with a smile in our voice. We also have to make our facial expressions in the same manner as they have, so that modulation is very necessary. You have to pay attention to modulation, sync, performance, and meaning.

This close attention to lip sync, performance, and meter is connected to a broader goal of making the dubbed film not sound or appear as if it were dubbed. Stating that while earlier films "looked and sounded dubbed," by which she meant that the vocabulary and syntax of the dialogues were stilted and lip movements out of sync, Acharya explained that currently the aim is to make dubbed content appear as natural and conversational as possible. She detailed how much effort dubbing professionals undertake to erase the traces of dubbing,

We try to make it as believable as possible, that this was the original work, which is why we also pay close attention to the closed lips: p-ph – b-bh. Wherever there is a close-up shot and somebody has said a word in closed lip, we try to match it with an equivalent in our language where there is a closed lip. Like if somebody is in danger and he says, "Please!" We can say "*bachao!*" ["help!"] there because it's a closed lip. If it's a close-up shot, we try as much as possible to match those closed lips so that it looks more natural, as if the person has said that, the very thing that has been dubbed.

*Acharya 2016*

With this meticulous attention to detail, dubbing professionals maintain that simply having a "good" voice is not enough to be successful as a voice artist. Sanket Mhatre, a voice artist who has frequently voiced for Matt Damon, Ryan Reynolds, and Brad Pitt, described the multitasking of physical and sensory skills involved in dubbing as being analogous to swimming. He related: "You're standing with a script in front of you; you have a headphone on; the left ear is listening to the original pilot that is being played; the right ear plays back what you're saying; you're reading off a script and you're trying to pause and talk along with the lips of the character that you're watching on screen" (Mhatre 2016). In addition to all of the sensory and mental coordination that is required to voice for audiovisual media, Mhatre also emphasized how voice artists have a harder job than conventional actors because voice artists have to act out scenes without the benefit of a process to get into character, having anyone to respond to, or anyone reacting to them. He explained:

> To extract a performance on the spot with what an actor must have done through a process on screen, is something that I think makes a voice actor kind of superior in a class of acting, because he's just essentially standing inside a dark room, but he's giving you the same emotions in another language or another voice.
>
> *Mhatre 2016*

What further complicates the dubbing process is the visual quality of films sent to Indian studios for dubbing. Since India is now part of Hollywood's day-and-date release schedule – films release in India on (or sometimes even before) the same date as in the United States – concerns about film piracy lead Hollywood studios to send visually redacted versions of their films to be dubbed. Mhatre explained:

> There are certain films which come completely black and white, with a flurry of water marks all over them, and there are some that come pre-special effects, so you actually have characters in green costumes walking around and they're doing their part.

Heavily watermarked films can pose a challenge for dubbing when the mark appears over a character's mouth, making it difficult for the voice artist to match the lip sync. Mhatre also pointed out how such anti-piracy efforts can constrain a voice artist's performance:

> It's a scale of difficulty with every kind of print. If it's like a war film, or if it has too many characters – the watermarked, greyed out version or the completely black screen version becomes tricky because then you're trying to figure out who said what and you're trying to respond to them.

Mhatre ended his discussion of the varied technical challenges faced by voice artists with his recollection of dubbing for Christopher Nolan's *Inception* (2010):

> I remember when I had done *Inception*, it was essentially, completely, a black screen, and you could only hear voices, and when your character would speak, there would be like a tiny circle that would emerge and so you could only see your voice's – your character's head. You didn't even know whether he was holding a mug of coffee or anything. We were so unsure of what was happening, because we had no clue! That movie is difficult to understand when you watch it, but when you're watching it completely blacked out with only a head popping out and you're trying to make sense out of it and you had to convert the dialogues to Hindi [it makes it that much harder]. That is how we ended up dubbing that film.
>
> *Mhatre 2016*

In addition to the challenges Mhatre describes, dubbing professionals also have to be ready to redo, add, or sometimes even jettison entire scenes if the final version of the film is different from the earlier iterations they received. Dubbing professionals, therefore, work within very tight timelines; the turnaround for dubbing a Hollywood feature film averages four weeks for a theatrical release, to a week – or even less – for non-theatrical (satellite TV, DVD, streaming) outlets.

Examining the dubbing process illustrates the tremendous amount of labor, effort, and skill that is involved in the production of dubbed content. In fact, "transcreate" is an apt term as dubbing a film includes many of the stages and steps involved in the production of a feature film: budgeting, scripting, casting, acting, sound mixing, sound editing, and trial screenings; dubbing also involves several categories of personnel – actors, writers, directors, producers, sound engineers – who are central to feature filmmaking. What further distinguishes the Hindi dubbing of Hollywood from other parts of the world where Hollywood films circulate in dubbed form is the reliance of Indian dubbing professionals on popular Hindi cinema. Bollywood provides a vast repertoire of catchphrases, quotable dialogues, iconic characters, and memorable music that serves as a resource for dubbing professionals in their efforts to localize and adapt Hollywood films for the Indian market.

## The significance of Bollywood and digital platforms for Hollywood

While dubbed versions of Hollywood films have been released in India since the late 1990s, it is only since 2012 that they have been making an impact at the box office and earning profits for their Indian distributors. YouTube and Facebook have been critical to expanding the presence of dubbed Hollywood films in the Indian media landscape by serving as key platforms for publicizing and promoting the films.[5] Dubbing studios receive trailers to dub into Hindi well before they receive the film and script to adapt. These trailers are released on YouTube through the official channels of the Indian divisions of the Hollywood majors in an effort to build up anticipation and interest for a film. The number of likes and comments posted about the trailer then become part of the marketing and promotion of the film.

In addition to official marketing and promotions on digital platforms and social media, there is an extensive presence of fan-generated content about dubbed Hollywood films online as well. During fieldwork in India in 2018, I had the chance to interview the administrator of the Facebook page – "Hollywood in Hindi." Vinay Kumar is a 26-year-old graphic designer with a mechanical engineering diploma who started watching Hollywood films around 2000 and the first one he saw was the Hindi dubbed version of *Jurassic Park III* (2001). While he can understand English, he preferred to watch films in Hindi and had started watching Hollywood films after he found that access to Hindi dubs became easier. Kumar's (2018) response to those who disparage dubbing is: "Watching a movie in the language you understand the most is not an insult, it means we actually enjoyed it." He started the "Hollywood in Hindi" Facebook page in October 2013 after moving to Jind, a small town in the northern Indian state of Haryana, where he discovered other people who were also big fans of Hollywood films and they started watching movies together. His initial motivation to create the page was as a forum for him and his friends to share their opinions and thoughts about movies. It then became a site to post news about upcoming Hollywood films that had a chance of being dubbed in Hindi. Information for the page is culled from a variety of digital platforms and social media sites: YouTube for trailers; Twitter for critics' takes; official Facebook pages of production houses and dubbing studios; news portals; and television channels. Kumar (2018) stated: "We can't consider this page as our personal page. It has become a social service now." By December 2020, "Hollywood in Hindi" had over 112,000 followers.

While it may be tempting to represent the growing presence and popularity of Hollywood films in small towns in North India as a sign of impending doom for Bollywood, the situation is more complex. As previously mentioned, when one examines the phenomena of dubbing, the boundaries between Hollywood and Bollywood appear blurred and porous. In fact, the main template for dubbing is to reshape the Hollywood film to be more similar to a Bollywood film. The Disney executives in Mumbai who decided to have *The Jungle Book* dubbed spoke at length about their decisions and strategies for the film, as well as their general brief for films they choose to dub. They mentioned that when they brief a writer about adapting a Hollywood film, they tell him that it should "be more like a Hindi film" with "localized humor" as the "local connect is very important" (Vice President 2016). Hence, their choice of writer is crucial to the localization process, which is why for *The Jungle Book* they chose to go with Mayur Puri, an established screenwriter from the Hindi film industry known for his flair with comedy, rather than a conventional dubbing script writer. Referring to the scripting discussions, one of the executives stated, "We treated it pretty much like a Hindi movie narration. How do we treat Baloo, how do we treat Bagheera, how do we treat Mowgli?" (Vice President 2016). Another one elaborated upon their efforts at local detailing such as deciding to render Baloo the bear as a stereotypical Punjabi through his speech and vocal mannerisms.

When I asked the Disney India team whether they have a fair bit of autonomy over creative decisions, one of them exclaimed, "We made a song. A song!" (Vice President 2016) (for *The Jungle Book*) as a way of indexing their level of autonomy. In response to my question about how a film like *Captain America,* which seemed like a quintessentially American story, could be localized, one of the Disney team members described the film as having had a "universal plot" of "good vs. evil." She continued,

> It was really taking that and seeing how we relate to it as Indians, which we do. I mean all of our stories right from *Ramayan* and *Mahabharat* etc. are all about good vs. evil and that resonates well. So, it's finding that local connect in whichever story.
>
> *Assistant to Vice President 2016*

An increasingly popular method of finding or generating that "local connect" undertaken by the Indian representatives of Hollywood studios is to hire Bollywood stars as the lead voices for a dubbing project. Recent examples include superstar Amitabh Bachchan voicing for the titular character in Spielberg's *The BFG*; Arjun Kapoor voicing for Buck, the weasel, in *Ice Age 5*; Varun Dhawan as Captain America in *Captain America: Civil War* (2016); Tiger Shroff as Spiderman/Peter Parker in *Spiderman: Homecoming* (2017); Ranveer Singh as the titular character in *Deadpool 2* (2018); Shah Rukh Khan as Mufasa in the live action version of Disney's *Lion King* (2019); and Priyanka Chopra and Parineeti Chopra as Elsa and Anna in *Frozen 2* (2019). Rather than melding seamlessly into the film, a star's voice, because of its familiarity, calls attention to the apparatus and artificiality of dubbing, even though dubbing professionals go to great lengths to efface the signs and traces of dubbing.

The main impetus for utilizing Hindi film stars is marketing and promotion, with the star's presence foregrounded rather than erased. This is in stark contrast with the prohibitions outlined in voice artists' contracts with Hollywood studios against publicizing one's role in voicing for particular animated characters or Hollywood actors. S. Kumar, Senior Vice President of Domestic Theatrical Distribution for Fox Star Studios India, stated that Hindi film stars were primarily hired for their PR value. He said, "We get a lot of mileage on the media so that helps a lot. It increases the reach" (Kumar 2018). When I asked executives at Disney India about their reasons for replacing the original voice artist with popular Bollywood star Varun Dhawan as the voice for Captain America in *Civil War,* they listed his "huge following with kids" and his "incredible mass appeal (Vice President 2016)." There are numerous promotional videos airing on YouTube where film stars discuss their experiences dubbing for a particular film combined with footage of them in the dubbing studio. The Indian news media also reports heavily on film stars who have voiced for Hollywood films. Therefore, executives of the Indian affiliates of the Hollywood majors attempt to market Hollywood content through Bollywood's star-centric frameworks. For them, a Hindi film star adds value in terms of name recognition, publicity, and fan mobilization. Hollywood's success in India is thus dependent upon Bollywood.

The critical role played by Bollywood in the dubbing and circulation of Hollywood films in India disrupts the standard narrative of Hollywood's global hegemony and inverts conventional hierarchies presumed by Euro-American media studies. In fact, the dubbing of Hollywood films into Hindi calls into question the conventional methods of constructing difference along national boundaries and problematizes the very notion of nation-state bound categories of industry and cinema. For example, how do we categorize the Hindi dub of Disney's *The Jungle Book*? The dubbing script was written by a mainstream Hindi screenwriter, voiced by popular Bollywood actors, and recorded in a studio in Mumbai. With the Hindi dub doing more business than the English original, the question arises, is the Hindi version of *The Jungle Book* a Hollywood film or a Bollywood film? As dubbed Hollywood films are part of the same distribution and exhibition network as Bollywood films, their commercial outcome is incorporated into the overall assessments of the health of the Hindi film industry. Distributors and exhibitors are indifferent to whether their profits are from a Bollywood film or a dubbed Hollywood film. A focus on dubbing, therefore, highlights the instability of categories such as Hollywood and Bollywood.

## The significance of translation for media industries research

Given the centrality of translation to the global circulation of media content, it is surprising that studies of audiovisual translation have been relatively marginal in media industries research.[6] A focus on audiovisual translation opens up many new and important research directions about media production. For example, does translation or the anticipation of translation determine what is greenlit by a studio? How are production decisions such as scripting or casting affected by the possibility of a media text being translated? What sort of audience classifications are produced through the circulation of dubbed content? How do media industries evaluate and make sense of audience response and commercial outcome with respect to the various linguistic versions of a media text? Is the "original" language privileged over dubbed versions in terms of industry feedback mechanisms? When dubbing, as "transcreation," creates an entirely new film, how do we think about questions of authorship as well as intellectual property? All of the above questions are examples of how language plays a critical role in the political economy of media industries and that translation practices are significant to understanding the global flows of media forms.

## Acknowledgments

Fieldwork in Mumbai in 2018 was supported by an American Institute of Indian Studies Senior Short-Term Fellowship. I would like to thank Divya Acharya, Mona Ghosh Shetty, Mayank Jain, Anju Jamwal, S. Kumar, Sanket Mhatre, and the team at Disney India for their insights and input which made this chapter possible. I am really grateful to Anupama Chopra, Datta Dave, Amit Khanna, Anjum Rajabali, Siddharth Roy Kapur, and Shyam Shroff who helped to facilitate crucial introductions and contacts within the dubbing world.

# Notes

1 Dubbing in India has a very long history, especially in the southern Indian film industries (Tamil, Telugu, Malayalam, Kannada), that predates the dubbing of Hollywood films. There are no systematically compiled statistics, but from my conversations with dubbing professionals, television probably represents the largest segment of this industry.

2 Examples include the *Avengers: Infinity War* (2018) – no major Hindi film was released on the same weekend – and *The Jungle Book* which was released a week earlier in India in order to avoid a clash with Shah Rukh Khan's *Fan* (2016).

3 For a much longer history of interaction between Hollywood and the Hindi film industry, see Govil (2015).

4 The term "transcreation" is also used by Indian scholars in their discussions of theories of literary translation that exist in Indian languages, which is beyond the scope of this article.

5 According to a 2019 Ernst & Young report about India's media and entertainment sector, at that time there were 512 million broadband subscribers in India, 96 percent of which were wireless users – 494 million people. The report also pegged the number of smartphone users at 340 million people. With some of the lowest data charges in the world, it is perhaps no surprise that India has among the highest per capita consumption of online video in the world – 8.46 hours per week while the global average is 6.75 hours/week and the United States is at 8.38 hours/week. Up to 70 percent of data used on phones is on entertainment.

6 The majority of attention to dubbing has been by scholars of translation studies, which has developed the subfield "Audiovisual Translation" to specifically investigate subtitling and dubbing. See Bernabo (2017) and Ferrari (2011) for examples in media studies.

# References

Acharya, D. (2016) Dubbing Director, Sound & Vision India, Interview with the Author, July 29, Mumbai, India.

Ascheid, A. (1997) "Speaking Tongues: Cinema as Cultural Ventriloquism," *The Velvet Light Trap*, (40): 32–41.

Assistant to Vice President (2016) Disney India, Interview with the Author, August 8, Mumbai, India.

Bernabo, L. E. N. (2017) *Translating Identity: Norms and Industrial Constraints in Adapting Glee for Latin America*, PhD Dissertation, University of Iowa.

Bhushan, N. (2016) "India Box Office: 'Jungle Book' Becomes Top Hollywood Release Ever," *The Hollywood Reporter,* April 20, available at www.hollywoodreporter.com/news/india-box-office-jungle-book-885950 (accessed December 8, 2020).

Bhushan, N. (2017) "Hollywood Film Revenue in India Rises 10 Percent, Boosted by Dubbed Versions," *The Hollywood Reporter,* March 21, available at www.hollywoodreporter.com/news/hollywood-film-revenue-india-rises-10-percent-boosted-by-dubbed-versions-987585 (accessed December 8, 2020).

Busch, A. (2016) "'The Jungle Book' Becomes Highest-Grossing Hollywood Release Ever in India." *Deadline Hollywood,* April 21, available at https://deadline.com/2016/04/the-jungle-book-highest-grossing-hollywood-release-ever-in-india-1201741499/ (accessed December 8, 2020).

Cain, R. (2016) "'Jungle Book' Rocks India's Box Office with Second Best Debut Ever for a Hollywood Film," *Forbes*, April 9, available at www.forbes.com/sites/robcain/2016/04/09/jungle-book-rocks-indias-box-office-with-2nd-best-debut-ever-for-a-hollywood-film/?sh=6c3d1dd122fe (accessed December 8, 2020).

Chatterjee, S. (1999) "The Dubbing Rub," *Outlook,* March 1, available at https://magazine.outlookindia.com/story/the-dubbing-rub/207074 (accessed December 8, 2020).

*The Economist* (2019) "Dubbing is Coming to a Small Screen Near You," December 21, available at www.economist.com/christmas-specials/2019/12/21/dubbing-is-coming-to-a-small-screen-near-you (accessed December 8, 2020).

Ernst & Young (2019) *A Billion Screens of Opportunity: India's Media and Entertainment Sector.* New Delhi: Federation of Indian Chambers of Commerce and Industry.

Ernst & Young (2018) *Re-Imagining India's M&E Sector*, New Delhi: Federation of Indian Chambers of Commerce and Industry.

Ferrari, C. F. (2011) *Since When Is Fran Drescher Jewish? Dubbing Stereotypes in The Nanny, The Simpsons, and The Sopranos*, Austin, TX: University of Texas Press.

Ganti, T. (2021) "Blurring the Boundaries Between Hollywood and Bollywood: The Production of Dubbed Films in Mumbai," in M. Mehta and M. Mukherjee (eds), *Industrial Networks and Cinemas of India: Shooting Stars, Shifting Geographies and Multiplying Media*, Abingdon: Routledge, 208–220.

Ghosh Shetty, M. (2014) Director, Sound & Vision India, Interview with the Author, August 8, Mumbai, India.

Goldsmith, J. (2019) "Netflix Wants to Make Its Dubbed Foreign Shows Less Dubby," *The New York Times*, July 19, available at www.nytimes.com/2019/07/19/arts/television/netflix-money-heist.html (accessed December 8, 2020).

Govil, N. (2015) *Orienting Hollywood: A Century of Film Culture Between Los Angeles and Bombay*, New York: New York University Press.

Gupta, P. (2015) "Hollywood is Turning Out to be Bollywood's Biggest Competitor," *The Times of India*, June 17, available at https://timesofindia.indiatimes.com/entertainment/english/hollywood/news/Hollywood-is-turning-out-to-be-Bollywoods-biggest-competitor/articleshow/47691269.cms (accessed December 8, 2020).

Jha, L. (2016) "The Jungle Book Crosses Rs140 Crore Mark in India." *Livemint*, April 27, available at www.livemint.com/Consumer/tdVkXkVZniYuaabuRQsHLP/The-Jungle-Books-success-heartens-Disney-to-boost-2016-rel.html (accessed December 8, 2020).

Jain, M. (2016) Scriptwriter, Interview with the Author, August 5, Mumbai, India.

Jamwal, A. (2014) Dubbing Coordinator/Co-Director, Mayukhi In-Sync, Interview with the Author, August 6, Mumbai, India.

KPMG (2017) *Media & Entertainment Industry Report: Media for the Masses: The Promise Unfolds*. New Delhi: Federation of Indian Chambers of Commerce and Industry.

Kumar, S. (2018) Senior VP – Domestic Theatrical Distribution, Fox Star Studios India, Interview with the Author, March 8, Mumbai, India.

Kumar, V. (2018) Creator/Administrator, Hollywood in Hindi Facebook Group, Interview with the Author, March 24, Jind, Haryana, India.

Lee, W. (2019) "Netflix and SAG-AFTRA Sign Contract That Includes Dubbing Work," *Los Angeles Times*, July 20, available at www.latimes.com/entertainment-arts/business/story/2019-07-20/netflix-and-sag-aftra-sign-contract-that-includes-dubbing-work (accessed December 8, 2020).

Mhatre, S. (2016) Voice Actor, Interview with the Author, August 6, Mumbai, India.

Parekh, K. (2016) Dubbing Director, Sound & Vision India, Interview with the Author, August 1, Mumbai, India.

Ramachandran, N. (2016) "Localization Makes 'Jungle Book' a Hit in India." *Variety*, April 21, https://variety.com/2016/film/news/localization-makes-jungle-book-a-hit-in-india-1201758157/ (accessed December 8, 2020).

Rapoza, K. (2016) "What Indians Are Really Saying About Disney's 'The Jungle Book.'" *Forbes*, April 10, available at www.forbes.com/sites/kenrapoza/2016/04/10/what-indians-are-really-saying-about-disneys-the-jungle-book/?sh=3533259e480b (accessed December 8, 2020).

Roxborough, S. (2019) "Netflix's Global Reach Sparks Dubbing Revolution," *The Hollywood Reporter*, August 13, available at www.hollywoodreporter.com/news/netflix-s-global-reach-sparks-dubbing-revolution-public-demands-it-1229761 (accessed December 8, 2020).

Sehgal, N. (2010) "Hollywood Reaches Out to India," *Tribune India*, April 25, available at www.tribuneindia.com/2010/20100425/spectrum/main9.htm (accessed December 8, 2020).

Vice President (2016) Disney India. Interview with the Author, August 8, Mumbai, India.

# 29

# THE HOLLYWOOD–CHINAWOOD RELATIONSHIP

## Continuities and changes

*Wendy Su*

This chapter is about the evolving relationship between the film industries of the two greatest powers as we enter the second decade of the twenty-first century. "Hollywood" is used to refer to the American film industry, and "Chinawood" refers to the mainland China-based film industry. The latter term originates from Hengdian World Studios, the largest film production base in China, located in Zhejiang Province, accordingly nicknamed "Oriental Hollywood." The relationships between the film industries of Hong Kong/Taiwan and Hollywood are beyond the scope of the chapter.

Film industries are considered to be market-based and profit-driven entertainment enterprises, especially Hollywood. Yet they are never purely entertainment businesses for they can never escape the constraints of the respective political structures, ideological and cultural value systems in which they are situated. Nor can they be free from the conditions of diplomatic relations and geopolitics. Both Hollywood and Chinawood are often caught in between these tumultuous relationships.

The Hollywood–Chinawood relationship is defined by an alternately competitive and collaborative partnership. By the first decade of the twenty-first century, China had cannily used Hollywood resources to modernize its film industry. Up to mid-2017, this partnership had even entered into an unprecedented honeymoon period, marked by a reverse flow of inpouring Chinese capital, the acquisition of Hollywood studio shares, and a record high number of film co-productions. This trend culminated in the first half of 2017 when 25 percent of Hollywood exports to China were funded by Chinese capital (Ha 2017). However, the seemingly smooth and fruitful relationship brewed the seeds of profound crisis and collapse.

During 2017, a turning point was marked in the Hollywood–Chinawood relationship. Newly appointed president Donald Trump and his administration drastically reversed the US's long-practiced policy toward China from engagement into confrontation, igniting a trade war. Among the hundreds of products listed in Trump's $200 billion tariff proposal announced in July 2018 were "motion-picture film of a width of 35 mm or more, exposed and developed, whether or not incorporating soundtrack" (Brzeski 2018). Hollywood is one of the few industries "where the US side commands a sizable trade surplus over China" (Brzeski 2018), and it had long hoped that China would increase its quota of Hollywood imports. At the same time, the Chinese government also made a strategic shift in its ambitions for global expansion,

DOI: 10.4324/9780429275340-34

veering from the previous Hollywood- and American-centered projects to the Belt and Road Initiative, a global infrastructure development strategy to invest in nearly 70 countries in the Asia Pacific area, Africa, and Central and Eastern Europe. Chinese investment in Hollywood dropped in 2017 to $489 million, down from $4.78 billion in 2016 (Han 2018). In 2018, the Chinese film industry was also besieged by a tax evasion scandal and a slowed-down domestic economy which drained its capital sources. Consequently, as the bilateral relationship and world politics stepped into an uncertain period, the two film industries were caught in the political crossfire.

In November 2019, the fraught US–China Relationship even pushed the Los Angeles-based Asia Society's annual US–China Film Summit to change its name to the "US–Asia Entertainment Summit" amidst the trade war and clashes between China and the US parts. The clashes included a message supporting Hong Kong twittered by one of the National Basketball Association (NBA)'s players, Quentin Tarantino's refusal to observe China's censorship requirements, and criticisms of China appearing in Comedy Central's animated series *South Park* (1997–) (Frater 2019a). Kevin Rudd, the former Australian Prime Minister, admitted at the Summit that "the US–China relationship has become increasingly fractious," and "there is a wider geopolitical competition between China and the United States." With a cautiously optimistic comment that "the overall fabric of continued significant economic engagement remains, all be it under significant and rising geopolitical pressure," he said in a flippant tone that "we're surrendering the US–China relationship now to Hollywood, it's over you to do some serious rethinking about how the hell do we manage this for the future" (Rudd 2019).

Shortly afterward, the COVID-19 pandemic ravaged the entire world, further deteriorating bilateral relations. Amidst anger, frustration, distrust, and hostility between the United States and China, bilateral relations plummeted to their lowest point since 1989. If in November 2019, Rudd had remained optimistic about "the overall fabric of continued significant economic engagement," 2020 brought fears of possible all-out de-coupling between the two countries. Under such gloomy circumstances, the questions to ask for media and film scholars naturally are: what will the future hold for the Hollywood–Chinawood relationship? Are there still prospects for collaboration? And, can Hollywood and Chinawood help towards bridging the two nations? In this chapter, I will provide an overview of the latest developments in the US–China film relationship, using 2017 as a demarcation line, specifying various factors that have impacted this relationship and discussing the future prospects.

## The Hollywood–Chinawood partnership up to 2017

The partnership between Hollywood and Chinawood has manifested through sharing market profits and funding productions. China's film market has been increasingly integrated into the global film market, becoming the major contributor to Hollywood's overseas box office. Equally, as Chinese capital has poured in, the country has become the industry's most important investor.

In late 1994, China introduced revenue sharing arrangements for an annual quota of ten blockbuster imports. After China joined the World Trade Organization (WTO) in 2001, that quota rose to 20 films, and from 2012 14 3D and IMAX movies were added. As the quota grew, so the Chinese box office increasingly constituted a significant portion of Hollywood's global box office, contributing to worldwide revenue growth. Data released by the Motion Picture Association (MPA) (until September 2019 the Motion Picture Association of America

(MPAA)), the trade association representing the collective interests of the major Hollywood studios, show consistent growth in the global market share represented by the Asia-Pacific region, primarily driven by the Chinese film market. The highest growth occurred in 2015 when global box office receipts (including the United States/Canada) reached $38.3 billion, mainly caused by a 13 percent growth in the Asia-Pacific region. In 2015, China's box office increased by 49 percent to $6.8 billion, surpassing the next largest international market of the United Kingdom by nearly $5 billion, and accounting for close to 50 percent of the Asia-Pacific box office. China's share of the global market increased to nearly 18 percent (MPAA 2016). In 2016, China contributed $1.8 billion in revenue to the 20 highest-grossing Hollywood films, whereas all US box office sales stood at $11.4 billion (Baker 2017). In 2017, global box office receipts reached a new record high of $40.6 billion, up 5 percent from 2016, with the international box office (i.e., excluding North America) up by 7 percent to $29.5 billion, accounting for 73 percent of total receipts. China's 2017 box office receipts were $7.9 billion, constituting 19.5 percent of the global total (MPAA 2018). But the trend reversed in 2018: of the $41.1 billion global box office receipts, the international box office decreased by 1 percent ($29.2 billion), while the US/Canada box office increased by 7 percent to reach $11.9 billion (MPAA 2019). However, 2019 witnessed once again the growth of the international box office to $30.8 billion, while the US/Canada box office decreased $11.4 billion. China remained the top overseas territory (MPA 2020), making China crucial to Hollywood's revenues. Between 2014 and 2016, China's market share of the top ten Hollywood exports was 17 or 18 percent, identical to its share of the entire global film market according to MPAA data.

Besides its share of the box office, China was also Hollywood's most important investor. Between 2014 and the second quarter of 2016, Chinese companies invested over $5 billion into the US film industry through 13 projects (anxininc.com 2017). The most remarkable cases included: the partnership formed between Jack Ma's Alibaba and Steven Spielberg's Amblin Partners to coproduce movies for global and Chinese audiences (Ryan 2016); Dalian Wanda's acquisitions of film production and media company Legendary Pictures for $3.5 billion and Carmike Cinemas for $1.1 billion, as well as its ambition to acquire one of the "Big Six" Hollywood studios (Brzeski 2016); and Bona Film Group's $235 million investment in a slate of 20th Century Fox movies (Frater, 2015). In 2015, TIK Films, a subsidiary of Chinese advertising and cable company Hunan TV & Broadcast Intermediary, and US-based Canadian company Lions Gate Entertainment, announced a $1.5 billion joint investment in 50 co-productions over the next three years. Among the hit movies TIK Films invested in were *Gods of Egypt* (2016), *Last Witch Hunter* (2015), *Now You See Me 2* (2016), and the Oscar-winning *La La Land* (2016). TIK invested $10 million in *La La Land,* or more than 25 percent of the total production cost (Guo 2017). Bona Film Group cooperated with Studio 8 and TriStar Pictures to invest in Ang Lee's *Billy Lynn's Long Halftime Walk* (2016). Bona also established a partnership with 20th Century Fox Film Corporation, part of which involved injecting $235 million into TSG Entertainment Finance LLC with whom Fox had a co-financing deal. Chinese investment in Hollywood blockbusters culminated in the first half of 2017, when 25 percent of Hollywood exports to China were financed by Chinese funders (see Table 29.1).

Aggressive investment by Chinese companies eventually drew the attention of China's state regulators and caused serious concerns for the US government. With the dramatically changing bilateral relationship and geopolitical concerns, the march of Chinese companies into Hollywood was abruptly interrupted in late 2017 and early 2018, and from late 2019 the COVID-19 epidemic further intensified tensions in bilateral relations leading to a standstill between the two countries.

Table 29.1 Chinese investment in Hollywood exports (2017)

| Hollywood exports | Chinese investors | US producer/distributor | Chinese box office (100 million yuan) |
| --- | --- | --- | --- |
| Wonder Woman | Wanda, Tencent | Warner Bros. | 4.9 |
| The Fate of the Furious | China Film Group | Universal Pictures | 26.7 |
| Ghost in the Shell | Shanghai Film Group, HuaHua Media | Paramount | 2.03 |
| Kong: Skull Island | Tencent | Warner Bros., Legendary | 11.61 |
| Assassin's Creed | Alpha Pictures | 20th Century Fox | 1.61 |
| La La Land | Hunan TV & Broadcast | Lions Gate | 2.48 |
| xXx: The Return of Xander Cage | Shanghai Film Group, HuaHua Media | Paramount | 11.28 |

Source: Ha (2017).

## Changes to the US–China partnership after 2017

Under the Trump administration, the severe turn in US foreign policy fundamentally altered the US–China bilateral relationship and subsequently changed the context and condition of the Hollywood–Chinawood partnership. For nearly four decades, the US and China had engaged in a "mismatched grand bargain in which China's desire to work with the US for its modernization coexisted with the US's desire to mold China's modernization in America's image" (Zhao 2019: 1). However "mismatched," the Hollywood–Chinawood partnership is a positive outcome of this grand bargain. Hollywood's hunger for the Chinese market and capital was met halfway with Chinawood's "going out" strategy to promote Chinese cultural soft power. Both sides thus entered into a marriage. This bargain began to collapse, however, as China defied the United States' expectation, and the Trump administration radically reversed US foreign policy toward China. Meanwhile, China's economy slowed down in 2017 and the government tightened control of overflowing capital, resulting in serious complications for the Hollywood–Chinawood partnership.

The US side had long expressed anxiety or even panic over "a Chinese Communist takeover of Hollywood" (Timberg 2016). As the two superpowers competed for world leadership, the United States increasingly feared China's rise and the Chinese threat and seems to be dragged into "The Thucydides Trap" (Allison, 2017). In the new cold war against China, especially launched across the digital frontier with US sanctions against ZTE, Huawei, and TikTok, the film industry could not evade politics and became a target as well. Vice President Mike Pence, Senator Ted Cruz, and Attorney General William Barr all joined the crusade. In his statement about foreign policy toward China, Pence (2018) pointed fingers at "Beijing's censors" and cited changes to the content of Hollywood movies *World War Z* (2013) and *Red Dawn* (2012) as evidence of how China's influence had manipulated Hollywood. In a so-called "Stopping Censorship, Restoring Integrity and Protecting Talkies Act," Cruz proposed to prohibit Hollywood studios from using US government funds for film production if they altered content to please Chinese censors (Davis, 2020a). Barr also criticized Hollywood for "kowtowing" to the Beijing regime (Hayden, 2020). Disney's 2020 remake of *Mulan* also fell prey to politics when the main actress Liu Yifei expressed her support for the actions of the Hong Kong police against the pro-democracy movement, and Disney's acknowledgment of assistance obtained from "publicity departments" in the city of Turpan and in the Xinjiang

Uyghur Autonomous Region where forced reeducation camps are located (Brzeski 2020a and 2020b). In September 2020, digital entertainment giant Netflix became the new target of this political crusade. A group of Republican senators criticized Netflix's high-profile plan to have *Game of Thrones* (2011–19) creators David Benioff and D. B. Weiss adapt Chinese writer Liu Cixin's bestselling sci-fi trilogy *The Three-Body Problem* because Liu openly supported China's mass internment of Uyghur Muslims in Xinjiang (Brzeski 2020c). In response, Netflix's VP of Global Public Policy Dean Garfield said Netflix "judges individual projects on their merits," and the company did not agree with Liu's comments which were "entirely unrelated to his book or this Netflix show" (quoted in THR Staff 2020). This new cold war is a profound battle between different ideologies and value systems. US politicians increasingly bring politics into business, maintaining the US entertainment industry is supposed to be a carrier of American values, and should not do its business at the expense of compromising those values.

On the other side of the Pacific Ocean, in late 2016 and early 2017 the Chinese government tightened its control over outflowing capital due to concerns over the slowdown in China's economic development and the weakening of the yuan. China's government was also worried that high-priced deals by entertainment companies could negatively affect China's stock market and so imposed significant restrictions on IPOs. These regulations prevented companies in other lines of business who had recently purchased entertainment assets from listing themselves as entertainment companies and collecting large sums of money (Moore 2017). In particular, the Dalian Wanda Group's overseas deals were considered overrated and insufficiently profitable. The company retreated from the global stage in 2017 after China's state-owned banks ceased loans to the company and re-examined its overseas purchases (Brzeski 2017).

Beginning in 2018, growth in China's film industry slowed. That year, the box office still grew by 9 percent over 2017, reaching RMB 60.98 billion ($8.87 billion), but this was considered moderate compared with the 13.5 percent the year before. A few Chinese domestic films performed well, such as *Hong hai xing dong* (*Operation Red Sea*) (2018) and *Wo bu shi yao shen* (*Dying to Survive*) (2018), boosting the box office share of homegrown movies to 62 percent (Tartaglione 2019). However, these encouraging signs and any sense of a triumphant atmosphere were soon overshadowed by harsh realities as film and television production in China entered a so-called "cold winter." The state's crackdown on tax evasion amongst celebrities saw the star Fan Bingbing fined 883 million yuan ($129 million) for tax fraud in October 2018, leading to the closure of tax havens. Further signs of the downturn crystalized in mid-2019. More than 80 percent of privately-owned film studios saw their profits drop by over 60 percent. China's top five private film companies – Huayi Brothers, Enlight Media, Wanda, Bona Film Group, and LeEco – all witnessed negative growth. For 2018, Huayi Brothers, the number one private film studio, documented a 231.97 percent reduction in net profits and a 1.4 percent decrease in revenue, with gross market value shrinking to 14.7 billion yuan from 80 billion yuan at its peak. The company's net loss in 2019 was estimated at RMB 3.9 billion (nbd. com.cn 2020). A total of 1,884 film and TV production companies closed in 2019 (Xie 2019). Even worse, the private cultural and entertainment funds that had supported film and TV production were leaving the industry, with 90 percent of funds predicted to drain out over the next two to three years (Wang and Feng 2019). Observers therefore pessimistically commented that "China's private film and TV companies have fallen to the most dangerous stage" (Jiang 2019). The domestic film market was temporarily boosted in 2019 by theater attendance on National Day for a few patriotic films such as *Wo He Wo De Zu Guo* (*My People, My Country*, *Zhong guo ji zhang* (*The Captain*), and *Pan deng zhe* (*The Climbers*), as well as the science fiction movie *Liu lang di qiu* (*The Wandering Earth*), elevating the year's total box office revenue to RMB 64.3 billion ($9.2 billion). On the other hand, the market share for Hollywood movies dropped to 31 percent or lower, defying Hollywood's original hope of taking the opportunity to enhance its prominence in China (Frater 2019b).

The outbreak of the COVID-19 pandemic dealt a devastating blow to China's film industry. By April 2020, 5,328 film and TV companies had closed or revoked their business registrations, 1.78 times the number for the previous year. Furthermore, there were less than 8,000 registrations of new movie theater companies in the first two months of 2020, down 25 percent from the same period in 2019 (Davis 2020b). During the first quarter of 2020, three major theater chains – Wanda, Jiyi, and Xingfulanhai – recorded a total financial loss of 800 million yuan (roughly $114 million) (Shenshu 2020). Similarly, the US business also suffered a loss of $7 billion over the six months from March 2020 (Rifaat 2020), and 93 percent of exhibition companies weathered losses of 75 percent in the second quarter of 2020. It was predicted that 69 percent of small- and mid-sized movie theaters would be forced to file for bankruptcy or close permanently, while it was predicted 66 percent of theater jobs would be lost if the pandemic was not effectively contained (McClintock 2020).

## Notable continuities in Hollywood–Chinawood partnership after 2017

The harsh reversal of US–China relations dramatically altered the conditions in which the countries' respective film industries operate, with the pandemic further ruining the financial health of both industries. However, because of how COVID-19 was handled by the two governments, the pandemic unexpectedly provided more opportunities for Hollywood to take advantage of the Chinese market. Notable continuities therefore remained to sustain a mutually dependent relationship.

One major continuity was Hollywood's increasing reliance on the Chinese market for profit gains before, during and maybe even after the pandemic. During 2018, the US domestic box office broke records thanks to blockbusters like *Black Panther*, but the international box office, and primarily China, is essential for Hollywood. Movies that underperform in the United States rebounded in China: for example, Dwayne Johnson's *Rampage* (2018) grossed $101 million in the United States but $156 million in China, while *The Meg* (2018), another monster movie, sold $530 million tickets worldwide boosted by its $153 million take in China. When it was released in China during November 2018, *Venom* was the box office champion for seven consecutive days. Despite a 28 percent Rotten Tomatoes critic score, *Venom* was the fifth highest-grossing movie in the world for 2018, taking $855 million at the box office, of which $270 million came from China. Similarly, Warner Bros.' *Aquaman* grossed nearly $190 million in the United States but $232 million in China thanks to a rare early overseas release ahead of the domestic debut. According to *Box Office Mojo*, nine Hollywood movies featured the top 20 at the Chinese box office during 2018 (Clark 2018).

Hoping to replicate the success of *Aquaman*, in 2019 a few superhero movies opened in China earlier than, or synchronously with, their US releases. *Captain Marvel*, *Shazam*, and *Avengers: Endgame* all secured early releases in China, followed by *Spider Man: Far from Home*, *Dark Phoenix*, and *Frozen II*. As 2019 marked the 70th anniversary of the founding of the People's Republic of China, however, and the entire nation was mobilized into a patriotic spree, nationalistic movies took the largest market share, reducing Hollywood's portion to roughly 31 percent; only two Hollywood movies – *Avengers: Endgame* and *Fast and Furious: Hobbs and Shaw* – featured among the top ten highest grossing titles in China that year (Frater 2019b).

Viewed from another perspective, the performance of Hollywood films in China testifies not only to their continuing attraction for Chinese audiences, but also the significance of Hollywood to the prosperity of the Chinese film market, industry, and national finance. With the arrival of the "cold winter," many Chinese film studios cut film production projects in order to recoup funds and survive, and the resulting austerity provided a better chance for Hollywood movies to enter the Chinese market. Alongside the annual quota limiting imports to 34 revenue-sharing films, China usually purchases another 30 movies at a flat fee every year. From the latter half of 2018, as the number of homegrown movies submitted for state approval significantly decreased, the price for each imported buy-out rose from $500,000 to $1 million (Gao 2018). Wang Xiaohui, director of China Film Administration, stated that Hollywood earned $2.8 billion on the Chinese market in 2018, whereas Chinese movies merely earned tens of millions overseas, testifying to the importance of Hollywood movies to the overall Chinese film economy (Liu 2019).

Unexpectedly but not surprisingly, China's tightened censorship became Hollywood's best opportunity for cashing on the Chinese market. Before the celebration of the 70th anniversary of the state, the Chinese government toughened its censorship of domestic movies, which in turn cleared space for Hollywood films and even negated fears about the consequences of the US–China trade war for the American movie industry. A market vacuum was created, as the release of *Ba Bai* (*The Eight Hundred*) (2020) was delayed for its portrayal of Kumingtang soldiers fighting against the Japanese invasion, and the release of *Wei Da De Yuan Wang* (*The Last Wish*) (2019) was also postponed due to sensitivities around representing a dying teenager's wish to lose his virginity. To fill this vacuum and meet audience demand, more Hollywood movies were imported, surpassing the annual quota with 40 and 42 in 2017 and 2018 respectively (Ma 2019).

COVID-19 made the Chinese market even more crucial for Hollywood's finances. Cinemas in China reopened in October 2020 with 75 percent seating capacity. When it was eventually released, *Ba Bai* became the biggest global epic of 2020, grossing over $460 million worldwide, nearly all of which came from ticket sales in China. Disney's live-action remake of *Mulan* skipped the North American theatrical market and premiered instead in China but performed disappointingly, grossing only $40 million. Meanwhile, Christopher Nolan's *Tenet* took $20 million in China compared with North American ticket sales of just $36.1 million (Brzeski, 2020d). At the global box office, North America remained the most valuable national territory, accounting for 28 percent of the worldwide revenues over the first nine months of 2020, while China ranked second with a 14 percent share (Tartaglione 2020). However, the balance was tipped in October 2020 when China overtook North America as the world's biggest box office (Brzeski, 2020e).

The economic significance of the Chinese market makes it a good venue for launching co-productions, leading to the third continuity in US–China collaboration. August 2018 witnessed the final arrival of a commercially successful US–China co-production, *The Meg*, co-produced by Warner Bros. Pictures and Chinese film companies including Apelles Entertainment and Gravity Pictures. Globally, the film grossed $530 million, with $153 million earned in China. Despite the political strife between the two countries, filmmakers continued to look forward to future collaborations. Speaking on the state of US–Chinese co-productions, Belle Avery, producer of *The Meg*, commented "I knew synergistically China would be the right place to do my co-pro," while John Penotti, President of SK Global, an independent developer-financier-producer of film, television and virtual reality content, remarked "there have been many peaks and valleys in the US-China co-pro market, but you can't focus on that. It's a continuum" (both quoted in Xinhua, 2020).

## New challenges and new trends

Although US–China collaborations continue, three challenges have already surfaced. First, Hollywood films remain popular in China, but their glamor appears to be fading. Chinese domestic movies, together with Korean, Japanese, Indian, and European movies, are competing for the Chinese market and challenging the domination of Hollywood films. The extraordinary market success of homegrown movies such as *Zhan lang II* (*Wolf Warrior 2*) (2017), *Liu lang di qiu* (*The Wandering Earth*), *Wo bu shi yao shen* (*Dying to Survive*) (2018), *Ba Bai* (*The Eight Hundred*) (2020) and *Ni hao, Li Huanying* (*Hi Mom*) (2021) illustrate Chinese people taking pride in the rising status of their motherland and their concerns over domestic social issues. Chinese audiences are no longer as fascinated by Hollywood films as they were 20 years ago, and they are increasingly embracing more diverse content. For example, the appeal of Korean and Japanese movies and animated films indicates a remarkable shift in the tastes and viewing habits of the Chinese audience. Furthermore, Indian film *Dangal* (2016) outperformed nearly every Hollywood film in China, grossing $189 million. For Hollywood, there is the good news that their exports still enjoy a favorable position in the Chinese market despite fading popularity. A survey conducted during 2020 by Maoyan Entertainment (2020), a leading Internet-based entertainment service provider in China, discovered that among 1,530 respondents, 72 percent were eager to return to cinemas when they reopened after the COVID-19 pandemic; of these, 55 percent were looking forward to watching new movies with positive word of mouth. Respondents reported their preference for domestic productions, but *The Avengers* series (2012– 2019) and *Harry Potter and the Sorcerer's Stone* (2001) were identified among the most popular foreign movies. As Alibaba Pictures director Zhang Wei noted in interview, "Chinese audiences have always loved Hollywood movies" but were wanting "more than the special-effects laden action or sci-fi movies that have been traditionally packaged and shipped off to the Chinese market to score extra box office value." Instead, with Chinese audience tastes becoming more sophisticated, "they appreciate stories that are relatable to them—not necessarily through subject matter, but through universal values and great stories" (quoted in Frater, 2019c).

Second, as the Hollywood-Chinawood collaboration moves beyond mergers and acquisitions to content generation and project-by-project cooperation, film co-productions continue to pose a big challenge for filmmakers of both countries. Replaying the unsuccessful story of their first coproduction *The Great Wall* (2016), Disney's live action *Mulan* also foundered in the Chinese market, testifying to the difficulty of appealing to international audiences. Both industries will need to experiment with new storytelling modes and techniques in order to better incorporate Chinese cultural elements into Hollywood-style blockbusters.

Finally, both sides will need to pay more attention to streaming services, digital production, distribution, and marketing. Digitalization of China's entertainment industry, and the extraordinary growth of online streaming platforms such as TikTok, have become a remarkable cultural and economic phenomenon. TikTok's expansion in the United States, and Netflix's exhibition of more Chinese movies on its own platform, are enhancing Chinese cultural power, challenging US domination and beginning to reshape the global power structure. As the COVID-19 pandemic has also fundamentally altered media consumption habits worldwide, profoundly impacting on cinema-going while also encouraging more online forms of viewing, then globally the practices and business models of the media industries are being transformed. To take its relationship with China forward, Hollywood must therefore face these digital challenges and find new ways of collaboration.

# References

Allison, Gr. (2017) "The Thucydides Trap," *Foreign Policy*, June 9, available at https://foreignpolicy.com/2017/06/09/the-thucydides-trap/ (accessed July 8, 2020).

Anxininc.com (2017) "zhongguo touzizhe wei haolaiwu dailaide shi jiyu erbushi youlv," ("Chinese Investors Bring More Opportunities to Hollywood, Not Concerns"), available at www.anxininc.com/index.php?cat=news&id=1023 (accessed August 4, 2017).

Baker, L. B. (2017) "Hollywood Effects Firm Deluxe Entertainment Looks to China for Deal," *Reuters*, January 26, available at www.reuters.com/article/us-deluxe-entertnmt-m-a-idUSKBN15B008 (accessed January 28, 2017).

Brzeski, P. (2016) "China's Wanda Planning Two Billion-dollar Film Deals this Year, Chairman Says," *The Hollywood Reporter*, August 23, available at www.hollywoodreporter.com/news/chinas-wanda-planning-two-billion-921985 (accessed August 24, 2016).

Brzeski, P. (2017) "Wanda Boss Signals Retreat from Hollywood Dealmaking," *The Hollywood Reporter*, July 25, available at www.hollywoodreporter.com/news/wanda-boss-signals-retreat-hollywood-dealmaking-1024144 (accessed July 26, 2017).

Brzeski, P. (2018) "Will Hollywood Get Caught in Trump's China Trade War Crossfire?" *The Hollywood Reporter*, July 13, available at www.hollywoodreporter.com/news/will-hollywood-get-caught-trumps-china-trade-war-crossfire-1126182 (accessed July 14, 2018).

Brzeski, P. (2020a) "#BoycottMulan Movement Gains Momentum in Hong Kong, Taiwan, Thailand," *The Hollywood Reporter*, September 6, available at www.hollywoodreporter.com/news/boycottmulan-movement-gains-momentum-in-hong-kong-taiwan-thailand (accessed September 10, 2020).

Brzeski, P. (2020b) "Disney Under Fire for Filming 'Mulan' in China's Xinjiang Province," *The Hollywood Reporter*, September 7, available at www.hollywoodreporter.com/news/disney-under-fire-for-filming-mulan-in-chinas-xinjiang-province (accessed September 8, 2020).

Brzeski, P. (2020c) "GOP Senators Send Letter to Netflix Challenging Plans to Adapt Chinese Sci-Fi Novel 'The Three Body Problem'," *The Hollywood Reporter*, September 24, available at www.hollywoodreporter.com/news/gop-senators-send-letter-to-netflix-challenging-plans-to-adapt-chinese-sci-fi-novel-the-three-body-problem (accessed September 24, 2020).

Brzeski, P. (2020d) "'The Eight Hundred' Becomes 2020's Biggest Film Globally, 'Mulan' Dissipates," *The Hollywood Reporter*, September 21, available at www.hollywoodreporter.com/news/china-box-office-the-eight-hundred-becomes-2020s-biggest-film-globally-mulan-dissipates (accessed September 22, 2020).

Brzeski, P. (2020e) "It's Official: China Overtakes North America as World's Biggest Box Office in 2020," *The Hollywood Reporter*, October 18, available at www.hollywoodreporter.com/news/general-news/its-official-china-overtakes-north-america-as-worlds-biggest-box-office-in-2020-4078850/ (accessed June 20, 2021).

Clark, T. (2018) "9 Hollywood Movies That Dominated the Chinese Box Office in 2018, Including Some That Underperformed in the US," *Business Insider*, December 31, available at www.businessinsider.com/top-hollywood-movies-at-china-box-office-in-2018-venom-aquaman-2018-12 (accessed January 3, 2019).

Davis, R. (2020a) "Ted Cruz Takes Aim at U.S. Studios and Chinese Censorship with New Bill," *Variety*, May 27, available at https://variety.com/2020/film/news/ted-cruz-china-script-act-1234617344/ (accessed May 28, 2020)

Davis, R. (2020b) "Coronavirus Puts 5,000 Chinese Film and TV Firms Out of Business," *Variety*, April 15, 2020, available at https://variety.com/2020/film/news/china-coronavirus-cinema-closures-1234581926 (accessed April 16, 2020).

Frater, P. (2015) "China's Bona Film Invests $235 Million in Fox Movie Slate," *Variety*, November 4, available at http://variety.com/2015/biz/asia/bona-film-fox-investment-1201633139/ (accessed November 6, 2015).

Frater, P. (2019a) "'Asians are Taking Their Rightful Place in Hollywood' Says Janet Yang," *Variety*, November 2, available at https://variety.com/2019/digital/asia/asians-taking-rightful-place-in-hollywood-janet-yang-wng-leehom-1203391049/ (accessed November 3, 2019).

Frater, P. (2019b) "China's Box Office Went Its Own Way in 2019, to Hollywood's Detriment," *Variety*, December 24, available at https://variety.com/2019/film/asia/hollywood-2019-setback-china-box-office-1203451505/ (accessed December 26, 2019).

Frater, P. (2019c) "China's Role in Hollywood is Changing, Says Alibaba Pictures' Zhang Wei," *Variety*, November 5, available at https://variety.com/2019/film/asia/zhang-wei-alibaba-pictures-china-hollywood-1203393854/ (accessed November 6, 2019).

Gao, H. (2018) "yingshi handong zhixia haolaiwu zhengjiu zhongguo shichang," ("Hollywood Saves Chinese Market in Cold Winter"), *Caijing*, November 16, available at http://yuanchuang.caijing.com.cn/2018/1116/4536904.shtml (accessed November 16, 2018).

Guo, Y. (2017) "cong aiyuezhicheng dao dazhentanhuosang, dianguangchuanmei ruhe yulanggongwu," ("From La La Land to Great Detective: How TLK Films Cooperates with the US's Lions Gate"), *D-Entertainment*, June 17, available at https://mp.weixin.qq.com/s/RgUoQY2ubRhK6G0Gt0yXdw (accessed August 10, 2017).

Ha, M. (2017) "Chanyeguancha: 25% haolaiwu dapian you zhongguo jinzhu touzi" ("25% of Hollywood Blockbusters Have Chinese Investment"), *I Kan Yingshi (I View Movies and TV)*, June 23, available at https://mp.weixin.qq.com/s/MgnTpJyA6CCFPPEaFc_jzQ (accessed June 24, 2017).

Han, F. (2018) "Yueledahengmen shi ruhe jiang zhongguo pengbo de dianyingshichang gongshouxiangrang de," ("How Chinese entertainment tycoons submit Chinese market to Hollywood?"), *Curiosity Daily*, January 12, available at www.entgroup.cn/news/Markets/1244615.shtml (accessed January 12, 2018).

Hayden, E. (2020) "Barr Criticizes Studios Over China Relationships, Singles Out Marvel, Paramount," *The Hollywood Reporter*, July 16, available at www.hollywoodreporter.com/news/barr-criticizes-studios-china-relationships-singles-marvel-paramount-1303474 (accessed July 17, 2020)

Jiang, Y. (2019) "minying yinshi gongsi daole zuiweixian de shike" ("Private Film and TV Companies Have Fallen to the Most Dangerous Stage"), *Dumou*, available at www.huxiu.com/article/297139.html (accessed October 30, 2019).

Liu, Y. (2019) "guojia dianyingju juzhang: zhengqu meinian piaofang guoyi yingpian chao 100 bu" ("Director of State Film Administration Says to Strive to Produce More Than 100 Movies Annually Each with Over 10 Billion Yuan in Box Office"), *People's Daily*, February 27, available at http://culture.people.com.cn/n1/2019/0227/c1013-30906250.html (accessed February 28, 2019).

Ma, A. (2019) "Hollywood Takes Advantage of China Censoring Its Domestic Movie Market," *Business Insider*, September 26, available at www.businessinsider.com/china-movie-censorship-gives-hollywood-advantage-2019-9 (accessed September 26, 2019).

Maoyan Entertainment (2020) "Maoyan Survey Finds Portion of China Movie Lovers Eager for Return to Cinemas Rose to 72%," *PR Newswire*, available at www.prnewswire.com/news-releases/maoyan-survey-finds-portion-of-china-movie-lovers-eager-for-return-to-cinemas-rose-to-72-301039832.html (accessed April 15, 2020).

McClintock, P. (2020) "Top Filmmakers Warn Congress That Movie Theaters Face Extinction," *The Hollywood Reporter*, September 30. Available at www.hollywoodreporter.com/news/top-filmmakers-warn-congress-that-movie-theaters-face-extinction (accessed October 1, 2020).

Moore, S. (2017) "The China Chill in Hollywood," *Forbes*, April 25, available at www.forbes.com/sites/schuylermoore/2017/04/25/the-china-chill-in-hollywood/#3918d84b2881 (accessed April 27, 2017).

MPA (2020) "THEME Report 2019," available at www.motionpictures.org/wp-content/uploads/2020/03/MPA-THEME-2019.pdf (accessed September 22, 2020).

MPAA (2016) "Theatrical Market Statistics 2015," available at www.mpaa.org/wp-content/uploads/2016/04/MPAA-Theatrical-Market-Statistics-2015_Final.pdf (accessed September 22, 2020)

MPAA (2017) "Theatrical Market Statistics 2016," available at www.mpaa.org/wp-content/uploads/2017/03/MPAA-Theatrical-Market-Statistics-2016_Final.pdf (accessed September 22, 2020)

MPAA (2018) "2017 THEME Report," available at www.mpaa.org/wp-content/uploads/2018/04/MPAA-THEME-Report-2017_Final.pdf (accessed September 22, 2020)

MPAA (2019) "2018 THEME Report," available at www.motionpictures.org/wp-content/uploads/2019/03/MPAA-THEME-Report-2018.pdf (accessed October 26, 2019).

nbd.com.cn (2020) "huayi xiongdi: yuji 2019 nian jingkuisun chao 39 yiyuan" ("Huayi Brothers Estimates Its 2019 Net Loss of 3.9 Billion Yuan"), January 23, available at www.nbd.com.cn/articles/2020-01-23/1402541.html (accessed January 23, 2020).

Pence, M. (2018) "Remarks by Vice President Pence on the Administration's Policy Toward China," *Foreign Policy*, October 4, available at www.whitehouse.gov/briefings-statements/remarks-vice-president-pence-administrations-policy-toward-china/ (accessed October 25, 2019).

Rifaat, H (2020) "How to Empower the Film Industry?" *China Global Television Network*, September 25, available at https://news.cgtn.com/news/2020-09-25/How-to-empower-the-film-industry--U49PLWQ16E/index.html (accessed September 26, 2020).

Rudd, K. (2019) "Kevin Rudd on Asia in 2020: A Year Full of Challenges for the Asia-Pacific," November 5, available at https://asiasociety.org/video/kevin-rudd-asia-2020-year-full-challenges-asia-pacific (accessed December 5, 2019).

Ryan, F. (2016) "Steven Spielberg's Amblin Partners, Alibaba Pictures Announce Partnership," *China Film Insider*, October 9, available at http://chinafilminsider.com/steven-spielbergs-amblin-partners-alibaba-pictures-announce-partnership (accessed October 10, 2016).

Shenshu (2020) "Shui shasile zhongguo dianyingyuan" (Who Kills Chinese Cinemas?), *shenshui yuleguancha*, April 20, available at https://mp.weixin.qq.com/s/5lsUGcFGpwqd4my-0bv9xA?utm_source=China+Film+Insider+Newsletter+Update&utm_campaign=db688679ef-Daily_Newsletter_2017_January_9_COPY_01&utm_medium=email&utm_term=0_9a066b9dc2-db688679ef-226863553 (accessed April 22, 2020).

Tartaglione, N. (2019) "China Box Office Growth Slows in 2018; Tricky Balancing Act Ahead for 2019," *Deadline,* January 3, available at https://deadline.com/2019/01/china-box-office-2018-growth-slows-2019-forecast-challenges-concerns-1202527834/ (accessed January 7, 2019).

Tartaglione, N. (2020) "With 'The Eight Hundred' Now 2020's No. 1 Global Grosser & As National Day Nears, Will China Box Office Top Domestic This Year? – Market Rankings Chart," *Deadline*, September 25, available at https://deadline.com/2020/09/the-eight-hundred-box-office-china-2020-best-beats-bad-boys-for-life-1234581827 (accessed September 25, 2020).

THR Staff (2020) "Netflix Responds to GOP Senators Critique of 'The Three Body Problem' Adaptation," *The Hollywood Reporter*, September 25, available at www.hollywoodreporter.com/news/netflix-responds-to-gop-senators-critique-of-the-three-body-problem-adaption (accessed September 26, 2020).

Timberg, S. (2016) "Hollywood's New China Syndrome: The Country's Enormous Audience Means Money for Movie Studios and Some Restrictions," *Salon*, September 25, available at www.salon.com/2016/09/25/hollywoods-new-china-syndrome-the-countrys-enormous-audience-means-money-for-movie-studios-and-some-restrictions (accessed September 28, 2016).

Xie, R. (2019) "yuleziben fengguangbuzai, niannei 1884 film and tv companies guangting," ("1884 Film and TV Companies Closed in 2019"), *Zhengjuan Daily*, November 27, available at www.zqrb.cn/stock/hangyeyanjiu/2019-11-27/A1574790176287.html (accessed December 12, 2019).

Xinhua (2020) "Hollywood Insiders Weigh in On Future of US-China Co-productions," July 26, available at www.china.org.cn/arts/2020-07/26/content_76313138.htm (accessed July 28, 2020).

Wang, F. and Feng, Y. (2019) "wenyujijin tuichangchao, 90% jiang daoxia" ("90% of Entertainment Funds to be Drained Out"), *PEdaily.cn*, March 21, available at https://tech.sina.com.cn/i/2019-03-21/doc-ihtxyzsk9332530.shtml (accessed February 2, 2020).

Zhao, S. (2019) "Engagement on the Defensive: From the Mismatched Grand Bargain to the Emerging US–China Rivalry," *Journal of Contemporary China*, 28 (118): 501–518.

# 30

# TV FORMATS

## Transnationalizing television production and distribution

*Andrea Esser*

A notable part of television's transformation during the first two decades of the twenty-first century, driven by the twin engine of digitization and globalization, was the radical growth and impact of the TV format trade. Program franchising became a systematized business and, for TV channels from around the world, a major form of sourcing content. Gradually, all entertainment genres came to be formatted, including game and talent shows, reality and lifestyle programs, comedy, and drama. To name but a few of the most successful formats – *Who Wants to be a Millionaire?* (1998–), *Miljoenenjacht* aka *Deal or No Deal* (2002–), and *Got Talent* (2006–) – spawn licensed adaptations in 115, 83, and 76 territories respectively. Colombian telenovela, *Yo soy Betty, La Fea* (*I am Betty, the Ugly One*, 1999–2001) has been adapted in 19 territories across the globe, with South Africa to be added as No. 20 in 2021 (Barraclough 2020; Vourlias 2020; Wallace 2015).

According to Jean Chalaby (2016: 8–13), one of the most prominent format scholars, a format can be defined in four dimensions: (1) a *licensed remake;* (2) a *recipe,* which combines immutable rules and principles with adaptable elements; (3) a *proven concept,* which helps both producers and broadcasters reduce risk, and (4) a globally shared *method of production,* which implies a significant transfer of expertise. Not everybody agrees. Tasha Oren and Sharon Shahaf (2012), Joseph Straubhaar (2012), and Albert Moran (2013) who first highlighted the growth in "copycat TV" in 1998, have criticized such trade-based definitions as too narrow. For a more nuanced theoretical understanding, they argue, a broader conceptualization is needed, one that includes unacknowledged and unpaid imitations, as well as "format types" – specific conventions pertaining to textual characteristics, production practices and audience address – that develop over time. Their objection is valid. However, a broad format definition goes beyond the affordances of a short book chapter. Moreover, it obscures the enormous changes that have transformed TV production and distribution during the past 20 years: the systematization of the format business, its tremendous expansion in scope and scale, and its transnationalizing effect on production and distribution globally. This chapter aims to illuminate these changes and to point the reader to pertinent scholarship.

The next two sections outline how and why the TV format business evolved, how formats are adapted in practice, and how this has been theorized. Subsequently, the chapter will argue and demonstrate how the format trade has contributed to changing the television sector in

DOI: 10.4324/9780429275340-35

three major ways: creating transnational production and distribution structures; producing a transnational tribe of TV executives, diffusing know-how globally on a scale not seen before, and with this transnationalizing production and distribution practices; and finally, multiplying, diversifying, and geographically expanding program flows.

## The emergence of the TV format trade in the twenty-first century

There is widespread agreement among format scholars on the history and periodization of formats. Moran (2013) speaks of four phases: early "trailblazing" program imitations (1935–55), "casual exchange" (1955–80), "the becoming of the format business" (1980–2000), and formats as a "significant worldwide business" (2000–present) (see Bourdon 2012; Chalaby 2012; Hallenberger 2002). Various early examples of licensed formats can be found between the 1940s and 1970s (Calbreath-Frasieur 2016; Chalaby 2012; Ferrari 2012; Keinonen 2016), but overall these were few and far between. The practice of franchising content grew markedly during the 1980s and 1990s, when television markets in Europe were expanding and commercializing, and broadcasters turned to US, Australian, and Dutch game shows, and in some cases soap operas, to meet their demand for popular programs. At the turn of the century, the exceptional popularity in multiple countries of *Who Wants to be a Millionaire?*, *Big Brother* (1999–), *Expedition Robinson* (1997) (turned into *Survivor*, 2000), and *Idols* (2001) caught the industry's attention as a systematized and increasingly recognized business in format sales began to develop and accelerate. In 2000, the Format Recognition and Protection Association (FRAPA) was set up to promote the trade in formats and to protect the format rights of producers and broadcasters around the world by offering registration and mediation services to members. In 2003, FRAPA launched the *Format Awards* to promote and cement the format business. Throughout the 2000s, references to TV formats in industry trade journals like *Broadcast* and *Variety* increased markedly. *Television Business International, World Screen* and *C21 Media* launched dedicated format publications, respectively *TBI Formats, TV Formats* and *Formats Lab*. In 2007, the Format Awards moved to one of the world's largest international program markets, *MIPCOM*, and in 2009, *MIPFormats*, a two-day format showcase preceding *MIPTV*, was launched and has been an annual fixture since.

The ongoing growth and commercialization of the TV sector globally boosted the demand for formats throughout the first two decades of the new millennium. Competition for both content and audiences rose steadily. Format acquisition was cost effective and enabled speedy production as the show was already fully developed and came with detailed production guidelines. Moreover, the latter meant that buyers benefitted from knowledge transfer. This was attractive for new, popular genres like sitcoms and soap operas in the 1990s, and lifestyle and reality TV in the 2000s. A further factor that spoke for the use of formats, particularly in the case of commercial operators, was proof of success. Evidence of a format's popular appeal in the form of audience ratings from previous markets satisfies risk management objectives. As a result, formats came to constitute a large share of program offerings of many, including major TV channels; and not just as cheap schedule fillers, as originally thought, but as popular primetime fare (Chalaby 2016; Esser 2013; Jensen 2013; Khalil 2017; Uribe-Jongbloed and Pis Diez 2017; Waisbord and Jalfin 2009).

Notably, it was not the commercially savvy US industry that moved to the forefront of the emerging format business, but rather small European producers. Throughout the 2000s, European countries accounted for a combined market share of over 60 percent of global format sales, in terms of both numbers and revenues (Jäger and Behrens 2009: 11, 17). The primary cause of this outstanding position was Dutch producer Endemol, who in the early 1990s had begun to focus on developing game, talent, and dating shows with cross-border appeal, grabbing the world's attention with *Big Brother* (Esser 2002). Moreover, a number of British independent production companies had come to realize the potential of developing and selling lifestyle formats internationally and successfully lobbied the British communications regulator, Ofcom, for the disaggregation of intellectual property rights (IPRs). Introduced in 2004, a new Code of Practice granted UK-based producers the right to retain IPRs for the international market, and with this cemented the country's enduring lead in the format business (Chalaby 2010: 685–686).

But by the middle of the 2010s, producers from many more countries had joined the format bandwagon. Between 2004 and 2014, the proportion of formats originating from the "rest of the world" grew from 26 percent to 48 percent (Figure 30.1). As Figure 30.1 reveals, format flows diversified especially from 2012 onward. Japanese producers were already successfully selling game show formats, including *Manē no tora* (2001–04) aka *Dragon's Den* (40 territories), *Fūun! Takeshi-jō* (1986–90) aka *Takeshi's Castle* (31), and *Tonneruzu no Minasan no Okage deshita* (1997–2018) aka *Hole in the Wall* (45) (Jäger and Behrens 2009; C21 Media 2017; Nippon TV 2020). Israel moved into the limelight with TV drama series *BeTipul* (2005–08), adapted by HBO in the United States as *In Treatment* (2008–10) and subsequently produced in 13 versions across Europe, South America, and Canada. This success was followed by *Hatufim* (2010–12), adapted as *Homeland* (2011–20) for Fox/Showtime in the US, and subsequently adapted in Russia (2015) and India (2016–17). The international franchise of Keshet's much-hyped musical talent show, *Rising Star/HaKokhav HaBa* (2013–), was less successful than hoped for (Shahaf 2016; Schiffman 2016), and South Korea moved into global headlines, when it sold reality show *Kkotboda Halbae* (2013–18), *Grandpa Over Flowers*, into the United States (adapted for NBC as *Better Late Than Never* in 2014), quickly followed by 16 further sales. Other countries from across the globe, too, increasingly succeeded in selling formats internationally (C21 Media 2017, 2019; Esser and Lee 2018).

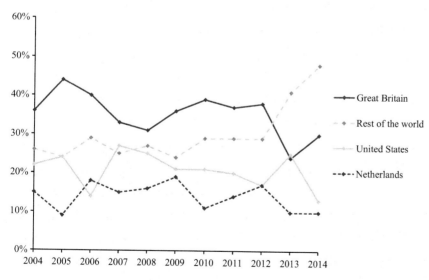

*Figure 30.1* Geographical origin (%) of TV formats (2004–2014).
*Source*: Wallace, Vasha/Fremantle Media (2015).

## The practice of format adaptation

One important aspect of the emerging format business was promotion of the idea that formats constitute intellectual property, which can and should be protected and exploited. Another key aspect was the form in which formats came to be sold, an instructive "production bible" accompanied by the services of a consultant. The bible includes key production information such as technical requirements, a shooting schedule and crew list, a sample budget, and casting and marketing tips. Sometimes it is complemented by graphics software, sounds or, where relevant, scripts. The consultant, or "flying producer," is someone intimately familiar with the original version and the growing count of adaptations. Typically, they oversee the early stages of a new adaptation but are available for consultation throughout the lifecycle of the production (Moran and Malbon 2006; Quigley 2017). This combination of detailed written instructions with consultancy support leads to the substantial transfer of expertise.

The flying producer has another important task, which is to protect the format brand. A balance has to be found between adapting the format to suit local needs and to ensure that the format is both successful and recognizable across the world. In other words, although changes are easy to make in principle, licensors aim to limit concessions as much as possible. This limited flexibility, Hallenberger argues (2002), is also what distinguishes the format business of the late 1990s and onward from earlier franchise deals. Even for formats that include scripts ("scripted formats") and are generally understood to require greater adaptation, examples of tight control exist. For instance, Dick Wolf, creator of the crime series, *Law & Order* (1990–2010), reportedly provided the producers of the French adaptation, *Paris Enquêtes Criminelles* (2007–2008), with a 1,000 page-long bible to ensure that nothing would be left to interpretation (Esser 2014). In practice, flexibility varies, depending on rights holders' market power and the desirability of the format in question. In either case, as Keinonen (2016) and Zeng and Sparks (2017) have argued and demonstrated with in-depth case studies, format adaptation involves a process of complex and ongoing negotiation between licensors and licensees.

Many format scholars contend that "cultural adaptation" and "national aesthetics" inevitably lead to palpable variation (e.g., Mikos and Perrotta 2012; van Keulen 2016). In fact, most scholars work on the assumption that it is primarily cultural factors that necessitate adaptation and that the culture in question is national – a result, they argue, of market structures as well as audience "preferences" for representations of the nation (e.g., Moran and Aveyard 2014; Waisbord and Jalfin 2009). However, a handful of studies have shown that the reality of adaptation is more complex. For instance, Martin Ndlela's (2013) work has shown that geopolitical, cultural, and linguistic factors have led to the predominance of either transnational or subnational format adaptations in Africa. Pia Jensen (2012) has argued that media-systems impact adaption, revealing differences especially between adaptations made by public-service or commercial broadcasters. Furthermore, Michael Wayne (2016) and Andrea Esser (2014) have found that channel identity and target audiences also count as key determinants. In a nutshell, there are multiple factors that impact adaptation and necessitate concessions, including media system, regulation, the budget and talent on hand, the brand identity and target audience of the licensing channel, the scheduling slot for which a format is adapted, and the time at which a format is launched in a given market. Considering whether to produce for national audiences and/or to represent the nation can play a role, but in today's predominantly commercial markets these factors are not as commanding as commonly assumed. Also, as the following will show, market realities make it increasingly difficult to demarcate national cultures of production.

Who carries out the adaption? In this respect, too, the industry has seen major changes over the past 20–30 years. Whereas throughout the 1980s and 1990s it was common practice for broadcasters or local production companies to buy the adaptation rights and adapt the format in-house, a new business model emerged during the 2000s: rather than sell the license for adaptation, some production companies with sought-after formats aimed to self-produce their shows in as many markets as possible, with the view to increasing their revenues and profit. A new corporate structure, combining multiple production outlets with one international sales outlet, evolved (Chalaby 2010; Nylund 2016). Endemol and FremantleMedia, the leading European format companies, had already begun to assemble production companies during the 1990s (the latter under the name of Pearson) and continued to do so in the new millennium. They were emulated by a number of small, independent European production companies which, backed by private investors, underwent rapid international expansion during the 2000s and became large transnational producer-distributors in the space of a few years (see Table 30.1). Both independent and vertically integrated companies continued their mergers and acquisitions activities during the 2010s, a frenzy too complex to detail here (see Chalaby 2016; Esser 2016). Suffice to say that this second decade was characterized by takeovers from the US majors. It ended, however, with the French-investor owned Banijay (Zodiak) Group announcing it was to buy Endemol from Disney. Following regulatory approval in 2020, this merger of the world's two largest transnational production-distribution groups created a network of around 200 production companies across 22 countries, with combined revenues for 2019 of approximately €2.7 billion (Banijay Group 2020).

## The transnationalization of production structures, know-how, and flows

The sheer scale and spread of these producer-distributors, plus many more informal networks of format production and distribution, have thoroughly transnationalized TV production. A fleet of flying producers, responsible for looking after individual formats rather than territories, interlink the globe on a daily basis. Working closely with flying producers and using the guidance of production bibles, local production personnel involved in format adaptation acquire format- and genre-specific production know-how, as well as expertise in how to sell formats (Khalil 2017; Zeng and Sparks 2017). In addition, local producers come together in annual format workshops to exchange knowledge of how a particular (big) brand, like for instance *Strictly Come Dancing* (2004–), sold internationally as *Dancing with the Stars*, fares across the world, and brainstorm how to innovate and keep it popular (Quigley 2017). The resultant transnational interconnectivity means that production practices, mindsets and genre fashions are converging globally.

Structures and know-how are further transnationalized when production is conducted through so-called "format hubs." The practice of filming multiple versions in one location began in the late 2000s/early 2010s when Endemol Shine Group (ESG) produced several versions of *Wipeout* (2008–) and *Fear Factor* (*Now or Neverland*, 1998–) in Argentina and Malaysia respectively. UK commercial broadcaster ITV built a hub for *I'm a Celebrity … Get Me Out of Here!* (2002–) in South Africa, and Banijay created two hubs for *Survivor*, each serving differing budget needs. During the late 2010s, ESG built regional production hubs in Poland and Brazil for its music talent competition *All Together Now* (2018–). The hub model is particularly attractive for island shows and gameshows with expensive studio sets, but it can also work for scripted formats. Disney, for instance, co-produced one Portuguese and two Spanish-language versions of *Desperate Housewives* (2004–12) in Buenos Aires. Highly cost efficient is also Netflix's sports competition, *Ultimate Beastmaster* (2017–). In this case, using a large obstacle course in Santa Clarita, California, and a set of competitors drawn from respectively six (season 1 and 2) and nine countries (season 3), US company 25/7 Productions creates

Table 30.1 European-led production groups with multiple outlets in at least two countries plus an integrated sales office (2010)

| Production group | Established | Ownership | Headquarters | No. of territories | No. of companies | Key subsidiaries |
|---|---|---|---|---|---|---|
| **Independent** | | | | | | |
| All3Media | 2003 | Equity fund Permira (majority owner) | London | 5 | 20 | IDTV, Lime Pictures, Lion Television, Maverick Television, MME Moviement, Optomen, Studio Lambert |
| Banijay Group | 2008 | Investment consortium | Paris | 8 | 10 | Air Productions, Banijay Finland, Brainpool, Bunim Murray Productions, Cuarzo, Nordisk Film TV |
| Endemol | 1994 | Investment consortium with Mediaset | Amsterdam | 31 | 80 | Gestmusic Endemol, Remarkable Television, Southern Star, True Entertainment, Zeppotron; mostly Endemol branded |
| Eyeworks | 2001 | Private shareholders (R. Oerlemans with venture capital) | Amsterdam | 17 | 4 (wholly owned) | At It Productions, Cuatro Cabezas, Egmont Film & Television, Touchdown Television; all Eyeworks branded |
| Shed Media | 1998 | Shareholders, AIM stock market listed | London | 2 | 8 | Richochet, Wall to Wall, Twenty Twenty, Outright Distribution |
| Shine Group | 2001 | Private shareholders (E. Murdoch, 53%) | London | 10 | 26 | Dragonfly, Kudos, Metronome, Princess Productions, Reveille, Shine Australia/France/Germany |
| Zodiak Media | 2007 | Investment consortium | Paris | 17 | 45 | Magnolia, Marathon, RDF, Zodiak TV; all Zodiak branded |
| **Vertically integrated** | | | | | | |
| BBC Worldwide | 1995 | BBC | London | 7 | 3 (wholly owned) | BBC Worldwide (London, Paris, L.A. Mumbai); plus, international equity stakes in GP Media, Freehand, Temple Street Productions, Tower Productions |
| FremantleMedia | 2001 | RTL Group/ Bertelsmann | London | 22 | 25 | Grundy-Ufa, Thames Television; mostly Fremantle branded |
| ITV Studios | 2009 | ITV | London | 7 | 3 (wholly owned) | 12 Yard, Granada Australia, Granada Germany, ITV Studios America; Shiver Productions; mostly ITV branded |
| Red Arrow Entertainment | 2010 | ProSiebenSat.1 Group | Munich | 8 | 3 (wholly owned) | Producers at Work, Redseven Entertainment, SnowmanProductions; plus, majority equity stakes in Kinetic Content, Sultan Sushi |
| Strix Television | 1988 | Modern Times Group | Stockholm | 4 | 4 | Strix Sweden, Norway, Netherlands, Czech Republic |

Source: Esser (2016: 3594).

different versions for the countries from which participants have been recruited (e.g., Japan, South Korean, Mexico, Germany, Brazil and the United States in season one). Each version is localized through commentary by two local hosts and highlighting local contestants. Cost saving is the most obvious benefit of the hub model, but there are other benefits, too, such as better utilization of show-specific expertise and greater brand consistency (C21 Media 2019; Jarvey 2017; Winslow 2006).

An interesting outcome of these transnationalized production-distribution structures is that many formats are no longer developed for a single home market and then licensed abroad; instead they are designed for global distribution from the start (Chalaby 2016; Nylund 2016). A program may also no longer be produced first in the country where it was created. Already in the 1990s, Dutch Endemol had begun developing entertainment shows for neighboring German commercial broadcasters. Today, increased transnational interconnectivity and spatial spread mean that the importance of geographical proximity further diminishes, and domestic buyers no longer carry the same importance they used to. In some cases, domestic markets might even be deemed suboptimal launch pads. To give an example, in 2016 LA-based creator-producer Kinetic Content developed the reality show *Buying Blind*. Rather than seeking a US launch, the company's Munich-based parent, Red Arrow Entertainment, convinced Kinetic to launch the show in Europe "in order to leverage the best international rights situation" (*Broadcast* 2017). As a result, Kinetic collaborated with another Red Arrow subsidiary, Snowman Productions, who produced the format for TV3 in Denmark. After its successful launch in 2017 on TV3, *Buying Blind* was produced for RTL in the Netherlands, Nine Networks in Australia, and M6 in France. Only in late 2018 did Kinetic finally produce its own homegrown version for US channel Bravo (*Broadcast* 2017; Formatbiz 2018).

It goes without saying that for various economic, structural, cultural, and other reasons, some of the world's markets are still more integrated and connected than others. Also, some are still more prominent than others and are likely to remain so. Much of Africa and parts of the Middle East have remained peripheral format markets, both as localizers and even more so as format originators. However, as Ndlela (2017) and Joe Khalil (2017) have shown, at least South Africa and some markets in the Middle East have become fairly integrated during the past decade, causing the launch of independent production companies in these countries, with some moving from format adaptation to format development. Enrique Uribe-Jongbloed and Ethel Pis Diez (2017) observe the same in several Latin American countries, whilst Michael Keane (2012) and Wenna Zeng and Colin Sparks (2017) have noted how Chinese producers have turned from "poachers," to format importers, to ambitious format developers. As both historical (The Netherlands) and more recent cases (Israel) have demonstrated, the most successful format developers in commercial terms are not necessarily those based in the largest markets, or with the largest production capacities, but those with a transnational commercial outlook plus favorable regulatory and market conditions (Chalaby 2016; Shahaf 2016; Uribe-Jongbloed and Pis Diez 2017).

The final argument of this chapter concerns program flows. By transnationalizing production and distribution, the TV format business has multiplied and diversified program flows globally. Old trade patterns, limited to countries that are close geographically, linguistically, or historically, have opened out, and TV programs no longer flow one way, from the United States to the rest of the world. For example, like many of the most successful formats before it, South Korea's musical talent show *Miseuteori Eumaksyo Bongmyeon-gawang* (2015–, MBC Entertainment, aka *The Masked Singer*) covers all continents with 37 adaptations to date (see Table 30.2) with reportedly another 13 to come (Middleton, 2020). In addition to factual entertainment, talent and game shows, South Korean producers have sold a growing number of scripted formats to

Table 30.2 International adaptations of South Korea's 미스터리 음악쇼 복면가왕 *(King of Mask Singer/ The Masked Singer)*, MBC (2015–)

| Region/Country | Local Title | Network | Launch |
|---|---|---|---|
| **Australasia** | | | |
| Australia | *The Masked Singer Australia* | Network 10 | 2019 |
| China | 蒙面歌王 | JSTV | 2015 |
| Indonesia | *The Mask Singer Indonesia* | GTV | 2017 |
| Malaysia | *The Masked Singer Malaysia* | Astro Warna | 2020 |
| Myanmar | *The Mask Singer Myanmar* | Channel ME | 2019 |
| New Zealand | *The Masked Singer* | Three | 2021 |
| Philippines | *Masked Singer Pilipinas* | TV5 | 2020 |
| Thailand | เดอะแมสก์ซิงเกอร์ หน้ากากนักร้อง | Workpoint TV | 2016 |
| Vietnam | *Mặt nạ Ngôi Sao* | HTV7 | 2017 |
| **Europe** | | | |
| Austria | *The Masked Singer Austria* | Puls 4 | 2020 |
| Belgium/Flanders | *The Masked Singer* | VTM | 2020 |
| Bulgaria | *Маскираният певец* | Nova TV | 2019 |
| Czech Republic and Slovakia | *Zlatá maska* | Prima TV JOJ | 2020 |
| Estonia | *Maskis laulja* | TV3 | 2020 |
| Finland | *Masked Singer Suomi* | MTV3 | 2020 |
| France | *Le Chanteur Masqué* | TF1 | 2019 |
| Germany | *The Masked Singer* | ProSieben | 2019 |
| Greece | *Masked Singer Greece* | Skai TV | 2021 |
| Hungary | *Álarcos énekes* | RTL Klub | 2020 |
| Italy | *Il cantante mascherato* | Rai 1 | 2020 |
| Latvia | *Balss Maskā* | TV3 Latvia | 2020 |
| Lithuania | *Kaukės* | LNK | 2020 |
| Netherlands | *The Masked Singer* | RTL 4 | 2019 |
| Norway | *Maskorama* | NRK1 | 2020 |
| Portugal | *A Máscara* | SIC | 2020 |
| Romania | *Masked Singer România* | Pro TV | 2020 |
| Russia | *Маска* | NTV | 2020 |
| Spain | *Mask Singer: Adivina quién canta* | Antena 3 | 2020 |
| Sweden | *Masked Singer Sverige* | TV4 | 2021 |
| Switzerland | *The Masked Singer Switzerland* | ProSieben Schweiz | 2020 |
| Ukraine | *Маска* | Ukraine | 2021 |
| United Kingdom | *The Masked Singer* | ITV | 2020 |
| **Middle East& Africa** | | | |
| Israel | במסכה הזמר | Channel 12 | 2020 |
| **North America** | | | |
| Canada | *The Masked Singer* | CBC | 2019 |
| United States | *The Masked Singer* | Fox | 2019 |
| **South America** | | | |
| Mexico | *¿Quién es la máscara?* | Las Estrellas | 2019 |
| Peru | *La Máscara* | Latina Televisión | 2020 |

*Source*: Author's analysis (2020).

Turkey, Russia, Thailand, and the Philippines (Esser and Lee 2018), breaking out of the Asian or East Asian regional markets highlighted by Keane, Fung, and Moran (2007). They have also sold scripts to the UK (*Hu-a-yu* (2013), aka *Who Are You?*), Italy, and Ukraine (*Noran Boksucho* (2012), aka *Ice Adonis*); and since 2016, EndemolShine, ITV Studios and Banijay have all actively sought and entered co-development deals with South Korea's major producers, CJ Entertainment, JTBC, and SBS (Esser and Lee 2018). Since *Gisaengchung* (2019, *Parasite*) became the first non-English language film ever to win a Best Picture Oscar in 2020, it looks as though further sales of Korean programs, both formatted and finished, are highly likely.

Finally, it shall be noted that program flows have not only multiplied and diversified because of the trade in formats, they have also become more intricate. Some shows travel as finished programs long before being adapted, as was the case with *Top Gear* (2002–) or some Hollywood classics, including Sony's *The Nanny* (1993–1999) and *Married … With Children* (1987–1997), or Buena Vista's *Golden Girls* (1985–1992). Others travel around the world simultaneously as finished tapes and local adaptations, sometimes in one and the same market. For instance, in Italy viewers can watch Italian, British, and US versions of UK-originated format *Don't Tell the Bride* (2007–) on different digital channels (Penati 2016). Where no local adaptation exists, as is often the case with scripted shows, program buyers might prefer an adaptation to the original. For instance, *Ugly Betty* (2006–10), the US adaptation of *Betty, La Fea*, was shown across the globe, including Australia, Britain, Germany, Italy, Japan, Spain, and Sweden. The German adaptation, *Verliebt in Berlin* (2005–07) was broadcast in Hungary, and – dubbed in French – in Belgium, Canada, France, and Switzerland, while the Russian adaptation *Ne Rodis Krasivoy* (2005–06) was broadcast in most former Soviet countries (Esser 2014). Like in the case of *Masked Singer*, where Asian buyers in China, Thailand, Vietnam, and Indonesia were the first to adapt, the role of language and traditional trade ties still shaped international circulation of the *Betty, La Fea/Ugly Betty* property. Equally, as that example shows, program flows are becoming increasingly complex and multifaceted: programs circulate either as canned exports, format adaptations, or both; and canned exports of formatted programs can include the original and/ or one or multiple adaptations, with the original not necessarily being the most successful in commercial terms.

## Conclusion and outlook

This chapter has argued that over the past 20 years, the creation of the format business and the accelerating trade in formats have significantly impacted television production and distribution across the world. The format business has expanded the scope and scale of program sales, and multiplied, diversified, and complexified international program flows. It has created transnational production and distribution structures and transnationalized production practices. Transnational interdependencies have grown and deepened, and as Paul Torre (2017) has rightly argued, make it increasingly difficult to demarcate the boundaries of national markets for content production and distribution.

Looking forward, two factors in particular are likely to affect the trade in TV formats in the years to come. Whereas the first 20 years of this thriving business were characterized by buyers across the world feeling pressured to quickly acquire what were believed to be "must-have" formats, resulting in international sales multiplying within a short period of time, evidence indicates that by the late 2010s international rollouts were decelerating. Data from format research company The WIT has revealed that in 2013, the five most licensed formats generated 64 adaptations between them, but in 2018 the top five had resulted in only 35 adaptations (C21 Media 2019). The most likely explanation for this drop is the larger volume of new and often similar formats developed in the much expanded and now thoroughly transnationalized market.

The second major factor impacting the future of the format trade is the growing interest among global streaming services in unscripted content. Subscription video-on-demand platforms like Netflix, which originally focused on acquiring canned fiction, are increasingly investing in the production of unscripted formats, including legacy shows such as *Queer Eye for the Straight Guy* (Bravo, 2003–07), rebooted as *Queer Eye* (Netflix, 2018–), or *Top Gear* (BBC, 2002–), which was reworked for Amazon Prime as *The Grand Tour* (2016–) by *Top Gear*'s producer and hosts. One reason for these investments is the hope that transnationally popular shows and hosts will attract subscribers. Other key reasons to invest in unscripted content are costs and local content quotas. In general non-fiction is significantly cheaper to produce than fiction; and using format adaptations helps global streaming platforms meet local content quotas, implemented in many countries to limit imports (usually from the United States) and support domestic production. In Europe, where content quotas have a long history, from 2018 EU regulation introduced content quota requirements for streaming services, stipulating that they must dedicate 30 percent of their future output to TV shows and films made in Europe. For producers across the world this demand for local investment by global video-on-demand players is good news. However, the rapidly growing status of global streamers could also bring bad news for format developers because the former will tend to push for global rights (C21 Media 2019). Global licenses undermine the tried-and-tested business model of territorial licensing upon which the television industry has been built, and upon which the format business was created and subsequently gained strength during the first two decades of this century. Reducing possibilities for generating revenues from selling adaptation rights across the world diminishes the format business. Arguably, the golden age of the format trade is gone.

# References

Banijay Group (2020) "Banijay Completes Landmark Deal to Acquire Endemol Shine Group," July 3, available at www.banijay.com/banijay-completes-landmark-deal-to-acquire-endemol-shine-group/ (accessed November 5, 2020).

Barraclough, L. (2020) "Simon Cowell Takes Full Control of 'Got Talent' Producer Syco," *Variety*, July 15, available at https://variety.com/2020/biz/news/simon-cowell-got-talent-syco-1234707143/ (accessed November 7, 2020).

Bourdon, J. (2012) "From Discrete Adaptations to Hard Copies: The Rise of Formats in European Television," in T. Oren and S. Shahaf (eds), *Global Television Formats: Understanding Television Across Borders*, New York: Routledge, 111–127.

*Broadcast* (2017) "Hot Picks: Buying Blind," *Broadcast*, October 12, available at www.broadcastnow.co.uk/international/buying-blind/5123179.article (accessed February 24, 2020).

C21 Media (2017) "C21's Formats Report. Global Trends and Programming Analysis," London, available at ww.c21media.net/products-page/reports/c21s-formats-report-2017/ (accessed February 25, 2020).

C21 Media (2019) "C21 Content Trends Report. International Formats," London, available at www.c21media.net/products-page/reports/the-c21-content-trends-report-international-formats-2019/ (accessed February 25, 2020).

Calbreath-Frasieur, A. (2016) "Localizing Sesame Street: The Cultural Translation of the Muppets," in A. Esser, M. Á. Bernal-Merino, and I. R. Smith (eds), *Media Across Borders. Localizing TV, Film and Video Games*, London: Routledge, 99–112.

Chalaby, J. (2010) "The Rise of Britain's Super-indies: Policy-making in the Age of the Global Media Market," *The International Communication Gazette*, 72 (8): 675–693.

Chalaby, J. (2011) "The Making of an Entertainment Revolution: How the TV Format Trade Became a Global Industry," *European Journal of Communication*, 26 (4): 293–309.

Chalaby, J. (2012) "At the Origin of a Global Industry: The TV Format Trade as an Anglo-American Invention," *Media, Culture and Society,* 34 (1): 36–52.

Chalaby, J. (2016) *The Format Age. Television's Entertainment Revolution,* Cambridge: Polity Press.

Esser, A. (2002) "The Transnationalization of European Television," *Journal of European Area Studies,* 10 (1): 13–29.

Esser, A. (2013) "The Format Business: Franchising Television Content," *International Journal of Digital Television,* 4 (2):141–158.

Esser, A. (2014) "European Television Programming: Exemplifying and Theorizing Glocalization in the Media, in R. Robertson (ed.), *European Glocalization in Global Context,* Basingstoke: Palgrave, 82–102.

Esser, A. (2016) "Challenging U.S. Leadership in Entertainment Television? The Rise and Sale of Europe's International TV Production Groups," *International Journal of Communication,* 10: 1–29.

Esser, A. and Lee, J. H. (2018) "Transnational Conglomeration and Cooperation in TV Format Production: The Europe-Asia Connection," conference paper, *Crossroads in Cultural Studies,* Shanghai University, August 12–15.

Ferrari, C. (2012) "'National Mike': Global Host and Global Formats in Early Italian Television," in T. Oren and S. Shahaf (eds), *Global Television Formats: Understanding Television Across Borders,* New York: Routledge, 128–147.

Formatbiz (2018) "Buying Blind to be Adapted in the U.S. and Finland," *Formatbiz,* April 17, available at www.formatbiz.it/dettNews.aspx?id=4277 (accessed February 24, 2020).

Hallenberger, G. (2002) "Fernsehformate und internationaler Formathandel," in Hans-Bredow-Institut (ed.), *Internationales Handbuch Medien 2002/2003,* Hamburg: Nomos Verlagsgesellschaft, 130–137.

Jäger, E. and Behrens S. (2009) *The FRAPA Report 2009: TV Formats to the World,* Cologne: FRAPA.

Jarvey, N. (2017) "How Netflix's 'Ultimate Beastmaster' Will Change Global Reality TV," *Hollywood Reporter,* February 20, available at www.hollywoodreporter.com/news/how-netflixs-ultimate-beastmaster-will-change-global-reality-tv-976142 (accessed January 22, 2020).

Jensen, P. M. (2012) "How Media System Rather Than Culture Determines National Variation: Danish *Idols* and *Australian Idol* Compared," in J. de Bruin and K. Zwan (eds), *Adapting Idols: Authenticity, Identity and Performance in a Global Television Format,* Farnham: Ashgate Publishing, 27–39.

Jensen, P. M. (2013) "The Use of Format Adaptation in Danish Public Service Programming", *Critical Studies in Television,* 8 (2): 85–103.

Keane, M. (2012) "A Revolution in Television and a Great Leap Forward for Innovation? China in the Global Television Format Business," in T. Oren and S. Shahaf (eds), *Global Television Formats: Understanding Television Across Borders,* New York: Routledge, 306–322.

Keane, M., Fung, A., and Moran. A. (2007) *New Television, Globalization, and the East Asian Cultural Imagination,* Hong Kong: Hong Kong University Press.

Keinonen, H. (2016) "Cultural Negotiation in an Early Programme Format: The Finnish Adaptation of Romper Room," in K. Aveyard, A. Moran, and P. M. Jensen (eds), *New Patterns in Global Television Formats,* Bristol: Intellect, 95–108.

Khalil, J. (2017) "From *Big Brother* to *Al Maleka*: The Growing Pains of the TV Format Trade in the Arab Region," *International Journal of Digital Television,* 8 (1): 29–46.

Middleton, R. (2020) "MBC's South Korean Format 'The Masked Singer' Reaches 50 Country Milestone," *Television Business International,* January 13, https://tbivision.com/2020/01/13/mbcs-south-korean-format-the-masked-singer-reaches-50-country-milestone/ (accessed November 9).

Mikos, L. and Perrotta, M. (2012) "Travelling Style: Aesthetic Differences and Similarities in National Adaptations of *Yo Soy Betty, La Fea*," *International Journal of Cultural Studies,* 15 (1): 81–97.

Moran, A. (1998) *Copycat TV: Globalization, Program Formats and Cultural Identity.* Luton: University of Luton Press.

Moran, A. (2013) "Global Television Formats: Genesis and Growth," *Critical Studies in Television,* 8 (2): 1–19.

Moran, A. with Malbon, J. (2006) *Understanding the Global TV Format,* Bristol: Intellect.

Moran, A. and Aveyard, K. (2014) "The Place of Television Programme Formats," *Continuum. Journal of Media and Cultural Studies,* 28 (1): 18–27.

Ndlela, M. N. (2013) "Television across Boundaries: Localisation of *Big Brother Africa*," *Critical Studies in Television,* 8 (2): 57–72.

Ndlela, M. N. (2017) "TV Formats in Anglophone Africa: The Hegemonic Role of South Africa in the TV Format Value Chain," *International Journal of Digital Television,* 8 (1): 47–64.

Nippon TV (2020) "Dragon's Den Reaches Milestone 40th Adaptation," press release, January 14, available at www.ntv.co.jp/english/pressrelease/20200114.html (accessed November 9).

Nylund, M. (2016) "Television Formats as a Transnational Production Model," in K. Aveyard, A. Moran, and P. M. Jensen (eds), *New Patterns in Global Television Formats*, Bristol: Intellect, 19–33.

Quigley, S. (2017) Lecture for students of the MA in Intercultural Communication, Roehampton University, London: BBC Studios, March 16.

Schiffmann, M. (2016) "'Rising Star': A Game Changing Format in a Dying Genre: The Highs and Lows of a Format's Birth," *VIEW: Journal of European Television History and Culture*, 5 (9): 43–47.

Shahaf, S. (2016) "Decentering Innovation: The Israeli Television Industry and the Format-driven Transnational Turn in Content Development," in K. Aveyard, A. Moran, and P. M. Jensen (eds), *New Patterns in Global Television Formats*, Bristol: Intellect, 245–262.

Straubhaar, J. (2012) "Telenovelas in Brazil: From Traveling Scripts to a Genre and Proto-Format both National and Transnational," in T. Oren and S. Shahaf (eds), *Global Television Formats: Understanding Television Across Borders*, New York: Routledge, 148–177.

Torre, P. (2017) "Television Formats and the United States: New Developments in Production and Distribution," *International Journal of Digital Television*, 8 (1): 117–141.

Uribe-Jongbloed, E. and Pis Diez, E. (2017) "The TV Format Market in Latin America: Trends and Opportunities," *International Journal of Digital Television*, 8 (1): 99–115.

Van Keulen, J. (2016) "Aesthetic Proximity: The Role of Stylistic Programme Elements in Format Localisation," *VIEW Journal of European Television History and Culture*, 5 (9), available at www.viewjournal.eu/articles/10.18146/2213-0969.2016.jethc105/ (accessed March 9, 2020).

Vourlias, C. (2020) "South Africa's 'Ugly Betty' Remake Stars Franchise's First Black Lead," *Variety*, available at https://variety.com/2020/tv/global/south-africa-ugly-betty-remake-1234809240/ (accessed November 7, 2020).

Waisbord, S. and Jalfin, S. (2009) "Imagining the National: Television Gatekeepers and the Adaptation of Global Franchises in Argentina," in Moran, A. (ed.), *TV Formats Worldwide, Localizing Global Programs*, Bristol: Intellect, 55–74.

Wallace, V. (2015) "International TV Distribution and Localisation," slides presented as part of an industry roundtable discussion at the Media Across Borders/ECREA conference *TV in the Age of Transnationalisation and Transmedialisation*, June 22, 2015, University of Roehampton, London, available at http://mediaacrossborders.com/wp-content/uploads/2016/02/Format-Distribution-slides_FremantleMedia.pdf (accessed March 9, 2020).

Wayne, M. L. (2016) "Critically Acclaimed and Cancelled: FX's The Bridge, Channel as Brand, and the Adaptation of Scripted TV Formats, *VIEW: Journal of European Television History and Culture*, 5 (9): 116–125.

Winslow, G. (2006) "'The Golden Girls' Goes Global. Studios are Remaking U.S. Hits Abroad," *Broadcasting & Cable*, December 29, available at www.broadcastingcable.com/news/golden-girls-goes-global-71492 (accessed March 5, 2020).

Zeng, W. and Sparks, C. (2017) "Localization as Negotiation: Producing a Korean Format in Contemporary China," *International Journal of Digital Television*, 8 (1): 81–98.

# 31

# FROM IDENTS TO INFLUENCERS

## The promotional screen industries

### *Paul Grainge*

The practice of promotion in the media industries is long established, linked to histories of advertising, branding, sponsorship, merchandising, and to marketing strategies developed by specific media industries to promote their wares. While distinctions are often made in academic criticism between "content" and "marketing," this boundary has become harder to maintain in the last two decades. From the teasers, trailers, websites, blogs, and bonus features that surround movies and TV shows, to the commercials, gifs, memes, and videos that are sought out and shared via social media, critics in media and advertising studies have examined how the status of "promotion" and "content" has become increasingly blurred (Gillan 2015; Grainge and Johnson 2015a; Powell 2013).

This blurring has occurred in response to shifts in the media environment where digitalization has enabled an increasing range of texts to circulate in more profuse ways across a greater range of screens and platforms. Leading to heightened competition for audience attention, media and marketing industries have had to rethink the way they engage audiences in a culture of connectivity (van Dijck 2013). This chapter examines the "promotional screen industries," a sector of media production that is highly visible in the audiovisual forms it creates (for media and consumer brands, corporations, universities, governments, charities, and other bodies), but that is far less visible in the attention it receives within media research. Briefly examining the hybrid nature of promotional content within film, television, and advertising, the chapter outlines the role that promotional screen industries play in the operations, and porous relations, of the media industries.

The blurred lines of content and promotion are exemplified in the film industry by the changing status of movie trailers. Although trailers have been a staple of the movie business since the 1920s, they have assumed a more prolific life in a digital world where trailers circulate across platforms: formally in terms of studio release through official websites, informally through sites like YouTube and Twitter, and occasionally figured as live events at fan conventions and through social media. Before the digital era, promotional campaigns for Hollywood movies would frequently originate with the premiere of the trailer in cinemas or on television. It is unsurprising that the first sustained analysis of movie trailers, Lisa Kernan's *Coming Attractions* (2004), focuses on trailers exhibited before the theatrical screening of feature films. In the contemporary period, blockbuster marketing campaigns often begin online and can involve anything from

DOI: 10.4324/9780429275340-36

"announcement trailers" lasting 10–60 seconds in length – what Carter Moulton (2019) calls the "teaser-for-the-teaser" setting expectations for the arrival of a film – to experiments in real-time "virtually live" trailer launches lasting 24 hours. While announcement trailers surfaced in the mid-2000s as a means of building anticipation for blockbuster spin-offs, remakes, prequels, and sequels, social media platforms like Facebook have provided film studios with new opportunities for elongating trailer events. In December 2016, for example, the Facebook page of the Warner Bros. film *Dunkirk* (2017) went "live," broadcasting real-time images of two beach locations. With no contextual information given about the beaches or the purpose of the live stream, the broadcast was layered every four hours with war-related audio cues, building to a crescendo after 24 hours that created a sense of foreboding ahead of the official trailer launch of Christopher Nolan's movie about the Dunkirk evacuation (see Stenson 2020).

Whatever duration, the digital environment has turned the trailer into valuable content sought out by viewers and platform owners alike. Expanding beyond the cinema screen, trailers have developed an aesthetic and circulatory life of their own, giving rise to new directions in "trailer studies" that have explored the mobility of trailers and their exhibition on DVD, online platforms, and through connected devices (Gray 2010; Johnston 2009; Stenson 2020; Tryon 2010). The new cultural status of trailers has led to parallel shifts in the culture of production. Rather than being a mere stepping stone to a role in feature film editing, trailer-making has increasingly become a discrete career choice, a professional craft within the work-world of "trailer houses" that make short-form content for film studios, videogame publishers, and other entertainment-based businesses (Grainge and Johnson 2015a: 148–177).

The digital environment has given rise to similar transitions within television promotion. According to Red Bee Media, a leading broadcast and digital communications agency based in the UK (with clients ranging from the BBC to NBC Universal and Netflix), the goal of television marketing is no longer simply to persuade people to watch programs on broadcast channels. Rather, it is to navigate audiences in rich visual environments and to "connect viewers to content" in a burgeoning multiplatform world (Red Bee Media 2012). This ranges from the design of broadcast "interstitials" that appear between television programs (channel idents, trailers, promos) to transmedia promotion where TV shows are extended across media platforms (via mobisodes, apps, and web shorts), through to personalized promotional messaging enabled by the new digital interfaces of online TV (Van Esler 2020).

For television marketing executives Andy Bryant and Charlie Mawer (2016), television is facing a "hybrid future" where data will increasingly be used to tailor promotion to the preferences of individual viewers, but where distinctive channel brands will continue to provide a beacon for large audiences. While personalized taste recommendations on services like Netflix have challenged TV business models, making channels less relevant, promotional screen work remains a key activity in the world of broadcast and digital television. This is evident in the creative application of traditional methods of producing idents, logos, promotional campaigns, trails, and title sequences, but also in harnessing social media to promote shows in digitally interactive ways. Examples of these strategies include a global mobile app that enabled fans of *Game of Thrones* (HBO 2011–19) to "Join the Realm" by creating their own family arms (attracting 1.2 million visits), and a second-screen app for the zombie series *The Walking Dead* (AMC 2010–present) (see Freeman elsewhere in this collection) that allowed viewers to predict the number of kills before each episode and post these on Facebook and Twitter to play along with friends.

The promotional media surrounding films, TV shows and videogames has given rise to the study of media "paratexts" (Brookey and Gray 2017; Gray 2010). Foregrounding materials such as trailers, spoilers, intros, mash-up, promos, bonus material, and merchandise, paratextual analysis helps make sense of the forms and artifacts that orbit and amplify the meanings of "primary" entertainment media. The focus on paratexts in media studies has enriched thinking about the relation of promotion to the textual construction of film and television, in particular. However, paratexts also invite questions about *production* and the specialized creative work that occurs in the crossover of media and marketing industries. Spot commercials and brand sponsorships are part of the blurring of "promotion" and "content" in this context and move paratextual analysis beyond the realm of film and TV franchises alone. Applying the concept of paratextual promotion to developments in contemporary advertising, Chris Hackley and Rungpaka Amy Hackley argue that "traditional TV 'spot' and print advertising remain relevant but … the fulcrum of creative advertising strategy is shifting from the brand, to the stories around and about the brand" (2019: 197). In this context, paratexts relate to the digital stories developed by the promotional industries more generally.

To take an example from the late 2010s, the premium UK satellite channel Sky Atlantic prefaced its season of 2019 shows with upcoming trailers and channel idents, but also hybrid channel sponsorships by the car manufacturer Volvo. The latter included 15-second sponsor messages that appeared before Sky Atlantic's roster of "exclusive US" and "original British" dramas, including *Game of Thrones, Big Little Lies* (HBO 2017–present), and *Chernobyl* (HBO and Sky Atlantic 2019). These interstitial "bumpers," to use industry vernacular, included two different sponsor sequences that depicted separate panoramic scenes: one of children running to the sea from a Volvo parked on a beach and another of two Volvos driving along a clifftop, coastline in view. Each carried the message "Watch the full film: search *The Unseen Ocean.*" This example demonstrates the way that commercial brands have embraced a mix of traditional and transmedia promotion in the development of "branded entertainment." In this case, the sponsor messages were themselves trailers for an online video series produced by Volvo telling stories of "defiant pioneers." Part of a range of digital shorts by the car brand, *The Unseen Ocean* focused on a primary school teacher who runs a program that involves driving to the coast (in Volvos of course) to teach inner-city children to surf and learn about the environment.

Branded entertainment became part of the advertising industry lexicon in the 2000s and 2010s, a term used for a diverse range of alternative, digital, and content marketing initiatives (Dzamic and Kirby 2018). Whatever the issues of "greenwashing" (Miller 2017) involved in the example of a car manufacturer telling stories about environmental sustainability, *The Unseen Ocean* (made by ad agency Grey London) illustrates the shift from "interruptive" to "engagement" advertising models that took hold within agency thinking at the start of the twenty-first century. Rather than depend on spot commercials that interrupt audience attention, brands have sought to experiment with the creation of entertaining or useful content that consumers are motivated to seek out.

By some accounts, such examples point to a deepening "promotional orientation" within everyday life (Cronin 2018; Davis 2013). From the brand initiatives of corporations and public bodies to the individual self-promotion encouraged by social media networks, the blurring of "content" and "marketing" has been associated with the extension of promotional logics in the cultural and media sphere. Rather than see this as a purely negative consequence of marketization, a body of work within media studies, cultural studies, and communication and advertising theory has sought to understand promotion as having complex meanings, functions, and pleasures, and as developing from particular discursive and industrial practices (Davis 2013; Grainge and Johnson 2015; McAllister and West 2013; Wang 2008).

In their short introduction to media industry studies, Daniel Herbert, Amanda Lotz, and Aswin Punathambekar eschew a "by industry" approach to their subject, suggesting that "an intellectual enterprise such as media industry studies should aspire to identify ideas or theory that offer insight to multiple industries" (2020: 11). They also point to the "blurring boundary" between different media industries, including the "artificial boundary assumed to exist between 'new' or 'digital' media and legacy television and film" (p. 119). The promotional screen industries are a pointed example of these blurring industrial configurations.

As the aforementioned trailers, interstitials, and forms of branded entertainment suggest, a range of companies, agencies, and intermediaries lie behind the production of promotional media. Operating in the fertile space between marketing and media, Catherine Johnson and I use the term "promotional screen industries" to encompass movie trailer houses, broadcast promotion specialists, film and television marketing departments, "content" divisions within advertising and media agencies, and digital media firms selling expertise in visual effects and experiential media (Grainge and Johnson 2015a). In addition, the term incorporates a wide range of freelancers and incumbent and upstart agencies with skills in promotional forms like online video, vlogging, and emergent digital media. As we suggest, the promotional screen industries are not a clearly defined sector, but a fluid site of industrial collaboration and competition, with companies and agencies from different fields moving into each other's territory.

The leaky territories of promotional screen work are marked in different ways. For instance, while trailer houses make pre-release teasers for game publishers and compete with digital design and animation companies for contracts, ad agencies, social media marketing firms, and TV promotion specialists all routinely pitch expertise in online video as a way of developing digital content strategies for media and consumer brands. The porous nature of promotional work extends within the production cultures of film and television. Notably, the scope of multiplatform work undertaken by the in-house marketing departments of movie studios and television broadcasters complicates distinctions between those responsible for "primary" film and TV content and the "secondary" or ancillary forms of media used to promote them. Marketing departments are increasingly involved in transmedia strategies from an early stage, developing media such as mobisodes and web-based content that anticipate, surround, and extend films and TV shows.

The fluidity between promotional intermediaries, in both sectoral and inter-divisional terms, complicates any sense of there being cleanly bounded production cultures in the media industries. For Aeron Davis, the term "promotional intermediary" designates those who work in promotional occupations (2013: 2). Applying his definition, the promotional screen industries "mediate" links between sectors in the process of identifying a saleable product, a potential audience, a communications medium, and a message. However, promotion is also a professional and creative discipline in its own right with a purpose that generates specific kinds of (screen) work within and between sectors. Promotional intermediaries who work in advertising, film and television, digital media design, and social media bring particular specialisms to bear. The expertise in strategy and media buying offered by media agencies is different to the skills in short-form editing provided by trailer houses, which is again different to the creative work of branding a TV channel or the data-driven knowledge required to maximize the algorithmic culture of online media. However, the complexities of promotional screen work often see professionals from different sectors competing for and collaborating in the production of the same work.

Promotional content can equally involve transaction between companies and professionals in adjacent media industry fields. Producers of ads, promos, trailers, and title sequences, for example, frequently collaborate with specialist firms and freelancers in music and sound design to provide soundtracks and soundscapes. Examining the use of music placements in advertising and television, Leslie Meier (2017) outlines the companies and in-house divisions of record labels dedicated to fostering "brand partnerships" and to licensing popular music for marketing purposes. In a different vein, TV producers and promotional specialists will often collaborate with composers to give title sequences and idents bespoke audio signatures, a feature of promotional design that has been increasingly taken up by music scholars (Brownrigg and Meech 2011; Davison 2013).

Within critical accounts of marketing in the media industries, promotion has often been regarded as a constraining force upon the creativity of directors and artists who make movies, television programs, games, music, and other popular cultural forms. Meier, for instance, provides a critique of the "possessive promotional logic characteristic of music branding" whereby "artists are playing by rules devised by brands" (2017: 122). In this tradition, "creativity" is often set against "marketing" as a default of promotional analysis. Rather than consider promotional work as a discipline requiring creative acumen (McStay 2013), marketing is often seen as limiting and vacuous in cultural and imaginative terms. While promotional content can certainly be crass, boring, and uninspired, it can also be beautiful, funny, and thoughtful. Picking up this theme, the cultural historian Joe Moran likens modern television idents to "visual poems" (2008: 184). According to one TV promotion specialist, idents necessitate

> a particular type of storytelling and a particular type of engagement that is possibly less about grabbing you by the front of your jumper and shaking you and is much more about giving you something you can sit back and be immersed in.
>
> *Charlie Mawer, cited in Grainge, 2011: 94*

A case in point are the channel idents made for Sky Atlantic in 2019 that appeared just before Volvo's sponsor messages. Using dynamic motion graphics and audiovisual tones (a stylistic feature of UK broadcast design), these short forms created arresting scenes based on a theme of urban noir that captured a mood for the channel's particular brand of transatlantic television.

The idents in question preceded program title sequences, synoptic short forms that have their own aesthetic pleasures. From the graphic "falling man" titles of *Mad Men* (AMC, 2007–15) to the traversal of the elaborate map that heralds *Game of Thrones*, title sequences epitomize the skill of producing content designed to be allusive, spectacular, and repeatable to watch. In a panel session on "The Dark Art of the Title Sequence" at a conference of the trade body of television marketers, PromaxBDA, a veteran title sequence designer (Richard Morrison) reflected on the creative "mind-wandering" needed to find ideas and the collaboration required to work with directors (Grainge and Johnson 2015b). Rather than make audiovisual content that film and television directors can just as easily produce, promotional screen forms require particular skills (in design, animation, editing, motion graphics) as well as a sophisticated appreciation of the nature of short-form media and the specific demands of screen-based marketing. The "dark art" of promotional screen work should not be seen as sorcery, in this sense, but rather as a discipline with its own creative vitality, with practitioners often required to be multidisciplinary and highly collaborative in their working practices.

PromaxBDA is one of a number of trade organizations that hold conferences to connect practitioners in the promotional screen industries. PromaxBDA sits alongside advertising festivals such as Cannes Lions, galas for movie marketing like the Key Art Awards, and ceremonies for design and art direction such as D&AD. These gatherings, which have their own accolades, provide a site where professional values are forged, specialist skills are put on show, and career capital is bestowed. This extends beyond the immediate creative design of promotional work to include other key areas such as strategy, planning, and account management.

Promotional work includes a spectrum of job roles. Trailer houses, for instance, typically organize work around the account handler/producer, who manages the relationship with a film studio's marketing department, and the editor who has overall responsibility for the creation of the trailer itself. Within advertising and media agencies, roles are often split between "account directors" who act as pivot points between clients and creative teams, "strategic planners" responsible for generating ideas based on data and research and who write briefs, "creatives" who develop content, and "operations managers" who oversee the management of production and resourcing. While hierarchies are often felt and debated within these socio-professional fields, trade bodies serve an advocacy role for promotional screen work. By its own account,

> PromaxBDA leads the global community of those passionately engaged in the marketing of television and video content on all platforms, inspiring creativity, driving innovation and honoring excellence [and is] … the leading global resource for education, community, creative inspiration and career development in the media and media marketing sectors.
>
> *PromaxBDA 2014*

As in other facets of the media industries, trade bodies and craft guilds provide a rich site for examining the rituals and values of screen work, promotion representing a type of creative labor with its own history, identity, structures, networks, and forms of best practice.

While large agencies, companies and in-house divisions dominate media and marketing sectors, freelance consultants and small-to-medium enterprises have carved out profitable niches in specific areas of promotional screen work. This includes making corporate films, infographics, product videos, and training films, to name just a few. Capitalizing on the growth of online video since the launch of YouTube in 2005, there has been a proliferation of agencies selling expertise in promotional videography. These range from boutiques specializing in video strategy to fully integrated film and video production agencies selling know-how in content planning, creative storytelling, production techniques (e.g., stop-motion, animation, tracking shots, aerial filming), and search optimization.

While the study of promotion and branding in the media industries has tended to focus on well-established industries such as film, television and music (see respectively Grainge 2008, Johnson 2012, and Meier 2017), online video points to a different vector of promotional screen work, often moving beyond media and consumer brands. In many cases, boutique video agencies are more likely to sell know-how to charities and universities than to film studios, and to produce digital shorts for "business-to-business" purposes than to meet the transmedia needs of TV networks or corporations venturing into branded entertainment. To take one example, the London-based film and video agency Spectrecom specifically targets the education market. With a staff base of 37 people (including two account managers for universities), Spectrecom is explicit in selling video expertise to higher education. Proclaiming to "understand the shifting patterns of viewing and content sharing for young people," Spectrecom pitches to universities directly, stating

> we will help you to find the right audience with the most relevant video content. Whether it's producing a cinema advert for a local catchment audience, or using social media to attract international students, we'll come up with creative film concepts that demand attention.
>
> *Spectrecom 2016*

Like other organizations operating outside the media industries, universities have placed growing emphasis on the development of digital shorts that tell stories to engage and involve their target audience. In this context promotional screen work has become as relevant to the public relations needs of educational, charitable, and governmental bodies as it is to the marketing demands of the media industries (Cronin 2018; Grainge 2017).

In a digital media environment that enables content to be spread and shared in new ways, calls on audience attention have led to emergent promotional screen practices. Stuart Cunningham and David Craig (2019) go as far as to posit an emerging "proto-industry" of content creators and intermediaries, which they regard as central to a new screen ecology of "social media entertainment". They describe this proto-industry as

> fueled by professionalizing, previously amateur content creators using new entertainment and communicative formats, including vlogging, gameplay, and do-it-yourself (DIY), to develop potentially sustainable businesses based on significant followings that can extend across multiple platforms.
>
> *p. 5*

Emerging in 2006, the new screen ecology has been driven by interactive platforms such as YouTube, Twitter, Facebook, Instagram, Snapchat, and Chinese equivalents like Youku, Weibo, and WeChat. A prominent feature of this ecology is "influencer marketing."

As part of the move from "interruptive" to "engagement" advertising models, influencer marketing moves from "push" approaches to promotion toward "pull" strategies whereby consumers are encouraged to seek out brands that provide engaging and valuable content relevant to their needs. In this case, the pull is provided by influential social media creators who engage with followers through vlogging – what Cunningham and Craig see as a core social media entertainment format "that deepens the effect of intimacy created between creators and their community" (p. 149). Influencer marketing has given rise to internet celebrities specializing in areas such as fashion, beauty, travel, lifestyle, design, and gaming. It has also facilitated the growth of intermediary firms that broker relations between social media creators and the brands they feature (Abidin 2018).

Like branded entertainment, there are historical precursors to the kinds of product placement, endorsement, and content–promotion hybridity represented by influencer marketing. However, Cunningham and Craig note that social media creators are distinct in the way they build individual brands based upon their personality and through "the intensely normative discourses of authenticity around vlogging" (2019: 13). The nature of "engagement" is particular in this regard as the dynamics of social media prioritize the way that creators sustain relationships with their fans, rendering "brand relationships subordinate to the dominant discourses of authenticity and community" (p. 183). Connecting the proto-industry of social media entertainment to the forms and networks of the promotional screen industries points to the fast-moving nature *of both* as hybrid industrial constellations responding to changes in the media and marketing environment brought about by digitalization.

The promotional screen industries are an amalgam, and in some sense a mess, of disciplines, practices, and categories of work in the space of interaction between media and marketing. The term is heuristic and does not refer to a fixed sector or list of agencies, intermediaries, and roles that can be easily mapped. Instead, it is deliberate in pointing to the porous nature of forms and practices that organize work in industries such as advertising, film, television, music, digital design, and social media entertainment. In critical terms, the scope of what is understood as "promotion" in the digital environment and what counts as "content" – including those who count as content providers, be it Volvo or vloggers – has pushed the traditional boundaries of the media industries. This does not mean to say that promotional screen work, or content–promotion hybridity, is a purely contemporary phenomenon. As critics from Janet Staiger (1990) to Jennifer Gillan (2015) have shown, advertising is integral to the history of media industries, and hybridity can be seen in the various forms of product integration, sponsor entwinement, and dramatized advertisement that have distinguished film and commercial television programming, in different ways, throughout the twentieth century. While paratextual approaches to such forms have tended to emphasize the textual and discursive function of promotional content, the study of promotional screen industries highlights different critical and methodological concerns. Whether historical in focus, or applied to the present, a media industries approach to promotion invites questions about cultures of production, the role of intermediaries, the specificity of professional and creative skills as applied to short-form media, the function of trade communities, as well as systems of regulation as these relate to promotional communication.

Moving forward, the era of "connected viewing" (Holt and Sanson 2014) will continue to invite new ways of conceiving the purview of promotion and the scope of promotional work. Beyond the creation of idents, trailers, webisodes, vlogs, and the like, the algorithmic nature of online culture has given new import to professionals with technological skills in software programming and data analytics. Notably, this includes digital specialists who develop and refine recommender systems that enable audiences to "discover" movies, TV shows, music, and videos on platforms like Netflix, Amazon, Spotify, and YouTube. The move toward personalization and programmatic promotion has become increasingly important within media and marketing industries. As a result, data science has emerged as a new dimension of promotional work, linked to the significance of content discovery within a "curatorial culture" where seeking, finding, and selecting has become the coin of the digital age (Johnson 2019; Robinson 2017). As a designation, the promotional screen industries is not simply a means of identifying a hidden or unbidden professional sector within media industry studies; it points to the way that blurring between "promotion" and "content" corresponds with industrial blurring within and between promotional intermediaries and occupations that produce, distribute, circulate, and locate audiovisual media.

# References

Abidin, C. (2018) *Internet Celebrity: Understanding Fame Online,* Bingley: Emerald Publishing.

Brookey, R. and Gray, J. (2017) "'Not Merely Para': Continuing Steps in Paratextual Research," *Critical Studies in Media Communication,* 34 (2): 101–110.

Brownrigg, M. and Meech, P. (2011) "'Music is Half the Picture': The Soundworld of UK Television Idents", in P. Grainge (ed.), *Ephemeral Media: Transitory Screen Culture from Television to YouTube,* London: British Film Institute, 70–86.

Bryant, A. and Mawer, C. (2016) *The TV Brand Builders,* London: Kogan Page.

Cronin, A. (2018) *Public Relations Capitalism: Promotional Culture, Publics and Commercial Democracy,* London: Palgrave.

Cunningham, S. and Craig, D. (2019) *Social Media Entertainment: The New Intersection of Hollywood and Silicon Valley,* New York: New York University Press.

Davis, A. (2013) *Promotional Cultures,* Cambridge: Polity Press.

Davison, A. (2013) "Title Sequences for Contemporary Television Serials," in J. Richardson, C. Gorbman and C. Vernallis (eds), *The Oxford Handbook for New Audiovisual Aesthetics,* Oxford: Oxford University Press, 146–167.

Dzamic, L. and Kirby, J. (2018) *The Definitive Guide to Strategic Content Marketing,* London: Kogan Page.

Gillan, J. (2015) *Television Brandcasting: The Return of the Content Promotion Hybrid,* New York: Routledge.

Grainge, P. (2017) "Ancillary Academia: Video Shorts and the Production of University Paratexts," *Critical Studies in Media Communication,* 34 (2): 184–192

Grainge, P. (2011) "TV Promotion and Broadcast Design: An Interview with Charlie Mawer", in P. Grainge (ed.), *Ephemeral Media: Transitory Screen Culture from Television to YouTube*, London: British Film Institute, 87–101.

Grainge, P. (2008) *Brand Hollywood: Selling Entertainment in a Global Media Age*, Abingdon: Routledge.

Grainge, P. and Johnson, C. (2015a) *Promotional Screen Industries*, Abingdon: Routledge.

Grainge, P. and Johnson, C. (2015b) "'Show Us Your Moves": Trade Rituals of Television Marketing," *Arts and the Market,* 5 (2): 126–138.

Gray, J. (2010) *Show Sold Separately: Promos, Spoilers and Other Media Paratexts*, New York: New York University Press

Hackley, C, and Hackley, R. A. (2019) "Advertising at the Threshold: Paratextual Promotion in the Era of Media Convergence," *Marketing Theory,* 19 (2): 195–215.

Herbert, D., Lotz, A. and Punathambekar, A. (2020) *Media Industry Studies: A Short Introduction*, Cambridge: Polity Press.

Holt. J. and Sanson, K. (eds) (2014) *Connected Viewing: Selling, Streaming and Sharing Media in the Digital Era*, New York: Routledge.

Johnson, C. (2019) *Online TV,* Abingdon: Routledge.

Johnson, C. (2012) *Branding Television*, Abingdon: Routledge.

Johnston, K. M. (2009) *Coming Soon: Film Trailers and the Selling of Hollywood Technology*, Jefferson, NC: McFarland.

Kernan, L. (2004) *Coming Attractions: Reading American Movie Trailers*, Austin, TX: University of Texas Press.

McAllister, M. P. and West, E. (eds) (2013) *The Routledge Companion to Advertising and Promotional Culture*, Abingdon: Routledge.

McStay, A. (2013) *Creativity and Advertising: Affect, Events and Process*, Abingdon: Routledge.

Meier, L. M. (2017) *Popular Music as Promotion*, Cambridge: Polity Press.

Miller, T. (2017) *Greenwashing Culture*, Abingdon: Routledge.

Moran, J. (2008) *Queuing for Beginners: The Story of Daily Life from Breakfast to Bedtime,* London: Profile Books.

Moulton, C. (2019) "'Announcement' Trailers and the Inter-temporality of Hollywood Blockbusters," *International Journal of Cultural Studies,* 22 (3): 434–449.

PromaxBDA (2014) "About PromaxBDA," available at www.promaxbda.org/about (accessed March 14, 2014).

Powell, H. (ed.) (2013) *Promotional Culture and Convergence*, Abingdon: Routledge.

Red Bee Media (2012) "Meet Red Bee Media," available at www.redbeemedia.com/work/meet-red-bee-media (accessed November 12, 2012).

Robinson, M. J. (2017) *Television on Demand: Curatorial Culture and the Transformation of TV*, London: Bloomsbury.

Spectrecom (2016) "Education video production", available at www.spectrecom.co.uk/student-recruitment-video-marketing/ (accessed December 5, 2016).

Staiger, J. (1990) "Announcing Wares, Winning Patrons, Voicing Ideals: Thinking About the History and Theory of Film Advertising," *Cinema Journal*, 29 (3): 3–31.

Stenson, R. (2020) *"Tune In/Join Us": Mobilising Liveness as a Promotional Strategy in Film Trailer Exhibition,* Doctoral thesis, University of Nottingham.

Tryon, C. (2010) *Reinventing Cinema: Movies in the Age of Media Convergence*, New Brunswick, NJ: Rutgers University Press.

van Dijck, J. (2013) *The Culture of Connectivity*, Oxford: Oxford University Press.

Van Esler, M. (2020) "In Plain Sight: Online TV Interfaces as Branding," *Television and New Media*, first published online, May 2020.

Wang, J. (2008) *Brand New China: Advertising, Media and Commercial Culture*, Cambridge, MA: Harvard University Press.

# 32

# BRANDED ENTERTAINMENT

## A critical review

*Katharina Stolley, Finola Kerrigan, and Cagri Yalkin*

Film, television, videogames, music videos, and other media forms provide worlds for us to escape into, to be inspired by, to learn from, to scare us, to thrill us, to represent us, to alienate us. In constructing these worlds, media producers provide credibility through setting their story worlds in various contexts. Conventionally, the story comes first, and what follows are actions focused on creating this story in the most credible way possible, through finding a place within which to tell the story, dressing the characters, giving them possessions, consumption activities, and so on. The role of audiovisual media to "sell" has long been understood. Whether this is selling ideology or selling fast food, positioning ideas, objects, and places within these stories can lead to positive perceptions among audiences. This capability has meant that audiovisual producers have been able to secure funding if they are willing to offer their film or television show as a shop window.

The contemporary media environment faces a number of challenges: production budgets are limited, film financiers can be risk averse, and the media landscape is fragmented. Similarly, brands have been looking for new ways to engage consumers and these combined challenges have resulted in the rise of branded entertainment. This chapter aims to introduce and redefine branded entertainment, an example of the collaboration between brands and creative producers. While branded entertainment exists in many media formats, we look specifically at the context of film and television. We examine the consequences of the development of branded entertainment in terms of collaboration between media companies and mainstream brands, and scrutinize the ethical debates surrounding it.

Placements remain prevalent today. Traditionally placements were rather basic (Karrh 1998) with objects being merely loaned or donated to the film production, or where essential items were simply being bought at local stores (DeLorme, Reid, and Zimmer 1994). Over time, the process of such placements has been elaborated, with movie studios and placement agents beginning to act as intermediaries. For several decades, placement agents have facilitated collaboration between advertisers and film or television producers. Agents would negotiate with production staff regarding opportunities for placements, including references to products in movie and television series scripts (Avery and Ferraro 2000). Major film studios generally had placement departments (Popeo and Price 2004) or engaged with placement agents to establish placement opportunities. More recent developments see various stakeholders involved in placements deals ranging from advertisers, creative agencies, brands, broadcasters,

DOI: 10.4324/9780429275340-37

and production studios, to talent and media agencies, demonstrating the complex field of partnerships. Even management consulting firms realize the potential of creative partnerships. Deloitte Digital, the creative consulting unit of accountancy firm Deloitte, acquired creative agency Acne in 2017 in order to capitalize on placement deals. Such deals are typically paid for by the advertiser or are based on a barter system with regard to products and/or services (Karrh 1998). As placements have become more elaborate so have the remuneration opportunities. Newell, Salmon, and Chang (2007: 591) state that "in a single program one product's on-screen appearance can be the result of cash payment, other products receive airtime in return for reciprocal advertising, whereas other products are included to save money on the purchase of props."

## Introducing branded entertainment

Drawing on O'Reilly and Kerrigan's (2013) work on the film marketing brandscape, it is clear that films (and television shows) are cultural products which carry and transmit meaning. The American Marketing Association defines a brand as "a name, term, design, symbol or any other feature that identifies one seller's goods or services as distinct from those of other sellers" (AMA 2020). Keller (2003) talks about brands as a way to provide meaning, through forming mental structures for consumers, to help them to interpret information, clarify consumer decision making, and create value for the firm. Brands provide shortcuts through the myriad of products and services on offer, to allow consumers to match their needs, wants, and desires to what is on offer. Through the film marketing brandscape, O'Reilly and Kerrigan (2013) propose that just as films themselves can be perceived as brands, the various elements such as actors, directors, the genre, and so on can be seen as brands collectively fighting for meaning within an overall film brand. Within this context, commercial placed brands can benefit from association with film brands, communicating a sense of realism by their presence in the brandscape. By moving from the idea of individual brands to brandscapes, it is possible to understand that meaning comes not just from a specific individual brand, but through locating that brand within a wider context. Preece, Kerrigan, and O'Reilly (2019: 331) draw on DeLanda (2006, 2016) to conceptualize brands as "dynamic assemblages of sociocultural artifacts that occupy simultaneously discrete and interacting nests of association and meaning." Following such a socio-cultural approach to branding allows us to understand why films as cultural brands can provide ideal places for other types of brands to be showcased, to reinforce or establish brand meaning. Film sets often need to mimic reality in order to draw the audience into the film, so particularly in the context of modern urbanscapes, where we live in brandscapes, an absence of expected local or global brands would deem the setting inauthentic.

Branded entertainment describes a rather new term that represents a comparatively modern, sophisticated implementation of product placement, where the brand is intrinsic to the storyline (Lehu 2007; Hudson and Hudson 2006). Hudson and Hudson (2006) define branded entertainment as "the integration of advertising into entertainment content, whereby brands are embedded into story-lines of a film, television program, or other entertainment medium" (p. 492). Other entertainment media may additionally comprise of novels, music videos, songs, plays, or shows (Lehu 2007; Molesworth 2006; Russell and Belch 2005; Williams, Petrosky, Hernandez, and Page 2011). Branded entertainment merges brands, entertainment, and media to allow co-branding, with companies forming partnerships to profit from the competences of each, which may accordingly reinforce the customer/brand experience. Indeed, many brands are moving toward producing, sponsoring, and being an actual part of films and other media.

Branded entertainment is transforming both marketing and the wider entertainment industries (Kirby 2016). While emerging hybrid messages draw attention toward influential media owners, advertising agencies and award organizers (e.g., D&AD, Cannes Lions), staking their claim in this profitable area, these developments have also spawned new vocabulary such as "branded content," "content marketing," "native advertising," "advertainment," and "entertainment marketing." However, the definition of branded entertainment is not thoroughly developed and requires further clarification (Arhio and Raunio 2015).

Following Hudson and Hudson (2006), we can usefully start by conceptualizing branded entertainment as a continuation of product placement. La Ferle and Edwards (2006) found that product placement is in a state of constant change, and this has resulted in the growth of branded entertainment as a related but discrete media category. Attempts to further differentiate branded entertainment from other forms of hybrid communications such as product placement, program sponsorships, and advertising was carried out by Kunz, Elsässer, and Santomier (2016) who describe branded entertainment as the greatest interweaving of editorial content and advertisement. Van Loggerenberg, Enslin, and Terblanche-Smit (2019) highlight that branded entertainment must use a convincing and authentic narrative to attain brand resonance. What we can conclude is that the distinction between product placement and branded entertainment is blurred, but that there is a need to unpack this toward understanding the concept from the perspective of brands, creative producers, and audiences.

## Product placement and brand placement

Balasubramanian, Karrh, and Patwardhan (2006) state that substantial growth in product placement occurred during the 1980s and 1990s after accelerating during the 1960s and 1970s. Indeed, public awareness as well as popularization of product placement applications became particularly apparent following Steven Spielberg's movie *E.T. the Extra-Terrestrial* (1982) in which Reece's Pieces became the alien's favorite candy (Law and Braun-LaTour 2004). Overall, the movie was a great success and Reese's Pieces sales rose by an impressive 65 percent (*AdAge* 2003). Subsequently, Hollywood has played a leading part in transforming the meaning and importance of product and brand placements, opening marketers' eyes to the potentials of placements, with many companies replicating similar advertising strategies to influence positive brand attitude (Brennan and Babin 2004).

Karrh (1998) expands the product placement definition by adding the term "brand," which he defines "as the paid inclusion of branded products or brand identifiers, through audio and/ or visual means, within mass media programming" (p. 33), thus highlighting the commercial aspect of placements. Instead of inserting certain product types, brand placements include specific brands for commercial intent. Moreover, brand placements are not exclusively regarded as discreet; certain brands can be also applied for promotional reasons to emphasize character specification or to fit the particular components of a scene. Placements of products may be integrated visually, verbally, or as a combination of both (Karrh, McKee and Pardun 2003). Based on a hierarchy of memory effects, audiences process brand placements differently, with the visual–verbal combination memorized the most, followed by a verbal-only placement, and lastly purely visual placements (Russell 2002; Karrh, McKee, and Pardun 2003). Russell (2002) suggests that if the placement is relevant and connected to the plot, the placement is memorized even more. In the same study, she investigated the relationship between different placement modalities in the television context based on potential multiple connections between plot, compatibility of the placement, and placement modality where the impact on attitudes depends on the congruency between brand and plot. Visual placements result in increased attitude change when plot and brand were barely associated, whereas audio placements performed well when plot and brand were closely related. Placement suitability is a crucial consideration, linking congruence theory in product and brand placements (Lee and Faber 2007). Acquiring congruent brand placements may facilitate placements being viewed as more welcoming as they are less irritating or prominent in an intrusive way (Lewis and Porter 2010).

Overall, the purpose of brand or product placement is to generate additional funding for the producer while at the same time allowing advertisers to integrate their offering in entertainment contexts (Russell and Belch 2005) for various marketing outcomes. From a marketing perspective, product or brand placement is a promotion tool, linked to the overall marketing communications, aimed at enhancing consumer awareness, recall, recognition, or preference of a brand or product toward fostering the intended or actual purchase of that brand or product (Kerrigan 2017).

## Placement effectiveness

Previous researchers have examined performance-related aspects (Russell 2002), economic value (Wiles and Danielova 2009), and cross-cultural differences in audience attitudes toward placements (McKechnie and Zhou 2003; Karrh, Frith, and Callison 2001; Gould, Gupta, and Grabner-Kräuter 2000). However, the most common method to measure the effectiveness of product placement is memory (Bressoud, Lehu, and Russell 2010), often determined with explicit or implicit memory measurements (Herrmann, Walliser, and Kacha 2011; Yang and Roskos-Ewoldsen 2007). Explicit memory relates to individuals attempting to intentionally and consciously remember a certain past event, whereas implicit memory occurs with no deliberate conscious recollection of that particular event (Schacter 1987). Explicit memory measurements relate to recall and recognition (Townsend and Ashby 1984) and implicit memory has been utilized as a complementary measure to evaluate brand placement effectiveness (Auty and Lewis 2004a).

Implicit memory is a central concept in advertising research (Duke and Carlson 1993, 1994; Krishnan and Chakravarti 1999) and has gained significant importance due to the perceived limitations of explicit memory measures (Shapiro and Krishnan 2001). This is because explicit memory measurements can uncover advertising effects available to conscious retrieval, yet advertising effects may also affect non-conscious memory processes (Krishnan and Chakravarti 1999). If no explicit memory of the placement occurred, it would be assumed that the brand placement was ineffective (Van Reijmersdal 2009). Consequently, Law and Braun-LaTour (2004) state it is vital to consider both explicit and implicit memory measurements as these are affected by various aspects of brand placements, producing more significant results through dynamic and thorough exploration where participants do not recognize the impact of placements.

## Differences between branded entertainment and product placement

Product placements can be described as messages designed to commercially support products by subtly embedding these in film or television programs in order to potentially influence the purchasing decisions of viewers (Balasubramanian 1994). Placements deliberately occur in non-commercial environments (Williams, Petrosky, Hernandez, and Page 2011) and so are not solely integrated into films or programs but also in other cultural products such as shows, plays, video games, books, songs, and music videos (Gupta and Lord 1998), social media (Colliander and Erlandsson 2015; Okazaki and Taylor 2013), online games (Dardis, Schmierbach, Sherrick,

Waddell, Aviles, Kumble, and Bailey 2016), virtual reality games (Wang and Chen 2019) and mobile phone applications (Confos and Davis 2016).

In contrast, branded entertainment vehicles have the promotion of a brand as the starting point for the creative storytelling. The narrative is developed around the need to position and promote the brand in question. This does not necessarily result in the production of a film or television show where the commercial intention is more overt than in the case of a film or show containing product placement. The difference is more evident through examining the power dynamics and creative decision-making behind the scenes.

The ultimate goal of marketing communications is to engage audiences to enable purchases (Fill and Hughes 2006). Thus, marketing communication aims at creating an overlap between what the sender (marketer) is trying to communicate and what the receiver (customer) understands. While product placement can be seen as a way to incorporate marketing communications within an existing media product, the evolution of branded entertainment sees this shifting to a context where the resulting program/film itself is a form of integrated marketing communications, with messages in and around a film or show complementing the broader communications paid for by the brand.

## Branded entertainment modalities and examples

While the distinction between product placement and branded entertainment can be understood mainly through examining the financing and control of the media production, the outcome of such a collaboration between a brand and a creative producer can take many forms. This section aims to highlight various modalities of branded entertainment that exist and provide examples in order to illustrate the prevalence across a range of genres.

Examples of branded entertainment in television and film are manifold and can be feature films or shorts, or a complete television series. Feature-length branded entertainment include the animated comedy-adventure *The LEGO Movie* (2014) and the documentary *Lo and Behold: Reveries of the Connected World* (2016) that explored how the Internet influences humans in their everyday lives and was directed by Werner Herzog. The latter premiered at Sundance Film Festival and was created by advertising agency Pareira O'Dell for the cyber security company NetScout. The British-Kosovan drama short *Home* was made in association with the United Nations for release on World Refugee Day in 2016. Responding to the discrimination and hate many refugees are confronted with, the 20-minute film follows a young British family of refugees who encounter humiliation and privation as they cross the border for freedom. The purpose of the film, which is not mentioned until the end, was to facilitate members of the public to sign the UN's #withrefugees petition to encourage decision makers to strive for shared responsibility and solidarity. *Home* won the 2017 award for British Short Film from the British Academy of Film and Television Arts (BAFTA).

Branded entertainment is also prominent within fashion as shown with the short film *Skirt*, a collaboration between *In Style* magazine and luxury fashion brand Mulberry. The film does not feature Mulberry products or branding, however at an event on branded entertainment held at BAFTA in 2011, Mulberry stated the film represented their brand and reflected their essence. Additionally, branded entertainment is increasingly integrated in television shows. In the UK, Channel 4 (2020) conducted a study about the effectiveness of branded entertainment in television formats, revealing that branded entertainment augmented brand engagement and stimulated positive viewer perceptions. For their award-winning documentary miniseries *Old Peoples Home for 4 Year Olds* (2017–18), Channel 4 collaborated with the charity Age UK. In the series, young children and older people living in a retirement home shared the same classroom to work and play together. This intergenerational experiment drew attention to current issues in social care to evaluate the impact on the health and happiness of the retired people. The show was a success and Age UK experienced significant changes in perceptions of their brand, with audiences viewing Age UK as an "uplifting brand" that is "caring and compassionate" (Channel 4 2020). Another example is *Nature Needs Heroes* by American outerwear brand Timberland. Timberland partnered with British musician Loyle Carner to create two 30-minute documentaries for MTV UK in which Carner visits his hometown Croydon in England to explore the concept of urban greening. Carner, a musician and social activist, visited multiple sites and consulted experts to promote the provision of green spaces by creating projects of benefit to Croydon's local community and the environment.

These examples illustrate the possible benefits derived by brands or organizations partnering with skillful storytellers. Equally, successful partnerships result in creative producers obtaining funding to develop content that has value as a film or television show, financed directly by a sponsor rather than via the sorts of complex deals that see many lower budget producers unable to sustain a career. However, the following section examines more problematic implications of the branded entertainment funding model.

## Critical appraisal of branded entertainment

Brand placement in feature films and other entertainment contexts has been criticized on aesthetic and public policy grounds. Aesthetically, there is a view from film critics that brand placement compromises artistic integrity. Many contend that films can become mere elaborate advertising vehicles to showcase brands (Wenner 2004). And, since marketers are more likely to prefer upbeat, positive contexts to promote brands, explorations of dramatic or controversial material could decline if producers rely on such funding to underwrite production costs.

Public policy critics maintain that brand placement is just subtle advertising (Eagle and Dahl 2018), interjecting a commercial message where no message is expected. The relaxed state of the viewer makes for effective selling. Research suggests that children under five cannot distinguish between regular program content and advertisements (Blosser and Roberts 1985; Butter, Popovich, Stackhouse, and Garner 1981; Levin, Petros, and Petrella 1982; McDowell and Palmer 1979; Stephens and Stutts 1982), and that children as young as six to seven years old are significantly more likely to choose a placed brand than the competitor brand after exposure to a branded clip (see Auty and Lewis 2004b). Adult consumers are also shown to have low resistance to product placement and branded entertainment if they are highly involved in the consumption experience (e.g., the visuals in an advertisement, or the plot line of a film, etc.) (Olsen and Lanseng 2012).

Some policy groups have suggested that brand placements be banned or identified in opening or closing credits. Due to the contested nature and effects of product placement, regulations exist around the globe, although not uniformly. For example, product placements on UK television were permitted from 2010; however, this excluded placements in news, religious and children's programming, and the placement of tobacco, alcohol, gambling, foods or drinks high in fat, salt, or sugar, medicines, and baby milk (Ofcom 2010).

In this chapter we establish the distinction between product placement and branded entertainment; however, from a regulatory perspective, branded entertainment is not governed by specific regulations. Guidelines for product placement act as a proxy for branded entertainment, despite the distinction in funding model. In the United States, legal scholars have also debated whether product placement should be considered as commercial speech, in the same way as advertising (see Synder 1992), which is subject to government legislation. Some countries like

Turkey have specific regulations regarding how many instances or minutes of branded content can be integrated into films and television programs, and they mandate the use of disclaimers to explicitly identify product placements (Radio Television Supreme Council 2011). The Advertising Standard Council of India (2019) holds product placement to the same standards as regular advertisements: any advertising promoting the production, sale, or consumption of tobacco, alcohol, and other substances is prohibited. However, there is no globally unified regulation that exists. For example, "in Canada there are no direct restrictions on the use of product placement; limits are set only on surreptitious advertising and via voluntary standards" (Ginosar and Levi-Faur 2010: 469). However, the European Union prohibits product placement in children's programs, unless a member state decides otherwise. The European Parliament rules that the presence of product placement must be clearly signaled at the start, end, and after any commercial breaks (European Parliament 2007). However, this legislation does not cover instances of branded entertainment such as the Lego movies where a brand is showcased in entire films.

Brand placements also appear in other contexts, including music videos and videogames. As virtual and expanded reality allow producers to develop fully interactive environments, further brand placement may be added. These practices raise specific concerns, such as the ability of the audience to distinguish the persuasion content from that of the regular experience. Therefore, there is a gap in checks and balances in terms of who is exposed to branded content and how.

## Concluding remarks

Use of entertainment media as a shop front for brands, or as a vehicle to highlight social issues, is not new. Further understanding is required, however, of the change from models of product placement where brands and ideologies were inserted into media, to current practices where entertainment is designed specifically with the needs of a brand or organization placed centrally in the creative storytelling. As shown above, producers faced with the challenges of accessing production financing can benefit from these options as they provide simpler solutions than the usual demands of piecing together a patchwork of public and private funding. Independent producers, who often supplement funding with personal loans and other precarious funding deals, can take advantage of this practice. Similarly, organizations facing the challenges of engaging audiences who are fragmented, hard to reach and who may be resistant to paid for advertising, can gain from the possibility of using long-form storytelling to present a brand/organization/idea in a positive light or to highlight issues of relevance. Thus, many entities in the entertainment and creative industries can profit from such forms of cooperation. This, however, means that relationships between different actors in the entertainment, brand management, and financing fields, and in turn, their relationships with audiences, will inevitably change.

As this mode of promotional entertainment evolves, there is a need for greater regulation. If such content blends into the entertainment landscape, audiences may struggle to understand that they are being targeted by commercial organizations. Unlike conventional advertising, where commercial breaks or program sponsorships still mark a boundary between being entertained, educated, thrilled, scared, and sold to, audiences have no way to discern or resist messages developed through branded entertainment. Therefore, the development of relevant knowledge will need to have its place in media literacy programs. Drawing on Klein (2000) in *No Logo*, it is possible to argue that increasingly, there may be fewer entertainment-scapes or entertainment formats that do not feature brands or organizations embedded within them. Evolution of this current landscape signals that in the coming years, more research into the consequences of branded entertainment and audience experiences will be required. This will also mean that branded entertainment will gain more prominence amongst audience reception and wider communication research.

# References

*AdAge* (2003) "Product Placement," September 15, available at https://adage.com/article/adage-encyclopedia/product-placement/98832 (accessed December 3, 2019).

The Advertising Standards Council of India (2016) "Principles & Guidelines," available at https://ascionline.org/index.php/principles-guidelines.html (accessed December 4, 2019).

AMA (2020) "Branding," accessed at www.ama.org/topics/branding/ (accessed December 4, 2020).

Arhio, T. and Raunio, M. (2015) "If You're Not At Least Thinking About Branded Content, You're Missing Out," *Adweek*, April 30, available at www.adweek.com/news/television/if-youre-not-least-thinking-about-branded-content-youre-missing-out-164378 (accessed December 3, 2019).

Auty, S. and Lewis, C. (2004a) "Exploring Children's Choice: The Reminder Effect of Product Placement," *Psychology and Marketing*, 21 (9): 697–713.

Auty, S. and Lewis, C. (2004b) "The 'Delicious Paradox': Preconscious Processing of Product Placements by Children," in L. J. Shrum (ed.), *The Psychology of Entertainment Media: Blurring the Lines Between Entertainment and Persuasion*, Mahwah, NJ: Lawrence Erlbaum; 117–133.

Avery, R. J. and Ferraro, R. (2000) "Verisimilitude or Advertising? Brand Appearances on Prime-time Television," *Journal of Consumer Affairs*, 34(2): 217–244.

Balasubramanian, S. K. (1994) "Beyond Advertising and Publicity: Hybrid Messages and Public Policy Issues," *Journal of Advertising*, 23 (4): 29–46.

Balasubramanian, S. K., Karrh, J. A., and Patwardhan, H. (2006) "Audience Response to Product Placements: An Integrative Framework and Future Research Agenda," *Journal of Advertising*, 35 (3): 115–141.

Blosser, B. J. and Roberts, D. F. (1985) "Age Differences in Children's Perceptions of Message Intent: Responses to TV News, Commercials, Educational Spots, and Public Service Announcements," *Communication Research*, 12 (4): 455–484.

Brennan, I. and Babin, L. A. (2004) "Brand Placement Recognition: The Influence of Presentation Mode and Brand Familiarity," *Journal of Promotion Management*, 10 (1–2): 185–202.

Bressoud, E., Lehu, J. M., and Russell, C. A. (2010) "The Product Well Placed: The Relative Impact of Placement and Audience Characteristics on Placement Recall," *Journal of Advertising Research*, 50 (4): 374–385.

Butter, E. J., Popovich, P. M., Stackhouse, R. H., and Garner, R. K. (1981) "Discrimination of Television Programs and Commercials by Preschool Children," *Journal of Advertising Research*, 21 (2): 53–56.

Channel 4 (2020) "Channel 4 Reveals Results from First of its Kind Study into TV Branded Entertainment," *Channel 4*, June 25, available at www.channel4.com/press/news/channel-4-reveals-results-first-its-kind-study-tv-branded-entertainment (accessed August 17, 2020).

Colliander, J. and Erlandsson, S. (2015) "The Blog and the Bountiful: Exploring the Effects of Disguised Product Placement on Blogs That Are Revealed by a Third Party," *Journal of Marketing Communications*, 21 (2): 110–124.

Confos, N. and Davis, T. (2016) "Young Consumer-Brand Relationship Building Potential Using Digital Marketing," *European Journal of Marketing*, 50 (11): 1993–2017.

Dardis, F. E., Schmierbach, M., Sherrick, B., Waddell, F., Aviles, J., Kumble, S., and Bailey, E. (2016) "Adver-Where? Comparing the Effectiveness of Banner Ads and Video Ads in Online Video Games," *Journal of Interactive Advertising*, 16 (2): 87–100.

DeLanda, M. (2006) *A New Philosophy of Society*, London: Continuum.

DeLanda, M. (2016) *Assemblage Theory*, Edinburgh: Edinburgh University Press.

DeLorme, D. E., Reid, L. N. and Zimmer, M. R. (1994) "Brands in Films: Young Moviegoers' Experiences and Interpretations," paper presented to the 1994 Conference of the American Academy of Advertising.

Duke, C. R. and Carlson, L. B. (1993) "A Conceptual Approach to Alternative Memory Measures for Advertising Effectiveness," *Journal of Current Issues and Research in Advertising*, 15 (2): 1–14.

Duke, C. R. and Carlson, L. B. (1994) "Applying Implicit Memory Measures: Word Fragment Completion in Advertising Tests," *Journal of Current Issues and Research in Advertising*, 16 (2): 29–40.

Eagle, L. and Dahl, S. (2018) "Product Placement in Old and New Media: Examining the Evidence for Concern," *Journal of Business Ethics*, 147 (3): 605–618.

European Parliament (2007) "New TV and Product Placement Rules Should Be Applied Before End 2009," November 29, available at www.europarl.europa.eu/sides/getDoc.do?pubRef=-//EP//TEXT+IM-PRESS+20071128IPR14028+0+DOC+XML+V0//EN (accessed December 13, 2019).

Fill, C. and Hughes, G. (2006) *The Official CIM 06/07 Marketing Communications*, Oxford: Butterworth-Heinemann.

Ginosar, A. and Levi-Faur, D. (2010) "Regulating Product Placement in the European Union and Canada: Explaining Regime Change and Diversity," *Journal of Comparative Policy Analysis*, 12 (5): 467–490.

Gould, S. J., Gupta, P. B. and Grabner-Kräuter, S. (2000) "Product Placements in Movies: A Cross-cultural Analysis of Austrian, French and American Consumers' Attitudes Toward this Emerging, International Promotional Medium," *Journal of Advertising*, 29 (4): 41–58.

Gupta, P. B. and Lord, K. R. (1998) "Product Placement in Movies: The Effect of Prominence and Mode on Audience Recall," *Journal of Current Issues and Research in Advertising*, 20 (1): 47–59.

Herrmann, J. L., Walliser, B., and Kacha, M. (2011) "Consumer Consideration of Sponsor Brands They Do Not Remember: Taking a Wider Look at the Memorisation Effects of Sponsorship," *International Journal of Advertising*, 30 (2): 259–281.

Hudson, S. and Hudson, D. (2006) "Branded Entertainment: A New Advertising Technique or Product Placement in Disguise?" *Journal of Marketing Management*, 22 (5–6): 489–504.

Karrh, J. A. (1998) "Brand Placement: A Review," *Journal of Current Issues and Research in Advertising*, 20 (2): 31–49.

Karrh, J. A., Frith, K. T. and Callison, C. (2001) "Audience Attitudes towards Brand (Product) Placement: Singapore and the United States," *International Journal of Advertising*, 20 (1): 3–24.

Karrh, J. A., McKee, K. B. and Pardun, C. J. (2003) "Practitioners' Evolving Views on Product Placement Effectiveness," *Journal of Advertising Research*, 43 (2): 138–149.

Keller, K. L. (2003) "Understanding Brands, Branding and Brand Equity," *Interactive Marketing*, 5 (1): 7–20.

Kerrigan, F. (2017) *Film Marketing*, 2nd ed., Abingdon: Routledge.

Kirby, J. (2016) "The Changing Landscape of Media and Marketing," presented at *Nottingham International Microfilm Festival*, October 21.

Klein, N. (2009) *No Logo: No Space, No Choice, No Jobs*, New York: Picador.

Krishnan, H. S. and Chakravarti, D. (1999) "Memory Measures for Pretesting Advertisements: An Integrative Conceptual Framework and a Diagnostic Template," *Journal of Consumer Psychology*, 8 (1): 1–37.

Kunz, R., Elsässer, F., and Santomier, J. (2016) "Sport-Related Branded Entertainment: The Red Bull Phenomenon," *Sport, Business and Management: An International Journal*, 6 (5): 520–541.

La Ferle, C. and Edwards, S. (2006) "Product Placement: How Brands Appear on Television," *Journal of Advertising*," 35 (4): 65–86.

Law, S. and Braun-LaTour, K. A. (2004) "Product Placements: How to Measure Their Impact," in L. J. Shrum (ed.), *The Psychology of Entertainment Media: Blurring the Lines Between Entertainment and Persuasion*, Mahwah, NJ: Lawrence Erlbaum, 63–78.

Lee, M. and Faber, R. J. (2007) "Effects of Product Placement in On-Line Games on Brand Memory: A Perspective of the Limited-Capacity Model of Attention," *Journal of Advertising*, 36 (4): 75–90.

Lehu, J. M. (2007) *Branded Entertainment: Product Placement and Brand Strategy in the Entertainment Business*, London: Kogan Page.

Levin, S. R., Petros, T. V., and Petrella, F. W. (1982) "Preschoolers' Awareness of Television Advertising," *Child Development*, 53 (4): 933–937.

Lewis, B. and Porter, L. (2010) "In-game Advertising Effects: Examining Player Perceptions of Advertising Schema Congruity in a Massively Multiplayer Online Role-Playing Game," *Journal of Interactive Advertising*, 10 (2): 46–60.

McDowell, C. N. and Palmer, E. L. (1979) "Program/Commercial Separators in Children's Television Programming," *Journal of Communication*, 29 (3): 197–201.

McKechnie, S. A. and Zhou, J. (2003) "Product Placement in Movies: A Comparison of Chinese and American Consumers' Attitudes," *International Journal of Advertising*, 22 (3): 349–374.

Miller, M. C. (1990) *Seeing Through Movies*, New York: Pantheon.

Molesworth, M. (2006) "Real Brands in Imaginary Worlds: Investigating Players' Experiences of Brand Placement in Digital Games," *Journal of Consumer Behaviour*, 5 (4): 355–366.

Newell, J., Salmon, C. T., and Chang, S. (2006) "The Hidden History of Product Placement," *Journal of Broadcasting and Electronic Media*, 50 (4): 575–594.

Ofcom (2010) "Rules for Product Placement on TV and Paid-for References to Brands and Products on Radio," available at www.ofcom.org.uk/about-ofcom/latest/media/media-releases/2010/rules-for-product-placement (accessed January 13, 2020).

Olsen, L. E. and Lanseng, E. J. (2012) "Brands in Texts: Attitudinal Effects of Brand Placements in Narrative Fiction," *Journal of Brand Management*, 19 (8): 702–711.

Okazaki, S. and Taylor, C. R. (2013) "Social Media and International Advertising: Theoretical Challenges and Future Directions," *International Marketing Review*, 30 (1): 56–71.

O'Reilly, D. and Kerrigan, F. (2013) "A View to a Brand: Introducing the Film Brandscape," *European Journal of Marketing*, 47 (5–6): 769–789.

Popeo, D. J. and Price, D. (2004) *Comments of the Washington Legal Foundation to the Federal Trade Commission Concerning Television Product Placement*, Washington, DC: Washington Legal Foundation.

Preece, C., Kerrigan, F., and O'Reilly, D. (2019) "License to Assemble: Theorizing Brand Longevity," *Journal of Consumer Research*, 46 (2): 330–350.

Radio Television Supreme Council (2011) "By-Law on Procedures and Principles of Media Services," November 2, available at www.rtuk.gov.tr/en/by-law-on-the-procedures-and-principles-of-media-services/5358/5175/by-law-on-the-procedures-and-principles-of-media-services.html?Keyword=product%20placement (accessed January 14, 2020).

Russell, C. A. (2002) "Investigating the Effectiveness of Product Placements in Television Shows: The Role of Modality and Plot Connection Congruence on Brand Memory and Attitude," *Journal of Consumer Research*, 29 (3): 306–318.

Russell, C. A. and Belch, M. (2005) "A Managerial Investigation into the Product Placement Industry," *Journal of Advertising Research*, 45 (1): 73–92.

Schacter, D. L. (1987) "Implicit Memory: History and Current Status," *Journal of Experimental Psychology: Learning, Memory, and Cognition*, 13 (3): 501–518.

Segrave, K. (2004) *Product Placement in Hollywood Films: A History*, Jefferson, NC: McFarland & Company.

Shapiro, S. and Krishnan, H. S. (2001) "Memory-Based Measures for Assessing Advertising Effects: A Comparison of Explicit and Implicit Memory Effects," *Journal of Advertising*, 30 (3): 1–13.

Stephens, N., Stutts, M. A., and Burdick, R. (1982) "Preschoolers' Ability to Distinguish between Television Programming and Commercials," *Journal of Advertising*, 11 (2): 16–26.

Snyder, S. L. (1992) "Movies and Product Placement: Is Hollywood Turning Films into Commercial Speech?" *University of Illinois Law Review*, 1992 (1): 301–338.

Townsend, J. T. and Ashby, F. G. (1984) *Stochastic Modeling of Elementary Psychological Processes*, Cambridge: Cambridge University Press.

Van Loggerenberg, M. J., Enslin, C., and Terblanche-Smit, M. (2019) "Towards a Definition of Branded Entertainment: An Exploratory Story," *Journal of Marketing Communications*, available at www.tandfonline.com/doi/abs/10.1080/13527266.2019.1643395 (accessed December 15, 2020).

Van Reijmersdal, E. (2009) "Brand Placement Prominence: Good for Memory! Bad for Attitudes?" *Journal of Advertising Research*, 49 (2): 151–153.

Wang, Y. and Chen, H. (2019) "The Influence of Dialogic Engagement and Prominence on Visual Product Placement in Virtual Reality Videos," *Journal of Business Research*, 100: 493–502.

Wenner, L. A. (2004) "On the Ethics of Product Placement in Media Entertainment," *Journal of Promotion Management*, 10 (1–2): 101–132.

Wiles, M. A. and Danielova, A. (2009) "The Worth of Product Placement in Successful Films: An Event Study Analysis," *Journal of Marketing*, 73 (4): 44–63.

Williams, K., Petrosky, A., Hernandez, E. and Page, R. (2011) "Product Placement Effectiveness: Revisited and Renewed," *Journal of Management and Marketing Research*, 7: 1–24.

Yalkin, C. (2019) "TV Series: Marketplace Icon," *Consumption Markets and Culture*, available at www.tandfonline.com/doi/abs/10.1080/10253866.2019.1669569?journalCode=gcmc20 (accessed December 15, 2020).

Yang, M. and Roskos-Ewoldsen, D. R. (2007) "The Effectiveness of Brand Placements in the Movies: Levels of Placements, Explicit and Implicit Memory, and Brand-Choice Behavior," *Journal of Communication*, 57 (3): 469–489.

# 33

# GATEKEEPERS OF CULTURE IN THE MUSIC VIDEO SUPPLY CHAIN

*Emily Caston*

The term "music video" arose in the 1980s to describe visual products mastered on physical videotapes for television broadcast. In fact, almost all of those products were shot on celluloid (16 mm or 35 mm) until digital technologies allowed high-definition (HD) video to become the norm in the 2000s. Music videos are, like pop promos, a type of musical short commissioned and released by record labels for mass audiences at the same time as an audio single. These video shorts comprise a copyrighted synchronized picture and audio track in which a percentage of the royalties accrue to the recording artist and/or record label. They are generally, but not always, produced out-of-house by independent production companies or sole traders working from home. This definition excludes a large number of unofficial videos made without any formal licensing arrangement with the artist or label. While sometimes regarded as a form of advertising, music videos have never been produced by advertising agencies, nor have they been broadcast on television using the advertising model in which agencies pay to purchase media time and space (Caston 2020).

In Europe, the independent production industry for pop promos emerged in the 1960s when bands such as The Kinks, The Who, Pink Floyd, The Beatles, The Rolling Stones, and the Dave Clark Five began to employ filmmakers to shoot conceptual films on location to promote their forthcoming single releases (Smith 2019; Caston 2020). These could be screened when bands weren't able to perform live on television due to touring or other commitments. Directors such as Peter Whitehead who owned their own 16 mm equipment would make the promos using either their own money or small sums agreed with a band's management. In the UK, from 1966 to 1976, independent production was conducted in a haphazard manner with no institutionalized procedures or trade agreements. Following a series of disputes regarding broadcast licenses between the BBC, the Musicians' Union (MU), and trade association the British Phonographic Industry (BPI), a distinctive tripartite structure emerged in the 1980s centered around the supply chain: music videos were commissioned and financed by the record labels (music industry), line-produced by independent video production companies (production industry), and viewed by audiences on a variety of exhibition platforms (constituted by a range of industries). By the late 1980s, with these legal disputes resolved, a standardized set of procedures fell into place for the commissioning, funding, production, postproduction, and exhibition of music videos on television. British production companies such as MGMM, Limelight, and Oil Factory established satellite companies in Los Angeles. North American

DOI: 10.4324/9780429275340-38

producers began to set up their own domestic production companies or purchased British companies such as Propaganda Films. This standardized set of procedures reigned until a period of transition (2001–2003), when the target youth audience moved to the internet, although it was not until 2014 that a new viable funding model emerged as a result of advertising revenue (IFPA 2014: 20).

## Music industry

Historically, in Europe and the United States, music video developed as a marketing device. From the early twentieth century, music marketing communicated genre distinctions through sheet music covers, album covers, posters, and other materials (Edge 1991; Jones and Sorger 1999). When music videos developed, they drew on earlier tropes, including generic styles of filming used for the presentation of live performances on music television in the 1960s. For example, John Maybury's video for Sinead O'Connor's *Nothing Compares 2 U* (1990) echoes the full-face portrait videos of the French 1960s Ye-Ye girls, evident in such clips as Francois Hardy's *Mon Amie La Rose* (1965) and *Voila* (1967). Music video genres emerged within a corporate culture organized around music genres such as Heavy Metal and Country & Western (Negus 1999). A loose correlation is observable between these genres and the threefold typology of performance, concept, and narrative videos used within the industry (Caston 2020).

The history of the music promo is intricately related to the history of the music single. By 1910, the 10-inch 78-rpm shellac disc was the most commonly used format, and songwriters and performers tailored their output to fit this. As the three-minute single remained the core product in the music market into the late 1960s, the conventions of the pop promo were formed. From the mid-1960s to the late 1990s, however, artists experimented with alternative formats and the multi-track album became the dominant form of recorded music expression and consumption for some. As a result, many "video albums" were produced by artists that included Annie Lennox and The The. Video albums remained a popular format into the digital music economy, with examples including Bjork's *Biophilia* (2011) and Beyonce's *Lemonade* (2016).

In the West, the so called "golden era" of music videos during the 1980s and 1990s was enabled by huge revenues from sales of the new CD format and the conviction that even larger revenues could be accrued from using videos as marketing tools. By 1998, the UK record industry spent £36.5 million on approximately 850 music videos (Caston, Parti, Walker, and Sutton 2000), a very substantial increase on the estimated £10 million spent in 1984 (Laing 1985). Production budgets were usually decided by the Head of Marketing and the Managing Director at a music label, with 50 percent of the cost recouped from artist royalties.

In Western economies, the commissioning of music videos has then generally taken place within the marketing departments of labels. By the 1980s, most major record labels had appointed a full-time in-house video commissioner, while labels such as Virgin and Sony would have a team of commissioners overseen by a Head of Video whose services would be used by the company's subsidiary and semi-independent labels. Since the early 2000s, it has become more common for labels to use freelance out-of-house commissioners. Today, video commissioners work closely with the digital marketing team to select the treatment most likely to go viral and be executed by an experienced director within the allocated budget.

A small, but significant, number of European music videos, however, have been made outside of these formal commissioning procedures. *The Queen is Dead*, for example, was a trilogy of short films released in 1986 made to accompany three songs by The Smiths. It was credited to Derek Jarman and premiered at the Edinburgh Film Festival before supporting Alex Cox's biopic *Sid and Nancy* (1986), and then was used by independent label Rough Trade for promotional purposes on the BBC's music chart show *Top of The Pops* (1964-2019). An important touchstone in the history of British art house and queer avant-garde cinema, the trilogy is the copyright of Basilisk Communications Ltd, not Rough Trade. Similarly, Jarman's *TG: Psychic Rally in Heaven* (Throbbing Gristle, 1981) is under copyright to the LUMA Foundation rather than the label. Recently, Klein's *Marks of Worship* (2016) was produced and partially funded by the director Akinola Davies who retained the copyright while creating the video in collaboration with Klein. Increasingly, funding for these types of videos is provided at least partially by the director herself or her production company.

In most cases where a record label has commissioned and financed a music video, the label will also be defined as the legal producer. This is because it not only provides the funding but retains all the copyrights and moral rights vested in the music video as an intellectual property. Since the early 1980s, music videos have functioned as an audiovisual product for generating income by record labels, musicians, and publishing companies through licensing fees charged to broadcasters and internet platforms for screening videos. Licensing revenues are managed by agencies working collectively on behalf of the industry such as VPL in the UK. In the 1970s, some labels, such as EMI, produced videos in-house at production companies such as PMI. Major record companies have always operated as audiovisual entities with an interest in generating as much visual back-catalog as possible – such as filming live gigs, tours, and behind the scenes documentaries – for future commercial exploitation.

Revenues generated from the commercial exploitation of music videos have been crucial for labels. Knopper argues that by stimulating further record sales, videos drove labels out of recession in the United States after the launch of Music Television (MTV): record sales in the United States fell during 1979 but then "wobbled up and down through the early 1980s, [before] jump[ing] 4.7 percent in 1983" (2009: xxxv). While in the 1980s, revenues generated from licensing music videos to broadcast television or for videocassette releases remained limited, income from music video exploitation in the digital era is viewed as rescuing labels from the recession caused by the decline in physical music sales. Furthermore, advertising revenues accrued from showing music videos on YouTube and other social media platforms are regarded as helping labels experience a period of economic recovery in 2013 (UK Music 2017).

## Production industry

In the United States and Europe, since the 1980s, music videos have generally been created and line-produced by independent production companies. These act as "service companies" in the sense that they provide the technical, craft, and creative expertise required but do not hold any rights in the videos they produce. The commissioner will invite a handpicked shortlist of directors (today up to 20 directors, but in earlier decades just one or two) to pitch an idea (called a "treatment"). Unlike in feature film and television production, companies act simultaneously as agents, so the commissioner will deal in the first instance with a director's representative. An executive producer will submit a production budget and a cost negotiation will follow. Production companies will normally be given between two and four weeks to shoot, edit and deliver a finished master to the label.

Music video production is horizontally integrated with other sectors of the screen production industries. Most countries will have between 20 and 100 micro companies engaged in producing music videos, with a handful of horizontally integrated small-medium enterprises (SMEs) simultaneously producing videos alongside high-end television drama or feature films. During the 1990s, in UK and United States, Propaganda Films Europe and its subsidiary

Satellite (both subsidiaries of PolyGram Filmed Entertainment (Kuhn 2002)), and Black Dog Films (a subsidiary of Ridley Scott Associates), dominated this sector of production. With these larger small and medium enterprises (SMEs), firms were able to strategically develop their directors' careers across a number of different sectors of the screen industries. In the UK today, few of the production companies who were at the forefront of music video production during television era (such as Oil Factory) have survived, and a new generation has emerged, including SMEs such as Pulse, Blink, Forever, Canada, Outsider, Academy, Pretty Bird, My Accomplice, most with satellites or partnership arrangements in Los Angeles and Paris.

Because music videos were produced by a service industry of film directors, often they not only drew on genres such as the musical, horror, comedy, and social realism (Caston 2020) but also on models of production from other screen producers and supply chains. Stubbs (2019) argues that Propaganda Films, which represented David Fincher and Spike Jonze among others, adopted a "Hollywood model" of production, normalizing a production culture in which music video directors were construed as auteurs. This construction of the music video auteur was further consolidated by a series of Directors' Label DVD releases, which each collated music videos from notable directors such as Jonze and Hype Williams. Railton and Watson, however, argue that the film auteur paradigm is problematic because "the formal, generic and commercial imperatives of music video" make it less likely that a director will be able "to develop a distinctive visual signature" (2011: 68). Videos are often a result of long-term creative collaborations between artists and filmmakers, such as Donald Glover and director Hiro Murai, David Mallet and David Bowie, Sophie Muller and Annie Lennox, Dom & Nic and The Chemical Brothers, and Jake Nava and Beyoncé. For production companies, music video directors can be considered – in terms derived from the Boston Matrix – as functioning as "stars," adding value through the talent development of other directors, peer acclaim, and creative kudos (awards), that is, unless they become "problem children" in which case they may be released from their contract.[1]

A key research question which has not yet been investigated is why certain regions and nations have been successful in developing constellations of music video directors. Two of the most notable are France (Michel Gondry, Jean-Baptiste Mondino, Romain Gavrais, and Stephane Sednoui) and Sweden (home to Jonas Akerlund, Johan Renck, Johan Camitz, Jonas Odell, and Lasse Hallström). Both countries have effective policies for supporting speculative, entrepreneurial, and experimental work in the creative industries through complex packages of artistic wages, paternity and maternity rights, tax-funded health care and schooling, meaning creative individuals from diverse backgrounds are able to invest time in artistic, scientific, technological, and business ventures. Music video production in France has been state-subsidized: in 1987 and 1990, Culture Ministers François Léotard and Jack Lang created a National Fund for "vidéomusiques," "managed jointly by the national Fund for Cinematography and the Fund for Musical Creation" (Hare 2003: 72). The French government also required the M6 channel to invest in French music video production (Hare 2003). Further research on music video production cultures in national contexts is much needed, such as the recent contributions presented by Tervo and Ridanpää (2016) on Finland, and Mazierska (2018) on Poland.

Within the screen industries, music video could be described as operating what Offer (1997) and Eisenstein (2011) describe as a "gift economy." Historically, production companies and directors have earned no share of the revenue arising from licensing, physical sales, or internet advertising fees accruing from the distribution of "official videos." All royalties from these are distributed entirely to the record company, music publishing company, writers, and musicians. At the same time, the flat fees paid to companies to produce videos are too low to cover their overheads or staff costs. These costs are instead borne by more lucrative commercial (advertising), corporate or digital divisions within the production company. As music video production companies may use the same suppliers and post-production houses as production companies making high-end television drama and film, then the gift economy is also evident when suppliers provide their services on a discounted basis in exchange for a contract on a sister company's upcoming high budget work. Within the screen industries, music videos historically functioned as an R&D sector in which VFX and post-production companies and suppliers trialed and develop new technologies such as telecine color-grading in the 1980s (Caston 2019).

In countries where a specialist production industry has been established over a number of decades, a professional trade body will have been set up to regulate legal, financial, and intellectual property contracts, lobby governments in the interests of its members, and to arbitrate in disputes. In the United States, the Music Video Producers' Association (MVPA) oversees contracts, and in the UK, a subsidiary of the Advertising Producers Association supervises arrangements. Alongside music video production companies, the APA represents companies working across multiple supply chains in the screen industries, including those engaged in post-production and VFX, such as The Mill, Framestore, MPC, and The Farm, all of which supply feature film and television drama content. Many regions also have award bodies. While the annual MTV Video Music Awards have the greatest international exposure, most countries have their own awarding bodies: for example, in Cuba, the Lucas awards, and in the UK, the UKMVAs. In addition, there are dedicated international festivals, such as the Oulo Music Video Festival in Finland and the International Music Video Festival in Ibiza.

## Exhibition and platforms

The third element of the tripartite structure lies in exhibition, and it is here that the industry has experienced most change. While some videos may be screened in art galleries, attracting an elite art audience is invariably a secondary goal for record labels. The primary objective is to exhibit the musical shorts through whichever output is judged most effective for reaching the label's mass target audience(s). In the 1930s, this was cinema, in the 1980s television, and in the 2000s the internet. Music videos are short, chameleon-like, and platform-neutral. As such they are ideal products for remediation across platforms. From the 1980s, production companies were issued contracts by record labels insisting all videos be cleared for all rights in perpetuity, across all media, and throughout the universe. Contractual terms insisted the potential moral rights of above-the-line film crew were waived and that the copyright remained with the label and other parties in the music industry. What this has meant is that cross-platform exploitation of music video has been not only aesthetically possible but legally and financially viable. By contrast, commercials, moving image works from artists, feature films and television drama, were produced on restricted legal clearances and so could not be remediated without entering into new rounds of rights negotiations.

Before the advent of youth television, music was promoted in cinemas. In Britain, for example, the Musical Film Revue (1933) and British Lion Varieties (1936) ran in cinemas as series of musical shorts (Mundy 2007). Developed at the end of the 1920s during the transition from silent film to synchronized-sound film, these musical shorts enabled audiences to see bands and singers when the songs were current and the artistes at the height of their popularity. In the United States, "Soundies" (1941–1947) were distributed to bars, restaurants, and other recreational centers to be played on a Panoram, a jukebox cabinet with a screen for patrons to watch three-minute musical films, one number for every 10 cents deposited (Herzog 2004; Kelly 2018). Also significant were Scopitones, created in the late 1950s and into the 1960s by a French division of Philips, 16 mm film shorts that played on coin-operated jukeboxes displaying recordings by contemporary artists performing their single releases. Competing visual jukebox technologies included the Italian Cinebox and American Color-Sonics (Herzog 2004).

Marketing in the television era increased with commercial TV and the emergence of youth music on television shows in the 1950s and 1960s. In the 1980s, music television displaced radio as the primary marketing vehicle for breaking new artists. In Western Europe during the 1980s, videos were sent to program editors by in-house pluggers or companies set up to promote tracks to radio and who subsequently took on the role of pushing videos direct to TV. In the 1970s, British labels harmonized release dates for singles in Europe to avert audiocassette piracy. Consequently, they began to make promos for sending to European shows as artists could not appear live on TV in all territories in the same release period. Smith (2019) documents the broadcast in Europe of British music videos in the 1960s. From the mid-1960s to 1980, British production companies were making music videos for US and UK labels to be broadcast on such shows as *The Ed Sullivan Show* (1948–71) (Inglis 2006) and *Top of The Pops* (Fryer 1997), when either the artists were unable to travel or unwilling to perform live on the show (the rationale attributed to the making of Queen's *Bohemian Rhapsody* (1975) (Caston 2020)).

As these developments show, promos were screened on television well before MTV was launched in 1981. Nonetheless, from 1980s onward, music video became progressively equated with the brand name of MTV as the company set up regional and national franchises across the world (Banks 1996; Roe and de Meyer 2016). Through its global expansion, MTV came into conflict with the culturally protectionist policies of some nation-states and the preferences of many audiences. In a significant number of countries, including the UK (Caston 2020; Smith 2017), audience rates for domestic music video channels and shows were higher than for MTV channels. The role of domestic music television shows and artists in relation to MTV has been examined in Germany (Adelt 2005), the Netherlands (Kooijman, 2017), and Britain (Smith 2017). In France, Channel M6 launched in 1987 for the under 35s as a dedicated music channel with a remit to ensure 50 percent of screened videos were in the French language (Hare 2003). States such as France sought to intervene to support domestic music artists and "national culture" against alleged Americanization by MTV. In response, MTV rolled out more regional franchises committed to protecting national culture, such as MTV India (1996), which "followed a market strategy of aggressive 'Indianization,'" programming "Indian film songs and music videos, and a vibrant promo culture featuring satirized and exoticized vignettes of Indian everyday life and film culture" (Juluri 2002: 369). MTV Base was launched in 2005 as a dedicated channel for sub-Saharan Africa, credited with stimulating demand and raising production standards in the continent, particularly in Nigeria's dynamic music industry.

Much of this changed in the internet era, generally marked in terms of music video history by the launch of YouTube in 2005 and its purchase by Google the following year. According to UK communication regulator Ofcom's *Media Nations* (2019: 14) report, 52 percent of those who use the internet consider a smartphone to be their most important device for going online (rising to 71 percent for 16- to 34-year-olds). In recent years, the video-sharing service TikTok has taken over as the main platform for unofficial fan-authored videos, with evidence that song writers and producers are creating music that invites fans to perform their own choreography and to facilitate sharing. Consequently, the direction of scholarship has steered toward enquiries into how music video has changed in the age of the internet (Hearsum and Inglis 2013; Vernallis 2013; Korsgaard 2017).

Since 2014, when labels saw revenues from online advertising pegged to music videos outstrip revenues from the official licensing of music videos (IFPA 2014), record labels have taken a portfolio approach focused on commissioning a variety of visual content rather than just traditional music videos (Haider 2018). Digital platforms have prompted a splintering of the music video such that now, when an act releases a new single, the record label will make a vertical video (optimized for viewing on smartphones), a lyric video (a label response to the surge in lo-fi fan-made lyric videos on YouTube), and an official video accompanied by a "making of" short. In the United States and UK, average budgets for official videos have fallen to around 10–20 percent of the rate seen in the "Golden Era" of the late 1990s (Edwards 2018). In addition, labels will issue licenses for content not commissioned by in-house marketing teams.

Scholars have, however, pointed out that global/local tensions have persisted with the internet (Spyridakis 2009), so that in many countries the nation state remains a key gatekeeper. In some parts of the world, music video has become equated with liberal consumerism and American imperialism. In Egypt, Shababi music with Western influences has been associated with controversial music videos banned by the government. State television channels instead favor traditional Arab music, which conventionally has a longer duration that does not fit the format of a short four-minute video clip (Aziz 2010). Protest music videos have played an important role in articulating critical political opinions that are not permitted in official news media (Kraidy 2013).

In South Korea, the state supported the K-Pop music video phenomenon to avert recession (Parc and Kawashima 2018). The government and industry acted much faster than Western economies to expand legal digital distribution when the data showed that pirated digital songs were distributed more rapidly and widely via the internet than physical copies through retail sales (Parc and Kawashima 2018: 133). Far from being an "add-on" to the music track, K-Pop videos are the central product, including "point choreography" consisting of repetitive key movements easily adoptable by fans to drive viral marketing. As well as producing coherent video shorts, K-Pop artists give fans a "tool kit" enabling GIFs to be made, memes and frames reinterpreted, and group member outfits to be purchased. The contents are parlayed into fan-led analytical discourse, usually presented in several hundreds of thousands of Twitter threads or theory videos (Suk-Young 2018).

While the music video form is often viewed as the product of capitalist music economies, music video has still played a key cultural role in countries operating by different economic models (Thomas 2017). In Cuba, for instance, advertising has been banned since the 1959 revolution, but music videos have formed a hugely popular part of popular culture and musical practice. In 1984, the Lukas Awards, a show dedicated to music videos was developed on Cuban television, and in 2019 the government announced an agreement with Google to facilitate downloads and streaming (Associated Press in Havana 2016). Cuba's experience, and that of Nigeria, demonstrate the role that music video can play for countries developing their own music industries.

Today, research on the music video industry focuses on the financial future of the sector. Having emerged from recession in the early 2000s, the music industry has now seen four years of growth (IFPI 2019). Globally, just under 50 percent of music revenues accrued from streaming in 2018, and 40 percent of that streaming is video based (IFPI 2019: 17). While high-end budgets for international artists such as Dua Lipa continue, "event videos" that support the brand value of artists toward securing lucrative product placement and fashion deals cannot sustain a production industry. Investment in commissioned video content by labels remains low, largely due to the plentitude of "free content" available online, composed of fan-authored material that generates advertising revenue for the labels, and archived live footage of bands and artists owned by the labels. Mass target audiences are no longer reached by broadcasting music videos to a captive television audience, but by viral marketing in which labels commission and license work strategically positioned for millions of internet users to share. This puts the financial strength of the production sector at risk. In the digital era, producers report that the demise of the TV producer gatekeeper has enabled greater freedom of expression for artists and filmmakers, enabling wider access to global audiences, but that freedom may have come at an unsustainable price.

## Note

1 Introduced almost 50 years ago, the "Boston Matrix," created by the Boston Consulting Group, is one of the most well-known strategic planning tools. Although questioned and often discredited by academics, the BCG Matrix has left an imprint on management education and many practitioners still view it as an important corporate portfolio planning technique (Henderson 1970).

## References

Adelt, U. (2005) "'Ich bin der Rock'n'Roll-Übermensch': Globalization and Localization in German Music Television," *Popular Music and Society*, 28 (3): 279–295.

Associated Press in Havana (2016) "Google and Cuba Sign Deal to Store Data on Island's Servers," *The Guardian*, December 12, available at www.theguardian.com/world/2016/dec/12/google-cuba-deal-data-servers (accessed November 26, 2020).

Aziz, M. A. (2010) "Music Videos and Their Implications for Arab Music and Media," in M. A. Frishkopf (ed.), *Music and Media in the Arab World*, Cairo: American University in Cairo Press, 77–90.

Banks, J. (1996) *Monopoly Television: MTV's Quest to Control the Music*, Boulder, CO: Westview Press.

Caston, E., Parti, N., Walker, N., and Sutton, C. (2000) "Report on the Music Video Industry in 1998 and 1999," *Promo*, May: 6–7.

Caston, E. (2019) "The Pioneers Get Shot: Music Video, Independent Production and Cultural Hierarchy in Britain," *Journal of British Cinema and Television*, 16 (4): 545–570.

Caston, E. (2020) *British Music Videos 1966–2016: Genre, Authenticity and Art*, Edinburgh: Edinburgh University Press.

Doyle, G. (2013) *Understanding Media Economics*, London: Sage.

Edge, K. (1991) *The Art of Selling Songs: Graphics for the Music Business; 1690–1990*, London: Futures Publications.

Edmond, M. (2014) "Here We Go Again: Music Videos after YouTube," *Television and New Media*, 15 (4): 305–320.

Edwards, G. (2018) "Algorithms, Product Placement and Shirtless Boys: Inside the Music Video Economy of 2018," *Billboard*, July 27: 7.

Eisenstein, C. (2011) *Sacred Economics: Money, Gift, And Society in the Age of Transition*, Berkeley, CA: North Atlantic Books.

Fryer, P. (1997) "'Everybody's on Top of the Pops': Popular Music on British Television 1960–1985," *Popular Music and Society*, 21 (3): 153–171.

Gershon, R. A. and Suri, V. R. (2004) "Viacom Inc.: A Case Study in Transnational Media," *Journal of Media Business Studies*, 1 (1): 47–69.

Haider, A. (2018) "Don't Tell the Label: The Artists Reinventing the Music Video," *Financial Times*, May 25: 3.

Hare, G. (2003) "Popular Music on French Radio and Television," in H. Dauncy (ed.), *Popular Music in France from Chanson to Techno: Culture, Identity, and Society*, Aldershot: Ashgate, 57–76.

Hearsum, P. and Inglis, I. (2013) "The Emancipation of Music Video: YouTube and the Cultural Politics of Supply and Demand," in J. Richardson, C. Gorbman, and C. Vernallis (eds), *The Oxford Handbook of New Audio-Visual Aesthetics*, Oxford: Oxford University Press, 483–500.

Henderson, B. D. (1970) "The Product Portfolio," Boston Consulting Group, January 1, available at www.bcg.com/publications/1970/strategy-the-product-portfolio (accessed November 26, 2020).

Herzog, A. (2004) "Discordant Visions: The Peculiar Musical Images of the Soundies Jukebox Film," *American Music*, 22 (1): 27–39.

IFPI (2014) *IFPI Global Music Report 2014*, available at www.medienorge.uib.no/files/Eksterne_pub/Digital-Music-Report-2014.pdf (accessed October 26, 2020)

IFPI (2019) *IFPI Global Music Report 2019*, available at www.ifpi.org/resources/# (accessed October 26, 2020)

Inglis, I. (2006) "The Ed Sullivan Show and the (Censored) Sounds of the Sixties," *The Journal of Popular Culture*, 39 (4): 558–575.

Jones, S. and Sorger, M. (1999) "Covering Music: A Brief History and Analysis of Album Cover Design," *Journal of Popular Music Studies*, 11 (1): 68–102.

Juluri, V. (2002) "Music Television and the Invention of Youth Culture in India," *Television and New Media*, 3 (4): 367–386.

Kelley, A. J. (2018) *Soundies Jukebox Films and the Shift to Small-screen Culture*, New Brunswick, NJ: Rutgers University Press.

Kent, J. C. (2017) "(Un)staging the City: Havana and the Music Film (2001–2005)," *Hispanic Research Journal*, 18 (1): 74–91.

Knopper, S. (2009) *Appetite for Self-Destruction: The Spectacular Crash of the Record Industry in the Digital Age*, New York: Simon and Schuster.

Kooijman, J. (2017) "I Want My MTV, We Want Our TMF: The Music Factory, MTV Europe, and Music Television in the Netherlands 1995–2011," *View: Journal of European Television History and Culture*, 6 (11): 23–49.

Korsgaard, M. B. (2017) *Music Video After MTV: Audiovisual Studies, New Media, and Popular Music*, Abingdon: Routledge.

Kraidy, M. M. (2013) "Contention and Circulation in the Digital Middle East: Music Video as Catalyst," *Television and New Media*, 14 (4): 271–285.

Kuhn, M. (2002) *One Hundred Films and a Funeral: The Life and Death of Polygram Films*, London: Thorogood.

Laing, D. (1985) "Music Video: Industrial Product, Cultural Form," *Screen*, 26 (2): 78–83.

Mazierska, E. (2018) "Polish Music Videos", in E. Mazierska and Z. Gyori (eds), *Popular Music and the Moving Image in Eastern Europe*, London: Bloomsbury Academic.

Mundy, J. (2007) *The British Musical Film*, Manchester: Manchester University Press.

Negus, K. (1999) *Music Genres and Corporate Cultures*, Abingdon: Routledge.

Ofcom (2019) *Media Nations Report 2019*, available at www.ofcom.org.uk/research-and-data/tv-radio-and-on-demand/media-nations-reports/media-nations-2019 (accessed October 26, 2020)

Offer, A. (1997) "Between the Gift and The Market: The Economy of Regard," *The Economic History Review*, 50 (3): 450–476.

Parc, J. and Kawashima, N. (2018) "Wrestling with or Embracing Digitization in the Music Industry: The Contrasting Business Strategies of J-pop and K-pop," *Kritika Kultura*, 30: 23–48.

Railton, D. and Watson, P. (2011) *Music Video and the Politics of Representation*, Edinburgh: Edinburgh University Press.

Roe, K. and De Meyer G. (2016) "One Planet–One Music? MTV and Globalization," in A. Gebesmair (ed.), *Global Repertoires: Popular Music within and beyond the Transnational Music Industry*, Abingdon: Routledge, 33–44.

Smith, J. (2017) "'Comparable to MTV–But Better': The Impact of *The Chart Show* on British Music Video Culture, 1986–1998," *Music, Sound, and the Moving Image*, 11 (1): 11–36.

Smith, J. (2019) "Absence and Presence: *Top of the Pops* and the Demand for Music Videos in the 1960s," *Journal of British Cinema and Television*, 16 (4): 492–544.

Spyridakis, I. K. (2009) "Multimedia and Culture: Globalization vs. Localization of World Music Videos in the Internet Age," *2009 IEEE International Professional Communication Conference*, July 19–22: 1–5.

Stubbs A. (2019) "Spike Jonze, Propaganda/Satellite Films and Music Video Work: Talent Management and the Construction of Indie-Auteurs," in K. Wilkins and W. Moss-Wellington (eds), *ReFocus: The Films of Spike Jonze*, Edinburgh: Edinburgh University Press, 213–230.

Suk-Young, K. (2018) *K-pop Live: Fans, Idols, and Multimedia Performance*, Stanford, CA: Stanford University Press.

Tervo, M. and Ridanpää, J. (2016) "Humor and Parody in Finnish Rap Music Videos," *European Journal of Cultural Studies*, 19 (6): 616–636.

Thomas, S. (2017) "Dancing Palimpsests: 'Bailando' and the Choreographing of Cuba's International Image," in F. R. Aparicio, M. I. C. Araya, J. Chindemi, G. Fernandes, J. P. González, R. R. Romero, S. Thomas, M. J. Van Hoose, and W. Vergueiro (eds), *Sound, Image, and National Imaginary in the Construction of Latin/o American Identities*, Lexington, MA: Lexington Books, 187–210.

UK Music (2017) *Measuring Music 2017 Report*, available at www.ukmusic.org/assets/general/Measuring_Music_2017_Final.pdf (accessed October 26, 2020)

Vernallis, C. (2013) *Unruly Media: YouTube, Music Video, and the New Digital Cinema*, Oxford: Oxford University Press.

# 34

# THE IMMERSIVE CINEMA EXPERIENCE ECONOMY

## The UK film industry's third sector

*Sarah Atkinson and Helen W. Kennedy*

In this chapter, we argue for the significance of what we describe as the immersive cinema experience economy (ICEEc) within the wider experience economy and examine its characteristics. Immersive cinema experiences are highly constructed and commodified live experiences based around a discrete film or media property which typically incorporate an element of augmentation to a central screening event. What we define as the immersive cinema experience economy is the emergent infrastructure through which these experiences are designed and delivered. This is a growing global phenomenon where we see augmented film experiences taking place in China, the United States, and Europe. While data capturing the value of this hybrid economy is yet to be recorded, we argue that it will continue to grow in economic scale and cultural significance.

The UK has been a global leader in this economy, mirroring the growth and influence of this territory in the film and screen industry more generally. For instance, the film and screen production industries are a key contributor to the UK GDP, worth £7.91 billion 2016, experiencing 73 percent growth since 2013 (BFI 2018). The value and significance of this sector is likely to continue to grow, with £800 million invested during 2020 to develop new film production studio spaces in the UK (Lumina Search 2020). This has been accompanied by a similar boom in the UK film and screen tourism sector, where visitors seek out film locations and participate in organized tours of significant sites featured in popular film and television series (e.g., *Downton Abbey* [2010–15]), or related to characters who have featured on-screen (e.g., Harry Potter, Sherlock Holmes). For 2016, the value of this sector was estimated at £266.2 million (BFI 2018: 73). In tandem with these developments, we demonstrate how over the past decade, the ICEEc has risen to prominence as a third "sector" of the UK film and cinema economy. We will present a model of both the sector and the experiences that it produces through a case study of a dominant and influential provider – Secret Cinema (SC).

Established in 2007, SC now has more than 50 productions in its portfolio, attracting over 600,000 audience members in the last five years alone. In 2019, SC established a number of high-profile partnerships signaling the company's growth and recognition on a global scale. First, they exported their *Casino Royale* experience for a three-month run in Shanghai, before collaborating with Netflix to stage a *Stranger Things* experience in the UK during November 2019, a partnership that continued with a socially distanced "drive into" experience launched

DOI: 10.4324/9780429275340-39

in October 2020 in Los Angeles. They have also signed a landmark deal with Disney to design experiences around both existing and new intellectual property. It is these factors that make SC an organization of considerable national significance for the UK as well as clearly indicating their global reach and ambition. In what follows, we therefore examine the characteristics of this emergent sector through three key common elements: the *places* of exhibition, the novel *practices* that lend these experiences their distinctive qualities, and the new kinds of *participants* involved in their creation.

## From the experience economy to the immersive cinema experience economy

Writing in the *Harvard Business Review* in 1998, Pine and Gilmore introduced the term "experience economy" to describe a significant shift away from a "service provider" model to an "experience stager" model in areas of the economy far removed from the entertainment sector:

> Economists have typically lumped experiences in with services, but experiences are a distinct economic offering, as different from services as services are from goods. Today we can identify and describe this [distinct] economic offering because consumers *unquestionably desire experiences*, and more and more businesses are responding by explicitly designing and promoting them.
>
> *emphasis added, Pine and Gilmore 1998*

To date, there has been very little application of the broader experience economy framework to the study of activity within the creative and cultural sectors, despite the fact that Pine and Gilmore clearly marked out Disney theme parks and cinema spaces as leading exemplars, demonstrating the value of an "experience-led" approach to communicating their provision. However, the critical economic shift they articulated – toward a marketplace where the design of memorable experiences is what enables brand differentiation – now has widespread recognition in the popular and industry press, and has also achieved adoption within economics, marketing, and leisure studies research and teaching. This contemporary model of commercialization and commodification of experience has been subject to critique within media studies, leading Fjellman for instance to proclaim: "Fantasy goes on the market, as the last remaining vestige of uncommodified life – the unconscious – is brought into the market system" (1992: 300). In our research and analysis of SC, we have also linked this commodification of experience to wider social and political issues. However, the experience economy, and its corresponding focus on the elaboration of memorable, unique, and personal experiences, is a very fruitful model through which to identify shifts across previously distinct domains of practice and so is well suited for identifying the expertise brought together in the formation of the emerging ICEEc.

We have established a model of the ICEEc, which builds upon Bille and Lorenzen's (2008) tentative demarcation of the experience economy where they have defined three groups of experience industries, differentiating between creativity in the domain of production, and experiences in the domain of consumption:

- *creative experience industries* that take the production of experiences as their primary goal and where artistic creativity is essential to production, for example, theater, music, visual arts, literature, film, and computer games.
- *experience industries* with the production of experiences as their primary goal, but where artistic creativity is not essential, for example, museums, libraries, cultural heritage sites, restaurants, and spectator sports.

- *creative industries* where artistic creativity is essential, but the production of experiences is not a primary goal, and rather than producing directly for the consumer market, they instead provide business-to-business services built into or around mixed products, for example, design, architecture, and advertising.

We have translated these three sectors into the screen, service, and creative industries respectively in our articulation of the ICEEc as a particular hybrid space, which also includes sub-sectors made up by three industry cross-overs – film tourism, immersive, and branding which are detailed in Figure 34.1.

As the model shows, the ICEEc is a distinct hybrid space bringing together the talents of the screen industries – including film, digital games, and television – but also elements from existing hybrids such as film tourism, which draws on wider infrastructures within the service industries. The ICEEc also utilizes expertise and innovations developed within what is described as the immersive sector (Immerse UK and Digital Catapult 2019), which is predominantly focused on the technologies of augmented reality (AR) and virtual reality (VR). Branding, and in particular experiential branding, is a key element of immersive cinema experiences (ICEx), with social media, online, and mobile media built into the marketing and audience engagement strategies of these experiences. Like the film industry, the ICEEc is a project-based sector in which numerous small organizations and freelancers are hired and temporarily come together to work on one project, although the production of ICExs fuses the inputs of professionals from across these three major industries and the cross-over fields. This emerging sector is constituted by collaborations between creatives in film production and exhibition, theater performers and professionals, brand developers, experience designers, live event/festival infrastructure specialists, construction, technology providers, caterers, security, and site-management professionals.

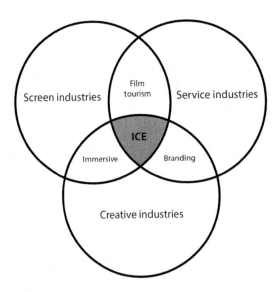

*Figure 34.1*  The immersive cinema experience economy (ICEEc) model.
*Source*: Authors' analysis.

## Immersive cinema experiences (ICEx)

Having now established the ICEEc model, we move into a closer examination of the design, configuration, and management of ICEx through the case study of SC as an exemplar organization shaping this hybrid space. From its modest beginnings in 2007, the company has been building its very own independent brand, starting off with small, underground, and clandestine events in non-traditional indoor and outdoor venues. SC now describe their offering as

> creating large-scale cultural experiences in abandoned spaces, we fuse film, music, theatre and installations. In our shows, audiences are assigned a character and step into the story. They explore richly-detailed, immersive worlds where fiction and reality blur. We achieve this by creating the world of a film, where the space is populated by a professional cast of actors and dancers. The experience culminates with a screening of the film.
>
> *Secret Cinema 2020*

We have written extensively about the distinctive brands that SC has elaborated around this core model (Atkinson and Kennedy 2015a, 2015b, 2016, 2017).

Over the years, SC productions have gradually begun to break box office revenue records and a number of their immersive events, often based around a cult classic movie that maybe more than 20 years old, have appeared alongside new releases in box office charts such as ComScore and Box Office Mojo (see Table 34.1 for detail). These box office successes are achieved through a pricing structure that maps on to gradations and augmentations of the experience: tickets can range from basic £49 to VIP level £175. The VIP experience includes exclusive access to performances, meals, drinks, and transport unavailable to other participants. VIPs are looked after by a team of in-character performers who escort them through the performance and smooth their access to the additional "content." We contend that these experiences are constituted by three essential and interdependent domains: place, practices, and participants (see Figure 34.2). These all play an equal part in the configuration of an ICEx but with varying levels of influence, as indicated by the strength of the arrows in the figure.

*Practices* refer to the relations, infrastructures, organization of labor, and interdisciplinary modes of working that exist between all sectors and stakeholders featured in the ICEEc. This domain has the most influence in shaping both the place and the participants' experience. *Place* and *participants* function interdependently: the place becomes populated and requires the participants to complete the filmscape – the recreated set or locations/scenes from the specific film – yet the place also functions to determine and control the movements and behaviors of these participants.[1]

## *Place*

For the purposes of this analysis, the domain of place brings analytical attention to the following:

- Access to large unoccupied spaces that can be completely repurposed for the duration of the "experience"
- "Occupation" and redesign of these spaces with specific consequences for the neighborhoods within which they are situated

*Table 34.1* Secret Cinema productions (2014–2020)

| SC Production | Capacity (duration) | Box office | Location |
|---|---|---|---|
| *Stranger Things* (2019-20) | 110,000 (16 wks) | n/a | Canning Town |
| *Casino Royale* (2019) | 120,000 (16 wks) | £8m | Dagenham East |
| *Romeo + Juliet* (2018) | 60,000 (13 nights) | £3m | Acton (outdoor) |
| *Blade Runner* (2018) | 70,000 (16 wks) | £4.8m | Canning Town |
| *Moulin Rouge* (2017) | 70,000 (16 wks) | £4.48m | Canning Town |
| *The Handmaiden* (2017) | 5,500 (1 wk/6 shows) | £159,295 | Troxy, Limehouse |
| *28 Days Later* (2016) | 22,000 (8wks/48 shows) | £1.33m | Canada Water |
| *Dirty Dancing* (2016) | 30,000 (6 nights) | £1.9m | Leyton (outdoor) |
| *Dr Strangelove* (2016) | 22,000 (24 nights) | £1.24m | Canada Water |
| *Star Wars: The Empire Strikes Back* (2015) | 100,000 (100 nights) | £6.45m | Canada Water |
| *Back to the Future* (2014) | 75, 000 (4 wks) | £3.5m | Olympic Park (outdoor) |

*Source*: Authors' analysis of ComScore, *Box Office Mojo*, and *Screen International* data.

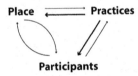

*Figure 34.2* Interrelations between the constituent domains of immersive cinema experiences (ICEx). *Source*: Authors' analysis.

- Repurposing and redesigning spaces, for it is the expansive nature of these spaces that allows for the creation of a filmscape and the spatialization of a film's narrative(s), and tight control of these spaces provides for but also determines the navigability of the experience.

Frequently staging experiences at sites in London, SC have used a number of distinctive environments for their productions, with a key characteristic being their temporary emptiness. SC's first production was in a disused railway tunnel (*Paranoid Park* 2007) and they have used empty former educational spaces (*Shawshank Redemption* 2012–13), the Olympic Park (*Back to the Future* 2015), and even occupied the faded grandeur of an out-of-use cinema (the Troxy for *The Handmaiden* 2017). As the experiences evolved, SC made repeated use of two key locations – a disused printing plant situated in Canada Water, and a series of connected warehouses near

Canning Town underground station. Both were reused for multiple productions, with Canning Town still in use at the time of writing (see Table 34.1).

Canada Water is a 14-acre decommissioned newspaper printing plant in a relatively run-down area with minimal cultural provision, and certainly very limited night-time provision. Use of this space has been a very significant "proof of concept" project for SC who commissioned an independent report by BOP Consulting (2018), the findings of which were used to argue for and demonstrate the cultural, social, and economic value of the "residency by Secret Cinema." BOP's report offered insight into the operating costs of SC experiences, stating the value of the investment in the site was £8.2 million over three key productions which brought 140,000 attendees into the area. Box office revenues for the three Canada Water experiences totaled £9.02 million (see Table 34.1). The report

> revealed that staging a spectacular production in a disused building awaiting regeneration, demonstrates the viability of future cultural and entertainment uses. It raises the area's visibility and can influence the future use of the building itself. The local economy benefits from millions of pounds of visitor spending (£4.2 million), and the local community's aspirations for the future of their neighborhood are raised.
>
> *BOP Consulting 2018*

SC's temporary redevelopment successfully established the Canada Water site as a significant cultural venue for the region, becoming a regular location for other activities, supporting the planning strategy for London's night-time economy in general and the regeneration of Canada Water in particular (Greater London Authority 2017). This "time-limited" occupation of such sites is described as "meanwhile use" (Entourage 2020b).

Development of the Canning Town site followed the same model, whereby SC identified a series of interconnected warehouses located near to the local underground station. Marked for redevelopment, the site was in a state of disuse while awaiting finalization of plans and permissions. Squatters had moved into the site and there were no longer any basic functioning services or amenities. For this location, SC worked with and developed an enduring partnership with consultancy firm Entourage, whose work on adapting the venue included the following.

> A new entrance was created; and lighting, plumbing, fire safety and power solutions were implemented internally to make the site safe to work in. The venue walls and roof were fully draped in black to provide an atmospheric theatrical space, and structural engineering was required to ensure that the roof could support the show rigging. Our administrative teams were also fully utilised, securing change of use planning permission, and premise licences for the space.
>
> *Entourage, 2020b*

As we see in the Canada Water example, the evidence gathered during this "meanwhile use" is significant in driving further planning and investment into the area in support of further cultural regeneration. We have seen this evolve even more successfully with new investment in Dagenham East, the site used by SC for their *Casino Royale* experience. This will now form part of a new film studio development, supported by a £300 million investment from a Los Angeles-based developer (Dunton 2019; London Borough of Barking and Dagenham 2020). As mentioned in the introduction, this forms part of a significant boom in the development of film production sites in the UK.

This interaction between novel forms of experience design, immersive cinema, and processes of regeneration aligns with the way in which the experience economy is conceptualized in Scandinavian creative industries scholarship. Economist Trine Bille (2012: 95) summarizes this approach as characterized by

- a sector [wide] perspective, including creative industries and other related industries such as tourism, sports, and public-supported cultural institutions;
- encompass[ing] the idea that the creative industries and cultural activities can create value for other industries besides themselves;
- [and] related to regional development … but also to the economic importance of tourism.

The "placemaking" activities central to the examples of Canada Water and Canning Town can clearly be understood within this framework. While the more enduring impacts remain uncertain, SC's annual summer offerings now appear in UK and London tourist guides as key "must do" attractions, and these experiences in general feature amongst the most significant attractions in reports on London's cultural tourism:

> London's top 20 attractions account for *90 per cent of visits* by tourists, but the success of events and attractions like Secret Cinema, which draws almost 50 per cent of its audience from outside the capital, and the weekend crowds heading to places like Brick Lane and Borough Market, indicates that tourists also have an appetite for more local and niche activities that will provide more "authentic" cultural experiences.
>
> *original emphasis, Greater London Authority 2020*

Alongside installing the basic electricity, water, waste management, and security infrastructures, SC adapt sites to become performative immersive film environments. For Canada Water, SC recruited Piers Shepperd, Technical Director of the London 2012 Olympic opening ceremony, to manage the transformation of the space for its first experience – a lavish and navigable recreation of the scenography from *Star Wars: The Empire Strikes Back* (1980) (see Atkinson and Kennedy (2016: 258–259) for a further discussion). The following year, in 2016 this site was then completely "redressed" for the Cold War setting of *Dr Strangelove* (1964) and again for the claustrophobic dystopic zombie thriller *28 Days Later* (2002). With Canning Town, in 2017 the site was developed first as the lavish Parisienne filmscape for Baz Luhrmann's *Moulin Rouge* (2001), then hosted the futuristic world of *Blade Runner* (1982) (complete with its own internal weather system in which rain constantly fell from the roof onto the crowd below), and most recently a version of the 1980s world of Netflix's *Stranger Things* (2016–). In each of these cases, a transformation from site to scene takes place as SC draw on stage and screen talents to create highly detailed reproductions of film sets as immersive filmscapes, complete with complex internal temporary architectures. These support what we have described elsewhere as the "spatialization of the film's story world through the actualization of the fictional locale of the film in which the chronological ordering of film's storyline is recreated through a carefully simulated topology" (Atkinson and Kennedy 2016: 257). This internal narrative architecture is accompanied by expansive light and sound design that are also highly significant in the distinctive shaping of each ICEx.

## Practices

Using the case study of SC, we can apply the ICEEc model to a specific ICEx. SC currently employs 11–50 core employees[2] consisting of a permanent team of lead creatives. Working within a project-based model of labor, each production commissions and hires its own temporary cast and crew to run and manage the complexity of the virtual and physical spaces of an experience. Full credit lists are not routinely and openly published for SC productions, and so hitherto we had only been able to identify key personnel through press articles and the social media accounts of individuals. There is, however, one exception that we have been able to locate – a credit listing for the 2018 production of *Romeo + Juliet*.[3] This took place in a West London park where each night 5,000 participants became members of the warring Montague and Capulet families in an expanded open-air "Verona beach" set. The single credit listing provides an exceptionally useful insight into the labor organization of an ICEx. As with all credit listings, it reveals a politics of production in its prioritization of departments and roles, and it is in this specific example that the convergence and interrelations between the three major sectors and three sub-sectors of the ICEEc model are most keenly illuminated.

In standard film end credits, the cast would almost always be listed first. However, this credit list starts with the specialist ICEEc Creative Team of 11 people, headed by a Creative Director, and includes a credit for a "Pre-narrative Producer." These are followed by Production credits that include a separate credit for Entourage, the organization mentioned earlier, who claim to "bridge the gap between brands who want unique experiences for their audiences, and the immersive theatrical world pushing the boundaries of interactive entertainment. With feet in both worlds, our teams deliver the unique and unusual, with style" (Entourage 2020a). Entourage is therefore situated in the *immersive* and *branding* domains of the ICEEc. Following this, further ICEEc specific personnel are credited – the SC Management including the founder and CEO – Fabien Riggall – the "Chief Creative Officer." Given the value placed on social media, it is interesting to see that what follows is Ops and Comms, Marketing, and a credit for Visible PR, a company specializing in "earned media strategies," earned media being the equivalent of online word of mouth used to increase brand awareness and reputation. Within our ICEEc model, Visible PR is situated in the *branding* sector.

Those responsible for Partnerships are then credited – a further crucial facet to the operation. All productions involve some form of brand integration – new partnerships are introduced for every production – from commercial brands to charitable organizations. Commercial brands are embedded and narrativized into the filmscape to enable more seamless financial "experiential exchanges" from the purchase of costumes, other merchandise such as badges, posters, and printed matter, and thematized food and drink. In fact, there is a dedicated, credited role assigned to this task – the "conceptual merchandise designer" – who describes their own role on LinkedIn as: "Working with creative directors to design, create/procure a high-quality costume and merchandise range that responds to the narrative story of our production. Designed to enhance the audience's immersion and enjoyment of the show." Such a role is a hybrid, and one that would be located squarely in the central sector of the ICEEc.

The site team are then listed (these include logistics and operations managers), followed by Performance (performance director, choreographer, action coordinator, global performance director, a Shakespeare consultant, and a cast of 47), which in our ICEEc model are all individuals from the *creative experience industries* (in this case – theater). Next in the list are stage management and production design. Again, these personnel are all from the theatrical domain. The VIP hospitality credits that follow relate to the team of performers who each play a named character and who are tasked with escorting their party around the experience.

Creative production teams feature high in traditional film production credits but low down in the credits for *Romeo + Juliet*. An extensive Art department – led by the art director, and including props buyers, set decorators, a model maker, carpenters, a scenic painter, a graffiti artist, concept artist, 3-D pre-visualizers, and graphic designers – combines expertise from across the creative industries. Organizations specializing in scenic construction and scaffold structures are also credited, representing inputs from the heritage, festival, and events sectors.

Site Services, Merchandise, Costume, Hair and Make-Up, Front of House (a substantial department which comprises 69 people), Health and Safety, Music, Gospel Choir, and Band are then listed. Those from the *service industries* are credited last – bars, first-aid, security, cleaning, and the 16 different food vendors. Themed food stalls align with the filmscape, so that in keeping with the Verona beach set, burgers, ice-cream, and churros are offered. At *Moulin Rouge*, the French food on offer featured croque monsieur, oysters, and champagne; *Blade Runner* was accompanied by pan-Asian fare; and *Star Wars* by Mediterranean and eastern flavors in keeping with the thematization of the bars and bazaars. Additionally, themed cocktails alluding to elements of the narrative are designed for every production. Finally, the role of the *screen industries* is confirmed through acknowledgments for 20th Century Fox (the film producer-distributor and rights holder) and Baz Luhrmann (the film's director). In total, 485 individual personnel are listed (not including all the food servers, bar staff, and volunteers). This prioritization of credits is revealing, with *marketing* and *partnerships* listed higher than cast members or those in creative production roles and providing the creative infrastructure.

In his chapter "The Smile Factory," Van Maanen examines worker hierarchies in Disneyland by applying class-based status and social weighting to the rankings of different workers (1991: 13). At the top, he places the Disneyland ambassadors and tour guides, with premium ride operators who undertake in-depth engagement with park visitors ranked second, operators of the more mundane rides third, "proletarian" keepers of the grounds in fourth, and finally the "sub-prole" peasant status of those offering food and drink. A similar hierarchy can be applied to SC by noting the relative positioning of roles in the credits and through our own first-hand observations of attending these events. Key cast performers play lead roles from the film, replaying scenes from the film around the site, and later augmenting the screening through mimicry and performance (Atkinson and Kennedy 2015). The second layer comprises the in-character stewards, that is, the front-of-house staff welcoming you in, setting the first "challenge" for participants, and marshalling attendees through the experience/activities, as well as the VIP hospitality team. Among this category are costumed stewards at train stations, ticket checkers, and security guards. There are other stewards in the venue who don't appear in character, plus the production team and stage management who *are* in costume but do not routinely interact with the participants. There is also security – inside the venue, costumed to suit the surroundings, and on hand to reprimand those who might attempt to take out their phone or to step over the boundaries of acceptable behavior (Atkinson and Kennedy 2016). There are also the food and drinks vendors who are usually costumed in theme appropriate attire but who only rarely interact in character. As we shall see, this performative hierarchy continues within the third domain of the ICEx.

## Participants

As our model acknowledges, participants play an equal part in the configuration of an ICEx, with their presence crucial to both populating and animating the filmscape. Participant expenditure is also essential in sustaining the high-cost productions, not only through ticket sales, but also additional purchases of costumes, merchandise, and refreshments. While crucial to the experience, participants have limited agency in shaping and influencing it, since both the place and the practices manage, control and limit how audiences can and should participate. To a certain extent, SC participants essentially play the part of "background artists" and extras, taking the kind of passive role observed of other forms of immersive experience; as Wozniak notes of immersive theatre, the audience had "only to 'complete' the performance because the performance was already written" (2015: 330). At the same time, ICEx participants more actively interact with immersive experiences than theme-park visitors. Kokai and Robson frame the Disney theme park experience as immersive theater (and the tourist as actor), claiming there is a blurring of spaces and roles within theme park spaces, suggesting this occurs "when the Disney guest speaks to a character performer, particularly when the interaction occurs in view of other guests" (2019: 14). Yet distinctions exist between ICEx and theme park attendance. ICEx participants tend to be costumed, and while some will take a passive (but importantly decorative) role and merely enjoy the spectacle of the surroundings, others assume a far more active role, playing out an alternate identity they have been given, such as those described in the example that follows.

In SC, the performative subjectivities of attendees firstly depend on the ticket they have purchased. In most productions, these are differentiated between "standard" and "VIP" entry: for example, for the 2019 production of *Casino Royale*, these were respectively priced at £49 and £175. As Kennedy (2017) notes with her analysis of the *Moulin Rouge* experience, different "grades" of audience participation were keenly pronounced, with attendees choosing between three distinct price bands – Creatures of the Underworld, the Children of the Revolution, and Aristocrats – overtly articulated in terms of allegiance to the film narrative. By their purchasing decisions, participants aligned themselves with characters within the film. The three price points led to markedly different experiences, with the implications of these distinctive bands only becoming apparent once the screening commenced. As Kennedy observed: "for those who attended as 'Creatures of the Underworld' the invitation of the title – 'Join a cast of 1000s, to sing and dance in the Revolution' – was also a direct *instruction*" (original emphasis p. 691). These participants, the lowest priced, were not provided with seating but were required to stand in front of the screen area and perform. They spent some 118 minutes standing, sitting, dancing, and singing to cue, and if they failed to comply, a "Zidler" character will insist they leave. These compliant "Creatures of the Underworld" played a critical role in animating the scene for other attendees. They significantly augment the screening for the Children of the Revolution, positioned in tiered seating around the stage, and the Aristocrats who enjoyed the best view and greatest comfort in a bounded seating area where they were also provided with "at table service" (see pp. 617–619 for further detail). This example underscores the critical role played by the participants; while integral to the immersive experience, their function was highly controlled within the overall design.

## Conclusion

In this chapter, we have argued that the ICEEc is a unique subsector of the wider experience economy and a growing third sector of the screen industries in the UK, with scope for income and value generation on a global scale.

SC now sits alongside other forms of mainstream entertainment as evidenced by distinct shifts in their audience engagement strategies. For example, where once the company resisted posting FAQs (see Atkinson and Kennedy 2015), these are now routinely produced to outline what attendees can expect from the experiences. Furthermore, the SC website also includes an "in your own words" video not too dissimilar from those screened at entrances to themed attractions, where audience members enthusiastically recount their experiences as a means of promoting the experience to others. On a macro scale, SC's impact and influence is felt through the new global partnerships built with Netflix through the *Stranger Things* experiences and Disney through a multi-title agreement signed in January 2020 for SC to adapt a number of

Disney films; their contribution to regeneration, new investment, and tourism; and their new management strategies that have been revealed in industry press (Gant 2019).

To summarize, we have characterized the immersive cinema *economy* as a project-based sector which integrates organizations and individuals from the screen, service, and creative industries, and from the sub-sectors of immersive, branding and film tourism in the creation and production of immersive cinema experiences. Our central case study provider, Secret Cinema, have already paved the way for and inspired numerous other companies, experience designers and immersive entertainment providers. Recent large-scale UK based examples include *The Wolf of Wall Street – Immersive Experience* and *Jeff Wayne's War of The Worlds: The Immersive Experience*, both running in London for extended periods. The global expansion, reach, and influence of the ICEEc is set to continue as the convergence of theme-park and immersive cinema comes ever-closer and the concept of a memorable brand or IP "experience" comes increasingly to the fore. The hybrid nature of this sector is such that we are likely to see increasing convergence of people and practices in the design of complex immersive experiences that draw on stories from beyond cinema. Punchdrunk, another highly influential UK based organization who have exported immersive *theatrical* experiences to both the United States and to China, are now partnering with games companies and broadcasters to innovate and evolve new storytelling experiences. Punchdrunk and Secret Cinema, while very distinctive in their approach to immersive experience design, have frequently drawn on a very similar talent pool as that described in our ICEEc model above. The future for the immersive sector more broadly is likely to continue to evolve along this hybrid, intersecting continuum.

## Notes

1 Issues of licensing and intellectual property negotiations are beyond the purview of this chapter but are discussed at length in Atkinson and Kennedy (2021).
2 As reported on the company's LinkedIn page, www.linkedin.com/company/secret-cinema/about/ (accessed March 4, 2020).
3 Located on the fictional pre-event "Truce of Two Houses" website www.veronaforpeace.org/credits (accessed March 4, 2020).

## References

Atkinson, S. and Kennedy, H. (2015a) "'Tell No One': Cinema as Game-space - Audience Participation, Performance and Play," *G|A|M|E: The Italian Journal of Game Studies|A|M|E: The Italian Journal of Game Studies*, 4: 49–61.

Atkinson, S. and Kennedy, H. (2015b) "'Where We're Going, We Don't Need an Effective Online Audience Engagement Strategy': The Case of the Secret Cinema Viral Backlash," *Frames Cinema Journal*, 8, available at http://framescinemajournal.com/article/where-were-going-we-dont-need-an-effective-online-audience-engagement-strategy-the-case-of-the-secret-cinema-viral-backlash/ (accessed March 2, 2020).

Atkinson, S. and Kennedy, H. (2016) "From Conflict to Revolution: The Secret Aesthetic and Narrative Spatialisation in Immersive Cinema Experience Design," *Participations: Journal of Audience and Reception Studies*, 13 (1): 252–279.

Atkinson, S. and Kennedy, H. (eds) (2017) *Live Cinema: Cultures, Economies, Aesthetics*. New York: Bloomsbury.

Atkinson, S. and Kennedy, H. (2021) *The Immersive Cinema Experience Economy: Industry, Audience and Aesthetics*, Manchester: Manchester University Press.

BFI (2018) *Screen Business: How Screen Sector Tax Reliefs Power Economic Growth Across the UK*, available at www.bfi.org.uk/sites/bfi.org.uk/files/downloads/screen-business-full-report-2018-10-08.pdf (accessed March 3, 2020).

Bille, T. (2012) "The Scandinavian Approach to the Experience Economy – Does it Make Sense?" *International Journal of Cultural Policy*, 18 (1): 93–110.

Bille, T. and Lorenzen, M. (2008) *Den Danske Plevelsesøkonomi: Afgrænsning, Økonomisk Betydning og Vækstmuligheder,* Copenhagen: Forlaget Samfundslitteratur.

BOP Consulting (2018) "The Value of a Residency by Secret Cinema: Assessing Local and Regional Economic Impact," available at http://bop.co.uk/projects/the-value-of-a-residency-by-secret-cinema (accessed March 4, 2020).

Dunton, J. (2019) "Council Injects £3.4m to Fund Film Studio Plans After Brexit Blow," *Room 151: Local Government Treasury, Pensions and Strategic Finance,* October 17, available at www.room151.co.uk/treasury/council-injects-3-4m-to-fund-film-studio-plans-after-brexit-blow/ (accessed November 1, 2020).

Entourage (2020a) available at https://entourage.live (accessed November 20, 2020).

Entourage (2020b) "Canning Town: Meanwhile Use Venue," available at https://entourage.live/case-study/creative-theatre-show-meanwhile-use-venue/ (accessed March 4, 2020).

Fjellman, S. M. (1992) *Vinyl Leaves: Walt Disney World and America,* Boulder, CO: Westview Press.

Francaviglia, R. V. (1981) "Main Street USA: A Comparison/Contrast of Streetscapes in Disneyland and Walt Disney World," *The Journal of Popular Culture,* 15 (1): 141–156.

Gant, C. (2019) "Secret Cinema Chiefs Talk Global Ambitions, Management Changes and 'Casino Royale'," *Screen Daily,* January 30, available at www.screendaily.com/features/secret-cinema-chiefs-talk-global-ambitions-management-changes-and-casino-royale/5136312.article?adredir=1 (accessed March 4, 2020).

Greater London Authority (2017) *Culture and the Night-time Economy: Supplementary Planning Guidance,* London: Greater London Authority, available at www.london.gov.uk/sites/default/files/culture_and_night-time_economy_spg_final.pdf (accessed March 4, 2020).

Greater London Authority (2020) "Cultural Tourism Vision for London," available at www.london.gov.uk/what-we-do/arts-and-culture/cultural-places-and-creative-spaces/cultural-tourism-vision-london (accessed December 8, 2020).

Immerse UK and Digital Catapult (2019) *The Immersive Economy in the UK Report 2019: The Growth of the Virtual, Augmented and Mixed Reality Technologies Ecosystem,* London: Immerse UK/Digital Catapult, available at www.immerseuk.org/wp-content/uploads/2019/11/The-Immersive-Economy-in-the-UK-Report-2019.pdf (accessed March 4, 2020).

Kennedy, H. W. (2017) "'Join a Cast of 1000s, to Sing and Dance in the Revolution': The Secret Cinema 'Activist' Brand and the Commodification of Affect within 'Experience Communities'," *Participations: Journal of Audience and Reception Studies,* (14) 2: 682–696.

Kokai, J. A. and Robson, T. (eds) (2019) *Performance and the Disney Theme Park Experience: The Tourist as Actor,* Basingstoke: Palgrave Macmillan.

London Borough of Barking and Dagenham (2020) "Mayor Gives Go-ahead to Major New Film Studios in Dagenham," August 14, available at www.lbbd.gov.uk/news/mayor-gives-go-ahead-to-major-new-film-studios-in-dagenham (accessed November 1, 2020).

Lumina Search (2020) "£800m Investment: The UK's New Studios," available at https://luminasearch.com/insights/800m-investment-uk-new-studios/ (accessed November 1, 2020).

Pine, B. J. and Gilmore, J. H. (1998) "Welcome to the Experience Economy," *Harvard Business Review,* 76: 97–105.

Secret Cinema (2020) available at secretcinema.org (accessed November 20, 2020).

Van Maanen, J. (1991) "The Smile Factory: Working at Disneyland," in P. J. Frost, L. F. Moore, M. R. Louis, C. C. Lundberg, and J. Martin (eds), *Reframing Organizational Culture,* Newbury Park, CA: Sage, 58–77.

Wozniak, J. (2015) "The Value of Being Together? Audiences in Punchdrunk's *The Drowned Man*," *Participations: Journal of Audience and Reception Studies,* 12 (1): 318–332.

# 35

# TRANSMEDIALITY AS AN INDUSTRIAL FORM

*Matthew Freeman*

Transmediality has become one of the dominant ways by which the flow of entertainment across media is now understood. As a practice, transmediality has gained wider relevance as emerging digital screen technologies have multiplied, with the so-called old media of film and television now experienced through online transmedia distribution practices (Evans 2018), whereby content becomes integrated with social media and apps. The connectedness of today's media industries – be it in terms of their digital platforms or across sectors such as digital and mobile communications, advertising, and marketing, and so on – is itself a defining underpinning characteristic of transmediality. While scholars such as Carlos A. Scolari (2017) suggest that "as of right now, almost everything is transmedial to some extent," this chapter aims to broadly conceptualize how transmediality operates as a dynamic within the media industries. The chapter brings together key research from across a range of media industry contexts so to define what I call the industrial form of transmediality, both as a mode of artistry and as a set of related production and distribution practices.

Specifically, having used the first part of the chapter to present a brief conceptual overview of what it means to characterize transmediality as a dynamic within and across media industries, I will use the remainder of the chapter to present a more focused snapshot of how this works in practice, focusing on how transmedia dynamics across the media industries have come to shape the use of mobile apps as a transmedia platform. In particular, I will consider the role of mobile apps in expanding the transmedia world of *The Walking Dead* (2010–), itself one of the most popular and well-known transmedia worlds of the past decade. As will be argued, the approach to transmedia storytelling taken by this example characterizes both the current trends and the future possibilities of transmediality in the media industries, and works to highlight the industrial presence, significance, and importance of transmediality.

## Conceptualizing the industrial form of transmediality

Let's, then, begin by attempting to conceptualize transmediality as a dynamic within and across media industries. Marsha Kinder (1991) first used the term "transmedia" to describe the multiplatform and multimodal expansion of media content. Henry Jenkins (2003, 2006) reintroduced the term within the context of digital change and "transmedia storytelling"

DOI: 10.4324/9780429275340-40

has subsequently seen widespread adoption and interrogation. Jenkins' (2007) definition of transmedia storytelling as "a process where integral elements of a fiction get dispersed systematically across multiple channels for the purpose of creating a unified and coordinated entertainment experience" emerged primarily in response to relationships between the commerce of industrially produced entertainment and cross-platform developments in digital media at that time. In my own *Routledge Companion to Transmedia Studies* (2018: 11), I redefined transmediality as the "building of experiences across and between the borders where multiple media platforms coalesce." But buried within this idea remains the almost synonymous relationship between transmediality and world-building. Jenkins famously argued that transmedia storytelling is itself "the art of world-building" (2006: 166) – immersing audiences in a story's universe and providing a comprehensive experience of a complex story across media. Echoing this idea of a "complex" or vast story structure, Scolari insists that transmedia storytelling's "textual dispersion is one of the most important sources of complexity in contemporary popular culture" (2009: 587). In essence, and according to Damon Lindelof, co-creator of the *Lost* (2004–10), the nature of transmedia storytelling – and indeed world-building – is "like building your Transformer and putting little rocket ships on the side" (quoted in Kushner 2008).

All transmedia phenomena, as a common ground, involve the richness of multiplatform media – it is, as Jenkins notes, "about a set of relationships across media" (2018: xv). Particular media platforms can emerge and disappear, can be in vogue or ostracized, can change and evolve, yet we cannot have transmedia dynamics without the support of multiple media platforms and the industries that align them together. Within this sphere, branding functions as a key practice for uniting multiple pieces of available content.

More to the point, the building of branded transmedia storyworlds is really about the folding in of text with paratext. Jonathan Gray (2010) conceptualizes the paratext – itself a kind of intertextual form found in the fuzzy threshold that exists between and around the textual storyworld and the intertextual cultural or promotional spaces around that textual storyworld – as lying in between products and by-products, between ownership and cultural formation, and between content and promotional material. Consider the Harry Potter storyworld as a case in point. To promote the film *Harry Potter and the Deathly Hallows – Part II* (2011) (i.e., the text), Warner Bros. created faux Facebook pages for a number of the film's characters, publishing paratextual snippets about the spells these characters have learned. These paratextual items exist simultaneously as both text and as promotion – at once operating to increase promotional awareness of the film while also working to develop the audience's understanding of the rules of magic governing that particular storyworld as a brand.

Indeed, much current research in the field – particularly that which comes from a media industry studies standpoint – points to the role of branding as a way of understanding the links between industrial or corporate activity, wider paratextual meaning, and that which occurs on the level of text, that is, in terms of story and character. In that sense, the notion of the media brand – traversing industrial, paratextual and textual phenomena – has been useful thus far in allowing researchers to account for the role of multiple pieces of text across multiple media. John Caldwell argues that media branding, much like transmediality, "has emerged as a central concern of the media industry in the age of digital convergence" (2004: 305). As Catherine Johnson adds, television "programmes are now being constructed as brands designed to encourage audience loyalty and engagement with the text beyond the act of television viewing" (2012: 1). Considerations of branding in this context work to evoke what Jenkins also calls brand extension, "the idea that successful brands are built by exploiting multiple contacts between the brand and the consumer" (2006: 69). For Jenkins, this too

> should not be contained within a single media platform, but should instead extend across as many media as possible. Brand extension builds on audience interest in particular content to bring them into contact again and again with an associated brand.
>
> *p. 69*

Following this logic, there is a distinct slippage between the concept of brand extension and that of transmedia storytelling. In fact, the industrial means through which transmedia storytelling occurs has considerable overlap with the concept of branding, for to maintain brand recognition across a range of media products itself requires a sense of textual or visual coherence across products so as to ensure each feels like it fits with the others.

Indeed, scholarship has tended to place emphasis on how a given media corporation coheres a given franchise's many fragments so as to present a consistent media-spanning brand. Scholars, for example, observe how IP-governing companies centrally coordinate transmedia storytelling within a given franchise, ensuring narrative consistency between texts produced for different media industries (Jenkins, 2006, 95–134; Harvey, 2015, 182–202). Disney-owned Lucasfilm's Story Group's tight regulation of *Star Wars'* transmedia storytelling is an example of this process (Harvey 2015). Scholars similarly observe how media companies engineer visual consistency between a given franchise's texts (Johnson 2007; Freeman 2014; Smith 2018). Previously, for example, I have shown how the noir-influenced visual style of *Batman: The Animated Series* (1992–1995) was designed to resonate with the gothic aesthetic of the Tim Burton-directed *Batman* (1989) and *Batman Returns* (1992) films, unifying the brand identity of the Batman franchise (Freeman 2014). In other words, both transmediality and branding are conceptualized in terms of extensions of content across media – working together via textual and paratextual elements to "produce a discourse, give it meaning, and communicate it to audiences" (Scolari 2009: 599).

Thinking about the significance and importance of transmediality from an industrial perspective, it is these dynamics of brand identity across media that encapsulates both how and why media producers engage in transmedia production. Strategically, whether operating in industries as diverse as film and television to journalism and comics, online or offline transmedia strategies can contribute to the growth in these industries, with the proliferation of content across media platforms building both new storyworlds and new job roles. At the same time, this kind of expansion speaks to the ways in which transmediality links to audience participation. In effect, if transmediality has become a means of understanding the flow of content across media, then this "circulation of media content – across different media systems, competing media economies, and national borders – depends heavily on consumers' active participation" (Jenkins 2006: 3). Scolari, Bertetti, and Freeman (2014: 3) suggest that there are different levels of transmedia participation, ranging from the consumer of a single medium to those who expand the storyworld by producing new content, typically via online platforms such as YouTube. Jenkins emphasizes that transmediality, especially in the context of converged digital platforms, has made this kind of participation possible, empowering audiences by giving them the "right to participate" (2006: 23).

However, it is not enough to assume that the creation of a coherent brand or the potential for participation is sufficient to explain the specificities and the reasons for why audiences choose to engage or not in transmedia activities. Elsewhere I have argued for the need to comprehend audience desires as migrating across multiple media platforms not solely in terms of notions of brand, story, or world, but rather to better interrogate the fact that many audiences base their decisions to cross media on values and themes. For example, based on research I conducted with Charlotte Taylor-Ashfield on the fans of Captain Marvel (Freeman and Taylor-Ashfield, 2018), it was discovered that many of the character's fans engaged in transmedia activity not based on the lure of interconnected stories or world-building, but instead on how closely the transmedia texts reinforced their personal preferences toward things like feminism and politics. Equally, the Internet and all digital technologies unequivocally play a crucial role in disseminating transmedia content, enabling a form of audience engagement based on immersively surrounding audiences with content.

When thinking about it in these terms, then, one can characterize the industrial form of transmediality – regardless of the type of specific transmedia project – according to two specific concepts: *participatory brand extension* and *personalized immersive experience*. Later in this chapter we will explore how these two concepts play out in a little more detail. But transmedia's prevalence is highly questionable and complex, and it is not particularly accurate to assume that transmediality exists across all creative and cultural industries. Indeed, as digital technologies and mobile devices continue to bring media interfaces into the workings of our daily lives, a salient question to consider is not only *what* is transmedia, but also *where* is transmedia? Jenkins' (2016) more recent writings on transmediality have begun to consider ideas of transmedia location, meaning "the context from which transmedia products emerge." There is thus a question in terms of for which industries transmediality is now an active part of, and what specific purposes it holds within and across them. When working on the *Routledge Companion to Transmedia Studies* (2018), it became evident that sectors as diverse as film, television, comics, publishing, games, music, journalism, sports, social media, and leisure attractions all embrace both fictional and non-fictional transmedia universes in their production, though each approaches the industrial form of transmediality in different ways, shaped by their industrial contexts. For example, in television, "notions of transmediality are at the heart of television and have merely become more prominent with the embracing of digital platforms" (Evans 2018: 243).

Let's, then, now explore how the aforementioned concepts of participatory brand extension and personalized immersive experience operate within the transmedia television industry. To do so, and as mentioned in the introduction, I shall analyze two app-based examples stemming from the world of *The Walking Dead*. First, I position the *Walking Dead* Story Sync facility – a double-screen application designed to enable audiences to post live comments about episodes and talk to other audiences via a chat platform – as an exemplar of participatory brand extensions. Second, I point to *The Walking Dead: Our World* – an augmented reality mobile game produced in 2018 – as an example of personalized immersive experience, focusing on the ways in which digital media technologies – as experiences across a multitude of screens – can work to engage audiences in a subjective and personal manner.

## Participatory brand extension

Even amidst the rise of technological convergence, describing a "hybridity that has folded the uses of separate media into one another" (Hay and Couldry, 2011: 493), it can be claimed that new media platforms such as apps – at least from a transmedia perspective – are largely about supporting traditional distribution models in the television industry, rather than forging entirely new paths for storytelling. As I will show, however, such technologies do offer rich sites for the development of transmedia narratives, mainly in terms of how the heightened communicative affordances of an app leads to transmedia experiences based on enhancing audience emotion – or, rather, on encouraging a kind of emotive reflection for the audience that is triggered by juxtaposing two temporally staggered digital media platforms.

In television, for instance, scholarly discussions often concern the multiplatform potentials of the digital media economy (Holt and Sanson 2014; Evans 2011; Doyle 2015). Jennifer Holt and Kevin Sanson (2014: 1) discuss "connected viewing," referring to "a multi-platform entertainment experience and relates to a larger trend across the media industries to integrate digital technology … with traditional screen media practices." From this, "second screen" practices have materialized, where a smartphone may be used alongside the television screen to access online material relating to televisual content.

Consider the *Walking Dead* Story Sync as an example, from 2012, which was to be used when new episodes of *The Walking Dead* were broadcast live. The app promised audiences the opportunity to "interact with the show while watching the premiere broadcast of the latest episode of AMC's *The Walking Dead*. Join the community of fans in weighing characters' decisions, rating the gore and rewatching intense scenes" (WalkingDeadWiki). The app included trivia questions, polls, exclusive videos, and pictures relating to the new episode being broadcast, affording immediate reaction and interaction. That the audience is now able to look across a variety of screens when engaging with, say, an episode of *The Waking Dead*, is important, for in transmedial terms the role of the app is partly to enable audiences to reflect on what they see. An episode may be "treated casually rather than concentratedly" (Ellis 1982: 128), with viewers glancing to and from the episode alongside other second-screen practices, but the narrative information gained while using the app carries significant transmedial value, working to reinforce or contextualize character choices.

Here's an example. The premiere episode of the season 7, "The Day Will Come When You Won't Be," was an intense experience for audiences, featuring as it did the death of both Glenn (Steven Yeun) and Abraham (Michael Cudlitz) at the hands of Negan (Jeffrey Dean Morgan). The episode sees Rick (Andrew Lincoln) emotionally tortured by Negan, almost being forced to cut off his own son's arm. Accompanying the broadcast of this episode, the Story Sync app gave insight into the motivations of the characters. The app begins, for instance, with a quote from a statement made by Rick in season 5: "There's a compound bow and a machete with a red handle. That's what I'm gonna use to kill you." This confident, threatening prediction is juxtaposed with the image of Rick during the season 7 opener, where he appears emotionally broken by the deaths of his friends and submissive to Negan's demands. When presented via the Story Sync app, the statement becomes a transmedial equivalent to having a flashback, denoting Rick's and Negan's motivations as the same. Features on the Story Sync are emotion-orientated by design, for example asking viewers to vote whether they are more frightened about what just happened or what is about to happen.

In another case, the Story Sync includes an actual "flashback" feature, which in this instance revolves around a set of black-and-white still images of the characters, scattered across the screen, and, crucially, depicting moments of laughter for characters such as Glenn and Abraham. Colin B. Harvey (2015) argues that memory is always important to transmedia storytelling, given that audiences are required to remember the specificities of characters and events when they migrate across multiple media. But in this case the images directly shape how viewers react emotionally to the deaths of Glenn and Abraham in the television episode, reminding audiences of previous happy moments that jar uncomfortably with the sight of their violent deaths. While the images dramatized on television prioritize emotions of shock, the still photographs available via the Story Sync encourage feelings of melancholy and loss. In other words, it is not so much a fictional narrative that is constructed transmedially across television and the Story Sync app, but rather the emotional reactions of the audience. As one fan, surveyed for the purposes of this chapter, asserted: "The second screen experience of the Story Sync lets you immediately contemplate what is happening on screen, that second." Encouraging such heightened emotional engagement is achieved by all sorts of strategies, such as designing features on the Story Sync that force users to empathize with a particular character. For example, accompanying the season 6 episode "No Way Out," the Story Sync asked users "who are you most like?" with images of the cast available to choose from.

Harvey's individualized idea of transmedia memory is based on audiences recalling aspects of plot during the process of migrating across media. Going further, the *Walking Dead* Story Sync app represents a form of transmediality based on the juxtaposition of narrative past and narrative present, such is the "reflexive and self-organizing potential of transmediality on the level of culture, [as] each additional version of a text or its fragment influences the ways in which we understand and remember the source text itself" (Ibrus and Ojamaa 2018: 90). This idea of transmediality as a relationship between past and present signals a key characteristic of how transmediality really works. Even as the contemporary television landscape is increasingly characterized by streaming and other online strategies that in many respects disentangle the watching of television from any particular temporality, such strategies still adopt inherently transmedial approaches to distribution that work to augment traditional television consumption. Evans (2011, 2018) emphasizes how relationships are formed between the linear temporality of conventional television viewing and the uses of transmedia television platforms, such as companion apps like the *Walking Dead* Story Sync. As my own brief analysis of this particular app demonstrates, the live and ephemeral affordances of app-based transmedia extensions can work to support the broadcast of a television series. This idea can apply more generally to characterize the tendency of media industries to use digital technologies to create participatory brand extensions of their IP. In artistic terms, the participatory digital affordances of these apps encourage one to think about how the media industries may use transmediality as a creative strategy for enabling audiences to reflect more profoundly on narrative and character dynamics, helping to build a more layered experience between, across and within multiple platforms and devices.

## Personalized immersive experience

This relationship between emotional experience and digital platforms is arguably at the core of how the media industries have development transmediality in recent years. Matt Hills (2018: 224) has called for the "need to consider transmedia not just as storytelling but also as a kind of experience," noting: "Given that transmedia extensions occur within a proliferating, ubiquitous screen culture, the issue of transmedia's locatedness in space and place has generally been under-explored" (2018: 224). While Hills is referring specifically to set tours and walkthrough experiences, my own approach to the term "transmedia experience" is less to do with ideas of "being there" (Hills 2018: 245) and more about the multifaceted ways by which the use of digital media across a multitude of screens and technologies work to engage audiences in a highly subjective, personalized and often immersive manner.

Indeed, perhaps the defining transformation toward the experiential design of transmedia worlds is immersive technologies, such as virtual and augmented technology. These technologies are a good example of how audiences are beginning to question their own subjective experience of a transmedia world. One example is *The Walking Dead: Our World*, a location-based AR mobile game developed by Next Games and released in 2018. On the official website, *The Walking Dead: Our World* is described as allowing users to "explore and defend your neighborhood: Get out in the real world to move your avatar in the game ... Collect stashes, find missions and rescue survivors with other players." But the key selling feature of the game is that it enables users to "immerse [themselves] in the zombie apocalypse by fighting off walkers in Augmented Reality!" Broadly, augmented reality (AR) refers to the display of virtual artifacts on screen once a user aims the camera of a mobile device at an object (see Petrucco and Agostini 2016). But what impact does AR technology have on the building of transmedia worlds, and indeed on enhancing subjective experiences?

In short, understanding the value of AR technology for transmedia world-building in *The Walking Dead: Our World* – and maybe the future of transmediality in the media industries more generally – means thinking about transmediality less as moving across distinct media, and more as the creation of an integrated experience based on a hybrid of media working together. As Gambarato and I put it elsewhere, transmediality is what happens when "the borders [of] multiple media platforms coalesce" to afford "immersive, emotional experiences that join up with the social world" (Freeman and Gambarato 2018: 11).

For example, the gameplay of *The Walking Dead: Our World* is dramatically enhanced by the fact the app is played in the real world, enhancing immersion and emotional impact as well as contributing new elements to the narrative world. Much of this stems from the game's visual style. The combat style is a first-person shooting experience with selectable (and discoverable) guns. This is where AR comes in. To use the AR in combat encounters, users tap an "AR available" toggle and point their phones at the ground. If the conditions are right, returning the phone to a central position shows the user's character companion superimposed in their real-world surroundings, with zombies lurking a few steps away. Morally, the affordances of AR in *The Walking Dead: Our World* work to distort the line between killing a make-believe zombie and hordes of "real" people: the latter become a kind of collateral damage in the act of killing the former, based on a user's subjective choice.

My reason for pointing to *The Walking Dead: Our World* is because it hints at the way transmedia experiences are increasingly blurring the line between digital and real-world environments, or between make-believe and real knowledge, by creating an extended reality. At any one moment, those engaging with *The Walking Dead: Our World* experience both real and virtual worlds on top of each other, with mobile devices and AR working to reinforce *The Walking Dead* as a world very closely related to our own. In doing so, users are drawn into the game's world by fictional images, narratives, and interfaces before being asked to perform the realities of that fiction in their own world.

In this sense, *The Walking Dead: Our World* is indicative of where transmediality, as an industrial form, seems to be heading: instead of escaping from reality by entering a fictional storyworld – which one assumes is the objective most major transmedia properties populating Hollywood and beyond in the present time – audiences are encouraged to believe in the imaginary virtual world as a reality they are willing to immerse themselves into. With its innate power to immerse audiences in interactive practices and shared, connected participation, transmediality is fundamental to this kind of storytelling experience across the media industries at large. For as Nataly Rios Gioco (2018: 478) argues, "one of the things about transmedia is that it allows you to associate virtual spaces and real spaces with a story ... We can expand the experience of the real world to the digital world, and vice versa."

## Conclusion

By looking at how transmedia dynamics across the media industries have come to shape the use of mobile apps as a transmedia platform, this chapter has conceptualized what I've called the industrial form of transmediality according to concepts of participatory brand extension and personalized immersive experience. Opening up analyses of transmediality to how the potentials of immersive technologies are becoming integrated with more established media forms and industry practices, enables researchers to explore the ways in which transmedia experiences constructed across the physical and virtual channels of the media industries are actively encouraging audiences to question their own subjective experience of storyworlds. The examples offered in this chapter show vividly how important transmediality is to understanding the media industries at large, for it operates as a lens through which to analyze and make sense of the deeply complex and often intertwined relationships between media texts, media industries, digital technologies, and increasingly participatory audiences. In this way, studies of transmediality become useful for studying the terrain of media industries.

# References

AMC Story Sync (n.d.) WalkingDeadWiki, available at https://walkingdead.fandom.com/wiki/AMC_Story_Sync (accessed September 2, 2020).

Caldwell, J. T. (2004) "Convergence Television: Aggregating Form and Repurposing Content in the Culture of Conglomeration," in L. Spigel and J. Olsson (eds), *Television After TV: Essays on a Medium in Transition*, Durham, NC: Duke University Press, 41–74.

Doyle, G. (2015) "Multi-platform Media and the Miracle of the Loaves and Fishes," *Journal of Media Business Studies*, 12 (1): 49–65.

Ellis, J. (1982) *Visible Fictions: Cinema, Television, Video*, London: Routledge and Kegan Paul.

Evans, E. (2011) *Transmedia Television: Audiences, New Media and Daily Life*. Abingdon: Routledge.

Evans, E. (2018) "Transmedia Distribution: From Vertical Integration to Digital Natives," in M. Freeman and R. R. Gambarato (eds), *The Routledge Companion to Transmedia Studies*, Abingdon: Routledge, 243–250.

Freeman, M. (2014) "Transmediating Tim Burton's Gotham City: Brand Convergence, Child Audiences, and *Batman: The Animated Series*," *Networking Knowledge: Journal of the MeCCSA-PGN*, 7 (1): 41–54.

Freeman, M. and Taylor-Ashfield, C. (2018) "'I Read Comics from a Feministic Point of View': Conceptualizing the Transmedia Ethos of the Captain Marvel Fan Community," *Journal of Fandom Studies* 5 (3): 317–335.

Freeman, M. and Gambarato, R. G. (eds) (2018) *The Routledge Companion to Transmedia Studies*, Abingdon: Routledge.

Gioco, N. R. (2018) "Afterword: The Present and Future of Transmedia Practices – A Conversation," in M. Freeman and R. R. Gambarato (eds), *The Routledge Companion to Transmedia Studies*, Abingdon: Routledge, 473–480.

Gray, J. (2010) *Show Sold Separately: Promos, Spoilers, and Other Media Paratexts*, New York: New York University Press.

Harvey, C. (2015) *Fantastic Transmedia: Narrative, Play and Memory Across Science Fiction and Fantasy Storyworlds*, Basingstoke: Palgrave Macmillan.

Hay, J. and Couldry, N. (2011) "Rethinking Convergence/Culture: An Introduction," *Cultural Studies*, 25 (4): 473–486.

Hills, M. (2018) "From Transmedia Storytelling to Transmedia Experience: Star Wars Celebration as Crossover/Hierarchical Space," in S. M. Guynes and D. Hassler-Forest (eds), *Star Wars and the History of Transmedia Storytelling*, Amsterdam: Amsterdam University Press, 213–224.

Holt, J. and Sanson, K. (eds) (2014) *Connected Viewing: Selling, Streaming and Sharing Media in the Digital Age*. New York: Routledge.

Ibrus, I. and Ojamaa, M. (2018) "Estonia: Transmedial Disruptions and Converging Conceptualizations in a Small Country," in M. Freeman and W. Proctor (eds), *Global Convergence Cultures: Transmedia Earth*, Abingdon: Routledge, 83–98.

Jenkins, H. (2003) "Transmedia Storytelling," *MIT Technology Review*, January 15, available at www.technologyreview.com/2003/01/15/234540/transmedia-storytelling/ (accessed April 3, 2020).

Jenkins, H. (2006) *Convergence Cultures: Where Old and New Media Collide*. New York: New York University Press.

Jenkins, H. (2007) "The Revenge of the Origami Unicorn: Seven Principles of Transmedia Storytelling," *Confessions of an Aca-Fan: The Official Weblog of Henry Jenkins*. December 12, available at http://henryjenkins.org/2009/12/the_revenge_of_the_origami_uni.html (accessed April 14, 2020).

Jenkins, H. (2016) "Transmedia What?" *Immerse*, November 15, available at https://immerse.news/transmedia-what-15edf6b61daa (accessed January 13, 2018).

Jenkins, H. (2018) "Foreword", in M. Freeman and R. R. Gambarato (eds), *The Routledge Companion to Transmedia Studies*, Abingdon: Routledge, xii–xv.

Johnson, C. (2012) *Branding Television*. Abingdon: Routledge.

Kinder, M. (1991) *Playing with Power in Movies, Television, and Video Games: From Muppet Babies to Teenage Mutant Ninja Turtles*, Berkeley, CA: University of California Press.

Kushner, D. (2008) "Rebel Alliance: How a Small Band of Sci-Fi Geeks is Leading Hollywood into a New Era," *Fast Company*, May 22, available at www.fastcompany.com/798975/rebel-alliance (accessed April 14, 2020).

Petrucco, C. and Agostini, D. (2016) "Teaching Our Cultural Heritage Using Mobile Augmented Reality," *Journal of E-Learning & Knowledge Society*, 12 (3): 115–128.

Scolari, C. A. (2009) "Transmedia Storytelling: Implicit Consumers, Narrative Worlds, and Branding in Contemporary Media Production," *International Journal of Communication*, 3: 586–606.

Scolari, C., Bertetti, P. and Freeman, M. (2014) *Transmedia Archaeology: Storytelling in the Borderlines of Science Fiction, Comics and Pulp Magazines*, Basingstoke: Palgrave.

Scolari, C. (2017) "Transmedia is Dead: Long Live Transmedia," paper presented at the *Transmedia Earth Conference: Global Convergence Cultures*, EAFIT University, October 11–13.

Smith, A. (2018) *Storytelling Industries: Narrative Production in the 21st Century*, Basingstoke: Palgrave Macmillan.

# 36

# SPORTS RIGHTS

## Global content, national markets, and regulatory issues

*Paul Smith*

The symbiotic relationship that exists between the media and sports industries is long established and well documented (Boyle and Haynes 2009; Rowe 2004). The term "mediasport" has even been coined as shorthand to describe the interdependent relationship that developed between sport and the mass media over the course of the twentieth century (Wenner 1998). On the one hand, top level professional sport provides valuable content for media organizations. On the other, the media (mainly television broadcasters) provide an important source of revenue for sports organizations (either directly from the purchase of broadcast rights, or indirectly via exposure for sponsors). Over the last few decades, the media and sports industries have become even more firmly intertwined and nowhere is this more evident than the burgeoning contemporary sports rights marketplace. In 2018, over a quarter (26 percent) of all content spend within the global television industry was accounted for by sports rights, at a value of nearly $38 billion (Dams 2019). At the same time, top-level sports organizations increasingly think of themselves as media companies. As put by Rafael de los Santos, global head of digital at the Spanish football giant Real Madrid, "we're a football club; we dedicate our activity to football, but in reality what we are is a content company" (quoted in Joseph 2017).

Using a range of national and international examples, this chapter examines the importance attached to sports rights within the contemporary media industries. The first part focuses on some of the main factors that explain why media organizations around the world, and particularly television broadcasters, have long been (and continue to be) willing to invest so heavily in the acquisition of sports rights. In doing so, this section also highlights the key characteristics of the contemporary sports rights marketplace. The second part of the chapter considers the growing use of the internet by US-based digital corporations, such as Amazon and Facebook, as well as a host of other media corporations and sports organizations, to deliver sports content "over-the-top" (OTT) to viewers online. Finally, the third section provides an overview of the main policy and regulatory issues raised in relation to the sports rights market, namely competition issues linked to the buying, selling, and distribution of premium sports content and legislation designed to safeguard coverage of certain national and international sporting events for free-to-air television, commonly known as major events or anti-siphoning legislation.

DOI: 10.4324/9780429275340-41

## The value of sports rights

The commercial value of the contemporary sports rights market is underpinned by the fact that live televised sport offers a highly popular and "unique form of mass entertainment," due to its explicit telegenic physicality; its innate competitive structure; its nurturing of deep-rooted individual identifications and loyalties; and, perhaps most significantly, its potential for generating visceral excitement created by the uncertainty, real or imagined, surrounding the outcomes of live sporting contests (Andrews 2003: 239). Measured in billions, global television viewing figures for major international sporting competitions, like the summer Olympic Games and the FIFA World Cup football tournament, are testament to the status of live sport as an enormously popular form of entertainment (IOC 2020: 25; FIFA 2018: 4). In turn, a defining feature of the contemporary sports rights marketplace is that it is the live rights that are by far the most commercially valuable, as distinct from delayed, or highlight coverage. For example, in the UK, the (domestic) live rights for English Premier League football (seasons 2019/20 to 2021/22) were valued at £5 billion, whereas the main highlights package sold for the comparatively low sum of £211.5 million (Bassam 2018).

While a number of international sporting mega-events have widespread global appeal, for the most part, it is local and/or national teams, athletes, and competitions that are most popular with television audiences. This leads to a second key feature of the contemporary sports right market, namely that for most, if not quite all, sports organizations the vast majority of revenue raised from the sale of media rights comes from domestic (i.e., national) markets. In Europe, for example, of the "big five" national football leagues, only the English Premier League has considerable cross-border appeal. In France, Germany, Italy, and Spain, between 80 and 90 percent of the total rights revenue comes from the domestic markets, whereas for the Premier League the ratio of domestic and international revenue is closer to 50:50 (Asser Institute 2014: 67). Some sports, perhaps most notably tennis and Formula One motor racing, benefit from a degree of popularity across a number of different countries/regions, but even here the value of rights tends to reflect the importance of a small number of key markets where the sport (i.e. Germany, Brazil, Italy and the UK for Formula One), or a specific competition (e.g., France for the French Open tennis tournament), are particularly popular. In this sense, the global sports rights market is, in fact, a host of different nationally, or regionally, focused markets, reflecting particular national/regional sporting traditions and preferences.

Also stemming from the national/regional popularity of particular sports and competitions, a third clearly discernible feature of the contemporary sports rights market is the disproportionately high value attached to the rights for one, or at most a handful, of sports and/or competitions, often referred to as premium content. For example, in most, if not quite all, of Europe, football is by far the most popular sport. As a result, football accounts for 79 percent of the spending on sports rights across the EU's five biggest markets (France, Germany, Spain, Italy, and the UK), with the acquisition of rights to domestic football leagues accounting for more than half of the total spend (Asser Institute 2014: 65). In contrast, representing just 4.4 percent of expenditure, Formula One is the second most valuable sport, followed by rugby (4 percent) (p. 65). Similarly, in India, cricket dominates, accounting for around 85 percent of total sports broadcasting revenues (SLPC 2018: 73). In other countries, such as the United States and Australia, preferences are spread more evenly between a handful of different sports, resulting in slightly less concentrated spending on rights. In the United States, for example, the NFL (National Football League), NBA (National Basketball Association), and MLB (Major League Baseball) are each able to command a sizeable share of the domestic sports rights market, with annual rights currently valued at $4.95 billion, $2.6 billion, and $1.5 billion respectively, although the value of these premium rights far exceeds those of other sports (Mance, Garrahan and Blitz 2015).

The final defining characteristic of the contemporary sports rights marketplace is the enormous value attached by media organizations to exclusive (live) coverage of certain sports events, or competitions. This stems from the fact that for many viewers there are few, if any, acceptable substitutes for being able to watch live coverage of a particular sporting event, team, or competition. For this reason, throughout the world, commercially funded free-to-air television broadcasters, such as Channel Nine (Australia), ITV (UK), Globo (Brazil), NBC and Fox (US), and e.TV (South Africa) have long relied on exclusive coverage of live sport to generate mass audiences and attract advertisers (Evens, Iosifidis, and Smith 2013). More significantly, since around the 1990s, pay-TV broadcasters across the world have, in Rupert Murdoch's much quoted phrase, used exclusive live sports rights as a "battering ram" to open up national pay-TV markets. With this approach, Murdoch's News Corporation established (and/or acquired) numerous national pay-TV services, most notably Sky (formerly BSkyB) (UK, Germany, Italy), Foxtel (Australia), and Star Sports (India). The same strategy has also been employed by a host of other pay-TV broadcasters, including Canal Plus (France), Mediaset (Italy), DStv (South Africa), and DirecTV (United States). More recently, telecommunications companies including BT (UK), Deutsche Telekom (Germany), Orange/France Telecom (France), Telefonica (Spain), Verizon (United States), and Optus (Australia), have adopted a similar approach, investing heavily in exclusive sports rights within their respective national markets as part of "triple play" strategies, which bundle together broadband, pay-TV and telephony services, in an attempt to ensure a competitive position in increasingly converged pay-TV and broadband markets (Smith, Evens, and Iosifidis 2016). In short, over the last couple of decades, exclusive premium sports rights have become a key source of market power within national pay-TV and wider communications markets in Europe and beyond.

The strategic importance attached to premium sport rights by pay-TV operators has led to a major escalation in value of sports rights since the 1990s. For example, between 1992 and 2016, the global value of television rights for the summer Olympic Games increased from $638 million to over $2.68 billion (IOC 2020: 27). In Europe, exclusive live rights for domestic football have experienced some of the biggest increases in value over recent years, most notably the Premier League (see Table 36.1). Even more starkly, in India, the cost of rights for the

*Table 36.1* The value of (UK) live Premier League football rights

| Years | Value (£m) |
|---|---|
| 1992–1997 | 191 |
| 1997–2001 | 670 |
| 2001–2004 | 1,200 |
| 2004–2007 | 1,024 |
| 2007–2010 | 1,706 |
| 2010–2013 | 1,773 |
| 2013–2016 | 3,018 |
| 2016–2019 | 5,136 |
| 2019–2022 | 4,815 |

*Sources:* BBC (2015); Sweney (2018).

*Table 36.2* Television rights for Indian cricket[1]

| Years | Broadcaster | Value ($m) |
| --- | --- | --- |
| 1995–1999 | ESPN–Star Sports | 30 |
| 1999–2005 | Prasar Bharati | 54 |
| 2006–2010 | Nimbus Communications | 612 |
| 2010–2014[2] | Nimbus Communications | 436 |
| 2012–2018 | Star India (Star Sports) | 750 |
| (June 2018 to March 2023) | Star India (Star Sports) | 945 |

*Notes:*
1. Data represents sales of rights for the national team's home matches.
2. This deal was terminated by the BCCI in 2011 following alleged non-payment by Nimbus Communications.

*Sources:* Smith (2016); Bassam (2018b).

Indian national cricket team has spiraled since the 1990s (see Table 36.2), while in the United States, current deals for the NFL, NBA, and MLB have increased by 60, 80, and 180 percent respectively since they were last sold (Mance, Garrahan, and Blitz 2015). In turn, this trend has meant that major sporting organizations have become increasingly reliant on the sale of live television rights for a significant proportion of their total income. For example, the International Olympic Committee (IOC) relies on the sale of television rights for 73 percent of its total income (IOC 2020: 6), while for clubs in Europe's big five football leagues, the sale of media rights accounts for an average of 51 percent of total revenue (UEFA 2020: 66).

## New players, new issues

The growing capacity to deliver sports content online poses a number of challenges for established pay-TV operators and leading sports organizations. To start with, both have become increasingly concerned at the use of the internet to illegally distribute live sports coverage, which it is feared could reduce viewing figures for official broadcasters and undermine the commercial value of rights. These fears are not entirely without foundation. While by its very nature the exact scale of illegal streaming is difficult to ascertain, survey evidence suggests the practice is widespread. A European Union Intellectual Property Office (EUIPO) survey revealed extensive illegal viewing, most commonly in Spain, with around 33 percent of respondents using illegal sources to access online content, including live football matches (Clancy 2016). In response, sports organizations and pay-TV operators have made full use of the courts to prosecute those involved in illegal streaming and/or remove illegal streams. For example, in Spain, since 2015, the top domestic football league, La Liga, claims to have removed over 268,000 videos, blocked 9,000 accounts, and taken down 140 mobile applications and 500 URLs, which shared illegal links to images of the competition (Holmes 2018). Such measures have ensured that any loss of value for leading sports organizations from breaches of copyright via illegal streaming has been relatively limited. There is little evidence to suggest that online copyright abuse will lead to a collapse in the value of contemporary sports rights market, with one notable exception. Since around 2017, control of sports rights has become part of an international political dispute between Saudi Arabia and Qatar. Pirate broadcaster, BeOutQ, has used online delivery, as well as the Riyadh-based satellite provider, Arabsat, to broadcast a whole host of high-profile sports events across Saudi Arabia and other Arab-speaking countries, despite (and perhaps even because) most rights were owned by the Qatari government financed broadcaster, beIN Sport. Following international pressure from the United States, the European Union and leading sports organizations, in 2019, BeOutQ officially ceased broadcasting, but widespread online piracy continues in the region, with beIN Sport claiming to have suffered over $1 billion in damages (Carp 2020a).

For most established pay-TV operators, a greater concern is the prospect of competition for premium sports rights from US-based digital media giants, most notably Facebook and Amazon. Both certainly possess the financial resources to outbid established pay-TV operators. For instance, Amazon's annual revenue of around £100 billion is around three times that of Sky and BT combined (Rumsby 2018). Over the last few years, Facebook and Amazon have looked to incorporate sports rights within their wider commercial strategies. In 2017, Facebook launched its new "Watch" tab as part of a plan to maintain/increase its popularity (and attract-iveness to advertisers) by greatly expanding its offering of audiovisual content, including sports. Meanwhile Amazon views sports rights as an important part of a drive to increase member-ship of Amazon Prime, which, for an annual fee, offers subscribers access to music, television/movies, and free next day delivery on home shopping purchases from Amazon. In the United States, Prime members have been found to spend almost twice as much per year as Amazon customers who are not Prime members (Hellier and Soper 2018).

Since around 2016, Facebook and Amazon have agreed an array of high-profile deals with leading US sports organizations, including the NFL, MLB, and Major League Soccer (MLS) for OTT coverage in the United States (Spangler 2018). Most of these have been either non-exclusive, or for a limited number of events. In 2017, however, Facebook's $600 million bid (albeit unsuccessful) for the exclusive global digital rights for Indian Premier League (IPL) cricket indicated a willingness to countenance major exclusive deals beyond the United States (Garrahan and Stacey 2017). Also, in 2017, Amazon agreed to an exclusive £50 million, five-year deal, with the Association of Tennis Professionals (ATP) to cover elite men's tennis (apart from Grand Slams) in the UK, followed by similar deals for the US and French Open tennis tournaments in the UK and France, respectively. Furthermore, in 2018 Amazon paid a reported £90 million for the exclusive UK rights to two rounds of Premier League football fixtures, starting with the 2019/20 season. Coverage of these matches attracted a record number of new subscribers to Amazon Prime and as a result has prompted much speculation over the possi-bility of a more significant bid from Amazon for Premier League rights in the future (Sweney 2019). By contrast, since its unsuccessful bid for IPL rights, Facebook has refined its sports rights strategy so as to maximize the impact of its global reach and avoid involvement in costly bidding wars. Specifically, Facebook has focused on acquiring rights for "niche sports" that are "under-served" by national broadcasters (e.g., La Liga across the Indian sub-continent), as well as investing in "clips rights" for high-profile sports, like the NFL (Goldbart 2019).

Subscription OTT service DAZN (pronounced da-zone), non-US new entrant backed by the billionaire Len Blavatnik, has arguably had a more significant impact on the contemporary sports rights marketplace. Focusing on national markets with relatively low levels of pay-TV subscription and high broadband speed capacity, in 2016 DAZN launched in German-speaking Europe. It has since expanded to other national markets, including Brazil, Canada, Italy, Japan, Spain, and the United States, with around 8 million subscribers worldwide (Impey 2019). In each of these markets DAZN, the self-proclaimed "Netflix of sports," has set about replicating the successful Netflix streaming model by offering an array of sports content for a relatively low monthly fee and with no long-term contract. This has meant focusing mainly on minority sports and/or non-domestic rights for popular sports, although DAZN has also invested heavily in the rights for more high-profile events and competitions in some markets, most notably

UEFA Champions League football in Germany, and a $1 billion eight-year deal with leading boxing promoter Matchroom Boxing in the United States (Bassam 2018c).

In response to competition from OTT new entrants, established pay-TV broadcasters have established their own OTT services, most notably, in Europe (e.g., the Eurosport player) in the United States (e.g., ESPN+). Control and/or access to established broadcasting infrastructure also remains a source of competitive advantage for traditional broadcasters. To deliver a high-quality viewing experience over broadband networks of variable speed and reliability is a significant technological challenge for new entrants using OTT delivery. Any delay in transmission during live sport is unlikely to be tolerated by viewers, in contrast to recorded content like drama and movies where withholding transmissions to allow for buffering is a more feasible option for OTT providers. Numerous OTT services have experienced complaints from viewers when offering live coverage of sports events. Most notably, during the 2018 FIFA World Cup, the Australian OTT provider, Optus, was forced to relinquish its exclusive rights to the competition and share matches with an established broadcaster, SBS, following public outcry over repeated "technical glitches" (Carp 2018).

For sports organizations, increased competition from OTT new entrants has enabled maximum value to be extracted from the sale of rights. In some cases, such as the UK rights to ATP tennis, an OTT new entrant (Amazon) has paid a significant increase on the previous fee paid by a pay-TV operator. In others, such as the 2016 auction for exclusive live domestic Bundesliga rights, competition from an OTT provider (DAZN) forced the incumbent pay-TV operators (Eurosport and Sky Deutschland) to significantly increase their payments. The continued high value of exclusive live sports rights is also underpinned by the potential for sports organizations to offer live coverage of their events and/or competitions directly to consumers by means of their own OTT services. At the very least, sports organizations are able to use this option to deter pay-TV operators (OTT or not) from reducing the value of their bids for rights, even when there is a lack of competition from pay-TV rivals. For example, in 2018, La Liga announced the launch of a multi-sport OTT streaming service, offering past La Liga games, interviews, and documentaries, but not live streams of matches. With pay-TV operators in mind, La Liga's President, Javier Tebas, commented he would not rule out live match coverage "in the mid to long term" and stressed that whether this is option is pursued will be "determined by the market" (quoted in Briel 2018). In other national markets, most notably the United States, major sports leagues already offer direct-to-consumer OTT services, albeit, to date at least, in partnership with established broadcasters, including the NBA (Turner Sports) and NFLSundayTicket.tv (DirectTV). These examples are also a good illustration of the "double game" played by sports organizations in the new OTT environment, whereby they look to explore potential new revenue streams, but at the same time without undermining the value of lucrative and guaranteed rights fees from established broadcasters (Hutchins and Rowe 2009: 356). For example, in 2016, the IOC launched the Olympic Channel, available OTT "anytime, anywhere and on any device," offering year-round live and recorded coverage of a range of different Olympic sports between the Summer and Winter Games but not the actual Olympics (Owen 2016).

## The regulation of sports rights

For as long as exclusive premium sports rights remain a key source of market power within contemporary national pay-TV/communications markets, competition regulators are likely to continue to take a keen interest in the sports rights marketplace. Prompted largely by the battering ram strategies of pay-TV broadcasters, since around the 1990s, one of the main concerns of competition regulators has been the anti-competitive impact of the collective selling of live rights by leading sports leagues and competitions (Evens, Iosifidis and Smith 2013). Critics argue that collective selling enables leagues to act like cartels so as to maximize the value of their rights, which, in turn, strengthens the market position of already dominant pay-TV operators, as they are the only ones able to afford to purchase the rights. In theory, if broadcast rights were sold by individual clubs/teams, there would be more possibilities for other broadcasters to obtain rights, which, in turn, would foster competition in (downstream) pay-TV markets. Alternatively, supporters of collective selling claim that the principles of competition law could/should not to be applied to sporting leagues, not least because the selling of rights by individual teams can lead to vast income discrepancies and undermine competitive balance within a league.

In most countries, perhaps most notably the United States (via the 1961 Sports Broadcasting Act), the collective selling of rights by major sports leagues has long been accepted (Smith, Evens, and Iosifidis 2015). In Europe, however, the issue has proved more controversial. In 2003, in a landmark case on the selling of media rights to the UEFA Champions League, the European Commission opted to allow collective selling, but only with the introduction of measures designed to ensure greater competition for rights, most notably the division of television rights into a number of smaller packages. The same approach was then adopted for the selling of top-level domestic football rights across the European Union (Asser Institute 2014: 78). However, this approach has proved to be only a partial solution. Competition for rights has increased, but for the most part national pay-TV monopolies have merely been replaced by duopolies, such as Sky and BT (UK); Canal Plus and beIN Sports (France); and DT and Sky Deutschland (Germany). The emergence of pay-TV duopolies has also contributed to rapid escalation in the cost of premium rights, which has then been passed on to consumers, who may now also require more than one pay-TV subscription. Paradoxically, for consumers, increased competition in the sports media rights market has led to higher prices (Smith, Evens, and Iosifidis 2016).

The issues raised by broadcasters seeking to use sports programming to ensure competitive advantage over their rivals are just as, if not more significant, than those related to collective selling by sports leagues. For sports channels, access to the most popular delivery platforms (e.g., local cable network) can be a prerequisite for commercial success, albeit less so since the potential for OTT delivery. Equally, in pay-TV markets where premium sports rights are also held by the owners of delivery platforms, rival distribution platforms require access to sports programming/channels in order to be competitive. Broadly speaking, competition issues related to the distribution of sports programming have predominately arisen in US broadcasting as a result of the former scenario (Zimbalist 2006), whereas in Europe's pay-TV markets and beyond, the latter issue has often prompted more concern from competition authorities, perhaps most notably in the UK, where a "wholesale must offer condition" was imposed on Sky during the 2010s, forcing the satellite broadcaster to offer its sports channels to rival delivery platforms.

From around the 1990s, the growth of pay-TV has also prompted policy makers in a number of different countries to introduce legislation designed to preserve coverage of major sporting events or competitions on free-to-air TV. In Europe, major events legislation has been facilitated by the EU and adopted by most of the largest member states, including Germany, France, and Italy, as well as the UK. Other countries, most notably, Australia, India, and South Africa have also adopted a form of major events legislation (Evens, Iosifidis and Smith 2013). Introduction of such legislation has been justified on the grounds that coverage of high-profile sporting events will otherwise tend to migrate from free-to-air broadcasting to pay-TV. There is certainly evidence to support this point of view. For example, during the mid-1990s, in New Zealand, live coverage of the matches of the national rugby team, the iconic All Blacks, moved from free-to-air (TVNZ) to pay-TV (Sky TV) (Scherer and Sam 2012). However, it should be emphasized that much of the sports coverage provided by pay-TV services does not consist of programming previously available via free-to-air broadcasters, but rather coverage of sports and sporting events that previously received little, if any, airtime.

The case for major events legislation is also based on its potential to promote (and/or preserve) "cultural citizenship" in two key ways (Miller 2014). First, legislation may be justified on grounds of equity, for low-income groups should not be excluded from access to major sporting events by their inability to pay. Second, one of the main benefits of ensuring that major sporting events are broadcast on free-to-air television is the generation of what economists refer to as positive network externalities, whereby the collective benefits that can result from the coverage of major sporting events on universally available free-to-air television are more significant than the benefits for any individual viewer, such as the "feel good" factor experienced in South Africa following its 2019 rugby world cup victory.

Opposition to major events legislation stems from an underlying commitment to free market principles. Many sports organizations resent legal restrictions being imposed on the sale of their rights, arguing that they are best placed to judge how to further the interests of their own sport, and in particular balancing the potential for increased revenue to be gained via pay-TV with the benefits of greater exposure through free-to-air television. However, the key argument in support of major events legislation is not that policymakers and regulators know better than individual sports organizations, but rather that the wider public interest in the form of cultural citizenship is best served by the availability of particular sporting events on free-to-air television. It is not particularly unusual in democratic societies for certain property rights to be subject to state regulation in the public interest. Planning laws, for instance, mean that those who live in heritage properties cannot do with them exactly what they want. To promote cultural citizenship, the same is true for sports organizations and listed events. With this in mind, it should be noted that while the growth of OTT subscription services may facilitate significant growth in the amount of sports content (live and recorded) available to viewers, access to much of this content is likely to be dependent on the ability or willingness to pay. Therefore, the challenge for policy makers in countries with major events legislation will be to resist pressure from (some) media and sports organizations to remove, or at least water down, such legislation.

## Conclusion

During 2020, the key characteristics of the contemporary sports rights marketplace identified in this chapter were underlined by the impact of the COVID-19 global pandemic on the media and sports industries. First, top-level live professional sport is (and remains) incredibly popular. During the pandemic, albeit for just a few months, the absence of live sports events was acutely felt by broadcasters around the world, resulting in reduced revenue from TV advertising and pay-TV subscriptions. Equally, the return of live sport witnessed record viewing figures, including for IPL cricket in India and Premier League football in the UK. Second, despite the fears of some industry observers, the commercial and strategic value of exclusive live sports rights for pay-TV operators remained largely unaffected. In Germany, for example, at the height of the pandemic, the rights the Bundesliga (football) sold for €4.4 billion, marginally short of the previous record deal (Carp 2020b). More generally, the value of rights continues to be underpinned by competition between established pay-TV broadcasters and new entrant OTT providers. Third, the pandemic also provided an acute illustration of the reliance of top-level sport on income generated from the sale of media rights. To secure revenue from rights holders, during 2020, various sports organizations around the world went to extraordinary lengths to ensure that their respective events could go ahead, even without paying spectators, including the US and French Open tennis tournaments, Formula One Grand Prix, and UEFA European club football competitions. Finally, key regulatory issues related to the sports rights market also increased in salience during 2020. Perhaps most notably, in various countries, including the UK and South Africa, additional public funding to support sports organizations during the pandemic prompted renewed political debate over the lack of availability of many top-level sports on free-to-air television. Clearly, the sports rights marketplace remains as commercially important and politically significant as ever.

# References

Andrews, D (2003) "Sport and the Transnationalizing Media Corporation," *Journal of Media Economics,* 16 (4): 235–251.

Asser Institute (2014) "Study on Sports Organisers' Rights in the European Union. Final Report for the European Union," available at http://ec.europa.eu/sport/news/2014/docs/study-sor2014-final-report-gc-compatible_en.pdf (accessed February 24, 2020).

Bassam, T. (2018a) "BBC Pays UK£211.5 Million to Renew Premier League Highlights Deal Until 2022," *SportsPro,* January 30, available at www.sportspromedia.com/news/bbc-renews-premier-league-highlights-deal-until-2022 (accessed February 28, 2020).

Bassam, T. (2018b) "Star Hits Rivals for Six with US$945m Deal for India Cricket Rights," *SportsPro,* April 5, available at www.sportspromedia.com/news/star-wins-india-cricket-rights (accessed February 25, 2020).

Bassam, T. (2018c) "Matchroom Lands on DAZN in 'Historic' US$1 Billion Deal," *SportsPro,* May 11, available at www.sportspromedia.com/news/matchroom-eddie-hearn-dazn-perform-group-billion-boxing (accessed February 29, 2020).

BBC (2015) "Premier League in Record £5.14bn TV Rights Deal," *BBC News,* February 10, available at www.bbc.co.uk/news/business-31379128 (accessed February 29, 2020).

Boyle, R. and Haynes, R. (2009) *PowerPlay: Sport, the Media and Popular Culture,* Edinburgh: Edinburgh University Press.

Briel, R. (2018) "Spanish La Liga to Launch OTT Sports Platform," *Broadband TV News,* February 19, available at www.broadbandtvnews.com/2018/02/19/spanish-la-liga-to-launch-ott-sports-platform/ (accessed February 29, 2020).

Carp, S. (2018) "Optus Gives World Cup Coverage to SBS After Streaming Blunders," *SportsPro,* June 28, available at www.sportspromedia.com/news/optus-world-cup-streaming-sbs-complete-coverage-australia (accessed February 29, 2020).

Carp, S. (2020a) "Saudi Arabia Criticised by European Commission over BeoutQ Inaction," *SportsPro,* January 28, available at www.sportspromedia.com/news/saudi-arabia-beoutq-european-commission-piracy-uefa-premier-league-la-liga (accessed February 29, 2020).

Carp, S. (2020b) "Bundesliga Pockets 4.4bn in Sky and DAZN Domestic TV Rights Deal," SportsPro, June 22, available at www.sportspromedia.com/news/bundesliga-sky-dazn-tv-rights-germany-value (accessed December 14, 2020).

Clancy, M. (2016) "EU: Piracy Rampant Throughout Europe," *Rapid TV News,* April 10, available at www.rapidtvnews.com/2016041042411/eu-piracy-rampant-throughout-europe.html?utm_campaign=eu-piracy-rampant-throughout-europe&utm_medium=email&utm_source=newsletter_914#axzz45REXH4UM (accessed February 29, 2020).

Dams, T. (2019) "Sports Rights Account for One Quarter of All TV Content Spend," *Broadcast Sport,* October 17, available at www.broadcastnow.co.uk/broadcasting/sports-rights-account-for-one-quarter-of-all-tv-content-spend/5143950.article (accessed February 26, 2020).

Evens T., Iosifidis P., and Smith P. (2013) *The Political Economy of Television Sports Rights,* Basingstoke: Palgrave Macmillan.

FIFA (2018) "2018 FIFA World Cup Russia: Global Broadcast and Audience Summary," available at https://resources.fifa.com/image/upload/2018-fifa-world-cup-russia-global-broadcast-and-audience-executive-summary.pdf?cloudid=njqsntrvdvqv8ho1dag5 (accessed February 26, 2020).

Garrahan, M. and Stacey, K. (2017) "Murdoch's Star Wins IPL With $2.6bn Bid," *Financial Times*, September 5: 11.

Goldbart, M. (2019) "Facebook Eyes Niche Sports," *Broadcast Sport*, October 23, available at www.broadcastnow.co.uk/broadcasting/facebook-eyes-niche-sports/5144077.article (accessed February 29, 2020).

Hellier, D. and Soper, S. (2018) "Amazon Plans Bid for Premier League Streaming Rights," *Bloomberg Technology*, January 5, available at www.bloomberg.com/news/articles/2018-01-05/amazon-is-said-to-plan-bid-for-premier-league-streaming-rights (accessed February 29, 2020).

Holmes, E. (2018) "Pro League Teams Up With La Liga to Fight Illegal Match-Streaming," *SportsPro*, March 20, available at www.sportspromedia.com/news/pro-league-la-liga-fight-illegal-match-streaming?utm_source=daily_deal&utm_medium=article&utm_campaign=pro-league-la-liga-fight-illegal-match-streaming (accessed February 29, 2020).

Hutchins, B. and Rowe, D. (2009) "From Broadcast Scarcity to Digital Plenitude: The Changing Dynamics of the Media Sport Content Economy," *Television and New Media*, 10 (4): 354–370.

Impey, S. (2019) "DAZN Up to 8m Global Subscribers," *SportsPro*, November 25, available at www.sportspromedia.com/news/dazn-subscribers-2019-streaming-global-growth (accessed February 29, 2020).

IOC (2020) "Olympic Marketing Fact File: 2020 Edition", available at https://stillmed.olympic.org/media/Document%20Library/OlympicOrg/Documents/IOC-Marketing-and-Broadcasting-General-Files/Olympic-Marketing-Fact-File.pdf (accessed February 29, 2020).

Joseph, S. (2017) "'In Reality, We Are a Content Company': Football Clubs Embrace the Role of Digital Publisher," *Digiday*, June 12, available at https://digiday.com/marketing/reality-content-company-football-clubs-embrace-role-digital-publisher/ (accessed February 25, 2020).

Mance, H., Garrahan, M., and Blitz, R. (2015) "TV Sports Rights: Show Them the Money," *Financial Times*, February 13, available at www.ft.com/content/91570e92-b369-11e4-9449-00144feab7de (accessed February 27, 2020).

Miller, T. (2014) "Before, During, and After the Neoliberal Moment: Media, Sports, Policy, Citizenship," in J. Scherer and D. Rowe (eds), *Sport, Public Broadcasting, and Cultural Citizenship: Signal Lost?* London: Routledge, 30–47.

Owen, D. (2016) "Olympic Channel to Launch on August 21," *Inside the Games*, July 27, available at www.insidethegames.biz/articles/1040035/olympic-channel-to-launch-on-august-21 (accessed February 27, 2020).

Rowe, D. (2004) *Sport, Culture and the Media: The Unruly Trinity,* Berkshire: Open University Press.

Rumsby, B. (2018) "Amazon Holds Talks Over Premier League UK TV Rights," *The Telegraph*, 4 January, available at www.telegraph.co.uk/football/2018/01/04/amazon-holds-talks-premier-league-uk-tv-rights/ (accessed February 29, 2020).

Scherer, J. and Sam, M. (2012) "Public Broadcasting, Sport and Cultural Citizenship: Sky's the Limit in New Zealand?" *Media, Culture and Society*, 34 (1): 101–111.

Smith, P. (2016) "Television Sports Rights Beyond the West: The Cases of India and South Africa," *Global Media and Communication*, 12 (1): 67–83.

Smith, P., Evens, T., and Iosifidis P (2015) "The Regulation of Television Sports Broadcasting: A Comparative Analysis," *Media, Culture and Society*, 37 (5): 720–736.

Smith, P., Evens, T., and Iosifidis, P. (2016) "The Next Big Match: Convergence, Competition and Sports Media Rights," *European Journal of Communication*, 31 (5): 536–550.

Spangler, T. (2018) "Big Media, Silicon Valley Battle for Multibillion-dollar Sports TV Rights," *Variety*, January 30, available at http://variety.com/2018/digital/features/olympics-rights-streaming-nbc-winter-games-1202680323/ (accessed February 29, 2020).

Sports Law and Policy Centre (2018) "A Wider Spectrum: Balancing the Many Interests in Sports Broadcasting Regulation in India," available at https://drive.google.com/file/d/1REYWMBxUErQFTos0CeKqGtSyQpwDF4Mp/view (accessed February 29, 2020).

Sweney, M. (2018) "Amazon breaks Premier League hold of Sky and BT with Prime streaming deal", *The Guardian*, June 7, available at www.theguardian.com/media/2018/jun/07/amazon-breaks-premier-league-hold-of-sky-and-bt-with-streaming-deal (accessed February 29, 2020).

Sweney, M. (2019) "Premier League Brings Record Number of Sign-ups to Amazon Prime," *The Guardian*, December 6, available at www.theguardian.com/technology/2019/dec/06/premier-league-brings-record-number-of-sign-ups-to-amazon-prime (accessed February 29, 2020).

UEFA (2020) "The European Club Footballing Landscape: Club Licensing Benchmarking Report Financial Year 2018," available at www.uefa.com/MultimediaFiles/Download/OfficialDocument/ uefaorg/Clublicensing/02/63/79/75/2637975_DOWNLOAD.pdf> (accessed February 27, 2020).

Wenner, L. (1998) *MediaSport*, London: Routledge.

Zimbalist, A. (2006) "Economic Perspectives on Market Power in the Telecasting of US Team Sports," in C. Jeanrenaud and S. Késenne (eds), *The Economics of Sport and the Media*, Cheltenham: Edward Elgar, 160–178.

# PART V

# Practices

## Doing media industries research and pedagogy

The previous chapters have set out a range of conceptual directions, industry formations, and contextual cases. To conclude this volume, the following chapters address the pragmatics of studying media industries, or the practicalities of doing work in this field. "Practices" therefore covers methodological procedures applied in media industries research but also broader issues regarding the production of knowledge in this field, including the politics of academic publishing and employment, reflexivity in ethical praxis, forms of interaction between media academics and media industry professionals, and strategies for enhancing student understanding of media as industries.

Initially, this part opens with two examinations of media industry historiography, the practice of writing industry histories. Andrew Spicer sees film industry historiography as tackling three core problematics. As media industry historians variously place their emphases on studios, technologies, or production, exhibition, and marketing practices, and at the same time debates continue over whether to see film as part of a wider media history, then questions arise over the object of study: how is "film" being defined or "industry" constituted in this context? Equally, selective uses of diverse types of source material, plus differences in conceptual perspective or methodological approach, necessitate querying what counts as historical evidence? Finally, as historical research is driven by multiple purposes and motivations, there is a persistent need to ask what is being explained here? Looking beyond film history, this tripartite set of problematics – object, evidence, explanation – might be applied more widely to not only interrogate the scope of media industry historiography but also the overall reach of the media industry research field.

Shifting discussion of industry historiography towards broadcasting, Jennifer Porst and Deborah Jaramillo analyze trends identifiable in recent scholarship on US radio and television. Surveying a decades' worth of books, articles, and dissertations in the area, they trace trends including the popularity of periods studied, recurring thematic preoccupations (e.g., foci on labor or programming output), and the types of sources and methods most commonly used. Situating this seam of enquiry within institutionalized conditions of knowledge production, Porst and Jaramillo conclude by encouraging consideration of how academic publishing, employment, and professional associations may filter and thereby circumscribe the value of historical research.

DOI: 10.4324/9780429275340-42

Two chapters then pose arguments for how our understandings of media industries will be enhanced by working between and beyond existing research silos. Studies of media policy (see Michalis in Part I) traditionally draw on methods from law and social sciences. Jennifer Holt and Steven Secular contend, however, that interdisciplinary insights and ways of working are needed to arrive at a more comprehensive critical evaluation of the forms of power embedded in policy, providing additional tools for articulating defenses of public interest, safeguarding privacy, and enlarging the range of perspectives and voices operationalized in policy debates. Advocating for interdisciplinary thinking and methodological plurality in media policy research, Holt and Secular propose historical, discourse, and ethnographic analyses as routes toward enhancing policy studies.

Reviewing the differences in perspective, method and outcome characterizing the traditions of media economics and media management research, M. Bjørn von Rimscha summarizes these as ways of conceptualizing and approaching optimization. While the former convention-ally using quantitative methods to arrive at findings directed at optimizing profits at the level of the firm, the latter employs qualitative empirical methodologies aimed at optimizing public welfare. Respecting the value of both, von Rimscha presents proposals for a multi-level and multi-method integrative research practice aimed at optimizing benefits for both the firm and society.

There follows three chapters evaluating the utility of different methodological tools. For Anna Zoellner, observing everyday working practices through immersive ethnographies of media production offers routes into compiling dense or "thick" interpretations of media cre-ation. Unlike interviews, observational methods generate data unfiltered by an interlocutor, yet Zoellner emphasizes ethnography does not create a direct, transparent window onto the phenomena observed. Media practitioners hold the status of exclusive experts, so researchers are dependent on their participation, yet preservation of professional discretion or business con-fidentiality, plus any lingering skepticism over the validity of academic media research, can lead participants to conceal information. Furthermore, among practitioners in research-centric areas of media production (e.g., news, documentary, and factual television), self-conscious awareness of investigative processes may lead to guardedness.

Interviewing industry participants generates rich data that can, as David Craig suggests, deliver valuable correctives to the presumptions or biases adopted by researchers. For Craig, micro-level insights obtained from interviews gain significance when synthesized into holistic multi-method, multi-perspective enquiries, potentially bridging persistent divisions between political economy and cultural studies traditions. To adequately recognize the collaborative work of media creation, Craig argues interview design must be led by a broad definition of roles identifiable as "producers". Yet mutual distrust between academia and industry may lead to media figures remaining hesitant or resistive to participating in academic research, possibly for well-founded professional reasons. Craig therefore offers practical strategies for accessing interview subjects.

Roei Davidson and Oren Meyers examine the application of unstructured interviewing in the collection of life histories. These involve media employees participating in extended in-depth conversations toward constructing personalized longitudinal narratives communicating thoughts and feelings about their occupational lives, and sometimes expanding to reflect on how these impact on their private lives. The prolonged temporality of these occupational tra-jectories captures experiences of institutional change and continuity, while the personalization of accounts illuminates heterogeneity rather than uniformity in how labor experiences industry transformations. Read symptomatically, individual accounts provide granular insights into how personal agency insects with higher-level structural or institutional conditions.

Dealing with the academia/industry divide, chapters by Stuart Cunningham and Annette Hill offer guidance for the forms of interaction or exchange that can be productively achieved between media industries scholars and practitioners. Drawing on his own extensive experience but also insights from other scholars, Cunningham poses a typology of ways in which academics interface with the media industries. These positions, characterized as a series of "personae," extend from communicating publicly on the conduct of the media, to engaging with policy makers to advocate for reforms, operationalizing academic independence to bring a fresh but expert voice to bear on industry related problems, undertaking research commissioned by industry, conducting enquiries through immersing oneself in an industry, and adopting governance or leadership roles by contributing to the work of industry or policy-related bodies.

Hill illustrates how an interface with industry was negotiated in practice. She focuses on a two-year funded multi-territory and multi-method project that bridged television production and audience research to examine how producers create content for audiences and how audiences then engage with that content. Amongst the insights emerging from the project were practical pointers for enhancing engagements between media producers and audiences. By accessing the voices of both categories of stakeholder, the project facilitated an "analytic dialogue" between producer interests and audience activity. One of the outcomes of this way of working was how audiences became humanized for producers by extending understanding of viewers beyond their conventional representation as ratings data or social media analytics.

Ethics govern the conditions in which research inquiry is performed, setting principles and standards by which participants will be engaged with, treated, and protected. For media industries research, particular ethical dilemmas come to the fore if gaining access to industry participants, data, or funding necessitates researcher and subject reaching agreements over consent and confidentiality. Yet noting tendencies in media industries research to elide reflections on ethics, Patrick Vonderau argues ethical questions are integral to the politics of inquiry. For Vonderau, this necessitates moving beyond merely assessing ethics on the basis of applying standard procedural requirements to fulfil a code of conduct, and instead exercising practical reasoning to assess balances between principles and practices attuned to the case-specific situational problems of a project. Rigor may therefore emerge not from rigidly repeating set procedures but rather by a continuing commitment to reflexive re-evaluation.

Of course, the practices of media research extend beyond the academic community, for media industries are themselves generators of research. Drawing on his own industry-insider experience, Justin Wyatt interrogates the work of market researchers in seeking to know and construct media audiences or users. Wyatt outlines the range of qualitative and quantitative techniques commonly employed to research audiences for film and television, and visitors to entertainment websites. Issues arise, however, over the status of this knowledge: producers may reject audience feedback if this is perceived to compromise creative autonomy; privileging the demographics valued by advertisers can weaken the representativeness and credibility of sampling; and while online surveys provide rapid means for large-scale surveying, concerns arise over non-completion rates, superficial results, and the tendency to abstract actual human subjects into "big data."

The status and value of data is a matter picked up by Jade Miller. Media companies and institutions but also academic researchers can frequently resort to numerical measures in the form of statistics or other quantitative data. Miller questions the representational currency of numbers. Citing statistics to evidence industry or market trends may aid media companies to justify investment decisions, while among academics this choice may be motivated by wanting to validate and substantiate the importance of the phenomena researched. For Miller though, this trust in numbers is flawed, for even in the most formally organized industries there are always elements of activity which are not or cannot be measured, while lack of bureaucratic auditing is a defining characteristic of informalized industries such as the Nollywood video film business.

For those working in academic contexts, knowledge production is a matter of research but also pedagogy. Yet the institutional environment of university education can frequently valorize research at the risk of downplaying or even devaluing teaching practice. At the end of this volume, it is therefore instructive to be reminded that if media industries research is to be outward facing in its objectives, pushing beyond talking to a closed – albeit globally extended – community of professional peers, then a basic principle must be to cultivate among students a utilizable understanding of, and critical engagement with, the media. Reflecting on her own teaching practice, Erin Copple Smith outlines experiential learning strategies for enabling students to develop first-hand insights into the operations of media institutions. By way of illustration, Smith poses selected exercises used to immerse students in some of the tasks and challenges confronting television professionals. Although focusing on the specifics of selling ad spots in television series, or designing pilots for new series, at the same time they act as vehicles for triggering broader consideration of how institutional structures and practices may privilege or stifle types of media content.

# 37

# WRITING FILM INDUSTRY HISTORY

## *Andrew Spicer*

Writing any form of film history necessitates addressing three basic questions: "What is the object of study, what counts as evidence and, finally, what is being explained?" (Elsaesser 1986: 247). This chapter explores how these issues have been tackled by a range of different scholars, discussing the ways in which they have conceptualized film industry history in what is a dynamic and shifting field populated by researchers from a variety of perspectives and disciplinary backgrounds with contrasting priorities and preoccupations. It discusses a selection of studies, chosen either because they have been influential, and/or they illustrate broad trends or shifts in approach. What follows is divided into four sections: the first discusses how film industry history has been defined and delimited (the object of study); the second outlines the customary sources used and the major methodological approaches employed (what counts as evidence); third, the chapter considers the purposes or intentions of film industry historians (what is being explained?); a brief concluding section then considers the possible future direction of film industry history.

## The object of study: establishing the field of film industry history

Although important pioneering work on film industry history already existed, including Tino Balio's edited collection *The American Film Industry* (1976a) and the first volume of his study of United Artists (1976b), Robert C. Allen and Douglas Gomery's *Film History: Theory and Practice* (1985) became the first attempt to explicitly and in a systematic manner define and reflect on both the purposes and practices of film historiography, including industry history. Allen and Gomery proposed four main approaches to writing film history: aesthetic, technological, economic, and social.[1] They define the object of economic film history as the industry's processes of production, distribution, and exhibition (the "basic descriptive model"). In American cinema this was organized through a "system of business operations" that controlled the allocation of goods and services (pp. 132–134). The task of economic film history, they contend, is to construct models, derived from more general economic analyses, which identify the industry's basic conditions of supply and demand and then evaluate its market structure, conduct, and performance. Although they recognize the importance of regulatory changes in shaping industry conduct, Allen and Gomery argue that technological changes should only be considered in so

DOI: 10.4324/9780429275340-43

far as they alter business practices and commercial operations. In contrast to aesthetic history, economic history regards films as commodities. Perhaps most contentiously, Allen and Gomery (p. 138) suggest that "industrial analysis" seeks only "to understand economic variables," thus "leaving questions of sociology and ideology to others" who pursue social analyses.

Allen and Gomery's study was part of a spate of important publications in the mid-1980s that redefined how the (American) film industry was understood: David Bordwell, Janet Staiger, and Kristen Thompson's (1985) *The Classical Hollywood Cinema*, Thompson's *Exporting Entertainment* (1986), Gomery's (1986) *The Hollywood Studio System*, and Thomas Schatz's (1988) *The Genius of the System*, plus Balio's updating (1986) of *The American Film Industry* and the second volume (1987) of his United Artists study. In *The Classical Hollywood Cinema*, Staiger's attention to shifting systems of production offered a way to understand how combinations of finance, labor, and physical means of production determine the nature of filmmaking at specific moments. Gomery's analysis of the studio system provided a broad historical overview of Hollywood's development as a commercial operation, while Schatz used André Bazin's contention that Hollywood must be understood as a whole organization – the "genius of the system" – to analyze the institutionally based craftmanship that constituted creativity as opposed to the then-dominant focus on auteur directors. These studies largely viewed the American film business in terms of production activity, but Thompson provided an incisive analysis of Hollywood's international distribution, lobbying, and marketing strategies for penetrating overseas markets, "exporting entertainment," while Gomery's *Shared Pleasures: A History of Movie Presentation in the United States* (1992) offered a systematic overview of the business strategies that shaped film exhibition from the beginnings to the widespread use of video cassette recorders (VCRs). Gomery not only drew attention to an area of the business frequently overlooked, but importantly reconceptualized the object of study as "cinema" rather than "film," an enlargement that most industry historians now accept.[2]

These foundational studies focused on the American industry. Although Hollywood remains the dominant focus for film industry histories, some histories analyze different national cinemas, for example Richard Abel's (1994) *The Ciné Goes to Town: French Cinema, 1896–1914*, while others take a regional focus, including Anne Jackel's *European Film Industries* (2003). Yongchun Fu's (2019) *The Early Transnational Chinese Cinema Industry* exemplifies transnational film industry studies, demonstrating the complex and shifting relationships between Hollywood and other film industries in which both engage in complex assimilations and reworkings of each other's characteristic modalities. Drilling down below the level of any particular industry, Christopher Meir's (2019) *Mass Producing European Cinema* illustrates the value of studying major non-US corporations, in this case the French film producer-distributor StudioCanal, which have different business models and commercial strategies.

For film history, work on non-US film industries offered an obvious but important extension of the object of study, showing – explicitly or implicitly – that Hollywood was *a* way rather than *the* way in which film industry could be organized. Another approach, reflecting the "spatial turn" in the humanities, focused on the importance of place in providing competitive advantage. Drawing on the influential work of the economist Michael Porter, Scott (2005: xi) demonstrates how part of Hollywood's industrial strength derives from an "organized ecology of specialized but complementary production activities." Scott argues that "Hollywood is neither just a metaphor nor a business model; it is also a unique geographical entity, with a very distinctive structure as a production locale" (p. 47). Brannon Donoghue (2017) extends this analysis to overseas production sites in which American companies work with indigenous talent to make locally inflected films and television shows that are often commercially successful.

Rather than extend the scope of existing approaches, other studies have sought to rethink what the film "industry" is. Govil (2013) argues that industry needs to be understood as a conceptual construct rather than simply as a form of production, created by policy decisions, coalescing spheres of practices (such as craft associations), and other forms of sociality and collective affinity. Similarly, John Caldwell (2013) argues that "the industry" should not be conceptualized as "a clear, self-evident sphere," an object ready to be researched, but as a discourse, constructed and reconstructed by intermediaries who manage and produce selective "data" that constitutes a "para-industry" surrounding the supposed object of study. Caldwell's major study, *Production Culture: Industrial Reflexivity and Critical Practice in Film and Television* (2008), examined the discourses of screen practitioners working in Hollywood, analyzing how they construct their own cultural and interpretive frameworks and their collective self-theorizing rituals that are central to how the screen industries operate.

Understanding "film" as a singular and separate medium has also been interrogated. Staiger contends that film "as a business and an art was never isolated from the other entertainments" but part of an interweaving mesh of leisure industries that were international in scope and reach (2004: 127). Understanding film as interwoven with other media and entertainment practices has become more insistent because the impact of digital processes has caused media to "converge," necessitating the replacement of film history with a wider media industry history (Staiger and Hake 2009). Jennifer Holt argues that rather than being technologically driven, convergence was the product of "globalization, deregulation and market concentration" (2011: 10), which, since the early 1980s, enabled the growth of horizontally and vertically integrated conglomerates that exploited their ownership of a range of entertainment outlets to maximize revenue. Film became subsumed into the wider entity of "media industries" (film, broadcast, cable, and video), whose histories are "no longer distinct but … fundamentally connected and contingent upon one another" (p. 7). Nevertheless, Schatz argues that these gigantic media conglomerates still have "film studios at the epicentre, and with 'filmed entertainment' as the key commodity" (2008: 27). Balio (2013) argues media conglomerates concentrate on the "tent pole" blockbuster (or the "event movie") that, ideally, forms part of a franchise operating across the proliferation of platforms and generating the huge growth of ancillary markets. Lower budget films have been farmed out to "independent producers," generating a connected but still separate American "indie" film industry organized on very different business models (see Tzioumakis 2017).

The object of film industry history has shifted. Analysis of production practices has expanded to include distribution, exhibition, and marketing strategies as film became a global industry dominated by the US studios. However, the focus on the international film industry has extended beyond documenting this dominance to include not only a recognition of the distinctiveness of various national cinemas but also, particularly studies of transnational cinema, their reciprocal relationship with Hollywood, now understood as itself a specific set of industrial and business practices that change in its various encounters and engagements with other forms of film. More broadly, "film" has been reconceptualized, not as a separate, singular practice but one that is positioned within a wider history of media forms and the term "industry" as a shifting set of practices and discourses rather than a given.

## What counts as evidence: Sources and approaches

As exemplified by the foundational work on the US business, film industry history emphasizes detailed empirical investigation of primary sources as forms of evidence, using available written records, archives, specific collections, personal papers and memoirs, the trade press, policy documents, and censor reports. Balio's two-volume study of United Artists (1976b, 1987), for example, was based on careful examination of the studio's internal production files and correspondence, including minutes of meetings, financial records, details of business transactions, and distribution data. Gorham Kindem's collection *The American Movie Industry* was composed of detailed case studies assembled by scholars who had examined "business records, legal proceedings, government and industry statutes, and trade papers" (1983: xiii). The professional scholarship of these studies contrasted with earlier impressionistic, mainly biographical, film industry histories – "tales of pioneers and adventurers" – and were characterized by their wide-ranging use of sources (Elsaesser 1986: 246). Subsequent scholarship has expanded the range of primary sources further to encompass previously disregarded or overlooked material, including ephemera and fan magazines (Chapman, Glancy, and Harper 2007: 7–8). Furthermore, archival analysis of unrealized films has demonstrated the value of studying aborted film production histories for what they reveal about the prevailing industrial conditions and constraints (North 2008; Spicer 2010; Fenwick, Foster, and Eldridge 2020).

However, while film industry scholars agreed on the centrality of primary sources and the empirical orientation of research, their approaches showed marked differences. The early collections edited by Balio and Kindem mixed neoclassical analyses of supply and demand with Marxist analyses; Kindem commented: "historical problems have been given contradictory or different explanatory models and emphasized different sets of economic, social, political, legal and aesthetic factors" (1982: xiii). Allen and Gomery (1985: 134–138) detected a similar split, contrasting the ideological neutrality of some film industry studies, with others such as Guback (1969) mounting a Marxist critique of how the American industry had used its commercial muscle to exploit European markets and thereby hindered the development of European film industries. By contrast, Waterman (2005) explains Hollywood's commercial success since the 1970s as arising mainly through segmenting markets across an expanded range of selling points without commenting on the wider consequences of this strategy.

The approach of economic historians such as Waterman is primarily quantitative, deploying microeconomic tools of analysis, including statistical data, tables, graphs, and mathematical modelling, to analyze industry practices. Perhaps the outstanding work of economic film history is Gerben Bakker's *Entertainment Industrialised* (2008), which analyses how film replaced theatre as popular entertainment, and the ways in which the United States became the dominant film industry. Bakker scrutinizes business innovations and the underlying forces that gave rise to them – increased leisure time and disposable income, urbanization, better transport networks, and significant population growth – and identifies film's unique commercial quality as its "tradeability," packed into cans of celluloid that could be easily and cheaply transported. As the industry developed, high production expenditure ("endogenous sunk costs") necessitated international distribution to recoup costs, which was economically viable because the costs of making additional sales were almost zero. He suggests that it was the size of America's internal market that enabled film entrepreneurs to risk high costs, leaving the smaller European countries unable to compete in the "quality race." Considered from a contemporary vantage point where Hollywood's dominance of the global film market is an established fact, Bakker's conclusions might seem unsurprising, yet through amassing the impressive range of detailed archival evidence on which his economic modelling is based, he demonstrates that America's commercial supremacy was far from inevitable.

However, the dominant approach to film industry analysis has been the forms of Marxist analysis adopted by Guback and others influenced by the critical political economy of the media, defined as "the power relations that constitute the production, distribution, and consumption of resources" and which focuses on "the fundamental forces and processes at work in the marketplace" (Mosco 2009: 2, 24). Political economy studies are characterized by their astringent critique of systems of ownership and control, advocacy for changes in public policy to curb or supplement market forces, and a concern for labor relations (Vasey 2008: 11). Commencing with her 1982 study *Movies and Money: Financing the American Film Industry*, Janet Wasko emerged as one of the most prominent and prolific political economists writing about film and media. In *Understanding Disney*, Wasko (2020: 117) analyses Disney's development of a "magic kingdom" produced by an organization which exhibits "the same goals as any profit-oriented company." She provides a detailed examination of Disney's "multiverse," encompassing all its entertainment activities from films to theme parks, looking at its corporate management and ethos, policies, and strategies, its divisions, products, services and properties, directors, shareholders, and employees. Wasko avoids the "great man" version of film industry history that dominated pioneering film history accounts (see Allen and Gomery 1985: 52–54, 110–114) by situating what she calls an "instrumental" analysis of key entrepreneurs, Walt Disney himself and his successors such as Michael Eisner, within the context of more general economic and political contexts, analyzing the "complex interplay of intentional action and structural constraint at every level of the production process" (p. 10).

Since 2008, the dominance of political economy has been challenged by production studies. Production studies scholars tend to adopt an ethnographic approach, combining interviews and field observations to generate "thick descriptions" of the minutiae of production cultures, the relationships in and between firms ("communities of practice") with a careful attention to less regulated networks and ecologies, thus emphasizing the media industries' cultural as well as economic dimensions. Interview sources are treated with caution, analyzed as situated utterances that need careful interpretation. This approach, it is argued (for example by Havens, Lotz, and Tinic 2009), has enabled a closer engagement with *agency*, the scrutiny of a wider selection of cultural workers performing a variety of roles including "below-the-line" screen workers, which highlights how more "menial" industry tasks are often performed by low-paid employees, often women and from minority ethnic backgrounds. In contrast to the assumptions of business, organizational, or economic analysts who emphasize the rational choices and "utility maximization" of self-interested individuals operating in competitive markets (Lipartito 2013), production studies recognize media workers have mixed motivations and values. Attention is paid to "the vagaries of human subjects or culture's thick complexities" (Caldwell 2013: 157), thus appreciating the potential importance of chance encounters, contingencies, and fortuitous circumstances in determining commercial processes. In contradistinction to critical political economy's focus on overarching patterns of ownership and global corporations, production studies examine small and medium enterprises (SMEs), which now form the overwhelming majority in the screen industries, and their variegated production cultures (Bakøy, Puijk, and Spicer 2017).

Although production studies has introduced a wider range of potential sources and practices within the purview of film history, the differences between the two approaches have been exaggerated. Critical political economy, as Wasko's analysis of Disney demonstrates, is fully capable of providing the detailed scrutiny of the minutiae of production cultures, and production studies retains a critical perspective on the media industries, derived from cultural studies, situating micro-level analyses within the macro conditions of power relationships and unequal flows of talent or finance found in international media industries (Holt and Perren 2009). Both approaches are characterized by rigorous analysis of sources, the "evidence" on which they base arguments and conclusions, drawn from detailed empirical investigations. They represent different emphases in the study of film history rather than more fundamental distinctions, though production studies, as currently constituted, is very oriented to the present and would benefit from more sustained attention to history, including the historical evolution of contemporary forms.

## Purposes: what is being explained?

Arguing that the study of film had become dominated by textual interpretation, film industry historians considered their primary purpose was to explain how the industry worked as a profit-seeking commercial operation. This was appropriate because, as Balio remarked, no other art has been "influenced so heavily by the predilections of the business world" (1976a: vii). Equally, Allen and Gomery (1985: 135) argued that business practices in the American film industry conformed to those deployed by other large US corporations, and so needed to be investigated "systematically" to explain the role of film in the American economy and to understand how that role changed over time. John Sedgwick and Michael Pokorny argue that economic historians attempt to "explain film business practices" pragmatically rather than ideologically (2005b: 6). Although the film industry conforms to general business characteristics as a "system of provision" producing a particular "commodity-type" (films), its success distinctively depends on audience approval, which is highly unpredictable. In an industry typified by extreme commercial volatility (huge hits and massive flops) and high risk, the Hollywood studios attempted to mitigate risk by pursuing a series of "empirical regularities": short-burst cycles of films initiated by highly successful originator; releasing portfolios of films and/or initiating franchises; attempting to guarantee audience appeal through high production costs, expensive stars, and substantial expenditure on marketing (pp. 16–19). Sedgwick and Pokorny, however, explain these "risk-attenuating" strategies cannot guarantee success in an industry that lacks a stable underlying business model and in which uncertainty is "integral" to the whole process of production and consumption. Gomery's (2005: 3, 5) account of the Hollywood studios attempted to explain their economic conduct ("How did they choose how many films to produce? How distribute them and exhibit them, at what price and in what order?") but also emphasized agency ("I seek to understand how and in what manner the studio corporation bosses fashioned ways to maximize profits, as do all corporations in the USA").[3] Economic accounts of Hollywood as a commercial practice serve as an effective counterpoint to the dominance of textual analysis, resituating films within their industrial context and accounting for the choices and strategies that led to what viewers see on the screen before any encounter or interpretation takes place.

However, the goal was not simply to explain Hollywood's internal operations, its studio chiefs, or even the industry's role in the US economy, but also how it achieved global dominance. As Ruth Vasey argues, "it is precisely Hollywood's enduring status as the world's most popular and financially successful cinema that requires analysis and explication" (2008: 287). Vasey contends she is not "interpreting Hollywood's world but trying to account for it" through an analysis of the "specific historical and industrial factors" that explain its global dominance (1996: 225). Vasey insists the Hollywood studios must be regarded as "profit-seeking corporations" rather than film-making entities, with their overall policy determined by corporate executives in New York rather than the much more high-profile subordinates who ran the production plants in Los Angeles. Industry historians also recognized that Hollywood's influence was not purely economic, but that "films, unlike other manufactured goods, have significant social, political, and aesthetic value" (Kindem 1982: xviii). Thus, Hollywood's historical importance has come through its ability to shape audience tastes across the globe, molding their expectations of what constitutes a film as a pleasurable experience. Understanding the history of Hollywood's cultural impact, therefore, necessitates emphasiz[ing] the economic/business dimensions of the industry, thereby broadening and deepening the context within which any cultural analysis takes place … to fully understand the cultural impact that Hollywood has had, and continues to have, it is also necessary to understand the economics and economic history of the industry.

*Sedgwick and Pokorny 2005a: 2*

Gomery argues that grasping the global dimensions of the industry can enable better understanding of how Hollywood has exercised "international *political and cultural* power" (emphasis added, 2005: 6). As noted, critical political economy seeks to explain in whose interests these global corporations work. Holt (2011) sees the present era of media convergence and conglomeration as the outcome of a longer-term neoliberal transformation in industrial politics in which market forces are deemed sovereign. Grieveson (2018) locates the origins of the present neoliberal compact between politics and the media in the interwar period, during which US government departments were reorganized to conform to corporate business practices, ideologies, and values. Similarly, analyses of other national film industries cinemas have to explain, not only how their different business models and industrial strategies are related to the specifics of national cultures and to precise historical moments, but also the ways in which those industries responded to Hollywood's commercial power. Such histories need to elucidate what has constituted a "national cinema" or an "indigenous film industry" in what became, from around 1907, an international marketplace that after the First World War was dominated by American companies.

Thus, while concerned with economics, the overall purpose of film industry historians should be to contribute to a broader analysis of cultural, social, and political processes, and so to explain film's "relationship to the development of modernity and its characteristic structures and procedures" (Garnham 2000: 38). Charney and Schwartz (1995) contended that film was not simply a new medium but central to how modernity was experienced and understood by a broad public. Similarly, Doane (2002) argues film was central to the development of "industrialized time," and so essential to the penetration of capitalist work practices into modern societies. While it has been argued that film's "disappearance" into digital multimedia offers a "threshold moment," in which the teleology of film's triumphant and inevitable emergence from a homogenized "pre-cinema" can be re-inspected (Mulvey 2007: xv–xvi), Charles Musser's (1990) meticulous research shows the emergence of what we can recognize as "film" was the result of commercial strategies adopted by entrepreneurs and largely determined by changes in exhibition practices, demonstrating the value of industrial history in these debates.

## Possible futures for film industry historiography

The three vectors of film industry historiography – the object of study, the status and types of evidence adduced, and the purposes of writing film industry histories – are undergoing significant change.

Hollywood, as the dominant global commercial entity, continues to be the central object of analysis. Although the old Hollywood studios may have morphed into "multiverses," "filmed entertainment" remains economically central to the huge, diversified media conglomerates even if film viewing is now distributed across a proliferation of different platforms. However, film industry scholars have also given detailed attention to the rise of the "new King Kongs," the rapidly growing financial muscle of online subscription- based video-on-demand (SVOD) companies such as Netflix, which have started to morph from distributor-exhibitors into commissioner-producers with huge resources, able to make feature films whose production values are indistinguishable from the Hollywood majors. Lobato (2019), for instance, analyses Netflix's sophisticated business strategy that exploits local variations demonstrating the continued importance of place, and which forms the latest phase of a longer history of US-based transnational commercial practices.

In a parallel development, increasing attention has been given to "other" cinemas, notably those from the Global South – India ("Bollywood") and Nigeria ("Nollywood") – that have become internationalized entities based on very different models of production, distribution, and exhibition. As Miller (2012) shows for example, Nollywood developed as a low-budget video industry by exploiting alternative, often informal, distribution networks. Her work meshes with that of Lobato (2012), who has extended the study of the film industry to include "shadow economies": spheres of economic activity generating value from film outside formally ordered and regulated markets.

Film industry historians continue to make use of traditional, if neglected, overlooked or recently discovered archival sources to provide evidence that revises conventional accounts. Jon Burrows' (2017) business history *The British Cinema Boom, 1909–1914*, for instance, analyses a period of rapid change in the UK film industry based on detailed scrutiny of surviving business and local government records, company accounts and box-office data situated as part of a scrutiny of Edwardian leisure activities and changing audience tastes, which challenges existing British cinema histories. An exciting development has been the increasingly sophisticated use of geocomputational methods that conducts spatial analysis using locational data. Representative of this work is Julia Hallam and Les Roberts' (2011) study of Liverpool, which constructs a moving image database to explore the evolution of spatial narratives of the city, using this case study to open out what they see as the cultural and historiographical implications for research into film, place and space, and from that to suggest how this might reshape national discourses of film industry historiography.

Turning to the purposes of writing film industry history, a noteworthy development has been the increasing attention given to environmental politics and sustainability, including media industries' often promiscuous use of energy, rare minerals, and other resources (see Herbert, Lotz, and Punathambekar 2020: 124–125). The growth of ecocritical approaches to film and other screen media is indicated by a recent dossier in the *Journal of Cinema and Media Studies* (Peterson and Uhlin 2019), and the formation of the *Journal of Environmental Media*. One of the journal editors, Hunter Vaughan, advocates "ecocriticism" focusing on the "geopolitics, industrial infrastructure, and material impact of media industries and practices" (2019: 10). This ethical focus is an appropriate place to end this overview, as it returns us to what has been argued is the central purpose of film industry historical research: to explain film's economic and commercial practices in detail but understood as part of wider social, cultural, and political processes.

## Notes

1 Allen and Gomery's divisions closely mirror the "explanatory frameworks" proposed by Thompson and Bordwell (2018): biographical, industrial, or economic (business practices), aesthetic, technological, and social/cultural/political.
2 This approach has been further advanced by the work of the History of Moviegoing, Exhibition and Reception (HoMER) group of scholars (see Maltby, Biltereyst, and Meers 2011). However, because their work focuses on exhibition in terms of the social experience of cinema (and so is representative of what Allen and Gomery (1985) regard as social film history) rather than economic/industrial organization, it is outside the scope of this chapter.

3 Gomery's explanation seems to ascribe the creation of the system to Adolph Zukor at Paramount and its reinvention in the 1960s to Lew Wasserman, the talent agent who took over Universal, which slides into "Great Man" causality.

# References

Abel, R. (1994) *The Ciné Goes to Town: French Cinema, 1896–1914*, Berkeley, CA: University of California Press.

Allen R. C. and D. Gomery (1985) *Film History: Theory and Practice*, New York: McGraw-Hill.

Bakker, G. (2008) *Entertainment Industrialised: The Emergence of the International Film Industry, 1890–1940*, Cambridge: Cambridge University Press.

Bakøy, E., Puijk, R., and Spicer, A. (eds) (2017) *Building Successful Film and Television Businesses: A Cross-National Perspective*, Bristol: Intellect.

Balio, T. (ed.) (1976a) *The American Film Industry*, Madison, WI: University of Wisconsin Press.

Balio, T. (1976b) *United Artists: The Company Built by the Stars*, Madison, WI: University of Wisconsin Press.

Balio, T. (1987) *United Artists, Volume 2, 1951–1978: The Company That Changed the Film Industry*, Madison, WI: University of Wisconsin Press.

Balio, T. (2013) *Hollywood in the New Millennium*, London: British Film Institute.

Bordwell, D., Thompson, K. and Staiger, J. (1985) *The Classical Hollywood Cinema: Film Style and Mode of Production to 1960*, London: Routledge.

Brannon Donoghue, C. (2017) *Localising Hollywood*, London: British Film Institute.

Burrows, J. (2017) *The British Cinema Boom, 1909–1914: A Commercial History*, London: Palgrave Macmillan.

Caldwell, J. T. (2008) *Production Culture: Industrial Reflexivity and Critical Practice in Film and Television*, Durham, NC: Duke University Press.

Caldwell, J. T. (2013) "Para-Industry: Researching Hollywood's Blackwaters," *Cinema Journal*, 52 (3): 157–165.

Chapman, J., Glancy, M. and Harper, S. (2007) *The New Film History: Sources, Methods, Approaches*, Basingstoke: Palgrave Macmillan.

Elsaesser, T. (1986) "The New Film History," *Sight and Sound* 55 (4): 246–251.

Fenwick, J., Foster, K., and Eldridge D. (eds) (2020) *Shadow Cinema: The Historical and Production Context of Unmade Films*, London: Bloomsbury.

Fu, Y. (2019) *The Early Transnational Chinese Cinema Industry*, Abingdon: Routledge.

Garnham, N. (2000) *Emancipation, the Media and Modernity: Arguments about the Media and Social Theory*, Oxford: Oxford University Press.

Gomery, D. (1992) *Shared Pleasures: A History of Movie Presentation in the United States*, London: British Film Institute.

Gomery, D. (2005) *The Hollywood Studio System: A History*, London: British Film Institute.

Govil, N. (2013) "Recognizing 'Industry,'" *Cinema Journal*, 52 (3): 172–176.

Grieveson, L. (2018) *Cinema and the Wealth of Nations: Media, Capital, and the Liberal World System*, Oakland, CA: University of California Press.

Guback, T. (1969) *The International Film History: Western Europe and America Since 1945*, Bloomington, IN: Indiana University Press.

Hallam, J. and Roberts, L. (2011) "Mapping, Memory and the City: Archives, Databases and Film Historiography," *European Journal of Cultural Studies*, 14 (3): 355–372.

Havens, T., Lotz, A., and Tinic, S. (2009) "Critical Media Industry Studies: A Research Approach," *Communication, Culture & Critique*, 2 (2): 234–253.

Herbert, D., Lotz, A. and Punathambekar, A. (2020) *Media Industry Studies*, Cambridge: Polity Press.

Holt, J. (2011) *Empires of Entertainment: Media Industries and the Politics of Deregulation*, Austin, TX: University of Texas Press.

Holt, J. and Perren, A. (eds) (2009) *Media Industries: History, Theory and Method*, Oxford: Wiley-Blackwell.

Jackël, A. (2003) *European Film Industries*, London: British Film Institute.

Kindem, G. (ed.) (1982) *The American Movie Industry: The Business of Motion Pictures*, Carbondale, IL; Southern Illinois University Press.

Lipartito, K. (2013) "Connecting the Cultural and Material in Business History," *Enterprise and Society*, 14 (4): 686–704.

Lobarto, R. (2012) *Shadow Economies of Cinema: Mapping Informal Film Distribution*, London: British Film Institute.

Lobato, R. (2019) *Netflix Nations: The Geography of Digital Distribution*, New York: New York University Press.

Maltby, R., Biltereyst, D., and Meers, P. (eds) *Explorations in New Cinema History: Approaches and Case Studies*, Chichester: Wiley-Blackwell.

Meir, C. (2019) *Mass Producing European Cinema: Studio Canal and its Works*, New York: Bloomsbury.

Miller, J. (2012) "Global Nollywood: The Nigerian Movie Industry and Alternative Global Networks in Production and Distribution," *Global Media and Communication*, 8 (2): 117–133.

Mosco, V. (2009) *The Political Economy of Communication,* 2nd ed., London: Sage.

Mulvey, L. (2007) "Foreword," in J. Lyons and J. Plunkett (eds), *Multimedia Histories: from the Magic Lantern to the Internet.* Exeter: University of Exeter Press, xv–xvi.

Musser, C. (1990) *The Emergence of Cinema: American Screen to 1907*, Berkeley, CA: University of California Press.

North, D. (ed.) (2008) *Sights Unseen: Unfinished British Films*, Newcastle: Cambridge Scholars Publishing.

Peterson, J., and Uhlin, G. (eds) (2019) "In Focus: Film and Media Studies in the Anthropocene," *Journal of Cinema and Media Studies*, 58 (2): 142–179.

Schtaz, T. (1988) *The Genius of the System: Hollywood Filmmaking in the Studio Era*, London: Faber and Faber.

Schatz, T. (2008) "The Studio System and Conglomerate Hollywood," in P. McDonald and J. Wasko (eds), *The Contemporary Hollywood Film Industry*, Oxford: Blackwell Publishing: 13–42.

Scott, A. J. (2005) *On Hollywood: The Place, the Industry*, Princeton, NJ: Princeton University Press.

Sedgwick, J. and Pokorny, M. (2005a) "Introduction," in J. Sedgwick and M. Pokorny (eds) *An Economic History of Film*, Abingdon: Routledge, 1–5.

Sedgwick, J. and Pokorny, M. (2005b) "The Characteristics of Film as a Commodity," in J. Sedgwick and M. Pokorny (eds), *An Economic History of Film*, Abingdon: Routledge, 6–23.

Spicer, A. (2010) "Creativity and Commerce: Michael Klinger and New Film History," *New Review of Film and Television Studies*, 8 (3): 297–314.

Staiger, J. and Hake, S. (eds) (2009) *Convergence Media History*, New York: Routledge.

Thompson. K. (1986) *Exporting Entertainment: America in the World Film Market, 1907–1934*, London: British Film Institute.

Thompson K. and Bordwell, D. (2018) *Film History: An Introduction*, 4th ed., New York: McGraw-Hill.

Tzioumakis, Y. (2017) *The American Independent Cinema*, 2nd ed., Edinburgh: Edinburgh University Press.

Vaughan, H. (2019) *Hollywood's Dirtiest Secret: The Hidden Environmental Cost of the Movies*, New York: Columbia University Press.

Vasey, R. (1997) *The World According to Hollywood, 1918–1939*, Exeter: Exeter University Press.

Vasey, R. (2008) "The Hollywood Industry Paradigm," in J. Donald and M. Renov (eds) *The Sage Handbook of Film Studies*, London: Sage, 287–311.

Wasko, J. (1982) *Movies and Money: Financing the Hollywood Film Industry*, New York: Ablex Publishing.

Wasko, J. (2020) *Understanding Disney: The Manufacture of Fantasy*, 2nd ed., Cambridge: Polity Press.

Waterman, D. (2005) *Hollywood's Rags to Riches*, Cambridge, MA: Harvard University Press.

# 38

# WRITING THE AIRWAVES

## Recent trends in histories of US broadcasting

*Jennifer Porst and Deborah L. Jaramillo*

In 2009, Michele Hilmes published the chapter "Nailing Mercury: The Problem of Media Industry Historiography," in Jennifer Holt and Alisa Perren's *Media Industries: History, Theory and Method*. By that time, research on the media industries, though robust, was still largely fractured along disciplinary and methodological lines and was just starting to coalesce into a more coherent field of study. In "Nailing Mercury," Hilmes charted the state of media industry studies by surveying the major publications on US broadcasting up to that point. Informed by Hilmes' work, this chapter assesses the contemporary state of the field by analyzing how it studies the past. We are interested specifically in the field's attention to histories of broadcasting and the degree to which the field has shifted that attention to the present moment. Our concern is not with presenting a thorough survey of US broadcasting research, but rather with producing an account of the methodological and practical matters that arise from doing history. Ultimately, the analysis of US broadcasting histories allows us to illuminate and explore the broader challenges and opportunities of writing histories of the media industries.

As Hilmes indicated in her title, conducting this type of study is a bit like nailing mercury. In identifying our focus for this chapter, we had to wrestle with the same challenges as scholars who undertake industry histories. First, we had to draw boundaries around the category of media industry studies, which encompasses audio and moving image media and has little regard for awkward academic naming trends that seek to remove cinema from the broader term, "media." Because the field is interested in people, institutions, and practices that operate around media texts, and which inform the construction and reception of those texts, it moves beyond historical rifts between film studies and television studies, or between approaches like political economy and cultural studies. Many industry studies employ mixed methods to analyze the relationship between industry and text, or industry and culture. Moreover, the convergent impulses of digital media have pushed scholars of different media to move swiftly in a more interdisciplinary direction that does not erase the peculiar circumstances of each medium, but that actively looks for areas of overlap and intersection. Today, we see a blending of multiple approaches as well as the continued blurring of lines between media in the streaming space.

Our second challenge was tied to our charge, which was to conduct a historiography of industry studies of US broadcasting. Broadcasting in the United States, unlike many other broadcasting systems around the world, developed within the structure of an often uneasy

DOI: 10.4324/9780429275340-44

public/private compromise. Private corporations would use the public airwaves for their private profit, while the government, primarily through the Federal Communications Commission (FCC), would regulate over-the-air radio and television according to how well they functioned in the public interest. This industrial structure meant that studies of broadcast regulation often fell within national borders, but the practices of the industry (e.g., international format marketplaces) often expanded beyond those same borders. Additionally, to isolate "broadcasting" within the larger pool of media industries research was a daunting prospect. For example, because historical studies of television bridge decades between the classic network era, the cable era, and even the streaming era, we had to grapple not only with what exactly is included in "broadcasting," but with what it means to conduct a "history," and accordingly, whether to consider studies that included or even started with the twenty-first century. Ultimately, we determined that erring on the side of greater inclusion would allow us to develop as big a picture as possible and to determine whether contemporary studies indeed are overtaking historical ones. The intended result is a more detailed understanding of the current state of media industry studies of US broadcasting, the opportunities and challenges faced by researchers, and the possible future directions of the field.

We begin by outlining our own methodology and the means by which we gathered our sample. Then we turn to analyzing that sample with an eye toward the foci, methodologies, and data featured in those works. We use that analysis to identify trends in the scholarship of the last decade, and ultimately, consider what those trends tell us about how that scholarship is valued.

## Our sample

Continuing the work started by Hilmes, we elected to restrict our sample to books, journal articles, and dissertations published between 2009 and 2019. We searched databases available through our institutions' libraries including Academic Search Complete, EBSCOhost, Project Muse, and ProQuest. Using a variety of search terms to capture the largest possible number of industry-focused publications, we ended up with a sample that includes 77 books, 62 journal articles, and 62 dissertations. The practical limits of the publication space we have for this chapter necessitated that we not single out works by title but, rather, elaborate on specific research in general terms. This also allowed us to identify trends across all publications rather than highlighting specific works. In order to sketch both the static and shifting contours of historical industry research, we adopted qualitative and quantitative approaches. Our qualitative analysis of trends and gaps in historical research complemented a quantitative analysis of temporal foci within and across publication types over time. A brief description of how we broke down our sample will indicate the various types of data we wanted to isolate.

While we focused on works that addressed twentieth-century US broadcasting, we included research on the twenty-first century when those works were in explicit conversation with history. This inclusion also allowed us to determine if there is a trend away from historical research within the study of the media industries. After noting the range of decades each study encompassed, we differentiated between the total number of works that focused on a single decade and those that used a particular decade as the starting point for a multi-decade study. For example, while 19 dissertations included the 1970s in their studies, only five of those began their studies in the 1970s, and 14 chose earlier decades as their starting points. Our goal in parsing time spans in this way was to see which periods of time, identified closely with key industrial moments, have garnered the most and least attention, and which remained stable across our sample. We were also interested in whether researchers embraced deep dives into brief spans of time or opted for longer, wide-ranging histories. Finally, by connecting these

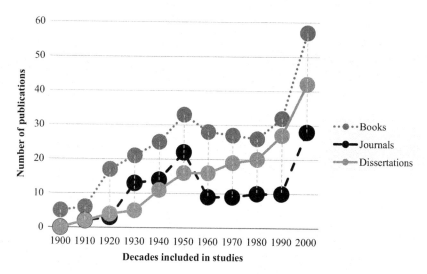

*Figure 38.1*  Decades included in publications (2009–2019).

research trends to their publication dates, we wanted to ascertain whether the field of media industry studies has drifted away from certain industrial moments and toward others.

Taken together, the books, journal articles, and dissertations in our sample showed two primary peaks: the 1950s and 2000s (for our purposes, the 2000s includes the 2010s) (Figure 38.1). Because the majority of research in our sample focused on television rather than radio, the midcentury peak, which relates to the period of television's commercial debut, makes sense. If we move away from the whole and break up the sample according to type of publication, we see some different emphases. Whereas books and journal articles prioritized the 1950s and 2000s over other decades, dissertations highlighted the 1970s, 1980s, 1990s, and 2000s.

When we dig deeper into the type of publication and identify starting points for studies, the 2000s were by far the most common starting point for books: 27 of the 77 books in our sample began in the 2000s (Figure 38.2). Many of these studies commenced in the 2000s as a means to connect contemporary industrial practices to those of the past. The 1920s were the second most common starting point, and the 1950s were not far behind. In both of those cases, we see a more traditional telling of history, starting with the widespread commercial adoption of radio and television, respectively. Less common starting points were the 1910s, 1960s, and 1970s, and in fact, those decades received the least attention overall. Turning to journal articles, the 2000s again were the most recurrent starting point: 20 of the 62 articles began in the 2000s. The 1930s and 1950s were second and third most common. The most infrequent starting points were the 1910s, 1920s, and 1990s, and the 1900s were not represented at all. Our analysis of dissertations once again painted a somewhat different picture. The 1940s, 1950s, and 1960s were key starting points, but the 1990s and 2000s were of greater interest for doctoral researchers, with 18 of the 62 dissertations starting their studies in the 2000s.

Organized by publication date, our sample reveals several trends that have emerged between 2009 and 2019. Overall, while the number of books that included the 1980s in their studies gradually decreased, the number of books that included the 1930s, 1940s, 1950s, 1960s, and 1990s increased. The number of books that included the 2000s showed the most significant increase in our time frame. Early twentieth-century studies appeared less frequently in journals than studies from the latter half of the century. Between 2009 and 2019, the decades that were

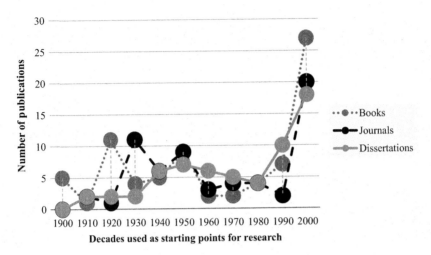

*Figure 38.2*   Starting points for research in publications (2009–2019).

most represented in journal articles were the 1980s, 1990s, and 2000s. However, between 2012 and 2016, and in 2019, articles covered a wider range of decades. For example, in 2014 and 2019, the 1910s, 1920s, and 1930s were represented along with later decades. Dissertations completed in 2014 spanned the 1910s through the 2000s, just as with journal articles published that same year, but in greater numbers. After 2014, however, we see the focus of historical research in dissertations shift primarily to the second half of the twentieth century and the 2000s. The amount of doctoral research focusing on the 1980s, 1990s, and 2000s saw the sharpest rise between 2009 and 2019, with the 1950s also well represented.

When we refine the data further and pair publication dates with each study's starting point, we see that the 1920s were a consistent starting point for books, even appearing more frequently in work published in 2017 and 2018. Few books published after 2014 began with the 1950s, while books with starting points in the 2000s outpaced all others. Journal articles published from 2009 to 2019 showed the 1930s to be a consistent starting point, but in 2015 and 2016, the 1950s and 2000s became more prominent. Between 2009 and 2019, the 1970s and 1980s became relatively common starting points, and by 2019, the 2000s had outpaced all other time periods. After 2014, dissertation starting points shifted to the 1950s and later (although the 1960s saw a decline). Between 2011 and 2016, the 1990s rose sharply.

Ultimately, our analysis revealed that journal articles, perhaps by virtue of their shorter length and tighter emphases, had more specific foci in particular decades or time periods. Books and dissertations, on the other hand, encompassed a broader span of time, and more often than not included some reference to the contemporary as either a framing device or as a point of comparison. Single-decade studies were rare overall, but were more frequent in journal articles and dissertations, and by far, the 1950s was the most frequently studied decade. The shift in emphasis to the latter half of the twentieth century and the early twenty-first century was evident across the entire sample.

## Trends

Tracking the quantitative data about periodization permitted us to take a snapshot of the landscape and assess the status of history in the field, but we also wanted to learn what subjects,

*Figure 38.3*　Recurring terms in publication abstracts (2009–2019).

themes, and concerns researchers had been drawn to over the past decade. Using a word cloud of terms found in the abstracts of books, journal articles, and dissertations immediately illustrates some of the most frequent preoccupations (Figure 38.3). Further, reviewing the content of these works draws out some of the key trends.

## Radio versus TV

For reasons that could range from the relative difficulty of accessing archival materials to the strength of the perceived audience for these studies, the number of television-focused publications outnumbered those attending to radio. Among the books and journal articles in our sample, television outnumbered radio almost four-to-one, and in dissertations, television outnumbered radio almost three-to-one. Although the numbers were small, books covering both media were more numerous than journal articles or dissertations covering both media. We should note that our sample did not include research on the podcasting industry, although our twentieth-century counts would not have been affected by the inclusion. This is potentially a contentious omission, and while we acknowledge that radio and podcasting scholars continue to debate podcasting's status in relation to radio, we wanted to direct our attention to studies of over-the-air and internet radio.

## Local versus national

At a moment when more scholars are thinking globally rather than nationally, the local persists as an area of inquiry and even increased between 2009 and 2019, particularly in books and dissertations. While certainly challenged, local radio and television institutions and professionals in the United States have not been erased by technological change. Consequently, although the number of publications devoted to local entities is small, these works appear consistently throughout our sample. Studies that bring local stations and broadcasting practices into focus underscore not just tensions between the local and the national but strong industrial ties between local broadcasters and national institutions *other* than the networks, such as satellite companies, record labels, and trade associations. Government regulation, a fairly constant presence in industry studies, plays a central role in local histories. Additionally, commercialism and corporate speech are positioned as both foundational for local media and detrimental to the aspirations of some stations.

Microhistories, or histories focusing on specific events or local contexts, offer ways of seeing how sweeping histories gloss over divergences between national and local industry practices. On their own, microhistories pose great challenges to researchers for reasons tied to the precarity of local archives and resources. But they also deliver great rewards, amplifying the stories of often marginalized broadcasters and their communities. When set alongside contemporary work, microhistories can temper discourses of newness or "disruption" by shining light on the conditions of sameness, continuity, and stability evidenced in discrete moments or localities.

## Culture, activism, and representation

Scholars' attention to the local creates room for histories of broadcasting tied to race, ethnicity, nationality, and religion. Studies of local radio, in particular, explore the intersection of industry, culture, and activism. Far from being incidental to these studies, *place* emerges as a marker of historical and sociocultural specificity, and assumes a key role in works that derive from production studies. When tied to cities or regions of the country, interviews with media professionals have allowed scholars to consider multiple articulations of the local apart from and in relation to the national and international communities.

## Programming

Although all of the publications in our sample fall under the industry studies umbrella, they do not cordon themselves off from cultural content and media texts. Select studies situate radio and television programs within frameworks that emphasize connections between industry and creative/cultural expression. In some cases, specific programs serve as case studies that bridge culture and industry, but more often than not, programming offers a path into the study of programming *entities* and trends. For example, works that analyze the practices of entire networks, cable tiers, or streaming platforms invariably engage with programming. Studies of radio and television genres trace not just trends but outliers, as well as commercial and regulatory issues. Programming is also shown to be a point of contention between rival media industries and between broadcasters, audiences, and regulators.

## Labor

The growth of production studies has placed workers at the center of many studies in our sample, and research on industry workers appeared more frequently after 2013. By far, studies of writers appeared more often in our sample of books and articles than any other type of worker in radio and television. Among the many possible reasons for this trend may be the practical fact that the Writers Guild of America maintains a stronger and more accessible archive than other Hollywood unions and guilds. Furthermore, the relatively high-profile position of writers in radio and television may mean that they are covered more frequently, and more prominently, in historical records like industry trade papers. That said, the diversity of workers represented, particularly in books and dissertations, indicates a growing acknowledgment of the many categories of labor supporting the radio and television industries. Within the dissertations we surveyed, we also found work linking labor to identity in the contexts of both nationally distributed television and local radio.

## Streaming

Since so many publications have focused on the 2000s, it is only natural that a great number study the ways radio and television have been challenged and changed by digital technologies. We also see works that use historical case studies as a means to understand contemporary industry phenomena. Since one of the primary challenges of studies of the contemporary media industries is the lack of reliable and accessible evidence, scholars can turn to evidence from comparable historical examples in order to provide insight into more recent industrial periods. Taken together, much of this work will help scholars make sense of how to define radio and television in the streaming era.

## Omissions

Books on the topic of advertising and commercial influence in radio and television appeared consistently in our sample, but their numbers were small. Journal articles had even fewer studies of advertising, with most published before 2015, and dissertations had the fewest. Since advertising has played such a central role in US broadcasting, this hole in the scholarship (also noted by Hilmes' 2009 survey) is noteworthy. Such an omission neglects the historical and contemporary significance of the primary economic engine of radio and television – a significance that includes but is not limited to sponsors' roles in creative production and content regulation. Transnational work is also lagging, although it has experienced a rise since 2016. Research by US scholars on links between the US broadcasting industry and the Latin American and UK industries has been relatively robust, but there remains a need for more work on transnational and international media industries. Such studies offer students and researchers pathways into industry paradigms and historical narratives that reveal larger patterns of continuity and change, and which have the potential to expose our own assumptions by revealing what we often take for granted as natural or unquestioned industry practice.

Additionally, while the regulatory, technological, and economic structures of broadcasting have in some ways confined the study of broadcasting to national borders, in the increasingly digital media industries, questions related to the flow of media texts and industries around the world become increasingly urgent. Perhaps as a result, research on streaming platforms delves into the transnational much more than research on traditional broadcasting. We are cognizant of the challenge of conducting transnational research for scholars who do not have access for whatever reason – including the lack of institutional support – to the broadcasting archives, systems, products, workers, and audiences of other nations, but, as media industries, texts, and audiences increasingly move beyond and between national borders, this is another significant area of the field that has been underexplored.

## The sources and methods of historical media industry research

Although media studies is a field with a distinct intellectual history, established professional organizations, and many well-regarded journals, the research conducted in the field of media industry studies draws from several disciplines. The media industries themselves are composed of multiple interests and agents, which means that industry researchers access knowledge produced by fields tied to business, law, and labor in addition to culture. Our survey of the works published over the last decade confirms that media industry researchers are uniquely positioned to employ multiple methods and a diverse array of sources. Studies in our sample that probe corporate practices and legal or regulatory maneuvers rely on textual documents from private and public archives. Researchers typically mine the wealth of trade magazines such as *Broadcasting* (1931–2002) and *Variety* (1933–) that are housed in libraries and archives around the United States and are digitized for online access by web resources like the Media History Digital Library. The open accessibility of websites like worldhistory.com and archive. org has been a boon to researchers who lack the institutional support to track down documents in physical libraries or archives. Increased digital access to historical archives can expand the range of topics available for researchers and facilitate the study of transnational broadcasting for scholars around the globe.

The dynamic digital media landscape has energized industry research, and it has also engendered the proliferation of new types of primary sources. Alongside the use of familiar archival print materials such as memos, letters, and reports, online sources such as blogs, tweets, and videos provided the researchers in our sample insight into audiences and creatives, alike. Of course, these sources inform research that is more contemporary in its focus, but research capturing these potentially ephemeral bits of information will be invaluable to forthcoming historical work. Interviews with living media professionals were one popular method in our sample, but archived oral histories and transcripts from legal trials offered researchers greater access to early periods of broadcasting, helping to ensure that work in industry studies is not beholden to the living, or restricted to the contemporary moment.

Access to early radio and television programming remains a challenge for broadcast historians, and perhaps as a result, few works in our sample explored early programming. Despite the tremendous efforts undertaken by archivists, activists, and scholars to preserve early and non-network broadcast media, the costliness of preservation and storage remains daunting. In all cases, the precarity of archives and access to historical evidence stands between researchers and their objects of study. As much as scholars and audiences might be interested in certain historical topics, areas of exploration will remain closed if no evidence is available. On the other hand, once scholars have access to archives, studies of those related topics become possible. While the areas and time periods covered in the publications we surveyed doubtless depended a great deal on the interests of scholars and the preferences of academic advisors and editors, the availability and accessibility of historical evidence also plays a significant role in the work undertaken.

## Reflections on our research challenges

As we reflect on the challenges faced by scholars who do these histories, we offer as case studies assessments of our own research and roadblocks.

**Jennifer**: Since making sense of contemporary media industries can be a challenge given the lack of access researchers have to documents or to gaining insights into behind-the-scenes processes that are not filtered through PR, my work has used historical media industry studies to understand contemporary phenomena. It has relied on archives created by virtue of the forced corporate disclosures that have resulted from legal action. Those materials have included transcripts from trials; internal corporate memos and minutes from meetings; union and guild newsletters; transcripts from Congressional hearings; internal memos from governmental entities such as the Department of Justice and the FCC; and correspondence submitted to government regulators in response to proposed legislation and ongoing legal cases. Even with a relative abundance of archival materials available, by the time I finished my most recent book project, *Broadcasting Hollywood*, I discovered that the National Archives had disposed of some of the case files from the 1940s and 1950s that I had used for my research. They, much like corporate entities, face the restrictions of physical, and even digital, space, and have to make decisions about what to keep based on their own perceptions of what is "valuable" at any given time. If the work produced by scholars is largely dependent on the evidence that can be found to support an argument, then what appears "valuable" is often a reflection not of real value, but of existence and access.

**Deborah**: I have joked from time to time that my research interests veer toward the "boring," that is, the industry practices that become routinized. But it is in this routinization that we see patterns of actions and reactions to things like scandals, technological innovations, and audience feedback. Studying routines can help us explain tactics and strategies, both historical and contemporary. My historical work tends, therefore, to focus on networks of private, corporate, and governmental actors that dwell on the margins of television but that have outsized influence on television. I envision this work as "micro" because it dives into a moment, a fuss, a failure, an outburst, a reaction – slices of a much longer history that our sample shows is not completely written. Unfortunately, some of my work relies on the same sources repeatedly mined by scholars because of their accessibility and, ultimately, because particular media companies have allowed their materials to live in archives. Even more unfortunately, as Porst points out, even those records are incomplete, having been pruned for reasons of acceptability or storage space. Fortunately, when one researches figures on the margins, one can wander into archived papers that are not accessed as frequently, if at all. As I benefit from the job that archivists do, I am compelled to think about how the histories I write can be woven into not only longer histories yet to come, but into the classroom. If they are not taught, are they valuable?

## On value to the field

Much of the responsibility for what work is accepted and published lies with faculty advisors, journal editors, peer reviewers, and academic presses. The particular interests of those influential persons have as much, if not more, to do with the types of work we see here than anything else, raising questions about what is valued in the field, how it is valued, and why. These systems of publication function as active, but unacknowledged, gatekeeping processes for the production of historical knowledge. The next phase in this project might then be a full accounting of academic family trees charting the research of advisors, their students, and their students' students to identify whether or not faculty engender within their students' certain foci, or if, continuing with the tree metaphor, they encourage their students to branch out. Such a project would also study which scholars assume editorial positions at academic journals, and what work they accept and reject. Finally, the decisions of editors at academic presses rely on what peer reviewers value and on what sells or not, so we can learn much from book sales and their fluctuations over time.

We acknowledge that research is limited by multiple factors, edited by a variety of hands, and influenced by many intellectual biases before it can become published work. The pressure to publish is not the exclusive domain of tenure-track and tenured individuals. Students and un/under-employed scholars experience the same pressure since the competition for full-time jobs, exacerbated by the preference of universities for part-time labor, has become fiercer. Our discussion of value, then, must turn to the topic of the academic job market. We must ask how historical industry research translates into peer recognition that further converts into full-time employment (or even promotion) for scholars in academia or in alt-academic jobs. To answer that, we have to determine which research is considered valuable by university presses, because they are the standard for university hiring and promotion. In our sample of 62 dissertations, as of 2019 we found that few had been published as monographs. Is this a result of the crisis in academic labor and the fact that graduates must spend years in adjunct and lecturer positions where heavy teaching loads make it difficult to swiftly translate a dissertation into a book? Or are the dissertation topics just not attractive to academic publishers? This situation brings to the fore questions about value, the diminished marketability of historical knowledge, and constraints on the production of that knowledge as a result of its devaluation.

For example, when considering local and microhistories in the context of value to the field, we must also ask if this type of research pushes back against the grander explanatory powers of large-scale studies, or if it asks to be folded into the larger histories. It is possible that these studies may get lost when (1) our data shows that industry research is increasingly grounded in the twenty-first century; (2) these presentist tendencies frame change in the media landscape and the pace of change as national and global issues; and (3) these discourses of change escort us away from studies of broadcasting, its histories, and the patterns and deviations that form those histories. Furthermore, we wonder how valuable this work appears to university presses. If the researcher is lucky enough to get their work published, will academics want, or be able, to proactively integrate the finished work into the longer histories of radio and television in their own classes?

Other metrics broaden our understanding of the construction of value. For example, which work receives acclaim in the form of awards recognition? A survey of some of the major awards in the field given over the last decade shows that organizations such as the Society for Cinema and Media Studies (SCMS), the International Communication Association (ICA), the International Association for Media and History (IAMHIST), and the Theatre Library Association (TLA), to name a few, have offered a surprisingly low number of awards to publications that fit our working definition of industry studies of US broadcasting. Many awards are given to works that focus on film, that utilize a more cultural or text-based analytical framework, or that study new forms of digital media. We also see an increasing recognition of research on all forms of media that is global or transnational in scope. This raises questions about the relative value of media industry studies and broadcasting in the larger field of media studies, and about whether the lack of awards recognition for these works points to a continuing bias against broadcasting in favor of the more prestigious medium of film, and against industry studies in favor of studies of art, theory, and culture.

For many scholars facing committees that will make hiring and promotion decisions, fund grant proposals, and even grant access to interviews and archival materials, value is often contextualized as impact in the field. As our survey has demonstrated, a great deal of research on the US broadcasting industries has been completed and published over the last decade. However, if a relatively small number of dissertations are published as books, and if an even smaller number are gaining awards recognition, what does it mean to have an impact? For those scholars needing to quantify their impact beyond citation numbers, how can we as a subsection of the field of media studies develop a stronger presence and impact?

## Challenges and opportunities for future research

We have found that the gaps Hilmes identified in her 2009 chapter remain. In addition to the need for work on the commercial influence of advertising on broadcasting, or on global and transnational broadcasting, our sample also reveals the need for more work on independent television production companies, the Hollywood studios as producers for television, comprehensive histories of the networks and their leading figures, and television's historical roots in radio – subjects that have steered the industry in consequential ways but whose histories have not received extensive critical examination beyond early, key pieces of research. Hilmes (2009: 24) also catalogued "ancillary industries that form a part of the media industry productive matrix" that deserve study, including:

> ratings and market research companies, the trade press, awards organizations, professional associations, craft unions, Congress, and the multitude of social and political organizations that have made the media part of their operations. These include political parties, parents and teachers groups, lobbyists, athletic associations, and religious organizations.

Although great strides have been made since Hilmes' intervention, our snapshot of the past decade shows that much historical work on US broadcasting remains to be done. This chapter shows that media industry researchers have indeed begun to shift their gaze to the twenty-first century at the expense of the early twentieth century, in particular. But as we urge our students and colleagues to fill apparent gaps, we should be mindful of the precarity of the historical archive and continue the struggle to preserve those records where possible. Additionally, the many challenges of academic publishing and the structures of academic labor have real consequences for the research that is conducted and ultimately published. Those who are able to should insist that their institutions recognize those challenges and push for positive change. We should remain hopeful that new generations of scholars, and the research opportunities made possible by digital technologies, will re-energize research on US broadcasting history within the paradigms established by media industry studies.

## Acknowledgment

The authors are grateful for the research assistance provided by Peter Arne Johnson and Anna Camp.

## Reference

Hilmes, M. (2009) "Nailing Mercury: The Problem of Media Industry Historiography," in J Holt and A. Perren (eds.), *Media Industries: History, Theory, and Method*, Malden, MA: Wiley-Blackwell, 21–33.

# 39

# POLICY STUDIES AND THE CASE FOR PLURALITY

*Jennifer Holt and Steven Secular*

We ask many questions in the course of our research, but the answers will ultimately depend on our method. It is the fundamental tool we use to define our object of study, formulate a vision for the project and its intervention, and locate evidence to support and contextualize our argument. In media industry studies, as in any field, there are myriad methodological challenges and issues that arise, as our choices ultimately privilege certain forms of knowledge at the expense of others. As a result, the list of considerations when conducting industry research includes many related to method. For example, when conducting first-person interviews, how does one sift through corporate spin and public relations, and reconcile contradictory perspectives and competing views of events? What are the most productive sources for our work and how do we go about identifying and finding them, particularly when so many primary materials are inaccessible to researchers? Which methods should be prioritized when doing interdisciplinary research and/or trying to write for scholars in multiple fields of study?

This question of interdisciplinarity has been especially relevant to the role of method in policy research. Manuel Puppis and Hilde Van den Bulck (2019: 6) have written that media policy "can be conceptualized as 'the broader field in which competing ideas and assumptions about the desirable structure, conduct, and performance of media systems circulate.'" In this definition, they are referencing Des Freedman (2008), who has further argued that policy is more than just an output, but it is also about the dynamic *processes* involved in arriving at such outputs, as well as the "interaction between different *actors*, the *institutional structures* within which they work and the *objectives* that they pursue" (original emphasis, p. 13). Historically, debating and defining such dimensions of policy as "desirable structure, conduct, and performance" has been the sole province of social scientists and those with law degrees. However, policy analysis demands much greater methodological interdisciplinarity in order to access its true spectrum of cultural concerns and stakes, and articulate insights that promote the best possible objectives. Policy scholarship has undoubtedly been enhanced by its engagement with media industry studies and the largely qualitative, often humanistic, lines of inquiry embodied by this field. This orientation has produced some of the most substantive, impactful work on policy advocacy and activist interventions (Perlman 2016; Lentz and Perlman 2016); public values in media policy and governance (Van Dijck, Poell, and de Waal 2018; Napoli 2019); and the longue durée of these histories (Pickard 2019: Igo 2018). Still, despite the fact that media policy affects so much of our daily life, our access to information, and our freedoms of expression,

DOI: 10.4324/9780429275340-45

it has not traditionally been conceptualized as central to humanities-driven scholarship and research, or vice versa.

This is a crucial shift for the discipline of media industry studies to make because, after all, media regulation cannot be simply about maintaining market competition from an economic or legal perspective. It must also be about preserving public interest values as defined by a wide variety of constituents, mitigating against unhealthy levels of consolidation and control in the news and entertainment industries, as well as safeguarding the rights to privacy and freedom from surveillance in the digital era. It must also be about ensuring broadband access for all communities, particularly the rural and underserved, and protecting the freedom of speech and of the press that is so essential for a functioning democracy. As such, media policy in democratic societies must be designed and constantly adapted to protect these values in changing technological and cultural landscapes. Articulating these stakes (among many others) is precisely what is necessary to preserve the core values of an independent media system. Such work requires a broad and eclectic methodology to illuminate how policies around media technologies, distribution, content, and industry behavior are evolving in ways that are not always immediately obvious or beneficial to most citizens. While many of the examples that follow are drawn from the US context, they illustrate methodological questions and approaches that are relevant to policy studies as a whole.

One of the most recent media policy battles in the United States – that over the preservation or eradication of net neutrality – is a prime example of why an interdisciplinary method is so crucial for media industry researchers. Net neutrality is the concept that all traffic moving through Internet pipelines should be treated equally and delivered with the exact same speed, somewhat akin to telephone calls. It is more than simply extracting more failed "promises" from Internet Service Providers (ISPs) that they will not throttle traffic and/or slow down Internet speeds for users who don't have "paid prioritization," or give faster service at a higher price for those who do. Installing this principle as law is also about protecting rural users, preserving affordable access to the Internet for all, and reducing the power of the middlemen (the heavily consolidated, profit-driven ISPs) to determine policy outcomes. It is also about how such battles are discursively framed, what evidence is utilized in the policy process, how users would be affected, and what interests ultimately become prioritized by policymakers. As Strover, Whitacre, Rhinesmith, and Schrubbe (2020) have demonstrated, at the heart of this issue is broadband access, and the social, economic, material, and environmental limitations on that access that disproportionately affect rural communities. Such research that combines an engagement with focus groups, literature on materiality and inclusion, and studies of broadband deployment and adoption is uniquely well-suited to investigate the "lived conditions of connectivity" while also addressing "meaningful routes toward digital inclusion" (p. 245) – critical dynamics that most net neutrality discussions ignore.

Unfortunately, as Becky Lentz (2009) has noted, the "sausage factory of policymaking" has developed the reputation for being "inherently boring" and most citizens are unaware of and uninvolved in such debates about one of the most important resources in contemporary life. Moreover, as talk show host John Oliver noted in his 2014 clarion call to save net neutrality, those in power (in this case, the cable and telecommunications companies) have figured out the great truth about America: "If you want to do something evil, put it inside something boring." It has become clear that rescuing the critical values of our media from the corporatized well of "evil and boring" requires a much more eclectic methodology than turning only to the economists and lawyers to determine the path forward. Along with data, we also need the methods of the humanists, the activists, the theorists, and the participation of a fully engaged citizenry to reclaim public values long forgotten in media policy.

Many policy scholars have called for shifting the methodological paradigm to a more inter-disciplinary one. One of the main reasons for this has been to more substantively interrogate the connections between media policy and various forms of power. Victor Pickard (2013b: 405), for one, has written about the dominant paradigm of the "media effects" methodological trad-ition that favored scientific approaches to media and "arguably has helped depoliticize media scholarship by relegating larger questions about ideology and power to the field's intellec-tual margins." Pickard concludes that "pluralistic approaches to media studies are necessary to encourage diverse conceptualizations of power" (p. 410). He built in part on the work of Herbert Schiller (1991: 137, 156), who developed a similar argument about the tragic flaw of effects research and methods as absolving those in power from accountability and removing the possibility of any structural critique. Christopher Ali and Manuel Puppis (2018: 271) have also called for a holistic approach to interrogating and theorizing media power, in order to fill the "significant gap [that] exists between the theoretical and empirical work being conducted under the auspices of media policy." They propose an original framework that views com-munication as a resource in and of itself which exposes the various "embedded dynamics of bias, silence, and capture within the policymaking process" (p. 286). Such biases, silences, and "captured" regulatory agents with inherent conflicts of interest (such as Ajit Pai, the current Chairman of the Federal Communications Commission (FCC) and a former lawyer for the telecommunications conglomerate Verizon) have long served to skew policy priorities in favor of corporations, to the detriment of the public.

Luzhou Li (2020: 2–3) has recently addressed silences in policymaking as a function of method, and in particular the result of framing issues "to the exclusion of others" as various interest groups and their concerns compete for visibility, resulting in "outcomes that are seen and those that are not." This is most commonly a result of the "festishizing of 'scien-tific' data" seen in policy circles that Freedman (2006: 921) has characterized as yet another means of "marginalizing the public from the public policy process and safeguarding it for the economists, lawyers and executives" who are the usual suspects when it comes to furnishing information for policymakers. This is a well-established habit in the United States, where defaulting to social-scientific methods and modes of thinking in policymaking has created a certain instrumentalist logic that prizes marketing research and quantified intelligence at the expense of values such as diversity, localism, and "the public interest" (Freedman 2006: 918). Thus, a more expansive methodology not only moves beyond the unrealistic faith in numbers and data as "objective" or "apolitical" but also allows for perspectives and voices previously silenced to be heard.

Accordingly, it is imperative to think beyond the unproductive quantitative and qualitative binary, and instead embrace an approach to answering one's research questions that allows for a more informed critique of policy's structural and cultural values. This necessitates a varied methodology that can incorporate, for example, historical perspectives, court documents, discourse analysis, and/or ethnographic research, or some combination thereof. Historical research and discursive inquiry frequently utilize similar materials, yet they reveal different insights into the policy process and evolution of the law in relation to industry studies. In places where the official record ends, moreover, interviews and ethnography may become crucial to understanding the full scope of regulatory decision-making. Deviating from "official" accounts and investigating "alternative" or less visible histories, as Allison Perlman (2016: 7) has done in her formative study of media advocacy, for example, also allows for a more comprehensive understanding of policy as not only a formalized, top-down process, but as "the result of a clash of interests, not of dispassionate reasoning." By drawing from a multiplicity of sources and methods, then, researchers are best positioned to recognize and articulate the range of political, sociocultural, economic, and technological concerns that are affected by policy and identify their very human costs and benefits.

Pickard (2019: 515) has highlighted historical research, in particular, as "an effective means by which to denaturalize present-day relationships, recover forgotten lessons and alternatives, and conduct well-informed policy interventions." Historical methods can ground policy developments in a series of clear human actions and decisions, whether they originate in a courtroom, a government office, or a corporate boardroom. Aaron Perzanowski and Jason Schultz (2016) follow this strategy in their discussion of digital media "property" and its own-ership, building out a timeline of foundational court decisions that highlight key aspects of its regulation as it evolved over time. In order to illustrate the emergence of digital rights man-agement (DRM), for instance, they cite and explain the series of legal battles beginning in 1984 that were waged against Sony over the VCR as a "piracy machine"; a 1992 case that pitted video game company Sega against Accolade, a third party developer that was creating unlicensed games for Sega's Genesis console; and a 1999 lawsuit brought by RealNetworks against Streambox, which translated DRM into an era of streaming media (pp. 126–131). They also emphasize the utility of primary documents such as contracts, Terms of Service (TOS), and End-User License Agreements (EULAs) in their chronicle.

Such lessons from the past, combined with materials from the present, allow historical scholars to highlight the details of a policy's origin and provide context for understanding its long-term impact, while also illuminating important truths about power in the current moment. Some scholars, such as Perzanowksi and Schultz, rely more on the judiciary and specific case law for this work. Others, such as Ithiel de Sola Pool and Robert Britt Horwitz, have focused more on issues and materials of legislation and governance. De Sola Pool, for example, charts the evolution of electronic communication leading up to and out of the Radio Acts of 1912 and 1927 and the Communications Act of 1934, as well as the "rejected options" of alternate legislative possibilities. De Sola Pool (1983: 109, 136) uses this history to address contempor-aneous "fears about the future of free expression" and provide greater context for "the erosion of traditional freedoms" that can result from the regulation of emerging media technologies (p. 4). Horwitz, too, identifies that a "historically rooted theory of regulation" is essential to maintaining "an adequate understanding" of policy issues (1989: 8–9). As a result, he charts the "mosaic of forces" that led to the deregulation of telecommunications by the close of the 1980s, building a history of government action that "accounts both for the genesis of agencies and for actual agency operations." In providing a context for specific judicial and/or legislative decisions over time, historical research serves to highlight the complicated arc of regulatory development, the cascading effect of one case on future cases, the alternative legal paths that once seemed possible, and the power relations between legal institutions and the public.

Research materials themselves often determine the methodological path of one's research, yielding particular and contingent truths. As such, relying upon congressional hearings, legis-lation, and agency reports usually leads to policy analysis highlighting the top-down mechanics of governance and regulation, while court documents, transcripts, and case law often provide insights into the judicial process, the legal strategies and actions of key participants, and the details of a case's "what," "how," and "why." Christopher M. Fairman (2009) and Lawrence Lessig (2004), for example, cite a wide range of court documents in order to build a histor-ical arc of a policy's development. Fairman (2009) in particular uses court transcripts to build out full scenes with dialogue relating to the use of the word "fuck" and its many derivatives. This method of citing the documents in full best serves his legal and cultural argument about the often absurd history of regulating "offensive" speech and "word taboos," and their critical connections to politics, censorship, and the First Amendment.

Lessig (2004: 7) employs a similar narrative-oriented approach, one that he describes as "not the usual method of an academic," since it begins with "a collection of stories that set a context" for issues of policy, rather than relying first on complex theories or legal references. Lessing opens *Free Culture*, for example, "on a windy North Carolina beach" with the Wright brothers, in order to frame a discussion of property ownership and vertical space, before jumping ahead to a federal case in 1945 "when North Carolina farmers Thomas Lee and Tinie Causby started losing chickens because of low-flying military aircraft (the terrified chickens apparently flew into the barn walls and died)" (pp. 1–2). Though the planes never touched the ground, Lessig explains, the Causbys sued the government for trespassing on their land; ultimately, the Supreme Court ruled that the airways were public and not private, a landmark decision in conceptions of property. For policy decisions that are not always immediately felt or understood by the very citizens most affected, colorful and descriptive scenes such as those bemoaning terrorized chickens can be highly valuable tools for animating law and policy, and an excellent method to engage readers and researchers less familiar with technical language. Court documents, therefore, are full of life for the policy scholar – they are texts that speak far more loudly and nuanced than the law itself. They reveal a wealth of details about the process of policymaking, as well as its alternate paths, roads not taken, and future legal possibilities.

While historical approaches, such as those noted above, seek to make legal concepts as accessible as possible by drawing on connections between past and present, some scholars have opted to delve deeper into the specific language of policy. Practitioners of *discourse analysis* begin by narrowing the focus to the text of legislative, judicial, or other primary documents, rather than by staging scenes or building a chronological narrative. As articulated by Frank Fischer and John Forester (1993: 6), it is a methodological project that asks "not only *what* an analysis claims but when it does, to whom, in what language and style, invoking what loyalties, and appealing to what threats and dangers." In another notable example, Thomas Streeter (1996: 15) describes the law as a "highly symbolic, interpretive activity; its raw materials are documents, rhetoric, and rituals." He calls attention to the "standard political and legal vocabulary" and how meanings have "shifted dramatically" over time (p. 32) in order to reveal the concurrent cultural politics bearing down on such definitions. Sandra Braman (2004:154) has also addressed how powerful and political such discourse around the identification of policy areas and concerns are; as she explains, "it determines who participates in decision-making, the rhetorical frames and operational definitions applied, the analytical techniques and modes of argument used, and the resources – and goals – considered pertinent." Discourse analysis thus examines policy vocabulary and its historical changes in order to uncover the evolving politics and ideologies embedded within the text itself.

Another method for obtaining knowledge of the legal and policymaking process is through interviews. In a study of film and television writers, Miranda Banks (2014: 548) explains the value of oral history as effectively allowing scholars to "verify" information "garnered from historical records, trade presses and other personal histories," "record how writers perceived particular events in the evolution of their profession," and "see shifts or trends in how writers define or even theorize their own work and position within the media industries" over the course of numerous interviews. These advantages are also true for the study of media policy, as interviews with experts, policymakers, and government officials can verify, record, and provide insights into a profession that is similarly in a never-ending state of change. Jennifer Holt (2016), for instance, emphasized the interpersonal relationships that can influence policy fights and decisions in an interview with Gene Kimmelman, the president and CEO of the nonprofit public interest group Public Knowledge. Kimmelman discusses his experience working with multiple FCC chairmen, for example, and how it is ultimately all about people. What are they really like? Not just their ideology or their philosophy, but also what kind of leaders they are: Will they get out front and lead? Are they consensus builders? Do they relish conflict and take it on because they believe in something or are they scared to death of conflict?

*cited in Holt 2016: 5806*

Such interviews impart scholars with a valuable perspective for understanding the mechanics of the policymaking process, providing a window into conversations that are entirely left out of any paper records or documents.

Susan Crawford (2013) also draws on conversations with executives, experts, and government officials in her chronicle of the 2011 Comcast–NBC merger and analysis of telecommunications monopolies in the United States. For example, she quotes one media executive calling the FCC's overall review process for communications industry mergers "just awful," noting "it will matter who is in the room," while government employees are similarly invoked describing the Comcast–NBCU merger, in particular, to Crawford as "the most intense review the FCC had ever run for a single transaction" (pp. 208, 213). Such interviews can reveal the mindset of personal and private experiences and conflicting perspectives on the same event; they can also provide colorful details that enliven regulatory processes and decisions while also accounting for human agency and the critical, yet often overlooked, interpersonal dimension of policymaking.

Interviews are often most valuable for their ability to capture knowledge that is not maintained in the official record. Tejaswini Ganti (2014: 17) has also cited the value of ethnography, which extends beyond interviews alone to include sustained participant observation, providing "an important contextual frame with which to understand media producers' self-representations and discourses about their practice." Ganti describes ethnography, moreover, as crucial for a context such as the Hindi film industry, which is "highly decentralized" and "does not render its structure or organization transparent" (p. 17). While the formal structure of the legal and policymaking system is somewhat more apparent, a great deal of decision-making occurs behind closed doors and away from the eyes and ears of the public. Where transcripts are scarce or unavailable, interviews become necessary to understand the full nature of the events and agents of change involved.

There are substantial benefits, therefore, to conducting policy research from outside the strictures of any one academic discipline, turning instead to a range of sources and methodologies. John McMurria (2009: 127) has described four distinct formal approaches to media regulation: legal liberalism, which is "principally focused on assessing regulation through First Amendment jurisprudence"; an institutional approach, which "considers the politics and everyday decision-making procedures within legal and regulatory institutions"; political economy, which "considers ownership structures and the capitalist ideologies that sustain them"; and lastly, a critical cultural citizen approach, which considers the role of regulation and the law in relation to consumer-oriented citizenship. The core issues reflected in and accessed through these perspectives – free expression, the politicization of the regulatory process, neoliberalism, and the protection of the public interest – offer a vivid argument for the value accrued from a varied and interdisciplinary approach to studying policy.

As C. Edwin Baker (2002: 6) has noted,

different methodologies are essentially different languages. Although the same question can be approached and the same "best" answer can often be reached using different languages, the different languages vary in their ability to shed light ... Each is a tool and should be sued to the extent it is useful; while it makes some things clearer, it is likely to obscure other important matters.

Moreover, Des Freedman (2019: 635) has argued that "methods are neither innocent nor self-sufficient and that what animates the methodological choices of academics are their chosen theoretical frameworks and preferred political commitments, in particular their willingness to press for change or to justify the status quo." Our materials and our methods are thus also our politics.

By utilizing historical, discursive, and ethnographic methods, as well as a broad range of materials and sources, scholars are able to best develop the strengths of each individual approach and overcome its weaknesses. *Primary texts*, such as court documents, case law, and congressional reports, are a crucial foundation for policy research, but can sometimes exclude important details that occur outside of the official record. *Interviews* can provide valuable perspectives that extend beyond the page, but they also necessarily include conflicting subjectivities and accounts. *Discourse analysis* offers a rich and nuanced understanding of the language of policy definitions, case law, and legislative materials, but can be enhanced by the chronology and context provided by *historical research*. While an historical method can be useful in making connections between policy's past and present, it also benefits from the animated nature of personal testimony, in order to make the events and details feel even more vital to the widest possible audience. A pluralistic approach to policy studies allows scholars to apply knowledge generated from a host of intellectual traditions to our objects of study, which in turn generates research that is itself is more complex and widely resonant. By embracing concepts and perspectives from across disciplinary boundaries and drawing upon all of the methodological tools at one's disposal, policy and its rich teachings can become accessible and meaningful for our scholarly community and, ideally, for our fellow citizens alike.

# References

Ali, C. (2017) *Media Localism: The Policies of Place*, Urbana, IL: University of Illinois Press.

Ali, C and Puppis, M. (2018) "When the Watchdog Neither Barks Nor Bites: Communication as a Power Resource in Media Policy and Regulation," *Communication Theory*, 28 (3): 270–291.

Baker, C. E. (2002) *Media, Markets, and Democracy*, Cambridge: Cambridge University Press.

Banks, M. J. (2014) "Oral History and Media Industries: Theorizing the Personal in Production History," *Cultural Studies*, 28 (4): 545–560.

Braman, S. (2004) "Where Has Media Policy Gone? Defining the Field in the Twenty-First Century," *Communication Law and Policy*, 9 (2): 153–182.

Crawford, S. (2013) *Captive Audience: The Telecom Industry and Monopoly Power in the New Gilded Age*, New Haven, CT: Yale University Press.

De Sola Pool, I. (1983) *Technologies of Freedom: On Free Speech in an Electronic Age*, Cambridge, MA: Harvard University Press.

Fairman, C. M. (2009) *Fuck: Word Taboo and Protecting Our First Amendment Liberties*, Naperville, IL: Sphinx Publishing.

Fischer, F and Forester, J. (eds) (1993) *The Argumentative Turn in Policy Analysis and Planning*, Durham, NC: Duke University Press.

Freedman, D. (2006) "Dynamics of Power in Contemporary Media Policy-Making," *Media, Culture and Society*, 28 (6): 907–923.

Freedman, D. (2008) *The Politics of Media Policy*, Cambridge: Polity Press.

Freedman, D. (2019) "Media Policy Activism," in H. Van den Bulck, M. Puppis, K. Donders, and L. Van Audenhove (eds), *The Palgrave Handbook of Methods for Media Policy Research*, Cham: Palgrave Macmillan, 627–640.

Ganti, T. (2014) "The Value of Ethnography," *Media Industries*, 1 (1): 16–20.

Holt, J. (2016) "Net Neutrality and the Public Interest: An Interview with Gene Kimmelman, President and CEO of Public Knowledge," *International Journal of Communication*, 10: 5795–5810.

Horwitz, R. B. (1989) *The Irony of Regulatory Reform: The Deregulation of American Telecommunications*, New York: Oxford University Press.

Igo, S. (2018) *The Known Citizen*, Cambridge, MA: Harvard University Press.

Lentz, B. (2009) "Regulation is Boring," *Flow*, October 30, available at www.flowjournal.org/2009/10/regulation-is-boringbecky-lentz-mcgill-university/ (accessed November 6, 2020).

Lentz, B. and Perlman, A. (2016) "Net Neutrality: Working for Internet Freedoms: Network Neutrality in the United States and the Labors of Policy Advocacy – Introduction," *International Journal of Communication*, 10: 5771–5778.

Lessig, L. (2004) *Free Culture: How Big Media Uses Technology and the Law to Lock Down Culture and Control Creativity*, New York: Penguin.

Li, Luzhou (2020) "How to Think about Media Policy Silence," *Media, Culture and Society*, available at https://journals.sagepub.com/doi/abs/10.1177/0163443720948004?journalCode=mcsa (December 4, 2020).

McMurria, J. (2009) "Regulation and the Law: A Critical Cultural Citizenship Approach," in J. Holt and A. Perren (eds), *Media Industries: History, Theory, and Method*, Malden, MA: Blackwell, 171–183.

Napoli, P. M. (2019) *Social Media and the Public Interest*, New York: Columbia University Press.

Perlman, Allison (2016) *Public Interests*, New Brunswick, NJ: Rutgers University Press.

Perzanowski, A. and Schultz, J. (2016) *The End of Ownership: Personal Property in the Digital Economy*, Cambridge, MA: MIT Press.

Pickard, V. (2013a) *America's Battle for Media Democracy*, New York: Cambridge University Press.

Pickard, V. (2013b) "Mending the Gaps: Connecting Media Policy and Media Studies," in K. Gates (ed), *Media Studies Futures*, London: Blackwell, 404–421.

Pickard, V. (2019) "Historical Analysis," in H. Van den Bulck, M. Puppis, K. Donders, and L. Van Audenhove (eds), *The Palgrave Handbook of Methods for Media Policy Research*, Cham: Palgrave Macmillan, 509–517.

Puppis, M. and Van den Bulck, H. (eds) (2019) "Introduction: Media Policy and Media Policy Research," H. Van den Bulck, M. Puppis, K. Donders, and L. Van Audenhove (eds), *The Palgrave Handbook of Methods for Media Policy Research*, Cham: Palgrave Macmillan, 3–22.

Schiller, H. (1991) *Culture, Inc*, New York: Oxford University Press.

Streeter, T. (1996) *Selling the Air: A Critique of the Policy of Commercial Broadcasting in the United States*, Chicago, IL: University of Chicago Press.

Strover, S., Whitacre, B., Rhinesmith, C., and Schrubbe, A. (2020) "The Digital Inclusion Role of Rural Libraries: Social Inequalities Through Space and Place," *Media, Culture and Society*, 42 (2): 242–259.

Van Dijck, J. Poell, T., and de Waal, M. (2018) *The Platform Society*, New York: Oxford University Press.

# 40

# MEDIA ECONOMICS AND MANAGEMENT AS OPTIMIZATION RESEARCH

## Toward a shared methodology

*M. Bjørn von Rimscha*

Media management research comes in two varieties that each have different aims and tools. One represents best practice research on the level of the firm. The underlying generic question in this context is usually how to make the organization more efficient and gain competitive advantage over competitors. This does not mean the research is necessarily only applied and atheoretical, but it usually does not account for the potential consequences of managerial actions beyond the boundaries of the firm. By and large, this kind of research can be realized using the tools from operational and strategic management science. The second variety considers exactly those societal effects beyond purely economic measures within the firm or industry. This is challenging in at least two ways. For one, it is difficult to pin down the economic performance of cultural activities such as media, and second, "Mainstream economic theories and assumptions do not always provide a made-to-measure framework for understanding and modelling cultural activities" (Doyle 2010: 248).

Both varieties of media management research have one thing in common: the ultimate aim is usually optimization; however, the scope and object of optimization differs as well as the measurability. In the following, I will describe the two strands of research, each with its typical research objects and methodological toolbox using examples from the literature. I will then point out how they differ and to what extent we might even trace the different results back to different methods used in different research contexts. Building from there, the chapter ends with a plea for research that recognizes the value of both traditions and tries to integrate the perspectives by using a more diverse methodological toolbox.

## Optimization for profit

Küng states that optimization in the media industry "requires critical mass and tight coordination" (2007: 34). This statement clearly illustrates an understanding of media management as an operational challenge: those who can reap the benefits of economies of scale and scope will be most profitable – that is as long as they solve the issue about how to deal with creativity. From this perspective, the objective of media management is to maximize profit. The effects of

458

DOI: 10.4324/9780429275340-46

media industries on society are by and large ignored, and the communality between different media sectors is only seen in "activities of content generation and the presence of regulation" (Küng 2007: 24). Thus, the job of media management scholars would simply be to identify which management theory – and corresponding method – would best address the respective challenges at hand for media managers.

Accordingly, several researchers simply apply methods developed for the marketing of fast-moving consumer goods to media goods. Kanuri, Thorson, and Mantrala (2014), for example, conducted a choice-based conjoint analysis to measure the content preferences of newspaper readers. Basically, they examine how to maximize use value in order to maximize profit (or retain profitability) and provide a real-life example where a newspaper has done just that. Similarly, Buschow and Wellbrock (2020) ask readers about their willingness to pay for journalistic content and not surprisingly deduce that publishers should focus on service journalism. Based on a time series analysis of the connection between content and financial performance of a news publisher, Li and Thorson (2015) suggest shorter and more diverse content to boost the financial performance. Collectively studies in this context seem to suggest journalism beyond public service media should put immediate customer needs first and forgo the very idea of journalism as a social institution.

However, immediate needs might not be the whole story, so optimizing for profit can lead to different outcomes depending on the time frame. While short-term strategies such as laying off editorial stuff will certainly cut costs, long-term success is likely a result of financial commitment toward content quality (Lacy and Martin, 2004). Even in complete neglect of the societal function of media, Mantrala, Naik, Sridhar, and Thorson (2007) still arrive at the conclusion that it is economically beneficial to invest in content quality. While intuitively comprehensible, the idea that content quality would be beneficial does not solve the underlying conflict of goals but merely shift the problem toward the issue of defining and measuring "quality". The term might be used in a normative way, simply referring to a property or – as common in economics – the superiority of a good in terms of fitness for purpose. Although falsehoods on social media platforms might not be considered as carrying normative quality, they might well be fit for the purpose of passing time and providing topics for follow-up conversations. Thus, the reference to content quality will usually point to a set of properties that are unambiguously measurable such as plurality of perspectives (see, for example, Forschungszentrum Öffentlichkeit und Gesellschaft 2020: 167–180).

Most of the research on success factors of media goods also fits in the perspective of optimizing for profit. In some cases, this is because the research simply takes for granted that success is necessarily measured in terms of revenue or profit (e.g., Chang and Chan-Olmsted, 2010; Schmidt-Stölting, Blömeke, and Clement, 2011); others, because it is notoriously hard to reliably measure success in terms of creative, artistic, or societal value (for a discussion, see also von Rimscha, Verhoeven, Krebs, Sommer, and Siegert 2018). For instance, the nomination of a film for a certain award is often but a weak proxy for non-monetary measures of success.

Albarran and Moellinger (2017: 19) examine media management and performance and find that the most common understanding of performance is "typically geared around financial and quantitative measures." Overall research in this field is dominated by quantitative methods that address assumed causal connections between metric data. The problem lies in the fact that the available quantitative data is often but an insufficient proxy and the causal relationships connecting cultural production and economic performance are seldom unambiguous. Verhoeven, von Rimscha, Krebs, Siegert, and Sommer (2018) have shown that the variables influencing success neither have a linear effect nor are they usually independent.

Thus, a multitude of possible explanations of success exist in parallel. Practitioners can regularly do without a theoretical underpinning of the casual relations between their "key perform-ance indicators" (Parmenter 2015), and instead they simply compare different versions of their product in so called A/B-tests, even if it is just about the wording of an article's headline (e.g., Hagar and Diakopoulos 2019). Optimization is therefore often focused on small aspects that might not seem all that relevant if regarded in a larger context.

## Optimization for welfare

It is generally accepted that media not only serve the economic interests of media owners but also the advancement of society at large, both in cultural and in economic terms. Media scholars have traditionally referred to this as "media responsibility" (see Bardoel and d'Haenens 2004) and focused on media functions beyond economics. Typical questions in this realm are whether media contribute to society by providing citizens the necessary input for informed choices on election day or how they might reproduce stereotypes and misrepresentations of minorities. Broken down to the individual firm, this relates to research on social (not-for-profit) enterprises where performance can be analyzed from a stakeholder perspective. Several authors have tried to apply the concept of corporate social responsibility (CSR) and how it is measured in relation to media companies (Bracker, Schuhknecht, and Altmeppen 2017; Tsourvakas 2016). Bachmann and Ingenhoff (2017) have shown how CSR and media responsi-bility can be conceptualized in parallel as ascriptions by managers or PR experts; however, their focus is on the strategic communication of that responsibility rather than its neutral measure-ment. All three studies just cited are purely conceptual and mostly just refer to other concep-tually focused texts, leaving empirical work in the field rather limited. Consequently, Peacock's observation in 1989 that empirical approaches in this field face practical problems in terms of available econometric data, and conceptual challenges when operationalizing content quality or recipient welfare, remain valid.

Welfare can also be understood in macroeconomic terms. Economic perspectives that ana-lyze the direct and indirect effects of media on gross domestic product (GDP) are scarce. As GDP per capita can be used as a measure for a person's welfare, optimizing media in order to produce as much of a positive effect on GDP as possible could also be considered as optimiza-tion for welfare. In this context, the main questions would be whether media can foster prod-uctivity in other sectors through a better information provision or whether media can foster consumption by creating demand. Albarran (2017: 8–17) offers descriptive data on the share of the media sector in GDP for a number of countries, but he does not analyze what drives the size of this share or whether the media can trigger economic activity in other sectors. Research that does try to draw such conclusions mostly focuses on the connection between advertising (as part of the media) and GDP (e.g., van der Wurff, Bakker, and Picard 2008) or analyzes the spillover effects of one media industry on behalf of its trade association. Seufert, Schlegel, and Sattelberger (2015), for instance, quantify how the music business triggers consumption in the travel sector as fans travel to concerts.

For public service broadcasters, the concept of public value (Moore 1995) gained much attention in their arguments for license fees and an inclusive mandate (e.g., Lowe and Martin 2014). The term has been used in many contexts and not always consistently. By and large, it resembles what Picard (2010: 61) calls "social value" and Flew (2013: 82) refers to as longer term collective needs in democratic societies. Early on in the debate, the BBC co-sponsored a report on how to measure public value (Hills and Sullivan 2006), and many other European public service media have followed and supported similar attempts. However, the results are limited. For example, even after ten years reporting and 23 publications from Österreichischer Rundfunk (ORF, Austria's public service broadcaster) on the issue,[1] no clear consensus has emerged on how to measure public value and thus the contribution made by public service media to societal welfare. Possible approaches range from the idea that an offer has public value if it meets a demand that no commercial provider is willing to serve, as in the German "Drei-Stufen-Test" (public value test) (Dewenter and Haucap 2009), to extensive lists of necessary traits of media organizations as in the "media for democracy monitor" (Trappel, Nieminen, and Nord 2011). Doyle and Frith (2006: 567) conclude: "Media output can be classified and quantified in numerous ways but translating this data into welfare impacts or utility is extremely problematic." Similarly, Wirth and Bloch have stated that "market performance is a multidimensional concept and therefore very difficult to define and measure for use as a dependent variable in multiple regression analysis" (1995: 18).

The implications of media economics for public welfare on the one hand and the difficulties in measuring this, on the other (Throsby 2001), have fostered the perspective of critical political economy with its largely normative approach (Doyle 2010: 247). It is widely used to analyze study topics such as media power, the potential implications of media ownership concentration, work relations in media industries, and inequalities of access to media among recipients (Flew 2020), all of which might be considered as aspects relevant to societal welfare. In contrast to the neoclassical approach in economics that focuses on individuals, the critical political economy approach conceptualizes markets as embedded in social institutions. This tradition usually takes capitalism as a starting point and discusses how this influences the production, distribution, and consumption of media content. Methods used in this perspective are usually not empirical, not least because direct links between macro institutions and micro behavior are almost impossible to measure.

Apart from calculating market impacts in the aforementioned public value test or the relationships between media advertising and consumption, empirical research into the public welfare dimension of media is methodically dominated by qualitative approaches such as guided interviews with media managers and editors, or case studies. Testing for causal relationships between certain variables are pretty uncommon. Doyle (2010: 256) mentions audience time spent as a potential proxy for an explained variable utility but points out its shortcomings at the same time. Thus, empirical work tends to focus on understanding the reasoning of involved actors rather than the measurable results of their actions.

Few studies try to reconcile optimization for profit with optimization for public welfare.[2] Abdenour and Riffe (2019) describe investigative journalism as socially beneficial addressing the monitoring and control function of the media. They find that the investigative quality of US local television stories drives audience ratings, while a higher quantity of these stories has no effect, and so conclude the quality of investigative reporting serves both objectives. This example, however, is an exception in the journalism literature. Regularly the objectives of optimization – profit versus public welfare – are described as mutually exclusive, from the seminal study by Underwood (1993) up to recent reflections on online audience metrics (Fürst 2020). Apart from journalism the question is regularly discussed in the context of film, whether it would be possible to optimize box office ($\approx$~profit) and artistic value ($\approx$~public welfare) (e.g., Holbrook and Addis 2008; Meloni, Paolini, and Pulina 2015; Simonton 2009). Results regularly point in the direction that it is possible for a film to be both economically successful and socially relevant, however, each objective is promoted by different influences. Using theaters as an example, Eikhof and Haunschild (2007) describe an unsolved paradox in creative production whereby economic logics would tend to crowd out artistic logics, and thus endanger the resources vital to creative production.

## How do they differ?

Certainly, the following description of differences does not apply to each and every work in the field, but in general, the respective research traditions have their distinctive shortcomings.

Optimization research at the level of the firm tends to neglect context. Humans are modeled as rational consumers, although it is obvious that their behavior is at times irrational and quite a few have needs other than short-term utility. Likewise, media producers and managers also do not always act rationally in neoclassic terms but also subscribe to alternative objectives such as peer praise, glamor, aesthetics, or truth. Integrating some understanding of the context in which these actions are taken might therefore show several objectives at work that might even be contrary or contradictory. Context is starting to gain more attention in general management research and multilevel analysis techniques are the tools of choice here (e.g., Bamberger 2008); however, although there have been calls for more context sensitivity (e.g., Picard and Lowe 2016), this trend has yet to trickle down to the field of *media* management research. Meanwhile, optimization research at the level of society tends to say a lot about how it should be but is less specific about how to get there, and why it is likely one path or the other might succeed. Some people might argue that public welfare perspectives are often paternalistic – maybe after all media users are not that keen on diversity, quality, and other hard to measure proxies of public welfare.

Optimization on the firm level subscribes to the assumption that if each and every actor, be it an individual or a collective actor such as a company, would pursue her own utility maximization automatically, the best possible result on an aggregate level will emerge. In contrast, optimization on the society level assumes that an objective optimum could exist and individuals might be guided in this direction. Thus, it is a bit like the differences between top-down or bottom-up approaches in management: the latter conducts research with a magnifying glass, focusing on the dependencies in the details, while the former takes a bird's eye view to see the whole picture.

Obviously, neither perspective can ever cover a situation in its entirety. And just as we know from top-down versus bottom-up management approaches, optimizations on one level might not be regarded as positive on the other. Doyle and Frith (2006: 567) point to the problem, that when regarded separately the two levels of analysis – firm and society – these might not be optimized at the same time. As their example, they refer to a broadcaster who reduces production costs by various means to allocate its resources more efficiently, yet it is hard to imagine this firm-level optimization will also deliver advantages on the society level as the decision will most likely be achieved by reducing output diversity or quality.

## Does the method determine the result?

The previous sections might give the reader the impression that there are two separate research silos, each with their distinctive worldview and connected methodological toolbox to underline this worldview. In a tweaked version of a famous aphorism, we could say, "If you are convinced the world is a nail the only tool you will ever need is a hammer." Or to put it more prosaically, it is likely that perspectives, methods, and results are closely connected.

Research results are never neutral, but rather the consequence of decisions made by the researchers along the way, most of them which are at least intersubjectively comprehensible, but some might just be arbitrary. There is a lively debate among methodology scholars how to deal with the problem of alternative results. Some suggest a rather radical approach: apply all possible data analysis methods to your data set and discuss the range of possible results (e.g., Simonsohn,

Simmons, and Nelson 2015; Steegen, Tuerlinckx, Gelman, and Vanpaemel 2016). This seems like a solution resting halfway between careful modesty (i.e., not overinterpreting one possible result) and capitulation where only after the data is crunched does a theory become necessary to provide a narrative toward selling the preferred result.[3] However, the problem is even bigger. If different methods of data analysis allow you to arrive at a multitude of possible results, the range of methods employed to gather the analyzed data in the first place exponentiate the realm of possible and justifiable results. Potential problems thus range from the scale that is used in a questionnaire (e.g., dichotomic answers vs. Likert scales) to issues of different levels of social desirability bias (e.g., between a content analysis or a participatory observation) or the fit of a proxy to stand in for a latent construct.

However, issues regarding the method dependency of research results are reinforced by separated research traditions. Journals and their reviewers have their distinct criteria when assessing the appropriateness of certain methods of data gathering and data analysis. The *Journal of Media Economics* will probably not publish a study on communicative practices in media brand management; as of 2020, the *Media Industries* journal has never published a time series analysis; and the *Journal of Media Business Studies* is unlikely to publish game theory-based modelling of certain media markets. The *International Journal on Media Management* used to demand a compulsory section on practical implication and recommendations for media managers at the end of each article, and therefore it is hardly the obvious outlet for research that takes a critical perspective on industry practices.

Thus, while the methodological toolbox does not directly determine the results of research in the field, it defines boundaries for the "space of possibility." For example, if research into media regulation routinely turns to the content analysis of texts produced overtime in the legislative process, it will provide a decent description of the common patterns of reasoning adopted by the respective actors in the process. However, we'll learn little if anything about how media workers interact with the resulting laws and regulations. Do they subscribe to the goals of the regulation? Do they cut corners? Do they use the rules to pursue different and seemingly unconnected objectives? Or in short: what is the practical effect of a regulation on the segregate level?

As media regulation scholars frequently use content analysis, be it the qualitative type that examines legislative texts, or the quantitative type focused on measuring the regulation result in a media content sample, chances are they will keep asking the questions that can be answered with this very toolkit. Furthermore, the logic of academic publishing can favor papers that build on each other in small steps but leading to ever better understandings of just one part of the story (the reasoning of actors in the lawmaking process) while neglecting others (e.g., the practical implication of the law for media workers). Thus, the reasoning and the agency of the companies or individuals concerned are not connected. Therefore, research does not help to assess the question whether the reasoning corresponds to the agency. We could say a great effort is done to answer a second order question (how a conviction about the media system is represented) while the first order issue (how to optimize the societal outcome of media system through effective regulation) is underserved.

## What could they learn from each other?

Research on welfare optimization on a societal level all too often remains at best conceptual and at worst anecdotal. Some authors rather describe how they believe things should be than actually identify the influences that might lead there and measure their respective effects. Now some readers might regard this critique as unfair since experiments with whole societies are not feasible and maybe also ethically questionable. But still theories that exclude themselves from empirical testing reduce their value. On the other hand, profit maximization on the firm-level or even beyond, all too often gets carried away by methodological details and micro adjustments that become irrelevant as soon as you zoom out: for example, what is the value of knowing how to optimize ad sales if the study does not take into account the effects of the proceeds on the recipient side? If we include external effects, the problem becomes even more obvious.

All too often, micro and macro perspectives are unconnected. This means results on the macro level are not founded on aggregate findings on the micro level, and researchers on the micro level miss out on the relevance of their findings and other influences on the macro level. Micro–macro links are not as intensively discussed as in sociology, for example (e.g., Buskens, Raub, and van Assen 2012). It should be noted though that micro and macro are far from clearly defined terms. While some scholars would surely put society on the macro level, others describe the macro level as "tactical choices [resulting from …] the perceptions and activities of senior managers" (Picard and Lowe 2016: 61). From a market perspective, the firm might be considered a micro unit, while from the perspective of an individual, it is already a macro unit. Independent from how and where you draw the line, however, each side could benefit from the other: for example, macro-level researchers could copy the smartness of micro-level researchers in identifying measurable proxies to model assumed causal connections; micro-level researchers might follow macro-level researchers in their preoccupation with discussing the question of what a research result actually implies in context. Micro-level researchers could eventually *test* rather than just assume whether individual utility maximization is actually contributing to the greater good. By actually confronting their ideas with data, macro-level researchers could eventually escape the prevalent allegation that they essentially produce armchair reflections.

Using multi-level analysis and research designs based on multi-method triangulation are worthy technical approaches to span the divide. A big advantage would be that they include two perspectives in one research design. Probably even more important, however, is to challenge the established triad of research object, method, and result for each tradition (see Hanson 2008). I believe only a few steps would be necessary to overcome the tendency for media economics and management research to form two separate silos. The first step would obviously be mutual recognition and approval by researchers from each tradition of the relevance of their respective objects of optimization. A second step requires the willingness of journal editors and research grant juries, authors, and reviewers to be more integrative. Journal editors and – even more important – grant juries, should welcome deviant perspectives rather than call for ever more detailed iterations of the same basic perspective. They could invite reviewers who are willing to take a critical but constructive look rather than just state this not how "we" usually do it. And of course, we need authors who in the first place dare to submit manuscripts and grant proposals bridging perspectives, and who then are willing to positively respond to the kind of reviewing preferences just mentioned. This would help create research projects and manuscripts relevant for readers oriented toward both micro and macro levels analyses.

This is of course a tall order and probably only really possible if authors from the different traditions work together, or more fundamentally, the training of future researchers provides them with a broader methodological toolbox that allows them to combine the strength of several methods while avoiding their respective weaknesses. This could lead to research results that gain attention in both camps and ideally provide indications on how media might be optimized to serve both individual *and* collective utility maximization.

# Notes

1 Interested readers can consult the reports at https://zukunft.orf.at/show_content.php?sid=129.
2 While neither a study nor in the context of media industries, Klamers' (1996) edited volume on the relationship between economics and arts provides useful insights here.
3 This is of course a bit cynical. More optimistically one could also argue that this approach enters data analysis as a tool for theory building.

# References

Abdenour, J. and Riffe, D. (2019) "Digging for (Ratings) Gold: The Connection Between Investigative Journalism and Audiences," *Journalism Studies*, 20 (16): 2386–2403.

Albarran, A. B. (2017) *The Media Economy*, 2nd ed., New York: Routledge.

Albarran, A. B. and Moellinger, T. (2017) "Examining Media Management and Performance: A Taxonomy for Initiating a Research Agenda," in K. -D. Altmeppen, C. A. Hollifield, and J. van Loon (eds) *Value-oriented Media Management: Decision Making between Profit and Responsibility*, Berlin: Springer International, 19–32.

Bachmann, P. and Ingenhoff, D. (2017) "Finding Common Ground: CSR and Media Responsibility," in K. -D. Altmeppen, C. A. Hollifield, and J. van Loon (eds), *Value-oriented Media Management: Decision Making Between Profit and Responsibility*, Berlin: Springer International, 147–157.

Bamberger, P. (2008) "Beyond Contextualization: Using Context Theories to Narrow the Micro-Macro Gap in Management Research," *Academy of Management Journal*, 51 (5): 839–846.

Bardoel, J. and d'Haenens, L. (2004) "Media Responsibility and Accountability: New Conceptualizations and Practices," *Communications*, 29 (1): 5–25.

Bracker, I., Schuhknecht, S., and Altmeppen, K. -D. (2017) "Managing Values: Analyzing Corporate Social Responsibility in Media Companies from a Structuration Theory Perspective," in K. -D. Altmeppen, C. A. Hollifield, and J. van Loon (eds), *Value-oriented Media Management: Decision Making Between Profit and Responsibility*, Berlin: Springer International, 159–172.

Buschow, C. and Wellbrock, C. M. (2020) "Paid Content, Plattformen und Zahlungsbereitschaft im digitalen Journalismus – Zusammenfassung und Handlungsempfehlungen für die Medienpraxis," in C. M. Wellbrock and C. Buchow (eds) *Money for Nothing and Content for Free?*, Baden-Baden: Nomos, 201–209.

Buskens, V. W., Raub, W., and van Assen, M. (eds) (2012) *Micro–Macro Links and Microfoundations in Sociology*, Abingdon: Routledge.

Chang, B.-H. and Chan-Olmsted, S. M. (2010) "Success Factors of Cable Network Brand Extension: Focusing on the Parent Network, Composition, Fit, Consumer Characteristics, and Viewing Habits," *Journal of Broadcasting and Electronic Media*, 54 (4): 641–656.

Dewenter, R. and Haucap, J. (2009) *Ökonomische Auswirkungen von öffentlich-rechtlichen Online-Angeboten: Marktauswirkungen innerhalb von Drei-Stufen-Tests*, Gutachten im Auftrag des VPRT e.V. Baden-Baden: Nomos, available at www.vprt.de/get_asset_file.php?mid=19&file=o_document_20090806 151124_studie_2009_07_29_VPRT_HaucapDewenter_DST_Gutachten_Oekonomische Auswirkungen_Zusammenfassung.pdf (assessed December 7, 2020).

Doyle, G. (2010) "Why Culture Attracts and Resists Economic Analysis," *Journal of Cultural Economics*, 34 (4): 245–259.

Doyle, G. and Frith, S. (2006) "Methodological Approaches in Media Management and Media Economics Research," in A. B. Albarran, S. M. Chan-Olmsted, and M. O. Wirth (eds), *Handbook of Media Management and Economics*, Mahwah, NJ: Lawrence Erlbaum, 553–572.

Eikhof, D. R. and Haunschild, A. (2007) "For Art's Sake!: Artistic and Economic Logics in Creative Production," *Journal of Organizational Behavior*, 28 (5): 523–538.

Flew, T. (2013) *Global Creative Industries*. Cambridge: Polity.

Flew, T. (2020) "Political Economy," in M. B. von Rimscha (ed.), *Management and Economics of Communication*, Berlin: de Gruyter Mouton, 87–105.

Forschungszentrum Öffentlichkeit und Gesellschaft (2020) *Jahrbuch Qualität der Medien 2020: Schweiz – Suisse – Svizzera*, Basel: Schwabe Verlag.

Fürst, S. (2020) "In the Service of Good Journalism and Audience Interests?: How Audience Metrics Affect News Quality," *Media and Communication*, 8 (3): 270–280.

Hagar, N. and Diakopoulos, N. (2019) "Optimizing Content with A/B Headline Testing: Changing Newsroom Practices," *Media and Communication*, 7 (1): 117–127.

Hanson, B. (2008) "Wither Qualitative/Quantitative?: Grounds for Methodological Convergence," *Quality and Quantity*, 42 (1): 97–111.

Hills, D. and Sullivan, F. (2006) *Measuring Public Value 2: Practical Approaches*, London: The Work Foundation.

Holbrook, M. B. and Addis, M. (2008) "Art Versus Commerce in the Movie Industry: A Two-Path Model of Motion Picture Success," *Journal of Cultural Economics*, 32 (2): 87–107.

Kanuri, V. K., Thorson, E., and Mantrala, M. K. (2014) "Using Reader Preferences to Optimize News Content: A Method and a Case Study," *International Journal on Media Management*, 16 (2): 55–75.

Klamer, A. (ed.) (1996) *The Value of Culture: On the Relationship between Economics and Arts*, Amsterdam: Amsterdam University Press.

Küng, L. (2007) "Does Media Management Matter?: Establishing the Scope, Rationale, and Future Research Agenda of the Discipline," *Journal of Media Business Studies*, 4 (1): 21–39.

Lacy, S. and Martin, H. J. (2004) "Competition, Circulation and Advertising," *Newspaper Research Journal*, 25 (1): 18–39.

Li, Y. and Thorson, E. (2015) "Increasing News Content and Diversity Improves Revenue," *Newspaper Research Journal*, 36 (4): 382–398.

Lowe, G. F. and Martin, F. (eds) (2014) *The Value of Public Service Media: Ripe@2013*, Gothenburg: Nordicom.

Mantrala, M. K., Naik, P. A., Sridhar, S., and Thorson, E. (2007) "Uphill or Downhill?: Locating the Firm on a Profit Function," *Journal of Marketing*, 71 (2): 26–44.

Meloni, G., Paolini, D., and Pulina, M. (2015) "The Great Beauty: Public Subsidies in the Italian Movie Industry," *Italian Economic Journal*, 1 (3): 445–455.

Moore, M. H. (1995) *Creating Public Value: Strategic Management in Government*, Cambridge, MA: Harvard University Press.

Parmenter, D. (2015) *Key Performance Indicators: Developing, Implementing, and Using Winning KPIs*, 3rd ed., Hoboken, NJ: Wiley.

Peacock, A. (1989) "Introduction," in G. Hughes and D. Vines (eds), *Deregulation and the Future of Commercial Television*, Aberdeen: Aberdeen University Press, 1–8.

Picard, R. G. (2010) *Value Creation and the Future of News Organizations: Why and How Journalism Must Change to Remain Relevant in the Twenty-first Century*, Lisbon: Media XXI.

Picard, R. G. and Lowe, G. F. (2016) "Questioning Media Management Scholarship: Four Parables About How to Better Develop the Field," *Journal of Media Business Studies*, 13 (2): 61–72.

Schmidt-Stölting, C., Blömeke, E., and Clement, M. (2011) "Success Drivers of Fiction Books: An Empirical Analysis of Hardcover and Paperback Editions in Germany," *Journal of Media Economics*, 24 (1): 24–47.

Seufert, W., Schlegel, R., and Sattelberger, F. (2015) *Musikwirtschaft in Deutschland: Studie zur volkswirtschaftlichen Bedeutung von Musikunternehmen mit Berücksichtigung aller Teilsektoren und Ausstrahlungseffekte*, Berlin, available at www.musikindustrie.de/fileadmin/piclib/presse/Dokumente_zum_Download/Musikwirtschaft_in_Deutschland_2015.pdf (assessed December 7, 2020).

Simonsohn, U., Simmons, J. P., and Nelson, L. D. (2015) "Specification Curve: Descriptive and Inferential Statistics on All Reasonable Specifications," *SSRN*, November 25, available at https://papers.ssrn.com/sol3/papers.cfm?abstract_id=2694998 (accessed December 15, 2020).

Simonton, D. K. (2009) "Cinematic Success Criteria and Their Predictors: The Art and Business of the Film Industry," *Psychology and Marketing*, 26 (5): 400–420.

Steegen, S., Tuerlinckx, F., Gelman, A. and Vanpaemel, W. (2016) "Increasing Transparency Through a Multiverse Analysis," *Perspectives on Psychological Science*, 11 (5): 702–712.

Throsby, D. (2001) *Economics and Culture*, Cambridge: Cambridge University Press.

Trappel, J., Nieminen, H. and Nord, L. (eds) (2011) *The Media for Democracy Monitor: A Cross National Study of Leading News Media*, Göteborg: Nordicom.

Tsourvakas, G. (2016) "Corporate Social Responsibility and Media Management: A Necessary Symbiosis," in G. F. Lowe and C. Brown (eds), *Managing Media Firms and Industries: What's So Special About Media Management?*, Berlin: Springer, 143–158.

Underwood, D. (1993) *When MBAs Rule the Newsroom: How the Marketers and Managers are Reshaping Today's Media*, New York: Columbia University Press.

van der Wurff, R., Bakker, P. and Picard, R. G. (2008) "Economic Growth and Advertising Expenditures in Different Media in Different Countries," *Journal of Media Economics*, 21 (1): 28–52.

Verhoeven, M., von Rimscha, M. B., Krebs, I., Siegert, G. and Sommer, C. (2018) "Identifying Paths to Audience Success of Media Products: The Media Decision-makers' Perspective," *International Journal on Media Management*, 20 (1): 51–77.

von Rimscha, M. B., Verhoeven, M., Krebs, I., Sommer, C., and Siegert, G. (2018) "Patterns of Successful Media Production," *Convergence*, 24 (3): 251–268.

Wirth, M. O. and Bloch, H. (1995) "Industrial Organization Theory and Media Industry Analysis," *Journal of Media Economics*, 8 (2): 15–26.

# 41

# BACKSTAGE OBSERVATIONS
## Studying media producers

*Anna Zoellner*

### Media production research and ethnography

Even though barriers to media production have become more porous in the wake of digital production and online distribution, the majority of media texts we encounter are produced by a relatively small number of organizations, placing those in control of this content in a position of significant power. In addition, media organizations are in the unique position to produce and distribute and therefore control representations of who they are and what they do (Caldwell 2008). Considering that the competitive, high-risk nature of the media industries encourages secrecy surrounding much of media production processes, these representations are unlikely to show the whole picture. Relying on the study of media representations and verbal statements from media producers alone creates a limited perception and understanding of what media producers actually do and for what reasons (Paterson 2008). Ethnographic immersion in the studied environment and direct observation of research subjects' activities provides this kind of information, helping us to explain why and how media texts take their specific form.

Inspired by the idea that anthropological methods can be useful for studying our own culture rather than the "Other," early production studies undertaken in the 1970s in the United Kingdom and United States helped to establish "ethnographically informed media sociology as a tradition within media and communication research" (Paterson, Lee, Saha, and Zoellner 2016: 4). At the forefront were scholars examining news and documentary production at national television networks in the United States and the United Kingdom (e.g., Gans 1979; Schlesinger 1978; Silverstone 1985; Elliot 1972), who were interested in bureaucratic routines and how power and ideology shape the resulting on-screen representations. Recent years have brought a revival and expansion of ethnographic investigations of media production not only in journalism (e.g., Paterson and Domingo 2008; Domingo and Paterson 2011) but across a range of media industries and genres (e.g., Banks, Conor, and Mayer 2015; Hesmondhalgh and Baker 2011; Born 2004). This growing body of research has drawn attention to the limitations of functionalist explanations of media production – such as gatekeeper theory and the concept of news values in journalism, for example – in addressing the complex and contested nature of media production and the perspective of media producers. If we understand media texts as

DOI: 10.4324/9780429275340-47

"ideologically loaded interpretations of the world (at the expense of other interpretations) that collectively shape what we all regard as 'real'" (Paterson 2017: 108–109), then it is important to examine the processes and conditions that lead to these interpretations on a micro-level.

Ethnographic methodologies, as a form of intensive research (see Harré 1979; Sayer 1992), can offer such in-depth and close-up examination based on immersion in the studied field. Intensive research designs enquire how processes work and what agents (individuals, groups, and institutions) do, revealing tensions, motivations, and causalities. The focus lies on explanation rather than on identifying generalizable distribution patterns of properties and characteristics as is the objective of extensive research methods (Sayer 1992). Extensive and intensive approaches are not competitive but rather they suit different research questions. In the case of media production research, which is concerned with the activities and opinions of media producers and what influences them, intensive methods such as ethnographic observation and interviews have several advantages: they offer direct access to the everyday social practices of media producers creating data that is not filtered through indirect and retrospective accounts; they provide data of exceptional depth and detail allowing for "thick description" (Geertz 1973: 6); and they enable causal explanations by studying actual connections between actors. In so doing, media production ethnography helps to reveal constraints, contradictions, and complexities to better understand how media organizations and producers operate and how they shape media representations. There are of course limitations to intensive research designs, perhaps most importantly the lack of representativeness and generalizability in research findings due to small sample sizes and the absence of interpersonal confirmation. But a lack of representativeness does not equal a lack of validity concerning casual explanation (Sayer 1992: 249). Ethnographers of media production do not seek to explain production in all its complexity but aim to reveal and translate "cultural meanings and social practices which are relevant to the subjects of the research" into comprehensive detailed interpretations (Paterson 2017: 110).

Nevertheless, this methodological approach involves challenges for researchers, which range from negotiating extensive access to the research site and securing funding to undertake resource intensive fieldwork, to managing distance during the immersion in the field. In this chapter, I focus on the particular nature of the research subject in media production research – media producers – and discuss the challenges arising from (1) media producers' status as exclusive experts, (2) their attitude toward media as a subject of academic study, and (3) the similarities between ethnographic research and media production processes. In the final section, I focus on potential responses to these challenges and argue for the value of a participatory approach and professional expertise to achieve access to and truthful disclosure in the field.

## Media producers as research subjects

Studying media production involves a diverse range of research sites and subjects across multiple industries and genres. There are many different types of media producers, by which I broadly mean workers who are directly involved in the creation and distribution of a media text in a creative, managerial, or organizational capacity, some of which are harder to study than others. In the following I focus mainly on professional producers employed/hired and paid by established, mainstream media organizations. I highlight three characteristics of media producers that have implications for research design and conduct: first, their status as exclusive experts for the research project; second, their skeptical attitude toward academic media research in general; and third, the impact of their occupational experience of observing and representing reality. The effects of these features on any given research project vary in their intensity depending on the specific research site, but they all influence the relationship between researcher and subject.

## Media producers as exclusive experts

By studying powerful gatekeepers, media production research differs from traditional anthropological research that focuses on giving voice to the marginalized (Ho 2012). Studying a social elite that has the power to shape media representations alters the power relations between researcher and subject. But aside from a clear association of power, the widely used concept of "elites" in research methodology is ambiguous and often poorly defined (Littig 2009: 99). Such research usually focuses on specific types of elites – frequently political or corporate in nature – with the objective to understand their culture as a social group (Harvey 2011). Media workers hold significant cultural power and occupy a relatively high status in the social structure (Dornfeld 1998). However, in the case of media production research, they are not studied as a social group but rather because of the exclusive knowledge inherent to their occupational position. In her discussion of qualitative interviews in media production research, Bruun (2016) suggests we consider media producers as "exclusive informants" rather than as "elite informants." She argues that media producers are not investigated in order to explore what characterizes them and their life-worlds but instead function as "means to gain insight" into the production of media representations (2016: 134). Building on the concept of the "expert interview" in German-speaking scholarship, in contrast to the prevalent notion of the "elite interview" in Anglo-American research (see Littig 2009: 98), I further recommend understanding media producers as experts rather than elites, as their exclusive knowledge is expertise specific to their occupational/professional role.

The exclusive and expert character of media producers as research subject increases methodological challenges typical for ethnographic research, such as gaining access to and managing relations within the field. Most media production involves backstage processes reliant on the collaboration of specific individuals, whose knowledge researchers depend on. Their exclusive often crucial knowledge makes research subjects hard to replace. Bruun (2016: 134) describes, for instance, how her study of the generic development of Danish television satire would have collapsed without the interview consent of one specific producer. This dependency heightens the importance of access requirements to research site and subjects. It further implies that research subjects may be easily identifiable and, therefore, hard to anonymize, which may lead to hesitation concerning their participation, or a lack of openness and honesty in their interaction with a researcher out of fear of reprisals within their organization or industry. This is less of a problem if media producers are investigated as part of a larger community, for example, as representatives of a workforce in critical cultural labor research. But it can become a significant challenge if the producers in question are holding key posts within a studied organization, or are centrally involved in the production process of a well-known media text. In my investigation of independent television production companies, access was granted on the condition of anonymity, which proved challenging to meet as anonymization extended from company name and location to producers' names and even program titles to prevent identification based on industry-specific insider knowledge (e.g., Zoellner 2009).

The interest of production studies scholars in the processes and conditions of media production goes hand in hand with a dependency on producers' exclusive expert knowledge. Combined with the reversed power imbalance of "studying up," this dependency makes access to organizations and people a central concern in the development of research question and design (see Bruun 2016: 139).

## *Media producers and academic critique*

Media producers are often skeptical about the value of media studies scholarship and have a tendency to disregard or even ridicule media studies as an academic subject. In the Anglo-American context, for instance, there are frequent examples of dismissive comments in news articles and television programs that refer to media studies as a "soft subject" or a "Mickey Mouse" course,[1] suggesting low levels of academic rigor and societal or vocational relevance. Historically, media producers have often been career changers who trained "on the job" and who, based on their own career trajectory, do not see the need for a dedicated media degree (e.g., Moodie 2016) and – by extension – dismiss the value of media research. Workers with such a career profile tend to be of an older generation and occupy senior roles in the media industries, making them particularly influential research subjects as they possess extensive experience, relevant knowledge, and – especially in managerial roles – the power to grant and deny researcher access. However, since the 1990s, there has been a substantial expansion of media and communication degrees and, consequently, a sharp increase in graduates, many of whom are working in the media industries.[2] This suggests at least the potential for a generational shift in producers' attitude toward greater openness about media scholarship in the future. For now, the persisting skepticism and disdain toward media scholarship create, unsurprisingly, barriers for collaboration between practitioners and researchers. Media producers' critical attitude may be attributed partially to a lack of familiarity with academic work and stereotypes of media studies as being out of touch with social reality, choosing obscure and insignificant subjects of study, or doing not much else but "watching films all day." For example, during my fieldwork in a television production company, the Head of Development questioned the academic validity of participatory ethnographic research and suggested (only half-jokingly) that "in that case, [she] should be a professor" due to her ten-year industry experience.

In other cases, it is precisely media producers' knowledge (or assumptions) of "what academics do" that can make them cautious about the research process and may lead them to deny access or conceal information (Radway 1989: 9). Rather than a perceived lack in value, it is fears of the potential economic and political consequences of the research findings that motivate the rejection of research collaboration and limited disclosure in the field. Media industries are highly precarious as commercial success is uncertain, production costs high, and competition pressing (Hesmondhalgh 2019). Their primary products are creative ideas and symbolic content, which are vulnerable to replication and hard to protect. Producers are therefore concerned about business confidentiality and losing competitive advantages by revealing details about business strategies and project ideas. Moreover, anxiety over the impact of research findings on public perception and their reputation can cause media producers to close their doors to researchers. Industry reputation and public image impact on audiences' media choices and on relations with fellow professionals. Bad publicity can, therefore, be harmful for an organization's or individual's future within the industry, making producers cautious of undesirable revelations as part of an academic study. In my investigation of independent television production companies, for instance, producers were concerned about the research damaging their relationship with commissioning editors and television networks, whom they depend on for income. Munnik (2016: 149) describes how the fallout of the Saville scandal[3] led to access for his ethnographic fieldwork being revoked, as BBC departments became cautious about external observers scrutinizing their organization and practices. His example shows how even public service media organizations, which in principle should be more open to researcher access based on their principles of transparency and accountability (Lindlof 1995: 107), are reluctant to participate in research. As political support and funding for public service media are waning, they are more than ever under pressure to justify their existence, which encourages a risk-averse approach to academic investigation.

Heightened competition and financial pressure in the current multi-platform media environment make economic and reputational concerns a priority for media producers. Combined with the skeptical attitude toward media and communication studies, this has negative consequences for academic researchers as their objectives are perceived either as irrelevant or potentially damaging. Such tensions can lead to the denial or restriction of access, and to confrontational or untruthful interaction in the field.

## Media producers as self-aware informants

The impact of media producers' knowledge of, or assumptions about, academic work and their resultant concerns about academic investigation are further increased by parallels between media production and ethnographic research in process and objective: to observe, study, and comment on aspects of society and its people. The resulting representations differ in style and may involve fictionalization and abstraction, but they are rooted in the basic principle of interpreting the world around us. Similarities between media production processes and ethnographic investigation both facilitate and complicate collaboration between media producers and academic researchers. On the one hand, media producers may offer sympathetic support and openness toward being studied. On the other, self-reflexive awareness of representational processes and practices may distort their actions and responses in the presence of a researcher. This can involve curated self-representation in participants' statements (e.g., self-censorship or pretense), restricted access within the field (e.g., meetings with high-status collaborators and funders), passive resistance by withholding information, or even intent to mislead through omission or misinformation.

Academic studies of the production of news, documentaries, and factual television, which bear particularly striking similarities not only in processes (the observation, recording, and interpretation of human behavior) but also in underlying principles (such as originality, impartiality, and ethics), are a good example to highlight the ambiguity in media producers' responses to being the subject of investigation (e.g., Silverstone 1985; Dornfeld 1998; Grindstaff 2002). While we could assume a generally sympathetic attitude among factual and news producers toward researchers' ethnographic quest, in practice producers are often not that forthcoming, and researchers have expressed their frustration about this lack of solidarity. After having tried unsuccessfully to gain access to documentary producers at the BBC, Silverstone, for example, describes how he felt "perhaps a little irritated with a group of people who spent their entire professional lives depending on others giving them access" but who in turn did not grant access to themselves (1985: 200). Dornfeld makes a similar observation in his investigation of a public television documentary series in the United States. He thought it "ironic that documentary producers who relied on their subjects' willingness to expose aspects of their life to an observer with a camera and recorder were unwilling to expose their own work practices to an observer with a notebook" (1998: 20).

I also struggled initially to gain access to production companies for my study of documentary television producers. In the end, it was my industry experience as a television producer, and recommendations from within the industry, that enabled initial contact and access rather than my academic credentials. However, one executive producer acknowledged the similarities between academic research and her own work, claiming this was a reason for her decision to support and participate in the study. During my fieldwork, producers were very conscious of, and frequently commented on, the fact that they were being observed. There was a sense of initial discomfort at "being studied," which can at least in part be ascribed to producers' familiarity with the subjective and selective nature of representing reality. In their own work-life, media producers experience how people's stories are framed, reduced, and potentially even distorted, making them self-aware and potentially cautious or resistant toward the research process. A development producer described how awareness of selectivity and manipulation in television representation is rising among the general public, making it harder to find participants for documentary programs as candidates are increasingly concerned that they are being "made to look bad" on television. The same fear of "being made to look bad" could be sensed among some of my research participants, especially in the early part of the observation period, leading to guarded conversation that belittled or denied production tensions and conflicts I observed for myself in the field. Although interest in the specific nature of my findings was limited, throwaway comments of my research participants, such as "You are listening to us!", "Are you still writing notes?" or "Don't write this down!" indicated their concerned awareness.

While similarities between ethnographic research and media production may inspire support for academic work, they also tend to increase the concerns of research subjects over participation and lead to self-awareness during data collection that may cause a lack of openness and truthfulness toward researchers.

The above described features of the relationship between media producers and media production researchers create challenges and barriers concerning access, field relations, and publication. The extent of such barriers differs across the various media industries depending on industry, institutional ownership and policies, genre, and the work role of the studied producers. While established mainstream media organizations, for example, newspapers and broadcasters, are reportedly the hardest to get access to (Paterson and Zoellner 2010: 102), producers in smaller, newer or more marginalized industries and organizations may well be more open to being at the center of an investigation, as Alacovska (2013) found in her study of travel guide book writers. In principle, publicly owned and non-commercial organizations may be more likely to participate in research projects as

> the more an organization or group is accountable to the public – usually conceived in terms of a public service mandate – the more likely it is to treat the researcher's inquiry with seriousness, and even welcome it in some cases. Commercial institutions usually keep their guards up very high, perceiving proposed research as an intrusion into the propriety nature of their activities.
>
> *Lindlof 1995: 107*

However, as mentioned above, current public funding cuts and political hostility toward public service media increase concerns over negative outcomes and reduce the willingness to participate. The challenges researchers experience also depend on the kind of genre or stage of production that is being investigated. Bruun (2016) noted stark differences in openness between producers of television satire and producers of political television talk shows, while Grindstaff (2002) highlighted the varied experiences of studying different kinds of talk shows. Finally, the specific professional role and hierarchical position of the studied media producers will also have an impact on their response to academic research. Their work role and relationship to the text matters as well as their hierarchical position and personal convictions. Producers in senior/

executive roles, for instance, possess valuable exclusive knowledge but are also more trained in public communication and deflecting critical questions. Producers involved in the managerial, legal, and financial activities of media production tend to have greater concerns about organizational confidentiality and propriety rights than producers primarily concerned with creative tasks. While these differences can make academic research more or less difficult, the above described challenges of access and self-representation persist to varying extents.

## Methodological strategies for studying media producers

Generally, people like to talk about what they do. They like to share their struggles and achievements and elaborate on the reasons and motivations behind their views and actions. They just don't always like to do so "on record." However, the exclusive nature of media producers as research subjects means that anonymization is often not a viable option. Production researchers, therefore, employ various strategies to overcome media producers' hesitation and build trust to secure access and cooperation. Here I focus on the role of active participation in the field and prior industry experience of ethnographers as research strategies and consider what these have to offer for access negotiation and field relations with media producers.

### *Participant observation*

To gain access for ethnographic fieldwork is a difficult and time-consuming process, and access conditions have consequences for the research experience. Frandsen distinguishes between access given as a trade or a gift (cited in Bruun 2016: 138), that is, whether access to a field site is offered with or without expectations of return services. While the latter is the most common, it also obscures expectations of the researcher due to the moral and symbolic dimensions of the gift economy and can make researchers vulnerable to access being suddenly restricted or withdrawn. Access as part of a trade relationship, on the other hand, involves clearer expectations and puts researcher and subject on a more equal footing, but it might involve restrictions concerning confidentiality and the publication of results (p. 138). Entering the field as a participant observer rather than as the traditionally passive observer presents a variation of the trade relationship. The researcher's contribution, usually in the form of free labor, can offset producers' arguments about the time and effort research participation demands from them and their colleagues, one of the main reasons given to deny access requests (Paterson and Zoellner 2010: 101). During fieldwork, being a participant observer can make the ethnographer less conspicuous, granting them colleague status that contributes to a sense of equality, helping build trust and encouraging openness through shared experiences. As Hesmondhalgh and Baker point out, this approach enables ethnographers to observe producers "off duty and/ or off guard" and to go "beyond language and discourse" (2011: 16). It further enhances access to people and documents since the ethnographer needs to be involved in meetings and communication as part of their industry-related activities. As Dornfeld describes:

> The ethnography of office work, in which subjects' primary activities are speaking on the phone and typing on computer keyboards, leaves little room for productive observation without conspicuously disturbing their work. (...) My revised stance as participant *and* observer afforded me a role in the production that made my visits to the office much more purposeful, provided me greater access to information, and resolved what sometimes felt like a duplicitous presentation of self.
>
> *original emphasis 1998: 23*

On the other hand, active participation increases the risk of "going native" and losing distance from the studied object. It also brings practical challenges as researchers have to balance two roles on site: as academic researchers and industry practitioners. Furthermore, interaction in the field affects the very processes and activities studied, such that we need to consider researcher activities as part of the data set and include (self-)reflection on this influence in data analysis.

## Industry knowledge and experience

Paterson and Zoellner's survey of media production ethnographers found that the majority had a professional media industry background, which in many cases prompted their research interest. Nearly all considered this background important for gaining access to media producers and had referred to it in access negotiations (2010: 101). Having prior professional experience in the industry studied is particularly useful in combination with participant observation. It helps researchers to dispel producers' concerns over the assumed demands on their time and the potential disruption of production activities by having a researcher on site because the ethnographer can perform as an insider who needs less explanation and training. As Newcomb claims,

> [p]rofessionals do not have the time and opportunity, for the most part, to teach researchers. They will be able to provide information about specific technical matters, work routines, and individual practices, but the researcher must have a high level of specific knowledge "going in."
>
> *1991: 100*

Existing knowledge of industry-specific jargon, processes and priorities furthermore serves as a means of better understanding and deeper questioning of the observed practices. Another argument in favor of industry experience is the fact that media producers rely on personal networks and contacts in production processes and employment decisions. They therefore "respond far more readily when approached through personal intermediaries" in the industry (Paterson and Zoellner 2010: 101). In other words, contacts from previous professional involvement in the media industries can help researchers to establish initial contact with their hesitant research subjects, as I found in my research of television production companies (see Paterson and Zoellner 2010: 100–101). Relevant industry experience reduces the distance between the researcher and subject, increases trust and consequently makes access more likely. The perception of the ethnographer not as an outsider but "one of us" further encourages greater disclosure and honesty from research participants during fieldwork. On the other hand, a high degree of familiarity with the studied field can also present a drawback as it carries a risk of "professional blindness", causing researchers to lose their distance to the research subject, potentially introducing a bias in data collection and analysis. Ethnographers, therefore, need to make a consistent effort to avoid the risk of accepting conditions as a matter of course and remain self-reflexive and open to unexpected connections to allow for alternative readings and explanations. On the other hand, prior professional experience may reduce the risk of going native compared to a participant-outsider, because researchers are less likely to be "taken in" by the explanations and claims they encounter in the field.

## Conclusion

Participant observation and prior industry experience have proven to be useful strategies for overcoming the resistance to participate in research that results from the particular characteristics of media producers described in this chapter. They make access more likely and can achieve greater levels of disclosure. There are, of course, other factors that influence the research experience and the quality of observational data, which need to be considered when developing research questions and designs: for instance, the length of time spent in the field, a participant observer's position in the organizational hierarchy, and the number and nature of research sites. In addition, the ethnographic approach in media production research usually involves a combination of methods including document analysis and the study of media texts and audiences. Complementary methods "allow the researcher to both describe the processes they seek to understand in richer detail and with greater nuance, and to 'triangulate,' comparing information discovered through one approach with information gleaned by another" (Paterson 2017: 110). In my research into television production, I found combining participant observation with professional experience while taking a mixed-method approach was helpful to overcome the barriers resulting from media producers' power as exclusive experts, their skeptical attitude toward academic research, and their knowledge of observational and interpretative processes. My prior professional experience and personal contacts in the television industry enabled entry to the field, while active participation in production (facilitated by my industry knowledge) provided me with greater access to data and helped to build relationships in the field. Finally, combining ethnographic observation, in-depth interviewing and document analysis enabled the verification of producer statements, revealing inconsistencies between observational and interview data.

In this chapter I have discussed the specificity of media producers as research subjects and outlined the resulting challenges for access and subjects' self-representations. I further debated potential approaches to counter these challenges and argued for the value of active participation and professional experience in the ethnographic study of media producers. In so doing, my aim was to show how the exploration of the particularities of media production as a site of ethnographic investigation and the development of strategies to address key challenges can help to strengthen the quality of empirical investigations and ensure the validity of research data and findings.

## Notes

1 The term was used, for example, in 2003 by the then Higher Education Minister of the UK, Margaret Hodge, who criticized the quality of university degrees in the context of Higher Education policy (BBC 2003). Although she did not specify individual degree courses, the term has since frequently been applied to media and communication studies.

2 In the UK, for instance, between 1996 and 2010 the number of higher education institutions offering media studies courses increased by 200 percent from 37 to 111. Courses in journalism increased by 325 percent from 16 to 68 institutions, and in publishing by 240 percent from 5 to 17 (Ramsden 2012: 27).

3 It was posthumously revealed that popular BBC television presenter Jimmy Saville abused his position of power to arrange sexual encounters with underage girls.

## References

Alacovska, A. (2013) *Genre and Autonomy in Cultural Production: The Case of Travel Guidebook Production*, Frederiksberg: Copenhagen Business School, PhD series, No. 21.2013.

Banks, M., Conor, B. and Mayer, V. (eds) (2015) *Production Studies, the Sequel! Cultural Studies of Global Media Industries*, New York: Routledge.

BBC (2003) "Irresponsible' Hodge Under Fire," *BBC News*, January 14, available at: http://news.bbc.co.uk/1/hi/education/2655127.stm (accessed October 18, 2019).

Born, G. (2004) *Uncertain Vision: Birt, Dyke and the Reinvention of the BBC*, London: Secker & Warburg.

Bruun, H. (2016) "The Qualitative Interview in Media Production Studies," in C. Paterson, D. Lee, A. Saha and A. Zoellner (eds), *Advancing Media Production Research: Shifting Sites, Methods, and Politics*, Basingstoke: Palgrave Macmillan, 131–146.

Caldwell, J. (2008) *Production Culture: Industrial Reflexivity and Critical Practice in Film and Television*, Durham, NC: Duke University Press.

Domingo, D. and C. Paterson (eds) (2011) *Making Online News – Volume 2: Newsroom Ethnographies in the Second Decade of Internet Journalism*, New York: Peter Lang.

Dornfeld, B. (1998) *Producing Public Television, Producing Public Culture*, Princeton, NJ: Princeton University Press.

Elliot, P. (1972) *The Making of a Television Series: A Case Study in the Sociology of Culture*, London: Constable.

Gans, H. (1979) *Deciding What's News: A Study of CBS Evening News, NBC Nightly News, Newsweek, and Time*, Evanston, IL: Northwestern University Press.

Geertz, C. (1973) *Interpretation of Cultures*, New York: Basic Books.

Grindstaff, L. (2002) *The Money Shot: Trash, Class, and the Making of TV Talk Shows*, Chicago, IL: University of Chicago Press.

Harré, R. (1979) *Social Being*, Oxford: Blackwell.

Harvey, W. S. (2011) "Strategies for Conducting Elite Interviews," *Qualitative Research*, 11 (4): 431–441.

Hesmondhalgh, D. and S. Baker (2011) *Creative Labour: Media Work in Three Cultural Industries*, Abingdon: Routledge.

Hesmondhalgh, D. (2019) *The Cultural Industries*, 4th ed., London: Sage.

Ho, K. (2012) "'Studying Up' Wall Street: Reflections on Theory and Methodology," in L. L. M. Aguiar and C. J. Schneider (eds), *Researching amongst Elites*, Farnham: Ashgate, 29–48.

Lindlof, T. (1995) *Qualitative Communication Research Methods*, Thousand Oaks, CA: Sage.

Littig, B. (2009) "Interviewing the Elite – Interviewing Experts. Is there a Difference?," in A. Borger, B. Littig, and W. Menz (eds), *Interviewing Experts*, Basingstoke: Palgrave Macmillan, 98–116.

Moodie, C. (2016) "'Mickey Mouse' Degrees Are a Waste of Time, Says Parky: Veteran Journalist Believes Many Students Would be Better of Learning on the Job," *Daily Mail Online*, November 25, available at www.dailymail.co.uk/news/article-3970084/Mickey-Mouse-media-degrees-waste-time-says-Parky-Veteran-journalist-believes-students-better-learning-job.html (accessed October 18, 2019).

Munnik, M. (2016) "When You Can't Rely on Public or Private: Using the Ethnographic Self as Resource," in C. Paterson, D. Lee, A. Saha, and A. Zoellner (eds), *Advancing Media Production Research: Shifting Sites, Methods, and Politics*, Basingstoke: Palgrave Macmillan, 147–160.

Newcomb, H. (1991) "The Creation of Television Drama," in N. Jankowski and K. Jensen (eds), *A Handbook of Qualitative Methodologies for Mass Communication Research*, London: Routledge, 93–107.

Paterson, C. (2008) "Introduction: Why Ethnography?," in C. Paterson and D. Domingo (eds), *Making Online News: The Ethnography of New Media Production*, New York: Peter Lang, 1–11.

Paterson, C. (2017) "The Ethnography of Digital Journalism," in B. Franklin and S. Eldridge II (eds), *The Routledge Companion to Digital Journalism Studies*, Abington: Routledge, 108–116.

Paterson, C. and D. Domingo (eds) (2008) *Making Online News: The Ethnography of New Media Production*, New York: Peter Lang.

Paterson, C. and A. Zoellner (2010) "The Efficacy of Professional Experience in the Ethnographic Investigation of Production," *Journal of Media Practice*, 11 (2): 97–109.

Paterson, C., D. Lee, A., Saha, A., and Zoellner, A. (2016) "Production Research: Continuity and Transformation," in C. Paterson, D. Lee, A. Saha, and A. Zoellner (eds), *Advancing Media Production Research: Shifting Sites, Methods, and Politics*, Basingstoke: Palgrave Macmillan, 3–19.

Ramsden, B. (2012) "Institutional Diversity in UK Higher Education," Report for the Higher Education Policy Institute, available at www.hepi.ac.uk/wp-content/uploads/2014/02/Institutional-diversity-in-UK-Higher-Education-final.pdf (accessed November 24, 2019).

Radway, J. (1989) "Ethnographies Among Elites: Comparing Discourses of Power," *Journal of Communication Inquiry*, 13 (2): 3–11.

Sayer, A. (1992) *Method in Social Science*, 2nd ed., London: Routledge.

Schlesinger, P. (1978) *Putting "Reality" Together: BBC News*, London: Constable.

Silverstone, R. (1985) *Framing Science: The Making of a Television Documentary*, London: British Film Institute.

Zoellner, A. (2009) "Professional Ideology and Programme Conventions: Documentary Development in Independent British Television Production," *Mass Communication and Society*, 12 (4): 503–536.

# 42

# BREAKING INTO HOLLYWOOD

## Strategies for interviewing media producers

*David Craig*

Interview methods pose an array of procedural and epistemological challenges for qualitative researchers, not least of which includes conducting replicable analysis and reliable interpretations of data. Yet, research that includes interviews with media and cultural producers can add even further levels of complication, whether securing access to what has remained a notoriously closed industry or challenging the veracity of their claims in an industry renowned for self-promotion. Still, these interviews may yield critical insider accounts of how media operate, complimenting other methods and analysis to expand vital networks for media scholars and aspiring media professionals. The following anecdotes reflect my own experience as a media industry professional, professor, and scholar on the challenges and rewards of pursuing interviews with media producers.

Within the academy, depending on the field and tradition, interview data secured from media producers may be held with little regard, if bordering on contempt. While conducting research for my dissertation about the cultural pedagogy of lesbian, gay, bisexual, transgender, and queer (LGBTQ)-themed TV movies, I consulted a leading media literacy scholar in my department. Along with content and reception analysis and secondary research, I explained that my project featured interviews with two dozen TV movie producers and network executives. With complete incredulity, the scholar asked, "Why bother? They only lie." The response left me dumbfounded, if also insulted, as I had confided that I had been a TV movie producer and network executive for decades. When I raised these concerns with a professor renowned for media industries scholarship, the response was that media scholars are weary of media producers due to their "anti-intellectualism." This response bore little relationship to the contempt held by the other scholar, if also my own experience after decades in the industry, reflecting more upon the pejorative biases of media studies scholars regarding their objects of study.

These methodological concerns regarding the veracity of information secured from interviews with media producers may be warranted. After all, Hollywood is an industry renowned for telling and promoting stories about the art and practice of storytelling, whether empirically true or not. However, a media industries research agenda without interview data may also expose the deep-seated subjectivities of the researcher, particularly operating from a critical stance regarding the (mis)abuse of media power. For an assignment in a cultural studies course, I conducted a multicultural analysis of the production of an acclaimed, if controversial,

DOI: 10.4324/9780429275340-48

television program – HBO's *The Newsroom* (2012–14). I scrupulously avoided interviews to avoid the risk of bias in my analysis and was granted permission from the producers to conduct ethnographic observations on the set. The goal was to assess whether criticism surrounding the lack of on-screen diversity was reflected by similar power dynamics within the production. However, upon sharing my findings with the producers, they cited numerous flaws in my analysis, not least of which was my profiling and misattribution of the gender and race of cast and crew. The producer then listed an array of diversity hiring strategies that the production employed throughout every stage of production from pre- to post-production, and above- and below-the-line. Not only was the research design a failure, so was the damage inflicted to my relationship with producers who had spent their careers generating content foregrounding multicultural identities and harnessing media to speak truth to power.

As reflected in the following cautionary tale, conducting interviews with media producers may prove precarious, particularly for scholars operating from research-based biases while lacking sufficient knowledge of production practices. Former ABC television executive Brandon Stoddard agreed to an interview for my dissertation. Known as "the father of mini-series," Stoddard was responsible for some of the most commercially successful and critically acclaimed television programs in history, including the race-themed mini-series *Roots* (1977), and post-apocalyptic drama *The Day After* (1983). I asked how often he had agreed to be interviewed by an academic.

> Only once. A doctoral student asked me to set aside the entire afternoon. When he arrived, the only question he asked was why *Roots* featured so much yellow-colored clothing. He was convinced the yellow was significant. I told him to contact the costume designer and asked him to leave.

Despite the challenges incumbent upon media scholars attempting to include interview data in their research, the benefits may extend beyond their own singular project throughout their career, whether as media scholars, pedagogues, or practitioners. In my graduate courses on a professional program at the University of Southern California (USC) Annenberg, I require that students secure an interview with a media professional for a research assignment in every class. I do not provide access to my own network; rather, I teach interview strategies for students to secure their own interviews, including harnessing a rich alumni network. Over 1,000 students have taken my courses and more than 90 percent have completed the brief. In addition to securing richer "insider" data for their projects, these interviews often contributed to a "snowball effect" of additional interviews with related media professionals introduced by the interview subject. In numerous instances, the interviews and the projects contributed to job offers for the students upon graduation. These benefits further reflect upon the heightened networked and interpersonal nature of the operations of and relationships within media industries.

While posing an array of challenges, limitations, and also unexpected benefits for media scholars, interviews with media producers can provide a more complex account of how power operates within media industries. As argued in this chapter, interviews with media producers align within a holistic and multi-methodological research agenda that may also bridge the divide within the media studies traditions of political economy and cultural studies. I further argue for a broader definition of media producers beyond industrial taxonomies, like those listed by awards programs or defined by Hollywood guilds. Rather, media producers include diverse practitioners who participate in the creative execution of the content throughout the production supply chain. These include above-the-line actors, writers, producers, and directors and below-the-line craft labor, talent agents and managers, creative development executives, personnel involved in physical production, and programming, production, marketing, and distribution executives at the studios and networks. Finally, I set forth an array of best practices and strategies for conducting interviews with media producers, which are informed by my experience as a veteran Hollywood producer, communication professor, and media scholar over four decades.

## Holistic media industries studies

Scholars may be "disciplined" against conducting interviews or, at the very least, advised to conduct them with the highest scrutiny, if also untenable skepticism. Nonetheless, despite these challenges, interviews represent a vital research method within the emerging subfield of media industries studies. As Herbert, Lotz, and Punathambekar (2020: 11) describe, "media industries use an array of methods and evidence, including industry and government data, archives of media organizations and individuals, trade publications, industry events, interviews, observation and, in some cases, participant observation and long-term ethnographic fieldwork".

Interview data can prove vital in generating a more rigorous and comprehensive account of the operations of media industries and assist with mapping the micro-social operations of media practices within production cultures. However, unlike social science methods, interviews with media producers may prove less viable as a prime source of factual, dispassionate information. Rather, they offer a means for triangulating secondary sources and securing data otherwise unobtainable through other methodological approaches. As advocated by prominent media industries scholars, interviews reside within a holistic multi-methodological research agenda. In describing his "synthetic" approach, Caldwell (2008: 4) conducts research across "four registers or modes of analysis: textual analysis of trade and worker artifacts; interviews with film/television workers; ethnographic field observation of production spaces and professional gatherings; and economic/industrial analysis."

In addition to multiple methods, a holistic media industries research agenda featuring interview methods compliments the approaches advocated by other media studies frameworks. In the multi-methodological research agenda they describe as critical media industries studies (CMIS), Havens Lotz and Tinic (2009) include interviews alongside case study work, ethnography, and industrial discursive analysis. These methods compliment if also mitigate the emphases placed by political economic analyses on markets and ownership that "elides the complex workings within the media industries where cultural workers negotiate every facet of the production process in ways that cannot be easily predicted by or read off from the interests of those who control the allocative resources of the industries" (p. 248).

While aligning with the mission within cultural studies surrounding power and ideology, interviews with media producers can bolster the claims about media producers missing from or limited by other methodological approaches, like textual analysis and reception studies. Borrowing from de Certeau (1984), who theorized how the less powerful deploy "tactics" to circumvent the "strategies" deployed by the powerful, CMIS methods allow scholars to understand how media producers are able to operate within the structural and material interests of industry to generate critical, progressive, and multicultural texts. Otherwise, as Havens, Lotz, and Tinic claim, "ignoring the logic of representational practices in entertainment production works to reinforce the relative invisibility or misrepresentation of those who often have the least power in the public sphere" (2009: 250).

## Redefining media producers

Failures to define media producers is reflective of how academic study of media industries can too easily presume, in Govil's (2013: 173) words, the "obviousness of its object." Researchers risk slipping into the aesthetic claims of auteurism that promote the notion of a singular creative vision, whether author, director, producer, or series showrunner. Yet, as Foucault (1991) notes, the "author-function" is as often the product of discursive strategies tied to legal and institutional systems including embedded power relations over who deserves credit or not. In addition to conducting interviews with media producers within a holistic media research agenda, in this section, I advocate for a broader definition of who qualifies as a media producer. This definition allows for a broader understanding of the critical, creative, and collaborative nature of media-making, if at risk of over-generalizing to all media practitioners.

While adding even greater complication and precariousness, securing multiple interviews across a diverse array of media producers throughout the media supply chain from inception to distribution affords deeper insights into the industrial process, especially for uncredited producers vital to either creative labor or management. For example, the Producers Guild of America narrowly defines and affords credit to producers according to a set of prescribed and vaguely determined, if often arbitrary, titles and duties. The guild's website (ProducersGuild.org) offers "Code of Credits" – a dizzying and iterative typology of producers, executive producers, line producers, etc. – that vary depending on medium (theatrical, television, new media), format (episode), and content (non-fiction). This amounts to a kind of taxonomic tyranny that renders many vital creative and industrial collaborators invisible, just as others are made visible and therefore eligible for award recognition and residual payments. Unit production managers may often fulfill the same functions of line producers while operating at a cheaper rate. More often uncredited, television programming executives not only commission, but may even conceive, of the project before hiring outside producers to creatively manage the project. Hollywood talent agents are licensed by the state and prohibited from taking credit on their client's projects despite delivering producer-like services, whether securing financing and talent or assisting with developing screenplays.

As the subfield of production studies has developed in the past decade, scholars have begun to address some of these discrepancies. Field-setting work by Mayer, Banks, and Caldwell (2009) considers media producers "up and down the food chains of production hierarchies" (p. 2), whether above- or below-the-line. Some accounts have extended well beyond physical media production work to recognize the multiple forms of labor found throughout the capitalist production of media. For some production scholars, broadening the definition of media producer can often expose the industrial hierarchies and myth-making around production, if risking over-generalization. Mayer (2011) includes the "twenty-two year old working the assembly line in an international electronics export zone" (p. 1) to highlight questions of media labor, even as these employees contribute little to the creative process prior to exhibition.

Yet, still missing from these frameworks and definitions for media producers are a vast network of media professionals operating critically and creatively throughout the rhizomatic structure of media industries and the complex, multifaceted nature of media production (du Gay 1997; Caldwell 2013). Borrowing from Deleuze and Guattari (1980), "rhizomatic" refers to multiple points of entry for conducting research in a system that is neither linear nor closed. In addition to credentialed producers and those involved in physical production above- and below-the-line, I define media producers as also including media professionals engaging in strategies of "creative media management." Following Johnson, Kompare, and Santo (2014: 2), this term describes media professionals who "create meaning, generate value, organize, or otherwise shape media work throughout each moment of production and consumption."

Examples of creative media managers include executives in the programming and production divisions of production companies, film studios, and television networks. For decades, these executives were either hired from or later segued into the role of media producer, as traditionally defined. Yet, while they may be as critical to the creative process as location managers, these producers are often systemically rendered invisible by the industry and, in turn, by scholars. They are frequently denied credit by the guilds or their employers, or cultural recognition through awards provisioners like the television or motion picture academies, and more often omitted from the personnel listed on a database like imdb.com.

Another set of media producers includes producer assistants and development executives, early career professionals hired by producers to fulfill producer-like duties, whether identifying media properties, securing rights, identifying screenwriters, developing the script, courting and packaging talent, or securing funding and distribution. These categories more often receive no credit while remaining egregiously underpaid, justified on the basis that they are paying their dues. Recent efforts by Hollywood assistants "in revolt" over pay and duties are just the latest in a long and notorious tradition of creative labor exploitation (Perlman 2019).

Working as a "development executive," I found, developed, sold, and supervised the production of projects for reputable producers, while often denied credit and paid an assistant's salary for nearly a decade. As a cable network programming executive, my responsibilities emulated the creative tasks I held as a development executive and executive producer, albeit without credit. As the only hire in charge of original scripted programming, I also contributed to the functions of other departments including business affairs, marketing, and publicity. Although I operated like a creative producer on my network projects, sometimes developing projects based on my original concepts or securing the rights before outside producers were hired, I initially declined any credit on the projects out of deference to outside producers. These producers operate independently of the network, often assuming more risk, including the financing of projects, or served a more critical creative role in a film's conception, development, and production. However, my network insisted that I take credit on these projects to ensure that the network would be acknowledged in the Emmy nominations awarded by the Television Academy. In prior years, the network's original programming had received awards, but producers and the press never even mentioned the network. Shortly after, I assumed the marketing role of running the first-ever Emmy campaigns for the network, which not only secured hundreds of Emmys for the network, but also for dozens for my programming colleagues who worked at the network, including two for myself. These developments not only reflect upon the diverse creative tasks that programming executives assume beyond those of outside creative producers, but also the complex stakeholder ecology of the industry where awards recognition can boost not only careers but network bottom lines through higher ad sales and increased distribution.

The Television Academy that produces the Emmy Awards further complicates these concerns by repeatedly changing the rules regarding who qualifies for credit or recognition, often with bewildering inconsistency. In 2006, I was nominated and then disqualified for producing a television movie. That year, the TV movie division of the Academy ruled broadcast and basic cable executives were ineligible but exempted public broadcasting (PBS) and premium cable (HBO) executives. Other branches of the Academy nominated my network colleagues in other program categories like documentaries and reality series. The following year, the TV movie divisions rescinded these rules to align with the others.

In my definition, media producers would include marketing and publicity executives within the studios and networks or even employed by outside firms contracted by the studios or networks. These professionals may be critical to crafting the marketing campaigns for projects, a function ever more vital in the digital age of atomized media audiences and content abundance. Other examples are distribution and advertising sales executives who are increasingly vital to securing financing before a project can be greenlit, and who are often tasked to participate in development of the project, including the casting of talent. Similarly, talent agents and managers may be vital to the execution of media projects, engaging in producer-like functions like identifying projects, developing screenplays, securing financing, and packaging talent. As intermediaries engaged in cultural brokerage to extend the value of their clients and properties throughout the creative industries, these professionals are vital to the creative success of media properties and many categories of cultural talent (Roussel 2017).

As reflected in these examples, a more expansive definition of the media producer can offer a richer account of critical and creative agency throughout the circuits of media production. If limited solely to industrial taxonomies, the vital and collaborative role of multiple media producers may go uncredited and unacknowledged by media scholarship. While on the one hand complicating our understanding of the creative processes of media production, broader definitions of media producers can also contribute to more diverse strategies for securing and conducting research interviews. Dating back to Rosten (1941) and Powdermaker (1950), interviews have featured prominently in media industries and production studies.

Nonetheless, interview methods remain one of the thorniest to practice. Lack of access to industry professionals has forced scholars to abandon their projects or pursue alternative strategies. Patterned after Powdermaker's work, anthropologist Ortner aspired to go behind-the-scenes of Hollywood, but due to lack of access, she pivoted to the independent film industry or, as she titled her book, *Not Hollywood* (2013). Scholars have mapped out alternative strategies for studying up, down, and sideways for circumventing these obstacles, whether by attending industry events in hopes of meeting interview subjects or conducting indirect interviews with production assistants to help identify the most relevant interview subjects. With greater emphasis on industrial discourses, Ortner (2010: 213) advocates for conducting "interface ethnography" – "doing participant observation in the border areas where [a] closed community or organization or institution interfaces with the public" – while Caldwell (2009) describes conducting research through industry "shoot-outs, bake-offs, and speed-dating." With modest redress for these formidable challenges, the following sections feature strategies and best practices for conducting interviews with media producers.

## Demythologizing Oz and a dialectic of no respect

Whether television series like *Entourage* (2004–11), or films like *The Player* (1992) and *Swimming with Sharks* (1994), Hollywood has populated the audience's imagination with loathsome and larger-then-life accounts of the culture of media production. These depictions serve to mythologize, if sometimes vilify, media producers. In turn, these images can strike fear in the hearts (and also handicap the efforts) of media scholars who may most benefit from industry interviews. Media scholars from all ranks can often invest in claims about the exceptionalism of media production cultures, and how the attitudes and representations by media producers are distinct from other industries and forms of labor. In describing the challenges with securing candor and transparency, Ortner (2010: 213) posits that,

There is also the fact that, because this is indeed a real community, people need to sustain their social relationships in good working order. One may hate someone, or think poorly of him/her, but this must not be allowed to circulate (unless there is some deeper reason for allowing it to do so).

Similarly, in his account of how producers "theorize," Caldwell (2009) likens the discourses conducted by practitioners to forms of spin and culture jamming.

This pattern grows more pronounced for scholars occupying a deeply critical and ideological stance. Through deep-seated subjectivities, they perceive media producers as singularly pre-occupied with commercial interests while offering little recognition of, or accountability for, their cultural influence. For example, in their account of the lack of and exploitative representation of people with disabilities in Hollywood films and television, scholars Kashani and Nocella (2010: 107) make provocative claims about media producers without evidence that

> some Hollywood executives knowing full well that cinematic representation is perhaps the most powerful means of communication … are having private conversations about the ways in which they can get a story about a "retarded" person or a "paraplegic", or a "freak", and so on, into a successful blockbuster for a great profit.

In describing centuries of struggles over cultural power between cultural critics and the consumers and producers of popular culture, Andrew Ross (1989) refers to a "dialectic of no respect." However, in my own experience, while equally blinded by my own industrial biases, this contempt proves one-sided. While they may understand "critical" as referring to those reviews listed in *Variety*, most media producers that I have known and interviewed present varying levels of self-reflective awareness about their media power. While not anti-intellectual, media producers may yield little regard for theorization. Focused more on industry discourses, they are less likely to have read high-level scholarship, often crafted in deep "academlish" and hidden behind more expensive academic firewalls than a subscription to *Variety*. Industry professionals may hold academics in high regard, whether they be former teachers who inspired them to enter the industry, or pedagogues training the next-generation of media professionals. Having navigated the transition from media professional to producer, and now in my capacity teaching in a professional media program, I am routinely approached by former industry colleagues desirous of opportunities to guest lecture and teach as a form of service, not a career or revenue stream. In the Los Angeles area, communication and media programs at research and teaching universities would not thrive without the support of media professionals willing to share their knowledge. Adjunct faculty, lecturers, and professors of practice may prove the first and best resource for securing interviews.

Mythologization or vilification of media producers can prove counterproductive for securing interviews, while also introducing biases into analysis. While occupying a critical stance, scholars may benefit by demystifying their subject and setting aside anxieties. Comparable to what Ortner (2010: 213) describes as "studying sideways" – that is, "studying people … who in many ways are really not much different from anthropologists and our fellow academics" – scholars are as likely to share the same social status and mutual affinities and interest as their subjects. Media producers may once have been media students who entered the industry out of deep regard for the industry and profound awareness of the power it yields. Referencing *The Wizard of Oz* (1939), scholars pursuing interviews should avoid becoming distracted by the ominous facade of the giant green talking head. Their job is to pull back the curtain. Odds are they may discover a nerdy, bald, overweight, white, middle-aged, gay, and/or Jewish man, much like this author, comparable to middle managers in most any industry.

## Network cultivation and strategic targeting

A feature of most media industries is a deeply networked production culture, in which jobs and opportunities may arrive out of both creative merit and interpersonal relationships, if also decades of nepotism reflected by the rise of scions into positions of influence at media institutions. As a consequence, interviews are more likely to be secured through these networks, whether directly or indirectly. Media scholars are well-advised if rarely instructed on how to cultivate their interview networks. Whether Facebook or LinkedIn, platforms may reveal degrees of separation from, and closer ties to, media producers that would best even Kevin Bacon's record. These pathways may lead to interview prospects through a colleague employed at their firms, connected through one of many school affiliations, or related through personal social networks. As mentioned previously, sideways or bottom-up interview strategies with lower-tier media employees may lead to interviews with the more relevant media producers and one successful interview with a media producer may result in a "snowball effect," gathering other interviewees while further expanding the researcher's network.

Cultivating networks ought to be considered in pre-meditative fashion. Just as I encourage students interested in media careers, I also urge early career researchers to pursue internships or paid positions in media firms. A year working within a talent agency would yield a vast network of professional relationships that could fuel an aspiring media industry scholar's career. Similarly, researchers hoping to secure industry interviews in Hollywood might consider post-doctoral funding, or taking a brief residency in Los Angeles. Local exposure to media professionals willing to be interviewed can occur as casually as waiting at a café for a latte, or through participation in media-related gatherings like local film festivals. I also encourage students and scholars to pursue informational interviews, a turn of phrase connoting a pre-job and pre-research interview, well before pursuing their career or position, or prior to the approval of a research project. Provided the meeting goes well, they should prompt their subject to supply possible additional interviewees before leaving the office.

Scholars are encouraged to map interview targets and harness a suite of platforms for their networking and contact affordances. To illustrate, I reference one of the projects in my graduate courses in visual storytelling. Students must conduct case studies related to the making of scripted films and television series across the entire circuit of production, tracing their development, production, marketing, distribution, and reception. They must also secure two interviews, one each from the producing and marketing ranks. In addition to accredited producers listed on the project, students should consider programming, production, and development executives at the networks, studios, or production companies. Additionally, they may consider employees at external creative and advertising agencies contracted by the studio or network. To secure credit, students must prove that their interview subjects were creatively involved in the film or series, whether through press accounts, industry award recognition, or listings in their LinkedIn profile.

## Circumventing gatekeepers and trust-building

Two Hollywood adages apply to our discussion of interview strategies: "You're only as good as your last project," and "the first thing you do after landing a job is update your resume." Whether on LinkedIn or IMDb, media producers and industry professionals must constantly update their profiles and credits. These practices are vital to securing their next job but may also prove a vital resource to media scholars. IMDb lists the names of accredited production members, above- and below-the-line, and through subscription to IMDb Pro – which is often available for free for a short period – researchers may discover contact information for their interview targets. Although rarely providing an email address or cellphone number, interview targets may list their agents, managers, lawyers, or business managers, in turn, placing researchers only two degrees of separation away from their targets.

Media producers, as broadly defined in the last section, may include creative media managers, who are often denied credit on IMDb. However, as media executives, they may list their projects and positions on LinkedIn. Here the features and affordances of LinkedIn can prove equally limiting and helpful. Through a paid subscription, the platform may expose more details about a media professional's career or even contact information, and may allow for direct messages to be sent. Media professionals may, however, disregard those contacting them outside their curated networks. As evidenced by my students' work, media professionals are unlikely to respond to direct messages or unsolicited emails. An alternative LinkedIn strategy is for scholars to identify alumni from their school that currently or previously worked at a media company. These alumni may be more inclined to assist with a research project, help with securing interviews with their colleagues, or provide a direct email or phone number.

Even with contact information, researchers must prove savvy at bypassing the gatekeepers. These may include assistants, agents, managers, interns, and publicists, who not only derive no value but may actually incur great risk by allowing access to their boss, client, or executive. As I remind my students, Hollywood is first and foremost a transactional culture, perhaps second only in quid pro quo expertise to ancient Rome or Washington, DC. What do gatekeepers or those they guard have to gain or lose by offering access or agreeing to an interview? Assistants and agents are more likely to be admonished or fired by their bosses or clients for taking up valuable time away from their never-ending duties. While scholars have offered a voluminous body or work on the precarity of creative labor, creative management may prove just as precarious. Even when well-intentioned, a research interview may inadvertently expose a producer, executive, firm, or production to a backlash, particularly in the social media age of call out culture.

One way to circumvent these concerns is to signal to the gatekeeper or target their recognition of the commitments and risks that can accompany the interview request. Offer to place the interview request or even the questions in writing. Set clear parameters around the amount of time needed. Solicit the meeting in person at the interviewee's convenience before settling for a phone call, Skype, or email exchange. Be as explicit and transparent as possible about the purpose of the interview, whether for a project or course, or as in the case of my own research, how data will be featured solely in scholarly books, articles, and chapters or presented at academic conferences.

Fostering trust with the interview target while securing approval from one's academic institution can prove complicated. Institutional review boards or ethics committees may demand interviewees sign release forms, but media producers are unlikely to do so. If approval is gained, I recommend scholars secure the permission of their interviewees to be recorded. It is a good idea to offer the interviewee a transcript of the discussion for review or, in light of their job demands, a summary or list of key quotes likely to be included in the scholarship. These practices may not only engender trust with the subject but contribute to greater candor. In the course of conducting hundreds of interviews with professionals working in social media entertainment, rarely did subjects object to this practice. The rare exceptions were an agent who reworded all of his responses, a journalist who preferred to go "off-the-record," and an executive no longer employed by the firm but now operating under a signed non-disclosure agreement.

## The social media entertainment and wanghong industries

As new media industries emerge, they pose yet another array of challenges and demand novel strategies for securing and conducting interviews with next-generation media professionals and producers. In this section, I describe these conditions with regards to the emergence of social media entertainment (or SME), a proto-industry that I have mapped alongside my co-author, Stuart Cunningham (who is also featured in this collection). SME refers to how a vast, diverse, and global wave of media producers – alternatively referred to as creators, influencers, youtubers, vloggers, gameplayers, Key Opinion Leaders (KOLs), and wanghong – are harnessing diverse social media platforms to generate commercial and cultural value (Cunningham and Craig 2019). Over the course of six years, we conducted over 300 interviews in ten countries with SME professionals, including over 100 in China where a competing Chinese social media entertainment industry, coined *wanghong*, has emerged. These interviews included creators, platform executives, and a diverse array of social media experts operating in established and emerging media organizations, whether multi-channel networks (MCNs), talent and influencer agencies, or third-party data firms.

Conducting interviews in the SME and wanghong industries proved as challenging as in established media, albeit with some variation. Interviews with platform executives were more often prohibited by platforms experiencing bad press in the wake of ongoing contestations over power. This "techlash" (i.e., negative reactions to the growing power of technology companies) has seen platforms adopt a reactive and defensive stance, demanding that employees remain out of the press, which is often undifferentiated from our status as academic researchers. Faced with these circumstances, the options for us as researchers included conducting interviews off-the-record or with former employees, although the latter may lead to charges of consulting disgruntled labor. Intermediaries working at multi-channel networks, platform data companies, influencer advertising agencies, and talent agencies were more willing to participate, if still hesitant to be forthcoming about the inner workings of their firm or a client's practices, business models, and revenue streams.

While we benefited from the knowledge of these platform executives and the representatives of creators, we hoped they would also prove a conduit to secure interviews directly with creators central to the success of this new screen ecology and, in turn, our research. Some of the executives, publicists, talent agents, and managers were remarkably helpful at introducing us to their clients. We found the success rate improved after first securing trust with these gatekeepers, more readily by convincing them of our less biased, if still critical, research position that neither celebrated nor vilified their work. Others proved more difficult, determined to protect their creator clients from any risk of exposure or critique.

Securing interviews with creators directly posed an array of challenges and demanded a new set of strategies. Most creators remain unrepresented, which meant neither managers nor agents could be useful. Some creators post direct email addresses or contact information on their social media channels, particularly the "about" page on YouTube, although only a few of them responded to our efforts to secure an interview. We tried other approaches that align with the adage "slipping into DMs," as in direct messaging them online through their various channels and platforms. In some instance, we had to confirm our identities and neutral bona fides by sharing prior scholarship with them, which is where earlier online commentaries that we had written about the political and progressive influence of creators proved useful. Even leading creators operate out of their homes and were unwilling to risk their privacy to allow us to visit, so interviews were often conducted in neutral spaces like coffeeshops. Some creators were underage, posing a set of critical ethical demands on the research, including institutional approval, and more often requiring parental supervision during interviews.

The psycho-social conditions for conducting creator-based interviews were unique from my experience interviewing other media professionals, whether behind-the-scenes producers to successful on-screen performers. In contrast to their confident online lives, many creators experience anxiety when interacting offline and IRL (in real life). If willing to be interviewed, the creators often proved awkward, being hard to elicit responses from, and often demanded that they be joined by their colleagues, representatives, spouses, and friends. Beyond the interpersonal, after years of contemptuous coverage in the press that may generate a withering online backlash, creators are particularly reticent to risk public disclosure. More readily, creators have constructed, curated, and commodified their online lives leaving little reason to provide any further exposure. Yet, creators present one future for media industries and for media industries research – a future driven by these sociocultural entrepreneurs who yield vital accounts of how power operates within these emerging platform economies and cultures.

## Peeking behind the curtain

Returning to the parable within *The Wizard of Oz*, behind even the most remarkable depictions of media spectacle, securing interviews with media producers allow scholars to pull back the curtain – to identify and critically reflect upon the role of human agency within the screen industries. As detailed in this chapter, interviews prove more useful in consort with a holistic media industries studies approach featuring diverse methods, including secondary online research and economic analysis. In expanding the definition of media producers to include a diverse array of creative collaborators, we may achieve richer insights into the complex operations throughout the media supply chain. Detailed here are strategies for securing interviews with media producers that demand networking skills, circumventing gatekeepers, and building connection through snowballing, among others. As discussed, the emergence of digital and social media industries era poses new complications and demand innovative strategies in order to secure value-rich interviews with these cultural and media producers.

## References

Caldwell, J. T. (2008) *Production Culture: Industrial Reflexivity and Critical Practice in Film and Television*, Durham, NC: Duke University Press.

Caldwell, J. T. (2009) "How Producers 'Theorize': Shoot-outs, Bake-offs, and Speed-dating," in R. Hammer and D. Kellner (eds), *Media/Cultural Studies: Critical Approaches*, New York, Peter Lang, 68–87.

Caldwell, JT (2013) "Para-Industry: Researching Hollywood's Blackwaters," *Cinema Journal*, 52 (3): 157–165.

Cunningham, S. and Craig, D. (2019) *Social Media Entertainment: The New Intersection of Hollywood and Silicon Valley*, New York: New York University Press.

de Certeau, M. (1984) *The Practice of Everyday Life*, Berkeley, CA: University of California Press.

Deleuze, G. and Félix, G. (1980) *A Thousand Plateaus: Capitalism and Schizophrenia*, London: Athlone Press.

du Gay, P. (ed.) (1997) *Production of Culture/Cultures of Production*, London: Sage.

Foucault, M. (1979) "What Is an Author?," *Screen*, 20 (1): 13–34.

Gitlin, T. (1983) *Inside Prime Time*, New York: Pantheon Books.

Govil, N. (2013) "Recognizing 'Industry'," *Cinema Journal*, 52 (3): 172–176.

Havens, T., Lotz, A. and Tinic, S. (2009) "Critical Media Industry Studies: A Research Approach," *Communication, Culture and Critique*, 2 (2): 234–253.

Hebert, D., Lotz, A., and Punathambekar, A. (2020) *Media Industry Studies*, Cambridge: Polity Press.

Johnson, D., Kompare, D., and Santo, A. (eds) (2014) *Making Media Work: Cultures of Management in the Entertainment Industries*, New York: New York University Press.

Kashani, T. and Nocella, A. J. (2010) "Hollywood's Cinema of Ableism: A Disability Studies Perspective on the Hollywood Industrial Complex," R. Van Heertum, T. Kashani, A. Nocella, and B. Frymer (eds), *Hollywood's Exploited: Public Pedagogy, Corporate Movies, and Cultural Crisis*, New York: Palgrave Macmillan, 105–114.

Mayer, V. (2011) *Below the Line: Producers and Production Studies in the New Television Economy*, Durham, NC: Duke University Press.

Mayer, V., Banks, M., and Caldwell, J. (eds) (2009) *Production Studies: Cultural Studies of Media Industries*, New York: Routledge.

Ortner, S. B. (2010) "Studying Sideways: Ethnographic Access in Hollywood," in V. Mayer, M. J. Banks, and J. T. Caldwell (eds), *Production Studies: Cultural Studies of Media Industries*, New York: Routledge, 175–189.

Ortner, S. B. (2013) *Not Hollywood: Independent Film at the Twilight of the American Dream*, Durham, NC: Duke University Press.

Perman, S. (2019) "Hollywood Assistants Are in Open Revolt. Here's Why," *Los Angeles Times*, November 2, available at www.latimes.com/entertainment-arts/business/story/2019-11-02/la-et-ct-hollywood-assistants-revolt (accessed March 26, 2020).

Powdermaker, H. (1950) *Hollywood, the Dream Factory: An Anthropologist Looks at the Movie-makers*, Boston, MA: Little, Brown and Company.

Ross, A. (1989) *No Respect: Intellectuals and Popular Culture*, New York: Routledge.

Rosten, L. (1941) *Hollywood: The Movie Colony, the Movie Makers*, New York: Harcourt, Brace.

Roussel, V. (2017) *Representing Talent: Hollywood Agents and the Making of Movies*, Chicago, IL: University of Chicago Press.

# 43

# HARNESSING THE LIFE HISTORY METHOD TO STUDY THE MEDIA INDUSTRIES

*Roei Davidson and Oren Meyers*

## What are life histories?

Life histories allow individuals to tell a longitudinal narrative of their experiences from their own, emic, perspective uncovering how media workers feel and think about the work they do, and the lives they lead (Meyers and Davidson 2017). These personal narratives provide a powerful prism for studying the media industries as social institutions, scaling up from individual experiences and recollections to an analysis of media organizations, whole industries, and their relationship with other social institutions. Researchers "read [the life histories] symptomatically, to uncover the deeper forces governing experience" (Morgan and Nelligan 2015: 69). Rather than detailing the particular life story of an individual, as commonly done in journalistic accounts or autobiographies of successful and famous cultural producers, life history research aims to illuminate the meeting point between structural and institutional conditions and personal agency. A life history narrative is co-produced by a participant telling her life story and a researcher who uses in-depth interviewing techniques to encourage the interviewee to narrate her story in a relatively unstructured manner. Life histories studies often focus on an aspect of one's life with occupational life histories being especially common.

While researchers can thematically focus on a particular aspect of a participant's life such as one's occupational history (Meyers and Davidson 2014), in telling their stories participants often consider other life domains such as family life, hobbies, formal education experiences and more. Thus, for example, Ofek (pseudonym), one of the interviewees in our large-scale occupational life history study of active and former Israeli journalists, recounted in detail how the intensive nature of broadcasting work strained his relationship with his spouse, contributing eventually to their divorce. Later, after Ofek left his broadcasting job to become a print editor, the newspaper in which he worked folded ("a horrible crisis"). Ofek evocatively recounted how "the day [the bank] in X neighborhood heard that Y newspaper had ceased publication, and I had an overdraft, I inserted my card to withdraw cash in Jerusalem and it swallowed the card". Later in the interview he told us how these painful experiences of familial and financial instability drove him to seek out an editorial position in a well-funded news organization to allow him to take care of a child of whom he now had custody.

DOI: 10.4324/9780429275340-49

When such connections between a project's occupational focus and other (personal, familial etc.) domains become apparent, the researcher should allow the interviewee to elaborate without interruption and might actively ask her to consider recounting experiences that extend beyond the study's putative focus. Such probing illustrates the co-productive nature of life history research. More generally, this vignette also highlights how the life history approach can identify the ways in which media production work is woven into the broader tapestry of people's personal, social, and economic lives. Finally, the presence of such segments in occupational life history narratives illustrate why media industry scholars should consider the fact that media producers increasingly do their work in an age of serial political, health and environmental crises that blur the lines between personal and professional realms.

In the remainder of this chapter, we will first survey recent advances in the use of life histories to study media industries labor. We will then consider how life histories could serve as a powerful tool to study the temporal dimension of media work, a dimension that has recently gained more attention among scholars studying media workers and especially journalists. We will then consider how analysis of detailed life histories accounts can help us identify the emergence of precarity side by side with the persistence of more stable employment arrangements. Hence, this method helps illuminate heterogeneity in labor experiences and especially variations in the levels of precarity workers experience in the media industries. Finally, we will consider the presence of life history-like accounts in the public domain – in the press, on crowdfunding platforms, and in the judicial arena – and the potential to study those to validate conventional life history research.

## Life histories and media industries research

Life histories of media industries workers document the unstable and casual nature of media careers, as the state and employers expect them to individually shoulder most of the economic risk they face. Most recent life history studies recognize that cultural producers often work simultaneously or sequentially in multiple industries and on multiple projects and hence these studies do not merely focus on a single cultural occupation.

A life history study of workers in the independent television production sector in England documented the precarious nature of such careers and the psychological (e.g., emotional burnout) and material costs workers must pay to secure the creative freedom they value. Deepening the longitudinal nature of life histories, this study notably interviewed workers twice in ten years documenting how the increased commercialization of British television had driven many to exit the industry because "it was no longer a space where one could have meaningful social impact" (Lee 2018: 117). Expanding this discussion, our exploration of life histories of active and former Israeli journalists (Davidson and Meyers 2016) found that in addition to the impact of external political-economic changes, life cycle changes, such as becoming a parent, drove some journalists to seek more stable and remunerative employment elsewhere.

The ways in which culture industries workers construct their life stories and frame them, delineate many of the fundamental dilemmas such workers face, and the rhetorical mechanisms they employ to ease career-related tensions. Hence, for instance, an exploration of the life histories of early-career graphic designers pointed at the ways in which interviewees drew boundaries between commercial and artistic work to contend with the commercial imperatives of the media industries. Some interviewees segmented their activities practically and rhetorically into artistic and commercial projects, presenting the latter as supporting the former. However, a significant minority of executives and entrepreneurs working in the culture industries recognized the boundary between commerce and art, but at the same time chose to integrate the two, arguing that grappling with commercial constraints actually required them to become more creative in their work (Rowe 2019). Following a similar route, successful Israeli screenwriters narrated the tension between commerce and art in their careers as a positive creative challenge, describing the pleasure they derived from "solving" (writing) a scene within given production constraints (Hagay and Davidson 2014).

As mentioned, occupational life histories reflect an ongoing negotiation between institutional or organizational settings and individual agency. Narration of such life histories, as a constant interface between macro and micro influences, becomes even denser when demographic and cultural factors are interwoven into the accounts. Thus, for example, a study of how young working-class Australians enter the media industries found gender and class differences in their ability to successfully secure a living. While women have an easier time adapting to the expectation to constantly network and socially perform, working-class men were more attracted to the craft aspects of their cultural trade, and rejected the need to invest in self-presentation. In contrast to many life history studies, that present their findings in the form of a narrative weaved out of interview snippets interspersed with interpretation from a large number of interviewees, this study chose to present extended case studies of five young people. Such an approach could potentially have the benefit of providing a thicker description of experiences in the media industries (Morgan and Nelligan 2015).

At the other end of the status ladder, exploring the occupational trajectories of senior culture industry workers helps further illuminate the challenges of promoting social mobility through culture industry labor: the life histories of senior men in the British creative and cultural industries suggest that those in positions of power (mostly white men from privileged social and educational backgrounds) recognize that there is racial and gender inequality in the makeup of these industries. However, these histories suggest that their narrators understand their relative success as a function of luck, rather than privilege. This tendency to ignore the role of inequality and foreground the role of luck in their own success could perhaps explain the interviewees' belief in their limited capacity to effect change in their workplaces, despite their prominent position in the organization and the wider field (Brook, O'Brien, and Taylor 2019).

## Examining temporality: the utility of life history research

Until recently, the temporal dimension of culture industry production was relatively neglected. This has been especially apparent in journalism studies. When time has been considered, the focus has often been on how time is invoked or represented in news stories, how time pressures relate to short-term deadlines shaping news routines (Schudson 1986; Zelizer 2018), and more recently, on how the affordances of different media shape the temporal dimension of news texts (Tenenboim-Weinblatt and Neiger 2018). Much less has been said about temporality as a key factor in shaping the occupational trajectories of those who cover the news; that is, how the work experiences of news producers evolve over time and, in turn shape the news. Some researchers have criticized this "presentism" and argued that life histories could be used to tell "us much about the nitty-gritty of everyday lived experience, which may often be unglamorous and unworthy of note, but is intrinsically tied to broader social, political, economic, and technological transformations" (Wahl-Jorgensen 2019: 672). Similarly, scholars have also argued that studies of news work should espouse "temporal reflexivity": an effort to evaluate "whether some phenomenon is indeed a break from what came before, a continuation of what has existed, or some middle-ground mutation" (Carlson and Lewis 2019: 644).

Considering how labor conditions and practices evolve over long time spans requires the use of methods that can account for the experiences of cultural producers over time. We would argue that life histories are uniquely suited to allow such a consideration. For example, in our examination of "tribes of professionalism," we found that even into the twenty-first century, relatively stable pockets of bureaucratic journalists working in public service broadcasting persist, alongside evidence of a novel type of entrepreneurial journalist rapidly moving sequentially and simultaneously between ventures (Davidson and Meyers 2015; Meyers and Davidson 2016). In this way, life histories can answer Carlson and Lewis' call to focus not only on institutional change, but also on continuity.

## Identifying heterogeneity: moving beyond precariousness

There are many examples of the potential utility of employing the life history logic to study media institutions and labor. One illustration of the methodological and conceptual advantages of life histories is the way they broaden the discussion about precariousness. A central finding regarding media industries work in recent decades is that workers tend to have precarious careers characterized by occupational instability, often working part-time for multiple employers with no tenure and limited benefits (Arnold and Bongiovi 2013; de Peuter 2014). Missing in much of this work is the fact that levels of precariousness vary considerably between workers who lead stable careers in particular organizations and entrepreneurs who by choice or compulsion switch constantly between projects and employers (Davidson and Meyers 2015). To identify this heterogeneity, we need to use methods suited to detecting differences in precariousness between people and across time. Life histories research is such a method. Identifying heterogeneity and comparing career trajectories allows us to outline mechanisms that make careers less precarious. Such studies are sensitive to the ways differing employment situations over time shape how workers experience and justify the work they do (Fine 1996). Decades into this age of precarity, practitioners and researchers can potentially learn from other practitioners how to contend with these many challenges, and what individual and collective strategies can be used to alleviate precariousness. As a result, life histories allow us to conduct a "geological" study of precariousness, constituting an opportunity to delve into the many layers and sediments of the unstable careers media workers now lead.

A life history approach could be especially useful to study the emergence of unionization as a collective strategy for coping with precariousness. News workers involved in the unionization of editorial employees at *Gawker,* a (now bankrupt) American digital news organization, made numerous temporal claims about how their career and employing organization had changed in the past and might change in the future. Union supporters cited past unionization experiences when considering present efforts (Prasad 2019). Such public unionization efforts that often aim to secure organizational change over time suggest a life history of union supporters and opponents in media organization would be a fruitful means for studying how workers cope with changing employment arrangements and attempt to shape them in the future. Hence, for instance, unionizing processes in the mobile communication industry in Israel which emerged after this industry became more competitive (Lazar, Ribak, and Davidson 2020) suggest that workers respond over time to changing conditions.

While in the unionization study, the professed aim of the inquiry was to identify changes of perception and experience across time, such phenomena could also be identified and studied through a retrospective reading of a life history corpus. For example, our study of the life histories of Israeli journalists did not feature gender-related questions as a primary analytical goal. And yet, a retrospective close reading of the narratives recounted by former and active female Israeli journalists illuminated a variety of experiences, related to themes such as the impact of having children on career choices and the various aspects of chauvinism within Israeli newsrooms.

In summary, a life history approach is especially suited for studying processes that necessarily unfold over time. Moreover, the tracking and exploration of such longitudinal processes could be aided through the implementation of a multiple wave design, entailing at least two life history interviews conducted with each participant, at distinct time points (Lee 2018).

## Triangulating life histories

While the life history approach enables researchers to co-construct together with interviewees a detailed longitudinal narrative of one's working life, and probe moments and experiences more deeply, labor narratives reminiscent of this method also occur outside of the immediate research context. In this final section, we will briefly discuss the ways in which an adoption of the life history logic could enrich the exploration of a number of other media labor narrative sites: third-person profiles, online first-person narratives on social media, crowdfunding pitches, and judicial processes. We will consider how life history sensibilities could be used to analyze these discourses and how such discourses can be used to triangulate and even validate interview-based life history research.

Third-person profiles of notable individuals have been a long-standing feature in journalism. In the mid-twentieth century, Leo Lowenthal famously analyzed these profiles and found a move from writing about "idols of production" in politics and business, to "idols of consumption" in the entertainment industries as the American economy became dependent on a large middle class of mass consumers. One of Lowenthal's essential observations pointed at the importance of lucky "breaks" in the narratives explaining the success of these idols (Lowenthal 2004). It is striking that the aforementioned life histories of twenty-first-century senior workers in the British media industries echo this same focus on luck, and disregard of structural limitations (Brook, O'Brien and Taylor 2019). This disregard in popular profiles and in these workers' life narratives might explain why both serve as agents of social stasis rather than of change. When media executives and workers consume popular accounts of the individual genius and luck cultural stars possess, they will be less likely to promote or demand organizational change because such accounts foreground chance and individual agency. Executives who lack an understanding of how uneven provision of social services such as education and health and endemic intergenerational economic inequality in capitalist societies provide some social groups such as their own with better occupational prospects than those of others, will not find it necessary to institute organizational policies (e.g., mentoring, affirmative action in hiring) that would provide workers from disadvantaged backgrounds with better occupational prospects.

A replication of the Lowenthal study (Duffy and Pooley 2019) finds that twenty-first-century accounts of celebrities in magazines, TV shows, and social media account profiles emphasize self-promotion, authenticity, and entrepreneurialism. It could be analytically worthwhile to analyze in tandem, using similar analytical categories, public narratives of celebrities and life history narratives of a diverse sample of cultural workers. This could allow scholars to consider to what extent media workers draw on common public tropes in their self-understandings of their work experiences.

In addition, crowdfunding is another prominent site of self-promotional work (Davidson and Poor 2015; Hunter 2016). In the frequent absence of an existing product, project founders, many of them cultural producers, rely on a presentation of their professional record side by side with the planned project to convince the public they can fulfill their promises. A parallel analysis of project founders' public self-presentation and personal life histories could uncover to what extent individual workers integrate market imperatives into their more private self-understandings of their careers.

Finally, we turn to the judicial arena, where information gathered from legal proceedings can illuminate covert or mundane aspects of cultural producers' work experiences, and corroborate life history accounts which must remain anonymous or are wholly dependent on the narrator's narrative choices and interests. While anonymity is ethically necessary in many ways, it can limit the ability to use life histories to study institutional practices rather than focus solely on individual perceptions or discourses of such practices. More direct reflections of daily work routines often documented in judicial processes in the form of public testimony and records of (normally confidential) organizational practices and communications submitted as evidence could be a valuable supplementary data source. Legal proceedings often force various actors to provide information they would rather have kept hidden, making the legal arena a useful journalistic source. Investigative journalists often rely on evidence discovered in litigation to originate a story, quantify the prevalence of a phenomenon, collect background details on individuals involved in a story, and corroborate existing information (Shapira 2018). In a similar manner, legal evidence can be used as data for research purposes. However, it is important to note that we are not advocating the use of legal evidence as a means of exposing research participants to whom we have promised anonymity. This would be a serious ethical breach. Rather, we are suggesting that legal evidence could be used to consider – in parallel with life histories – institutional mechanisms rather than the activities of particular individuals which are seldom of interest in social science research.

To illustrate the potential for validation, we will triangulate the life histories of Israeli journalists we collected, demonstrating the extensive political and economic pressures they contend with and to which they often succumb (Meyers and Davidson 2014), with evidence of journalists' daily work experiences collected as part of the indictment of Israeli Prime Minister Binyamin Netanyahu (The State of Israel V. Binyamin Netanyahu 2019) on suspicion of trading regulatory favors for positive journalistic coverage. In our life histories corpus, Idan (pseudonym), an editor in an Israeli daily newspaper, was one of a number of senior journalists who recounted how higher-ups in the news organization often channeled external pressures from political and economic actors as well as publisher demands to reshape their coverage in ways that serve those actors' interests, producing a general "sense of resignation." Idan noted: "There are all kinds of interests you have to take in account, all kinds of sensitivities from within the newspaper and from the outside … You always need to lie, you always regret some things" (cited in Meyers and Davidson 2014: 1001).

One of the central accusations in the Netanyahu indictment revolves around the relationship between Netanyahu, a number of his advisors, Shaul Alovitz (owner of a large media conglomerate which includes a major Israeli news site, *Walla!*), *Walla!* CEO Ilan Yeshua, and several of the website editors. The indictment claims Alovitz pressured his news site employees to ensure positive coverage of Netanyahu in return for the government taking regulatory decisions benefiting his other business interests. In a long appendix to the indictment, the Justice Ministry included extended excerpts from WhatsApp correspondence, mostly between Alovitz and Yeshua. These related to demands made to include particular flattering stories and headlines and demote or delete stories that were not supportive of the Prime Minister. The pressures seem to illustrate the constant compromises contemporaneous Israeli journalists mentioned in the occupational life histories we collected. For example, paragraphs 41–42 in the appendix focus on demands made through a media advisor to publish two stories glorifying Netanyahu and recounting the cultural pursuits of his wife. The appendix quotes the acerbic response of the news site's acting editor: "The story will be published as Kim is recounting it in less than an hour … I am absolutely certain you understand the gravity of inventing journalistic stories at the regime's behest. Another good day for all of us." Here, the editor assigns the Israeli Prime

Minister the name of North Korea's Supreme Leader, Kim Jong-un, illustrating his belief that these practices stray far from liberal democratic ideals. The ironic reference to "another good day" validates the constant compromises Israeli journalists recounted in their life histories.

Using qualitative data analysis software (e.g., Atlas.ti, Dedoose, etc.) researchers could load for joint analysis a corpus of documents – transcribed life histories, judicial documents and more – and carry out thematic analysis of these texts using a common set of analytical categories. Hence, in the above case, researchers could examine indications of how external pressures compromise professional autonomy in both transcripts and judicial texts. Were we to identify such commonalities across data sources, we would be able to leverage data source triangulation (Denzin 1978) to validate the existence of such a professional and civic pathology.

## Conclusion

In this chapter, we surveyed recent life history studies of culture industries workers, and especially journalists. Many of these studies provide granular representations of the discourses and practices of cultural producers, as they relate to their work experiences and career structure. In their attempt to construct biographical narratives, life histories allow scholars to consider more closely how industries evolve over time and how workers experience this evolution, moving away from more static accounts that ignore temporal change and heterogeneity. Further, we argue that the granularity of life histories might allow media industries studies to go beyond evidence of occupational precarity and identify the varying levels of instability workers experience. Finally, we suggest that the sensitivity life histories engender to the ways cultural producers recount their careers could be harnessed toward the analysis of public narratives of cultural work. When appropriate, life histories can be triangulated with public narratives allowing media industries scholarship to tell more analytically complex stories of media industries as crucially important social institutions.

## References

Arnold, D., and Bongiovi, J. R. (2013) "Precarious, Informalizing, and Flexible Work: Transforming Concepts and Understandings," *American Behavioral Scientist*, 57 (3): 289–308.

Brook, O., O'Brien, D., and Taylor, M. (2019) "Inequality Talk: How Discourses by Senior Men Reinforce Exclusions from Creative Occupations," *European Journal of Cultural Studies*, available at https://journals.sagepub.com/doi/full/10.1177/1367549419886020 (accessed December 4, 2020).

Carlson, M. and Lewis, S. C. (2019) "Temporal Reflexivity in Journalism Studies: Making Sense of Change in a More Timely Fashion," *Journalism*, 20 (5): 642–650.

Davidson, R. and Meyers, O. (2015) "Toward a Typology of Journalism Careers: Conceptualizing Israeli Journalists' Occupational Trajectories," *Communication, Culture and Critique*, 9 (2): 193–211.

Davidson, R. and Meyers, O. (2016) "Should I Stay or Should I Go?" *Journalism Studies*, 17 (5): 590–607.

Davidson, R. and Poor, N. D. (2015) "The Barriers Facing Artists' Use of Crowdfunding Platforms: Personality, Emotional Labor, and Going to the Well One Too Many Times," *New Media and Society*, 17 (2): 289–307.

de Peuter, G. (2014). Confronting Precarity in the Warhol Economy. *Journal of Cultural Economy*, 7 (1): 31–47.

Denzin, N. K. (1978) *The Research Act: A Theoretical Introduction to Sociological Methods*, 2nd ed., New York: McGraw Hill.

Duffy, B. E., and Pooley, J. (2019) "Idols of Promotion: The Triumph of Self-Branding in an Age of Precarity," *Journal of Communication*, 69 (1): 26–48.

Fine, G. A. (1996) "Justifying Work: Occupational Rhetorics as Resources in Restaurant Kitchens," *Administrative Science Quarterly*, 41 (1): 90–115.

Hagay, H. and Davidson, R. (2014) " 'It's Difficult to Dream': The Career Structure of Screenwriters in the Israeli Film and Television Industry," [Hebrew], *Media Frames*, 13: 63–84.

Hunter, A. (2016) "'It's Like Having a Second Full-Time Job: Crowdfunding, Journalism and Labour'," *Journalism Practice*, 10 (2): 217–232.

Lazar, T., Ribak, R., and Davidson, R. (2020) "Mobile Social Media as Platforms in Workers' Unionization," *Information, Communication and Society*, 23(3): 437–453.

Lee, D. (2018) "Working in the Indies: Precarity, Value and Burnout," in D. Lee (ed.), *Independent Television Production in the UK: From Cottage Industry to Big Business*, Cham: Palgrave Macmillan, 97–126.

Lowenthal, L. (2004) "Biographies in Popular Magazines," in J. D. Peters and P. Simonson (eds), *Mass Communication and American Social Thought: Key Texts, 1919–1968*, Lanham, MD: Rowman & Littlefield, 188–205.

Meyers, O. and Davidson, R. (2014) "The Journalistic Structure of Feeling: An Exploration of Career Life Histories of Israeli Journalists," *Journalism*, 15 (8): 987–1005.

Meyers, O. and Davidson, R. (2016) "Conceptualizing Journalistic Careers: Between Interpretive Community and Tribes of Professionalism," *Sociology Compass*, 10 (6): 419–431.

Meyers, O. and Davidson, R. (2017) "Interviewing Interviewers: Collecting, Analyzing and Generalizing from Occupational Life Histories of Journalists," *The Communication Review*, 20 (4): 1–19.

Morgan, G. and Nelligan, P. (2015) "Labile Labour: Gender, Flexibility and Creative Work," *The Sociological Review*, 63 (S1): 66–83.

Prasad, R. (2019) "An Organized Work Force is Part of Growing Up: Gawker and the Case for Unionizing Digital Newsrooms," *Communication, Culture and Critique*, 12 (3): 359–377.

Rowe, M. S. (2019) "Boundary Work and Early Careers in Design and Media," *Poetics*, 72: 70–80.

Schudson, M. (1986) "Deadlines, Datelines, and History," in R. K. Manoff and M. Schudson (eds), *Reading the News*, New York: Pantheon, 79–108.

Shapira, R. (2018) "Law as Source: How the Legal System Facilitates Investigative Journalism," *Yale Law and Policy Review*, 37 (1): 153–226.

Tenenboim-Weinblatt, K. and Neiger, M. (2018) "Temporal Affordances in the News," *Journalism*, 19 (1): 37–55.

The State of Israel V. Binyamin Netanyahu (2019) (indictment), available at www.gov.il/BlobFolder/news/28-1-2020-01/he/files_cases_and_verdicts_case-1000-2000-4000.pdf (accessed December 4, 2020).

Wahl-Jorgensen, K. (2019) "Challenging Presentism in Journalism Studies: An Emotional Life History Approach to Understanding the Lived Experience of Journalists," *Journalism*, 20 (5): 670–678.

Zelizer, B. (2018) "Epilogue: Timing the Study of News Temporality," *Journalism*, 19 (1): 111–121.

# 44

# INTERFACING WITH INDUSTRY

*Stuart Cunningham*

There is too little public debate in our discipline field about the academic interface with industry. After all, what we study is called media *industries*. In conversation, my colleague at Queensland University of Technology (QUT) Amanda Lotz calls it a "perennial conference colloquium topic" without that much, we agreed, being actually published around the topic. When we as a discipline seek, or are asked, to be expansive, reflective, or metacritical, such as on the occasion of the launch of the *Media Industries* journal, the topic can come up (see Patrick Vonderau's (2014) "Industry Proximity" or Des Freedman's (2014) "Media Policy Research and the Media Industries" in the inaugural issue of that journal). Vonderau warns us, for example, that "the imperative of getting 'close' or 'inside' the field often poses more challenges than opportunities." A recent book such as Matthew Freeman's (2016) *Industrial Approaches to Media: A Methodological Gateway to Industry Study*, a guidebook that "provides direction in ways best suited to collaborative dialogue between media scholars and media professionals," is an unusual centralization of the question of the interface with industry for the academy. Examples of the case for the wider contribution to the public good made by communication and media scholarship has been recently passionately argued by Philip Napoli and Minna Aslama (2011) and Silvio Waisbord (2019). The times may be with those who would seek to make the relationship between media industries scholarship and the industries we study a closer one.

First, I will situate myself personally in this topic together with my theoretical and national context. The alternative to a personal approach to a topic like this is a hectoring how-to tone. I would rather show than tell. I then suggest there are three main drivers for engagement with industry: the motivations of media industries scholars themselves and the different means of activating them; the institutional nudge, or mandate, for interfacing with industry; and a pedagogical ethics that supports engagement beyond the academy.

## Formative background

It's important to situate any attention to the practicalities and contingencies of engagement with industry in a larger normative framework of political economy and public culture and polity. I use the word "industry" as a short-hand for engagement with the media industry itself, but

DOI: 10.4324/9780429275340-50

also bodies which represent their interests, as well as the governmental "industries" of public policy and public agencies which subvent, regulate, and develop policy for the media industries.

The broader public culture which was a formative influence on my development as a researcher and teacher of media and communication studies from the 1980s was one characteristic of so-called semi-peripheral nations in the center-periphery model developed in Immanuel Wallerstein's (2004) world systems theory. This was, broadly speaking, a cultural nationalist model, which stressed the potentially positive role of the state in such semi-peripheral, settler-colonial nations as Australia in mitigating and managing some of the effects of the cultural and media hegemony of both the United States and the UK. This normative framework formed the basis for textual and industrial analysis of semi-peripheral nations' cultural legitimacy and vibrancy in complicity but also managed dialogue with, and resistance to, culturally hegemonic forces. I wrote my PhD dissertation (and first book – *Featuring Australia*) on Australia's greatest cultural-nationalist filmmaker from the early period (Cunningham 1991). Working in collaboration, there followed *Australian Television and International Mediascapes*, a study of Australian television export during the first wave of European broadcasting liberalization and US cable expansion (Cunningham and Jacka 1996), and *New Patterns in Global Television*, a general study of peripheral nations' "striking back" at US–UK global television dominance (Sinclair, Jacka, and Cunningham 1996). The broader normative position in interfacing with industry was to support its efforts for cultural definition and advancement of the national cultural "project" – not a position easy for media scholars in the United States, UK, or Western Europe to adopt, given their nation-states' histories as imperial and global hegemons.

A further fundamental formative influence was working outside the academy for a period as a policy analyst and adviser in a not-for-profit public interest advocacy unit, the Communications Law Centre, which was based on US models of public interest advocacy into the policy process. There, the interface with industry and policy actors was daily and direct, leading to my book, *Framing Culture* (Cunningham 1992), which advanced a controversial argument against left tendencies favoring a default internationalism and cosmopolitanism against state action and national cultures as those tendencies are played out in practical cultural and media policy positions in everyday national jurisdictions. This was applied cultural nationalism focused on the legitimacy and sustainability of the industries producing representations.

Together, these two formative influences have combined to shape a couple of decades of my industry- and policy-oriented research agenda, and my interface with industry. Most recently, the largest frame for this research has been the role of creative industries, especially digital media applications, in national innovation systems. Debates around creative industries have certainly attested to their controversial status in the academy – while being treated as an oftentimes welcome addition to the contemporization of cultural, industry, and innovation policies in several policy jurisdictions and industry sectors around the world. While some (Miller 2009; for a rebuttal, see Cunningham 2010) would argue for an "epistemological break" between cultural policy (potentially progressive state and local action) and creative industries (neoliberal capture by corporate interests), my investment in the creative industries idea was driven very much by recognizably cultural-nationalist goals to shore up the sustainability of small business in the emerging and expanding digital media field against the power and influence of Big Culture and Big Media.

A key feature of creative industries discourse is an "enterprise" approach to business development. This seeks to take account of the vast preponderance of small business or small business-like entities that populate the sector in most countries and builds theory around what we might call the "economic subalterns" in our midst. This is a sector running on tight margins and facing high rates of failure, in need of flexible and in many cases experimental forms of state facilitation, and which rarely figures on governments' cultural policy radar. The point is that much of the independent media enterprises sector (games, design, web development, music, audiovisual) is organized in this way and spans the commercial and the subvented, complicating the binary thinking that seeks to exclude the commercial from anything other than critique, and marks out the distance of these sectors from most official state cultural policy. Small business enterprise or entrepreneurship, and policies to support it, often has to run the gauntlet against much more powerful vested interests – Big Culture, Big Business, and Big Government. These concerns culminated for me in running for nine years a multi-university, multidisciplinary, publicly funded research center of excellence, with sufficient public and industry funding to more programmatically engage with these issues and with industry stakeholders affected by these issues (see "ARC Centre of Excellence for Creative Industries and Innovation," Wikipedia (n.d.)). With this background established, I now turn to the three drivers of engagement with industry.

## Motivations of critical media industries scholars

Media industries scholars, particularly those who identify as "critical," embrace normative frameworks that guide and inform their research and which, in principle, may motivate them to wish to see reform and improvement in the media systems they examine. To see how these motivations might play out in practice, I will suggest six different but mostly complementary positions, or "personae" (Marshall, 2015), scholars can adopt as they engage outside the academy and give one or two examples of each: the public communicator; the advocate; the independent expert; the researcher in collaboration with, and funded by, industry; the immersive researcher; and governance and leadership roles.

First, we can engage in *public communication*, writing, speaking, and being interviewed on matters of public import about the media industries. This is perhaps the most common approach, and the one most closely aligned with the habitus of the academic. At the least, it requires our preparedness to translate our concerns out of "academlish" and being available and open to media interest in our work. It can also involve proactive placing newsworthy perspectives arising from our research. The avenues for this sort of interface with the news industry and generally beyond the academy have increased as a result of digital disruption of the information media. The need for evidence-based public communication is also arguably greater, with the rise of fake news and systematic attempts to hack the public spheres of Western democracies. What have come to be called "amplifier" platforms – academic voices amplified beyond academia – are now numerous and include *Salon*, *Medium*, and *The Conversation*. *The Conversation* is a site (begun in Australia, now operating in the UK, United States, Canada, France, South Africa, New Zealand, and Spain) dedicated to professionalizing and disseminating public academic communication. *The Conversation* self-reports that 82 percent of its readership in Australia is non-academic (*The Conversation*, 2018).

Kim Osman and I (Osman and Cunningham 2020) surveyed and interviewed scholars across career stages, disciplines, and institutions in a research project investigating the increased role of amplifier platforms in academic and public spheres. We found that scholars frame engagement as an ethical imperative integral to their practice. They are not only interested in seeing their own research amplified, but in amplifying other quality research, and this benefits their other academic activities. But they often remarked that institutional support for engaging on amplifier platforms is uneven and underdeveloped. Our research has identified numerous media scholars who are committed to making a contribution to this post mass media journalism.

Second, there is *advocacy* and *industry activism*. This often takes the form of engaging with policy bureaus and the methodologies of engagement can typically take the form of reports and briefs. I spent a period outside the academy as a policy analyst and advocate in a not-for-profit public interest advocacy unit, the Communications Law Centre. There, the interface with policy and industry led me to experience directly the structural tension between tactically achievable, highly focused and technically precise, reformist advocacy and the universalizing principles and revolutionary rhetoric that often guide academic debate (cf Cunningham 1991).

Pat Aufderheide, a veteran scholar, advocate and activist based at the American University in Washington, DC, is perhaps best known for the depth of her engagement with industry around the maximization of fair use affordances for media and cultural workers (Aufderheide and Jaszi 2018). But this work is the tip of the iceberg: her advocacy and activism has taken in telecommunications reform, cable access policy, and community media in the United States, and has been practised in Brazil and Australia (see Aufderheide, Pappalardo, Suzor, and Stevens 2018) – the latter two on Fulbright scholarships. A particularly telling example of assistance to documentary filmmakers through advice to a major foundation is retold in a personal communication from Professor Aufderheide:

> The MacArthur Foundation, which was interested in learning about how to fund in the area better, gave me funds to address the topic of threats facing filmmakers who make investigative/journalistic docs. What emerged was *Dangerous Documentaries: Reducing Risk While Telling Truth to Power*. The report got wide coverage in the field, influenced MacArthur's funding choices, triggered a new project to increase funder awareness of the funding needs to cover risks, and initiated a project at the Reporters' Committee on Freedom of the Press to offer pre-production risk-avoidance legal advice for filmmakers.

Third, *independent expertise*. The academic tradition of tenure is meant to protect scholars so they can speak truth to power based on independent expertise. Leading US media and cultural studies scholar Henry Jenkins gives a trenchant account of his engagement with the corporate world in a personal communication about the origins of two of his most notable books:

> We developed a consortium of multiple corporate partners which had a shared interest in thinking about how the media industry engaged with its fans and consumers in the Web 2.0 era. And this involved the production of white papers, consulting and speaking inside their organizations, and student internships. The *Spreadable Media* book emerged from these kinds of interactions with industry. Both *Convergence Culture* and *Spreadable Media* have been widely read within creative industries around the world, sometimes with constructive results, sometimes less so, depending on how its insights were taken up and understood by the corporate leaders. Often, I have seen our work as empowering counter voices within the room – that is, I am often told by younger executives that we are supporting arguments for corporate reform they have advocated but which are not absorbed until someone outside the organization delivers a similar message. We've found that corporations, far from silencing us or buying us off, want us to critique what they are doing because they do not get those perspectives

within their organization. I rarely feel as political as when I am standing in a corporate boardroom questioning the decisions they have made. It's hard to speak truth to power when you aren't speaking to power.

It is instructive to compare media industries and policy with a discipline it shares much with – law. I think we can learn a lot from law, and I turned to my QUT colleague Nicolas Suzor to explain, in a personal communication:

> The strong connection to the legal profession provides academic scholars with a strong motivation to influence law and policy reform as well as established channels through which to reach policy audiences. Engaging directly with parliamentary processes, government departments, professional associations of practitioners and judges, and independent law reform bodies is often part of the routine work of legal scholars, and the work of translating research outputs for these audiences is increasingly routinely expected. We typically choose research problems that not only address a scholarly gap in knowledge, but have serious implications for justice. The explicit commitment to justice as a normative goal – however different scholars tend to define it – underpins all but the most black-letter formal scholarship in legal academia. In our research training we learn how to communicate our research to policy and legal audiences through formal submissions to law reform processes, direct consultation with government, amicus briefs or interventions to courts, and continuing professional education to lawyers.

There is a case for reform of academic incentives to make substantial contributions to public life of the sort Suzor outlines (these can be article length and often much longer) better recognized through inclusion in performance assessment and reward systems.

Independent expertise can support new, emerging elements of the born-digital media industries. Our global study of "social media entertainment" (Cunningham and Craig 2019a) saw David Craig and I speaking at creator forums and assisting in the development of a pop-up creator space, but also arguing that, instead of deconstructing the claims of online creator culture, we could be assisting its progressive elements through conceptually constituting it *as* an emerging industry sector with labor, contract, and terms of trade rights (Cunningham and Craig 2019b). We were repeatedly told by those inside the new industry that independent research, disseminated widely, would help their proto-careers.

Fourth, we can engage through *research commissioned or otherwise funded* by industry and policy agencies. Here is where most of the academic debate about needing to have a long spoon to sup with the devil comes in. There is a long and strong tradition warning of the dangers of compromising academic independence through taking money from industry. Jennifer Holt (2013), in her look at "the future of academic-industry engagement," rehearses the well-known concerns that industry-funded research may be subject to "charges of instrumentality and ideological bias, or even of veering into applied research" (2013: 186). But, as Holt shows herself with the outstanding example of the Media Industries Project at University of California Santa Barbara's Carsey-Wolf Center (e.g., Holt and Sanson 2014), funded by Warner Bros, it is possible to produce substantial independent research that is both academically original and useful to industry.

A fully institutionalized model that confronts Martin Luther's vivid metaphor, or Goethe's Faustian pact problem, is media industry research conducted at Microsoft Research New England (MSR-NE). MSR-NE is one of Microsoft's ten basic research labs worldwide, bringing together "core computer scientists and social scientists to understand, model, and enable computing and online experiences of the future" (Microsoft 2020). The need for research and development (R&D) space for pure math in a global software engineering corporation was obvious and fully recognized. But R&D leader at the Redmond headquarters, Jennifer Chayes, could see the value of social science in the tech industry, and championed that interdisciplinary build-out in Boston. danah boyd, a key interdisciplinary crossover figure from engineering to social science, was hired in part to facilitate the growth of a node of leading critical media and social media scholars. From 2012, with the recruitment of leading critical media scholars Nancy Baym, Kate Crawford, and Mary Gray, and then scholars of social media like Tarleton Gillespie, MSR-NE has become one of the world powerhouses of research at the critical juncture of traditional media and social media industry studies (Social Media Collective n.d.).

There is another fully institutionalized variation of this model – that I have found particularly fruitful – which addresses the Faustian pact problem. The Linkages Program, a research funding support scheme run by the Australian Research Council, facilitates research–industry links by matching public research funds with combined cash and in-kind commitments from industry partners. It offers, under competitive conditions, the opportunity to leverage the actual cash contributed by a partner by up to 400 percent, making this a very cost-effective means of conducting research of value to industry which is also rigorously peer-reviewed. I've won a total of sixteen of these kinds of grants over a couple of decades, with partners ranging from screen companies, to government departments, and public health charities. One partnership investigated the ongoing effects of the global economic downturn of 2007–09 on the Australian games industry. It involved several games companies which had survived the downturn and included practical workshops with the companies exploring creative inputs that they may have been otherwise unable to afford or consider relevant to innovation in their practices. This resulted in a report to industry, a number of academic publications, op-ed articles, and a submission to, and verbal evidence before, a parliamentary inquiry into the future of the games industry. These kinds of projects can be excellent ways to provide properly paid graduate and postgraduate training and industry networking opportunities. If you don't have such research programs in your country, whereby government facilitates the interface with industry, advocate for them!

*Immersive research* is an intriguing, and deeply methodologically challenging, model of engagement, drawing on anthropological-ethnographic traditions that have always subtended the field of media industry studies. This is autoethnography – becoming what we study. Two of its most esteemed proponents in our field are Brent Luvaas (2019) and Hector Postigo (2016). To research the street-style fashion blogger, Luvaas became one, and to really get inside the genre of video gameplay commentary in social media entertainment, Postigo trained up and became a passable version of such. Autoethnography, or what Postigo calls immersive research methods, provides embodied ways of knowing the industry you are studying that no other form of social scientific research can provide. That takes interfacing with industry to another level.

Finally, *governance and guidance roles for industry*. Opportunities to chair not-for-profits, or sit on governance or advisory boards, can be an important part of academic service, but also can bring you much closer to industry and its associated opportunities. Sonia Livingstone, based for some time at the London School of Economics and Political Science (LSE), is outstanding is this regard. In 2014, she was awarded an Order of the British Empire (OBE) "for services to children and child Internet safety." Her work hardly stops at the university gate. She's served on the Executive Board of the UK's Council for Child Internet Safety, the Department of Education's Ministerial Taskforce for Home Access to Technology for Children, the Home

Secretary's Taskforce for Child Protection on the Internet, and the boards of the Voice of the Listener and Viewer and the Internet Watch Foundation. In a personal communication, Livingstone writes that these commitments mean

> translating research complexities into more straightforward language, for sure, but I have learned that it need not mean either simplifying or omitting critical analysis. I have learned a lot in the process – how to ask telling questions, which concepts or findings have an impact, which arguments don't hold water, how evidence can be misinterpreted, what industry does or doesn't know, what is achievable.

Livingstone offers a model of ongoing industry engagement steered by principles of reform and evidence-based guidance, while ensuring those whose interests are not usually heard in industry and policy fora, such as children and families, have a voice.

## The institutional nudge, or mandate, for closer relations

There are now stronger institutional incentives for scholars to engage outside the academy. In some higher education systems, this comes as merely a "nudge" (through indirect suggestions and possibly some positive reinforcement – see Thaler and Sunstein 2008) but in others it is a little closer to being mandated. The so-called Impact (or Engagement and Impact) agenda, as it is evolving in the UK and Australia, is an adjunct to nationally coordinated audits of research quality (the Research Excellence Framework (REF) in the UK, and Engagement and Impact (EI) as part of Excellence in Research Australia (ERA)). As Mats Benner (2018) points out, there are few university systems worldwide that are not engaged in debates about, or deeply embedded in, engagement and impact – although it is the "gift" of the Anglosphere, and currently and particularly UK and Australia, to wish to seek to measure it in country-wide assessment exercises conducted independently of university jurisdiction. Accompanying these exercises are urgings when drafting applications to bodies administering public funds for research to build engagement and impact into the conceptualization of research in advance rather than add these considerations *ex post facto*, with the chances of success being at least part dependent on convincingly forecasting impact.

Such exercises have seen a range of published case studies of how academic research engages with and benefits industry. In the UK, among the numerous impact case studies submitted to REF2014 were projects entailing "Supporting Digital Media and the Creative Industries" (University of Ulster), a framework improving player experience and agency through video game design (Brunel University), collaboration with a publisher to enhance digital news production capabilities (University of Central Lancashire), developing sustainable models, partnerships and co-production models for local digital news production for public service broadcasters (University of West of England, Bristol), and assessing the efficacy of digital platforms in fostering creativity and influencing the commerciality of media businesses (University of Westminster). All – and there are many more – provide arresting examples of interfacing with industry.

The first iteration of the EI in Australia in 2018 saw QUT submit an impact case study on "Creative Industries Mapping: Establishing the Significance of the Size and Scope of the Creative Economy." This reported on 15 years of work, partnering internationally with UK body the National Endowment for Science, Technology and the Arts (NESTA), to propose and demonstrate ways to deal with the fact that Standard Industry Classification (SIC) and Standard Occupation Classification SOC codes (the international standards by which industries and occupations are classified by governments) are subject to change far less frequently than changes in industries and occupations. We mapped much of the dynamic change in media industries by combining hitherto separate SIC and SOC codes that bring "culture and leisure" data together with "computing services" data. Modelling these methodologies and publishing internationally contributed to the Australian Bureau of Statistics creating the first Cultural and Creative Activity Satellite Account in 2014. Satellite accounts allow an expansion of the national accounts for selected areas of interest where those interests are not defined in international statistical standards. Our research therefore contributed to stabilizing a statistical basis for measuring the economic significance of dynamic change in the media and creative industries.

## Pedagogical ethics

Working for a majority of my academic career in an applied technology university such as QUT has shaped my pedagogical ethics. QUT takes seriously a mission to address the vocational aspirations of its students: its motto since its starting in 1989 has been a "university for the real world." This hasn't stopped QUT from being ranked first among Australian institutions in the QS world rankings for media and communication over the last few years. At the same time, this has meant that it is a matter of core pedagogical ethics to refine critical stances in the disciplinary traditions of media and communication studies traditions to take account of vocational aspirations, workplace trends and the broader structure of the industry sectors into which students will be moving and will be looking to try to build a career.

The nature of work in the media industries – including the destruction of journalism and analog publishing jobs, and their partial replacement by contingent work as freelancers, casuals, or contractors, mostly in digital media – are fields typical of much knowledge work today. Media industries see an increasing occurrence of contract labor, multiple career pathways, increasingly global opportunities and challenges, and the diminution of the market organizer roles played by many large (outside the United States – often public sector) agencies in mentoring, providing apprenticeships for, and structuring, whole-of-career pathways of progression for media workers. In most cases, "learning-by-doing" apprenticeships, such as these organizations used to provide, have declined significantly. Many media careers – often better remunerated and more stable, such as journalists becoming public relations (PR) agents for corporates, government or the third sector –will be forged outside the media industries. And in a few cases, such as social media entertainment – which I canvassed briefly above – quite new modes of media careers have emerged.

It is important to engage students in the nature of media labor, including the option or necessity of portfolio careers, sole trader or self-employment status, and the expected multiplicity of career directions in any one person's working life. The conditions of precarious, "flexible" labor – such an established focus of research in media and communication studies – needs to be addressed as a current reality, all the while providing knowledge, strategies, and resources to deal with that reality.

It seems to me that building into media industry studies curricula both analytical *and* practical skills (including "left" knowledge and skills, for example about rights at work and critical knowledge of corporate citizenship or lack of it, but also "right" knowledge and confidence of global "creative class" opportunities, entrepreneurial, and personal brand strategies) is self-evidently necessary to achieve a balance between critique and vocational realism. For that to happen, scholar-teachers must interface with industry, maintaining currency as the media industries continue to be one of the canaries down the mine of digital disruption.

There is a similar rationale for a pedagogical ethics for media policy. A generation ago, I wrote *Framing Culture*, a book which called on media and cultural studies to frame their research agendas to take much greater account of policy. I did this, not to turn students into technocrats, but on the contrary to focus attention on the deeply normative roots of policy debate and action. For it is in policy debates and action that we find people wrestling with questions of what constitutes the public interest, weighing up and balancing competing and sometimes irreconcilable interests, and practising the art of the best-possible rather than sitting in the splendid isolation of the ideal. With committed training, students can be stimulated and excited to engage with policy debates that really matter to more people than academics – to citizens, to audiences, to producers, and to the political class.

## Acknowledgments

In addition to those whose personal communications have been quoted, I would like to thank Nancy Baym and Jean Burgess for backgrounding me on MSR-NE.

## References

Aufderheide, P. and Jaszi, P. (2018) *Reclaiming Fair Use: How to Put Balance Back in Copyright*, 2nd ed., Chicago, IL: University of Chicago Press.

Aufderheide, P., Pappalardo, K., Suzor, N., and Stevens, J. (2018) "Calculating the Consequences of Narrow Australian Copyright Exceptions: Measurable, Hidden and Incalculable Costs to Creators," *Poetics*, 69: 15–26.

Benner, M. (2018) *The New Global Politics of Science: Knowledge, Markets and the State*, Cheltenham: Edward Elgar Publishing.

Cunningham, S. and Jacka, E. (1996) *Australian Television and International Mediascapes*, Cambridge: Cambridge University Press.

Cunningham, S. (1992) *Framing Culture: Criticism and Policy in Australia*, Sydney: Allen and Unwin.

Cunningham, S. (1991) *Featuring Australia: The Cinema of Charles Chauvel*, Sydney: Allen and Unwin.

Cunningham, S. (2010) "Aligning Communication, Cultural and Media Studies Research and Scholarship with Industry and Policy: Australian Instances," *Media International Australia*, 136 (1): 13–19.

Cunningham, S. and Craig, D. (2019a) *Social Media Entertainment: The New Industry at the Intersection of Hollywood and Silicon Valley*, New York: New York University Press.

Cunningham, S. and Craig, D. (2019b) "Creator Governance in Social Media Entertainment," *Social Media + Society*, 5 (4): 1–11.

Freedman, D. (2014) "Media Policy Research and the Media Industries," *Media Industries*, 1 (1), n.p.

Freeman, M. (2016) *Industrial Approaches to Media: A Methodological Gateway to Industry Study*, London: Palgrave Macmillan.

Holt, J. (2013) "Two-Way Mirrors: Looking at the Future of Academic-Industry Engagement," *Cinema Journal*, 52 (3): 183–188.

Holt, J. and Sanson, K (eds) (2014) *Connected Viewing: Selling, Streaming, and Sharing Media in the Digital Era*, New York: Routledge.

Livingstone, S. (2013) "'Knowledge Enhancement': On the Risks and Opportunities of Generating Evidence-based Policy," in B. O'Neill, E. Staksrud and S. McLaughlin (eds), *Children and Internet Safety in Europe: Policy Debates and Challenges*, Goteborg: Nordicom, 91–107.

Luvaas, B. (2019) "Unbecoming: The Aftereffects of Autoethnography," *Ethnography*, 20 (2): 245–262.

Marshall, P. D. and Barbour, K. (2015) "Making Intellectual Room for Persona Studies: A New Consciousness and a Shifted Perspective," *Persona Studies*, 1 (1): 1–12.

Microsoft (2020) "MSRNE 10th Anniversary Symposium," available at www.microsoft.com/en-us/research/event/msrne-10th-anniversary-symposium/ (accessed July 31, 2020).

Miller, T. (2009) "Can Natural Luddites Make Things Explode or Travel Faster? The New Humanities, Cultural Policy Studies, and Creative Industries," in J. Holt and A. Perren (eds), *Media Industries: History, Theory, and Method*, Malden, MA: Wiley-Blackwell, 184–198.

Napoli. P. M. and Aslama, M. (eds) (2011) *Communications Research in Action: Scholar-activist Collaborations for a Democratic Public Sphere*, New York: Fordham University Press.

Osman, K. and Cunningham, S. (2020) "'Amplifier' Platforms and Impact: Australian Scholars' Use of The Conversation," *Australian Universities Review*, 61 (2): 41–49.

Postigo, H. (2016) "The Socio-Technical Architecture of Digital Labor: Converting Play into YouTube Money," *New Media and Society*, 18 (2): 332–349.

Sinclair, J., Jacka, E., and Cunningham, S. (1996) *New Patterns in Global Television: Peripheral Vision*, Oxford: Oxford University Press.

Social Media Collective (n.d.) "About," available at https://socialmediacollective.org/about/ (accessed July 22, 2020).

Thaler, R. and Sunstein, C. (2008) *Nudge: Improving Decisions About Health, Wealth, and Happiness*, New Haven, CT: Yale University Press.

*The Conversation* (2018) *The Conversation 2018 Stakeholder Report*, available at https://cdn.theconversation.com/static_files/files/395/TCSR_2018singlepagesupdated.pdf (accessed March 31, 2020).

Vonderau, P. (2014) "Industry Proximity," *Media Industries*, 1 (1): 69–74.

Wallerstein, I. (2004) *World-systems Analysis: An Introduction.* Durham, NC: Duke University Press.

Waisbord, S. (2019) *The Communication Manifesto*, Cambridge: Polity.

Wikipedia (n.d.) "ARC Centre of Excellence for Creative Industries and Innovation," available at https://en.wikipedia.org/wiki/ARC_Centre_of_Excellence_for_Creative_Industries_and_Innovation (accessed July 22, 2020).

# 45

# MEDIA INDUSTRIES AND AUDIENCES

## An analytic dialogue

### Annette Hill

This chapter focuses on the value of dialogue across media production and audience research. Focusing on dialogue highlights the value of listening and respect (Sennett 2002) across creative production and audience practices. Researchers listen to the voices of producers and the values they create alongside the voices of audiences and their engagement with cultural artifacts and live events. As such, researchers become a bridge across the producer–audience divide, identifying, through a process of mutual recognition, the ideals and practices of media industries, and audience engagement and experiences. We can see an analytic dialogue as having a double value within media industries research: first, it is a method for productively bridging the interests of producers and audiences in academic and industry research; and second, through the product of exchanges between these two actors, we find an understanding of media engagement as relational. Drawing on this insight, the research explores the meaning of engagement as relationships, looking to capture the subjective positions of varieties of people, such as producers creating content that engages us, professionals promoting and marketing content for mass and niche audiences, and fans as producers and users.

The type of research exemplified by an analytic dialogue between producers and audiences aims to make an intervention in media industries to humanize audiences so that alongside ratings performance and social media analytics, producers can get a sense of engagement as cultural resonance. We can engage with a television series on a personal level, for example character engagement, or emotional engagement with a narrative, in the moment of viewing; and we can also engage at a collective level, suggesting how a series resonates with us, sparking conversations and becoming part of cultures of viewing. This means media engagement is a nexus of relations that operate at both the individual and collective level.

This way of researching media engagement sees the sites of analysis across media structures, content, and processes as difficult to identify and research but significant to our sense of the media producer–audience relationship. In particular, the role of academic research can be to creatively explore engagement in varieties of forms. Indeed, by considering the value of media for both creative producers and audiences, inside and outside the media industries (Corner and Roscoe 2016), academic research can be a form of public engagement, where we as academics can potentially open up the meaning of media engagement beyond a pragmatic definition used in the media industries.

DOI: 10.4324/9780429275340-51

Thus, an analytic dialogue is a new concept that can enhance critical thinking on media producers *and* audiences, not as separate spheres of study but as a product of exchange, dialogue, and collective engagement. For example, an analytic dialogue can enable the researcher to ask questions about how producers craft creative content for their intended audiences with particular values in mind. An analytic dialogue is both a concept and a method in that it can generate evidence-based arguments through the use of original data on creative producers and audiences, which is a means of thinking through ideals and practices, for example the concept of engagement and how this is defined and used in media industries and by audiences in their everyday lives.

## The *Media Experiences* project

The basis for this chapter is an industry–academic collaborative project between Lund University and the television producer-distributor EndemolShine (now Banijay). The *Media Experiences* project (2014–2016) conducted production and audience research on a range of drama and reality entertainment during a three-year period in several countries, primarily Sweden, Denmark, and the UK, with smaller offshoot research in Japan, Colombia, the United States, and Mexico, and with one case study, which included transnational audiences from around the world. The project was funded by The Wallenberg Foundation, a charitable organization in Sweden; some of the ideas for this chapter are addressed in further detail in the book *Media Experiences* (Hill 2018).

In brief, the project was designed to look at the connections across media industries and creative production, genre, and audiences. It builds on an innovative approach where production research intertwines with the crafting of genre and aesthetics within particular texts and live events, and crosses over into audience research that explores people and their experiences of these genres, texts, and events. This way of conducting multi-site and multi-method research is a means of focusing on production values for creative content, such as the various ways people craft sonic and visual scapes; and it is a means of taking into account everyday lives, such as the various ways people engage and disengage with these texts, and embed their engagement with entertainment into the fabric of their lives.

EndemolShine Group was a European producer and distributor of factual and entertainment content, including reality entertainment formats such as *Big Brother* (1999–) and *MasterChef* (1990, 2005–), drama formats such as *Broadchurch* (2013–17), *The Bridge* (2011–), and *Utopia* (2013–). Certain formats were identified as of particular relevance to the project, and the case studies chosen on the basis of how audiences were cast and included in the programs. *MasterChef*, a typical reality food talent show designed for family viewing, offered the possibility of researching entertainment audiences at home, including transregional audience research for Northern Europe. The *Got to Dance* (2009–15) talent format offered the possibility of examining participants in a reality talent competition together with live audiences and crowds at media events, plus audiences at home reacting, interacting, and voting. In this case, several performances by audiences and participants would be observed in relation to one show, in particular the live experience of an entertainment event. Nordic noir *The Bridge* offered audiences in different territories, forming a transregional audience for original drama viewing adaptations made by public service and commercial broadcasters. Including the conspiracy thriller *Utopia* directed the project toward examining cult drama audiences, in particular transnational audiences who accessed the drama both through the formal media channels of national broadcasters and informal streaming. In all, the range of audiences included reality entertainment audiences at home, reality talent show participants, live audiences and fans at entertainment events, crime drama audiences and fans in transregional viewing cultures, and conspiracy drama audiences and fans in transnational online cultures of viewing.

With the *Media Experiences* project, we asked a simple question: "How do creative producers craft content for audiences and how do audiences actually engage with this content?" We primarily used qualitative, flexible research (e.g., a fit-for-purpose design for each case study) to explore this question across production practices and cultures of viewing. The research analyzed drama and entertainment formats from particular production companies, including *The Bridge* (made by Filmlance International and Nimbus Film), *Utopia* (Kudos), *MasterChef* (Shine), and *Got to Dance* (Princess). The insights were cross-referenced with quantitative evidence from EndemolShine on global audience research trends, led by Douglas Wood, Director of Audience Research and Insight, and the key industry partner in the project.

The project used multi-method and multi-site research where each television series was treated as a fit-for-purpose study. We used a range of qualitative interviews, focus groups, and participant observations, but also social media analytics and analyses of scheduling and ratings. In total, we completed: 108 production interviews with creative and executive producers, actors, performers and below-the-line workers; 25 days of production observations; 33 interviews with reality television performers; 336 interviews with audiences and fans; and participant observations of live events with crowds reaching up to 6,000 at venues. For a project such as this, perhaps one of the most important values of qualitative research is pragmatism and flexibility, allowing researchers to iteratively design and collect data, and to observe and reflect on this data along the way. This pragmatic approach to the fieldwork enabled us to develop the concept of an analytic dialogue as a way of offering multiple perspectives on qualitative research in the production and audience studies. The ability to use multiple methods and to situate and contextualize research design, data collection and analysis made space for the researchers to observe, listen, and understand the meaning and value of engagement and subjective human experience.

## Analytic dialogue: establishing the concept

An analytic dialogue involves media producers, researchers, and audiences in meaningful relationships about the media. For example, the dialogue of creative producers of a reality series are multi-directional. Such a way of thinking about an exchange of ideas, opinions, or feelings is somewhat different to the traditional way of imagining broadcaster–audience communication, for example producer *to* audience; a message to receiver model can reduce opportunities for dialogue and label audiences as listeners, or spectators, not actors in a multi-party conversation. If we focus on dialogue as multi-directional, then we recognize producer *and* audience working together in meaningful relationships.

By using the term dialogue in relation to production, we can see a dialogue as an exchange of ideas among creatives in the making of a reality entertainment show, for example, regarding the casting of participants or the use of music as a form of emotional engagement. The dialogue between creatives and executive producers about these ideas further serves to represent key values for the show, the genre, the production company, and the channel it will be broadcast on. These values may include discussion about a passion for the arts, or participation by the public in television. A dialogue can also involve executive producers, the commissioning editor responsible for a show and its performance for a broadcaster, the schedulers who choose when and how to transmit the show to the public, and distribution platforms handling live transmission, on-demand services, availability in archives, and as social media content. The flow of dialogue can be understood and shared, or it may become stuck, misunderstood, and even ignored by various actors and structures in this production–distribution–reception environment.

By using the term dialogue in relation to audiences, we can infer a dialogue between the creative producers and their imagined audience (see Litt 2012) who they hope to be in conversation with when they cast, script, or edit a show. Producers usually have a particular demographic in mind regarding age, gender, region, class and so forth, and so shape their content to invite a certain kind of conversation, say, about dancing as self-expression, or the dance profession. If there is a targeted marketing campaign, in particular with social media, then there will be a more direct kind of conversation where a participant or judge in a reality competition, for example, will have live chats with their real, no longer imagined, audience. This brings us to a vital part of the dialogue, which is that listeners also have a voice. Audiences will find various ways to articulate their experiences in the home, while travelling to work, in the lunchroom, and through social media. Again, the flow of dialogue can be understood and shared by audiences, fans, and users, or it may become stuck, misunderstood, and even ignored by various actors and structures in both public and private, mediated and real-world spaces.

This way of seeing producers and audiences as participants in cultural conversations is important to how we think about media engagement. A multi-directional and multi-party dialogue about a reality series is going to involve several conversations, internal and external to the series. Such conversations may be about casting by the casting director and the contestants in the early stages of a reality talent show production, thus signaling the internal conversations taking place, and these conversations can be happening alongside talk among the executive producers about the ethical treatment of young dancers, or amateur and semi-professional dancers in the competition. These various conversations can contribute to a common topic of dialogue regarding people who are passionate about dance – a key production value of this reality entertainment format. In turn, external conversations will be occurring about the new cast for a returning reality series by audiences and fans, and these conversations, say about talent, personality, dance school training, and so forth, can also contribute to a common topic of dialogue about passion for dance – a key cultural value for audiences of this format. Sometimes these conversations can be at odds with the overall dialogue; so, we might see criticism by fans about casting choices for example, or how contestants are treated when auditioning and being judged by the expert panel. Here it is important the judges mirror the cultural value of audiences about passion for dance and motivate their scores and comments regarding dance skills as opposed to personality. Audiences and fans of this format are highly attuned to the genre's tendency to promote personality over talent, and they value this format for being different; indeed, this is what sets it apart from other talent shows.

What we can begin to detect in the concept of an analytic dialogue is that conversations by several actors, inside and outside of television, coalesce in a broader thematic dialogue, or dialogues, for, of course, a series can generate several dialogues of varying intensities and tones. It's worth underscoring the way an analytic dialogue, as method and process, can signal value for a TV series, production brand, or audience and fan culture. Corner and Roscoe point out that notions of value and quality circulated inside media industries, such as television, are contingent on production aesthetics and commodity values, but also on other meanings of value formed outside television, including social and political values (2016: 158). Here we see how conversations inside a television production that coalesce into broader dialogue(s) about production aesthetics and economics can contribute to, and challenge, other meanings relating to the value of television in people's lives. Such a perspective is crucial to redefining media engagement, not only as a metric of consumer attention, but also as cultural resonance. A television series can score highly in terms of economic targets, or brand recognition in advertising campaigns, but to get at the cultural value of a television series we need to look beyond economic logics and toward how content means something to people, where a series generates conversations, becoming part of people's cultural memories and a resource for public dialogues about popular culture.

Notions of television and broadcasting more generally as a dialogue have been addressed, not least, by public service media with reference to an idea of public engagement. Public service media have a special remit to inform, educate, and entertain citizens, with attention given to the diversity of citizens in a national context through providing news services in different languages or representing different ethnic groups in media content. The remit for public service media holds up the notion of dialogue as a value in its own right. Here, specifically analytic dialogues are required if producers as well as audiences are to have opportunities to articulate what is important to them, having a voice and being recognized in broader political and cultural conversations.

An understanding of public engagement as a form of dialogue is not confined to public service media. Commercial broadcasters and production companies can adopt an explicit aim to invite their audiences into a cultural conversation: soap operas, for example, are a popular genre that engages audiences in sociocultural issues, such as domestic abuse. Some commercial content, especially popular documentary series and consumer series, is commissioned specifically with the value of public engagement in mind. Other content may have a more explicit entertainment remit, but still implicitly spark a dialogue between producers and audiences about sociocultural issues. Perhaps one of the biggest challenges inside television is to find business models that offer financial rewards for the industry and also address the symbolic power of television in a democratic cultural context. Such a model can be an ideal rather than reality. Nevertheless, academic research on media producers and audiences can position values "within the larger framework of political and social values and both within the flows of 'everyday' life and within the existing flows of power" (Corner and Roscoe 2016: 163). Corner and Roscoe's point suggests values internal to television production can be positioned in dialogue with wider social, cultural and/or moral values.

## Analytic dialogue: establishing the method

The focus on dialogue came about because of a difficulty early on in the research collaboration, where the research team was having trouble explaining the project to various local producers within the parent company. The biggest obstacle to overcome was the absence of qualitative research as a regular part of organizational working. Priority was given to understanding audience engagement through quantitative measurements of interest, with performance metrics for ratings and social media, and internal surveys for specific series. Creative producers were unfamiliar with academic qualitative audience research, and the research team lacked the language necessary to make this work seem accessible to professionals within the media industries.

There was a moment in the research process when an analytic dialogue started to take shape as a method. Ann Gray (2001) argues that subjective human experience is part of a process through which we articulate our identities. So, attention to how people account for themselves in relation to their experiences can produce new knowledge. As Gray points out, this creates knowledge about other people but also of ourselves as researchers. She quotes the cultural scholar Raymond Williams who says that experience is a useful term if we want to "locate those specific and definable moments when very new work produces a shock of recognition" (1979: 164). On the project, this moment occurred when talking to Julie Donovan, the industry consultant for the research. I was on a call while walking in the Swedish winter forest where I lived. I had climbed to a hotspot to get a 3G signal and listened to Julie tell me that I needed to change my language if I wanted to be heard – in essence she encouraged me to listen more. Re-tracing my route through this white and silent landscape, I realized that at its core the research project was about listening, really listening closely to producers and the values they create in their work, and then listening closely to audiences and their actual engagement with this content.

To start a dialogue, then, is to begin with the basic approach of listening and respect for creative production as well as cultures of viewing. An additional benefit may be to encourage mutual respect for academic research by producers and within cultures of viewing, something that is not a given and is related to relationships of trust by all parties in the conversations. The role of academics on the project was to bridge the two, analyzing where dialogue flows, or breaks down, when producers are listening to audiences, and when audiences feel ignored, or sense a disconnection. In essence, the academic role was to humanize the audience for creative producers, which is to say see the faces of viewers, normally only visible to producers as numbers in a chart. An analytic dialogue, thus, is a means to explore and critically analyze the meaning of audience engagement in different settings, across media industries and everyday life, which can widen our horizons when understanding engagement.

As academic-industry scholar Jane Roscoe notes: "there are often different languages and value systems at play, such as pragmatism in the industry and creative explorations in academia" (Hill, Steemers, Roscoe, Donovan, and Wood 2017: 3). Academic research can identify some of the gaps and some of those shared moments where we can expand and explore engagement further. The value of the research for Endemol Shine was explained by Douglas Wood, the Head of Audience Research and Insight:

> In the commercial world you rarely have the opportunity to do this type of research, typically in our research you go in with a problem that needs to be answered – "why isn't this storyline working?" We would never analyse the creative process itself: it's alien to us. So, it was fortunate to have a third party come in and explore this process of talking to creatives and audiences. It was a unique opportunity to understand what we do internally and how that relates to our audiences, and to think about the future of those audiences and where they may be in five or ten years' time.
>
> *p. 2*

Julie Donovan, the creative content consultant in the project group, noted:

> The conversation from the academic perspective was to listen more and ask less questions, "We are looking into this, and how do we find it?" There is a different language. If you are going to maintain relationships across academic and industry sectors, then you have to make sure the conversation is dynamic and fluid.
>
> *p. 3*

The additional feedback we received from the producers supports the value of industry–academic dialogue for stakeholders in both the commercial and public service media sectors. Here are a couple of illustrative comments on the collaborative work:

> You are the person in the whole machine who has the most contact between the producer and the audience. We need you ... It is really hard to know what signals you communicate to the audience ... what is it in storytelling that moves us?
>
> *Austen 2014*

It is so nice to have everything that you think and hope that you are doing right actually confirmed. It is exactly what you want to hear. All the ideas we have, that we fight over, we are right! And the viewers actually get it. It is so nice to get this, rather than statistics where you are told your viewer is a 47-year-old woman from Jutland [region of Denmark]. This is really, really, really helpful.

*Velling 2015*

Note how terms like "the machine" or "statistics" suggest the way audience data de-humanizes audiences, rendering them as numbers rather than people who can communicate what they think or how they feel about television. Use of qualitative methods is precisely designed to deliver these kinds of insights into the subjectivities of audiences.

From a research perspective, relationship management is central to both dialogue(s) and the analyses supporting them. At each step in the process, it was evident that relationships between the creatives, within the production teams, and with audiences were a constant presence. As such, we can begin to understand that engagement within the industry is about relationships, the collaborative experiences of creatives working together to produce content, that is to say relationships formed between professionals, and the relationships of academic researchers with these writers, directors, or actors and extras, that is to say engagement between academia and industry. Then, we can also understand the tensions surrounding relationships between the creatives and the executive producers and broadcasters, where trust can be broken by decisions from on high about marketing, or scheduling. And finally, engagement within the industry connects with audiences, fans, and consumers, as the relationships across the production and reception contexts make or break the overall success of a show.

The project highlighted how among industry participants there is an ongoing reevaluation of the meaning of engagement. According to Douglas Wood:

We are moving away from a single currency of engagement … we are in a situation where engagement may mean a very different set of criteria depending on how you judge success. Faced with this audience fragmentation, as producers we are increasingly being asked for platform defining content, something that is unique, something that will find a voice and have cultural impact.

*Hill, Steemers, Roscoe, Donovan, and Wood 2017: 3*

The playoff between engagement as performance metric and as cultural resonance, that is, why media matters to us, is a sign of the tensions around the very meaning of the term engagement within media industries. If we see engagement as a quantitative performance indicator for economic targets, then this is a one-dimensional understanding of the term. In cultural production, media industries have dominated the definition of engagement as economic targets, and it is time we changed the conversation to include the sociocultural value of engagement as well. Creative producers themselves experience the tensions between these kinds of targets all the time. There is the cultural value of their work, which they know and understand – it is a language of facts and knowledge, or emotion, storytelling, and aesthetics – and then there is the economic value placed by the industry on their work, which is communicated by ratings in a way that is often hard to understand.

To consider the cultural values that feed engagement, take for example the cookery format *MasterChef*. We found local audiences loved homegrown versions of the series. So, in Denmark, *MasterChef* follows the brand and the building blocks of this competitive cooking show, but what audiences valued most about the local version was its focus on Danish food and national traits that place significance on using all the leftover scraps. People talked a lot about how the show was relevant to them because it symbolized a down-to-earth approach to food in family life. Accordingly, we spoke with the production team about this kind of engagement as embedded in families' everyday lives. For these viewers, food comes first and the competition second. On the value of food, a crucial issue is that the program promotes "decent and honest food" (30-year-old Danish self-employed male (2014)). A woman added: "the food is the most important part to me … It is not what kinds of funny things are said along the way, it's the result on the plate, you could say" (45-year-old Danish female secretary (2014)). This attention to honest food makes the amateur version of the series have strong cultural resonance with Danish viewers. A father summed up the position:

> Food means a lot to me. It really does. It has to be proper food and by that I mean good ingredients. It doesn't have to be gourmet or fine dining but it has to be honest food. And that means something to me because I know that everything we put in our mouths matters. If you put diesel in a car running on gas that doesn't work either. It needs to be suitable for us humans. I just had a boy and I think a lot about what he eats. Food is what sows the seeds for everything we do and become. That's what it means to me.
>
> *48-year-old Danish male IT consultant (2014)*

One food blogger reflected on how a series like *MasterChef* can be part of a collective dialogue about an economic crisis:

> I think when the crisis started this *do it yourself* trend emerged. We realize we could go back to home cooking and save money … There has been a shift in focus from quantity to quality … and in the process I think people realized just how delicious it is, how cool real, home-cooked, authentic food can be
>
> *30-year-old Danish male musician (2014)*

All of this was in stark contrast to the celebrity aspect of the format, which viewers felt was overly commercial and not honest at all. They informed producers: do not underestimate us, a rallying cry for a more inclusive and participatory approach to creative production and reception. Repetition of the phrase "do not underestimate us" signaled how audiences wanted a clear invitation to engage in broader dialogue, in this instance regarding food, family, and the environment, indeed to participate in a national debate about sustainable lifestyles.

The type of research exemplified by an analytic dialogue across creative production and cultures of viewing aims to make an intervention into media industries so that we open up the language of engagement to include sociocultural as well as economic values. As work on media industries and engagement emerges (see Evans 2019 among others), such academic research questions the strategic use of engagement as a performance indicator for economic targets. Quantitative values offer a rather reductive meaning of the term, with engagement seen as something to capture and measure in specific places (platforms, channels, or influencer profiles) and at certain times (hourly, daily, or weekly leaderboards). Engagement is more than capturing the attention of audiences; it is about making a relationship. Thus, we can understand engagement as a nexus of relations that operate at both the individual and collective level; often there is a dynamic that renders the two levels mutually supportive. We develop relationships with media that are not solely about consumption and economic value, but that also enable us to recognize the values of media in our lived experiences (see Dahlgren and Hill 2020 for further details).

## Conclusion

To sum up, the term analytic dialogue can include a double meaning of dialogue as a noun and a verb. Dialogue as a noun refers to the way academic research involves conversations with producers and audiences directed toward the meaning of media engagement. As a verb, the term refers to the way academic–industry research can provide a space to exchange ideas on public engagement. These dialogues are contingent on the uneasy relations between media producers and audiences, and public service and commercial values. Analysis of these dialogues encourages a sociological perspective on the various values of the media and the existing flows of power inside and outside media industries (Corner and Roscoe 2016).

This chapter has shown how combining production and audience research can illuminate the flow of dialogue, along with the problems or absences of dialogue, across moments of creative production, distribution and marketing, and audience engagement. The key points in this chapter highlight the value of collaboration between media industries and academic research for how this can offer fruitful insights into the ways engagement is conceptualized and researched today. Within the media industries and academic research, we can see how a new currency of engagement holding both economic and sociocultural value is emerging. As such, we can research media engagement as both a measurement of attention and as cultural resonance. Overall, research into media engagement that combines production and audience perspectives can offer valuable data on public engagement and disengagement with media. Here, then, by moving beyond conventional quantitative understandings of engagement, academic research can highlight the long view of engagement, with media positioned as cultural resources for lived experiences.

## References

Austen, P. (2014) Editor, *The Bridge*, Interview with the Author, January 22, Lund, Sweden.

Corner, J. (2011) *Theorising Media: Power, Form and Subjectivity*, Manchester: Manchester University Press.

Corner J. and Roscoe, J. (2016) "Outside and Inside Television: A Dialogue on 'Value,'" *Journal of Media Practice*, 17 (2–3): 157–167.

Corner, J. (2017) "Afterword," *Media Industries*, 4 (1): 1–6.

Dahlgren, P. and Hill, A. (2020) "Parameters of Media Engagement," *Media Theory*, November, available at http://mediatheoryjournal.org/peter-dahlgren-annette-hill-parameters-of-media-engagement/ (accessed June 16, 2021).

Danish male IT consultant (2014) Interview with Tina Askanius for the *Media Experiences* project, December 10, Århus, Denmark.

Danish male musician (2014) Interview with Tina Askanius for the *Media Experiences* project, December 15, Silkeborg, Denmark.

Danish self-employed male (2014) Interview with Tina Askanius for the *Media Experiences* project, December 11, Århus, Denmark.

Danish female secretary (2014) Interview with Tina Askanius for the *Media Experiences* project, December 12, Charlottenlund, Denmark.

Evans, E. (2019) *Understanding Engagement in Transmedia Cultures*, Abingdon: Routledge.

Gray, A. (2001) *Research Practice for Cultural Studies*, London: Sage.

Hill, A. (2017) "Reality TV Engagement: Reality TV Producers and Audiences for Talent Format *Got to Dance*," *Media Industries*, 4 (1): 1–17.

Hill, A. (2018) *Media Experiences: Engaging with Drama and Reality Television*, Abingdon: Routledge.

Hill, A, Steemers, J., Roscoe, J., Donovan, J., and Wood, D. (2017) "Media Industries and Engagement: A Dialogue across Industry and Academia," *Media Industries*, 4 (1): 1–15.

Litt, E. (2012) "Knock, Knock. Who's There? The Imagined Audience," *Journal of Broadcasting and Electronic Media*, 56 (3): 330–345.

Sennett, R. (2002) *Respect*, London: Penguin.

Velling, T. (2015) Series Producer, *MasterChef* Denmark, Interview with the Author, May 15, Copenhagen, Denmark.

Williams, R. (1974) *Politics and Letters: Interviews with the New Left Review*, London: NLB.

# 46

# ETHICS IN MEDIA INDUSTRIES RESEARCH

*Patrick Vonderau*

Do ethics matter? For many scholars in our field, the issue evokes professionalism as much as procedures, reputation as much as the review board.[1] To act "professionally" means adhering to appropriate codes of practice and general ethical principles, with most of the latter adopted from clinical research involving human subjects. We all aim for accountability, trust, and transparency. We worry about whether or not our research subjects have consented in a truly "informed" manner to our study, and if both the law and public interest have been respected. Beyond that, however, there is little public reflexivity on ethics in media industry scholarship. No specific guidelines exist. Introductory textbooks often all but ignore ethical considerations (e.g., Lotz, Herbert, and Punathambekar 2020). Researchers relegate them to footnotes or, less frequently, to method confessionals and epilogues hidden in the back of their books. Occasionally, research ethics are brought up in reviews or cautionary conference asides, but overall there is no sustained debate. In media industries research, ethics matter primarily in relation to professional routine, standard methods, value neutrality, and other tenets of a positivist paradigm, that is, as a problem to be anticipated or silently solved. In consequence, ethical considerations usually remain external to the process of knowledge production itself, confined to a seemingly depoliticized sphere of deliberation separated from historical and social context.

The reasons for such an instrumental notion of ethics are not specific to media industry studies. Across disciplines, higher education has been economized to a degree that even peer assessment and gatekeeping processes are seen to be affected. As anthropologist Marilyn Strathern (2000) and others have observed, the language of ethics has long proliferated in relation to academic "audit cultures," used to manage public opinion. Such language is what Stephen Hilgartner calls a "technology of trust," employed in the construction of public credibility (2000: 11). Since the 1980s, with the spread of new public management at universities in the United States and Europe, a depoliticized, decontextualized ethics has become an effective instrument for minimizing the risk that research always incurs for both the scholar and her subject. Institutional and professional pressure to conform to routinized forms of research and not to pursue innovative or risky projects has led to an "industrial mode" of knowledge in which "the process guarantees the product" (Burawoy 1998: 28). At the same time, however, research cannot be routinized completely and must always allow some space for exploratory work and the unpredictable, as it remains a dynamic process that works against "compulsive

DOI: 10.4324/9780429275340-52

tidiness in methodology" (Calvey 2017: 456). It is not possible, in other words, to completely decouple reflexivity on ethics from the politics of the actual research process, and from the often-spontaneous method choices to be made by the researcher. Neither are ethical considerations confined to research, of course; some of the more controversial issues relate to other areas of academic practice, most notably publishing (e.g., Mayer, Press, Verhoeven, and Sterne 2018).

In addition, while risk-taking may not have increased among scholars in the humanities and social sciences, risk certainly has. Risk has increased with changes in our understanding of the values of science and growing public skepticism regarding the "ideology of scientific neutrality" (Mills 2003: 39). Over the last decades, alleged or actual failures of accountability have repeatedly been publicly exposed and denounced as unethical. At the center of these scandals were social and natural scientists analyzing data for companies such as Cambridge Analytica, Theranos, and most recently during the COVID-19 pandemic, Surgisphere.[2] Simultaneously, positivist and hard science scholars have staged or defended hoaxes to similarly expose the "unscientific worldview" and "highly dubious ethics" of the humanities, especially cultural studies (Pluckrose, Lindsay, and Boghossian 2018; see also Sokal 2009). Discussions of "nonsense in academic research" now regularly prompt calls for ethical "responsibility to establish the meaning of what we do and demonstrate its social value beyond our narrow self- or tribal interests" (Alvesson, Gabriel, and Paulsen 2017: 9). Media scholars may now aim to establish such meaning through critical work on today's digital media industries and infrastructures, given the latter's social relevance, yet such work remains prone to risk, especially when depending on these very organizations for access and data.

This chapter advocates for more public reflexivity on ethics. Media industry scholars may want to join an ongoing conversation on ethics and methods that so far has largely been driven by other disciplines, most notably the social sciences, alongside (digital) media companies themselves. The main contention of this chapter is that ethics cannot be separated from the politics of the scientific process. Ethics and epistemology are indivisible, and to this end, reflexivity on ethics has everything to do with inventive methods and critical analyses. The problem lies not in how we police our ethical codes, but in the politics of what knowledge we should be aiming to produce. While scholars recently have argued for a more "positive conceptualization of method as creative act" (Sandvig and Hargittai 2015: 4), we still lack such a positive attitude when it comes to ethics. Given that "ethics is method, method is ethics" (AOIR 2020: 4), ethics ought not to be seen as a tedious tool just to be taken up in defense of attacks on status and credibility, but as part and parcel of knowledge production itself.

## Devising a framework

Media industry studies has come to thrive over the past decades in part because it remains a heterogeneous field of scholarship. Situated at the interface between the humanities and the social sciences, the field is set up to make tensions between different academic cultures productive. As historian Peter Galison once observed in regard to science more generally, "it is precisely the disunification of science that brings strength and stability" (1997: 781). Varying disciplinary backgrounds from film history to computer science make it difficult to formalize codes of conduct and ethics statements that would apply to all. Researchers have a number of conceptual frameworks from which to choose, some of which are considered mutually exclusive in regard to methods and ethics. For instance, "contextual" political-economic approaches are sometimes pitched against "celebratory approaches," as critical "macro"-perspectives on industries in capitalist economies seem opposite to "micro"-scaled, more sympathetic industry studies of specific companies or workers (Wasko and Meehan 2013). Drawing on the political economy of communication as a normative science, researchers in the first area may primarily rely on their reading of trade press articles, while those in the second may gain direct access in exchange for "sustained engagement" with a particular company (Corrigan 2018; Grainge and Johnson 2015: 9). For the latter, brand reputation might be an ethical issue, while for the former, public interest in a brand's hitherto undisclosed malpractices might outweigh other considerations.

One-size-fits-all ethical requirements are of little help also because researchers often face complex, non-standard ethical situations. Policies, technologies, industry strategies, organizational forms, and cultural practices change; norms remain inconsistent and debated; research is sometimes mixed into other contexts such as journalism, activism, or business analysis. In addition, getting access to industries comes with many caveats, requires ad hoc adjustments, and continually has to be renegotiated. Given these difficulties, the few field-specific discussions that exist usually take a *procedural perspective*, focusing on the terms of academy–industry engagement that accompany funding or review board applications (e.g., Freeman 2016: 47–62). In the absence of binding rules, procedural ethics help to establish a transactional framework for researchers and companies to interact. The procedure is transactional insofar as it rests on a trade-off, and the ethics consists in making this trade-off explicit and justifiable for both sides. For instance, scholars may benefit from funding, access to data, insider status, and increased public visibility, while providing a company with commercially disinterested, comprehensive, and comparatively inexpensive insights not to be gained elsewhere. Terms of engagement can take on various forms – from short and limited encounters to trust-based "partnerships" between "co-researchers" (Freeman 2016: 51) – but the idea of course is that once a procedure is established, it then is followed through.

Occasionally, procedural ethics are turned into *models* in the sense of exemplary, institutionalized infrastructures for collaboration between industry and academia. One very successful model was the Connected Viewing Initiative, a multi-year research collaboration (2011–2015) coordinated by the Media Industries Project, Carsey-Wolf Center at the University of California at Santa Barbara that supported an international team of researchers exploring global changes in digital media distribution in conjunction with and funded by the Warner Bros. Home Entertainment Division. In the words of Jennifer Holt, Director of the Media Industries Project,

> We were very committed to doing basic as opposed to applied research, and creating an independent, collaborative model as opposed to a more typical "sponsored" model where researchers solve specific problems for the funders. Our research questions were generated and designed by the scholars themselves, and they were funded to pursue their projects as they wished. Our researchers retained the rights to all of their work, and they presented their results with various audiences of Warner Bros. executives who had exclusive first-look rights for six months before the work was made public.
>
> *Holt 2020*

With the expansion of the field from legacy media to Internet industries, however, such terms of engagement are increasingly formalized. A controversial "new model" exemplifying this trend is Social Science One, initiated in 2018 in the wake of the Cambridge Analytica scandal. This "partnership" between Facebook and academia "enables firms to enlist the scientific community to help them produce social good, while protecting their competitive positions," barring any research on internal corporate policies, decisions, or product development (Social Science One 2018; Bruns 2019).

Formalized data access models like the latter illustrate the potential downside of procedural ethics for media industry research, especially where research is conducted on or via Internet platforms. The move from analog to digital considerably alters consent transactions. Informed consent, a legal requirement and ethical imperative adopted from clinical research that has long guided scholars in conceiving their relation to the researched, is what researchers usually obtain from their research subjects. Where access is framed via a platform's Terms of Service, however, it is the scholar who has to consent first. Internet companies establish legalistic frameworks for engagement and regularly research the behavior of their users without consent rules acknowledging the bilateral nature of the consent transaction (Grimmelmann 2015: 246). Using metrics or tools for data collection found on platforms further increases "troubling relations of dependency with the infrastructures and organizations that make them available" (Marres 2017: 182). Scholars may be aware of these limitations but still face risk. For instance, some may want to study the Netflix catalog in various countries, but such work with catalog data may fall within a gray zone when larger volumes of data are scraped or archived, or when virtual proxy networks (VPNs) are used. Good faith violations of Terms of Service are a common issue reported by ethics committees. Any research done digitally increases informational risk, or the potential harm from the disclosure of information, even when the information is freely available, because such seemingly non-sensitive information can turn out to be sensitive at some point. In 2006, Netflix released data related to 100 million movie ratings, and researchers were able to trace those data back to individuals, resulting in a class-action suit by users against Netflix (Salganik 2019: 310).

Procedural ethics thus are an important but insufficient framework to guide the research process because ethical issues are neither confined to nor solved by establishing formalized research agreements. A common observation among scholars is that the questions which need to be answered in order to get approval differ from the everyday ethical issues that arise in the doing of research. Such "ethics in practice" are not the alternative to procedural ethics, but another ethical "dimension" (Guillemin and Gillam 2004) to be taken into account, similar to general codes and principles such as Respect for Persons, Beneficence, Justice, and Respect for Law and Public Interest (e.g., Salganik 2019: 294–300; Israel 2015: 24–44). Consequently, I would like to suggest that ethical judgment in media industries research ideally rests on a *nexus between primary ethical norms, procedural arrangements, and forms of case-based, practical reasoning*. Making ethical decisions means, in other words, to draw together professional codes of practice, the respective terms of engagement, and responses to specific situated dilemmas, in a similar fashion to how we draw together a set of conceptual premises with an approach and specific methods in our research when trying to solve a problem. In this view, it is neither purely rules-based nor ad hoc judgment, neither formulaic ethics nor mere casuistry that benefit the field, but the realistic, continuous assessment of the relation between principles and practices in context of a given research procedure. The remainder of this chapter briefly develops this suggestion, focusing on my main area of expertise within the field, production studies.

## A research perspective

When it comes to research ethics, production studies is an instructive area of media industry studies for three reasons. First, production scholars have traditionally taken a *holistic view* on their subject. From the early projects of Leo C. Rosten or Hortense Powdermaker in the 1930s and 1940s to the present day, a basic tenet of research in this area has been to study production not in isolation, but as part of a system or "maze of intricate relationships" where "no one aspect is intelligible except as part of the whole," as Rosten's collaborator Mae D. Huettig put it back in

1942 (cited in Phillips 2015: 139). This always included acknowledging capitalism as forming the context for both production and its study, yet without the aggressively biased normative predisposition informing political economy of communication. Scholars within production studies consider the ethics of media work, how workers manage their occupational identities in response to the normative meanings shaping a given industrial culture, and how "production culture" in itself constitutes a nomos, or normative universe, through continual acts of industrial reflexivity and critical practice (Caldwell 2008; see also Cover 1993: 95). Engaging in ethnographically informed "behind-the-scenes-scholarship" (Banks 2009: 89), the approach also considers how the norms of the field relate to the ethics of research itself, anticipating by decades today's worry among Internet researchers on how to "produce valid, ethical research in an ecosystem of capitalist production, while being under pressure from private industry" (Poletti and Gray 2019: 266). Production studies thus invites us to re-contextualize ethics, and to understand *ethics as a politics of method*, a direct consequence of which has been to focus on "below-the-line" technical crafts and labor involved in production, rather than above-the-line talent, for instance.[3]

Second, the long genealogy of production research suggests that an alleged historical split between "administrative" and "critical" research does not hold up well within the context of media industry studies. Although this supposed split is regularly mobilized to construct opposing ethical and ideological positions vis-à-vis "the industry," it is historically inaccurate to claim that the field developed from a controversy between Paul F. Lazarsfeld and Theodor W. Adorno, or the tension between on the one hand a positivist, utilitarian interest in business-oriented, problem-solving quantitative research on audiences and effects, and on the other, problem-oriented, disinterested, qualitative critical analysis of the general role of media, their organization, and institutional setup. Seemingly unbeknownst to Lazarsfeld, who famously laid the grounds for this distinction in a 1941 article, production research already had begun to better integrate these two traditions. While Lazarsfeld had embarked on the Rockefeller Foundation–funded "Radio Research Project" in 1937, Leo C. Rosten started the "Motion Picture Research Project" in 1939, also funded through a Rockefeller (and Carnegie) grant, with the express aim to relate Hollywood's coordinated set of economic structures and practices to their impact on moving pictures and their audiences (Rosten 1939, 1941; Lazarsfeld 1941).[4] *Relating "administrative" to "critical" research interests, methods, and ethics has always been a core productive dynamic of the field*, from Powdermaker's book on Hollywood's "social system" and its impact on the movies' "content and meaning" (1951: 3) to the later work of Newcomb and Alley (1983), D'Acci (1994), Born (2005), or Caldwell (2008). Put the other way around, binaries do little to help articulate ethical positions. It is possible to conduct critical research within administrative research arrangements, as the model of the Connected Viewing Initiative has shown. Furthermore, ethical judgment in general means addressing issues that sit on a "sliding scale" between "ethical dilemmas" and "etiquette questions," thus involving "continuous cultural and other work of translation, in real time" (Malkki 2007: 178–179).

Third, in a marked difference to other areas within media industry research, production scholars emphasize *reflexivity*. This is largely due to the ethnographic orientation and immersive impulse of this research tradition, which, unlike most desk research, resists the notion of a privileged vantage point for observation, recognizes the participatory dimension of the researcher's role, and encourages experiments with research methods and publishing practices. To practice reflexivity is to contextualize ethics, rather than to treat ethics as an autonomous sphere separated from historical, social, and cultural context. In line with the problem-oriented design of ethnographically informed research, production studies follows a *situative approach* to ethics, making ethical judgment integral to a process of grounded theorizing. This includes attending to ethically important moments in a given research situation. It also includes departing from the positivist cliché of an "administrative" approach, which sees research ethics depend on the strict division between a researcher's opinions, desires, and social orientation on the one hand, and the research object on the other, positioning the dispassionate observer and interpreter of facts against the normatively bounded critic. In contrast, production studies always walks a "fine line between intimacy and detachment," as ethnographic fieldwork does generally – a unique process in its often unforeseen trajectories and its use of ethnographic detail to produce theoretical insights (Grindstaff 2002: 278). While the positivist tradition often bases *ethical rigor* on rigid procedure and replicability, rigor in this more qualitatively oriented area stems precisely from reflexivity. Here, "good" research practice is marked by ethical revisionings and the need for researchers to be recursive in their thinking and actions, making ethics an engaging dialogue and negotiation with multiple stakeholders.

## Engaging in reflexivity on ethics

I have taken a closer look at one particular area of media industries research to substantiate my previous assertion that in making ethical judgments, we usually don't resort to more abstract ethical frameworks and also don't need to. This is a departure from standard introductions to research ethics, which develop guidelines by working through the dominant ethical paradigms of deontology and consequentialism, or "means-oriented" versus "ends-oriented" frameworks (Israel 2015: 9–13). Guidelines do so because primary ethical norms may take on a different character depending on the framework. Respect for Persons, for instance, implies that researchers receive informed consent from participants. A consequentialist argument here is that the requirement for informed consent may be waived in a setting where there is no risk, while a deontologist would underline the researcher's imperative to respect the autonomy of her participants under any circumstances. Again, such binaries are of little help, given that most research situations are considerably more complex. As production scholar Laura Grindstaff notes, consent is "more developmental than contractual," and always part of an "ongoing series of research bargains" that leaves open the question "at what point the fieldworker stops being accountable to subjects since the reception of the final text [...] can significantly influence, after the fact, a participant's sense of having been adequately informed" (2002: 285).

Hence the more realistic suggestion made in this chapter to situate ethical considerations within specific research areas of our field, and to balance key ethical principles such as those above against the ethics of a given pre-agreed research procedure on the one hand, and the area-specific ethics-in-practice on the other. It is difficult to evaluate a method without taking into account the premises and approach it is based on. In making this suggestion, my point is to move beyond a negative connotation of research ethics as plugging holes or settling debts. Ethical considerations are interesting finds in themselves. To illustrate this point, consider how one standard ethical concern – obtaining informed consent from industry – may prompt us to further develop our conceptual premises and approach by asking questions.

To begin with, how does a key ethical norm grounded in biomedical research relate to a subject that is not human but organizational? If national laws or a given firm require the researcher to approach said firm as a person, implying it has moral agency, do consent transactions publicly hold this firm accountable for its decisions? How do we properly differentiate between the various, often conflicting actions within such an organization when attributing accountability, without giving in to a "normative impulse" (Nader 1972) that may have prompted the research? How do we balance consent informally obtained from vulnerable persons within an organization against formal consent rules imposed by the latter? Why and how do organizational cultures differ in ways that require some researchers to sign non-disclosure agreements for information that is in the public domain, while others get sensitive information without obtaining formal consent? For instance, reflecting on her acclaimed study of Hollywood talent agents, sociologist Violaine Roussel notes that "Interestingly, when I did in situ observations at the agencies, each time I offered to sign a confidentiality agreement, but they never made me sign anything. Of course, the relevance or irrelevance of these ethical norms in the world we study says a lot about this social world" (Roussel 2020).

While matching research ethics to the "informational norms" of a given field is widely recommended (Nissenbaum 2004), does this support covert or "gonzo" methods when researching bad actors, and if yes, for how long? How do we determine that breaking consent rules is in the public benefit without breaking the rules? Finally, in moving from field to archive, how does time modify consent rules? Does historic uniqueness justify hacks and other illicit means to obtain data (Connor 2015), and when should we consider papers (or algorithms, for that matter) as persons, too?

## Conclusion

Organizational environments, with their inbuilt instrumentality, might predispose us to think about methods and ethics in empiricist terms, as an essentially technical affair, something to be "applied" or "taken up" as one would a hammer from a toolbox. Formal ethics tempt us to tick off the boxes and to minimize using our full judgment. This chapter has made a case for moving beyond a utilitarian rationale where ethics is partly public relations, partly legal concern. In my assessment, doing critical media industry studies means to resist a convenient, but unproductive tendency of reducing ethics issues to professional or procedural matters, thus potentially giving in to what are attempts by Facebook and other digital media companies to establish their own, self-serving ethics standards. What has been said of methods also applies to ethics, namely, that they are "not indifferent or external to a problem" and "require their user to reflect critically upon the value, status, and significance of knowledge today" (Lury and Wakeford 2012: 3). Not all such reflections ought to be public, of course, but debate certainly may benefit media industry scholars in situations of enculturation and crisis. Debate also might help to more properly weigh ethical concerns about research against ethics issues in other areas of academic practice, such as teaching, supervision, and especially publishing. Even mundane ethical issues in research are quickly addressed as major dilemmas, while misconduct in publishing is usually treated as a question of etiquette. Company data may be collected according to rules, but its use as evidence, or as part of a self-positioning, may defy appropriate codes of practice. As I see it, reflexivity on ethics not only contributes to our understanding of the social worlds we study, it also sheds light on how research communities – and *our* research community in particular – evaluate the credibility of knowledge claims.

## Notes

1 I would like to thank a number of colleagues for sharing their (much farther reaching) insights and observations, most notably John Caldwell, Bridget Conor, David Craig, Stuart Cunningham, Maria Eriksson, Adam Fish, Jennifer Holt, Alisa Perren, Violaine Roussel, and Petr Szczepanik. The financial support of the Swedish Research Council/Vetenskapsrådet (D07310500) is gratefully acknowledged.
2 Aleksandr Kogan, a psychologist at Cambridge University, is considered a protagonist in the Cambridge Analytica scandal, in which Facebook data collected for academic research was used for commercial political micro-targeting during the 2016 US elections. Theranos was a highly valued American health technology corporation that falsely claimed to have revolutionized blood testing. Surgisphere

is an American healthcare analytics company which used unverified data on COVID-19 in an article published in renowned British medical journal *The Lancet.*

3 This exemplary recommendation relates to research on the US-based film and television industries and is not meant to be prescriptive for the area as a whole. As Caldwell puts it, below-the-line crafts "provide a better – or at least different – understanding of the complex fabric of the production culture" than executives whose viewpoint "inevitably brings with it top-down perspectives and pressures" (2008: 118–20; cf., Banks 2009: 89–90).

4 Lazarsfeld extensively quotes Harold D. Lasswell (1947: 3–8) who acted as Rosten's project adviser, using the quote to outline what he then came to define as administrative research.

# References

Alvesson, M., Gabriel, Y., and Paulsen, R. (2017) *Return to Meaning: A Social Science with Something to Say,* Oxford: Oxford University Press.

AOIR (2020) "Internet Research: Ethical Guidelines 3.0," available at https://aoir.org/reports/ethics3.pdf (accessed August 4, 2020).

Banks, M. (2009) "Gender Below-the-Line: Defining Feminist Production Studies," in M. Banks, V. Mayer, and J. Caldwell (eds), *Production Studies: Cultural Studies of Media Industries,* New York, Routledge, 87–98.

Born, G. (2005) *Uncertain Vision: Birt, Dyke and the Reinvention of the BBC,* London: Verso.

Bruns, A. (2019) "After the 'APIcalypse': Social Media Platforms and their Fight Against Critical Scholarly Research," *Information, Communication and Society,* 22 (11): 1544–1566.

Burawoy, M. (1998) "The Extended Case Method," *Sociological Theory* 16 (1): 4–33.

Caldwell, J. (2008) *Production Culture: Industrial Reflexivity and Critical Practice in Film and Television,* Durham, NC: Duke University Press.

Calvey, D. (2017) *Covert Research: The Art, Politics and Ethics of Undercover Fieldwork,* London: Sage.

Connor, J. D. (2015) "Data and Decision in the Contemporary Studio," *Media Industries* Journal, 2 (2): 41–58.

Corrigan, T. (2018) "Making Implicit Methods Explicit: Trade Press Analysis in the Political Economy of Communication," *International Journal of Communication,* 12: 2751–2772.

Cover, R. (1993) "Nomos and Narrative," in M. Minow (ed.), *Narrative, Violence, and the Law: The Essays of Robert Cover,* Ann Arbor, MI: Michigan University Press, 95–172.

D'Acci, J. (1994) *Defining Women: Television and the Case of Cagney and Lacey,* Chapel Hill, NC: University of North Carolina Press.

Freeman, M. (2016) *Industrial Approaches to Media: A Methodological Gateway to Industry Studies,* London: Palgrave Macmillan.

Galison, P. (1997) *Image and Logic: A Material Culture of Microphysics,* Chicago, IL: University of Chicago Press.

Grainge, P. and Johnson, C. (2015) *Promotional Screen Industries,* Abingdon: Routledge.

Grimmelmann, J. (2015) "Law and Ethics of Experiments on Social Media Users," *Colorado Technology Law Journal,* 219 (13): 221–270.

Grindstaff, L. (2002) *The Money Shot: Trash, Class, and the Making of TV Talk Shows,* Chicago, IL: University of Chicago Press.

Guillemin, M. and Gillam, L. (2004) "Ethics, Reflexivity, and 'Ethically Important Moments' in Research," *Qualitative Inquiry,* 10 (2): 261–280.

Hilgartner, S. (2000) "The Sokal Affair in Context," *Science, Technology, and Human Values,* 22 (4): 506–522.

Holt, J. (2020) Personal correspondence with the Author, June 12.

Israel, M. (2015) *Research Ethics and Integrity for Social Scientists,* Los Angeles, CA: Sage.

Lazarsfeld, P. F. (1941) "Remarks on Administrative and Critical Communications Research," *Studies in Philosophy and Social Science,* 9: 2–16.

Lotz, A., Herbert, D., and Punathambekar, A. (2020) *Media Industry Studies,* Cambridge: Polity.

Lury, C. and Wakeford, N. (2012) "Introduction: A Perpetual Inventory," in C. Lury and N. Wakeford (eds), *Inventive Methods: The Happening of the Social,* Abingdon: Routledge, 1–24.

Malkki, L. (2007) "Tradition and Improvisation in Ethnographic Field Research," in A. Cerwonka and L. Malkki (eds), *Improvising Theory: Process and Temporality in Ethnographic Fieldwork,* Chicago, IL: University of Chicago Press, 162–188.

Marres, N. (2017) *Digital Sociology: The Reinvention of Social Research*, Cambridge: Polity Press.

Mayer, V., Press, A., Verhoeven, P., and Sterne, J. (2018) "How Do We Intervene in the Stubborn Persistence of Patriarchy in Communication Scholarship?," in A. Shaw and D. T. Scott (eds), *Interventions: Communication Research and Practice*, New York: Peter Lang, 54–63.

Mills, D. (2003) "'Like a Horse in Blinkers': A Political History of Anthropology's Research Ethics," in P. Caplan (ed.), *The Ethics of Anthropology: Debates and Dilemmas*, London: Routledge, 37–52.

Nader, L. (1972) "Up the Anthropologist: Perspectives Gained from Studying Up," in D. H. Hymes (ed.) *Reinventing Anthropology*, Ann Arbor: University of Michigan Press, 284–311.

Newcomb, H. and Alley, R. (1983) *The Producer's Medium: Conversations with Creators of American TV*, New York: Oxford University Press.

Nissenbaum, H. (2004) "Privacy as Contextual Integrity," *Washington Law Review*, 79 (1): 119–158.

Phillips, W. D. (2015) "'A Maze of Intricate Relationships': Mae D. Huettig and Early Forays into Film Industry Studies," *Film History*, 27 (1): 135–163.

Pluckrose, H., Lindsay, J. A., and Boghossian, P. (2018) "Academic Grievance Studies and the Corruption of Scholarship," *Areo*, October 2, available at https://areomagazine.com/2018/10/02/academic-grievance-studies-and-the-corruption-of-scholarship/ (accessed August 4, 2020).

Poletti, C. and Gray, D. (2019) "Good Data Is Critical Data: An Appeal for Critical Digital Studies," in A. Daly, S. K. Devitt, and M. Mann (eds), *Good Data*, Amsterdam: Institute of Network Cultures, 260–276.

Powdermaker, H. (1951) *Hollywood. The Dream Factory*, New York: Little, Brown & Co.

Rosten, L. C. (1939) "A 'Middletown' Study of Hollywood," *The Public Opinion Quarterly*, 3 (2): 314–320.

Rosten, L. C. (1941) *Hollywood: The Movie Colony*, New York: Harcourt Brace.

Roussel, V. (2020) Personal correspondence with the Author, June 27.

Salganik, M. (2019) *Bit by Bit: Social Research in the Digital Age*, Princeton, NJ: Princeton University Press.

Sandvig, C. and Hargittai, E. (2015) *Digital Research Confidential: The Secrets of Studying Behavior Online*, Cambridge, MA: MIT Press.

Social Science One (2018) "Building Industry-Academic Partnership," available at https://socialscience.one/ (accessed August 4, 2020).

Sokal, A. (2009) *Beyond the Hoax: Science, Philosophy and Culture*, Oxford: Oxford University Press.

Strathern, M. (2000) *Audit Cultures: Anthropological Studies in Accountability, Ethics and the Academy*, New York: Routledge.

Wasko, J. and Meehan, E. (2013) "Critical Crossroads or Parallel Routes?," *Cinema Journal*, 52 (3): 150–156.

# 47

# APPRECIATING THE COSTS AND BENEFITS OF MEDIA MARKET RESEARCH IN THE DIGITAL ERA

*Justin Wyatt*

## Who is the viewer?

Sitting at the weekly update meeting, the television cable network team pondered the question. Each person at the table imagined a different possibility. For the network president, the viewer is simply whomever could be counted on as being loyal in their viewership, trying out new shows and watching more of the network over time. For the marketing chief, the viewer is the ideal sales demographic, comprising the magical mix of characteristics appealing to the widest number of potential sponsors. For the research head, the viewer is the most recent television ratings supplier Nielsen's composite of who was watching the network most of all. For others in programming, scheduling, and digital, the viewer might be a specific friend, focus group participant, or online commenter who made a vivid and lasting impression. Regardless, the most basic of questions yields a multitude of responses.

The "simple" goal of understanding the viewer is asked often by an array of television media industry "insiders," from programming and marketing executives to schedulers and ad agencies. This question is, of course, at the basis for the entire set of media industries in the United States. While it may seem like a straightforward empirical query, marketplace events since the 1990s have rendered it increasingly relevant and difficult to unravel. Of course, technology and media consumption patterns have shifted dramatically in this time period. Suddenly, the industry is scrambling to understand exactly who the potential audience for their product(s) can be.

While this question is at the center of so much academic and industry research, like Alice down the rabbit hole, the more time and effort spent investigating, the further we seem to be from the answer. First, we need to keep in mind that media research is split into scholarly/academic work, either quantitative or qualitative in nature, and market research/industry work, also quantitative or qualitative and usually designed to help answer a business question. Inevitably, industry research studies for television are focused on either two issues: how to get people to watch a show or how to get them to stay watching longer. These, of course, just boil down to the single question – how can we make more money?

DOI: 10.4324/9780429275340-53

Academic/scholarly work has been more far-reaching, to say the least. On the one hand, poststructuralism has heralded the death of the author, the deconstruction of the individual, and the difficulty of assigning a single meaning or coherence to media texts. Critical theory has created an environment in which to speak of "the viewer" is to unpack immediately a barrage of cultural, social, political, and economic factors at play in the construction of this figure. Media market research, originating specifically by/for use within the media industries, has largely been exempt from these critical inquiries. Industry practitioners have been goal-directed in their use of primary and secondary media research, attempting to understand media viewers, the mass audience, and the options for entertainment in mostly proprietary individual studies and occasionally co-sponsored studies.

While this approach may have sufficed in the last millennium, the rapid shifts in technology, delivery systems, and entertainment options have created a wider gap between media industry research and academic/scholarly research practice. Both industry practitioners and the academy are invested in the same basic questions: mainly identifying audiences, factors in entertainment decision-making, and, ideally, understanding the "next step" for audience members in their choices. Increasingly, there is a division in the ways through which the viewer has been constructed. Academics have theorized ways to understand media consumption through a variety of perspectives (transmedia storytelling, convergence culture, wired TV). Industry practitioners have either been playing catch up with marketplace/structural changes through studying the impact of new technologies/delivery options or through suggesting that "big data" will prove to be the panacea for understanding audience and media consumption moving forward.

As an industry practitioner (a media market researcher) slash academic (each for about 15 years), I've been able to see both sides of the debate over audiences and consumption. My goal in this chapter is to offer a model for media market research in terms of typical projects enacted within the industry. With this framework in mind, I will then identify key challenges and issues facing media market research. Although answers to these issues are not as readily obvious or available, it is worth considering some of the challenges to media market research. These factors impact many of the market research parameters, including the efficacy of the research method, the ability to construct an adequate sample for research purposes, and the ability to reconcile market research data with other data streams. Media market research is a first step for understanding audiences by foregrounding viewer attitudes, perspectives, and behavior. As a former Senior Vice-President of Program Planning and Scheduling at ABC describes it though, "It's not an exact science. It's one element in the scheduling-setting process, and it's flawed" (Stanley 1996: 22).

## The model of market research: setting the parameters

Market research studies within the media industries follow different paths based on the medium: film, television, and online sites. At the most basic level, projects across all media can be divided into qualitative and quantitative research studies. Qualitative research, focused on a small number of respondents (even one-on-ones), allows for exploration of a topic in depth. Frequently, qualitative media research takes the form of focus groups: eight to twelve respondents recruited by a focus group faculty for a one- or two-hour discussion led by a moderator. While focus groups may yield useful attitudinal information, the small sample size means that one cannot extrapolate the findings far beyond this limited number. Quantitative market research studies, on the other, are designed around a respondent sample that mirrors a larger population, such as the broader national (or international) market for an entertainment product. In many instances, media research clients will employ a combination of qualitative and quantitative research projects. The qualitative project can help researchers understand the vocabulary and range of attitudes and behaviors. These findings can then be utilized to craft a useful quantitative research survey to yield results that may be extrapolated to the larger market. Quantitative studies are done most frequently online with respondents culled from sample providers, web site visitors, and other third-party sources. Other methods, such as mail or telephone surveys, are occasionally utilized, but the online method is very attractive for ease of completing the survey and for lowering costs compared to alternatives. Sometimes the order of studies is reversed. For instance, a quantitative study could be used to identify different viewer profiles for a network. These survey answers yielding these profiles could then be used to recruit focus groups composed of these different segments. In this case, the qualitative focus groups would be conducted to give greater depth and texture to the quantitative results.

Film market research typically involves a discrete stimulus, the film, being assessed for overall audience enjoyment and/or fine tune editing given the audience's reaction. Film market research often involves recruited audience screenings with audience members completing simple two-sided surveys at the end of the screening (James 1988). A subset of the audience is selected to participate in a focus group led by a moderator. This focus group is used to understand the audience's reaction in more detail. Trying to comprehend the whys behind the survey scores often motivates one fruitful line of inquiry in these groups. In-theater surveys and focus groups are used to identify any narrative issues or confusions and to assess the audience's reaction to the film and its constitutive parts.

Market research on entertainment web sites can take a variety of forms, from concept testing an idea for a new site, to usability studies in which respondents navigate a site so that developers can understand site functionality and appeal. These usability studies are enacted by user experience/design (UX) professionals who are well versed in the protocols of effective site design. In these studies, a respondent is asked to navigate through a site with the researcher taking note of the path(s) chosen and any confusions. In addition, usability studies are frequently task-based, meaning that a respondent is asked to achieve a particular task (e.g., on a network site, a question might be "how would you watch a recap from last week's episode of 'show X' on the site?") with the facilitator gauging the route used to successfully achieve the task. So web site market research relies a great deal on these kinds of hands-on research studies. Once the site is live, online metrics are used to understand the appeal and the stickiness (factors encouraging the visitor's time on and frequency of visiting the site). In addition to baseline metrics on usage, there is considerable attention paid to user-generated comments and assessing the sentiment (positive, neutral, negative) of these comments.

Market research within the television industry typically tends to rely on a greater range of studies compared to film and digital sites. This derives from the more far-reaching aspects of television as a medium. Instead of a single stimulus, like a film, television research seeks to understand the relationship of the TV viewer to the medium, the ways that series can be maintained across a lengthy time frame, and the factors for creating series, personalities, and segments that appeal to viewers. As a result, networks and content providers are often engaged with several different research studies across the life of a television show. Apart from awareness/interest tracking surveys, the television industry enacts more substantial studies such as talent testing, pilot testing, and exploratory testing. All three may require a combination of both qualitative and quantitative research, and are directly connected to the green light decision for a new show. As with any market research, the utility of these studies must be seen in the context of other factors (e.g., production cost, scheduling, competing shows).

The talent research project starts with the most basic of links between audience and industry: connecting to talent on-screen. Certainly, viewers connect with human characters, leading them to bond and become enmeshed in conflict and drama. The link is even more significant in the specific realm of news and information programming. A viewer watches an on-air journalist present a story, whether light news or breaking news, and their reaction is impacted, in some way, by who is delivering the information. Traditionally, networks distinguish between news presenters and news journalists, although viewers mostly have no concept of whether the on-air talent has authored the story or whether they are simply reading the teleprompter. Before committing to an on-air talent assignment, broadcast and cable news operations frequently engage in the process of talent testing, or understanding the emotional connection of the viewer to on-air talent. Even today, the process of conducting market research for news/information programming is largely met with hostility within the journalistic community. As former ABC News executive Tom Bettag (2000: 105) describes it, the move to "focus groups and research" led simply to news becoming "what people say they want to know more about." In other words, market merely yields "news" that people want to see rather than what journalists and editors designate as valid news.

The market research portfolio of talent testing involves a blend of qualitative and quantitative research. On the qualitative side, viewers in a variety of settings (focus groups in a local facility, at-home ethnographies, one-on-one online interviews) evaluate talent. This evaluation is framed in terms of specific personal and professional attributes held by the talent. Watching clips of the talent "in action" (interviewing, hosting, reporting, analyzing news and issues, bantering), the respondent rates them on individual skills and, more globally, on both their personal and professional attributes. If this testing is conducted in a setting allowing for a follow-up discussion, a focus group would be used to probe on the reasons behind the ratings and for an overall assessment of the talent. Alternately, an ethnographic approach is used, with a moderator watching a news show during broadcast at a respondent's home. The goal would be to get unguarded reactions to talent and content in an environment of "normal" show viewing.

Historically, both the broadcast and cable universes have been ruled by a most concentrated period of viewer testing during April each year in which pilot episodes for the fall season are evaluated. The task of pilot testing is direct and deliberate: what do people think of this pilot episode for a potential new series? The input from respondents is used to inform decisions over whether the pilot should, in fact, be picked up for a full series commitment and premiered in the fall. As John Caldwell (2014: 153) points out, this testing has ignited large debates within Hollywood on the "research versus intuition" division. Rather than take a middle road of using the testing in conjunction with creative and financial input, Jordan Levin, then president of the WB network, decided to scratch pilot testing altogether in 2004. "What 60 random people think about a show can be a huge distraction," proclaimed Levin during pilot testing season (quoted in Barnes 2004). "We want to filter all that noise out," said Levin. "We're investing in the management team to make tough decisions and trust their guts" (quoted in Ryan 2004: 3). Tellingly, by 2005, Levin had exited his role and the WB committed to pilot testing again for data on a pilot's demographic appeal, character development, and cast chemistry. Pilot testing and its results were safe again. In the years since this brief experiment, all the broadcast and cable networks have engaged in pilot testing which has become, if anything, even more pervasive.

In describing the process of gauging viewer enjoyment, James Webster (2014: 47) talks of "the puzzle of preferences," that is, the difficulty of understanding viewer actions because their preferences cannot be adequately modeled. Admittedly, preferences are volatile and contradictory. Market research of television pilots should not be seen as a way to understand viewer preferences in a global sense. At its best, this testing reveals only what the respondent thinks of this individual episode, nothing more, albeit in moment-to-moment readings if the respondent is part of a pilot test dial testing study (i.e., the respondent conveys their enjoyment of the pilot by turning the dial from 0 to 100 based on their reaction in the instant). In practice, pilot testing is best used to identify red flags: unlikeable characters, narrative confusion(s), negative comparisons to other series, unlikely plot twists and other elements. Pilot testing can shine a light on these issues, although it is unlikely that respondents can or will be able to explain how these individual issues could impact a show or a series. As such, pilot testing is more useful not for predicting hits, but rather for identifying red flags that could negatively impact the enjoyment of the show.

Since even niche networks have a national footprint, pilot testing is usually conducted so results can be extrapolated to the national viewing population. This requires a quantitative sample so that the key demographics (age, gender, household composition and ethnicity) can be disaggregated with statistical reliability. Traditionally, networks want to mirror the home viewing experience as much as possible in their pilot testing. The logic is that a tested show would be closer to real-world ones if the viewing context matched the typical viewing environment. What does this mean in practice for testing? Networks screen their pilots on available cable channels ("cable testing") for in-home viewing, provide a link to watch the show streaming, or send a digital versatile disc (DVD) to the respondent for watching in-home at their leisure. In all these instances, the respondent then completes a questionnaire, either by phone or online, gauging their reaction to the pilot and its individual elements. More cost-effective variations on this approach would be using dial tests online or in a focus group facility to measure moment-to-moment reactions to the pilot. The attractive aspect of the dial testing approach is the wealth of data, including dial "traces" mapped across the entire show moment-to-moment and a battery of closed-end questions on overall reaction as well.

Exploratory media market research centers on the creativity and analytical powers of the viewers. Rather than the traditional stimulus/response model of market research, these exploratory studies are based on the ideas, attitudes, and opinions of the viewer. During the session, the respondents, solo and in groups, develop and discuss ideas and concepts that matter personally to them. Conducted over several hours in a single day, the ideation session usually begins with a homework assignment. During the week prior to the session, 20–25 respondents are asked to collect a media artifact set (e.g., website listings, news headlines, logos, brand images, hashtags) of items that have personal meaning to them. The choice of items is eclectic, but all have some emotional resonance for the respondent. Crucially, respondents are not informed about the goal of the study beforehand. The study is framed in terms of getting in-depth information about their daily lives. On site, the respondents are asked to use their media artifacts to build an impressionistic representation of a new TV show, series, or segment on a poster board. The only real constraint is that the person must construct a show concept that would appeal to them – meaning a show that they would actually watch.

This type of study is used within networks to identify and mold new concepts or show ideas. Through empowering the viewers to focus on creative execution and development, the studies offer a new way for market research to interact with viewers. When enacted with care and with moderation that is both challenging and supportive, these ideation studies can generate useful and provocative material to stimulate the creativity of the respondents, the television production team, and even the network executives.

All of these studies – talent testing, pilot testing, and exploratory testing – are focused on the content of a television show. It should be noted that another important study across media is marketing testing, that is, qualitative or quantitative research addressing individual marketing and advertising executions or the overall brand impressions, expectations, and assumptions for an entertainment product. Brand assessments may be gathered unaided or in response to specific marketing and advertising stimuli. Print ad testing (film or television), television promo testing, movie trailer testing, radio spot testing (film or television), and, for lifestyle brands and networks, brand trackers, assessing image and favorability of the brand, are among the more prominent marketing/advertising testing conducted within the media industries.

## Issues with media market research

Perhaps the most pervasive argument against market research in the media industries is based around the efficacy of testing a creative product with consumers (Wyatt 2014: 256). Entertainment creators – from screenwriters to producers and directors – can bristle at the idea of market testing their film or television show. Usually this argument is based, at least in part, on not wanting to adjust a creative product on the basis of either qualitative or quantitative audience research. While these concerns have diminished since the 1980s, there is still a contingent resistance to the idea of viewer/consumer feedback. Most often this is manifested in simply ignoring the market research results since these people know that open rejection of the process would cause concern with senior executives and stakeholders. Passively ignoring the results and their potential impact on audience enjoyment is just a much simpler route to follow for those creatives uncomfortable with the process of market research helping to shape their film or television show.

Even with this provision, market research does pose some challenges, some of which are unrelated to the entertainment industry. Constructing an appropriate sample is one of these foundational issues. For much of the North American television industry, the advertising sales demographic falls between 18 and 49 years of age. As a result, many television studies use this demographic as the sample parameters for their study. While this correspondence makes it easier to sell advertising spots, it may not actually reflect the viewing audience of the show. Broadcast news shows tend to skew older in age so setting the range at 18–49 years may not capture a significant percentage of the viewership. The alternative is to adjust the age range to higher numbers, but this may not happen since the sales department wants to highlight the accepted sales/advertising demographic. The other issue with constructing the sample is "guesstimating" the sample parameters (e.g., age range, ethnicity, household composition, urban/suburban/rural breakdown) for a study. Often a media researcher may not have accurate data on these viewer parameters, perhaps due to the show pilot being tested or because the Nielsen household data is not discrete enough for these purposes. The result is using either generic viewer parameters associated broadly with the television landscape or adopting estimates for the viewer parameters based on shows past of the same genre. Of course, both methods can be flawed by specifying sample viewer parameters that do not fit with actual real-life viewers. Although clients, and sometimes researchers, can be fascinated with data, asking the hard question of how the sample was screened and recruited is an absolute necessity.

The method for collecting data is also worth evaluating when considering the efficacy of the data findings. Prior to the new century, many media surveys were conducted by phone. This method allowed for rich qualitative comments from the respondent. As with any research study though, given busy lives, the length of the survey needed to be manageable (ranging from 15 to 30 minutes). With the online environment gaining precedence in the early 2000s, surveys began to appear online. These were fostered by sample providers who offered an easy location for survey takers who could qualify for sweepstakes prizes or other incentives by completing their responses online. Additionally, the speed and lower cost of online surveys proved attractive to researchers, clients, and respondents. The form of the online survey facilitates easy answering through grid questions and scales.

Despite these advantages, online surveys do have vulnerabilities, as do all research methodologies. One of the biggest concerns is the completion rate by respondents. As would be expected, the longer the survey, the more likely that respondents will either simply discontinue or start giving false answers. The latter could be sticking to one side of the scale or, more deviously, by selecting a diagonal pattern, with no reaction to question content, through the survey. Market researchers have developed algorithms to identify these (and other) patterns of invalid responses. With these algorithms in place, the respondent and associated data can be eliminated from the study.

Discontinuation is a more perplexing problem. Many surveys, however, test the respondent's patience given the length; clients and researchers are usually looking for a battery of questions to identify the respondent apart from those questions at the core of the survey. As would be expected, there is an inverse relationship between the length of the survey and the percentage of respondents completing it. The response rate can be impacted by several other factors, including incentives, sweepstakes entries, and other means to foster survey completion. The length of a survey and a general ennui with taking online surveys impact the ability to conduct in-depth research online. Keep in mind that in our digital era, people are asked to do surveys of all kinds as part of routine consumer purchases and behaviors. The culture of instant feedback presents a challenge to those quantitative market research projects requiring more in depth and reflective responses. A media research project, for example, assessing the breadth of a respondent's leisure time activities and choices could seem daunting after completing numerous one- to three-question consumer satisfaction surveys. Substantive media research therefore faces a new challenge in our current digital environment: how to conduct research on viewers/consumers media attitudes, behaviors, and usage in a culture deadened by endless customer satisfaction surveys and polls.

In a business known for catch phrases and savvy taglines, media industries have been associated with one of the salient phrases of the past decade: "big data." John Cheney-Lippold characterizes our contemporary era as one where we produce (and consume) data: "Across this data world, we participate in a colossal ecology of data production. We make data, we signify to algorithms what that data means, and what we do differently allows those measuring types to change" (2017: 89). Big data refers to the many data streams available within our digital environment. For the television industry, the relevant data derives from connected viewing, that is, the cross-platform usage of media outlets in a household. Paul Clemens Murschetz and Dimitri Prandner (2018: 56) list some of the possibilities for connected viewing: TV sets with Internet connectivity, set-top boxes delivering audiovisual content "over-the-top" (OTT), connections offered to social media and networking services ("Social TV") and viewers with the ability to interact with gestures and voice commands or use multiple screens ("Multiscreen-TV"). The challenge for researchers is how to conform these different streams into an aggregate picture. Whereas the traditional broadcast and basic cable model was advertising-centric, meaning that Nielsen was measuring the potential viewers for an advertising spot, the new digital environment suggests a radical modification to this model. One way to move forward would be to align quantitative and qualitative research with the data streams on cross-platform usage and other consumer/viewer data available now. For samples recruited through a third-party provider this can be arduous and often simply not feasible. Even with respondent-level data, the challenge of big data can be realized by considering the many different data streams that can be measured: viewer metadata, device-level data, distribution-level data, web traffic data, geolocation, and third-party data sources (Murschetz and Prandner 2018: 64). As Cheney-Lippold

(2017: 87) suggests, big data also moves researchers further away from the actual viewer, leaving instead only profiles "at the intersections of categorical meanings."

Nielsen, the primary provider of ratings data, has offered a couple of alternatives. First, quantitative samples in a custom research project recruited from their panel can be matched with external data profiling their respondents. This can allow for greater profiling in terms of background and cross-platform behavior. Second, Nielsen produces syndicated reports (i.e., reports sold to multiple television clients rather than exclusive to one client) analyzing the overall cross-platform viewing environment: in 2020, Nielsen issued the Total Audience Report measuring the consumer usage of a variety of entertainment options including devices and services in the household, cross-platform usage, media time used by select demographics and weekly reach across platforms. That a syndicated report of this type could still be considered useful in 2020 speaks to the difficulty in creating custom research projects really addressing cross-platform usage and choice decision-making between the many entertainment options in our current environment. It should be noted that Nielsen's different ratings modalities fail to capture adequately streaming viewing and particularly the viewership attached to portals (Porter 2019).

With the existing concerns about online survey research and the difficulty of understanding how big data can be mobilized to enhance our understanding of media consumption, we may seem further away from explaining the viewer than where we were before the beginning of this century. Certainly, online surveys by themselves are not adequate to characterize the contemporary media consumer. Our relationship to viewership had altered considerably given new technologies and the development of "portal television," to use Amanda Lotz's (2017) useful term for the internet-distributed television "channels." Cross-platform usage can be considerable, as can watching simultaneously on more than one device. As the options for viewing have expanded so much over the past two decades so have the ways of watching. By this, I mean to suggest that the days of appointment viewing for network and cable shows are largely absent. With the advent of social media, fandom has also shifted a great deal, with direct access to stars and the solidification of fan sites as community building (Stein 2015). Even with this burst of activity, a lack of racial diversity is present in the world of portal television (Christian 2018: 249). A low-budget alternative to conducting primary research is to analyze sentiment and volume of social media posts. At best, social media measurement can give you a very rough view of feelings toward a show, personality, or brand. It cannot, however, replace either customized qualitative or quantitative research projects recruited for the correct sample population.

With multiplying options for viewing and a fractured universe of entertainment choices, market research would appear to be more important than ever before: in this context, the key challenge for networks and portals becomes how to locate and secure a viewing audience in this quickly changing media environment? Media market research needs to delve deep into the contexts of viewing, the habits of viewing by key demographics, and the decision-making on the part of the viewer. The days of stimulus/response testing of shows, talents and brands are now looking as outdated as your VCR in the attic. Market research needs to start addressing method, context of viewing, and connections to shows or talent afresh. In this new world of media consumption, market researchers must be prepared to speak to these changes and to anticipate the future of media entertainment consumption.

# References

Barnes, B. (2004) "Trusting Gut Instincts, WB Network Stops Testing TV Pilots," *The Wall Street Journal*, May 3: B1.

Bettag, T. (2000) "Evolving Definitions of News," *Harvard International Journal of Press/Politics*, 5 (3): 105–107.

Caldwell, J. (2014) "Post-Network Reflexivity: Viral Marketing and Labor Management," in D. Mann (ed.), *Wired TV: Laboring Over an Interactive Future*, New Brunswick, NJ: Rutgers University Press, 140–160.

Cheney-Lippold, J. (2017) *We Are Data: Algorithms and the Making of Our Digital Selves*, New York: New York University Press.

Christian, A. J. (2018) *Open TV: Innovation Beyond Hollywood and the Rise of Web Television*, New York: New York University Press.

James, C. (1988) "Test Screenings of New Movies Put Demographics Over Creativity," *The New York Times*, March 9: C17.

Lotz, A. (2017) *Portals: A Treatise on Internet-Distributed Television*, Mountain View, CA: Maize Books.

Murschetz, P. C. and Prandner, D. (2018) "'Datafying' Broadcasting: Exploring the Role of Big Data and Its Implications for Competing in a Big Data-Driven TV Ecosystem," in D. Khajeheian, M. Friedrichsen, and W. Mödinger (eds), *Competitiveness in Emerging Markets: Market Dynamics in the Age of Disruptive Technologies*, Cham: Springer, 55–71.

Porter, R. (2019) "TV Long View: A Guide to Ever-Expanding World of Ratings Data," *The Hollywood Reporter*, October 5, available at www.hollywoodreporter.com/live-feed/tv-ratings-explained-a-guide-what-data-all-means-1245591 (accessed November 30, 2020).

Ryan, L. (2004) "WB Abandons Testing of Pilots," *Television Week*, March 29: 3, 34.

Stein, L. (2015) *Millennial Fandom: Television Audiences in the Transmedia Age*, Iowa City, IA: University of Iowa Press.

Stanley, T. (1996) "Fate by Focus Group?" *Mediaweek*, July 8: 22.

Webster, J. (2014) *The Marketplace for Attention: How Audiences Take Shape in the Digital Age*, Cambridge, MA: MIT Press.

Wyatt, J. (2014) "Market Research in the Media Industries: On the Strategic Relationship Between Client and Supplier," in D. Johnson, D. Kompare, and A. Santo (eds), *Making Media Work: Cultures of Management in the Entertainment Industries*, New York: New York University Press, 254–274.

# 48

# NUMBERS AND QUALITATIVE MEDIA INDUSTRIES RESEARCH

*Jade L. Miller*

From ethnographic production studies research of film workers, to interviews with high-level media executives, critical media industries research is often qualitative in nature. Yet, while engaging in everything from micro-level site observations to macro-level critical political economies, qualitative critical media industries researchers are at times compelled by readers and editors to include quantitative measures in their studies as a means to justify their industry as worthy of analysis. This chapter examines the inherent fuzziness that girds the production of such statistics across media industries, particularly in studies of industries involving extended degrees of informality. How can we best understand media industries as worthy of investigation without relying on murky statistics and haphazardly generated numbers? How do even critical qualitative researchers contribute to the creation of a market for quantification of that which cannot be reliably counted? How can we instead rely upon qualitative measures to indicate the importance or influence of any media industry we study?

## Demand for statistical measures

Whether citing statistics on the number of titles produced per year or the profits made, there are many offhand ways in which media researchers are asked to justify their research using quantitative measures, even as the core of their study is qualitative. In the course of pursuing research questions on everything from production and distribution to textual analysis, researchers often refer in offhand ways to specific figures. Common statistical measures of media industries include the volume and value of sales and budgets, number of titles produced annually, market shares, number of jobs created, and contributions to gross domestic product (GDP), among others.

The global English language movie industry known as Hollywood, for instance, is widely considered to be the world's dominant global film industry based on figures including its revenue, the size of its budgets, and receipts from cinema attendance the world over. Hollywood is also the industry with some of the most rigorous public accounting of such numbers, due to the formality of its distribution. Major studio Hollywood films are regularly screened at multiplexes and other theaters around the world known to document their ticket sales in a fairly transparent fashion. Every time a film enters theaters, statistics on ticket sales are produced and largely released publicly.

DOI: 10.4324/9780429275340-54

Researchers and investors can be relatively certain that sales figures produced during opening weekends accurately reflect trends in global attendance and can be extrapolated to produce at least a sense of the popularity of a film. A movie can be deemed a hit or a disappointment in the very first weekend of its release. The transparency and reliability of this data is widely taken for granted. While unmeasurable watching also occurs via everything from online pirated torrents to unauthorized public screenings, and while some theater receipts may be obscured or inflated (particularly in international markets) (Ulin 2019, pp. 200–202), interested observers can generally assume cinema receipts for Hollywood films have a very strong correlation to how many people are globally watching a new title. When writing about a Hollywood movie from a critical media studies perspective, one can quickly and quantifiably justify a claim that a film is popular, by referring to publicly available cinema receipts largely considered to be reliable.

The assumption that such statistics can be taken as a given applies across media industries, even as levels of formality in compiling and reporting these numbers varies wildly. When encountering research on a non-Hollywood movie industry, researchers are frequently expected to have answers to questions regarding how many titles are produced per year, cost per title, or the gross revenues of an industry per year. In other words, researchers are expected to indicate the importance of the industry they work on by indicating its size and it is assumed that measures of size derive easily from reported data.

## Obscuring data as standard media industries practice across contexts

Every media industry falls in a gray area along a continuum between formality and informality. The placement of an industry on this continuum, as understood in this chapter, is based on the scale of documentation of industrial practices and level of reliance on external structures (courts, for example) for industrial governance (see Miller 2016, p. 32). In other words, the production of industrial statistics and the work of measuring and documentation is a key mechanism in an industry's formalization.

Even Hollywood, one of the most formal and documented film industries in the world, is informal in significant areas of its distribution, production, and accounting practices (Lobato, 2012). Furthermore, despite the apparent precision of reported figures, meticulousness in accounting should not be mistaken for accuracy (Poovey 1998). So-called creative accounting (Karim, Shaikh, Hock, and Islam 2016) has been a hallmark of Hollywood productions, transforming hit blockbusters into losses on balance sheets, thereby ensuring minimal returns are shared with those promised a percentage of a film's profits (Thompson 2011; Sisto 2003; Sparviero 2015). Warner Bros. hit *Harry Potter and the Order of the Phoenix* (2007), for instance, reportedly grossed $983 million in global box office receipts. Studio accounting practices, however, documented for creditors a $167 million overall loss, based in part on the studio showing a cost of $350 million in full-cost distribution, prints, marketing, and promotion, with much of this work performed in-house by the company's own salaried employees (Thompson 2011).

The reason this type of accounting manipulation is so well-known to outside observers (and has even become a model for accounting in other industries)[1] is in part because the Hollywood studios have furnished their official accounting documents to the Motion Picture Association (MPA)[2] (Epstein 2005). Additionally, documents have been made publicly available as part of lawsuits in US courts when attempting to demystify the definition of a movie's profitability and to spread profits more evenly among non-studio participants (Sisto 2003). Filing documents with courts and trade organizations loosens the flow of publicly available data, allowing researchers and other onlookers to make their own observations of film budgets and profits.

External assessments of profitability can be performed by creative quantitative and qualitative researchers eschewing studio accounting of profits and instead basing their calculations on estimates produced by information publicly available on industry tracking services such as *Box Office Mojo* (a website reporting official box office figures for all films at the end of every opening weekend), in-depth economic analyses of trends in Hollywood film studio costs based on trade publications like *Variety*, access to proprietary data from industry analysis firms, and interviews with industry executives (see Epstein 2010; Sparviero 2015; Ulin 2019; Wasko 2003). This mix of vetted court documents, independent trade publications, reliable trade organizations, and film studio workers revealing trends can help create a relatively reliable picture of budgets and profits in Hollywood, though one can still not call Hollywood a fully transparent nor fully formal industry: the formal production of data may obfuscate the true opacity of industry finances, a characteristic more closely associated with informal economies.

Due to the mass trackability of viewers, online distribution has the potential to create even more reliable accounting of views, profits, and geographic trends in distribution. Yet, major online distributors (most notably global giant Netflix) are well known for their guarding of this data, rendering it private and inaccessible, though it does exist internally (Lee 2019). While researchers and industry investors and analysts are stymied by this lack of access, companies like Netflix track this data in a calculated and accurate fashion, maintaining opacity by hoarding this information from outside eyes (Lee 2019). As Netflix do not release lists of program and film titles, Lobato (2018), for instance, has attempted to calculate the size of Netflix's catalog of global offerings using data from an analytics firm (Veed), backdoor analysis through direct URL investigation, and third-party search engines like Netflixable. The motivation for this obfuscation is to limit the ability of outsiders to assess the company's business model, allowing only Netflix to benefit from analysis of this information. In contrast, smaller online distributors, such as iROKOtv, the leading streaming service for Nollywood (Southern Nigerian) movies, mark themselves by the visibility of similar data, something they hope makes them more "investible" in than other entities in their industry (Miller 2016). Jason Njoku, CEO of iROKOtv, for instance, regularly posts to Twitter and Medium the sorts of internally produced figures that researchers and investors crave in order to stimulate external investment in his company, though the release of this data is limited and strategic as well.

Strategic use of data obfuscation has been documented in movie industries worldwide. Bollywood, the Hindi language movie industry based in Mumbai, has been studied most closely in this regard. Ganti (2015) has written extensively on the use of opacity, ambiguity, and fuzziness in this industry as a tool for allowing Bollywood producers to manipulate their own profits. A policy change in 2000 granted the Indian film industry official industry status, thereby making it investible for major banks and other formal investors. As Ganti illuminates, this policy revealed the ways in which Bollywood moviemakers manipulate data to their benefit. Prior to the policy change, producers attempted to make movies seem less profitable than they were, feeding manipulated information to industry publications to make it appear that less profits had been made, leaving them less liable to investors and creative workers seeking a share of profits (p. 459). After the policy change, Ganti described an elaborate symphony of exacting numbers released in which producers sought to show growth quarter after quarter in order to encourage formal investment from banks, major multinational corporations (MNCs), and other institutional investors (p. 461). These numbers were portrayed as accurate and concrete, despite their emergence from an industry that cannot track nor predict sales to the level of certainty portrayed (Ganti 2015; Govil 2016). Studying conferences promoting investment in Bollywood, Nitin Govil (2016: 106) described numbers so precise they could hardly be taken seriously (for example, a prediction that domestic box office would increase by specifically

10.2 percent over the next five years). Yet, these numbers hold weight: their production is, essentially, a necessity for formal investment.

Govil (2010: 107) suggests statistics perform three functions in film industries. First, they make the industry "legible" and comprehensible to investors. Second, they enable the operations of diverse individual producers to be grouped together under a single label, enabling them to be understood as a single group following a specific trend. Finally, they indicate to outsiders that the industry is willing and able to translate itself into the language of formal investment: that industrial actors have the capacity and will to produce numbers that appear transparent, rendering them worthy of serious investment, no matter what direction those numbers indicate nor their precision. In this way, the official numbers produced and displayed to outsiders are *performative* more than they are informative, as each statistic has varying levels of manipulation feeding its production. As informative as the numbers may be, their production alone justifies investment by outsiders.

Movie industries worldwide produce numbers for outsiders, but capacity to verify these numbers varies from industry to industry. As discussed above, even with its apparent transparency, Hollywood is able to manipulate and obfuscate numbers to its own advantage, just as Bollywood has done before and after the 2000 policy change. A major difference between industries, however, is whether the numbers are known by insiders. Netflix, for instance, can track the viewing habits of every subscriber (though not how many people are watching at once in group versus solo, or how many people may share the same profile) and this data is calculated and analyzed internally (Lee 2019). In instances like the 2014 Sony Pictures hack, when hackers leaked a trove of internal documents belonging to the Hollywood major, an industry becomes more transparent due to the illicit exposure of confidential accounting information (Siegel 2014). Industries that are more heavily reliant on less trackable distribution, such as physical sales at private informal distribution hubs like stalls at open-air markets, managed by a disperse group of small-scale entrepreneurs rather than a handful of major studios, are more of a mystery to outsiders, as there can be no sureness that accurate ledgers even exist. There is no potential for such information to even be leaked if it is not first gathered and accounted internally.

Nollywood, the Nigerian movie industry, is a prime example of this sort of sphere. Not only does the industry not systematically disclose film budgets or the wages paid to workers, but, with most viewers acquiring movies as physical copies purchased from open-air markets and street vendors, where there is little differentiation between official and unauthorized copies, there is little ability for external observers to determine the sales volume, viewership, or profitability for individual titles or the industry as a whole (Miller 2016; Lobato 2012). The opacity of this distribution is theorized to be intentional, performed by the large and diverse number of small-scale producers known as marketers (Miller 2016: 52). Between creative personnel and government representatives seeking a share of profits, and foreign and formal investors interested in corporatization processes that would exclude most of these producers from power they currently hold, there is no real incentive to share figures with outsiders or even among one another (Miller 2016). Held together by ethnic ties[3] and a powerful guild comprising a vast network of producer-distributors with direct control over networks of open-air marketplaces handling physical distribution, producing verifiable numbers is seen as a source of weakness rather than potential power (Miller 2016).

A newer subset of Nollywood, known as New Nollywood (Haynes 2014; Ryan 2015) prioritizes the most traceable distribution outlets, including cinema screenings and sales to online distributors. But, in Nollywood, these can be ciphers for clout more than profitability. Producers can lose money on cinema screenings, as the handful of multiplexes in Nigeria screening Nollywood movies as opposed to foreign (often Hollywood) blockbusters, charge producers a fee for their films to be screened, and sales to online distributors are negotiated as a flat fee. Even so, these higher profile Nigerian movies must rely on physical distribution in open-air marketplaces to make the core of their sales. As the bulk of the movies produced in Nollywood follow this original business model, assessments of this largely undocumented distribution activity are inaccessible or illegible to investors, journalists, and researchers. Illegibility to outsiders, then, is a product of informality (Guyer 2004; Meagher 2010; Govil 2016), and, in many cases, this is intentional (Ganti 2015; Meagher 2010; Miller 2016).

## Institutions producing industrial statistics

As mentioned above, Hollywood studios release many of their own distribution figures publicly, yet they too are reticent to provide transparent accountings of profitability and full budgets including marketing costs. Other producers have similar reticence to publicly provide data on viewing and distribution to external investigators, from Netflix's opacity, to Bollywood's suspiciously shifting figures, and the lack of data generated by Nollywood's marketers. Despite the fuzziness (Ganti 2015: 453) of distribution figures across industrial contexts, a number of public institutions and private companies still produce numbers measuring audiovisual entertainment industries. They do this because of the hunger for such data from a variety of stakeholders. Banks and independent investors want numbers to justify which industries and companies they should invest in. Governments want these figures to plan taxation and film funding schemes alike. But we should also interrogate our own position as researchers in the demand for such fuzzy statistics. Journalists and qualitative researchers alike rely on the offhand citation of industrial figures to justify reader interest in their topic, from the number of movies produced per year, to the industrial gross per year, to the number of people employed by an industry.

Take, for instance, a 2015 article by Landé Pratt, in which she assesses the potential implications of increasing online distribution in Nollywood. The abstract opens by referring to Nollywood as the second largest film industry in the world based on UNESCO's figure for numbers of films produced per year in 2012. She follows by noting that Nigeria was totally excluded from a 2013 UNESCO study of film markets due to the non-theatrical release and "semi-professional production" (p. 70) of most titles. In these ways, UNESCO statistics are consumed and reproduced, though their production is also analyzed as of varied reliability due to the different formulas used from report to report to produce the numbers (p. 70).

Taking a different angle, Moradewun Adejunmobi refers to Nollywood as "the largest film industry in Africa" (2011: 68), and to DStv, a prominent satellite provider of Nollywood content, as "DStv, a South African satellite television station that is perhaps the dominant satellite television provider in many parts of the African continent" (p. 68). She doesn't present DStv's statistics to back this up, as she is aware of their lack of verifiability, due in part to sharing of satellite subscriptions, unauthorized reception of DStv signals, and other unmeasurable popularity. She asserts that one can assess Nollywood's and DStv's vast presence in sub-Saharan Africa by qualitative assessments of their visibility alone, based on time the researcher spent in communities, and hedged with phrases like "perhaps" and "many parts", without recourse to misleadingly specific figures. On one hand, these hedged phrases can be critiqued as "verbal counting," a practice in which qualitative assessments disguise their lack of precision and generalizability (Sandelowski 2001). I argue, however, that it *is* possible to use words like "perhaps" or "many parts" without overstating specificity. Having spent years researching media in sub-Saharan Africa, Adejunmobi can report upon the experienced pervasiveness of DStv and Nollywood as observed in community after community in which she has done research. This is a qualitative assessment of popularity, based in local knowledge, without overstating the certainty the researcher can possess.

One reason to trust qualitative assessments of popularity, such as Adejunmobi's, more than figures produced by intergovernmental organizations is embodied by the UNESCO statistics mentioned above. As part of their charge to stimulate and promote industrial growth, a number of intergovernmental and governmental organizations produce statistics every year, often on a haphazard basis, neither measuring the same statistics every year, nor utilizing the same methodologies for operationalizing terms used year after year, or country by country. For instance, the World Bank, headquartered in Washington, DC, annually releases single reports by external analysts on a long series of topics, sometimes covering audiovisual media. These reports measure only that year, enabling no commensurate longitudinal analysis. The European Audiovisual Observatory (EAO), based in Strasbourg, releases much more consistent statistics on audiovisual industries in the European Union or loosely bordering it.

UNESCO's Institute for Statistics (UIS), located in Montreal, is a hub for producing free global figures on creative industries and they are the source of the statistics referenced by Pratt in the example above. These statistics, which report Nollywood as the second largest movie industry in the world based on number of titles produced annually, have been cited innumerable times in an offhand way by the popular press and scholarly articles. As Bud (2014: 92) points out, this particular statistic was gathered by the UIS asking national governments to self-report titles per year produced in their country. In 2009, there was a change in reporting procedures at the National Film and Video Censors Board (NFVCB) of Nigeria, and they decided to announce the number of video films released that year instead of just the number of cinema releases. This change caused the output-per-year statistic for Nigeria to increase exponentially, giving the misleading perception that there had been a sudden boom in production. All other national film boards reporting to UNESCO continued reporting only cinema releases, maintaining their exclusion of domestic video releases. Accompanied by no acknowledgment of this increased incommensurability between Nigeria's and other nations' reporting, Nollywood achieved international fame, and film festivals, investors, and academic conferences alike were compelled to acknowledge and incorporate the output of the industry (Bud 2014: 91). While 2009 does not mark a year of increased output by Nollywood (in fact, it marked a year of shrinking production, see Miller, 2016), it marks the year in which the statistics released by a respected intergovernmental organization (the UIS) commanded the world to pay attention to this industry (Bud 2014).

Although intergovernmental organizations like the EAO and the UIS lead the charge in producing statistics on audiovisual industries, these statistics are usually initially produced by the national agencies of governments reporting to these organizations. This obscures data about industries not measured at the national level, such as Flemish language production coming out of Belgium (Verheul 2018), and nations differ in the reliability of the data they supply to the EAO (see Papadimitriou (2018), for example, regarding Greece's EAO data production). The very question of *what* data is measured by national statistics boards tends to stem from perceived intersection between these domestic measures and international development indicators such as the UN's Millennium Development goals (Jerven 2013) and is often predicated upon figures already commonly measured by national government agencies, obviating the employment of further expensive measurement tools (Merry 2016). As the case of Nollywood's rapid rise to second largest film industry in the world (in terms of titles produced per year) shows, decisions made by these national statistics boards can have real power.

Outside of governmental and intergovernmental organizations, interested observers have further recourse to investigate industries not known for reliably producing statistics. Those looking to justify investment in so-called "emerging" audiovisual industries may sometimes be compelled to commission a report by an international accounting firm like PricewaterhouseCoopers (PwC) or KPMG. In the case of iROKOtv, the Nollywood streaming service headquartered in New York and Lagos, their quest for an uptick in venture capital compelled them to commission a KPMG report to show investors, creating data points unavailable elsewhere. Similarly, industry advocacy groups in India commissioned reports from all Big Four accounting firms (Arthur Andersen, KPMG, PwC, and Ernst & Young) to hype the industry to potential investors (Govil 2016: 223).

In both these cases, those seeking investment in their industry have turned to major accounting firms to make themselves legible, legitimate, and generalizable to investors (Govil 2016: 228). These qualities are also welcomed by researchers as they seek to investigate an industry, laying it bare for outsiders to view. For both parties, the impulse is to uncover the obscured, to enable analysis of an industry that is otherwise impenetrable, even if this cloaking has been intentional.

## Discussion

The commissioning of audits from one or all of the Big Four accounting firms by media companies or advocacy groups is symptomatic of our collective citizenship in "the audit society" (Power 1997) or "audit culture" (Shore and Wright 2015). Such terms refer to an age in which nearly everything and everyone can be tracked and accounted for, from personal credit scores, to audits of governments, businesses, and institutions like universities. In this era, that which cannot be counted is not only illegible but also suspect as a result. Consequently, those relying on informal transactions, from undocumented workers paid under-the-table, to industries without verifiable statistics, are ineligible for participation in established systems of credit and influence.

This chapter encourages a critical look at the weight given to counting in audiovisual media industries. Rather than being neutrally inquisitive, this impulse toward quantifying hopes to translate the world into a language that is palatable to the external glance, to foreign investment, to bank investment, to corporatization, and to be made understandable by global actors. As a means of justifying an industry as worthy of attention, critical media industries researchers are often compelled by readers, editors, and other interlocutors to include quantitative measurements in qualitative studies. In this way, academic researchers join investors, tax authorities, and intergovernmental organizations as both demanders and producers of manipulated statistics.

Media industries researchers should, when possible, take inspiration from those documenting or analyzing other "fuzzy" phenomena on a global level. In their work on informal trade in Africa, for instance, Ellis and MacGaffey (1996) propose combining micro-level case studies of individual trading businesses with meso-level market studies, in which a researcher would track prices and connections between traders visible at the market level. This is a qualitative approach to economic analysis that is dependent on time spent with producers and distributors. By involving intensive time spent on-site with industry workers, the approach shares some common ground with the observational work undertaken in production studies of media industries, though such research is not usually employed in pursuit of economic analysis. At heart, this is research based in intensive local knowledge instead of manipulated statistics reported by national agencies. Merry (2016) echoes this approach in her work critiquing global indicator culture (the assumption that everything from unemployment to infant mortality can and should be measured by globally commensurable numerical indicators), noting the superiority of quantitative analyses produced by local knowledge over those that attempt to produce globally commensurable data. In both these ways, one can see qualitative critical researchers as particularly well-poised to investigate the obscured in informal media industries.

To be sure, qualitative research is not always the best way to understand media industries. Small-scale case study work, even when rigorous, long-term, and wide-reaching, can sputter when assessing macro-level trends. The contested generalizability of samples in qualitative research, as well as its labor-intensive research practices are not fit for every research goal. Quantitative research can illuminate the wider operations of media industries in ways qualitative research is not always equipped to do. However, qualitative media industries research has wide explanatory potential, and it is the aim of this chapter to encourage those engaged in such research to guard against their unnecessary utilization of manipulated statistical measures in the course of their research. One can argue for the importance and even dominance of particular industries without leaning on such measures.

After referencing the UNESCO statistic, Pratt's piece goes on to include number-based assessments, which could best be referred to as an interview subject's *perception* of frequency as opposed to a measure that could ever contribute to correlational statistical analysis. For example, she notes "the director Tunde Kelani estimates that there are now five or ten pirated copies of films in the market for every legitimate one" (2015: 73). While this is an example of an individual high-profile filmmaker producing exact-sounding numbers for the purpose of filling in the blanks in scholarly and journalistic articles, we can also think of this as a number meant to express the general shape of one prolific filmmaker's knowledge based on his own experiences distributing movies rather than the product of a precision-focused accounting. We can think of this number as contributing to a qualitative analysis that is based on in-depth investigation of multiple distributors' experiences, as opposed to institutionally produced statistics from which to draw direct conclusions. Micro-level knowledge of the industry would lend the researcher a window on which informants would have the most thorough perspective on the industry and least incentive to over- or under-estimate. Given the uneven and incommensurable nature of statistics generally cited in quantitative and qualitative media industries research, close qualitative work with producers, distributors, fans, and others at the heart of an industry can be the motor not only of production studies but of all analyses of media industries across global contexts.

## Notes

1 When used in manufacturing and other industrial sectors, this accounting practice is sometimes referred to as "Hollywood accounting," due to the ways in which Hollywood is known as the genesis and most prominent and persistent user of this strategy (Karim, Shaikh, Hock, and Islam 2016).
2 The MPA releases these only as averages and other generalizations, as opposed to supplying the micro level data about individual films that they receive.
3 The marketers largely hail from the Igbo ethnic group, a traditionally stateless society that has dominated long-distance trade in the region dating back to pre-colonial times via networks of trust and personal connections (Meagher 2010).

## References

Adejunmobi, M. (2011) "Nollywood, Globalization, and Regional Media Corporations in Africa," *Popular Communication: The International Journal of Media and Culture,* 9 (2): 67–78.
Bud. A. (2014) "The End of Nollywood's Guilded Age? Marketers, the State and the Struggle for Distribution," *Critical African Studies,* 6 (1): 91–121.

Ellis, S. and MacGaffey, J. (1996) "Research on Sub-Saharan Africa's International Trade: Some Methodological and Conceptual Problems," *African Studies Review*, 39 (2): 19–41.

Epstein, E. (2005) "Hollywood's Profits, Demystified," *Slate*, August 8, available at www.slate.com/articles/arts/the_hollywood_economist/2005/08/hollywoods_profits_demystified.2.html (accessed September 22, 2020).

Epstein, E. (2010) *The Hollywood Economist: The Hidden Financial Reality Behind the Movies*, Hoboken, NJ: Melville House.

Ganti, T. (2015) "Fuzzy Numbers: The Productive Nature of Ambiguity in the Hindi Film Industry," *Comparative Studies of South Asia, Africa, and the Middle East*, 35 (3): 451–465.

Govil, N. (2010) "Size Matters," *BioScope*, 1 (2): 105–109.

Govil, N. (2016) "Envisioning the Future: Financialization and the Indian Entertainment Industry Reports," *South Asian Popular Culture*, 14 (3): 219–234.

Guyer, J. (2004) *Marginal Gains: Monetary Transactions in Atlantic Africa*, Chicago, IL: University of Chicago Press.

Haynes, J. (2014) "'New Nollywood': Kunle Afolayan," *Black Camera: An International Film Journal*, 5 (2): 53–73.

Jerven, M. (2013) *Poor Numbers: How We Are Misled by African Development Statistics and What to Do About It*, Ithaca, NY: Cornell University Press.

Karim, A. M., Shaikh, J. M., Hock, O. Y., and Islam, M. R. (2016) "Creative Accounting: Techniques of Application-An Empirical Study Among Auditors and Accountants of Listed Companies in Bangladesh," *Australian Academy of Accounting and Finance Review*, 2 (3): 215–245.

Lee, E. (2019) "Netflix Looks Abroad as Growth Slows in the U.S," *The New York Times*, December 16, available at www.nytimes.com/2019/12/16/business/media/netflix-us-subs-slowing-down-international-subs-growing.html (accessed September 22, 2020).

Lobato, R. (2012) *Shadow Economies of Cinema: Mapping Informal Film Distribution*, London: British Film Institute.

Lobato, R. (2018) "Rethinking International TV Flows Research in the Age of Netflix," *Television and New Media*, 19 (3): 241–256.

Meagher, K. (2010) *Identity Economics: Social Networks and the Informal Economy in Nigeria*, Woodbridge: James Currey.

Merry, S. (2016) *The Seductions of Quantification: Measuring Human Rights, Gender Violence, and Sex Trafficking*. Chicago, IL: University of Chicago Press.

Miller, J. (2016) *Nollywood Central*, London: British Film Institute.

Papadimitriou, L. (2018) "Researching the Greek Film/Screen Industry: Challenges and Opportunities in the Study of a Crisis-ridden Sector," paper presented at *Media Industries: Current Debates and Future Directions*, King's College London, April 20.

Poovey, M. (1998) *A History of the Modern Fact: Problems of Knowledge in the Sciences of Wealth and Society*, Chicago, IL: University of Chicago Press.

Power, M. (1997) *The Audit Society: Rituals of Verification*, Oxford: Oxford University Press.

Pratt, L. (2015) "Good for New Nollywood: The Impact of New Online Distribution and Licensing Strategies," *International Journal of Cultural and Creative Industries*, 3 (1): 70–84.

Ryan, C. (2015) "New Nollywood: A Sketch of Nollywood's Metropolitan Style," *African Studies Review*, 58 (3): 55–76.

Sandelowski, M. (2001) "Real Qualitative Researchers Do Not Count: The Use of Numbers in Qualitative Research" *Research in Nursing and Health*, 24: 230–240.

Shore, C. and Wright, S. (2015) "Audit Culture Revisited: Rankings, Ratings, and the Reassembly of Society," *Current Anthropology*, 56 (3): 421–444.

Siegel, T. (2014). "Sony Hack Reveals Top-Secret Profitability of 2013 Movies," *The Hollywood Reporter*, December 5, available at www.hollywoodreporter.com/news/sony-hack-reveals-top-secret-754491 (accessed September 22, 2020).

Sisto, J. (2003). "Profit Participation in the Motion Picture Industry," *Entertainment and Sports Lawyer*, 21 (1): 1–21.

Sparviero, S. (2015) "Hollywood Creative Accounting: The Success Rate of Major Motion Pictures" *Media Industries Journal*, 2 (1), available at https://quod.lib.umich.edu/m/mij/15031809.0002.102/--hollywood-creative-accounting-the-success-rate-of-major?rgn=main;view=fulltext (accessed September 22, 2020).

Thompson, D. (2011) "How Hollywood Accounting Can Make a $450 Million Movie 'Unprofitable,'" *The Atlantic*, September 14, available at www.theatlantic.com/business/archive/2011/09/how-hollywood-accounting-can-make-a-450-million-movie-unprofitable/245134/ (accessed September 22, 2020).

Ulin, J. (2019) *The Business of Media Distribution: Monetizing Film, TV and Video Content in an Online World*, 3rd ed., Burlington, MA: Focal.

Verheul, J. (2018) "Lack of Data: Researching a Small Media Industry in the Absence of Screen Regulation," paper presented at *Media Industries: Current Debates and Future Directions*, King's College London, April 20.

Wasko, J. (2003) *How Hollywood Works*, Thousand Oaks, CA: Sage.

# 49

# TEACHING MEDIA INDUSTRIES THROUGH EXPERIENTIAL LEARNING

## Pathways to engagement and understanding

*Erin Copple Smith*

Inescapability. That's what I focus on when I speak to my undergraduate students about the value of Media Studies courses to their college experience and lives. Because media are omnipresent – the music playing over the speakers in a Target store, the TV scrolling behind the bar, the phones in our pockets – it behooves all of us to gain some critical thinking skills regarding what we encounter daily. Key to those skills is a sense of where all that media comes from. As I tell students, media texts are not created in a vacuum, they're the product of industries and those industries have an imperative to generate profit. In order for them to understand the texts they encounter in the world, they must understand the conditions of their production, distribution, and exhibition. Media is not unlike a magic show in this way: audiences get distracted by the trick when we should be focusing on the magician.

At the small college where I teach, most of the students in my classroom are not majoring in Media Studies; they're there to broaden their horizons, to acquire skills like critical thinking, close analysis, and writing within the context of their liberal arts education. At my institution and many others, I am sure, most of our students enter into Media Studies because they're interested in media texts. They want to study them, they want to understand them, they want to make them. They find texts fascinating. And of course, they are! But the truth is that one cannot fully understand media texts without understanding the industries that made them. I'm certain that my students don't enter my classroom expecting to spend weeks interrogating the role of the media industries. They're expecting to watch films, talk about TV series, or perhaps discuss the power of the news media, but they're surprised at how much time we spend talking about the institutions that create those texts. We explore how media industries have developed and shifted over time, their ownership structures, and the intricacies of media economics (and why creating and selling media isn't like making and selling widgets). Most importantly, I want students to understand that media industries are complex, ambivalent, contradictory, and contested. There are no straightforward answers to why these companies do what they do, and they can do everything "right" and still fail (or do everything "wrong" and succeed). As Harold Vogel notes in *Entertainment Industry Economics*:

DOI: 10.4324/9780429275340-55

It is *economic forces* – profit motives, if you will – that are always behind the scenes regulating the flows and rates of implementation [of new ideas]. Those are the forces that shape the relative popularity and growth patterns of competing, usually inter-dependent, entertainment activities and products.

*original emphasis 2001: xviii*

In short: media are omnipresent and influential cultural and social forces, and by tracing the origins of the texts we encounter we can better understand why we get the media content (and its attendant messages and meanings) that we do.

The key questions I ask students to keep in mind are: what do media industries do; why do they do it; and what is the potential impact of those decisions on media content? This, of course, leads to other questions: why do the same stories get told over and over again; why are certain representations privileged; why are other representations missing entirely; and what's the potential impact of those decisions on society? We can perhaps understand why an institution would make a particular choice, but that should not let those folks off the hook when it comes to the consequences of that choice. All of these questions are complex and interrelated, and the processes of understanding how media industries operate can feel overwhelming to undergraduates for whom most of this material is new. They've spent their lives with media texts, but very little time thinking deeply (or often at all) about media industries.

So the crucial questions for us as teachers become: how can we best help our students understand the complexity of these industries and their operations; what are the many and varied factors that influence their decision-making processes; and what roles are played by the countless individuals who participate in creating, distributing, and exhibiting media texts – all of whom leave fingerprints on that text in some way? The strategy I've found most successful in making this complexity real and meaningful for students is to engage them in experiential learning. In my case, this requires them to operate as though they were members of one of these institutions by engaging in activities during class. In doing so, the complexity, ambivalence, contradiction, and contestation present in all institutional practice is truly felt by the student as they try to navigate the tasks I've laid out for them. And once they've experienced it, they're better equipped to make sense of it. Because the student is role playing as a member of a media company, they're actively thinking through a decision-making process. They're experiencing it, not just reading about it or being told about it. This allows them to achieve a different type and level of understanding. They "get it" because they've done it.

Media industries, after all, are made up of people who make decisions based on multiple factors considered in conjunction with one another. Asking students to make similar decisions forces them to experience the decision-making process in all its complexity and ambiguity. As students occupy these roles (however briefly), their reflections on these concepts become much richer because they're able to actually consider their own experiences rather than abstract concepts. Because students have something concrete to discuss, their reflections on the experience and what it reveals about the activities of media industries are richer and more meaningful.

In this chapter, I lay out some specific strategies for designing activities for use in teaching media industries, including careful consideration of the following: what do you want students to learn; how much time do you have; and what do students need to know in order to do the activity properly? The chapter concludes with a case study of the institutional analysis unit of my introductory course in which I walk students through a deep dive of the American broadcast TV industry, culminating in an activity in which they roleplay TV networks building schedules and TV production studios developing and pitching pilots. Throughout, I hope to inspire you to design thoughtful and meaningful opportunities for your students to engage with the concepts related to understanding media industries by occupying industry roles in order to experience the complexity and tensions innate to the operations of these industries.

## Strategies for activity design

It's one thing to decide to develop and integrate in-class activities for your students and it's another to figure out what those activities should include. Often the prospect of creating experiential learning opportunities for students feels daunting for us, particularly when we have many other things clamoring for our attention. Where to start? What to include? How to design materials? And to what end in terms of student learning and engagement? There are several strategies I've found that work well in designing activities for the classroom: consideration of what you want students to learn, allotting the appropriate amount of time to the activity, thinking through what students will need to know, avoiding overcomplicating the experience for students, and building in time for meaningful reflection. In what follows, I explain each of these strategies in further detail and provide examples from my own classroom to illustrate.

There are a few things to keep in mind when designing in-class activities around media industries. First, consider what you want students to learn. This needs to be clear to you as the instructor so that you can make it clear to them. Is there a particular portion of that day's reading that you think would lend itself well to an activity in order to illustrate a key point? In my course on popular music, students read Keith Negus' (1998) article "Cultural Production and the Corporation," which discusses risk management in the music industry. Negus does a good job explaining his point, but it's hard for students to fully understand why risk management is important and what it actually looks like. In other words, how do the strategies of risk management apply to the actions of people working at music labels? To illustrate Negus' explanation, I ask students to do their own risk assessment and corporate management. In small groups, they imagine themselves as heads of a music label developing corporate strategies for managing risk. For example, what changes should a small indie label make to its portfolio of artists in order to bring its budget under control? Groups have to decide which artists/departments/genres to keep and grow, and which to cut. After they discuss and then share, we consider why they made the decisions they did. In so doing, they realize that each group made different decisions based on a variety of factors (e.g., genres that are particularly well-liked by members of the group, or a purely financial decision based on the popularity of individual genres and/or artists). In reflecting on their choices, students realize there's no clear "right" or "wrong" answer to the questions posed – it's just a matter of considering assets, weighing choices, and ultimately personal taste.

Next, consider how much time you have to devote to the activity. Be sure to factor in time necessary for distributing materials and explaining the basics of the activity at the outset, as well as time for wrap-up and discussion afterward. In my class on television, I ask students to participate in an activity around product placement. Half the students roleplay TV writers, the other half advertisers. They're given existing sitcom scripts and have to separately come up with suggestions for how to work the product into the script. In planning for the activity, I have to factor in enough time for everyone to read their script in addition to time for them to discuss with their partner and then with the other half of their team. After the activity, it is valuable for you as a tutor to ask the students about what happened and to make note of things that you noticed as you circulated during the activity, too. Ask students to reflect critically on what happened with questions like, "Why did you do that?" "When that happened, how did you respond and why?" and "How do you think this compares to how a similar experience would happen in reality?"

Perhaps most importantly, be sure to think carefully about what students need to know in order to do the activity properly. It's difficult for us to remember that students don't know everything we know, so step back and think about the component parts of the activity you are planning. Be explicit with your instructions and guidelines during the activity. If students are role-playing, be specific about their role so they know who they are and what they're supposed to be doing. In my introductory course, students' role play either ad agencies or networks as they negotiate ad prices on current TV series. Each group is given a packet of papers that includes a brief explanation of who they are role playing and what they're doing (see Box 49.1 for an example).

---

**Box 49.1  Specific and detailed instructions for the "networks" to use for the advertising activity**

You and your partner(s) represent CBS. You will be attempting to sell ad space during three of your series to the agencies who come around shopping. Below is important information about these series that will help you. Before shopping begins, you should discuss how you can best sell each series to make it attractive to advertisers. Are you going to focus on how many viewers it has (ratings)? How well it does in its timeslot compared to the competition (share)? Are you going to focus on the audience the show attracts?

Your goal: sell as many ad spots as you can for as much money as you can. You are negotiating with the agencies to sell them a single ad spot on a single series. You need the advertisers more than they need you – be prepared to sell your series to them!

---

As you put the materials together, be sure to provide any additional information they may need to do the activity. For example, in this TV advertising activity I ask students to negotiate ad prices during popular TV shows, but I realized that students had no idea where to start their negotiations. Is $50,000 for a 30-second spot reasonable? Or $5 million? They had no frame of reference. Now I tell them the current average price for a 30-second primetime spot so they can then consider whether to negotiate up or down from that number. Additionally, whenever possible, I use real-life examples because it makes things more meaningful to the students. Rather than having the sense that they're "playing," they can see that the practices they're engaging in are very similar to the ones encountered by workers within the industry. For the aforementioned TV advertising activity, students are "buying" and "selling" ad time on current TV series. This means that ratings data is made readily available along with information about the average price of an ad on those series. After the activity, I distribute a handout that lists the current ad price for each series they negotiated with, and the students always enjoy seeing how close they got to the actual ad price amid shouts of, "I knew you screwed us over!" and "Ha! We got that so cheap!"

Throughout designing the activity, be sure not to overcomplicate things. As this chapter has already discussed, media industries are complicated institutions, but a single in-class activity designed for undergraduates cannot account for all of that complexity. In the advertising activity, I could easily overcomplicate things by having students consider putting together packages by giving them information about ongoing partnerships or by asking them to consider the possibility of product integration. But all of this would make things more confusing for students and would detract from what I want them to get out of the experience: a sense of what factors make TV shows attractive to advertisers, the various kinds of audiences that are valued by the industry, how in fact it is the audience that is bought and sold during these negotiations, and so how the audience gets to be created as a necessary fiction. So just focus on the factors you really want them to learn and leave out the rest.

Most importantly, be sure to build in time for meaningful reflection. For short activities, this can be done in class after the activity has wrapped up. Begin by asking students to explain what happened during the activity: what did they do? In my course on independent media, I have students work together to design a film festival. They're asked to develop a general theme for their festival and are provided with a long list of films they could include. If there's time, they begin planning a preliminary program. Afterward, I ask students to tell us about their festivals – what's the festival's mission? Name? What films did you admit (and not admit) and how did you choose? Were there any films your group couldn't agree upon? Why or why not? Once the basic recap has concluded, I push students to think more deeply about their experiences by connecting them to the larger concepts I want them to consider. I ask questions including: for the films that were chosen by multiple festivals, why do you think they were so popular; what do they have in common; were you choosing to canonize films just because they fit the theme of your festival; or did you choose films because they sounded particularly interesting to you? We then move in for the deep reflection designed to bring home the point of that day's materials: how do you see your process of selection informing "indie film" as a cultural category? For longer, more involved activities, you may want to ask students to reflect on their experiences in writing. The case study explored below provides an example of that type of reflection. In all cases, you don't want to leave students hanging at the end of an activity – you need to provide them time to debrief and discuss their experiences as you move them toward applying those experiences toward a deeper understanding of the concept(s) you want them to understand.

Thoughtful design of in-class activities needn't be complicated or time consuming. By thinking through these various strategies, it's possible to develop activities that support student learning without overtaxing yourself. Just concentrate on the resources available and what you want students to learn. The more narrowly you can focus your goals, the greater the outcome for students, and by incorporating meaningful reflection, students are asked to apply their own experiences in the activity toward a clearer understanding of the operations of media industries more broadly. Their insights are keen, and the impact can be long-lasting, as students are much more likely to remember haggling with their classmates over the price of an ad than a particular course reading.

## Case study: TV industry and scheduling activity

My introductory course, Elements of Media Analysis, is structured as a primer on Cultural Studies and an integrated approach to studying media. In each unit (ranging in length from three to six class sessions), my goal is for students to understand the basic components of doing a particular form of media analysis – textual, institutional, social context, and audience analysis. We then finish up the class by talking about how those four forms of analysis are not actually distinct, but rather used in combination to provide a more comprehensive view of how media works in the world. Over the course of teaching the course regularly, I've worked hard to refine and focus each unit to provide students with a useful basis for understanding these components and applying them to the media they encounter. Because the class covers so much ground, we move through units fairly quickly, so I've designed each to be as efficient as possible. Key to this efficiency has been achieving clarity on what, precisely, I want them to learn in each unit. What are the concepts, techniques, vocabulary, and experiences that students most need to have in order to understand each type of media analysis? Below, I walk through the processes behind my design of the industry unit of the course and the activity that comprises the final project for that unit in order to illustrate the strategies and suggestions addressed above.

In my first iteration of the course, the content of the industry unit was entirely too broad. Because industry analysis is my area of expertise, I wanted to expose the students to a little bit of everything, so they read about the film industry, broadcast TV, streaming, and so on. The result was a very disjointed experience for them and for me. I was unable to build knowledge because we were working in an entirely different institutional context each day, so the knowledge felt broad but very shallow. I decided I needed to reverse engineer this segment of the course. I stepped back to consider what it was that I most wanted students to understand after this unit and settled upon the following: institutional analysis is valuable because it allows us to better understand why we get the media texts and experiences that we do and understanding that relationship involves interrogating the actions of people working in the media industries and also the logics that govern those actions. Once I was clear on the learning outcomes of the unit, the path became more obvious. By focusing on a single media industry as narrowly as possible, I would be able to give my students greater depth of understanding of those logics and practices. My hope was that, in providing a deeper understanding of this specific industry, I could better equip students to think through the strategies and logics that govern all media industries. In short, once students had the intellectual "muscle memory" for performing industry analysis, I hoped they could then apply those same muscles to different industries in the future. Ultimately, I chose to focus exclusively on the American broadcast television industry because it is one I know very well.

Once I had a clear sense of what I wanted students to learn, I considered how much time I had to devote to the unit. For the Institutional Analysis unit, I have only six 50-minute class sessions, so each meeting has to be jam-packed with the information students need – there's no time for extras. The process of designing those six 50-minute class meetings required a good bit of reverse engineering: I had to think about what knowledge students needed to have in order to participate in the scheduling activity. This requires students to know the following concepts: the financing and ownership structure in American broadcast TV, the role of advertising as a funding mechanism, the development of target demographics, scheduling strategies, and the way that all of these components are brought to bear in developing new series. These concepts became the backbone of the overall unit.

Throughout the unit, we spend time talking about why institutional analysis is valuable, and what makes media industries different from other types of industries including the immense risk that media makers take in producing media of all types. This foundational understanding of risk underpins everything the broadcast television industry does, as all of their actions must be first understood from the perspective of minimizing or managing risk. The unit makes use of Michael Curtin and Jane Shattuc's (2009) *The American Television Industry*, which provides students with a consistent and clearly explained introduction to some of the core concepts related to the broadcast TV industry. Building on the Curtin and Shattuc text, we engage in discussion of the differences between broadcast, cable, premium cable, and streaming TV, as well as an explanation of the structure of production, distribution, and exhibition in broadcast TV. The unit includes an explanation of TV's financing structures, including the three-party market model and the role of advertising. The students participate in the advertising activity mentioned above in order to better comprehend the various factors that determine ad prices. We consider various scheduling strategies (e.g., block scheduling, lead-ins and lead-outs, tentpoles) and look closely at current TV schedules to see them at work. Students then apply their knowledge of these various practices and logics to a new broadcast TV series to consider why they think it made it to air. Only by focusing specifically and narrowly on broadcast TV can students develop both breadth and depth of understanding. The unit is not comprehensive, but we cover a lot of ground so that students have a general sense of how broadcast TV works and why.

The unit wraps up with an in-class activity that asks them to draw on all of this knowledge. In the activity, half the class is assigned to work as schedulers in an imaginary broadcast TV network. These students work in small groups to design a weekly prime time schedule, drawing on their understanding of scheduling practices to select from a list of series I've provided for them. That list includes existing TV series that each network has exclusive access to as well as the price of producing an episode for each series. They're also given a list of syndicated series options that are available to all networks (for a lower price, naturally). Concurrently, the other half of the class works in small groups to role play a TV production studio. Each studio is given a brief logline (two- to three-sentence description) for two imaginary TV series, as well as the price, it would cost the studio to produce each episode (see Box 49.2).

---

### Box 49.2 Loglines for two imaginary series concepts for use by the "TV studios" during the culminating activity

#### *Pilot 1:* **Roll Your Own**

(Comedy) A sitcom centered on a combined marijuana dispensary and sushi restaurant.
  30 Minutes; Production Cost: $550,000/episode

#### *Pilot 2:* **The Fracks of Life**

(Dramedy) A single father and owner of a natural gas company in east Texas has to navigate the legal landscape, dealing with reminders of life lessons from his now-deceased environmentalist father as he struggles to balance company profits with his social responsibility.
60 Minutes; Production Cost: $850,000/episode

---

Each studio also has to design their own pilot as a combination of two existing series drawn randomly from a deck of cards. So, for example, a studio might have to design a mash-up of *The Walking Dead* (2010–) and *South Park* (1997–). Studios are encouraged to embroider on the basic setup they've been provided (e.g., including stars, famous showrunners, gimmicks) and then consider how they'll negotiate with studios to get their series to air. After some planning and discussion, the studios pitch their original series to the network schedulers, negotiate prices, and eventually come to agreements for as many of their series as they're able to sell. These include an agreed price per episode, ownership rights for the series, and timeslots within the networks' schedules.

Throughout the process, students are required to draw upon the knowledge gained in the unit. Students at networks think through scheduling strategies, drawing and maintaining an audience throughout the night, and building a brand identity. Students in studios consider target audiences, including what factors of series design are likely to be appealing to audiences that are attractive to advertisers and thus networks. All groups engage in a fairly creative process, whether developing concepts for new series or thinking about how to arrange programs into a weekly schedule. In all cases, they're constantly thinking about the commercial interests of the larger industry. And all students also consider ownership structures – why they might want to retain ownership rights, or why they're willing to give them up in whole or in part based on the likelihood of a TV series being successful in aftermarkets. The activity gets them thinking by applying the knowledge they've gained throughout the unit to a specific example. Rather than simply reading about scheduling strategies, they've now applied them to an example. Instead of just hearing me talk about how target audiences are determined, they've actually defined an audience themselves and then sold that audience to a network. As an alternative to sitting through a lecture on the tension between creative and commercial interests in the media industries, they've actually experienced that tension themselves as they designed new TV series.

Following the activity, students reflect upon their experiences by responding to a series of prompts (see Box 49.3).

---

### Box 49.3 Instructions for student reflections on their experiences during the culminating activity

1. Describe *one* strategy your group used during the activity. What is *one* thing you did? Explain why you utilized that strategy. *Why* did you do what you did? What were the *logics* behind your decisions? You should make connections here to what you know about the economics of the television industry. How do TV networks make money? How were your specific strategies of either selling programming (for those of you acting as production studios) or buying and scheduling programming (for those of you acting as network schedulers) designed to maximize profit for your (fictional) company? *You are required to use Curtin and Shattuc to help justify your logics and actions.*

2. Describe a *second* strategy your group used during the activity. What is *a different* thing you did and why? The two strategies you describe in your responses should be *distinct and separate*. In crafting your response, you should follow all the advice given to you in the prompt above, including the *required use of Curtin and Shattuc.*

3. What did you learn about the way institutional structures and practices in media privilege and/or stifle certain types of content? In other words, what did you learn about the relationship between media industries and media content? How does your understanding of these practices (e.g., scheduling strategies, financing models, what makes a series attractive to buyers) give you a better insight into what kinds of TV content are most (or least!) likely to be produced and aired and *why*?

---

The course assignment requires them to more deeply interrogate their own experiences, mining those experiences for meaning by finding connections. In a traditional institutional analysis, I would ask students to look at a specific case study to consider what that industry did and why. In this exercise, they're asked to turn that critical lens on themselves when I ask: what did *you* do? Why did you do it? This shift has several advantages: first, that the experience is made more meaningful for students because they feel a part of it rather than separate from it. Second, rather than hypothesizing about what the nameless, faceless media industry did, they have actual answers – they are able to think through their own decision-making process. And once they've examined their own strategies, logics, and practices, they're asked to extrapolate to the larger industry by considering the broader impact of their decisions on content.

Unsurprisingly, students process and absorb this understanding at variable rates and depths. Still, they are nearly all able to articulate that the assignment helped them to see that the content they consume doesn't just arrive by magic, that there are multiple and complicated factors at work determining what content gets produced. As one student noted in their assignment,

> every program a studio creates is tailor-made to be the most appealing for a net-work to buy, and every program a network chooses is selected based on what they think will bring in the largest/most reliable audience and in turn the most number of advertisers. All interactions between studios & networks are based around this co-dependent relationship.
>
> *Thomas 2020*

This revelation is particularly well-phrased, but most other students reach similar insights throughout the process of the unit, the activity, and the final reflection assignment, seeing (often for the first time) the complexity of the media industries. The strongest students use this understanding as a launching point for deeper insight into how institutional practices shape content and in turn society. Here's one example of a student making these connections between industry practice, content, and sociocultural impact:

> You often hear people say that all TV or movies feel the same nowadays, very cookie-cutter and not unique. This is by design, there are formulas that these networks have found that work, and they stick to them religiously in order to ensure that the money they are spending is spent wisely and with the most assurance they can afford that their money will be made back [...] Unfortunately, this idea of what "works" is often based on old ideologies or prejudices. For example, advertisers prioritize the "majority," which is apparently seen as straight white males ... therefore the networks and studios make shows that prioritize the values and ideas that represent this [...] This paves the way for a multitude of problems, starting with a lack of representation of minorities because they can be harder to market to on a larger scale because they are seen as, well, minorities.
>
> *Armstrong, 2020*

And occasionally, students take a moment to consider the way the structure of the unit, activity, and assignment provide them with experiential learning opportunities that deepen their know-ledge. Another student concluded:

> Getting to do a role-playing activity and actually acting as a network was a really helpful way for me to learn about the relationships between studios and networks. Scheduling programming was also a great way for me to learn about the kinds of things that networks think about when maximizing profits. And learning about audiences and how to manipulate audiences into watching more TV gave me an idea of what kinds of shows networks greenlight. [...] Overall, I really enjoyed how this assignment was hands-on and experiential learning. This type of activity makes it really easy for me to understand how this process works, and so that is pretty awesome.
>
> *Weatherby, 2020*

In the end, my students have a deeper and more meaningful appreciation for the complexity of the broadcast TV industry because they've experienced (in small part) what it's like to work in that industry. In one response to prompt 3 (Figure 49.3), a student commented,

> I see now that TV producers are wary of taking big risks because they know that networks want to make safe choices in order to guarantee advertiser support. But at the same time, they can't make their content *too* safe because then it's boring, so they try to find a middle ground.

A student is able to see this because they've done it – having developed a series to pitch to networks, they "get it." Rather than parroting a conclusion or insight back at me, they're actually coming to that conclusion on their own based on their experiences. Though our focus in this unit is fairly narrow, students who have a deep and broad understanding of broadcast TV develop muscles for institutional analysis that they can then apply to other industries and situations in the future. In short, through exploring a specific example, they are able to gain the knowledge I wanted them to get throughout the unit: institutional analysis is valuable because it allows us to better understand why we get the media texts and experiences that we do, and understanding that relationship involves interrogating the actions of people working in the media industries and also the logics that govern those actions.

## Conclusion

Teaching critical media industry studies provides students with an appreciation for the complexity of these industries. By engaging in (admittedly simplified) practices performed by workers within the American broadcast TV industry, they are invited to begin imagining themselves in similar roles. In the process, they start to internalize the various and competing forces that influence decision-making within that industry – they develop an awareness that these choices are never straightforward but always complicated by multiple factors. The appreciation for the complexity of the broadcast TV industry developed by this activity allows them to more deeply understand that these industries aren't faceless monoliths but are populated with people who are trying to get their jobs done in the best possible way. They're not evil or benevolent, they're just people. This understanding brings in the hard-core economists who argue that capitalism allows for anything and also the students with deep distrust of Hollywood. Both groups start to see that the truth is more complicated than either of those positions allows – and isn't that complexity at the heart of Cultural Studies as a discipline? By engaging in these activities, students' reflections on the operations of media industries become much richer because they're able to consider their own experiences. Students who participate in an activity designing product placement opportunities can more fundamentally understand the way in which TV is both a creative and a capitalist enterprise because the concept is no longer abstract—it's made (at least somewhat) concrete.

The Media Studies classroom can be among the most dynamic and engaging on any campus as students encounter materials that they can immediately apply to their everyday lives. Their preexisting fondness for movies, TV series, video games, and social media and popular music (and so on) can quickly blossom into an appreciation for not only the texts themselves but also for the ways in which they emerge from and shape our culture. Understanding how media industries operate is a key part of that process. As we pull back the veil on the structures of these industries, their goals and strategies, their processes and procedures, we simultaneously diminish and enhance the magic of the media. Activities invite our students to become a part of that magic – by learning the magicians' tricks and trying them out themselves, they can begin to understand why they matter.

# References

Armstrong, T. (2020) *Institutional Analysis Reflection Assignment*, Elements of Media Analysis, Austin College: unpublished.

Curtin, M. and Shattuc, J. (2009) *The American Television Industry*, London: British Film Institute.

Negus, K. (1998) "Cultural Production and the Corporation: Musical Genres and the Strategic Management of Creativity in the US Recording Industry," *Media, Culture, and Society*, 20 (3): 359–379.

Thomas, A. (2020) *Institutional Analysis Reflection Assignment*, Elements of Media Analysis, Austin College: unpublished.

Vogel, H. (2001) *Entertainment Industry Economics*, 5th ed., Cambridge: Cambridge University Press.

Weatherby, L. (2020) *Institutional Analysis Reflection Assignment*. Elements of Media Analysis, Austin College: unpublished.

# INDEX

Note: page numbers in *italics* indicate a figure and page numbers in **bold** indicate a table on the corresponding page.

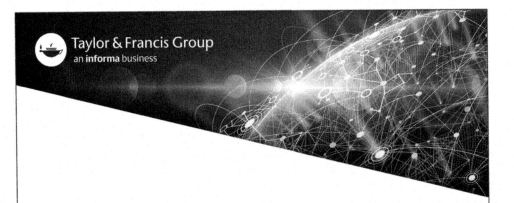